DATE DUE

Tommaso Campanella and the Transformation of the World

Tommaso Campanella and the Transformation of the World

John M. Headley

PRINCETON UNIVERSITY PRESS
PRINCETON, NEW JERSEY

B785.C24 H43 1997
Headley, John M.
Tommaso Campanella and the
transformation of the world

Copyright © 1997 by Princeton University Press
Published by Princeton University Press, 41 William Street,
Princeton, New Jersey 08540
In the United Kingdom: Princeton University Press,
Chichester, West Sussex

All Rights Reserved

Library of Congress Cataloging-in-Publication Data
Headley, John M.
Tommaso Campanella and the transformation of the world /
John M. Headley.
p. cm.
Includes bibliographical references and index.
ISBN 0-691-02679-3 (cloth : alk. paper)
1. Campanella, Tommaso, 1568–1639. I. Title.
B785.C24H43   1997
195—dc21   96-37931

This book has been composed in Times Roman

Princeton University Press books are printed on
acid-free paper and meet the guidelines for permanence
and durability of the Committee on Production
Guidelines for Book Longevity of the
Council on Library Resources

Printed in the United States of America

1 3 5 7 9 10 8 6 4 2

For P.I.K., G.M.M., R.G.W.

Ptolemy, who was a great man, had established the limits of our world; all the ancient philosophers thought they had its measure, except for a few remote islands that might escape their knowledge. It would have been Pyrrhonizing, a thousand years ago, to cast in doubt the science of cosmography, and the opinions that were accepted about it by one and all; it was heresy to admit the existence of the Antipodes. Behold in our century an infinite extent of terra firma, not an island or one particular country, but a portion nearly equal in size to the one we know, which has just been discovered. The geographers of the present time do not fail to assure us that now all is discovered and all is seen. . . . The question is, if Ptolemy was once mistaken on the grounds of his reason, whether it would not be stupid for me now to trust to what these people say about it; and whether it is not more likely that this great body that we call the world is something quite different from what we judge.

Plato holds that it changes its aspect in all regards: that the sky, the stars, and the sun at times reverse the movement that we see in them, changing east to west. The Egyptian priests told Herodotus that . . . the sun had four times changed its course; that the sea and the land change alternately into one another; that the birth of the world is undetermined. Aristotle, Cicero, say the same. And one of ours [Origen] says that it goes through an eternal and frequently recurring cycle of death and rebirth; calling to witness Solomon and Isaiah to avoid these objections: that at one time God was a creator without a creation; that he had been idle and then renounced his idleness and set about his work; and that in consequence he is subject to change.

In the most famous of the Greek schools, the world is held to be a god made by another, greater god, and is composed of a body and a soul that dwells in the center of it, spreading by musical numbers to its circumference; divine, very happy, very great, very wise, eternal. —Montaigne, *Essays*, II, 12

[M]uch I learned . . . how the eclipses in Aries and Libra (equinoctial signs) that will follow upon the great conjunction, together with the renewal of anomalies, will do stupendous things to confirm the decree of the great conjunction and transform the world completely and renew it.
—Campanella, *City of the Sun* (1981), 125–27

> Dream not of other worlds, what creatures there
> Live, in what state, condition, or degree,
> Contented that thus far hath been revealed
> Not of earth only but of highest heav'n.
> —Milton, *Paradise Lost*, VIII, 175–78

I believe the world grows near its end, yet is neither old nor decayed, nor will ever perish upon the ruins of its own principles. As the work of creation was above nature, so is its adversary, annihilation, without which the world hath not its end, but its mutation. —Sir Th. Browne, *Religio Medici*, I, 45

CONTENTS

List of Illustrations	xi
Abbreviations	xiii
Preface	xvii
PROLOGUE Naples and Europe in 1601	3

PART ONE: *Biographical Context*

CHAPTER I Toward the Making of a Prophet	9
CHAPTER II The Prophet Bound	26
CHAPTER III The Celebrity Faded	103
INTERMEZZO	139

PART TWO: *Engaging the Major Issues of the Emerging Modern World*

CHAPTER IV The Controversy with Aristotle	145
CHAPTER V The Controversy with Machiavelli: On the Rearming of Heaven	180
CHAPTER VI Universal Monarchy: On Identifying the Arm of God	197
CHAPTER VII Universal Theocracy and the Ecclesiastical State: The Figure of Melchisedech	247
CHAPTER VIII Naturalistic Religion, America, and World Evangelization	315
EPILOGUE Campanella and the End of the Renaissance	339
Select Bibliography	355
Index	383

ILLUSTRATIONS

Following page 138

Tommaso Campanella by Francesco Cozza. (By permission of the Ministero per i Bene Culturali e Ambientali, Rome)

Map of Spanish Naples. (Reprinted with permission from *Naples: An Early Guide* [New York: Italica Press, 1991])

Title Page of Campanella's *Philosophia sensibus demonstrata*. (By permission of the Houghton Library, Harvard University)

"Ferrante Imperato's Museum." (Frontispiece from Ferrante Imperato's *Historia naturale* [Venice: Presso Combi & L. Nou, 1672], by kind permission of Special Collections Library, Duke University)

Andrea Sacchi's *Divine Wisdom*. (By permission of John Beldon Scott and Barbara Bini)

"Plots of Jesuites," 1653. (By permission of the British Library, Shelfmark E715 [19] G19577.2)

"A Composite Portrait of Philip IV of Spain." (Fotografia del Archivo Fotográfico de Espasa Calpe by kind permission)

ABBREVIATIONS

UNLESS otherwise stated, all translations are my own. The Latin or Italian original will only be provided in the notes when a readily available modern edition does not exist. All biblical references are to the Vulgate: *Biblia Sacra iuxta vulgatam versionem*, ed. Robert Weber, 2 vols. (Stuttgart, 1969).

AESC	*Annales, Économies, Societés, Civilizations*
AFP	*Archivum Fratrum Praedicatorum*
AHSI	*Archivum Historicum Societatis Iesu*
Amab., *Cast*.	Luigi Amabile, *Fra T. Campanella ne'castelli di Napoli in Roma e in Parigi*. Naples: Murano, 1887.
Amab., *Cong*.	Luigi Amabile, *Fra T. Campanella, la sua congiura, i suoi processi e la sua pazzia*. Naples: Murano, 1882.
Amab., *Doc*. I, II	Luigi Amabile, *Fra T. Campanella: Documenti*, I (= Amab., *Cong*., III) and II (= Amab., *Cast*., II). Naples: Murano, 1882, 1887.
ASI	*Archivio Storico Italiano*
BeC	*Bruniana e Campanelliana*
BHR	*Bibliothèque d'Humanisme et Renaissance*
BU	*Biographie Universelle ancienne et moderne*
CHR	*Catholic Historical Review*
COD	*Conciliorum Oecumenicorum Decreta*
CT	*Concilium Tridentinum. Decretorum, Actorum etc.* Freiburg i. Br., 1901– .
DBI	*Dizionario Biografico degli Italiani*
DHI	*Dictionary of the History of Ideas*
DTC	*Dictionnaire de Théologie Catholique*
GCFI	*Giornale Critico di Filosofia Italiana*
GG	*Geschichtliche Grundbegriffe: Historisches Lexicon zur politisch-sozialen Sprache in Deutschland*. Ed. Otto Brunner, Werner Conze, and Reinhart Kosselleck. Stuttgart: Klett-Cotta, 1972–92.
GSLI	*Giornale Storico della Letteratura Italiana*
IPP	*Il Pensiero Politico*
JEH	*Journal of Ecclesiastical History*
JHI	*The Journal of the History of Ideas*
JWCI	*The Journal of the Warburg and Courtauld Institutes*
LF-*Autobi*.	Luigi Firpo et al., eds., *Autobiografie di filosofi*. Turin: G. Giappichelli, 1982.
LF-*Bibl*.	Luigi Firpo, *Bibliografia degli scritti di Tommaso Campanella*. Turin: Vincenzo Bona, 1940.
LF-*PP*	Luigi Firpo, "I primi processi campanelliani . . ."

LF-*RC*	Luigi Firpo, *Ricerche Campanelliane*. Florence: G. C. Sansoni, 1947.
LF-*Suppliz.*	Luigi Firpo, ed., *Il supplizio di Tommaso Campanella*. Rome: Salerno, 1985.
LF-*Tutte*	Luigi Firpo, ed., *Tutte le opere di Tommaso Campanella*. N.p.: Arnoldo Mondadori, 1954.
Mers.	Correspondance du P. Marin Mersenne, *Religieux minime*. Ed. Paul Tannery, Cornelis de Waard, and Réne Pintard. Paris: CNRS, 1936.
MPG	Migne, *Patrologia Graeca*
MPL	Migne, *Patrologia Latina*
NBG	*Nouvelle Biographie Général*
NDP	*Nuovi Documenti sui Processi di Tommaso Campanella*
NZfMW	*Neue Zeitschrift für Missionswissenschaft*
Op. GG	*Opere di Galileo Galilei*
Pauly-Wissowa	*Paulys Real-Encyclopädie der classischen Altertumswissenschaft*. Neue Bearbeitung begonnen von George Wissowa. Stuttgart, 1937
PP	*Past and Present*
RCSF	*Rivista Critica di Storia della Filosofia*
RF	*Rivista di Filosofia*
RFNs	*Rivista de Filosofia Neo-scolastica*
RQ	*Renaissance Quarterly*
RSF	*Rivista di Storia della Filosofia*
RSI	*Rivista Storica Italiana*
SCJ	*Sixteenth Century Journal*
SS	*Studi Storici*
TC-*AfP*	*Aforismi Politici con sommari*
TC-*AP*	*Articuli prophetales*
TC-*Apol.*	*Apologia pro Galileo*
TC-*Astr.*	*Astrologicorum libri vii*
TC-*AT*	*Atheismus Triumphatus seu Reductio ad religionem per scientiarum veritates . . . contra Antichristianismum Achitophellisticum*
TC-*AV*	*Antiveneti*
TC-*CA*	*Consultationes Aphoristicae*
TC-*Comm.*	"Commentaria." In *Opere letterarie di Tommaso Campanella*. Ed. Lina Bolzoni. Turin: UTET, 1977.
TC-*CS*	*La Città del Sole*
TC-*De gent.*	*De Gentilismo non retinendo*
TC-*DG*	*Documenta ad Gallorum nationem*
TC-*DMI*	*Idee politiche di Tommaso Campanella nel 1636, Due memoriali inediti*
TC-*DPI*	*Discorsi ai principi d'Italia*
TC-*DPLC*	*Dialogo politico contro Luterani e Calvinisti*. Lanciano: Carabba, 1911.

TC-*DSCM*	*Del senso delle cose e della magia*
TC-*DUGE*	*Discorsi universali del governo ecclesiastico per far una gregge e un pastor*
TC-*LASP*	"Liber apologeticus contra impugnantes institutum scholarum piarum"
TC-*Lett.*	*Tommaso Campanella: Lettere*
TC-*Med.*	*Medicinalium iuxta propria principia libri septem*
TC-*Meta.*	*Universalis philosophiae, seu Metaphysicarum rerum* . . . Paris, 1638. Repr., Turin, 1961.
TC-*Meta I–III.*	*Metafisica.* Ed. Giovanni di Napoli. 3 vols. Bologna, 1967.
TC-*Misc.*	*Tommaso Campanella (1568–1639): Miscellanea di studi nel 4° Centenario della sua nascita.* Naples, 1969.
TC-*MM*	*Monarchia messiae*
TC-*MM-Disc.*	*Discorsi della libertà, e della felice suggettione allo stato ecclesiastico*
TC-*MN*	*Le monarchie delle nationi*
TC-*MS*	*De monarchia hispanica*
TC-*MS*[1]	*La monarchia di Spagna: Prima stesura giovanile*
TC-*OC*	*Gli opuscoli del Tommaso Campanella*
TC-*Op. in.*	*Opuscoli inediti*
TC-*Op. Lat.*	*Opera Latina. Francofurti impresa annis 1617–1630.* 2 vols. Turin: Bottega D'Erasmo, 1975.
TC-*P*[1–3]	P^1 = "Poesie," P^2 = "Poetica," P^3 = "Poëtica," in *Tutte le opere di Tommaso Campanella*
TC-*Po*	*Poetica*
TC-*PR*[1]	"Disputatio in prologum instauratarum scientiarum ad scholas Christianas," in *Philosophiae realis libri quatuor*
TC-*PR*[3]	"Quaestiones super tertia parte suae philosophiae realis, quae est De politicis," in *Disputationum in quatuor partes suae Philosophiae realis libri quatuor*
TC-*PSD*	*Philosophia sensibus demonstrata*
TC-*QR*	*Quod reminiscentur et convertentur ad dominum universi fines terrae*
TC-*RC*	"Risposte alle censure dell'Ateismo Triunfato," in *Opuscoli inediti di Tommaso Campanella*
TC-*Risp.*	Risposte alle censure dell' "Ateismo Triunfato"
TC-*RPE*	*Realis philosophiae epilogisticae Partes Quatuor* (see TC-*OP. Lat.*, vol. 2)
TC-*Syn.*	*Syntagma de libris propriis et recta ratione studendi*
TC-*T*	*Theologia*
TC-*US*	*Gli ultimi scritti politici di Tommaso Campanella*
WA	*Luthers Werke.* Weimar, 1883– .

PREFACE

SINCE the nineteenth century and the perfervid period of nationalism, research on Campanella has pursued a few fairly discernible paths. First, scholars, particularly in the field of literature, have continued to worry the question as to the meaning of Campanella's apparent masterpiece, *The City of the Sun*, and the place it occupies in the corpus of his writings. Second, the more philosophically inclined have come to focus on Campanella's *Metaphysics*, the formal, systematic presentation of his thought, all in an effort to suggest its unity and even modernity. But a still more all-embracing question has come to confront students of the Calabrian reformer: that of his orthodoxy and to what extent a natural philosopher, perhaps a deist, was really a Christian. Here in this last respect the publications of the systematic statement of his theology, composed from 1613 to 1624, seem to have laid to rest the earlier doubts of those who place their confidence in a formal, comprehensive presentation of ideas as the most reliable expression of a man's thought. To the satisfaction of one school of Campanella's interpreters he emerges as thoroughly orthodox.[1]

In considering the vast corpus that constitutes his writings, we need to be clear as to our own intention regarding the approach we choose to pursue. Our desire is not to focus on the masterpiece or on either the systematic philosophical or theological statements in order to define what he may have meant in toto or in part, or as the part relates to the whole. Although an informed judgment must be made as to the unity or disunity, the catholicity or heterodoxy, the sincerity or dissimulation in Campanella's thought, the investigator is here not desirous of distilling the philosophical content out of his writings and thereby identifying him with a particular ideology or intellectual tradition. In contrast, historians inevitably ask a less abstract, more extrinsic question in their effort to situate and understand their subject within its historical context. The historian cannot identify the human subject as pure intellect nor its work

---

[1] Here especially as editor of the *Theologia* Romano Amerio, *Il sistema teologico di Tommaso Campanella* (Milan/Naples, 1972) and Giovanni di Napoli, *Tommaso Campanella filosofo della restaurazione cattolica* (Padua, 1947). While Amerio admits an earlier period of incredulity on Campanella's part, ending with a conversion in 1603, Di Napoli argues persuasively for his orthodoxy throughout and specifically against any period of juvenile waywardness. See his "L'eresia e i processi Campanelliani," in *Tommaso Campanella (1568–1639): Miscellanea di studi nel 4° centenario della sua nascita* (Naples, 1969), 169–258. For an example of the *Metaphysics*' importance, see its usage in Bernardino M. Bonansea, *Tommaso Campanella: Renaissance Pioneer of Modern Thought* (Washington, D.C., 1969). The most recent systematic study of the *Metaphysics*—Ruth Hagengruber, *Tommaso Campanella: Eine Philosophie der Ähnlichkeit* (Sankt Augustin: Academia Verlag, 1994)—came to my attention too late to be incorporated in the present study.

as an abstract monument of cerebration. Rather, he must view that subject as a thinking person expressive of will, passion, and commitment, as well as intellect, reacting to and perceiving his world with an intensity depending upon the particular individual and problem at issue. Thus, if we are to capture the synchronic meaning of Campanella for his age and how he reflects options and potentialities that ultimately failed to bear fruit, we must go beyond the diachronic meaning that would associate him with a particular philosophical tradition; we need to look more to his correspondence, his tracts, his occasional writings and statements wherein he engages and enters into controversy with his age.

In a letter of 1635 Campanella will himself make the distinction between his own formal, comprehensive intellectual statement represented by the *Metaphysics*, which he continued to prize as his enduring legacy, and all his other writings that he here designates as *aforistici*.[2] In short, we seek to confront Campanella where he emerges, in places less of his own choosing than that afforded by the formal philosophical statement. In doing so, we prefer to consider the engaged rather than the contemplative thinker. Neither the brief, enigmatic masterpiece nor the monumental, systematic statements, represented by both the *Metaphysics* and the *Theology*, can be ignored; yet they can be temporarily left to one side, their central import or particular details used as a reference or check to confirm, control, or contrast, all in order to permit a focus upon the extensive body of occasional, unsystematic writings that are at once more revealing of the engaged reformer both in a specific instance and of his historical context. Thus, if it is true that something more than intellect describes the meaning of a man for his age, then a fortiori such pertains to our present subject, Campanella, *l'eterno imprudente*,[3] the born propagandist in the most profound and original sense of the word, a man who is at once all passion, all communication; in the assessment of money, sword, and the tongue for the shaping of human affairs he will characteristically assert the supremacy of the last, the tongue or language, in every instance. In short by weighing the repetition of images, issues, and themes, by sensing the personal commitment to an argument, by appraising the sustained vectors in his overall

---

[2] TC-*Lett*., 320. In the course of the sixteenth century the aphoristic mode enjoyed a revival first with Guicciardini and then later with the rising tide of Tacitism, reflecting the interest and dissimulation of princes. The very use of the term here for purposes of definition and Campanella's earlier incremental musings on past political practices, *Aforismi politici*, together prove revealing. For the word signifies a defining statement, a distinctive feature, a clue. Aphoristic literature attempts "to formulate evaluations of man and society on the basis of symptoms and clues, a man and a society that are sick, *in crisis*," wherein even "crisis" as a Hippocratic term reaffirms the medical analogue and source. See Carlo Ginzburg, *Clues, Myths, and the Historical Method* (Baltimore, 1989), 124; Richard Tuck, *Philosophy and Government, 1572–1652* (Cambridge, 1993), 34, 43–46, 65–66, 76.

[3] Di Napoli, "L'eresia," 233.

thought, we hope to arrive at a more accurate appreciation of the man's relationship to his age. For it is not what a philosopher formally states and includes within his system of thought that must prevail in our judgment of his work and intent, but what he repeatedly and functionally affirms.

Not reflection and contemplation, productive of the formal philosophical *summa*, but rather assertion, persuasion, indeed proclamation distinguished the majority of Campanella's writings in his engagement with the issues and problems of the age. Yet this is not to deny that he aspired to and realized a formal, abstract, intellectual statement, promoted not only by his comprehensive mind and surging drive for unity but also by the accidents of his own tragic existence, allowing him half a lifetime for reflection in prison, withdrawn from society. Nevertheless his commitment to freedom, most immediately his own personal freedom and, more generally, freedom of thought, shifted the import of his work to the "aphoristic." In this irrepressibly aspiring personality the life of his age is seen as an intersection of crises astronomical and intellectual, political and religious. Prison afforded this Prometheus a vantage point from which to reflect and pass judgment upon the issues that beset European civilization as it approached what in fact proved to be the great watershed in its own development, yet what appeared to Campanella as an ideal, universal fulfillment. And while in Campanella's mirror, that enchanted glass of the mind, the great forces of the age move each to a critical turning point, he defined each often with cunning insight, yet his Christian apocalyptic stance did not allow him to see beyond the turn. Instead, it provided him with a telos. This study seeks to comprehend the interaction between the trajectory of Campanella's questing, perceptive vision and the West at its own most decisive juncture in the first third of the seventeenth century. Through the lens of his mind may be brought into focus the salient issues of the age to be analyzed in terms of a universalist imperative.

Our line of approach is dictated by a question that is historical, not philosophical. We are asking not for the precise definition, coherence, or validity of Campanella's total corpus or part thereof but, rather, how this profound, encyclopedic mind identifies, understands, and relates to his age. This perception of early modern Europe and how Campanella impinges upon his times constitute the goal of this study. His thought reflects and expresses the crisis of the West at the beginning of the seventeenth century on five different levels as major issues: (1) the dismantling of the Aristotelian establishment and the reconstruction of science; (2) an anti-Machiavellism that seeks the revitalization of the Christian religion in its political role; (3) the realization of universal empire through the vehicle first of Habsburg Spain and then later of Bourbon France; (4) the capping of this world order with the Roman universalism of papal theocracy and the ecclesiastical state; and (5) the opportunity afforded by the intersection of America's discovery with the invention of the printing press to pursue world evangelization on a total, global scale and thus to realize that haunting Johannine prophecy (John 10:16) with its apocalyptic/eschatological ring that there will be one sheepfold and one shepherd.

Of the five contemporary problems that will be defined as major issues or crises the economic/social dimension has not been numbered. There are several reasons for such an exclusion. First, a German Marxist study has exhaustively and quite effectively treated this largely submerged aspect of Campanella's thought.[4] Here Campanella appears less the dreamer than tradition has made him out to be; not only was he the leader of the Calabrian revolt of 1599 but its goals were more expressly social and economic, less astrological, religious, and even political than we have been led to believe. The extremely scattered and oblique nature of the evidence, however, suggests that if economic and social concerns constitute a major issue for Campanella, they belong to another order than the five more obvious ones that we have already defined, and that we are justified in subordinating and assimilating the economic/social to the five. Second, and more substantively, no matter how great and fundamental the economic and social issues are for understanding Campanella and the Europe of his time, they do not constitute a crisis as it is considered here: as a growing tension concerning a fundamental problem that achieves a discernible resolution in the course of the century.

Beginning in 1599 with his arrest and imprisonment, a new period of protracted suffering intrudes upon Campanella wherein perforce he must surrender his role of actor and agent for that of critic and prophet. The validity of this distinction draws support from the generally recognized belief that there is in fact a watershed in Campanella's life dating to the years 1599–1602/6 from the Calabrian rebellion through his trial to imprisonment and to a possible conversion or, at the least, accommodation to the powers of this world. While disagreement prevails as to the exact nature and meaning of his apparent conversion in 1606, most scholars now agree that there occurred a conversion to a more explicit Christianity and certainly to a more prudential posture. Such a shift suggests, as the main line of contemporary scholarship argues, that prior to his trial and imprisonment, the Christianity of the youthful Dominican was nominal, his temperament rebellious, and his preeminent intellectual interests those of the natural philosopher. In the trauma of his own life crisis these qualities did not suddenly disappear but were transformed into a new intellectual amalgam, gradually imparting a different attitude toward the world. With the failure of force to bring in the new aeon, a strategy of persuasion, exhortation, and admonition was to be pursued together with an updated astrology.

Consequently the present study will focus on Campanella and his work after 1599—the mature Campanella—but will not ignore the earlier develop-

---

[4] Gisela Bock, *Thomas Campanella: Politisches Interesse und philosophische Spekulation* (Tübingen, 1974).

ments in his thought. Likewise his social/economic critique will be considered but as an undercurrent to the larger, more expressed issues of the political and the religious. The embattled European world upon which the Calabrian gazed constituted for him a whole, a unity adumbrating a universal oneness on the eve of its actual shattering and dissolution. The total import of Campanella's life and thought represents a massive effort to drive to a new and consummate level the realization of a unified European political/ecclesiastical order, its expanding learning, and the global extension of the Catholic religion.

More difficult than the problem of the texts to be emphasized and the period of our concentration is the question of the prisoner's credibility, his precise intention. Is he truly a Christian convert or an arrant dissembler? Furthermore, is he to be seen preeminently as a magician, a patriot, an astrologer, an orthodox Christian, or a deist? In varying degrees he could be all of these. Here whatever perspective is adopted must be based upon an informed judgment of the man, as his ultimate priorities emerge from the context of his engaged writings. Scholarship has come to transcend the view that Campanella's works after 1599 are but a continuous simulation. If laced with opportunism, they reveal an adherence to a number of long-range principles in keeping with the integrity of the man's life: the realization of a single, evidently Christian world order; the dismantling of Aristotelianism; the fusion of religion with politics and of religion with science; and the *libertas philosophandi*. Ultimately it is his self-understanding as a new messiah that will establish his essential and continuing integrity. For whatever his role-playing and simulation, they are always controlled and justified, in his own terms, by a transcendent sense of mission and by the continuities and essential consistencies of his beliefs.

The picture emerging is that of a friar who never lost his confidence in and fascination for a natural philosophy of his own devising—a philosophy with dimensions religious, astronomical, and magical to which Christian theology and the Roman Catholic Church might provide an obvious shell and shortly a meaningful sounding board whereby it might resonate and enfold all men. The resulting Christian heterodoxy is an amalgam of science and religion, an expression of late Renaissance thought. But which predominates—the new philosophy or the weight of theological tradition? Or is this "une question mal posée"? The analytic, compartmentalized mind of a later age would force choice and subordination upon what the early seventeenth century experienced as a synthetic, single reality. Perhaps Frank Manuel, in his treatment of utopias, is not far off the mark when he claims that Campanella appears as a Christian in the universal spirit of the current pansophic tradition wherein science and religion strive to achieve a new synthesis for the spiritual renovation of humankind.[5] Yet in context the hard question must still be asked.

---

[5] Frank E. and Fritze P. Manuel, *Utopian Thought in the Western World* (Cambridge, Mass., 1979), 288.

Briefly, a further query. Beyond the abundance of material and the intense, sustained argument with its own essential coherence, why the strangely bewitched mirror of Campanella's mind in which to consider early-seventeenth-century Europe at the crossroads? For all its obscurely magical and astrological intricacies, so difficult for a modern reader to appreciate, Campanella's entire intellectual endeavor expresses an effort to impose a distinctive order and direction upon the major issues and forces of the age different from that which was shortly to prevail with the new Galilean science and the Leviathan state. In the process of identifying and engaging these issues and imparting in some instances something of his own, he manages to mobilize and deploy for the last time many of the salient principles of late medieval and Renaissance culture, often cast in a curiously modern hue and aligned with the new forces of the age. Indeed modern and antique, new and old juxtapose violently in the person of this reformer, who combines an encyclopedic comprehensiveness of intellect with an amazing intensity of will. He strives to destabilize the regnant forces of what he identifies as tyranny, sophistry, and hypocrisy and to shake the world into a new order.

Yes, the world—both as the universe astronomically conceived and as the given order of all things, globally evident and contemporaneous with our author in the present envelope of time—would be transformed, but on very different lines from those envisaged and sought by Tommaso Campanella.

Only after this work was fairly much completed along the lines of contextualizing the five major issues did it begin to become apparent that the subject required some chapter or section of a biographical nature in order to provide background. For while the Italian intellectual world can hail Campanella as the most outstanding philosophic mind between Ficino at the end of the fifteenth century and Vico at the beginning of the eighteenth, in the English-speaking world he is less than a household word: perhaps because he occupies a position that is so late in the Renaissance and yet strongly suggestive of the baroque, he falls through the interstices of academic programs. Indeed he is hardly known through his important, recognized utopia even by scholars in the field. Thus what we have sketched here almost as an afterthought cannot begin to claim the status of a formal biography. Such an undertaking would need to address more fully the magical, the dissimulative as well as those millennial dimensions, evident in a Fra Dolcino, a Jan of Leyden, even a David Koresh, dimensions that inevitably inhere in varying degrees to any leader of an apocalyptic community. At least, however, the present, relatively conservative portrayal may provide the agent of all this cerebration with a measure of flesh and blood and at the same time afford a context as well as a degree of continuity for the complex development and reception of his thought.

• • •

Besides acquiring an expectable number of debts in the course of living with Campanella, I have also experienced the ground changing beneath me in the long trajectory of this work's composition. For what had started as a rather lonely, curious pursuit has at its end been drawn into a confluence of intellectual, scholarly interests that gives new attention to the Calabrian. For although not entirely neglected in Anglophone scholarship, as evinced in a notable chapter by the Manuels and another by Frances Yates,[6] Campanella missed the opportunity of being presented to an English-speaking readership by such a distinguished scholar as Paul Kristeller, who decided to omit him from his *Eight Italian Philosophers of the Renaissance* as too political and too diffuse in his philosophy;[7] similarly and more recently Robert Bireley also chose not to include Campanella in his *The Counter-Reformation Prince: Anti-Machiavellianism or Catholic Statecraft in Early Modern Europe* as being again too idiosyncratic, utopian, and universalist for this historian's more restricted purpose. Yet in roughly the same period outside Italy Campanella's politics, medicine, and natural philosophy have been the subjects of individual, extensive treatment.

In Italy modern interest in Campanella has, however, never languished. Here anyone attempting to treat the unencompassable thought and career of Campanella must address the immense, if very different, achievements of two giants of scholarship—Luigi Amabile and Luigi Firpo. While not a professional historian, Amabile provided in the late nineteenth century that vast quarry of Campanellan materials through an impressive mining of European archives, which any prospector on this difficult terrain needs to study carefully; his rendering of an exhaustively detailed biography nevertheless lacked structure and suffered from the overly extended claims as to Campanella's dissimulation. But even more considerable is the contribution of the late Luigi Firpo, who in a long life of devotion to Campanellan scholarship, through his formidable bibliographical talents, mapped out the otherwise impassable landscape of Campanella's tangled productivity in manuscript and early imprints, thus providing the necessary guide for any others venturing upon the subject. So great here is the debt to his *Bibliografia* alone, whatever the need for its *aggiornamento*, that this writer at one point contemplated dedicating the present work to him, in memoriam, only to reject the act as too presumptuous. The continuity and advance of Campanellan studies within Italy and the recovery of interest in Campanella on an international scale draw sustenance from Firpo's splendid enterprise.

Yet what has most contributed to the abrupt burst of scholarly attention

---

[6] Frances A. Yates, *Giordano Bruno and the Hermetic Tradition* (Chicago/London, 1964), 360–97.

[7] Personal communication, May 23, 1992, and two conversations.

derives from the impressive talents and energies of two young scholars—Lina Bolzoni and Germana Ernst. Through her profound appreciation of and insight into Campanella's poetry Lina Bolzoni has given new dimensions to the subject and in her forthcoming edition of the *Commentaria* she will present that longest single work of Campanella. For her part Germana Ernst through her relentless archival, critical, textual studies has blazed a luminous trail of scholarly achievement beginning with the *Articuli prophetales*, proceeding to a number of archival discoveries, and culminating most recently with a shortly to appear critical edition of the *Monarchia di Spagna*, considered by the present author at the inception of his own studies as something inhumanly demanding and impossible to expect. In short my indebtedness in this respect remains considerable, although she has had no part in whatever inaccuracies and misjudgments occur in this book. Despite her own protests Dr. Ernst has more than anyone else inherited, through her archival sleuthing, the mantle of Luigi Firpo. The growing momentum in Campanella studies culminated only this past year in the founding of the new review *Bruniana e Campanelliana* with Germana Ernst and Eugenio Canone as coeditors, but its first number appeared too late for this study to benefit.

In ways direct and indirect I have benefited from the conversation and counsel of my own immediate colleagues Lucia Binotti, Melissa Bullard, Lloyd Kramer, and Michael McVaugh. From my former student, John McManamon, I have ruthlessly plundered an unpublished paper whose subject I had earlier suggested. I am indebted to Ross Ettle Pemberton, current graduate student in Renaissance history, for bringing initial order to the bibliography and abbreviations and to George Garrett in Classics for commenting upon my Latin translations. I continue to be grateful for the generosity and interest of William J. Bouwsma, who volunteered to read the body of the book even before I had thought of adding a biographical section. I owe special thanks to Frances Huemer and to John Beldon Scott for their valuable advice and assistance with the illustrations. To Michael J. B. Allen for his willingness to read section 3 of chapter 7 and to T. C. Price Zimmermann for guidance at a critical moment, I remain indebted. In more than one instance, I appreciated and benefited from the prompt responses of Dr. Leonard E. Boyle, prefect, Biblioteca Apostolica Vaticana. To my two readers, one unknown and the other Anthony Grafton, I wish here to express my gratitude.

I wish to acknowledge the kind permissions of those journals and publications in which earlier versions of chapters have previously appeared as articles: *Journal of Medieval and Renaissance Studies* for "Tommaso Campanella and the End of the Renaissance," 20 (1990): 157–74; *Renaissance Quarterly* for "Tommaso Campanella and Jean de Launoy: The Controversy over Aristotle and His Reception in the West," 43 (1990): 529–50; *Central European History* for "'Ehe Türckisch als Bäpstisch': Lutheran Reflections on the Problem of Empire, 1623–28," 20 (1987): 4–8, 12–17; the Johns Hopkins University Press for "On the Rearming of Heaven: The Machiavellism of Tommaso Campanella," *Journal of the History of Ideas* 49 (1988): 387–404; Gutersloher Verlagshaus Gerd Mohn for "Tommaso Campanella's Military Sermon before Richelieu at Conflans—8 June 1636," in *Die Reformation in Deutschland und Europa* (Göttingen, 1993), 553–74; the University of North Carolina Press for "Campanella, America, and World Evangelization," in *America in European Consciousness 1493–1750* (Chapel Hill, 1995), 243–71; Istituti Editoriali e Poligrafici Internazionali (Pisa/Roma, 1997) for "Campanella on Freedom of Thought," *Bruniana e Campanelliana*, 2 (1996): 165–77.

On two occasions I have enjoyed grants from the history department at UNC/CH as well two grants from our Institute of the Arts and Humanities on campus, two grants from the John Carter Brown Library, one summer grant from the Newberry Library, and a one-term grant from the Folger Shakespeare Library. I also wish to thank the staff of Davis Library (UNC/CH) and especially its Interlibrary Loan/Borrowing under the careful direction of Rebecca Breazeale. And without the stalwart efforts and sustained patience of Mattie Hackney the manuscript would have never emerged.

Finally, for their long friendship, supportive collegiality, and ever reliable criticism on various aspects of this and other work, in all matters and at all times, I wish to recognize Peter Iver Kaufman, G. Mallary Masters, and Ronald G. Witt. To them I dedicate this book.

Tommaso Campanella
and the Transformation
of the World

Prologue

NAPLES AND EUROPE IN 1601

IN A CELL of the Castel Nuovo in Naples, June 4–5, 1601, the long ordeal of a Dominican friar that had begun with his arrest twenty months earlier and had seen repeated interrogations and tortures at last reached its climax—a climax marked by the dreadful *la veglia* or "awakener": the victim is suspended in such a way that only his arms and shoulder muscles prevent his body from coming to rest on a set of wooden spikes; eventually, however, he tires and must allow the spikes to gash his buttocks and thighs until he can once more raise himself. Thus between these positions he must move back and forth. In this instance the torture was being applied in order to determine whether the prisoner was actually mad or simply feigning madness. After forty hours, near death, yet spiritually unbroken, his simulation of madness undiscovered, our prisoner was cut down. According to canon law his insanity had been established: therefore he could not be executed. He was safe—quite safe, for he would remain in prison to write and think for the next quarter century. The man was Tommaso Campanella.

Of what was the prisoner accused? Inspired with messianic purpose and apocalyptic expectation, Campanella had led against the Spanish authorities a popular revolt that included peasants as well as a handful of displaced nobles and at one point involved the cooperation of the Turkish fleet, all in an effort to establish an ideal state, a democratic/theocratic republic as harbinger of a new aeon. The imminence of the year 1600, as well as 1603, the occurrence of a number of natural disasters, the deep-seated popular mood of miracle, magic, and divine expectancy had all contributed to the momentary success of the revolt—one in a series of popular uprisings in the Kingdom of Naples that would be suppressed by the Spanish authorities. The locus of this one had been Calabria.

Calabria is not the first place a historian considers when reflecting upon Europe at the beginning of the seventeenth century. Constituting the toe of the Italian boot, the province could nevertheless claim a glorious past: land of the apocalyptic prophecies of Joachim of Fiore, Calabria was also the country of Pythagoras and Parmenides—the source of truly the first philosophy. Since the early sixteenth century the province together with Naples, the most populous city of Europe, and the so-called Kingdom of the Two Sicilies, had come to be included in the burgeoning global empire of the Spanish Habsburgs. It was a world of dynastic politics, aspiring principalities, and creaking empires, far removed from the national states of a later era. Nor did the Spanish presence in the Italian peninsula limit itself to the Neapolitan lands but included the duchy of Milan in the central Lombard plain. From thence the Spanish imperial tentacles extended northward down the Rhine and eastward into the Germanies of the Holy Roman Empire to link up with and affirm the Madrid–Vienna axis of family relations between the Spanish and Austrian branches of the Habsburg dynasty. Madrid's effort to involve its Austrian cousins in its own protracted struggle to suppress the Dutch revolt, Spain's Vietnam, would prove abortive.

The resources of Habsburg hegemony with its Castilian core and global reach were to be found in the finest infantry of Europe (when it was not mutinying for lack of pay), the Jesuits in their inner European mission to reconquer the Continent for Catholicism, and the returns from the American mines whose receipts would reach their peak in the course of the decade. The enemies of the Habsburg hegemony were the Turk, the Protestants, and France. The last of these, France, the most consolidated of territorial states, seemed encircled by the Spanish/Habsburg colossus; yet the French realm dislocated this encirclement at several points. In 1600 France was beginning to recover from almost forty years of civil/religious wars. This recovery was first registered in Rome, the barometer of European political life, in those successive conclaves which, when selecting one cardinal from their midst to the vicariate of Christ, now recognized in France an effective counterweight to Spanish bullying: the signal went out to the rest of Europe that henceforth Madrid was not to have everything its own way.

Between Spanish Milan and Spanish Naples sprawled the ecclesiastical state of the popes, a territorial state among other European territorial states as Thomas Hobbes himself would shortly recognize. The Rome of the high Counter Reformation breathed a mood of restored confidence in its universal mission. The intellectual/political context of the ecclesiastical capital was hardly conducive to the promotion of a self-critical review and revision of the prevailing philosophy. Indeed the atmosphere of Rome conveyed a peculiar mixture of triumphalism laced with a hard defensiveness only a few years earlier made manifest in a reaffirmation and recommitment to the preeminence of Aristotle.[1] Among the casualties were Pucci, Patrizi, and the poet-philosopher Giordano Bruno, who suffered the spectacular death of being burned at the stake in the Campo dei Fiori on February 17, 1600. The only eyewitness report that we have of his execution related that when, in his last moments before expiring, a crucifix on an extended pole was presented before his gaze, he averted his face in contempt.[2] Linked in the same condemnation

---

[1] On this point and the purge of Platonists in the last decade of the century, see Luigi Firpo, "Filosofia italiana e controriforma," *RF* 41 (1950): 150–73.

[2] Mario D'Addio, *Il pensiero politico di Gaspare Scioppio e il Machiavellismo dei Seicento* (Milan, 1962), 25–31, esp. 29.

of Bruno's works were those of another poet-philosopher as well as Dominican friar, Tommaso Campanella.

Imprisonment represented no new experience for Campanella, nor would the present detention even be the last occasion for his confinement, yet it certainly proved to be the longest—a period of twenty-seven years. Shifted among Naples' worst dungeons, sometimes in chains, often in darkness, the man survived. His very survival not to mention his immense productivity remains a monument to the will's triumph and the mind's freedom, whatever the obscurities and tergiversations of his formal philosophy. The astonishing literary output of these years attests to a prodigious memory, a comprehensive, questing mind, and the porous nature of seventeenth-century European prisons. Five decades later another literary giant of an entirely different sort, suffering from a different kind of confinement, would convincingly affirm that the mind is its own place and in itself can make a hell of heaven, a heaven of hell. Similarly, in his own soaring affirmation of the mind's power and place Campanella reveals a transcendent confidence:

> Man lives in a double world: according to the mind he is contained by no physical space and by no walls, but at the same time he is in heaven and on earth, in Italy, in France, in America, wherever the mind's thrust penetrates and extends by understanding, seeking, mastering. But indeed according to the body he exists not, except in only so much space as is least required, held fast in prison and in chains to the extent that he is not able to be in or to go to the place attained by his intellect and will, nor to occupy more space than defined by the shape of his body; while with the mind he occupies a thousand worlds.[3]

[3] TC-*Meta.*, III, 156 (XV.ii.v).

PART ONE

Biographical Context

Chapter I

TOWARD THE MAKING OF A PROPHET

OF THE *REGNO*: CALABRIA AND NAPLES

The traditional *Regno* of the Italian peninsula had decayed over the centuries from being possibly the foremost state of medieval Europe when under the Hohenstaufen emperor, Frederick II, *Stupor mundi*, to the feudal confusion suffered under the Angevins, followed by an apparent rally under the Aragonese after 1442. Subsequent to 1503 under a Spanish viceroy, the *Viceregno* comprised all of the Italian boot south of Rome; in the 1590s it had a population of approximately two and a half million. The richest and most agriculturally productive of the kingdom's nine regions or twelve provinces hovered around the city of Naples; the poorest, most rock-ridden, and most pastoral was Calabria in the toe of Italy. As in the papal states, banditry thrived throughout the kingdom and seems to have peaked in the early 1590s. In Calabria the communes could not meet the fiscal quotas imposed, and the ever-menacing Turks raided the province in 1595. For Calabrians the magnetism of the big city with its allurement of apparently cheap food and ready employment came to be exercised less by Naples than by Messina and Palermo. At the turn of the century one-fifth of the kingdom's total population could be found in impoverished Calabria, where overtaxation figured as a factor in the decline of the silk industry.[1]

At the turn of the century Naples represented the supreme case in Europe of a city undergoing massive urbanization without development or industrialization. The concentration of population, bloated by provincials escaping baronial aggrandizement, promoted and announced a growing tension between city and country.[2] Beginning in 1530 an exploitative baronage, general to the kingdom, started to forsake their country estates for their Neapolitan town houses in order to live near the court of the viceroy; when the expense of urban existence proved too much, they would return to their country estates to oppress more effectively their peasantry and tenantry. The city's most renowned captive would refer to this rhythm in their lives as "running round in the same

[1] Peter Burke, "Southern Italy in the 1590s: Hard Times or Crisis?" in *The European Crisis of the 1590s: Essays in Comparative History*, ed. Peter Clark (London, 1985), 177–90, esp. 178–85.

[2] John A. Marino, "Economic Idylls and Pastoral Realities: The 'Trickster Economy' in the Kingdom of Naples," *Comparative Studies in Society and History* 24 (1982): 211–34, esp. 226–27.

circle."[3] Yet at least for the more prudent members of the nobility, aristocratic families usually lived in Naples only when their children were of marriageable age or when litigation required their presence. Otherwise their forceful presence on their fiefs remained in evidence.[4]

By whatever account, Naples, Neapolis, the "New City," founded originally by Greek settlers, was one of the greatest cities of late Renaissance Europe and for that matter of the world. Its population exceeding three hundred thousand, Naples rivaled Paris and with Constantinople represented the two most densely populated cities of the Mediterranean—urban monsters, great gorging parasites. Braudel characterizes Naples as being in its simmering disorder, in its excessiveness evident in consumption, in poverty, and in sewage, "the most astonishing, the most fantastically picaresque city in the world."[5] More sedately and reassuringly, a contemporary guidebook for the many avid visitors and tourists who flocked there, the *Descrittione del regno di Napoli* of Enrico Bacco, first published in 1616 and passing through six subsequent printings by 1671, celebrated the classical past, the many kings of diverse nations, the gardens, the churches, and above all the fortresses of what had by then become a baroque city.[6] Of all the architectural delights of the great city, Castel Nuovo most commanded the eye of any visitor. Crouched at the bay's edge, its massive walls seemingly evoked from the watery depths, Castel Nuovo had been built by the first Angevin ruler, Charles I, and became the royal residence. Situated nearby directly to the south and again at the bay's edge stood the supporting fortress of Castel dell'Ovo. Beyond this complex of the two fortresses and the intervening arsenal, the greatest of Spanish viceroys, Pedro de Toledo, had in the first third of the sixteenth century extended the city westward, rebuilt the walls, paved most of the streets, and built the avenue named after him, Via Toledo. Along with this enterprise he expanded the ramparts of the city up the slopes of the Monte S. Martino to Castel San Elmo;[7] enlarged and strengthened, the fortress, glowering downward, sought more to control than to defend Naples. San Elmo constituted the fearsome third of that triangle of pain which would define a life.[8]

For the impact of this splendid city and its nether provinces upon the strenuous, late sixteenth-century visitor we are not dependent upon the contriving of the informed imagination. That oft-quoted, observant traveler, Sir George

[3] Burke, "Southern Italy," 178–87.

[4] Tommaso Astarita, *The Continuity of Feudal Power: The Caracciolo di Brienza in Spanish Naples* (Cambridge, 1992), 234.

[5] Fernand Braudel, *The Mediterranean and the Mediterranean World in the Age of Philip II* (New York, 1972), 1:345–47.

[6] Ronald G. Gusto, "Preface" and "Historical Introduction" to Enrico Bacco et al., *Naples: An Early Guide* (New York, 1991), xiii–xv, liii–liv.

[7] Bacco, *Naples*, 19, explains that Elmo or Ermo, a corruption of Erasmo, obtained its name from its close situation near an ancient church dedicated there to S. Erasmo.

[8] Ibid., xl, l.

Sandys, youngest son of the archbishop of York, in his return to Europe from the Levant by way of Sicily during July 1612 provides us with contemporary impressions of the area. To the young, fastidious English gentleman no people on earth professing Christ seemed more uncivil than the vulgar Calabrians. The omnipresent tarantula that left its victim hooting and dancing; the thieves and murderers stifling overland travel; the pervasive mulberries, infinite in number, which made the province the chief silk producer of Italy; the popular interest in magic; the watchtowers, alert to the threatened incursions of the Turks, ever lurking off the coast—all made a not altogether favorable impression upon the visitor. Whatever the dangers presented by the Turkish presence, prudence dictated ordinary passage to be by sea and as Sandys' galley nosed its way up the coast first to Paola and then to Salerno, he was brought to the Bay of Naples.[9]

First of man-made features to capture the eye of our traveler, the triangle of fortresses presented itself, knitting together the shore, the ramparts, and the surrounding arc of mountains, each of its three members reworked within recent memory.[10] Thereupon he quickly senses the pulse of Naples:

> But now the onely regall Citie of Italy, her royall Court is completely furnished with Princes and Commanders: her Tribunals are pestered with clamorous aduocates, and litiguous clients: her streets with citizens and forrainers, in pursuite of their delights and profits: whose eares are daily enured to the sound of the drumme and fife, as their eyes to the bounding of steeds, and glistering of armours. So that she seemeth at this day to affoord you all things but her former vacancy. Being first the receptable of Philosophie, then of Mules, and lastly of the souldiery.[11]

And again he appreciates the dignity of the city's architecture, the rhythms in its life, and the predilections of its population:

> Naples is the pleasantest of Cities, if not the most beautifull: the building all of free stone, the streetes are broad and paued with bricke, vaulted underneath for the conueiance of the sulledge; served with water by fountaines and conduits. Her pallaces are faire, but her Temples stately, and gorgeously furnished; whereof, adding Chappels, and Monasteries within her walles, and without, (for the suburbes do equall the City in magnitude) she containeth three thousand. It is supposed that there are in her three hundred thousand men; besides women and children. Their habite is generally Spanish: the Gentry delight much in great horses, whereupon they praunce continually through the streets. The number of carosses is incredible that are kept in this City, as of the sedges not unlike to

---

[9] George Sandys, *A Relation of a Journey Begun AD 1610* (London: W. Barrett, 1615), 250–53.
[10] Ibid., 253–55.
[11] Ibid., 256.

horse-litters, but carried by men. Thefe waite for fares in the corners of streetes as watermen do at our wharfes, wherein those that will not foote it in the heate, are borne (if they please vnseene) about the City. None do weare weapons, without speciall admittance, but the souldiery. Their women are beholding to Nature for much beauty, or to cunning arte for a not to be discerned impostury: howsoever, they excell in favour which arte can have no hand in. They are elegantly clothed, and silke is a work-day weare for the wife of the meanest artificer. They are not altogether so strictly guarded as in other places of Italie: perhaps lesse tempted in regard of the number of allowed Curtizans, there being of them in the City about thirty thousand.[12]

While briefly noting such destabilizing factors as a faction-ridden nobility and the involvement of popes in the election of Neapolitan kings, Sandys found most sinister the strategic garrisoning of a considerable Spanish soldiery upon the kingdom's population, "who may obey perhaps with as much love, as gally-slaves obey those that have deprived them of their fortunes and libertie."[13]

But such outward features failed to conceal the more profound, long-current political, social, and economic forces that determined the life of the *Regno*. Accompanying the repeated revolts, ominously associated with the explosive energies of the huddled, urban masses of Naples itself, developed the constant slippage of wealth and power to a well-established landed aristocracy. For with the possible exception of Pedro de Toledo's viceregal regime (1532–53), the Spanish government acquiesced in the already existing predominance of the Neapolitan aristocracy and effected no basic social or economic changes. Whereas elsewhere in western Europe public officials were coming to prevail, in the *Regno* Neapolitan landlords grew in their exercise of judicial and administrative powers. The public sale of lands in the form of villages and towns, the alienation of taxes, the disposal of titles, jurisdictions, and shares of public revenue all enhanced the position of the landed aristocracy. From 1590 to 1620 fiscal pressures increased but not upon the nobility. Indirect taxes grew on both exports and internal consumption to the virtual extinction of Neapolitan exports by the late seventeenth century. Habsburg needs, increased by the Thirty Years' War, intensified this fiscal pressure, accelerating and complicating the downturn in the entire southern Italian economy evident since 1580.[14] Most taxes had to be approved by the General Parliament of the kingdom, which comprised only the barons and the representatives of the city of Naples. Both Parliament and city council remained thoroughly under the control of the baronage. Of this last, constituted by six *Seggi*, only one was

[12] Ibid., 259.
[13] Ibid., 257.
[14] Antonio Calabria, *The Cost of Empire: The Finances of the Kingdom of Naples in the Time of Spanish Rule* (Cambridge, 1991), 130–32.

representative of the people and could always be outvoted by a simple majority of four of the five aristocratic members. While the Church and its clergy enjoyed their traditional exemptions, the inhabitants of the city of Naples paid no direct tax, which helps explain the demographic explosion that the city experienced during the Spanish period. The fiscal burden fell on the merchant, the peasant, and the ordinary consumer. Almost masterfully, by its compromises with the nobility and by its increasing fiscality at the very time of growing depression, the Spanish government served to draw money away from the more productive enterprises and redistribute it upwards in the social hierarchy, thereby accentuating injustices and inequities.[15]

Beginning in the last decades of the sixteenth century and culminating in the great explosion of 1647, Naples suffered a number of revolts. Such uprisings were usually the result of popular reaction to an increased tax or shortage of bread—a distemper more social than of political or constitutional significance, which could normally be cured by alternate, imported doses of Sicilian grain and Spanish soldiery. In the insurrection of 1585 popular violence came to focus on the people's representative, the master of the merchant guild, accused of private speculation in the city's grain supply. To him fell the grim fate of being lynched, mutilated, and ritualistically cannibalized. In this instance the uprising had manifested an ominous ability on the part of the people to mobilize themselves and even to articulate a political demand for equality of representation on the city council. Thus the authorities had all the greater reason to effect their brutal suppression. The ferocious reprisals and punishments of the restored government evoked from the Venetian ambassador the exclamation: "Such is the terror among the people . . . that I don't think anyone will try anything new for any reason whatsoever."[16] Both for Naples and for the *Regno* in general, events would shortly disprove the judgment of the Serenissima's agent.

Calabrian Beginnings

Stilo, Catanzaro, Nicastro, and all Calabria itself—of Byzantine and Norman, of Saracen and Angevin intrusions compacted—how many centuries of strife, contention, bitter hatreds, and spiritual exaltation therein layered: the land of Pythagoras, Timaeus, and Abbot Joachim, once fertile and abundant, now harsh, austere, savage, yet capable of nurturing still other sons of intellectual passion.

To Geronimo and Caterina Martello on Sunday, September 5, 1568, in a humble dwelling outside the walls of Stilo, a son was born, who seven days

---

[15] Astarita, *Feudal Power*, 9, 14, 203, 217–31; Rosario Villari, *The Revolt of Naples* (Oxford, 1993), 7–8.
[16] Villari, *Revolt*, 26–27; idem, "Naples: The Insurrection in Naples of 1585," in *The Late Italian Renaissance, 1525–1630*, ed. Eric Cochrane (New York, 1970), 305–30, esp. 315–23.

later would be baptized in the parish church of S. Biaggio, Giovan Domenico Campanella, but shortly better to be known by his Dominican name, Tommaso. Although his father was an illiterate cobbler, the child early manifested a keen intelligence, a thirst for learning, and an astonishing memory; he readily absorbed the rudiments of grammar and the catechism as well as fitful exposures to available scraps of learning. According to local legend the boy, too poor to pay for his studies, would eavesdrop at the school window and when one of his more fortunate playmates should falter in his recitation, the young, irrepressible Tommaso would seek to prompt him. Distinguished by both precocity and poverty, he would later in a letter to a high-placed ecclesiastic contrast the crushing adversity of his early circumstances with the rich and full endowments of a Pico della Mirandola to whom he had been compared.[17] Indeed his Calabrian roots and context in the last third of the sixteenth century richly endowed the lad with the long-standing evils of the province: "feudal exploitation, Spanish oppression, Turkish incursions, prevalence of monkish idleness, the record of recent Waldensian massacres, recurrent famine, earthquakes, misery."[18]

Both an important event and an important decision marked his passage to puberty. In his thirteenth year he struggled for six months with a quartan fever. Did it occasion his first exposure to the magical arts of a witch?[19] This extended experience of illness, however, had its constructive effects upon the impressionable youth. For as one who would later write on physiology and medicine and continued to take an active interest in pharmaceutical and medical lore, Campanella early developed an acute awareness of the changes and ailments of his own body, which from this moment became an object of reflection, perception, and experience, and a source for his biomedical knowledge.[20]

At the same time with his family's removal to Stignano his parents considered his joining a paternal uncle in Naples for advancement in the law; Campanella in the following year, 1582, apparently reacting negatively to the allurements of a legal career, took the fateful step of entering the order of St. Dominic and began his year of probation before the novitiate in the small, ancient convent of Placanica, a mile west of Stignano. After taking his vows and assuming the name of Tommaso in 1583, the young novice found himself transferred to the more important convent of the Annunziata in San Giorgio Morgeto. Ever since its foundation at the beginning of the thirteenth century the Dominican order had been central in the teaching and operation of the Church. It had recently received further recognition with Pius V having declared in 1567 St. Thomas Aquinas a doctor of the Church by which time the

[17] TC-*Lett.*, 133.
[18] *DBI*, 17:372–73; Amab., *Cong.*, I, 1–2.
[19] *DBI*, 17:373.
[20] Michael Mönnich, *Tommaso Campanella: Sein Beitrag zur Medizin und Pharmazie der Renaissance* (Stuttgart, 1990), 52–53.

Angelic Doctor's theology had come to replace Peter Lombard's *Sentences* as the basic structure of the Church's theology. But before St. Thomas, the young Dominican's future ultimate reference and resort, there was Aristotle: Campanella entered upon a triennial course in dialectic, philosophy, and metaphysics, which exposed him to the *Logic*, the *Physics*, the *Metaphysics*, and the *Soul* by the Master of Those Who Know. Just how long it took Campanella to realize his dissatisfaction with Aristotle—whether in this first three-year period or shortly thereafter—remains uncertain, but it would appear not too long. He must have seemed overly curious, intellectually aggressive, even combative to his teachers, pressed to answer the questions and many difficulties with which their less than docile charge harried them. In quest of more solid fare Campanella began to turn to a broad consultation of the works of Plato, Pliny, Galen, the Stoics, and the atomists, culminating with Telesio.[21] Most probably at this early date he first engaged the potent idea of a plurality of successive worlds, their recurrent conflagration, their structure, if not their nature, periodically destroyed and renewed, the resolution of each in the Divine Fire, which afterwards reconstructs it—themes prevalent among the Stoics, mediated principally by Seneca to Christian thought, to Origen, and most recently to a distraught Christendom by Justus Lipsius.[22] By 1587 Campanella had achieved his philosophical formation in his completion of the triennial, but from 1588 he would abandon the subsequent quadrennial course in theology for the composing of his own first published work.[23]

Transferred for purposes of his studies from San Giorgio Morgeto to the convent of the Annunziata in Nicastro in the fall of 1586, Campanella drafted his first work, a methodological treatise called *De investigatione rerum* (since lost) in 1587. Here he became acquainted with a fellow friar, Dionisio Ponzio, with whom he seems to have found common ground in discussing the impending renewal of the world; a freedom and spontaneity, apparently missing in their formal instruction, marked their conversations together. Campanella's extracurricular readings, pursued confusedly and ill-digestedly in great gulps, culminated when in being transferred again, this time to San Domenico di Cosenza, a friend placed in his hands the first books of Telesio's *De rerum natura iuxta propria principia* in its initial edition of 1565.[24] The very title

---

[21] LF-*Autobi.*, 273–74; M. P. Lerner, "Campanelle, juge d'Aristote," in *Platon et Aristote à la Renaissance*, XVI Colloque international de Tours. (Paris, 1976), 336–37; *DBI*, 17:373.

[22] Gabriel Naudé's *Thomae Campanellae De libris propriis et recta ratione studendi syntagma* [Paris, 1642], ed., Vincenzo Spampanato (Florence, 1927), 12–13: "statui ipse libros omnes percurrere Platonis, Plinii, Galeni, Stoicorum et Democriticorum, praecipue vera Telesianos, ac cum mundi codice primario conferre." On the Stoic idea of recurring worlds, see Jason Lewis Saunders, *Justus Lipsius: The Philosophy of Renaissance Stoicism* (New York: Liberal Arts Press, 1955), 127, 202–10.

[23] Lerner, "Campanelle," 337.

[24] Luigi De Franco, "Nota al testo," in Tommaso Campanella, *Philosophia sensibus demonstrata*, ed. Luigi De Franco (Naples, 1992), 738; *DBI*, 17:374. On the Dominican convent at

proved inviting: the elucidation of nature according to its own principles ("iuxta propria principia"), divorced from Aristotelian hylomorphism, could not help but be captivating. Toward the end of his life, looking back upon this fateful encounter, Campanella would register his youthful delight with the *libertatem philosophandi* and with a system springing from the nature of things rather than the opinions of men.[25] Apparently so moved by this new philosophy, the enthusiastic tyro hastened in October 1588 to seek out the octogenarian philosopher, but arrived only in time to be able to affix an elegy to Telesio's coffin, exposed in the cathedral of Cosenza.[26]

Among his extracurricular authors, Telesio had the enormous attraction of being a living contemporary, a near neighbor at Cosenza, and one who in defying the traditional authorities, presented a coherent alternative system to all those who might be suffering from the suffocating pervasiveness of Aristotle's philosophy. Even in its earliest stage of development *De rerum natura* represented by its largely cosmological emphasis one of the first efforts to replace Aristotle's natural philosophy with an original, satisfying philosophic statement of reality. Telesio claimed that Aristotle's doctrine conflicted with the senses as well as with Scripture and that his own teaching based itself on sense perception and nature alone. He set forth two active principles of all things (heat and cold) and a passive principle (matter). At this stage in the development of Telesian doctrine as first received by Campanella, the bold, incisive criticism of Aristotle and the assertion of an independent, sensate philosophy proved immediately appealing to the young student. Only in the 1586, final edition of Telesio's great work, which developed in its last five books the biological and psychological issues, would Campanella's own extreme sensationalism, his exposure to the influence of the Stoic/medical tradition of *pneuma* (*spiritus*), and the distinction between two souls, one material, the other infused and immortal, reveal the fundamental impact of Telesio upon his intellectual formation.[27]

Possibly on account of his perceived excesses, Campanella's superiors now

---

Cosenza, since 1525 a *studium generale* and together with the Accademia cosentiana constituting the preeminent intellectual center for the southernmost provinces of the Mezzogiorno at this time, see the useful article of L. Guglielmo Esposito, O.P., "La biblioteca di S. Domenico di Cosenza," *AFP* 47 (1977): 439–73, which includes in an appendix (464–70) the sixteenth-century catologue of the library's holdings, thus providing a fair conspectus of the theological culture available to Campanella at this stage of his development: e.g., item 47—*In Averroistas de eternitate mundi libri quattuor*. I am grateful to Dr. Leonard E. Boyle, O.P., prefect of the Vatican Library, for bringing this article to my attention.

[25] From the *Syntagma* 13, quoted in Luigi De Franco, *Introduzione a Bernardino Telesio* (Messina, 1995), 385–86. I want to thank the author for once again sending me a copy of his latest scholarship.

[26] *DBI*, 17:373–74.

[27] Paul Oskar Kristeller, *Eight Philosophers of the Italian Renaissance* (Stanford, 1964), 97–104.

had him transferred to the small, remote convent of Altomonte, there ostensibly to cool off. Developments proved otherwise. The recent convert to Telesio soon learned of the publication in Rome in 1587 of a work by a Neapolitan jurist, Giacomo Antonio Marta, championing Aristotle over against the principles of the Cosenzan philosopher. Outraged, Campanella ran to the latter's defense in eight books entitled *Philosophia sensibus demonstrata*, composed between January and the end of August 1589.[28]

The importance of the *PSD*, written in his twenty-first year, derives not only from his formal, pronounced break with and condemnation of Aristotle and the Aristotelian tradition but also from his express effort to define a countervailing philosophic tradition—eclectic, diverse, but largely to be found among the Platonists. Consequently, philosophy's current affliction he attributes to a tendency to excuse the errors coming down from the ancients, as if our captors, and to deny our own sensible experience. The source of this difficulty lies with Aristotle's books on dialectic from which proceeds a vast confusion of abstract names and obscure terms. Aristotle's philosophy makes claims to divinity and its practitioners refuse to discuss with those who dissent from it. They have no eyes for reality but only for what they find written in his pages. Rather than complacently gargling vapid words, science proceeds by way of things, not names.[29] Campanella appeals to another philosophic tradition that lies with Plato, Pythagoras, Hermes Trismegistus, the Neoplatonists, including the Arabs, coming down through the recovery of Greek texts in Florence to Ficino, Pico, and Patrizi. But Campanella as a Dominican must explain so as to explain away the Aristotelianism of St. Thomas Aquinas. This he now accomplishes at the outset of his tormented career in a way that persists throughout. The Angelic Doctor lived in a world addicted to Aristotle, in which the pullulating Aristotelian doctrines made contradiction or disentanglement impossible. He transformed the sense of these texts in the interests of the faith so that an erring or about to err world might properly understand them. In a vein similar to Telesio Thomas is seen as opening up these texts, twisting them back and restraining them from their Aristotelian errors. For the saint was not a follower of Aristotle but of Christ and of the holy theologians ("Christi et sacrorum theologorum") by whom Campanella intends here the patristic Christian Platonists—Augustine, Pseudo-Dionysius, and Origen.[30] He will conclude his redrafting of philosophy—less as a history of Western intellectual development and more as a supplement and support to his own emerging controversy with Aristotle—by rooting this First Philosophy with Timaeus, Philolaus, Pythagoras, and the Crotonists of ancient Calabria.[31] His patriotism for Calabria as the birthplace of Greek philosophy, his efforts to

[28] De Franco, "Nota," 735 in TC-*PSD*².
[29] TC-*PSD*², 4–6.
[30] Ibid., 13–15.
[31] Ibid., 19–20.

define philosophy beyond the long shadow of Aristotle, and his enthusiasm for the contemporary philosophy of Telesio as a revival of that earlier philosophy articulated in Magna Graecia—the emerging parts of his program adumbrated in 1589—will come into focus a decade later in a sonnet immediately following the abortive conspiracy.[32]

Beyond the preface to the *PSD*, which first announces Campanella's program that will be later elaborated and developed, the value of the total work is considerable for providing us with an appreciation of Campanella's philosophic culture and his textual practices at this formative stage of his intellectual odyssey. Campanella speaks of being visited at Altomonte by two medical doctors, who not only engaged him in extensive philosophical discussion but brought him books of the Platonists and Peripatetics, of Galen and Hippocrates, all to be pressed into service for the defense of Telesio.[33] He draws frequently upon Averroes, Galen, Simplicius, Plato, Plotinus, Albertus Magnus, Ficino, and Nifo, as well as Pico, Hermes, Hippocrates, Philoponus (through Simplicius), Cardanus's *De subtilitate*, and of course Aquinas.[34] In his pursuit of a proof he can be irresponsible and casual in the quoting of his texts. While he correctly observes an absolute fidelity in his citing of Telesio, with Aristotle and other authors he can be general and vague, and compress his own personal considerations into his summaries of their positions. Yet even here there are constraints upon his arbitrariness: in order to make his case he must quote accurately those texts of Aristotle taken over from Telesio. And with Albertus Magnus there are the least instances of distorting the sense of the passage quoted.[35] Through a display of a diversity of texts in this tour de force Campanella manifests a dangerous, youthful exuberance for philosophic independence.

But the import of the months spent by Campanella at Altomonte did not exhaust itself with this single composition. It is here that he came to indulge in Hermetic texts, divination, cabala, and magic, apparently under the guidance of a dark, obscure figure known as Abraham, a young rabbi whom he had encountered and befriended in the populous Jewish communities in this region of Calabria and with whom he would flee from Altomonte at the end of 1589.[36] Campanella's association with this important figure dates according to some later writers from his days at Cosenza, now carrying over to his stay at

---

[32] TC-P^1, 258/115, 1347/115, 1332/61 (January to February 1600). The practice followed here and henceforth: the first number refers to the page; the second, following the virgule, to the particular item, poem, or document.

[33] TC-PSD^2, 7–8.

[34] De Franco, "Nota" at 741; cf. 62, n. 73 and 799–801.

[35] Ibid., 741–43.

[36] Giacomo Oreglia, "Campanella in Svezia," in *Studi politici in onore di Luigi Firpo*, ed. Silvia Roti Ghibaudi and Francio Barcia (Milan, 1990), 2:55–91, esp. 65.

Altomonte. The two maintained long discussions together from which the young Calabrian Dominican obtained not simply a fresh and more sympathetic look at astrology, divination, and the occult, but from which he was to receive a far more precious endowment: his calling, the vocation as well as the instrument of prophecy. The Hebrew himself prophesied that one day Campanella would become Monarch of the World.[37]

In the Naples of the Della Portas

Happiness—never a measurable commodity and indeed so chimerical as to have no serious place in the estimates and expectations of a life—seems universally inappropriate to the human condition, but most peculiarly inappropriate to the life of Tommaso Campanella. Insofar as it has any relevance, however, it may be understood as assuming some form of self-affirmation or self-fulfillment through the nurturing and advancement of one's own interests and concerns within a meaningful context. It is in this sense of self-fulfillment through the sharing and exchange among like-minded individuals regarding mutual interests and pursuits that the two years from the end of 1589 to the beginning of 1592, constituting the period of Campanella's first stay in Naples, can be considered the only happy period in an otherwise peculiarly tormented life. Not that this period lacked its setbacks and darker aspects: in the summer of 1591 Campanella suffered hugely from sciatica and rheumatism, attributed to the elegant fare that he received from his patron's table; and in the following year, beginning in May with his being denounced, occurred his first trial and the imposition of penance that would lead to his abrupt removal from the circle of Neapolitan associates.[38] Otherwise this period allowed the already renegade friar the unique opportunity for research and reflection, for writing and reading, for discussion and experimentation plus the pleasure of learning and sharing with some of the best minds of the age, constituting the culture of one of the foremost cities of Europe. The conjunction of several factors made this fruitful condition possible for the wayward Calabrian visitor: principally and most substantively the very open cultural world created by the Della Porta brothers—the Naples of the late Renaissance, a subject that is gaining but demands more attention from historians (a re-creation is impossible here).[39] But more immediately and materially for Campanella any appreciation of this charmed moment requires some recognition of the status of the

---

[37] Amab., *Cong.*, I, 18–19.

[38] *DBI*, 17:374–75.

[39] For a most recent situating of the Della Portas and their Naples in a larger context, see William Eamon, *Science and the Secrets of Nature: Books of Secrets in Medieval and Early Modern Culture* (Princeton, 1994), 194–233.

Dominican order in Naples at the end of the sixteenth century and the role of patronage as it affected at this juncture the deportment of the friar.

Arriving in Naples, possibly by sea, in late 1589, Campanella first stayed at the principal convent of the Dominicans, San Domenico Maggiore. Scholars have been quick to note that the splendid library of San Domenico afforded Campanella opportunities similar to those of Giordano Bruno a generation earlier. Would that we might know more about that library's exact contents at this time.[40] Nevertheless we have already seen that its new visitor had already been exposed to a dangerous medley of authors and that in the formulation of his intellectual bearing he also benefited from extensive conversations and simple observation. Thus while he may have profited from the library's probable holdings of Lucretius and Ficino and further reinforced his reading of that bizarre Neoplatonist, Ocellus Lucanus,[41] we must not envisage him solemnly turning pages in the quiet remove of a great monastic library. The very fact that as a disobedient, virtually renegade friar he could attend the convent at all and continue to wear the habit speaks to the relaxed conditions of the Dominicans in Naples in the last decade of the sixteenth century.

A number of factors contributed to heightening the radicalism of these Neapolitan Dominican houses. No matter how august the traditions of learning and piety dignifying the great convent of San Domenico Maggiore, graced with the lecture hall of Thomas Aquinas, the bubbling life of Naples seems to have engulfed most of its members as well as those of the ten lesser unreformed Dominican convents in the city.[42] The convent's great library was in the same structure as that of the lay culture of the university, thereby inviting intellectual exchange and a freedom of thought that had already produced a Giordano Bruno—indeed an atmosphere and context that the heresiarch himself had later praised as having afforded him eleven years of free study, thought, and discussion.[43] The uncloistered nature of Dominican life in Naples at this time can be assessed from the frustrations of the newly appointed papal nuncio, Jacopo Aldobrandini. In being appalled on arrival in 1592 at what seemed to Counter Reformation clerical eyes as the licentious life of the friars, he wrote to Rome asking for powers to correct the situation. Not until 1595 was he able to undertake the necessary remedial action. Beyond the nine or more conventual Dominican houses there were six others belonging to the Reformed Dominicans, of which Santa Maria della Sanità was the largest. Sixty of its reformed brethren were now transferred to San Domenico and the

---

[40] F. Russo, "Gioachinismo e Francescanismo," *Miscellanea Francescanea* 41 (1941): 71–73, indicates that the library possessed Joachimist materials in 1240. But were they still available 350 years later?

[41] On Ocellus Lucanus, see chap. 7, n. 217, *infra*.

[42] Bacco, *Naples*, 50; Amab., *Cong.*, I, 25.

[43] Villari, *Revolt*, 44; Bock, *Campanella*, 80.

more unworthy members of that convent evicted. But not for long. The sixty evicted inmates returned with staves, knives, and pistols, manfully, if not altogether piously, took the convent by assault, expelled the sixty newcomers, and proceeded to fortify and entrench themselves defiantly for the next three months. Such defiance would have been impossible without the broad support of the Neapolitan populace, which apparently took pride in the learning and reasonable worldliness of its monastic establishments. Both secular and ecclesiastical authorities hedged, unwilling to press the matter. In the subsequent settlement that reaffirmed the old order at the monastery only the leading instigators suffered imprisonment—among them Fra Serafino Rinaldi da Nocera, who soon emerged as the prior of San Domenico Maggiore and who would remain a lifelong defender of Campanella.[44] For his part the nuncio, writing to Cardinal San Giorgio at the end of his term of office in 1604 and reflecting upon the Dominicans, sighed: "I want you to know that there is no religious order (*Religione*) in this kingdom more relaxed than this one."[45]

While religious relaxation certainly worked to the benefit of Campanella at this time, he could do and did do better for himself by seeking the patronage of a great aristocrat who could advance him in learned circles and the cultural life of the capital. Such a person was Mario del Tufo, baron of Matina and Minervino and second son of Giovanni Geronimo, second marquis of Lavello. The Del Tufos traced their ancestry back to Norman origins in the kingdom and the family's members came to populate the highest offices of church and state. Campanella's initial encounter with the family dated from his first years in the Dominican order, during his triennial at San Giorgio Morgeto, when in 1585 Giacomo II Milano, who had married Isabella del Tufo, came to take possession of his fief; on the occasion of this always solemn ceremony, annually renewed, the young Campanella composed and recited an oration in hexameter and a sapphic ode for good measure. In the intervening half decade the association, presumably cultivated, allowed Campanella in 1590 to transfer himself "to the household of the marquis of Lavello with the patronage of his son, Mario del Tufo," as he later explained in his *Syntagma*.[46] More than two decades afterwards, in reflecting upon Tufo's hospitality he could praise it affectionately but also present it as an example of dangerous expenditure and his host as the imprudent householder inevitably begetting parasites.[47] The new ambiance afforded Campanella more than simply greater comfort and freedom. For good reason he dedicated to the younger son his *PSD*, which Orazio Salviano, Telesio's printer, published in 1591.[48] In his association with

---

[44] Villari, *Revolt*, 42–46.
[45] Amab., *Cong.*, I, 26–28.
[46] LF-*Autobi.*, 276.
[47] TC-*Op. Lat.*, II, 1078–79. See also chap. 3, n. 67, *infra*.
[48] Pietro Manzi, *La tipografia napoletana nel'500. Annali di Orazio Salviani, 1566–1594*

Mario del Tufo he accompanied him at one point to his fief of Minervino, where the friar took careful note of the practice of systematic horse breeding. Could not similar controls be applied to human copulation? To one who was currently reading Ocellus Lucanus on the imagination's transfer of images for the purposes of eugenics, practice and theory would unite under the auspices of Plato to constitute the seed for his later program of procreation in the *City of the Sun*. But the patron's support and advancement of his protégé proved far more fundamental and pervasive. Mario del Tufo and his illustrious father had been closely supportive of Telesio, and the son had taken instruction in philosophy from their *devotissimo*. Little wonder that Del Tufo would patronize and promote the Cosenzan's defender and potential reincarnation in the young, wayward Dominican. Through such support Campanella would gain direct access to the highest circle of Neapolitan cultural life.[49]

Since midcentury the town house of the Della Porta brothers, situated on the Via Toledo near the Piazza Carità, the most elegant central section of the city, had become the obvious resort of the lettered, both local and foreign. Coming there the visitor entered into one of the most splendid learned circles of Europe, succulently expressive of the best of the overripe late Renaissance culture. The three brothers in order of age and eminence—Gian Vincenzo, Giambattista, and Gian Ferrante—had through tutors, amplified by celebrated visitors, been exposed to the expectable humanistic curriculum but with a heavy component of medicine and mathematics, especially the last of which being in its contemporary understanding closely associated with magic. The eldest of the three, Gian Vincenzo, had built up a collection of books, statues, ancient marbles, and medals. Drawn more to the library than the laboratory, he seemed content to preside over gatherings and place his considerable knowledge at the disposal of his more enterprising younger brother, Giambattista. The latter, a more dramatic and articulate personality, would achieve in the long run greater attention and renown, but he benefited from the sedate, learned elder brother, drawing upon Vincenzo's liberally deployed superior knowledge of astrology and classical methods for prognostication. The youngest brother, Gian Ferrante, shared and reinforced his elders' interests, adding his own particular pursuit of collecting geological specimens.[50]

Before the better known Academy of the Linceans G. B. della Porta had organized a scientifically oriented academy in his home since the 1560s. The Accademia dei Segreti seemed to have been based on an earlier society of the 1540s expressly founded for conducting experimental research. It consciously

---

(Florence, 1975), 160. Unfortunately the rarity of surviving copies does not allow Emerenziana Vaccaro to include its printer's mark in her *Le marchi dei tipografi ed editori italiani del secolo xvi nella Biblioteca Angelica di Roma* (Florence, 1983).

[49] Amab., *Cong.*, I, 9, 28–32; *DBI*, 17:374–75.

[50] Louise George Clubb, *Giambattista Della Porta, Dramatist* (Princeton, 1965), 4–11; Amab., *Cong.*, I, 33–35.

pursued a primitive sort of experimentation with the intent of producing a book of "secrets" or recipes comparable to what one would later find in Della Porta's *Magia naturalis*, first published in 1558. This experimentation as *venatio* or hunting can be understood as a stage in the development of the concept of experiment. Following Agrippa of Nettesheim, Della Porta saw the natural magician not just as an observer but as a doer, mediating between two worlds; "he joins together those inferior things with the marvelous gifts and virtues of superiors . . . [sending] forth into public notice the secrets that lay hidden in the innermost bosom of nature." Technical recipes came to be linked with scientific discovery.[51] Yet in the contemporary context of celebrating the wondrous and the marvelous, the hunt inevitably emphasized *meraviglia* to the detriment of empirical proof. In contrast to the Aristotelians' concentration upon the normal and the quotidian, Della Porta's natural magic focused on the exceptional, the unusual, the apparently miraculous.[52]

It is easy, however, to focus on Della Portan research as exclusively in the terrain of the empirical. But this very experimentation rested upon philosophical assumptions and premises, making fact and theory inseparable. A firm belief in the harmony of the cosmos—not just in numbers or music but even *in rebus ipsis*—made possible his scientific pursuits. The contemporary Hermetic and Telesian currents, nurtured in the learned circle, had the effect of transcending or of cutting across the traditional Aristotelian dichotomy between the substance of the heavens and that of the earth. Telesian celestial heat and terrestial cold constitute those very intrinsic principles of life for that great animal that is this world. As the *Magia naturalis* tells us: "All the parts of the world, like the limbs of a single animal . . . are mutually joined together by the connection of a single nature. . . . All the bodies of the world being connected in like manner change their nature mutually and are mutually changed, and from a common affinity derives a common love and from love a common attraction." The imagery here is less mechanical than organic, even chemical, pointing to the most typical fonts of the chemical/medical culture of the late Renaissance.[53]

---

[51] William Eamon and Françoise Paheau, "The Accademia Segreta of Girolamo Ruscelli: A Sixteenth-Century Italian Scientific Society," *Isis* 75 (1984): 327–42, esp. 328–33; William Eamon, "Arcana Disclosed: The Advent of Printing, the Books of Secrets, Tradition and the Development of Experimental Science in the Sixteenth Century," *History of Science* 22 (1984): 111–50, esp. 134–37.

[52] Clubb, *Porta*, 12; Eamon, *Science*, 210–11.

[53] Nicola Badaloni, "I fratelli Della Porta e la cultura magica e astrologica a Napoli nel'500," *SS*, 1 (1959–60): 677–715, esp. 679, 683, 698–703. The Latin original to this important statement noted by Badaloni reads as follows: "Platonici Magiam vocebant attractionem unius rei ab altera, ex quadam naturae cognatione. Mundi autem huius partes, ceu animalis unius membra, omnes ab uno authore pendentes, unius naturae coniunctione invicem copulantur: . . . id est omnia mundi corpora connexa similiter mutuant invicem naturas, & mutuantur & ex communi cognatione, communis nascitur amor, & ex amore communis attractio. Haec vere magica est." *Magia naturalis* (Frankfurt: Andr. Wechel heredes, 1597), I.ix, p. 22.

Campanella entered this learned circle at its peak. Della Porta had published in 1586 the second edition of his influential *De humana physiognomonia* and in 1589 the definitive second edition of the *Magia naturalis*; the same year also saw the printing of his first play, *L'Olimpia*. In touch with the most learned and the most powerful, Della Porta seemed to be on the verge of discovering the philosophers' stone for an expectant European culture. His own continuing investigations would soon impinge upon the invention of the telescope and the camera obscura. It is both ironic and worthy of note that Campanella came to partake of what was currently considered the most up-to-date and viable science just shortly before its eclipse and that abrupt rerouting of science effected by Galileo subsequent to 1610.[54] In the magico-astrological reaches of the academy's intellectual range the young Dominican could find food for thought in the speculations of Colantonio Stelliola (Stegliola), Giulio Cortese, and Giovanni Paolo Vernaleone; all three of whom promoted the idea of an impending public and religious *mutazione*.[55] In his conversations with Stelliola, who seems to have absorbed a good deal of the thinking of Giordano Bruno, Campanella found himself debating world systems and taking issue with the principles of infinity and plenitude. Both now and as he debated related issues later in his *Physics* and *Metaphysics*, Campanella showed himself less receptive than Stelliola to both Copernicus and Bruno.[56]

He also encountered here the considerable figure of Ferrante Imperato, whose celebrated museum in the style of a *Wunderkammer* gave Campanella hope of greater specificity and control for the strivings of Della Porta in the field of natural history. Campanella attributed great importance to this museum and tended to prefer Imperato's empiricism, based on the direct *experientia* of the Book of Nature and evinced in his collection, to the more formal use of it by Della Porta as a philosophical category.[57] Imperato's own work, *Dell'historia naturale*, would be published at the century's end. It was in the supportive context of this learned group that Campanella, substantially inspired by Della Porta, composed possibly his most influential work—*Del senso delle cose e della magia*; when together they examined the *Physiognomonia*, he acknowledged that in conversation with Della Porta the latter claimed the sympathy and antipathy of things to be inexplicable.[58] In an even more intimate recorded encounter with the Neapolitan virtuoso, Campanella

---

[54] Clubb, *Porta*, 20–29; this last point finds its implicit support in Eamon, *Science*, 229–33.
[55] Badaloni, "I fratelli," 683.
[56] Badaloni, "Il programma scientifico di un bruniano: Colantonio Stelliola," *SS*, 26 (1985): 161–75, esp. 163–64.
[57] Amab., *Cong.*, I, 41; TC-*DSCM*, 221–22. See also the perceptive remarks of Paula Findlen, *Possessing Nature: Museums, Collecting and Scientific Culture in Early Modern Italy* (Berkeley/Los Angeles/London, 1990), 228.
[58] LF-*Autobi.*, 276.

will later speak of a time when before a group of associates and students Della Porta cured Campanella's afflicted eye by introducing with his own hands a marvelous collyrium.[59] Of the Dominican as likewise of the Nolan, Bruno, we hear nothing in the letters and many writings of Della Porta, for he had had his own fearsome brush with the Inquisition and in experiencing intermittently its hot, unsettling breath, maintained a prudent distance from compromising associates.[60]

Campanella's attendance upon the Della Portan circle reveals the formidable and initially preeminent role of natural philosophy and the science of the age in the intellectual formation of one who is too often identified as principally a political thinker. In the emerging prophetic element and an overwhelming sense of a personal role in *mutazione*, world transformation, Campanella differed significantly from his host. In contrast, and fortunately for his own good, G. B. Della Porta, ever in pursuit of the immediate and the tangible, lacked his young admirer's taste for philosophical and theological speculation. For Campanella's own problems with the ecclesiastical authorities had been heating up not only as a result of his flight from Altomonte but also from the recent publication of the *PSD*. Rome was decisively turning away from the Platonists to an even more pronounced embrace of Aristotle. By flight Campanella had arrived in Naples; by flight he would now save himself from being recloistered. Henceforth all his major movements would be by fleeing or, apprehended, by being transported in chains, up to the final resort in Paris.

Della Portan magic, now added to Telesian naturalism and the rabbinical astrology of Abraham, began to promote a total, comprehensive, and pervasive view of reform and renewal—something cosmic as well as just locally political. The exposure to members of this circle, especially Colantonio Stelliola in 1590–92, to be reinforced and elaborated in 1597–98, would prove decisive in providing Campanella with the intellectual sources and ideological goals for the later conspiracy of 1599.[61]

[59] Mönnich, *Campanella*, 54; cf. TC-*Med.*, 395.
[60] Clubb, *Porta*, 33–34; cf. 15–19.
[61] This apparently straight line of development has been recently laid out by William Eamon, "Natural Magic and Utopia in the Cinquecento: Campanella, the Della Porta Circle, and the Revolt of Calabria" [to be published].

Chapter II

THE PROPHET BOUND

The Earlier Trials and Incarcerations

With the publication of the *Philosophia sensibus demonstrata* in the spring of 1591 a new and most ominous stage develops in the young friar's life. It is one that sees his descent through a series of legal trials, repeated detentions, and ever-harsher incarcerations to the penultimate and most terrible confinement in the dungeons of Naples, following the abortive Calabrian uprising. A more prudent, less restless soul might at any earlier stage in the progress of the decade have taken notice and stepped out from the closing grip of the authorities by means of some nice accommodation. But with Campanella, *il eterno imprudente*,[1] there is evident during these years an almost ruinous restlessness, thirst for knowledge, and mastering pride, all of which find expression in his early attained self-perception and understanding of himself as a prophet.

The first legal process would suggest that the young Dominican's brilliance and arrogant deportment had generated envy and enmity among his own brethren and most certainly among the friends of Giacomo Antonio Marta. Since the hard-line Aristotelians did not deem him assailable for simply the opinions expressed in his recent book, they could nevertheless manufacture charges that might gain wider support in both university and juristic circles as well as within clerical circles. In May 1592 Campanella was imprisoned in the convent of San Domenico, Naples, after being denounced on two accounts: for harboring a familiar demon under the nail of his little finger and for having shown contempt regarding the Church's power of excommunication. It was an in-house affair, pertaining to discipline. Now occurred the exchange between Campanella and his judges: to the question how one who had learned so little should know so much, he replied all too promptly with the old adage used by St. Jerome as well as Demosthenes that he had been consuming more oil than wine.[2] The proceedings turned soon enough upon his Telesianism, which could not help but be an offense to a Church whose position was rapidly crystallizing upon Aristotle during these same months. An attack upon Aristotle could only be interpreted as an attack upon St. Thomas and all of Church doctrine no matter how strenuously Campanella was seeking to unsolder the church father from the Stagirite. There was never any question of heresy, either convicted or confessed. According to his sentence on August 28, 1592,

---

[1] Di Napoli, "L'eresia," 233.
[2] TC-*Lett.*, 107, according to his own account written to Kaspar Schoppe in 1607.

following an imprisonment of eight months, he was called upon to renounce Telesio specifically for St. Thomas Aquinas and given eight days to remove from Naples to his native province. The trial remained throughout a disciplinary matter internal to the Dominican order.[3]

Campanella now arrived at a fateful decision that could only deepen his troubles and complicate his future: rather than turn south to rejoin his community in his native province, on September 5 he moved north to Rome and Florence. Accustomed to the rich intellectual fare of Naples, the twenty-four-year-old philosopher appeared unwilling to submit to the cultural isolation of his home province and to be afflicted by the nasty factionalism of his brethren. Instead, lured by the hope of an appointment to a chair of metaphysics at a Tuscan university, perhaps Pisa or Siena, he traveled northward. Certainly at this time Pisa offered the greater attraction as a university that had benefited from the efforts of Cosimo I and Francesco I (1574–87) to build it into one of the best in Europe: its strong occult element in the teaching of mathematics and astronomy could reinforce current tendencies of Campanella; and the distinctive commitment of the Medici to the Platonic tradition could serve to enhance developing interests in the young friar.[4] After visiting with friends and fellow members of the order in Rome, he proceeded to Florence, where he had an audience on October 2 with Grand Duke Ferdinand I, who remained noncommittal; apparently finding entanglements with the regular clergy an embarrassment, he urged Campanella to transfer to the secular clergy. Nevertheless the dissident friar did not abandon his habit and would remain loyal to his order. Continuing northward he would persist in his pattern of staying at convents as he had in Rome and Florence, now Bologna and Padua. In not abandoning his identity as a Dominican he distinguished himself from the earlier practice of Giordano Bruno.

Campanella stayed in Bologna for the remainder of 1592 in the convent of San Domenico. The vigilant Inquisition confiscated all his manuscripts, some of which still remain unrecovered. Barely had he arrived in Padua than he was charged with sodomy, apparently in order to discredit the general of the Dominicans. It amounted to no more than an inquest, and the charges were quickly dismissed. Nevertheless, clearly Campanella had become a marked man subject to constant observation.[5]

Living wretchedly at the convent of St. Augustine in Padua, he enrolled at the university as a Spanish student, perhaps giving private lessons while studying medicine and attending anatomical dissections. The milieu for a few months offered a stimulating environment. It was here that he met Galileo, apparently missed Paolo Sarpi, and resumed his friendship with Della Porta,

---

[3] LF-*PP*, 5–43, esp. 7–14; Di Napoli, "L'eresia," 169–258, esp. 176–87.
[4] Charles Schmitt, "The Faculty of Arts at Pisa at the Time of Galileo," *Physis* 14 (1972): 243–72, esp. 250–63.
[5] LF-*PP*, 14–18; Di Napoli, "L'eresia," 187–89; *DBI*, 17:375–76.

who himself sought relief from the annoyances of the Inquisition in Naples. In 1593 all three were together when Campanella resided in Padua.[6] Much later he would attest to their conversations being saturated with Democritus and regretting that flight prevented his communicating with Sarpi.[7] Did they ever convene at the prized library of Pinelli in Padua?[8] Certainly Pinelli's Neapolitan origins and contacts would have recommended Campanella to him. It would appear that during his stay in Padua he began his most unfortunately unrecovered *De philosophia Empedoclis*, no doubt drawn to the pre-Socratic idea of panpsychism and the grounds for the succession of worlds and cosmic palingenesia.[9]

Campanella also composed at this time the since lost *Monarchia Christianorum*, in which he would later claim to have shown the true republic at Rome as established by the apostles—what no philosopher had been able to depict before.[10] In August he represented himself in a letter to the grand duke as an expert on political theory and would shortly receive back from the Medici prince a negative response conveyed by Galileo himself.[11] Concomitant with his medical and scientific training the year provided further evidence of his growing political preoccupation: a renewal of the Church's structure and clergy in the *Discorsi universali del governo ecclesiastico* together with the probable outlining of his *Discorsi ai principi d'Italia* calling for a neo-Guelph federation under the pope.[12] Thus 1593 saw the rather abrupt emergence and rapid maturing of the political or at least for his philosophy some major political themes that would now amplify and pervade his total intellectual stance.

It is fair to imagine that during these hectic months the sensuous succulence of the Venetian mood cast something of its seductive spell over the struggling friar. A decade later, from the depths of a Neapolitan cell, Campanella would represent Venice as a great miracle illuminating the world.[13] Indeed he would never renounce his warm admiration for the splendid maritime republic. Nevertheless forces were at work in preparation for the third and far more serious legal proceeding against Campanella. In July 1593 the Congregation of the Index cast its pall over Telesio's *De rerum natura* along with two minor works, but then moved on to the examination of all Campanella's works con-

---

[6] Luigi Firpo, "Appunti Campanelliani," *GCFI* 35 (1956): 545–46.

[7] See Germana Ernst and Eugenio Canone, "Una lettera ritrovata: Campanella a Peiresc, 19 giugno 1636," *RSF* 49 (1994): 353–66, esp. 363–64.

[8] On the library of Pinelli at Padua, see Marcella Grendler, "A Greek Collection in Padua: The Library of Gian Vincenzo Pinelli (1535–1601)," *RQ* 33 (1980): 386–416.

[9] LF-*Bibl.*, 173/58. On the later correlation with Origen regarding world renewal, see TC-*Meta.*, III, 336–46.

[10] TC-*Lett.*, 107.

[11] LF-*PP*, 21–22; cf. TC-*Lett.*, 6–7.

[12] *DBI*, 17:376; Di Napoli, "L'eresia," 192–93.

[13] TC-P^1, 103, madrigale 6.

fiscated in Bologna.[14] By the beginning of the following year, 1594, it struck: the Inquisition in Venice arrested Campanella for having disputed *de fide* with a "Judaizer"—who had lapsed from Christianity—without having denounced him to the Holy Office. Beyond this accusation a whole ragbag of charges accumulated against Campanella: author of the atheistic book *De tribus imposteribus*, thereby joining a line of august culprits from Emperor Frederick II to Voltaire; but more seriously author of an impious sonnet against Christ; possessing a book on geomancy; disapproving the rule and doctrine of the Church; and sustaining the opinions of Democritus to the extent that his own sensism could be identified with that of the philosopher of Abdera.[15] Amidst this motley assortment one may pause to note that Campanella seemed to be having problems with the Second Person of the Trinity—difficulties that certainly bore watching. Whatever the merits of Firpo's observation that Campanella's Telesianism worked to deny every form of transcendence,[16] it overlooks the Platonic/Pythagorean component already evident since 1592 and among the papers of the Bolognese confiscation.[17]

Included in the arresting reach of the Holy Office was Campanella's medical friend Giambattista Clario along with Ottavio Longo of Barletta. On February 8 the Holy Office after appropriate deliberation had Campanella and Clario tortured, with the former being submitted to further and more severe torture in July by which time the case had been revoked to Rome. By October 11 the three entered the Roman prisons of the Holy Office, where Giordano Bruno and Francesco Pucci lingered. The Inquisition now deployed the several charges against Campanella. The friar defended himself skillfully but in the end had to submit along with his friend Clario to an abjuration *de vehementi* on May 16.[18] However, he remained in detention in the Dominican convent of Santa Sabina, there to write, most probably with an eye to achieving his freedom, the *Dialogo politico contro Luterani, Calvinisti e altri eretici*. The work betrayed more political fervor than doctrinal zeal, the heretics being assailed for fragmenting the political unity of Christendom rather than for dogmatic dissent.[19] Dedicating the work to Cardinal Michele Bonelli, protector of the order, Campanella obtained further mileage by sending it with a covering letter to Alberto Tragagliola, the commissary general of the Holy

---

[14] Di Napoli, "L'eresia," 193–94; Firpo, "Filosofia italiana e controriforma," 391.
[15] LF-*PP*, 23.
[16] Ibid., 26.
[17] LF-*Autobi.*, 277.
[18] LF-*PP*, 30–32; *DBI*, 17:376–77. In the Church's scaling of religious crimes that moved from slight suspicion of heresy through vehement suspicion of heresy to the charge of formal heresy, Campanella had thus here scored a solid "two." See Maurice A. Finocchiaro, *The Galileo Affair: A Documentary History* (Berkeley/Los Angeles/London, 1989), 14–15.
[19] LF-*PP*, 37.

Office, who had shown sympathy for the impetuous friar and seemed convinced of his substantial innocence.[20] Shortly his *Poetica* would follow in 1596, dedicated to Cinzio Aldobrandini, Cardinal S. Giorgio.[21] In the earlier, harsher confinement Campanella had composed one with the significant title *Apologia pro philosophis Magnae Graeciae ad S. Officium*, where the Magna Graecia would suggest that in his defending Telesio, he was associating him with that emerging idea of Calabria as being the seat of truly the first philosophy:[22] in the struggle against Aristotelianism recourse would be had to the ancient Calabrian philosophy.[23] The limited liberation that he enjoyed for eighteen months at Santa Sabina (May 1595–December 1596) while awaiting the final determination of his case can probably be attributed to the toll that imprisonment had taken on his health, for he suffered from hernia, sciatica, consumption, and paralysis. Certainly the early composition of these political writings had contributed to mitigating the severities of his detention. It raises the issue of his simulation and dissimulation in order to contend with the dangers and pitfalls resulting from his deportment. While judgment of this thorny issue may be suspended for the present, it will need to be addressed after more evidence and in greater perspective.

In the same years that saw the sledgehammer blows of the Holy Office falling upon Pucci and shortly thereafter upon Bruno, Campanella attracted the benevolence of some persons in high places, as he enjoyed first the better conditions of Santa Sabina and then in the final stage, before his being absolved and liberated, the heightened cultural and political attributes of Santa Maria sopra Minerva, the citadel of the Dominican order in Rome.[24]

Liberty was becoming an ever more precarious matter for our dissident friar. Within two months of his release he found himself by the beginning of March 1597 back in the worst prisons of the Inquisition, there to remain until the middle of December. He had been denounced by a compatriot as a heretic. This period surely strengthened some of his heterodoxies, for at this time he became the cellmate of that restless, bold, free thinker Francesco Pucci. In the amazing conversations that were allowed to occur for a period of three months between the condemned heretic, ripe from the fields of Polish Anabaptism, and the questing, although heterodox, Dominican, there were nurtured and promoted those sprouts of free thought that must perforce struggle to survive in an authoritarian garden. The correspondences in the mature thought of each are too considerable to deny influence of some sort, whether actual nurturing of seeds already present in the mind of the younger party or reinforcement of barely developing tendencies: religion as a natural light present in all human-

---

[20] Di Napoli, "L'eresia," 201–2; *DBI*, 17:377.
[21] LF-*PP*, 34–35.
[22] Ibid., 34; Di Napoli, "L'eresia," 195; LF-*Bibl.*, 179–81.
[23] Nicola Badaloni, *Tommaso Campanella* (Milan, 1965), 109–10.
[24] Di Napoli, "L'eresia," 202–3.

kind; from natural and rational sources the salvation of all humankind; the aspiration to a general reform of the Christian commonwealth through dogmatic and liturgical simplification; personal messianism and the prophetic stamp. It is significant, however, that in terms of their idea of the total political life and the perfect state the two would part company. Here Campanella's ideas appeared to be maturing more rapidly than some of the rest of his philosophy. Rather than Pucci's emphatic laicism Campanella was diverging toward a return to a medieval catholic theocracy of Spanish-papal amalgam. But he would pick up on such Puccian themes as the strong unitary sense of the common, the appreciation of republican, elective institutions, eugenic prescription, and disinterested matrimonial unions because they reinforced already existing notions. While Pucci would be beheaded and then have his body burned, his young friend would remain to celebrate in sonnet form the flight of a soul heavenward to its redemption.[25]

Yet it is in another sonnet, "In the Dungeon" ("Al carcere"), from this same period of imprisonment that Campanella gives vent to his impatience and rebelliousness regarding his confinement and his passionate longing for free thinking. With Dantesque force and reference—"the strait dead sea of sophistry" (*morta gora*, *Inf*. 8.31)—he reviles that dark oppressiveness of his sacred confinement, expressive of a secret tyranny.

> As to the centre all things that have weight
>   Sink from the surface: as the silly mouse
>   Runs at a venture, rash though timorous,
>   Into the monster's jaws to meet her fate:
> Thus all who love high Science, from the strait
>   Dead sea of Sophistry sailing like us
>   Into Truth's ocean, bold and amorous,
>   Must in our haven anchor soon or late.
> One calls this haunt a Cave of Polypheme,
>   And one Atlante's Palace, one of Crete
>   The Labyrinth, and one Hell's lowest pit.
> Knowledge, grace, mercy, are an idle dream
>   In this dread place. Nought but fear dwells in it,
>   Of stealthy Tyranny the sacred seat.[26]

Have we not here during this return engagement to the prisons of the Roman Inquisition the making of an intellectual dissident? Have we not also here that

---

[25] Luigi Firpo, "Processo e morte di Francesco Pucci," *RF* 40 (1949): 371–405, esp. 390–93; on Pucci in general, see Miriam Eliav-Feldon and Élie Barnavé, *Le périple de Francesco Pucci: Utopie, hérésie et verité religieuse dans la Renaissance tardive* (Saint-Amant-Montrond Cher, 1988).

[26] John Addington Symonds, *The Sonnets of Michael Angelo Buonarroti and Tommaso Campanella* (London, 1878), 166; cf. TC-*P*¹, 129/60, 1221–22.

very Campanellan motif of monstrous intellectual aspiration within a power system that temperamentally can never be forsaken—temperamentally because the twin paradox of love and power, of science and authority must be lived out in tense and terrible association?

Although the accusation against Campanella was withdrawn, his situation remained extremely precarious. As a *lapsus* he could not afford to run further danger of becoming a *relapsus*. In mid-December 1597, after participating in a collective abjuration, he received his sentence: all his books would be prohibited and he would be consigned henceforth to his native province. Again for such an active spirit it must have seemed another form of imprisonment. Now as a marked man, well-noted and observed by the Inquisition, he could not afford any repetition of his former departure for northern parts. Yet at least in his movement south from Rome he could interrupt his trip with an extended visit in Naples among friends and intellectual groups from the end of March to the middle of July before his return to Calabria. There he would complete the first part of his *Epilogo magno*, the nucleus of the later *Philosophia realis*.[27] There also he resumed those contacts—mathematical, astrological, and philosophical—with such luminaries as Giulio Cortese, Giovanni Paolo Vernaleone, and above all Colantonio Stelliola, who reinforced the Empedoclean, Pythagorean, and Origenist tendencies of the Dominican miscreant with their powerful implications for *mutatione di stato*.[28]

THE CONSPIRACY

We will probably never begin to understand the confluence of forces that led to the Calabrian explosion of 1599 with its abrupt shunting, torquing, perduring effect upon our still youthful friar's life. If the Roman authorities reasoned that by sending their dissident child to his home province, he might find there a neutral, stabilizing environment, events would shortly prove their decision to be without foundation. For in the multilayered dislocation of an antique environment where ecclesiastical, viceregal, and local/feudal authorities wrangled over the last ounce of wealth that might be drained from an impoverished countryside, itself infested by bandits and violated by Turkish incursions, the tinder lay at hand for all the confusions of an abortive uprising against an accumulation of injustices and disorders.

Beyond Rome and Naples, in the countryside, the lawlessness that normally prevailed had reached epic proportions by the last decade of the sixteenth century. At the root of the social disorder was a growing downturn in the economy. The disruption most immediately manifested itself in the dislocations experienced by the tenant farmers, engaged in grain production and

[27] LF-*PP*, 37–43.
[28] Badaloni, *Campanella*, 92–93; Villari, *Revolt*, 60–61.

sheep farming. Hitherto this group served as a stabilizing element, providing a damper on the darker, primitive energies of the peasant world. Presently threatened and increasingly undermined, they found themselves unable to pay their rents and labor services, thereby provoking the protests of clergy and landlord. Unrest ramified and with the loosening of the normal ecclesiastical and feudal bonds, the peasant became more susceptible to other currents of a more dramatic or even fantastic sort that might fill the spiritual/emotional vacuum. In the general anarchic struggle against rents the main source of booty and the focus of depredation was the landlord, who thus found himself squeezed often in the interests of a more equitable, if extralegal distribution of wealth. The most prominent bandit, Marco Sciarra, a sort of Robin Hood who operated mainly from the Abruzzi into the Roman Campagna (1585–93), gave to his followers a sense of rough justice, discipline, and esprit de corps; he managed to draw into his net a diversity of supporters and enjoyed the sympathy, connivance, and often outright aid of large segments of the rural population. While the primitive ferocity of the peasant world could respond amiably, if aimlessly, to such banditry, the consolidation of these energies into anything like a political program was lacking. In the absence of a political ideology the unfocused currents of indignation against the oppressiveness of the existing regime actually invited by their very ideological vacuity an authoritative, transcendent impulse that only the resort to the apocalyptic and prophetic could offer to the rebellious urges of a sixteenth-century populace. In the return of a native son, who conjoined prophetic vocation to the beginnings of a political program of populist dimensions, these explosive undercurrents would now obtain confused expression.[29]

Having been absent from his homeland for a decade, Campanella disembarked in July 1598 at Sant' Eufemia in Calabria and promptly settled into the small Dominican convent of S. Maria di Jesù at Stilo. Even if he wanted a retreat, the place hardly afforded him one, for he immediately found himself involved in a jurisdictional controversy between the secular authority and the bishop of Nicastro in which Campanella showed his ecclesiastical colors. The altercation brought him into conspicuous opposition to the *fiscal* or local state prosecutor, Luis de Xarava, later to prove compromising. Also during this early period he wrote as drama and tragedy a play on Mary Queen of Scots, perhaps after his *Monarchia Christianorum* the greatest loss among his unrecovered works. It is hard to believe that the drama did not possess strong

---

[29] Villari, *Revolt*, 35–39, 49–52; on the potential crystallization of a rudimentary populist program in the political thinking of Campanella at this time, the chief evidence can be found in the *Monarchia di Spagna* and its criticism of the Neapolitan nobility. See Bock, *Campanella*, passim. After 1599 the populist element became more explicit. See the present author's "On Reconstituting the Citizenry: Campanella's Criticism of Aristotle's *Politics*," *IPP* 24 (1991): 28–41.

political and religious implications, for the subject gave ample opportunity to depict in the wake of the invincible armada's failure a heroic, if impractical champion of Catholicism in northern Europe.

Both the context provided by a province of the Spanish *monarquía* and his own prior political writings allowed the restless friar to turn his mind to that most signal political fact of his day, the mighty amalgam of Spanish-papal universality. For whatever the very real ongoing tensions and disagreements between successive popes and the king of Spain, the combined weight of these dual authorities was an everyday reality to Campanella. Indeed it would appear that during his first Roman imprisonment he had drafted an earlier, compressed version of what would become the notorious *Monarchia di Spagna*. Now in his withdrawal to Calabria, in the relative quiet afforded by the convent of S. Maria di Jesù at Stilo, he returned to the manuscript of this work to expand it. In chapter 17, "On the Love and Hatred of the People and of Conspiracies," he brooded longer upon the latter problem, now bringing the issue of social justice more to the fore and giving attention to the dangers faced by conspirators.[30] Regarding the work as a whole, two points need to be recognized at this stage. First, although the treatise clearly seeks to present high expectations for the realization of Spanish universality, it is not without forthright criticism of the Spanish—both their social attitudes and technological inadequacies. Second, the priority and preeminence of the clerical partner, the papacy, is never in doubt: the awaited universal *pax hispanica* is but an instrument and function of papal hierocracy.[31]

In his *Dichiarazione*, written immediately after the catastrophe and replete with compromising admissions, Campanella provides a more than usually fresh, essentially ingenuous, statement of his activities at this time—the first months of 1599. His initial self-identification warrants attention: for fifteen years a Dominican, he has become conversant in several *professioni de scienza*, but especially prophecy, so much recommended by St. Paul in Corinthians ("potestis omnes prophetare" 1 Cor. 14:31). He continues:

> Consequently when I consulted the old histories concerning the kingdom of Naples, which always had upheavals [*revoluzione*] with beginning, middle, and end in short under diverse families, it occurred to me that revolution [*mutazione*] ought to happen soon; furthermore when I spoke to the people, they seemed to complain of the ministers of the kingdom. . . . Afterwards when reasoning with several astrologers—especially with the Neapolitan Giulio Cortese, Col' Antonio Stigliola, great mathematician, and Giovan Paolo Vernaleone—all in Naples

---

[30] Comparison is here being made between the recent publication of an earlier version of the TC-*MS*, determined and edited by Dr. Germana Ernst, *La Monarchia di Spagna: Prima stesura giovanile* (Naples, 1989), and the unpublished typescript of the forthcoming definitive, critical edition of the later expanded work, both made available to me by the kindness of Dr. Ernst.

[31] Di Napoli, "L'eresia," 207–12; Bock, *Campanella, passim*; Ernst, TC-*MS*.

three years ago—I understood from them that political revolution [*mutazione di stato*] ought to occur for us.[32]

Beyond the reasonable probability that the authorities would have been leveraged out of their seats in digesting the bland, appalling candor of this statement, for our purposes here it requires careful examination.

The modern sense of revolution is absent from early modern Europe. The idea of a comprehensive shift is associated with astronomy and the heavens, whose shifts may or may not have political-social involvement.[33] The contemporary Italian or more precisely Neapolitan/Calabrian term for such an astronomical shift or revolution is *mutazione*. In using it Campanella leaves his readers in no doubt as to potential political involvement. Significantly, however, he grounds that reality of his perception in his appeal to astronomy, to the findings of the astrologers, and he will continue these reflections by referring to the Bohemian astronomer, Cipriano Leowitz (1521–74), and the Ferrarese astrologer, Antonio Arquato. In doing so Campanella was quite traditional in recognizing the concurrence of Christian time and astrological time—a recognition that Western medieval theology had absorbed ever since the influx of Arab astrology in the twelfth century.[34] In the present passage the historical, the political, and the astronomical stand firmly together and move in accordance with a prophesying promoted by the dreadful imminence of the year 1600. Obscurely, yet decisively, *mutazione* connoted a far more than political transformation; drawing upon Empedoclean and Origenistic cosmological themes, it pointed toward a total transformation, comprehensive and cosmic in scope: *propter melius*, the conflagration of this present world, would lead on to another, magically purified and more lasting.[35]

It would be at least fifteen years later during the decade-long composition of his *Theology* that at one point Campanella revealingly addresses the arresting problem of the unbelieving preacher: not granting an inner assent to what one is mouthing. Impressive is the very candor with which he treats this issue regarding such a preacher's own doubts and disbelief as to the claims being publicly asserted in his preaching. Even though St. Thomas may have pro-

---

[32] Campanella, "Dichiarazione rilasciata a Castelvetere (1599)," in *Autobiografie di filosofi: Cardano, Bruno, Campanella*, ed. Luigi Firpo, Mariarosa Masoero and Giuseppe Zaccaria (Turin, 1982), 144.

[33] See Reinhart Kosellek's article in *GG* on "Revolution," 5:653–788, esp. 714–22; for the more Italian sources and aspects, see Felix Gilbert in *DHI*, 4:152–53, who finds the political notion in Machiavelli and Guicciardini. For the emergence of the term *mutatio* in political literature, see Arist. *Pol.* 5.12.1316a3–11 and subsequent translations, especially those of Bruni and Ficino given in M. J. B. Allen, *Nuptial Arithmetic*, 11–13, n. 19 and 210–11.

[34] LF-*Autobi.*, 144–45, but greatly reinforced in its astronomical associations by Copernicus as well as by contemporary belief in the influence of the stars; Tullio Gregory, "Temps astrologique et temps chrétien," in *Le temps chrétien de la fin de l'Antiquité au moyen Age, IIIe-XIIIe siècle* (Paris, 1984), 557–73.

[35] Badaloni, *Campanella*, 197–98, 201, 327–29; cf. TC-*Meta.*, III, 258, 344–46.

vided for this eventuality and dissolved to his own satisfaction the difficulty, nevertheless the existential reality cracks the logic of the Angelic Doctor: "For someone is able with certain arguments to be moved to propagating without his own assent doctrines that may be undoubted to them to whom he preaches, but not to himself. And this I have often experienced. . . . Yes, he, who in his heart does not believe, seems even able to effect miracles for the establishment of faith."[36] Here Campanella's supporting examples are interesting: one is able to persuade others of astrology while not believing in it oneself; Patriarch Theophilus of Alexandria, often alluded to, impugned Origen while believing in him and reading his books. Indeed according to Philippians 1:15–18, whether in pretence or in truth, Christ is preached and advanced. But for our purposes here the question remains: when did Campanella have anything like a sustained experience of preaching during his entire life, wherein such doubts might be harbored? Only in the fourteen months leading up to the rebellion. Most likely in the very summer of 1599 he experienced the doubts and disbeliefs of an apocalyptic preacher amidst his confident assertions. Passionate astrological convictions and prophecies jostled traditional doctrinal positions. Not that the conspiracy was all a hoax and simply another clear example of simulation. Rather it was a genuine expression of human nature and of the human condition caught up in the context of anxious expectation.

In a series of sermons preached from February to April 1599 Campanella publicly announced in the church at Stilo the imminence of grave, worldly upheavals. When the bishop of Squillace intervened, the friar moved out among the people, sharing reports and beliefs and finding sufficient support among all groups, lay and clerical, nobles and bishops, artisans and peasants to encourage him in his claims. Indicative of the rising level of expectation, the conspiracy would drag within its net the complicity of some high-placed ecclesiastics, the bishop of Mileto, himself a Tufo.[37] Among the most enthusiastic followers numbered fellow Dominican Dionisio Ponzio and the noble landowner Maurizio De Rinaldis, who undertook the negotiations for enlisting the services of the Turkish fleet, ever cruising off the coast and apparently willing to be helpful.

In the goings and comings to his cell Campanella reports to his own advantage the following contretemps with one of his more obstreperous associates, Giulio Contestabile. The latter, seeing on the wall of Campanella's chamber, which also sported pictures of the Transylvanian prince Stephen Bathory and the Turkish sultan Muhammad III, the effigy of King Philip III of Spain, said: "It displeases me that the king [Philip II] has died and the Turks or the French have not yet come to take this kingdom [of Naples]." Campanella: "You there-

---

[36] This important text is presented as an appendix by Romano Amerio, "Un'altra confessione dell'incredulità giovanile del Campanella," *RFNs* 45 (1953): 76–77; cf. also TC-*T*, XIV, 24.

[37] LF-*Autobi.*, 151–52.

fore consider some new things!" Breaking into a rage Contestabile removed the effigy from the wall and stood upon it, proclaiming, "Behold to whom we are subject! To the king of the birds!" claiming him to be an overgrown child, short on governance. Somewhat embarrassed and seeking to report the episode to his own advantage, Campanella dismissed the matter.[38] Whatever the balance of emotions, the encounter suggests that Campanella's apocalyptic preaching appeared in a heavily charged context that was already out of control.

The grandiose exuberance of the movement's intellectual claims beggared only further the meagerness of material support and the poverty of the planning. Yet if the stars were propitious, little else mattered. Even as Brother Dionisio began to preach rebellion at Catanzaro "secondo la profezia mia," as Campanella later explains, the uprising was coming apart in the background, each party going its own way.[39] Beyond the idea of some sort of republic to be presented to the pope, the whole weight of the rebellion fell on the Spanish viceregal regime. On August 10 two defectors divulged the conspiracy to the Spanish public prosecutor, Xarava, and four days later a fellow Dominican denounced Campanella to the Holy Office, a reidentification—for the attention of that body—which our friar did not need. In his subsequent flight from the convent at Stilo Campanella, disguised as a layman, was betrayed into the hands of the secular authority and by September 13 found himself translated to the castle of Squillace, where the Calabrian phase of the trial began, only to be transferred shortly to Gerace. In the scramble of the less compromised to divest themselves of blame, making deals and seeking immunity in exchange for testimony, there ballooned a motley collection of claims and accusations. The depositions provided a thick harvest of charges for later consideration. By the end of October 156 prisoners, among them Campanella, chained in couples, moved in long files on foot to Montelcome, thence to Bivona where they embarked on four galleys. When on November 8 the laden boats came within sight of the triumphant arc of Naples' port, four from the dismal cargo were hanged from the yardarm of each galley in order that all might enter into the spirit of things. And in case the point had not been made with sufficient clarity two others were quartered on the wharf for good measure as a warning to the good folk of Naples.[40]

The Trial

On November 23, 1599, in the fortress of the Castel Nuovo Campanella submitted to the routine examination for purposes of identification. This prelimi-

[38] Ibid., 146–47.
[39] Ibid., 151–52.
[40] Di Napoli, "L'eresia," 216–20; *DBI*, 17:378–79.

nary deposition provides us with a sort of sixteenth-century version of the "mug shot" of the leading conspirator.

> There has been examined a certain young man with black beard, clothed in lay habit, with black cap, black overcoat, leather trousers, and a mantle of that wool commonly called cheap Morano. With his hand on the Bible, having sworn to tell the truth to the relevant questions of the Auditor Antonio Perio he gave the following deposition: [Having sworn and been interrogated regarding his name, place of birth, parents, profession, and permanent domicile, to the last two of these he replied] "my occupation is that of the religious—to recite the office, the Mass, to preach, hear confession; my abode is in Stilo at the convent called Santa Maria di [J]esù of the Dominican order; and if I find myself so garbed in this manner, it is because I fled the wrath of my enemies who persecuted me, namely the public prosecutor Don Luis Sciarava [Xarava] and Giovan Geronimo Morano who oppressed me." Asked as to how much time had passed since he had entered the convent and assumed the habit of the order, he replied, "In the year 1581 it appears to me that I entered the religious and first became a cleric."

At this point the auditor interrupted the interrogation, apparently with the intention of returning to it later.[41]

Campanella's struggle for mere survival now began in violent earnest. Confined to the Castel Nuovo, he busily composed poems and anxious slips to maintain the spirits of his comrades and to urge their retraction of earlier confessions. Meanwhile the wheels began to turn for his own trial. On January 11, 1600, Clement VIII, having failed to obtain the transfer to Rome of those suspected of heresy, constituted the tribunal for judging the clerics involved in the uprising; it included among others the Dominican Alberto Tragagliola, the commissary general of the Inquisition, who had earlier shown some sympathy and understanding for Campanella. Nevertheless the tribunal promptly applied to Rome for permission to use torture; when on its being granted, Campanella was subjected to several rounds first of the *coccodrillo*'s week-long solitary, subterranean isolation, then the more forceful *polledro*, designed to rupture veins and tissue; the prisoner succumbed to a confession of having wanted to create a new sort of republic, but denied having plotted the rebellion. His own defense seems to have been devised now as proceeding on two tracks: a justification of his own role that came to be set forth in the *Prima* and then *Se-*

---

[41] *Il supplizio di Tommaso Campanella: Narrazioni, Documente verbali delle torture*, ed. Luigi Firpo (Rome, 1985), 67–71. On Campanella's initial interrogation, see also the anonymous report coming from Reggio, October 8, 1599, published by J. Kvačala, "Thomas Campanella und Ferdinand II," *Sitzungsberichte der philosophisch-historischen Klasse der Kaiserlichen Akademie der Wissenschaften* 159 (1908): 29–32; "d'età d'anni 35 in circa, di statura alta, faccia pallida, pilo negro, e denti rari . . ." which ends on the alarming note that "haveva pensato pigliarsi per moglie otto o diece titulate delle prime della provincia, ammazzando prima lor mariti, e tener un seraglio nel Castello di Stilo designato per sua residenza."

cunda delineatio defensionum; and his feigning madness—an act evinced by his setting fire to the contents of his cell on April 2.[42]

In the first of these justificatory statements Campanella sought to present himself, somewhat naively, as one without malevolence toward the Spanish regime but guided rather by prophecy, human and divine. Of course it is to his interest to claim the *Monarchia de Spagna* to have been written in the months immediately prior to the uprising, a probability that can now no longer be disallowed.[43] Apocalyptic expectations increase with the accumulation of evidence: preaching the gospel in the New World, the coming of the fateful year 1600, a great comet seen in the sky.[44] The genuinely messianic emerges in a familiar note struck from the developing Campanellan repertoire: "And although some Fathers sustain by means of an anagogic interpretation that only in heaven will be realized the reconciled future community, nevertheless the Fathers cited above with whom I agree allow for a literal interpretation according to which some sort of prelude of the heavenly city is already to be realized on earth."[45] By seeking shelter under the reputation of the Dominican order, for which he claims a central role in the new ordering, he denies that such *mutazioni* should occur to the prejudice of the king of Spain.[46] He strives to distance himself from Maurizio de Rinaldis and his Turkish involvements.[47] Confessions under torture naturally implicate the innocent.[48] In denying any heresy on his part he avers that it is not possible to establish heresy in Calabria without disposing of the forces of the nobility.[49] He alludes to the accomplices of Catiline, convicted and confessed of having conspired— neither of which Campanella had as yet done—yet they had still proved able to engage the support of some members, led by Caesar, of an otherwise most hostile senate that they be imprisoned and not executed.[50] Campanella represents himself as a fly in the maelstrom of a movement out of control, merely guided by prophets and the stars![51] Pleading clerical privilege and the office of a prophet, he claims not to have been alone in desiring to institute the republic.[52]

The prophetic element defines even more decisively the second *Delineatio*, which would constitute the outline for his impending *Articuli prophetales*. Again he prefers the historic to the anagogic sense in interpreting the millen-

[42] "Prima delineatio defensionum . . . (1600)," in LF-*Autobi.*, 156–57.
[43] Ibid., 160–61.
[44] Ibid., 163–66.
[45] Ibid., 166–67.
[46] Ibid., 169–70.
[47] Ibid., 176.
[48] Ibid., 179.
[49] Ibid., 180.
[50] Ibid., 182.
[51] Ibid.
[52] Ibid.,182–84.

nium and claims for support not only the usual assemblage of early church fathers but now Dante, Petrarch, and Abbot Joachim.[53] The republic's imminence signified the elimination of all *principati* and authorities, which will be reduced to Christ Himself governing the world in the person of the pope[54] under whom and in the Church's interest Spain's king, the Catholic, hence universal king, beginning with the New World, will establish the Church throughout the terrestrial circumference. It is interesting to note that in this sacerdotal republic the Turks will come to learn that their paradise, which included eating and marriage, does not pertain to heaven but to earth in this earthly "preludio del Paradiso celeste."[55] Amidst the rich messianic-millenarian lore one may stop to appreciate those signs that must have impelled Campanella to take the fatal step that he did in the spring and summer of 1599, signs that amount to a distillation of early modern European experience:

> Indeed eclipses, inundations, venereal diseases, the discovery of America, the reform of the calendar at the time of Gregory XIII, death, pestilences, past heresies, the observed stellar motions, the census of the Kingdom of Naples, the impending division of the Turkish empire, the lack of faith, the monstrous invasion of locusts into Italy all augur changes in human affairs. But if a general transformation [*mutazione*] should impend for us, certainly it will happen on a crucial date, thus in the next seven-year period following the year 1600.[56]

Especially when it comes to the arguing of his own prophetic orthodoxy,[57] based largely on the earliest of the church fathers, Campanella suggests for his part a vehement naivete and a terrifying sincerity. To an official of any worldly order the two defenses would have proved less than reassuring. Indeed from the distance of four hundred years and shorn of the clerical and millenarian dimensions that so profoundly pervaded the culture of Latin Europe in 1600, one can only marvel at the Augustinian wisdom of the Western Church in late antiquity, when it preferred the anagogic to the historical reading of apparently apocalyptic biblical texts. Or, differently expressed, one may appreciate the wisdom of any establishment that would keep such a destabilizing influence as this Dominican friar under lock and key.

Along with his apparent claims to being a messiah Campanella seems to have endowed himself with the aura of a divine or charismatic person or at least projected the qualities of a holy man. Twenty years after the event, in writing that part of his extensive theology called *Vita Christi*, he will slip into a parallelling of his own self-presentation with that of Christ. Then in reflect-

[53] "Secunda delineatio . . . (1600)," in LF-*Autobi.*, 192–93.
[54] Ibid., 194.
[55] Ibid., 200.
[56] Ibid., 210.
[57] Ibid., 192.

ing upon the conspiracy of 1599 and its failure, he allows that as with the soldiers trying to partake of Christ's benefits by touching His clothing, so did the king of Spain's soldiers, in afflicting him as heresiarch and rebel, secretly seek his blessings and *arcana* for their own betterment; while publicly execrating him, secretly they besought him.[58]

Apart from these parenthetical musings the real question needs to be asked: how guilty was Campanella? Did he fairly represent his own complicity? Beyond the fact that the prophetic note provided the most obviously inflammatory element for any contemporary uprising seeking to enlist all groups, beyond this torch in the arsenal, the expressly anti-Spanish dimensions to Campanella's personal perception of the enterprise might well have been minimal. In fact apart from some well-founded criticisms of Spain, his most explicit hostility fell upon the Neapolitan nobility. Were there not other aspects to the uprising, however, that Campanella could readily accept on his own terms yet exclude from admission? It is not that his justificatory pieces in explanation of his conduct are false. What may Campanella have chosen to omit from the accounts of his own motivation and participation in the affair?

In the aftermath of the abortive conspiracy the participants scrambled to divest themselves of responsibility by denial, silence, or charges directed toward its fallen leader. From the depositions, often extreme and outrageous in their claims, Campanella emerges as the target of accusations ranging from free love and naturalistic religion to atheism. In any assessment of the conflicting evidence one may be encouraged to associate Campanella with those ideas that have either appeared earlier or will reappear in his expressed thought. Ideas that repeatedly recur in the charges of the depositions without clear confirmation in any of Campanella's writings may be understood as a product generated by the collective excitement, expectation, and aspirations of the moment, which in the disenchantment following its dissolution tend generally to flow as accusations in the direction of the thwarted messiah. Such accusations cannot be rejected out of hand as inapplicable to Campanella, for more than anything else his was the messianism that had made the movement and, given the intricate recesses and instabilities of his personality, they are not to be entirely divorced from what he would later admit to Galileo as being "the sins of his youth."[59] Finally, as some sort of control over the refuse of charges, nothing can be admitted as authentically Campanellan that stands clearly opposed to a radical Christian view of the realized, apocalyptic republic.

Among several accusations of atheism attributed to Campanella stands one that envelops an important issue and position in the Dominican's thought. At the beginning of a long summary statement of the trial drawn up by the bishop of Caserta we learn from a secondhand report originating with his fellow friar,

---

[58] TC-*T*, XXI (*Vita Christi*), 118.
[59] TC-*Lett*., 178.

Dionisio Ponzio—possibly the most violent and erratic of all his accomplices and one who would shortly abscond to Islam—that Campanella did not believe in God's existence. Indeed to him it seemed incredible that Christians, constituting but a mere fraction of the human race, comparable to a fingernail (*un'ongia*) of the human body, should be saved and all the rest of humanity damned.[60] Despite the unreliability of Friar Dionisio as a source attesting to Campanella's "atheism" at this particular moment, we can afford to entertain the possibility, even probability, that the new messiah could have been overheard denying the Christian God. For there are many levels to sixteenth-century atheism. Such a denial does not entail his principal understanding of God as identical with nature.[61] More important and clearly more enduring than the uncertainties of his atheism appears its basis in the anguish that he experiences over the limitations to Christian salvation. This continuing anguish would come to operate in his theology so that despite his occasional anti-Molinist posturings he will end by marching with the Jesuits on this issue in express opposition to the latest "Calvinistic" developments within the camp of his fellow Dominicans.[62] And in the decisive statements stemming from the defense of his own position in *Atheism Conquered* he will repeatedly allude to that same, small Christian fingernail of the entire human body that represents the saved from all humankind.[63]

Repeated charges mount to construct the picture of a community and its leader naturalistic in aspiration and far removed from traditional Christianity. Indeed the prophetic evidence and inspiration for the millenarian aeon is more astrological than scriptural, pertaining more to a republic than to a kingdom. Against a backdrop of anticlerical denunciations[64] two issues stand out: denial of the sacraments and the sexual freedom advocated by the self-styled messiah. Individual accomplices attest to Campanella's cavalier dismissal of the sacraments, which he claimed to be the result of reasons of state or inventions of the apostles in order to spread the faith.[65] Repeatedly throughout his writings Campanella will reiterate that Christ is but the Primal Reason and that Christianity adds nothing new to the basic prevailing rational religious naturalism but the sacraments.[66] Although by the time he writes on *sacri segni* in his *Theology* around 1616, he is formally correct enough, yet it would have been quite possible for him in the right context and atmosphere to assume a

---

[60] Amab., *Doc.*, I, 421/393.

[61] Ibid., 261/311.

[62] "Compendium de praedestinatione," in *Opuscoli inediti*, ed. Luigi Firpo (Florence, 1951), 128–30; cf. also TC-*DPLC*, 101–3, 119–20.

[63] TC-*AT*, 9–10; TC-*T*, XVIII, 30; TC-*Risp.*, 12.

[64] Amab., *Doc.*, I, 196/269, 200/278, 229/296, 255/307.

[65] Ibid., 200/278, 204/279, 229/296, 310/343, 431/393, 456–57/394.

[66] TC-*Lett.*, 15; TC-*AT*, 126; TC-*T*, XXIII, 11; cf. also TC-*AP*, 134; TC-*AT*, 74, 79; and TC-*MM*, 42.

much more casual, dismissive stance toward the sacramental system together with much of ecclesiastical ceremony.

It is equally possible that, given the excitement of the apocalyptic moment, the naturalistic impulses of the community's experience should have spilled over into sexual license and a denunciation of clerical celibacy. Two separate witnesses among the assemblage of clerical culprits attest that Campanella had announced that the venereal act is perfectly licit; just as man is able to use his arm or foot for a natural function so he is able to use the virile member.[67] One of the two fellow friars, Domenico Petrolo, hostile to Campanella, asserted that one of his sisters had become enamored of Campanella and they had sinned together.[68] In a similar vein Petrolo later claimed that Campanella, while announcing the pope and prelates to be usurpers and tyrants, rejected monasteries as mere devices for preventing the procreation of the species.[69] In the *City of the Sun*, written shortly after these events, the priests, presumably less spirited than the rest, would be compensated with the best women.[70]

One could go on examining this highly ambiguous material. It is not that we can here be more clever than the Neapolitan Inquisition, which sought apparently to dismiss most of the more extreme and exaggerated accusations or simply rap them up in a bundle designated "heresy." The Church's apologists had always represented heresy as a seamless garment, something totally corruptive and all of one piece. On the other hand its defenders in the legal prosecution of heresy were perfectly adept at drawing distinctions.[71] Yet any effort to understand Campanella's mind and actions during the summer and early fall of 1599 needs to take into account a number of factors militating toward the credibility, even veracity, of many of the accusations leveled against him: (1) as a constrained, thwarted, highly intellectual friar, he came to this event after a decade of repeated detentions, investigations, and incarcerations; (2) the excitement of the chiliastic moment and of the prophet turned messiah worked to dissolve all the normal rules and distinctions; (3) there is enough preparation in Campanella's prior thinking and resonances in his later writings to prevent any easy dismissal of these accusations. Later in a letter to King Philip III of Spain he probably spoke the truth when he allowed that the movement had had its violent wing identified with Dionisio Ponzio and Maurice de Rinaldis.[72] Regarding the expressly violent and extreme aspects of

---

[67] Amab., *Doc.*, I, 261/311, 434/393. For further radical statements bearing on the sexual, see Blanchet, *Campanella*, 39/n. 2.

[68] Amab., *Doc.*, I, 378–79/371.

[69] Ibid., 508–9/408.

[70] *La città del sole: Dialogo poetico*, trans. and annot. Daniel J. Donno (Berkeley/Los Angeles/London, 1981), 56–57.

[71] On *proposizioni eretricali*, see John Tedeschi, *The Prosecution of Heresy: Collected Studies on the Inquisition in Early Modern Italy* (Binghamton, N.Y., 1991), 99, and the related chapter, 89–126.

[72] TC-*Lett.*, 77.

the uprising Ponzio surely qualifies for a double share of the guilt. Indeed one witness who had known Campanella at Santa Sabina averred that he had always considered Ponzio as an unstable, restless rascal, while affirming the basically good character of Campanella.[73] Nevertheless without Campanella the Calabrian conspiracy of 1599 would never have had its apocalyptic force and brief release of terrifying energies.

Campanella's case came before an overworked inquisitorial tribunal. All four in the Roman system reached their highest level of activity in the late sixteenth and early seventeenth centuries. Naples' business peaked in the 1590s with over four hundred accused, followed by three hundred for the 1601–10 period.[74] By the beginning of January 1601 the tribunal for heresy had distilled five specific charges against Campanella out of the medley of accusations deriving from successive depositions: (1) sexual liberty, including sodomy, does not constitute sin; (2) Turkish doctrine is better than the Christian; (3) Mass celebrated by a priest in mortal sin or requested by a person in mortal sin is not valid; (4) all the existing religious orders are not necessary; (5) eternal salvation is possible even without baptism. Only the last three have some resonance within the theology of the prisoner. But what of those pertaining to his behavior and to claims that might have been made at the time of the uprising? Lurid and monstrous as some of the five appear, collectively they register a considerable reduction from the grab bag of twelve drawn from the Calabrian depositions taken at Castelvetere. While there is no need to rehearse them all here, a few and their comparison with the later distillation of charges against Campanella invite attention.[75] The first two deny the Trinity, Christ as God incarnate, His miracles, and the institution of the sacraments. The ninth charge ("sexual liberty is licit") has an authentic ring to it and even more so the eleventh ("community of goods and of women is licit and advisable"). While this distinctively Campanellan idea would achieve fruition in the *City of the Sun* and some of his later writings, its practical root goes back to the horse breeding of his friend Mario del Tufo in the summer of 1591 and would have achieved nourishment and development in the Dominican's conversations with Francesco Pucci in 1597.[76] On the other hand despite its authentic ring and later development in Campanella's thought, community of women could be seen as a natural outgrowth of most extreme, communitarian efforts. The vagrant charges of personal sexual promiscuity leveled against Campanella by his accomplices under pressure can never be entirely dismissed. The importance of this issue here lies in the fact that it served as a significant

---

[73] Amab., *Doc.*, I, 217/284.
[74] Tedeschi, *Prosecution*, 92.
[75] See here Di Napoli, "L'eresia," 221–24.
[76] Firpo, "Processo," *RF* 40 (1949): 392.

ingredient in the rebellion; Campanella knew it, yet barely hinted at it in his defense.[77]

The most reliable of Campanella's writings deriving from the early spring of 1600 is his *Appendix ad amicum pro apologia*. Written in the form of a letter to one of the major accomplices in the conspiracy, most probably Dionisio Ponzio, it could not afford to misrepresent the facts. Campanella begins by admonishing Fra Dionisio that he ought to be mad at himself, not Campanella, for "you spoke what you little understood." To his disenchanted fellow Dominican Campanella reasserts the credibility and validity of his preaching—preaching directed toward the breakthrough of a new aeon and a new community. He reviews the signs, the comments, the words of prophecy from pagans as well as Christian and Jew attesting "rempublicam sanctam a prophetis, et philosophis, et gentibus expectatam." The entire clergy has been bought by the secular powers. Do you not see what our brethren impose on us? Against the world's accusation of rebellion and heresy Campanella proceeds to align the great Jewish prophets with an assortment of classical philosophers and stalwart republican conspirators, including among others Socrates, Lucan, Thrasea Paetus, Pythagoras, and Plato in the *Apology* all combatting this most perennial accusation of the world. With unshakable confidence in this desired republic that he had preached, Campanella, seeking to classify and justify the confession that had been forced from him so recently, asserts that he confessed not to heresy or rebellion but to having wanted to educe good from a bad event. Here, interestingly, he appeals to the example of the Venetians who, with Aquilea attacked by Attila, as rebels from the empire, withdrew to the lagoons and constituted a new and free republic from the empire, thereby turning a bad situation to good. And, yes, when he speaks of the reformation of the Dominicans it is for having wanted to prepare for the expected republic.[78] Thus he again reasserts the centrality of prophecy (the expectation of *magna mutatio* for bringing in the promised community), its definitive role in his thought as well as in the recent uprising, and the validity of his own prophetic credentials.

If 1600 had been the year in which Campanella composed his widely read *Monarchia di Spagna*, he would have written it under less than ideal circumstances. After April 2 the prisoner had embarked upon a plan to simulate madness. Three successive interrogations, conducted May 17, 18, and 20, failed to break him, although the torture of the cord had been applied in the second instance for an hour. To Tragagliola, the commissary general of the Inquisition, fresh from the experience of Bruno's burning in Rome, Campanella was by now well known. If convinced of the irregularity of the Cal-

[77] LF-*Autobi.*, 182.
[78] Firpo, "Una autoapologia del Campanella," *RF* 32 (1941): 96–110, esp. 97–99, 103–8.

abrian trials and persuaded of the insubstantial nature of some of the present accusations, Tragagliola together with the nuncio apparently had no doubt as to the considerable enormity of Campanella's heresy. Both wrote several times to the Holy Office, expressing reservations and urging greater efforts to have the case extradited to Rome. In his letter of late December 1599 to Cardinal Aldobrandini the nuncio expressed the issue succinctly: a case of human rebellion must not be allowed to outweigh and displace one of divine rebellion.[79]

Nevertheless the ecclesiastical efforts to extradite the case and its clerical leadership to Rome, reasonable, even most appropriate as they appeared, proved vain. For the Spanish viceroy, the count of Lemos, remained adamantly opposed to any loosening of the monarchy's grip upon the unhappy friar and company. His correspondence with the king of Spain strikingly reveals the government's perception of Campanella's character, his intentions in the present instance, and the nature of the revolt itself. Campanella is introduced as the principal conspirator, preeminent in the sciences and claiming miraculous, even diabolical works according to some such as Cardinal Aldobrandini. The rebellion had as its target the king and the insupportable evil of his ministers, who by usurpation and tyranny burden the sweat of the poor and tyrannically occupy Naples, a kingdom belonging to the Holy Church. Indeed they claim that all the kings of Spain have usurped the states of the Church. Their own action thus seeks to remedy this injustice toward the Church's vicar and to dispense with such slavery and tyranny, releasing the people from their present calamity in order to realize the pristine liberty of a republic as earlier existed; they would recognize the Holy Church as lord merely by giving their free consent to the pope and a modest tribute.[80] Significantly, the viceroy will shortly add to this picture by informing his king on September 11 that as the chief mover of the rebellion, the knave Campanella sought to include the pope in this dance, and if the fruits of its success were to accrue to anyone, it would have been to the pope and not to the Turk.[81] Given thus the traditional Spanish sensitivity to papal interference with Naples and impressed by the enormity of Campanella's horrendous heresies,[82] the viceroy went to unusual lengths to secure the royal detention of the chief conspirator.[83] By May 26 of the next year, despite the huge efforts of the nuncio and the bishop of Termoli to have the case removed to Rome, Lemos could crow to his master that he was hanging tough ("yo e tenido tiesso") and would only let the lot of culpable friars depart northward as hanged corpses or in ashes

[79] Amab., *Doc.*, I, 59/78; Di Napoli, "L'eresia," 223–24.
[80] Amab., *Doc.*, I, 15–17/7.
[81] Ibid., 22/14.
[82] Ibid., 25/17.
[83] Ibid., 42–43/37.

("ahorcados o quemados").[84] Campanella's prospects dimmed further: by the first day of the new year Tragagliola had died.[85] The much more severe Benedetto Mandina, bishop of Caserta, now succeeded to the tribunal.

Campanella could hardly have been in a more dangerous position. Because he was a *lapsus* who had abjured in 1595, any further suspicion of heresy could send him down the slippery slopes to the condition of *relapsus* and thus make him a candidate for being relaxed to the secular authorities for burning. Little wonder he was now seeking to establish his madness and thereby according to canon law unable to be punished as an impenitent heretic, when unable to experience that ultimate qualifying penance. Nevertheless the fact that Campanella had been provided legal counsel for his defense signified a concession impossible for an obvious heretic. Furthermore his lawyer blew holes during the spring of 1601 in the last three of the five charges against Campanella, charges pertaining to baptism, the Mass, and the irrelevance of the religious orders, in other words the most theologically sensitive issues, while the remainder, consisting of sexual license and the preference for Turkish over Christian doctrine, seemed mildly insubstantial compared to the rich possibilities lurking in the friar's thought.[86]

From Rome on May 31 came the order to ascertain definitively whether the prisoner's madness was real or feigned. The frightful torture of *la veglia* or "the awakener" would serve as the instrument for determination. The supreme moment in Campanella's life had arrived: failure to sustain the punishment and thereby end it through admission of simulating madness warranted death; the practical enjoyment of the torture won survival through a saving madness, legally established.

The ordeal would last a total of forty hours, thirty-six of them unremitting; it took place in the bowels of the Castel Nuovo on June 4–5, 1601. The written account of the event offers a mixture of curial Latin, salted with Italian, interspersed by splutterings of Calabrian dialect, suggesting the incongruities of the situation. The exquisite concern of the examiners as they duly pursue the legal process contrasts with the shattering torment of their prisoner, steadied only by a fierce, terrible determination: the smothered shouts, plaintive cries, disjointed references—"ten white horses," "I am slaughtered," "Enthrone and shut up"—hour after hour, one day following the next, all without sleep; the terrible monotony of pain interrupted only by an escorted visit to the adjoining latrine; and then at one point the sound of the trumpet from a trireme as it drew up to the mole of the Castel Nuovo. When asked to neglect the now lost body and to give thought instead to the salvation of his soul, there flashed

---

[84] Ibid., 45/41.
[85] Di Napoli, "L'eresia," 223–24.
[86] Ibid., 224–29.

back from that broken heap of mortality the fierce assertion: "The soul is immortal!"[87]

It was over. He could be declared officially mad. The taurine strength and adamantine determination of a single man had prevailed in defying the most impressive procedures this world could inflict. In our natural rush to sympathy and admiration for the victim we tend to forget the endurance of Campanella's august inquisitors and the faithful, illiterate, but well-meaning jailer, Giacomo Ferraro, who also stayed the forty hours.[88] Posterity can afford to celebrate them also in this mortal game of being tested, enduring, surviving. One thinks of Giordano Bruno's statement to his judges on hearing the terrible sentence to a death by burning: perhaps his judges had experienced more fear in pronouncing the sentence than he in hearing it.[89] As the jailer gathered up the remains of the tortured prisoner to help him back to his cell, there to render some basic salves and wrestle his limbs back into their appropriate sockets, he heard Campanella whisper: "Did they really think that I would be enough of a blockhead to speak?"[90]

On January 8, 1603, the Neapolitan tribunal summoned the prisoner to hear the sentence that the Holy Office in plenary congregation had formulated in Rome two months earlier: that "pro causis haeresis" he was condemned to perpetual imprisonment for life without any hope of liberation. The sentence proves puzzling because if a heretic, then he was a *relapsus* subject to death by burning, if impenitent; or death by decapitation, if penitent, followed by relaxation of the body to the secular power for burning. Apparently the legally established madness of the prisoner, although the simulation of madness had been dropped since "the awakener," had had the effect of gumming up normal procedure.[91] For the question had been one of heresy, not disbelief or atheism on the part of the prisoner, who in successive memorials to Paul V, Rudolf II, and Philip III would proclaim that he was neither a heretic convicted or confessed. The deflation of the earlier Calabrian charges as they moved to the Neapolitan trial and the successful defense of Campanella by his lawyer had apparently left no specific charge in place. And even after Tragagliola's demise there remained the vague sense of sympathy and potential support in high places—a sympathy that the prisoner would now proceed to probe. If one considers the number of statements and issues in Campanella's writings up to this point that possessed a heterodox ring, it seems puzzling that no specific

---

[87] LF-*Suppliz.*, 13–14, 205–27. At the end of his life Campanella would tuck into his *PR* (Ethica, Qu.1) 8 his own description of the torture, the forty-hour ordeal, and the moral implications. See the Intermezzo herein.

[88] On the divergence here from Roman practices, see Tedeschi, *Prosecution*, 58, 145.

[89] Quoted in Luigi Firpo, "Il processo di Giordano Bruno," *RSI* 61 (1949): 49.

[90] LF-*Suppliz.*, 229–33.

[91] Di Napoli, "L'eresia," 226–29.

charges were developed against him.[92] "Pro causis haeresis" indeed. It would appear that the Holy Office in its greater wisdom had decided to detain the intellectually and politically restless prisoner on the basis of his past performance and for good measure. From the perspective of the established authorities it was a sound, commendable decision.

As for the prisoner in his newly defined liberty, no matter how straitened the physical circumstances, he would now have ample opportunity to pursue the mind's ponderings in the enforced privacy of his cell and of his skull.

Prisons and the Prisoner

For the next quarter century Campanella remained a prisoner. He would be juggled among the three Neapolitan prisons of Castel Nuovo, Sant' Elmo, and Castel dell'Ovo, each with its peculiar features, the second being easily the worst. To attempt to measure the intellectual vitality and courage of the man, manifest in the torrent of writings poured forth from his respective cells, we need to consider something of the nature of an early-seventeenth-century European prison.

Recent historiography has turned with increasing interest to the study of the early modern European prison, not only as a manifestation of the emerging state, but also as an expression of larger cultural, legal, and moral realities. At the outset, there existed from the long medieval experience a curiously revealing relationship between the monastery and the prison. Beyond the issue as to how many monks and nuns perceived their abode as a prison, both ecclesiastical and secular judges sentenced the condemned to monastic imprisonment. Thus religious establishments served as the first places where penal imprisonment occurred as the result of a judicial decision by trial. Not only did monastery and prison interrelate but also charity with workhouse, imprisonment with poor relief, love with repression, even the government-related brothel, where, according to one author considering government regulation in fifteenth-century Languedoc, prostitutes lived "virtually cloistered." What the monastic model provided in an otherwise unruly world was order, regimentation, and the golden bond of discipline all within the citadel of love.

In the process of secularizing the carceral, Venice, among Italian cities, had begun by the mid-fourteenth century to make extensive use of penal servitude. At the same time in Florence, there began to emerge the secular prisons of the Bargello and Stinche, the first largely for political prisoners, the second largely for debtors. The prisoner was usually expected to provide his own means of support. Alms, state support, and sometimes even the creditors themselves contributed to the maintenance of the impoverished offender.

---

[92] On some of the parameters of inquisitiorial practice, see the excellent analysis in Tedeschi, *Prosecution*, 144–45.

While detention seemed to serve more the purposes of the trial process rather than the punishment itself, for the more punitive purpose of incarceration, the southern European, Catholic countries enjoyed a considerable advantage over the more Protestant north: the Mediterranean, which offered superlative outdoor relief to the overcrowded prisons of southern Europe in the form of those galleys plying its waters by means of chained oarsmen. Indeed the very words *galera* and *prigione* would become almost synonymous. In concluding these preliminary observations we may note one further feature that could bear directly upon the long ordeal of our Calabrian prophet: at least in the Dutch, Protestant pattern evident at Haarlem and at Delft, visitors to inmates purchased entrance tickets.[93]

Prisons varied enormously in their amenities and conditions. At the upper end of the scale running from best to worst stand most probably the prisons of the Holy Office in Rome, housed in the Palazzo Pucci.

> [C]ells were commodious and well lit, and could be furnished by prisoners at their own cost with a bed, table, sheets, and towels. The Inquisition itself was only expected to provide a straw pallet, a single sheet, and a long cloak or blanket. Prisoners had access to a barber, bathing facilities, laundry service, and mending and were permitted a change of clothing twice weekly. All this was at their expense, if they could afford it. In the case of the indigent, public charity would be expected to support them (more modestly), while religious were considered the burdens of their orders. Prisoners appeared periodically before the Congregation to testify concerning their material needs and the cardinals, in turn, were obliged to inspect conditions in the prisons. As for prohibitions, prisoners could not converse with their fellows in other cells; they could not attempt to read or write about matters that did not immediately concern their cases; nor could they converse privately with their jailers or use them to communicate with the outside world. These optimum conditions were clearly not met in the provinical tribunals. There, facilities were frequently inferior, when they existed at all, as we learn from prisoners' appeals and from the repeated attempt by Rome to remedy the situations.[94]

Since one's maintenance as a prisoner depended upon one's rank and order in the universally hierarchicalized societies of the age, everything turned upon the individual's recognized status and perceived importance; a great noble could live most agreeably, holding court with his friends and retainers and generally enjoying comforts comparable to a modern Colombian drug lord. Here possibly the "Wizard Earl," Henry Percy, ninth earl of Northumberland,

---

[93] Peter Spierenburg, *The Prison Experience: Disciplinary Institutions and Their Inmates in Early Modern Europe* (New Brunswick/London, 1991), 14–16, 26, 43, 57, 83, 90–93, 110–11, 274; John K. Brackett, *Criminal Justice and Crime in Late Renaissance Florence, 1537–1609* (Cambridge, 1992), 40–42, 51–56.

[94] Tedeschi, *Prosecution*, 148–49.

represents the most extreme case. During the sixteen years (1605–21) of his sojourn in the Tower, Percy enjoyed a well-stocked personal library, one of the best-appointed tables in England, a bowling green, and a distillery for alchemical experiments (these last two in the lord lieutenant's garden), not to mention the pleasant company of his pensioners and friends among whom could be numbered the incomparable fellow prisoner, Sir Walter Raleigh.[95] All this was of course very English and quite exceptional. For ordinary mortals imprisonment could be expected to be considerably less agreeable.

At the other end of the scale the indigent were as always out of luck; they had to depend upon public charity or the barest minimum for maintenance. Survival would hinge upon one's wits and a form of networking. A friar, ostensibly armored to require the least and to thrive spiritually on less than the least, could ultimately look to his own religious order for maintenance, provided the context was European or Spanish-American. Far the most appalling case at the remotest end of the scale derives from the experience of the Dominican missionaries to Japan, persecuted, imprisoned, and martyred at Nagasaki in the 1617–22 period. Again, following the natural reaction of admiration for the superhuman courage and endurance of the friars, one's heart goes out in commiseration toward the Japanese *daimyos* on seeing their authority shattered upon the reefs of Western religious zeal and determination. Beyond its very contemporaneity the Japanese example proves instructive in another respect: the mystery of communication or how individuals held in apparently close confinement may nevertheless release important writings and testimonials to the outside world.[96] At least prior to the Panoptic State, prisons, it would be fair to speculate, depended for their security upon the fragile morality of the bribable jailor. Even the grimmest seventeenth-century prison represented ultimately a permeable affair.

Only the most skeptical and unsympathetic reader of Campanella's repeated appeals would deny that the Calabrian friar's living conditions, especially at San Elmo, left something to be desired. Castel Nuovo, where Campanella was first incarcerated until his effort to escape in 1604, offered conditions that were only less than tolerable. It is during the first years at San Elmo that we recover, ascending from the dark depths of his fetid cell, the repeated supplications, concentrated in the first stay (1604–8) rather than the later one (1614–18). For in the earlier instance the harshness of his conditions coalesced with the very real possibilities of his liberation, raised by his ostensible friend, Kaspar Schoppe, to make all the more painful those pleas, cries, and laments coming from the abyss of his imprisonment. Writing to Paul V in mid-August 1606 Campanella sends up a cry to be released from "questa fossa

---

[95] John William Shirley, "The Scientific Experiments of Sir Walter Raleigh, the Wizard Earl, and the Three Magi in the Tower," *Ambix* 4 (1949): 52–66.

[96] C. R. Boxer and J. S. Cummins, "The Dominican Mission in Japan (1602–1622) and Lope de Vega," *AFP* 33 (1963): 5–85, esp. 47–57.

orrenda." He reports how the captain of the guard had shown the visiting nuncio the prison from the outside and well out of reach of its occupant, making the solicitous ecclesiastic believe that all was well, without ever bothering to descend the twenty-two steps to that cell where the walls oozed water, the ground was always damp, and the rain frequently entered, thus adding to the ever-present slime. And always pervasive stench and all-enveloping darkness prevailed.[97] A month later the straitened friar will inform the pontiff how he had overheard the prison barber chatting with the guards whereby he learned that the papacy had excommunicated Venice. Amidst all his opportunism, dissimulation, and simulation Campanella will feel compelled to inflict some frank advice and hard criticism upon the current papacy, culminating in a quotation from an earlier, most vehement critic of the contemporary papacy in the mounting denunciation of greed and subversion placed in the mouth of Marco Lombardo. But he will not follow the great exile up the path of a purely pastoral papacy.[98] With March 1607 the complaint comes to be reiterated from darkest depths to the same: "for eight years most Holy Father I have been in a dungeon where I see neither light nor sky, always chained, suffering from bad eating and worse sleeping, with headaches, pain in the chest."[99] A month later to Philip III of Spain he describes himself as "existing within the lowest depths [sto intra un calaboso] in consuming, fetid darkness, never seeing sun or air, receiving neither sacrament nor Mass [certainly an exaggeration] with water oozing through the walls summer and winter, eating little and badly, sleeping night and day with the crickets, ever in the power of a lieutenant, the friend of his enemies."[100] To Antonio Querengo in July he will describe his subterranean existence in the same terms, adding that shackled upon a foul, sweat-ridden straw mattress, never seeing light or human persons other than three hours of light in the afternoon when he pursues his writing secretively and a little in the morning for saying the office, he nevertheless can thank God for allowing him clandestinely to communicate with friends outside, working for his release. Perhaps most mind-numbing is his further claim that he has not for the past eight years spoken seriously in his own tongue to anyone from the outside world. Then from the depths of his Caucasus come three words summing up his condition: a living death (*Sto quasi morendo*).[101]

While a private individual could expect to have the expenses of maintenance in prison paid out of his own estate, a member of a religious order would look to the good offices of the local provincial. The records provide

---

[97] TC-*Lett.*, 18; Firpo, "Appunti campanelliani: Un memoriale inedito dalla fossa di Castel S. Elmo," *GCFI* 32 (1953): 482–87.
[98] TC-*Lett.*, 38, 44; on Marco Lombardo, see *Purg.* 16.101–3.
[99] TC-*Lett.*, 52.
[100] Ibid., 78.
[101] Ibid., 132, 135–36.

occasional notice as to the supply of hose, mantle, and other necessaries,[102] as well as complaints from the supplier regarding excessive expenses rung up by the friar in his final Roman imprisonment: let monthly allowances for such needs be limited to ten *scudi*![103] Access to books and writing materials was at worst furtive, at best intermittent and uncertain. We know that Antonio Persio, his friend from Paduan days, sent him in 1611 Galileo's *Sidereus Nuncius* and the writings of Tycho Brahe, and Gilbert's *De magnete* arrived the next year from Tobias Adami.[104] Shifted from the more relaxed Castel dell'Ovo in October 1614 to San Elmo for four more years, Campanella early suffered the removal of his manuscript copy of the emerging *Atheismus Triumphatus* and, according to the instructions given by the Holy Office to the Neapolitan nuncio, the withdrawal of all materials for writing.[105] With time and a shift of incarceration back to Castel Nuovo his situation moderated so that by July 1624 he would be writing to the distinguished antiquarian and polymath Cassiano dal Pozzo, exulting in the freedom of the mind in its pursuit of wisdom; he thanks him for the support of his study and asks that books be sent in sufficient abundance as well as his own publications promoted.[106] From Rome and the Consistory of the Holy Office in mid-July 1626 Bellarmine himself interceded for Campanella, urging that every effort be made to improve the conditions for his writing and communication. Apparently at least one person in Rome had begun to realize the truth articulated by some friends, interceding for Campanella exactly twenty years earlier: he was too useful to the Church and its revival to be so confined.[107] Indeed during the last years of his Neapolitan confinement our prisoner was afforded the opportunity to carry on tutorials, give lectures to small groups of admirers, and receive visiting notables, who often sought to have him autograph their copies of his books.[108] As one of the sights to see, if visiting Naples, Campanella had not only survived; he had become possibly the first European celebrity.

Nevertheless we must return to the problem of the prisoner maintaining his sanity. The experience of imprisonment threatens the psychic survival of the individual personality. Only one with a powerful sense of self-identity can surmount the numbing succession of days, weeks, years that merge into a senseless continuum. The ordinary, even educated layman is unprepared for the grinding, relentless passage of undifferentiated time that beyond the provi-

---

[102] Enrico Carusi, ed., "Nuovi documenti sui processi di Tommaso Campanella," *GCFI* 8 (1927): 321–59, nos. 5 and 31.
[103] Ibid., no. 86.
[104] TC-*Lett.*, 163; TC-*AP*, 300; TC-*DSCM*, 25.
[105] *DBI*, 17:386; *NDP*, no. 67.
[106] TC-*Lett.*, 202–3.
[107] *NDP*, no. 76; cf. *GCFI* 32 (1953): 485.
[108] Firpo, "Appunti Campanelliani," *GCFI* 29 (1950): 85–91.

sion of meals reduces itself to a temporal vacuum. Here a cleric and especially a member of a religious order is at an advantage, having access to an interior life and reality through methodical prayer. Here through even the most fractured observance of the offices, the canonical hours, he can keep some handle on time and his own personal identity. And here especially any claim to a messianic calling can work to secure one's self-identity against the invisible passage of the years. Finally, writing itself, the vehement commitment to literary/intellectual expression, and even better, the trumpeting of a new program, as if by the constant ringing of a small, internal bell, will serve to reinforce continually the prisoner's identity and dispel those shades of oblivion that press upon him. More than anything else Campanella early came to understand himself as a prophet. Yet given his proclivity to amalgamate the expressly Judeo-Christian tradition with the classical, he readily identifies with the intellectual luminaries (*sapientes*) of the Graeco-Roman past. Writing violently defines itself as his only vocation, his only work: it provides his lifeline to sanity and the means of appealing to the outside world, thereby maintaining hope. The extreme duress of his condition will warp his writings in the interests of first survival, then liberation, to constitute an intellectual product for specific purposes as so many counters in the game of liberation. Simulation and opportunism? Yes, but never to the displacement of the prophetic and the transcendent commitment of the prisoner.

In the autumn of 1606 and again in the spring of 1607 Campanella deployed a cluster of letters in successive salvos to cardinals, pope, king of Spain, and emperor, calling attention to his plight and offering a list of intellectual goods ranging from works on world monarchy to conversion of heretics and infidels, from astronomy to biblical exegesis.[109] Repeatedly, there runs throughout all these letters the association of Amos with his prophesying of Jeroboam and Plato and Xenophon on Socrates. At his trial and afterwards Campanella continued to reject the charges of rebellion and heresy.[110] Thus all the more significant that to the current powers of the world he should represent his action as that of Amos against whom the false prophets and officials, the *satrapes* of this world, raised their finger in accusation.[111] For concurrent with the figure of Amos and accompanied by the heavy advertisement of the list of books to be produced all within twenty-five months, satisfaction guaranteed, there appears repeatedly the figure of Socrates.[112] With Amos and the other great Hebrew prophets, Socrates reflects that perennial charge directed against *li sapienti*, those born to illumine the people to a better life. This group includes all the holy philosophers on the law of nature, extending to Pythagoras, Anax-

---

[109] TC-*Lett.*, 9–88.
[110] Firpo, "Autoapologia," 96–100 [n. 78, *supra*].
[111] TC-*Lett.*, 13, 33, 51.
[112] Ibid., 25–29, 35–36, 80–81.

THE PROPHET BOUND   55

agoras, Seneca, and Lucan.[113] This matter of self-understanding and representation loomed so significantly for Campanella that he would write a treatise, since lost, whose long title conveys the point at issue: "Why almost all the sages and prophets of all peoples in great crises are marked as if by the peculiarly composite crime of rebellion and heresy, are subjected to violent death, and afterwards return to live on through religion's practice." Elsewhere he includes in this group "all prophets, apostles, Our Lord Christ, even the good philosophers and sages of all nations—as Plato notes and I compose a treatise on it—they will die in the great crisis of the age under this title of heretics and rebels through the political zeal of princes and priests."[114] Thus although Campanella betrays something of the self-consciousness and ambiguity of circumstances characteristic of the intellectual, such dispositions are heavily entangled in the traditional images of the prophet, now supplemented by select philosophers from antiquity—an image moreover torqued by the terrible needs and constraints of his imprisonment.

* * *

From the start of his imprisonment the twofold struggle for sanity and liberty presented itself to the badly maimed prisoner: first the retention of mental stability through intellectual labor; then the exploration and promotion of the possibilities for his own liberation. One is struck by the early resort to poetic composition, a solace indeed, but more than any solace a mastering impulse to the mind's activity. For poetry better than prose required a compression of language, an intensity of feeling, a transcendent, yet informing intellectual vision, each feeding upon and promoting the other. Poetry offered that creative distraction, that avenue of forceful expression, that release from the ruins of his life which the captive craved. Poetry would now provide that leverage, that freedom, that transcendence whereby he could from the depths of his cell in the bottommost pit of Christendom come to look down upon a world of crawling men; shunning all pettiness whether in poetic fashions, political constraints, or theologic limitations, now flesh-torn and manacled, he could achieve a much needed philosophic posture.

He had had recourse to poetry before especially in his earlier Roman imprisonment. Indeed it would appear that as a precocious child of nine years, later given as thirteen, he had first taken to composing poetry.[115] Now it would bulk larger, inspiring, firing, illuminating through the incandescence of creation the darkest of periods during his extensive incarcerations—the first years at Castel Nuovo and then, after July 1604, the subsequent four years of

---

[113] Ibid., 22–23, 67, 76.
[114] LF-*Bibl.*, 187/76.
[115] TC-*P*¹, 197/81, 1338–39.

dreadful San Elmo. While still in the former and prostrate upon his cot he dictated his poetry and with the help of a friend and fellow conspirator, Pietro Ponzio, eighty-two poems managed to be transcribed. Years later in composing a sort of autobiography, the *Syntagma*, Campanella will describe laconically his resort to poetic composition as immediately following upon the clashing shut of that door which would seal him away for the next twenty-seven years: "Denied books, I composed many poems both Latin and Tuscan (*Hetruscaque*) about the primal wisdom, and power, on primal love, on the good, the beautiful and such—all written only when opportunity furtively allowed."[116] The mighty triad of *Potestas, Sapientia, Amor*, a triad with an august heritage having powerful outcroppings from St. Thomas to Ficino,[117] Campanella would have most likely taken from Dante's Gates of Hell, there to incorporate into his philosophy as the monotriad during this early period of his Neapolitan imprisonment.

Except for a few sonnets written during his captivity in Rome (1594–98) and some occasional sonnets in 1613 to Bünau and Tobias Adami, and omitting the Eclogue to the dauphin at the end of his life, the overwhelming bulk of Campanella's poetic productivity, amounting to 146 of a total 164 separate sonnets and madrigals, occurred in the 1599–1608 period. The remarkably clear definition to this period that coincides with the first decade of his Neapolitan imprisonment and the mysteriously abrupt end to his poetic composition in 1608, except for some stray sonnets to his German admirers in 1613, the distichon for Louis XIII, and the great Eclogue for the future Louis XIV, present a problem and require some explanation. While Firpo explained the limitation of his vernacular poetic endeavors to these years as a result of Campanella's lack of books, Ducros more satisfactorily argues that poetry served as a means for Campanella to struggle with truth, in short, as a way to work out his most intimate problems. Building on Ducros's thesis and taking account of the eroding effect of imprisonment on the integrity of the self and all sense of temporal succession, one may suggest that poetic composition with its combination of intense intellectual and emotional concentration worked to salvage the identity of the prisoner. This same period constitutes the time of his greatest intellectual productivity both philosophical and political. His boundless creativity seems to defy and transcend the very horrors of his confinement: from the depths of suffering a soaring vision.

In the first part of this period emerging from his feigned madness at Castel Nuovo, then later removed to San Elmo, chained, manacled, buried from the light of day and from the sun that he hails, Campanella addresses profound themes, raising his song to the question of immortality, to beauty, to love, and

---

[116] LF-*Bibl.*, 40; LF-*Autobi.*, 282.

[117] On some of the sources for this triad, see *DTC*, 2:235; *Summa theologia*, Q. 27.2.2; Ficino, *Comm. on Banq.*, end.

will pass on to the exposition of his philosophic Trinity, the monotriad of Power, Wisdom, and Love, and to the presence of evil that seems to mock any divine Providence; above all he treats his own mission, his prophetic vision, and his spiritual crisis. Expectably his sonnets are rough-hewn but massive in emotional force, intellectual depth, and perception. Radically departing from prevailing conventions, he turns to the Psalms and above all to Dante. In his admiration for that "holy poet David," whom he claims to have expressed more exalted and beneficial words than all the others, Campanella studies and translates in order to appropriate and emulate such Psalms as 49, 87, 111, and 128.[118] Strongly influenced also by Dante, at one point he expresses his preference for the *Inferno* over the *Paradiso*, claiming the former to be more appropriate to perceived reality.[119] Yet he draws as much if not more from the latter, especially when struggling to express the mystical reality of the soul's divine symbiosis. This consciousness, "this handful of brain" that is the self, so tiny, yet so ferocious in its craving to know all things, becomes the image of its divine source in His immensity, merging in God, as God in him.[120] In his struggle to contend with the ultimates of human existence and in his huge effort to seize and express the divine essence, we are reminded of his model's more elegant and successful achievement in attaining to the ineffable and expressing in words the inexpressible.

It would appear that during this very period he forges that mighty triad that would run its course throughout all the rest of his metaphysical speculations: Power, Wisdom, and Love. He seems to arrive at each principle gradually and in reverse order. His early quest for immortality causes him to address the two Venuses of Plato's *Symposium*. Shortly Love posits Wisdom and both together require Power, which he formally and explicitly recognizes in his "Della Prima Possanza" of July 1607.[121] Or is the montotriad implicitly realized in the "Fede naturale del vero sapiente," which seems to provide through poetic compression the distillation of that later philosophic troglodyte, the *Metaphysics*?[122] Worth noting, however, is Campanella's early turning to both papacy and Spain, shortly after the failure of the conspiracy, in the recognition of the more practical need for power. In his praise of Spain, composed during the first weeks of January 1600, he depicts the imperial eagles of Austria bearing the fasces.[123] This recognition of Spain concurs with his writing of the *Mon-*

---

[118] Firpo, "Versioni poetiche campanelliane," *GSLI* 153 (1976): 230–42, esp. 237–40.
[119] TC-P^2, 401–2; cf. 1324 at n. 5.
[120] TC-P^1, 17/5, 1319/n. 3; 135/66, 1333/n. 2; cf. Dante, *Par.* 9.73, 81. For Dante's influence upon Campanella's poetry, see the telling arguments of Lina Bolzoni, "La *Poetica* latina di T. Campanella," *GSLI* 149 (1972): 481–521, esp. 495–99.
[121] TC-P^1, 197/81–203, 1339.
[122] Ibid., 10–15/3.
[123] Ibid., 246/111/13–14. Briefly may it be signaled here the riches available in the first fascicle of *Bruniana e Campanelliana*. In the first article (11–20), Germana Ernst has published

archia di Spagna; his apparent opportunism does not detract from the basic sincerity of both the sonnet and the political tract. For Campanella's fascination with power, its apotheosis at his hands, becomes the keystone to his thought and his personality. That he should renounce the explicitly Christian religious idiom of Father, Son, and Holy Spirit for a philosophic, metaphysical one, emphasizing power, has ultimate significance for the nature and intent of his thought and for his spirituality. As "Della Prima Possanza" sings: from Power derive Being, Love, Wisdom; and where absent, suffering and all evils abound.

A series of sonnets pursues the theme of the Pater Noster's "Thy kingdom come":[124] that age of innocence, which Adam lost, will be piously empowered.[125] In that happy golden age "mine" and "thine" will be transcended.[126] The conjunction of terrestrial omens and disasters that seems to have encouraged Campanella in his conspiracy of 1599 will now have their astral counterpart in the great conjunction that he predicts for December 24, 1603.[127] It is given to him to preach these wonders.[128] Campanella's tocsin, "My Campanella," together with the Eternal Reason calls all human kingdoms to compose themselves to one.[129]

In the development of Campanella's spirituality during these years of his early Calvary we need to linger momentarily over his perception of Christ. He is reported by his fellow conspirators and enemies at the time of the abortive plot to have expressed himself most negatively about the Crucifixion—it cast a pall over his spirit. Indeed we have his sonnet of Easter 1601 on the Resurrection of Christ, in which he takes implicit issue with the piety of humility distinctive of the Counter Reformation; trumpeting his aversion for such devotion, Campanella shifts the emphasis to the triumph and glory of Christ in His Resurrection.[130] Yet Campanella entertains real doubts as to the divinity of Jesus. In his "Pious Exhortation," dating from the conspiratorial period of 1599, he charts the Passion of Christ from the Crucifixion through the Descent into Hell but ends abruptly on the stunning note of denial that Jesus is the son of the eternal Father.[131] In fact the rejection of the doctrine of the Trinity

---

five hitherto unrecognized sonnets of Campanella; the second of this collection, "A Spagna," constitutes a distillation of all the filohispanic themes—global, prophetic, providential, technological—regarding this encircling *Monarchia del mondo . . . Meraviglia di Dio*. Nevertheless closely associated with these materials in the manuscript lurks a bitterly anti-Spanish pamphlet. Thus the worm of ambiguity persists.

[124] TC-*P*¹, 114–17/46–48.
[125] Ibid., 118/49.
[126] Ibid., 121–22/52–53.
[127] Ibid., 125/56.
[128] Ibid., 126/57.
[129] Ibid., 244/108/26–29.
[130] Ibid., 37/22.
[131] Ibid., 238–39/102.

figures in the articles against Campanella at this time. Moreover in the *City of the Sun* the effigy of Christ with those of the apostles, while being given the most distinction, is still grouped as one among other divine emissaries. Closer examination of this passage in its successive reworkings indicates that the determinant of greatness and of such recognition remains throughout that of being a preeminent inventor of laws, sciences, or arms, for they are all *legumlatores*.[132] The designation is strongly reminiscent of the Paduan school and Pomponazzi in the understanding of Christ as a *legifer*, bringing in another religion according to the periodic eight hundred-year shifts of the astral cycle.[133] Then in the final development of Campanella's thinking on the matter, Christ emerges as the supreme principle of rationality pervading the universe.[134]

Given Campanella's fascination with and dependence upon the universalizing structures of the Roman Church, it is hardly surprising that this cleric should take such a cool philosophical attitude toward the Redeemer. By equating him with universal reason Campanella attempts to make Christianity thereby more accessible to an enlarged humanity in this age of the Church's global expansion. Indeed the absorption of Christ into a rationalistic framework would suggest that Campanella came to perceive God preeminently not as a Newtonian mechanic but as a supreme, impersonally immanent, power. For the present, however, from his dungeon in the Castel Nuovo the sonnets that Campanella raises to God are at best to the Father but more often to Eternal Reason, to the sun, to a philosophic abstraction, manifesting a justifiable impatience, an unrepentance, to some even a lack of religious feeling.[135] Shifted to the horrors of the cell in San Elmo, Campanella, writing in the summer of 1604, will address the Omnipotent God, announcing that if there were another God, to that he would resort.[136] And with respect to his specifically invoking an other than Christ-centered Deity one of his greatest poems,

---

[132] Christ and the apostles are grouped first with Moses, Osiris, Jupiter, Mercury, and Muhammad as "tutti l'inventori delle leggi e delle scienze e dell'armi" according to the early Italian version (TC-*CS*, Donno 36–37); then in 1623 with the first four again plus now Lycurgus, Numa Pompilius, Pythagoras, Zalmochis, and Solon (TC-*Op. Lat.*, II, 422); and finally in the 1637 Paris versions of the *Philosophia realis* (II, 148), two lesser lawgivers, Charondas and Phoroneus, have been added. In both later Latin versions Muhammad has been ostentatiously expelled and those remaining described as "depicti omnes Inventores scientiarum & armorum & legumlatores."

[133] With *lex* understood as formally established religion, see the section introduced by the gloss entitled *Legum mutatio* in Petrus Pompanatius, *De naturalium effectuum causis sive de Incantationibus* (Hildesheim/New York: George Olms, 1970; reprinted from *Opera* [Basel, 1567], 283–97).

[134] On Christ as *razionalita universale*, see the excellent expositions of the matter by R. Amerio, "Ritrattazione dell'ortodossia campanelliana," *RFNs* 21 (1929): 3–23, and idem, "Le dottrine religiose di Tommaso Campanella," *RFNs* 22 (1930): 3–29.

[135] TC-P^1, 134–35/65–66.

[136] Ibid., 145/73/7–8.

"Al Sole" (To the Sun), dates significantly from the Easter season of 1605, 1606, or 1607. Let us hearken to its paean:

> I address my righteous prayer to you, Phoebus. . . . I see you in the sign of Aries, risen to glory, and every vital substance now strives to approach you. You exalt, revive, and call to new energy every hidden thing, languishing, dead, and ugly. Alas! with all other things, O powerful god, revive me, to whom more than to others you are dear and worthy of love. If I honor you, Great Sun, more than all others, why should I, more than all others, be condemned to cold and darkness? May I come forth from my prison at this season when from the deepest roots the green crown of leaves is springing! You draw out the virtues hidden in the trunks of trees and convert them into flowers and sweet fruit. The hidden, frozen springs dissolve into pure water, which overflows and fertilizes the earth. The moles and the dormice throw off sleep; you give life and movement to the meanest worms. The pale snakes turn to life at the touch of your rays; I, in my misery, envy their wanton play. In Ireland the birds die, frozen, for five months in every year, but now even they rise into flight. All these are the works of your holy energy, refused to me alone, your most fervent lover.[137]

From July 1604 to April 1608 Campanella existed Prometheus-like in his "Caucasus," the bowels of San Elmo. Possibly from as early as the tenth century but certainly since 1275 the prison fortress of San Elmo had been associated with a charterhouse, the Certosa of San Martino, which, beginning in 1578, had been undergoing remodeling and expansion for an increased monastic population. Under Giovanni Antonio Dosio until his death in 1609 and then with Felice De Felice (1617–22), culminating in the intarsiated polychrome marbles of the pavement to the choir and chapel by Cosimo Fanzago, the cloister would be expanded and the church made among the most splendid of a confident, revived baroque Christendom.[138] Meanwhile in the dungeons of the fortress Tommaso Campanella gasped out a horrible existence. Imposingly linked, the Certosa of San Martino and San Elmo, together they announced the bonds associating love with power, spiritual aspiration with enforcement.

We need to focus on those poems of the first half of this most dreadful period leading up to Campanella's ostensible conversion early in 1606. At first he considers opting for death, but then rejects this choice as simply that of exchanging present woes for new ones in other worlds that are also sensate and thus resonate a universal scream. Somehow patience must be sought even within the terrible, divine silence.[139] Vainly addressing the Omnipotent, he doubts that he will be heard; centered in the weight of all the ruins of the

---

[137] Ibid., 228–30; on its dating, 1341; for the translation, Anthony Blunt, *Nicolas Poussin* (New York, 1967), 329–30.

[138] Raffaelo Causa, *L'arte nella Certosa di San Martino a Napoli* (Naples, 1973), 15–18, 28–49.

[139] TC-*P*¹, 140/71.

world, he finds himself among a Dantesque damned ("delle perdute genti").[140] Between oblivion and perdition he contends with a God deaf to his pleas and with eyes averted.[141] Exhausted by his own unheard pleas before a deaf, dark God, he claims that if there were another, to Him he would run. For words apparently do not exist that might move a divine benevolence to him whom He has destined from all eternity not to love.[142]

Interestingly Campanella understands his present imprisonment in 1604 as the twelfth year of a period that began with his first Neapolitan trial of 1591–92.[143] Unable to fly without the wings of divine grace, may God grant them to him.[144] He begins to enter into direct controversy with his God: following Jeremiah's (12:1) "You are indeed just, O Lord," he contends that Dionisio Ponzio has been freed and his enemies and betrayers have been allowed to thrive. Conquered, weary, spent, he nevertheless disputes with God; yet like the worms in our body that we kill without hearing their pleas, so God deals with us.[145] Then shortly thereafter, while invoking his monotriad and denouncing ignorance, tyranny, and hypocrisy, he comes to flaunt in a very revealing madrigal his own apocalyptic credentials: the seven bumps on his head with their ostensible planetary resonances and the white horse of Revelation that he associates with his Dominican order. He makes claims somewhat reminiscent of that earlier apocalyptic figure, Thomas Muentzer, that the present time is most pneumatic in that numinous, prophetic events are today more potent than at the time of Elias.[146] At this stage Campanella apparently understands himself as still specially equipped to herald the New Age.

The four *canzoni* constituting the "Dispregio della morte" provide an interesting analysis of the Platonic body/soul dichotomy. We are all prisoners within the human cell of the body. The soul's prison is all opaque except for two transparent apertures that see things not as they are, but tinged, altered. Not only are we unable to see things in their reality; we also fail to perceive the subtler air and the circumambient angels on account of the grossness of this fleshly tunic. We can know only semblances, not things in themselves. Every man wishes to arrive with the body wherever his thought goes, yet he is unable to internalize within himself the things that he wants to know. This great swaddling, this mortal coil (*fascia*), balks at following nor is able to internalize what is needed. Thus this tenebrous weight holds all gladness, desires, senses grounded. Soul and body stand each in separate darkness, ignorant of each other.[147]

---

[140] Ibid., 141/72/madr. 2/5.
[141] Ibid., 142–44/72.
[142] Ibid., 145–46/73.
[143] Ibid., 147/73/madr. 3/13–14, 1335/n. 3.
[144] Ibid., 148/73/madr. 5/8–9.
[145] Ibid., 153–56/74.
[146] Ibid., 167/75.
[147] Ibid., 169–74/76.

Pursuant to the same theme Campanella examines the conjunction of soul and body to the enhancement and affirmation of the latter. He is led to consider demonic evocations and in this respect it is worth noting that at this time the *Atheismus Triumphatus* was largely written in the spring of 1605 and completed by early 1607.[148] More than relevant is the affirmation of Christ as true religion warding off the demons and their deceptions.[149] Yet as is true for a good part of the European seventeenth century, Campanella's world is a demonically ridden one; the very struggle with demons and with this invisible world assures him that he is immortal and there is another life.[150] While these rhymes made in a *fossa* may be stillborn, he can nevertheless exhort his fellow men to change their life of distrust, for he is persuaded not by some chance reason but by experience as well as by divine and natural law.[151]

Our consideration of the poems culminates inevitably in the famous, if puzzling, "Canzone a Berillo" of early 1606. It registers a decisive shift of mood, if not of total orientation. Reiterating the earlier timeframe Campanella asserts that he has suffered fourteen years, always with increasing error. As excuse for so many errors he had accepted so many punishments. Although unworthy, he longs to be remade. He seeks but an end to this torment, not the great content of the prodigal son. Then in notable contrast to his earlier claims to messianic/prophetic credentials he avers that none ought to preach novelties or betterment of the human lot unless armed with miracles, proofs, and countersigns, all of which he has been unworthy. Otherwise such innovators are not sent by God but by the devil or their own malevolent cleverness (*astuzia*). Rather than applying novelties one must endure tyrants as God's flail. The message now coming across: suffer tyrants; avoid novelty; recognize the rules; admit of a future justice.[152] Then reminiscent of Augustine's ascending plaints "Sero te amaui . . . sero te amavi" in the *Confessions*: "How late, Father, do I return to your counsel; how late do I invoke the doctor. . . . Among the impious I am the worst."[153] With soul parted from body he confesses his great fault: "Air, heaven, sacred stars and you spirits volant among them, hearken to me, . . . pray for us!"[154]

The precise import of the elusive "Canzone a Berillo" assumes major significance for assessing any shift or development in Campanella's religious stance. Dedicated to his confessor, Don Basilio Berillari of Pavia, the poem gives vent to a new humility and patience, painfully developing and recently attained, that for some interpreters has signified a turning point of real repen-

---

[148] Ibid., 1338/79/n. 4.
[149] Ibid., 187/79.
[150] Ibid., 187–88/79.
[151] Ibid., 159/74.
[152] Ibid., 190–92/80.
[153] Ibid., 194–95/80/madr. 9–12; cf. Aug. *Conf.* 10. 27. 38.
[154] TC-P^1, 195/80/madr. 12/7–11.

tance and even conversion.[155] If so, a conversion to what? Certainly still not the God of Catholic orthodoxy in 1600. Yet it would seem to be more than an internal accommodation, prudential, if unsimulated, an adjustment to his condition, but rather something having a genuine measure of religious import. For the "Three Psalmodic Metaphysical Prayers," written in the summer of 1604 at the beginning of his San Elmo incarceration, in that very prayer which would have him abscond to a more merciful God, he comes to recognize that he cannot avoid the dreadful chalice (*il calice orrendo*) of his own Gethsemane.[156] And in a gloss to the second of these psalmodic prayers he admits to having previously been a poor Christian—"Christian" to be understood in its religious and doctrinal sense rather than having that moral import acquired during subsequent centuries.[157] In "Canzone e Berillo" emerges this awareness of a terrible pride in having believed that he held God in his hand, rather than following His lead.[158] Scattered subsequent statements in his *Metaphysics* accrue to suggest a growing awareness of this ruinous pride and some shouldering of the harness of Christ, some accommodation, which is not without specific Christian import. This strain—and it is one of several strains—will later culminate in the "Oratio pro Deo" inserted into the beginning of the *QR*.[159] In the shadow of a Paul or Augustine conversion would thus suggest too much; more than any breakthrough to Christ, there is rather a growing awareness of the inadequacies of his past self, sometimes, now seen in the light of Christ. Less acquired at one moment, this moment, but slowly, painfully won, a decisive threshold had nevertheless been attained and was in the process of being crossed during these first years at San Elmo.

Whatever the shift, it is not from heresy to orthodoxy, nor from revolt to complete submission. If this shift is, as Ducros has argued,[160] from a revolutionary millenarian vocation to one reformative for all the sciences, the millennial vision may have lost its violent edge, but has not disappeared; it nevertheless awaits developments both divine and natural and remains integral to the intellectual alchemy of the prisoner. That vision has become more complex and nuanced. His concurrent political writings, hailing the temporal power of Spain in its global march and the political as well as spiritual power of the papacy in its universal structures, would seem here to have their philosophic and emotional counterparts in the slowly attained but firmly held recognition of the preeminence of Power amidst Wisdom and Love and the cele-

---

[155] Ibid., 190–96/80.
[156] Ibid., 151/73, madr. 9/10.
[157] Ibid., 153/74.
[158] Ibid., 191/80, madr. 4.
[159] I have here been guided by that extraordinary assemblage and distillation of texts presented by Romano Amerio, "Un'altra confessione dell'incredulità giovanile del Campanella," *RFNs* 45 (1953): 75–76. Cf. also Badaloni, *Campanella*, 303.
[160] Franc Ducros, *Tommaso Campanella poète* (Paris, 1969), 416.

bration of the Resurrection in its glory and triumph rather than the Passion of Christ. As Ducros has observed, Campanella wants not only to be the Amos and Isaiah of his time but also the David and Solomon of the imminent *renovatio*.[161]

* * *

In considering Campanella the poet, one must take up in the very same breath Campanella the astrologer and the magician, for the latter are not simply associated with his poetic endeavor but most integral to it. Indeed astrology and magic constitute the necessary coefficients of a pansensist/panpsychic, Neoplatonic view of the world. *Vates*, legislator, *astrologus*, *magus*, *poëta* become one in creating that prophylactic against the obliteration of identity and for the survival of his world purpose.

For Campanella words are not flat names, pale substitutes for the thoughts they represent, exercised to tickle the reason; rather they are analogues of the divinized cosmos, communicable by an informing *spiritus*—evocative, charmed, incantational, productive. Thus poetizing for him involves a sort of gnosis and requires a transcendental gift on the part of the poet, rendering him an instrument of supernatural inspiration. In his emerging understanding of poetry, Campanella breaks significantly with the current Aristotelian rules by which poetry had become entangled in pretty techniques of imitation. Building upon the proclivities of Telesio, Bruno, and Patrizi, Campanella conceived of poetry as a divine gift having a moral/political force as its immediate import and proper focus. While part of his gnosis involves the Christian revelation, there are other revelations—the ontologies of the Neoplatonists, the astrological/magical scales of Hermes Trismegistus, the prophecies of Joachim of Fiore, St. Bridget, and Catherine of Siena—all to be turned to the celebration not of classical mythology, Greek fables, but to contemporary heroes—Columbus, Magellan, Cortés, Galileo.[162] This force, this sense of wondrous achievement, this perception of grandeur and of the universal, this true *terribilità* leads to a recovery of the Dantesque and a fresh perspective upon the totality of things.[163]

In his *Del senso delle cose e della magia*—initially composed in the first Neapolitan period, then confiscated at Bologna, to be recomposed in Italian during the commencement of his study in the dungeon of San Elmo, beginning

[161] Ibid., 495.

[162] Dennis Costa, "Poetry and Gnosticism: The *Poetica* of Tommaso Campanella," *Viator* 15 (1984): 405–18, esp. 406–7; see also Brian Vickers, "Analogy versus Identity: The Rejection of Occult Symbolism, 1580–1680," in *Occult and Scientific Mentalities in the Renaissance*, ed. Brian Vickers (Cambridge, 1984), 95–163, esp. 105–8, 122–23, 126–30, 134, 149–51, 155–56.

[163] Lina Bolzoni, "La *Poetica* latina di T. Campanella," *GSLI* 149 (1972): 481–521, esp. 495–503.

July 1604[164]—our prisoner explains that words and sounds as signs and motions possess magic force, both wonderful and certain, having the effect of impressing motion upon us and arousing sensations in us.[165] For the air itself is a sentient medium upon which we impress words hortatory, evangelical, amatory, thus moving the spirit.[166]

Admittedly, in the *DSCM* Campanella suggests a progressive naturalization of magic whereby what had before been apparently demonic in its practice becomes transformed into a positive activity of man, a recognized feature of public knowledge and use: therefore gunpowder, the printing press, the compass, once considered magical, now become public phenomena of current usage.[167] Yet such a statement hardly exhausts Campanella's view of and recourse to magic, as evinced by his affirmation a few chapters later regarding the magical power of words. But even more so almost in the same year (1603–4) he engages in what has been characterized as a "particular spiritualistic magic rather perilous and uncertain." In an effort to communicate with demons and angels he managed, while still at Castel Nuovo, to put a fellow prisoner into a trance that he might serve as a medium.[168] In gaining the cooperation of his youthful companion, Felice Gagliardo, Campanella apparently played upon the youth's excessively superstitious nature and loaded him down with astrological lore—a science that our Dominican had first eschewed, but after his encounter with the obscure rabbi, Abraham, he achieved a proficiency that glittered convincingly at the time of the conspiracy. Its application to magical contrivances in the interests of effecting a supernatural escape from prison only led to his transfer in July 1604 to the far harsher confinement in the dungeon of San Elmo.[169] It is in this developing context that poetry, magic, and astrology coalesce to advance the prophetic.

At the beginning of the fourth book of the *DSCM* Campanella directly addresses the nature of magic as being the investigation of the occult aspects of God and of nature, whereby marvelous things may be effected and applied *all'uso umano*. He associates its original practitioners with the ancient wise men of the Orient, especially the Persians. But magic had fallen into disrepute and the word had come to connote merely superstition. Astrology, also exercised by inept practitioners, had come to partake of magic's bad reputation. Yet Campanella hastens to add that most recently Della Porta and Imperato have done much to restore magic, although only *istoricamente*, by which he

---

[164] LF-*Bibl.*, 67.
[165] TC-*DSCM*, 292, 296.
[166] Ibid., 182–84.
[167] Ibid., 237–42.
[168] D. P. Walker, *Spiritual and Demonic Magic from Ficino to Campanella* (London, 1958), 228–29.
[169] Luigi Firpo, "Il Campanella astrologo e i suoi persecutori romani," *RF* 30 (1939): 200–215, esp. 200–201; TC-*Op. in.*, 42–44; LF-*RC*, 137–38.

clearly means the narrowly empirical, lacking in the understanding of the more basic causes.[170] For theory Campanella would turn increasingly to the very font in the Renaissance's recovery of magic cum astrology—Marsilio Ficino, specifically the third book of the *De vita*. Precisely a century separated the *De vita coelitus comparanda* (*On the Celestial Instituting of One's Life*), that "founding charter of the new natural magic," published in 1489, from the definitive edition of Della Porta's *Magia naturalis*, appearing in 1589.[171] Campanella appears to have absorbed the *De vita* with its Plotinian-Proclan as well as Hermetic strains, including an anxious concern for distinguishing demonic from spiritual magic, in short, between a magic that evokes and worships demons and one that ostensibly uses them as agents for a higher purpose.[172] Just as Ficino believed to find astrology an indispensable part of the medicine he practiced, so magic and astrology were closely associated.[173] Even though the two disciplines might conflict in terms of their inner logic— astrology tending to determinism, magic to playful experimentation and manipulation—natural magic was inseparable from astrology: correspondences with the planets and with the signs of the zodiac defined the occult qualities of animals, herbs, and their appropriate combinations.[174]

From Origen and other Christian apologists down through the Middle Ages to the Renaissance a long-established interest in the apparently independent corroboration of Christian mysteries had persisted. As with the pagan poets and philosophers, so also the astrologers could be mobilized to support the faith. In their astrological conjectures on the difficult question regarding the nativity of Christ Albertus Magnus and Cardinal Pierre D'Ailly could both affirm that the Incarnation was in part due to heavenly and stellar influences.[175] Ever since the invasion of the West by Arab astrology in the twelfth century there had emerged the need to coordinate Christian time with astrologic time. While Latin theologians worked to reduce astral causation to inclination or mere signification, the spook remained regarding the superior celestial motions curtailing or even eliminating the direct action of God in time. The issue of the horoscope of Christ, cast in the ninth century by Albumasr, the impresario of the new Islamic invasion, recurs constantly in all the astrological and theological literature. In his efforts to head off the violation of free will Aquinas will grant celestial bodies only an indirect and incidental influence.

[170] TC-*DSCM*, 222–23.

[171] Paola Zambelli, "Le problème de la magie naturelle a la Renaissance," in *Magia, astrologia e religione nel Rinascimento*, Convegno polacco-italiano, Warsaw, 1972 (Wroclaw/Warsaw/Cracow/Danzig, 1974), 48–82, esp. 52; Marsilio Ficino, *Three Books on Life*, ed., trans. and annot. Carol V. Kaske and John R. Clark (Binghamton, N.Y., 1989), 54.

[172] Ibid., 52.

[173] Ibid., 31–38.

[174] Zambelli, "Le problème," 61.

[175] Stephen M. Buhler, "Marsilio Ficino's *De stella magorum* and Renaissance Views of the Magi," *RQ* 43 (1990): 348–71, esp. 360–61.

Again, D'Ailly will direct his anxiety to composing a *Concordantia astronomiae cum historica narratione*, coordinating the two times. In all this cerebration the big issue was never the prediction of individual destinies but rather the doctrine of the grand conjunctions that constituted the keystone in the vault of the astrological science, where the superior planets of Saturn and Jupiter or Mars and Saturn played out their dark purposes and in which major historical events assumed a pattern of great conjunctions, celestial motions, and corresponding terrestrial occurrences.[176] Indeed Ficino had seen in the fateful conjunction of Saturn and Jupiter the conjoining of wisdom and power, the veritable precondition for a golden age.[177] And the end of the sixteenth century could certainly expect to evoke more than the normal share of conjunctions. Ficino and Campanella both had frequent recourse to the authority of St. Thomas Aquinas, dipping defensively, if generously, into the rich lore of astrology.[178]

By the last decades of the sixteenth century astrology had come to permeate the mental processes of high and low alike; from cardinals, popes, and princes to the meanest artisans the grammar of astral conjunctions, the houses, the trigons, watery and fiery, had become the furniture of people's thinking, emotions, expectations. For good reason had Cardanus specified 1583 as the year for cataclysmic change. Indeed the astrological uproar of that year and its aftermath in England particularly had been based on the calculations of the most authoritative astrologers in an emotional marketplace thirsting for prophecy. Any conjunction or meeting of planets in the same degree of a given sign of the zodiac became a portentous event, especially when it involved the two highest planets, Jupiter and Saturn, whose conjuction occurred every twenty years in cyclic ascent to ever higher degrees of significance. The cycle depended upon one of four trigons or triplicities—a set of three signs, each 120° distant from each other, thus forming an equilateral triangle with lesser conjunctions occurring every twenty years, the greater recurring every 240 years, and the greatest coming at the end of the complete cycle of the four trigons after 960 or even 800 years. This most critical of all conjunctions occurred at the end of the watery trigon and in the new sequence of the fiery trigon of Aries, Leo, and Sagittarius. Such an event was truly epoch-making, ushering in new empires or religions, mutations of enormous import that amounted to a new period of history, new worlds, possibly the end of the world. Such expectation of prophetic fulfillment had convulsed English life, awaiting the year 1583, but when the year had passed without having produced even a ridiculous mouse, not even by its extension to 1588, some could well snort that

---

[176] Tullio Gregory, "Temps astrologique," 562–64, 566.

[177] Hankins, *Plato*, 1:302–4, quoted with valuable additional evidence by Michael J. B. Allen, *Nuptial Arithmetic*, 82, n. 1.

[178] Giorgio Scrimieri, "Sulla magia in Tommaso Campanella," in *Studi in onore di Antonio Corsano* (Mandaria, 1970), 709–46, esp. 734.

astrologers "had made themselves ridiculous to the whole world." Yet others could anxiously begin to plot ahead to 1603.[179] In fact despite the skepticism of a few the astrological saturation of the European consciousness would continue for at least another century.

During these very first years of Campanella's imprisonment poetry, magic, and astrology coalesced in the interests of prophecy. Although the composition of his own formal presentation of astrology would have to wait at least another decade, his practical astrology had by 1603 reached a sufficient maturity to allow that science's integration into his larger purposes. In two sonnets Campanella announces the sun's presence in the house of Capricorn and gives great significance to the most rare conjunction of planets in the apogee of Mercury in Sagittarius during the expected imminent conjunction of December 24, by which stupendous event the present "sons of death" shall be confounded and the new aeon ushered in.[180]

At this time Campanella's overwhelming sense of a total change derived from the same expectation of a great conjunction that had led to the abortive conspiracy. In this expectant mood he was not alone, for among other important star gazers no less an astrologer/astronomer than Johan Kepler in 1600 prepared for the eighth age that would last until the year 2400. In his *Articuli prophetales* Campanella writes of a shift from the watery trigon or triplicity, namely, the conjunction of the planets in the signs of Pisces, Cancer, and Scorpio, to the fiery trigon, marked by the signs of Aries, Leo, and Sagittarius—a shift that will open the new eight-hundred-year epoch in world history.[181]

Neither is it accidental nor a matter of mere passing note that the prisoner had a year before written his powerful artistic rendering as well as programmatic statement of the impending society, *The City of the Sun*, that distillation of Campanella's learning, aesthetic, and aspirations. Astrology plus Neoplatonic-Hermetic magic inform the conception of this city, divided into seven circles corresponding to the seven planets, the four avenues converging on a temple upon whose altar is a huge celestial globe depicting all the heavens, and a comparable one for the earth. Through the constellation of images on its walls and cupola the temple becomes a detailed, abbreviated model of the universe.[182] In a cosmos of sympathies and correspondences, the

---

[179] Margaret E. Aston, "The Fiery Trigon Conjunction: An Elizabethan Astrological Prediction," *Isis* 61 (1970): 159–87, esp. 161–62, 180.

[180] TC-*P*[1], 125–26/56–57; cf. 1330–31.

[181] Germana Ernst, "From the Watery Trigon to the Fiery Trigon," in *Astrologi Hallucinate: Stars and the End of the World in Luther's Time*, ed. Paola Zambelli (Berlin/New York, 1986), 265–80, esp. 266–67, 273; J. V. Field, "A Lutheran Astrologer: Johannes Kepler," *Archive for History of Exact Sciences* 31 (1984): 189–272, esp. 229–31.

[182] TC-*CS*, 30–31; Scrimieri, "Sulla magia," 742–43.

operation of this temple and its officialdom—poetic, magical, astrological—suggests some sort of harmonic, celestial computer.

Poet/magus, poet/astrologus, but always poet/prophet, Campanella bent his immense energies to mobilize the only instrument at his command, language, for the evocation and proclamation of the new age. In this focusing of his prophetic powers he massively affirmed and secured his self.

German Efforts at Liberation

The prisoner's unflagging efforts to draw attention to himself and to his work searched for some form of leverage from outside to achieve liberation. In this respect the unique receptivity of Germans and their varied and protracted attempts to come to his aid are striking. What made some in German lands more susceptible to Campanellan ideas than those in other parts of Europe? Admittedly, our prisoner had a bag full of tricks for all occasions, and given the encyclopedic range of his mind plus the elasticity of his emotions he could provide something for almost any party. Nevertheless the very divisiveness of the empire made it more vulnerable than France or certainly Castile to a diversity of intellectual currents and enterprises. More precisely the hardening and attenuation of Lutheran Orthodoxy by the end of the sixteenth century, coupled with the recent Catholic revival, created a volatile context of hopes, anxieties, and aspirations as the empire slipped ominously toward confessional strife. Germanic awareness and interest in the Neapolitan prisoner would come in two waves: the first from Catholics in the 1607–11 period, motivated by confessional and political interests; the second from ostensibly Orthodox Lutherans, first evident in 1612–13 but with a long aftermath lasting until at least 1623, promoted and nurtured by broadly philosophical and religious interests. And again the inevitable political dimension would be present.

Numbered among the German Catholics seeking the prisoner's release were first and foremost Kaspar Schoppe, a Lutheran who converted to Catholicism after reading Baronius's *Annales*—noted humanist, emerging controversialist, and one who had been attendant at the burning of Bruno, he would move from initially avid admirer of Campanella to tepid friend to harsh traducer;[183] Johann Faber, chancellor of the new Lincean Academy, medical doctor, and distinguished botanist, who maintained a significant correspondence among the learned both within and beyond the Italian peninsula; Georg Fugger, scion of the great Augsburg banking family, who commanded a broad network of financial agents and prompt to employ his wealth in the efforts to release the captive; Mark Welser, imperial counselor and learned patrician, who attracted the dedication of Galileo in the Florentine *mathematicus*'s *Letters on Sunspots*

[183] D'Addio, *Scioppio*, 14–50.

and served along with Faber as an intermediary for the forwarding of Campanella's letters to friends in the Germanies; finally, Archduke Ferdinand, Jesuit educated, soon to become most fatefully Emperor Ferdinand II and one briefly attracted to the theocratic ideas of the prisoner.[184] Indeed an impressive group exercising a variety of talents and a number of connections.

Manipulative, self-centered, and self-seeking, Schoppe worked to obtain from Campanella writings that he could adapt to his own agenda for hardening the lines of Catholicism against the dangers of Protestantism and winning over the Lutheran nobility. Fresh from the bruising experience of the papal imbroglio with Venice, Schoppe strived in Rome to advance his own interest at the curia and to cooperate with Johan Faber in the promotion of conversion and Catholic polemic. A fellow German, Christoph Pflug, had managed to get himself imprisoned in Naples since 1603 and it had been through his letters that Schoppe had first learned of Campanella. It is conjectured that the Germans may have even participated in the latter's attempt at flight in 1604.[185] Yet inauspiciously early in the considerable effort mounted by the German Catholic juggernaut to save Campanella, Mark Welser, the coolest head throughout among those sharing at least an initial enthusiasm for the Neapolitan philosopher, confessed to Faber in a letter of mid-January 1608, written from Augsburg, that he entertained doubts regarding Campanella and was simply not able to believe certain things that were said of him. But he would go along for the companionship.[186]

To study the correspondence between Campanella and his would-be liberators proves worthwhile on several accounts: it reveals an arc of friendship shaped by the changing perception of interests and possibilities by each party; it reminds us of the simulative pressures conditioning all of Campanella's writings; it reveals some of the less attractive, yet human features of his character; it provides a view of some of the problems confronting publication in Catholic Europe that contrast with those of Protestant Europe at this time.

Writing to Faber on April 26, 1607, Schoppe expresses eagerness to speak with Campanella and to take away whatever he wanted, especially *A Venezia*, whose title he will promptly change to the more expressly combative *Antiveneti*. It would seem that he wished to use the work as an instrument for advancing himself with the pope.[187] During the spring of the same year he obtained leave from Rome to attend Campanella in Naples. He caught the prophet-prisoner at the peak of his creativity, no doubt made more productive

---

[184] *Nuovi documenti su Tommaso Campanella tratti del carteggio di Giovanni Fabri*, ed. Domenico Berti (Rome, 1881), 11–13; Giuseppe Gabrieli, "Bibliografia Lincea: IV Scritti di Giovanni Faber Linceo," *Accademia Nazionale dei Lincei*, Classe di Scienze, Morali storiche e Filologiche. Rendiconti. Roma. ser. 6, 9 (1933): 276–334.

[185] D'Addio, *Scioppio*, 57–58.

[186] Amab., *Doc.*, II, 33/117.

[187] Ibid., 25/107.

by the extremities of his harsh confinement and by the apparent gleam of liberation. Although after the event he will speak of having had an audience with the prisoner, his communications were most probably by letter.[188] More important during this period (April 17–May 18) he quarried and removed for his own purposes a veritable mine of manuscripts that Campanella entrusted to him—the *Monarchia di Spagna, Discorsi ai principi d'Italia, Il prognostico astrologico, Epilogo magno* (*De sensu rerum, Dialogo contro Lutherani, Aphorismi Politici*), *Articuli prophetales, Monarchia messiae, Antiveneti, De regno ecclesiae*, and the *Atheismus Triumphatus*—thereby acquiring for himself, among other things, a corpus of political doctrine lacking in his own training. There he would be introduced to Machiavelli and the politics of the age.[189] Meanwhile the plans for Campanella's release went forward, Georg Fugger spreading his largesse, Faber standing as intermediary, Schoppe drawing upon his new role as a counselor to Archduke Ferdinand, and the whole network resonating with hope.

The prisoner's hopes ran high—too high. For his part Campanella looked to Schoppe as the lifeline for his liberation from captivity and ultimately as the means for the translation of his writings into German to confute the Lutherans. In a flurry of letters during the subsequent months Campanella emitted prophetic, astrological, magical sparks in extravagant statements that would ill-serve his credibility in higher circles. Now arrogant, now servile, now boastful he prepared himself to go into Germany and in ten days convert the Count Palatine and two other princes, being equipped with every type of science both new and recondite that with God's help he might win over Germans and Indians.[190] A letter in late spring provides important insight, however, into what for succeeding generations became his most problematic and controversial work, the *Recognoscimento filosofico della vera universale religione contro l'anticristianesimo e macchiavellismo*, which at this point would suffer its first major refraction by Schoppe's pompous retitling as *Atheismus Triumphatus* (*AT*). Campanella now selected it for consideration from the bag of manuscripts, as if it bore the ultimate import of his message to the outside world. Apparently projecting his own bodily imprisonment upon the current condition of the human intellect, politicized, walled about as worms in a cheese, unknown to each other, Campanella depicts the present darkness of this Antichristic age. Christianity (*Christianismu[s]*), which used to occupy almost the entire earth, now finds itself reduced to the two corners of Italy and Spain. And yet even these suffer the wretched poison of Machiavelli, who believes religion to be the cunning of friars and clergy for the domination of peoples. Indignantly Campanella believes to see in his Promethean condition of help-

---

[188] Ibid., 26/109.
[189] TC-*Lett.*, 110; D'Addio, *Scioppio*, 62–63.
[190] TC-*Lett.*, 93–95; cf. 96–99.

less suffering the proliferation of sects.[191] In this work he avers to show the Catholic faith to be that of Roman Christianity and to demonstrate that religion is the natural *virtus* endowed in us by God from which it follows that God is, that He exercises care on things, that man is immortal and fit for another life. As he explains in his letter of June 1607 to Schoppe:

> You are mistaken, Schoppe, if you plan to preach to your Germans the new article: "I believe the Holy Church," for it is fitting to begin with "I believe in God" and [proceed] by means of natural philosophy, not authority. For none puts his faith in the Bible, the Koran, Luther, or the pope except insofar as it is useful. Indeed the common people believe in them. But the learned and almost all princes are political Machiavellians using religion as an art for dominating. . . . If [the German Lutheran princes] believed in God, they would also believe that God serves but one school of truth on earth. Then through the laws of succession, the amassed weight of other laws and the observances of the Fathers they would recognize that school to be the Roman Church. But because they see the clergy to be of little piety, although more than their own, and Peripateticism to dominate with its mortality of souls, eternity of the world, and ridicule of paradise and hell, and the astronomers connive by obscuring the heavenly evangelical signs of truth and of Aristotelian falsity, thus all the worst are conjectured and the authority of leaders, fomented by our very own [members], eradicates from their hearts the authority of the gospel; thus rules a certain tacit consensus of mutual deception. This is the preparation only of the Antichrist: behold the papacy virtually prostrate.[192]

The passage is important for it not only expresses what amounts to the central idea governing the recently composed *AT*, but it also serves to link Campanella's essentially apologetic efforts therein with the current confidence entertained by Catholic theology in a *praeambula fidei*; namely, that belief in God's existence was essentially a natural preamble to the faith and not an article of the faith and that it was rationally demonstrable by natural lights.[193] In the very special role exercised by the *AT* among the manuscripts, Campanella now commended as his monument to Schoppe that it particularly should be translated into German.[194]

In a more personal vein the prophet-reformer casts himself in the role first of Christ, then of Socrates, while arguing that he should not go unheard when

---

[191] Ibid., 101–2.

[192] Ibid., 103; cf. TC-*AT* (1636), "*Praefatio*," sig. ciiii, where the crucial passage of his letter to Schoppe has been incorporated into the more abbreviated preface of the *AT*'s second edition as "oportuit incipere non a Credo sanctam ecclesiam, sed a Credo in Deum."

[193] On the *praeambula fidei*, see Alan Charles Kors, "Theology and Atheism in Early Modern France," in *The Transmission of Culture in Early Modern Europe*, ed. Anthony Grafton and Ann Blair (Philadelphia, 1990), 238–75, esp. 242, 266–67.

[194] TC-*Lett.*, 110.

one considers how many benefits he offers the Church.[195] Continuing in this same vein, which could only serve to compromise him with ostensible liberators as well as with any ecclesiastical review of his case, Campanella will in late October again overplay his hand: the self-proclaimed devotee of Aquinas attacks current theologians for reading only St. Thomas, his disciples, and Aristotle; whatever not found in these books they deem heretical. "But if I may seize the attention of Rome for a month you will see a new heaven and a new earth."[196]

Proceeding northward with this rich haul of manuscripts, Schoppe imprudently stopped in Venice, where he soon reported being relieved of all Campanella's writings by the authorities; the *Monarchia di Spagna* and predictably the *Antiveneti* proved particularly disturbing to the Serenissima. All but the last would in good time be returned to him.[197] Schoppe announced to Faber his intentions to have the *Monarchia messiae* and the *Discorsi* published in Bologna, the dialogue against the Lutherans published by Fugger in both Latin and German, and the rest appear with the Venetian printer Ciotto.[198] Negotiations lapsed. Arriving in Ratisbon, Schoppe announced that he was unable to extract the *Antiveneti* from the Venetian authorities and feared that Ciotto had failed him for none of Campanella's writings entrusted to him had appeared.[199] In actual fact Schoppe was far less desirous of publishing these materials than he proclaimed, for he wished to appropriate them for his own purposes while requiring from their author clarifications on such matters as distinguishing St. Thomas from an Aristotelianism represented as the source of atheism. Schoppe appropriated Campanella's emphasis upon religion as the prime reason for guaranteeing society its unity, harmony, and order.[200] His *Ecclesiasticus*, begun in 1609 and completed for publication in 1611, would be based upon Campanella's *Aforismi Politici*, *Monarchia messiae*, and *De regno ecclesiae*. He did not hesitate to incorporate whole passages from the *Antiveneti*, especially the identification of the pope not with the Levitical priesthood but with that of Melchisidech, thereby far more ecclesiastically theocratic in its implications. Even the Campanellan primalities were pressed into service. Thus while their author remained in prison, his ideas entered the currency of Catholic propaganda and became part of the political ideology of the Counter Reformation.[201]

Meanwhile the program for the prisoner's liberation went forward at first, only to falter for reasons that are revealing. Georg Fugger proved especially

---

[195] Ibid., 108–9.
[196] Ibid., 136.
[197] Amab., *Doc.*, II, 30/112.
[198] Ibid., 26/110.
[199] Ibid., 33/118.
[200] D'Addio, *Scioppio*, 95, 147.
[201] Ibid., 384–415.

solicitous: in Naples his agents, armed with *scudi*, prodded and poked for any weakness in the system of detention; he pursued initiatives in Madrid in 1608 for the captive's liberation; he continued to furnish Campanella with money and materials for writing and to have letters and books sent from outside through the cooperation of Faber. For his part Schoppe called the attention of his patron, Ferdinand of Styria, to the opportunities for Catholicism and Habsburg imperialism in the release of Campanella. Early in January 1608 the archduke wrote the viceroy of Naples, asking that the prisoner be transferred from the harsh conditions of San Elmo to a context more commodious for allowing his completion of works on mathematics and religious controversy.[202] Actually Campanella had already been transferred in August of the previous year to an ordinary cell in San Elmo. The present effort led to his shift to the Castel dell'Ovo and thus to a considerably more commodious ambiance. In October the archduke once more interceded, asking the viceroy for the liberation of Campanella; his letter represented the rare learning of the prisoner, which could be of great profit for the Catholic religion, and emphasized that the request had the backing of many other personages. Still another letter followed from the archduke in May 1609, this time representing the importance for both Spanish and Austrian branches of the dynasty that Campanella be given free access to books that might allow his most rare genius and subtle intellect to expedite the completion of the *Mathematics*, *Prophetic Articles*, and *Metaphysics*. To all these requests the viceroy responded that the prisoner's freedom was not within his power to grant. By this time the flood tide of opportunity for Campanella's release was clearly subsiding.[203]

The ebbing of momentum for the prisoner's release can be measured in the correspondence of the key player, Schoppe. Returned to the empire in early January 1608, Schoppe crowed from Ratisbon to Faber that his books could serve as the effective antidote to Luther's poison. If not, certainly other authors would be encouraged to provide the remedy and "if our Campanella should come and pass the Danube dry shod, he would render the old ladies young."[204] At least to Faber he claimed still to see in the prisoner a powerful source for the conversion to Catholicism: "if we could liberate Squilla [Campanella] and have him with us, we might effect more easily the conversion of [the prince of] Anhalt."[205] For a while the idea was entertained of sending Campanella northward in chains for service in the deepening polemical trenches of the empire.[206] To Campanella himself in the same month of Febru-

[202] Amab., *Doc.*, II, 33/228.
[203] Berte, *Nuovi doc.*, 19–27; Amab., *Doc.*, II, 48/158; *DBI*, 17:383. See also the early treatment of this subject by Jan Kvačala, "Thomas Campanella und Ferdinand II," *Sitzungsberichte* 159 (1908): 1–48, esp. 42–44.
[204] Amab., *Doc.*, II, 32–33/116.
[205] Ibid., 34/123.
[206] Ibid., 37/128.

ary Schoppe urged patience and sought to impress him with growing difficulties, some self-created: his fabulous promises to all brought only smiles and even his friends believed that his unbridled desire for freedom had pushed promises well beyond prospects for performance. Nothing could be expected from the emperor, yet Archduke Ferdinand gave every indication of being helpful.[207] Wanting more from the prisoner during 1608 and still persuaded as to his ultimate effectiveness for the specific purpose of Catholic controversy, Schoppe, while urging the usual patience, asked Campanella in June for the composition of political commentaries on the scriptural books of Kings.[208] To Faber he could report that it was believed he had no equal in all Italy in true philosophy and the secrets of nature.[209]

By the following spring Schoppe showed clear signs of growing disenchantment with the whole enterprise the group had embarked upon two years earlier. To Faber he imparted his exasperation with Campanella's "tired old songs," his unrealistic importunities, and the deaf ears of otherwise potential patrons. In fact Campanella was becoming so self-discrediting as to be a distinct liability to his earlier advocates: to grant him liberty would no longer be safe, for he believed himself to be the chosen legislator of God for a new world, nor did he hesitate to prefer himself to Christ who had only five planetary lumps on his head, while Campanella has seven in the ascendant.[210]

To the importunate prisoner the signals emitted by Schoppe must have seemed exasperatingly ambiguous. For while the ostensible German liberator repeatedly urged him to moderate his promises to avoid being discredited,[211] he could also coach the captive at apparently critical moments to make a special effort. For one who knew no moderation, desperate, operating between extremes, such advice could well have elicited anguished bewilderment. Such a situation arose in April 1609, when Schoppe informed Campanella of the game plan to persuade Ferdinand to petition his cousin Philip, king of Spain, to grant a pardon. Campanella would need to send a pleasing letter, expressing and giving prayers for him and here the archducal counselor attempts to instruct the desperately guileful captive on what to say. He then deviates into a perceptive criticism of Campanella's inconsistencies, requiring his clarification: St. Thomas as only an expositor of Aristotle, presumably not an adherent; Aristotle as precursor of the Antichrist; and if his coming impends, why bother to propagate the Habsburg *monarchia*? And if in the last time the Church flees to America, will the forty-five days of Daniel 12 allow enough time to constitute the monarchy of the saints? Then comes the suggestion that would seem to prepare for the unraveling of the preceding cautionary instruc-

[207] Ibid., 35–36/125.
[208] Ibid., 39/134.
[209] Ibid., 41/144.
[210] Ibid., 45–46/153.
[211] Ibid., 35/125.

tion: Schoppe asks the prisoner to incorporate in his letter some *arcanum* useful to his patron.[212] When the following month Schoppe in writing to Faber observed that nothing more could be expected from Georg Fugger and that twenty *scudi* should be forwarded to Campanella, the German controversialist still sought from the prisoner his *Metaphysics*.[213] A year later Welser and Schoppe could agree that Campanella was precisely where he should be and that his extraction could only prove damaging personally as well as generally for the larger public.[214] Thus Campanella had now come to be seen as a menace if free, and an embarrassment for those having past or present contacts with him. In June 1611 Schoppe remarked to Faber that he had no time for Campanella's dirges and claimed that he had lost credit among too many.[215]

During the course of 1613 and thereafter the group of German Catholics confirmed their withdrawal from efforts to liberate the prisoner. In surveying a recently acquired list of titles of Campanella's works, provided by "a certain Tobias Adami," Welser confided to Faber that he held out little hope for the suppliant; judged from the extravagance of their titles, his works would do him more harm than good. And furthermore a new edition of Tommaso Costo's *History of Naples* presented the Calabrian affair much to the disadvantage of Campanella.[216] For his part Schoppe admitted to Faber that he would not want Campanella free and that he gradually and willingly lost touch with him.[217] Faber gingerly obliged Archbishop Federigo Borromeo with a list of Campanella's works as presumably the first step in that library builder's efforts to include the writings of the Neapolitan philosopher in what would become the Ambrosiana.[218] Schoppe became increasingly derisive regarding the poor captive: if he could get money to rain from heaven, then our pitiless critic would follow him;[219] "I am more Tommaso than he, for unless I see, I shall not believe."[220] Yet writing from Madrid in the 1614–16 period, where he had managed with the complicity of the English ambassador to get himself mugged, Schoppe mentions encountering the hostile deportment of one Rudolf von Bünau despite their apparent common interest in trying to alleviate Campanella's condition. For as late as September 1616 Schoppe could represent himself to Faber as promoting the old enterprise and in fact had commended Campanella personally and by letter to Quevedo.[221] And in March 1617 he claimed affection for him, that his letters to him were being

[212] Ibid., 46/155.
[213] Ibid., 47–48/157.
[214] Ibid., 49/163.
[215] Ibid., 50/165.
[216] Ibid., 50/167.
[217] Ibid., 51/169.
[218] Ibid., 51–52/173.
[219] Ibid., 52/175.
[220] Ibid., 54/180.
[221] Ibid., 50–51/168, 52–53/177; D'Addio, *Scioppio*, 119.

seized by the Inquisition and blamed the Jesuits for preventing Campanella's as well as his own works from being published. In this last respect he noted that Bünau and Adami, Campanella's presumed champions, rendered him no assistance and as Lutherans it is no wonder that they should forsake their pledged word to the prisoner.[222]

In fact, however, the two Lutherans had not forgotten that most unforgettable prisoner and were moving toward the publication of his writings. Thus just as the German Catholic effort to liberate Campanella subsided, the German Lutheran effort now moved forward to effect the only sort of liberation possible at this time—namely, the publication of his thought.

• • •

At the turn of the century developments within Lutheranism plus political alignments within the empire allowed the penetration of Campanellan ideas into the Germanies to become a much more profound and upsetting matter under the auspices of Protestants than had their earlier entertainment in Catholic circles. For Lutheranism had not lost its prophetic/apocalyptic edge, which had only been sharpened during the course of the previous century and which afforded the ground for a development in contrast to the mainline of formal Lutheran theology, hardening since the Formula of Concord into dogmatic Orthodoxy. Besides its imminent eschatological expectations the prophetic strand came to draw with it a variety of Paracelsian, Hermetic, and alchemical occult beliefs, aligning science with theology, magical discovery with the expectation of radical spiritual transformation. Thus the appearance at Kassel of the *Fama fraternitatis* in 1614 and the *Confessio fraternitatis* in 1615, the original Rosicrucian manifestos, ushered in a new, heightened idealism that seized upon youthful minds at the chief Lutheran theological center at Tübingen.[223] Rosicrucianism, brief as the bubble lasted, would release tremors not only in the empire but in France also, where Mersenne and his group would recognize its cloudy, generous occultism as the enemy to be crushed.[224] By the century's second decade the excitement, expectation, and utopianism would engage some of the most prominent figures in Württemberg. At Tübingen students of Johann Arndt, representing a pietistic search to escape the straitjacket of Orthodoxy and a repressive church order, quaffed, for a charmed moment, the enticing brew. In this Rosicrucian context Tobias Adami and Wilhelm von Wense, returning from Italy, added the exhilarating nourishment deriving from a Neapolitan cell. While Adami sifted Cam-

[222] Amab., *Doc.*, II, 53/178.
[223] Robin Bruce Barnes, *Prophecy and Gnosis: Apocalypticism in the Wake of the Lutheran Reformation* (Stanford, 1988), 186, 216–20.
[224] Enrico DeMas, *L'attesa del secolo aureo (1603–1625): Saggio di storia delle idee del secolo XVII* (Florence, 1982), 211–26, 232.

panella's works into the press, Johann Valentin Andreae translated some of his poems, Christoph Besold rendered the *Monarchia di Spagna* into German, and some anonymous editors prepared fragments of his political writings for publication.[225] The philosophical-religious and then the political aspects of Campanella's reception in the empire will require separate consideration.

Adami's publication of Campanella's *Compendium de rerum natura*, appearing in Frankfurt in 1617 under the title of *Prodromus philosophiae instaurandae*, marked only the second work of the Neapolitan philosopher in print, following distantly upon the *Philosophia sensibus demonstrata* over a quarter of a century earlier. Originating in the months of Roman imprisonment (1594–95), the *Compendium* explores Pythagorean, Timaean, and Copernican themes concerning the motion of the earth and the corruptibility of the heavens.[226] In his preface to his friend's work, "Ad philosophos Germaniae," Adami emphasized the coincidence of Campanella's thought with the present Hermetic/alchemical features of Rosicrucianism; in this as in all his later Campanellan publications the papal-theocratic and the anti-Lutheran polemics were carefully omitted.[227] While Adami developed strong associations with the Württemberg group, he himself was a Saxon trained not in theology but in law, medicine, mathematics, and the languages (including Hebrew), all of which made him something of a polymath susceptible to a governing philosophy. This scholarly training would recommend him later for service in the Saxon ducal government but at the outset of his career for service as tutor to the young noble Rudolf von Bünau.[228]

The instruction of his charge, which had begun in 1607, culminated in a six-year grand tour that started from Nuremberg in the spring of 1611 and proceeded by way of Venice to the Holy Land with the return by way of Malta, Sicily, and finally Naples, where their stay came to be protracted for eight months from August 1612 to March 1613. The incarceration of the Dominican conspirator, now something of a celebrity and a tourist attraction, had passed its thirteenth year and presently found him at Castel dell'Ovo. It is possible that at some personal risk, the generous, enthusiastic Adami actually penetrated the system of detention to meet with the prisoner. Communication, however, appears to have limited itself to the letter and came to be regularized by daily correspondence, amounting to perhaps as many as two hundred missives, none of which has survived. Part of this correspondence undoubtedly

---

[225] Firpo, "Appunti campanelliani," *GCFI* 41 (1962): 374; John Warwick Montgomery, *Cross and Crucible: Johann Valentin Andreae (1586–1654) Phoenix of the Theologians* (The Hague, 1973), 1:233–36.

[226] Badaloni, *Campanella*, 79–81; TC-*Op. Lat.*, I, 34–35, 50.

[227] DeMas, *L'attesa*, 139–42, 302.

[228] The following paragraph is based largely on Luigi Firpo's "Tobia Adami e la fortuna del Campanella in Germania," in *Storia e cultura del mezzogiorno: Studi in memoria di Umberto Caldora* (Cosenza, 1978), 77–95.

dealt with the confessional divide between the two parties; the articulation of Campanella's polemical position at this time with respect to Lutheranism will figure as the "Epistola antilutherana," an integral part of his great missionary work, the *Quod reminiscentur*. Yet Adami imparted a moral probity, philosophical earnestness, and larger religious commitment that managed to transcend the confessional divide between the two men. Campanella entrusted him with copies of works, some earlier consigned to Schoppe: *Metaphysica*, *Philosophia realis*, the *De sensu rerum*, and now part of the *Cantica* and the *Prodromus*. That part of the *Cantica* will appear as the eighty-nine poems constituting the *Scelta d'alcune poesie filosofiche* published in 1622, possibly in Paris. In the *Antilutheran Epistle* Campanella speaks of committing as well to Adami the *Physiology*, *Ethics*, and *Politics*. Adami's sojourn in Naples during these months proved of decisive importance for the European reception of Campanella. Following a visit to Galileo in Florence, the two Saxon gentlemen continued their tour to Cadiz, Madrid, Paris, the Netherlands, and England, reaching Saxony again in 1616.[229]

In the preface to his first Campanellan publication, addressed to the philosophers of Germany, Adami broadly surveys the philosophical landscape to discover three groups: the pure materialists; the biblical literalists never philosophizing beyond Scripture; and those finding attestations of the Creator in His work, the physical universe, by discovering the correspondences between nature and divine authority with truth permitting no conflict.[230] Adami prefers the third, where the words and the works of the divine artificer coinhere *ad trutinam Harmonicam*.[231] This harmonic balance, equivalence, agreement between the written Book and the Book of Nature is best evident in Telesio and more recently Campanella in their recovery of the principles of Parmenides and Pythagoras. In the Calabrian's *De sensu rerum* the principle that the machine of this world is but the living image of God (*Dei vivam statuam*) brings into focus this salutary philosophy.[232] In his review of Campanella's writings Adami offers a notable reading of the author's *AT*, which he renders as *The Triumph over Atheism* (*Triumphum Atheismi*) "or the Recognition of the Christian Religion from the secrets of nature, where he teaches against the Jews, Mohammedans, Atheists and all other sects of philosophers and heathens that nothing in Christianity is able to be found beyond reason [*irrationabile*]."[233] In his praise of the solid work of Gilbert, Brahe, Galileo, and Kepler along with the fantasies of Bruno, Hill, Patrizi, and Postel, as a sort of second string, Francis Bacon remains conspicuously absent at this time from the mental horizon of Tobias Adami. Yet he will allow a certain agreement

[229] TC-*QR*, 128.
[230] TC-*OP. Lat.*, I, 7–8.
[231] Ibid., 10–11.
[232] Ibid., 12–15.
[233] Ibid., 16; cf. Firpo, "Tobia Adami," 100.

between the alchemy of Paracelsus and the philosophy of Campanella.[234] Amidst the mud of the Platonic cave we are summoned to aspire toward the light.[235] As portal to the ostensibly new philosophy Adami placed the sonnet that his imprisoned friend had addressed to him.

> Holding the cynic lantern in your hand,
> Through Europe, Egypt, Asia, you have passed,
> Till at Ausonia's feet you find at last
> That Cyclops' cave, where I, to darkness banned,
> In light eternal forge for you the brand
> Against Abaddon, who hath overcast
> The truth and right, Adami, made full fast
> Unto God's glory by our steadfast band.
> Go, smite each sophist, tyrant, hypocrite!
> Girt with the arms of the first Wisdom, free
> Your country from the frauds that cumber it!
> Swerve not: 'twere sin. How good, how great the praise
> Of him who turns youth, strength, soul, energy,
> Unto the dayspring of the eternal rays![236]

Repeatedly during 1617 Adami asked Galileo for news of Campanella.[237] With a never-failing solicitude for his friend Adami brought out in 1620 the *De sensu rerum* accompanied by a preface celebrating his twenty years of suffering and dedicated to the two Bünau brothers, Henry and Rudolph. During these months prior to the political crisis at the year's end Adami worked more closely with his friends in Tübingen. Fortified with Campanellan manuscripts, Adami pursued a schedule of publication that could only enhance the idea of *Societas Christiana* culminating in the lives and work of Wilhelm von Wense and J. V. Andreae at this time. A certain equivalence could be drawn between their ideal, projected City of Christ and the Neapolitan's *City of the Sun*, which the two German Rosicrucians read in manuscript and which served to influence Andreae's *Christianopolis* published in 1619.[238] The same year saw the appearance in Strassburg of a small collection of Campanella's poems translated by Andreae into German.[239] Ostensibly from Paris in 1621, but most probably from a Württemberg press, Adami would offer to his friends Wense, Besold, and Andreae the *Scelta* of some of Campanella's philosophical poems, bearing the publication date of 1622. In that year Adami also

---

[234] TC-*Op. Lat.*, I, 20.
[235] Ibid., 21.
[236] Ibid., 25; cf. Symonds, *Sonnets*, 176.
[237] Amab., *Doc.*, II, 68/188; *Le opere di Galileo Galilei*, ed. Antonio Favaro (Florence, 1966), 12, 304, 352.
[238] Cf. Montgomery, *Andreae*, 1:49–50, 129, 215, 221.
[239] LF-*Bibl.*, 43–45.

published through his Frankfurt printer the *Apologia pro Galileo*, written in 1616 and forwarded to him probably through the network of the Linceans in Rome and Florence;[240] in the preface Adami would sound the characteristic Campanellan note represented by the image of the cheese and the worms: that men live out their lives in intellectual isolation.[241] In 1623 he brought out the *Realis philosophiae epilogistica*,[242] which included among its four parts the first edition of the *City of the Sun*.

In the preface to the comprehensive compendium Adami engaged the challenge presented by Francis Bacon, copies of whose *Novum organum* had been distributed by the British ambassador to Venice, Henry Wotton, in 1620 to some of his German connections.[243] Having set forth the two conflicting Telesian principles of heat and cold, so intensely perceptible to our senses ("sensibusque nostris valde cognoscibiles"), preferring their sovereignty and empire ("maiestatem & imperium") to the Peripatetic four causes or the Paracelsean elements of sulphur, mercury, and salt to which principle they have an affinity,[244] Adami shortly comes to the English chancellor's *Instauratio magna*. For his own Campanellan philosophy Adami claims that it too proceeds by sense and experience of what must be investigated through even more attentive inductions ("per inductiones diligentiores"), but staring out from this passage is the assumption that through the guidance of sense and the irrefragible attestation of the Artificer concord will be revealed between what His finger has effected in His works and His voice in His letters.[245] In seeking to harmonize Baconian inductivism with Campanellan sensism, which trails magical and metaphysical assumptions, Adami almost intentionally makes light of the differences. For although Campanellan experience refers continually to nature, it operates in a hall of mirrors, reflecting and affirming the same basic reality. The crushing force of the true scientific message will be to purge the concept of experience from all its metaphysical and alchemical incrustations, trailing from remote antiquity.[246]

Although Adami would bring to an end his editorial project in 1630 with the publication of the *Astronomiae libri VII* from the same Frankfurt press of

---

[240] Cf. *Op. GG*, XII, 277, 285.

[241] Firpo, "Adami," 105–10.

[242] Giorgio Spini, "Christianopolitanae nugae," in *Studi politici in onore di Luigi Firpo*, ed. Silvia Rota Ghibaudi and Franco Barcia (Milan, 1990), 2:37–53, picking up on Adami's bringing Campanellan MSS. to Wende, Andreae, and Besold in Württemberg, deals splendidly with this Campanellan/Andreaen seed in England, Germany, and America, and notes that the *Realis philosophia epilogistica* is registered among the books of Harvard College in one of its earliest catalogues (1732).

[243] DeMas, *L'attesa*, 153–54.

[244] TC-*Op. Lat*., II, 539–47.

[245] Ibid., 554.

[246] DeMas, *L'attesa*, 164–66; cf. also Étienne Gilson, "Le raisonnement par analogie chez T. Campanella," in *Études de philosophie médiévale* (Strasbourg, 1921), 125–45, esp. 143–44.

Gottfried Tampach, it would be in the latter part of the same preface of 1623 that he directly addresses his great friend for the last time. The matter pertained to Adami being won over to the Copernican view of the universe by Galileo himself during that fateful trip northward before his departure from Italy; recourse to the telescope convinced him as to the truth of the heliocentric view. Because the sun's heat nourishes and animates the moving earth, he argues that the Copernican view would serve to confirm the Telesian-Campanellan dichotomy between the sun's heat and the otherwise cold earth. Adami, invoking Campanella's own *Apology for Galileo*, now invites his unfortunate friend to reconsider his position regarding the two great world systems. The sensory factor of vision augmented by the new instrument of the telescope would argue against the traditional view. But his poor friend, without telescope and bound to the evidence of the senses, is left indecisively between the two systems.[247]

At the time, 1623, there was nothing self-evident or inevitable about a heliocentric view of the universe. It may appear surprising that for one who had argued so forcefully in defense of Galileo, he should never have accepted Copernicus. But in the *Apologia* Campanella argued for Galileo's right to inquiry and freedom of thought, not for any particular world system. In fact except for a possible fleeting acceptance in 1591 with Stelliola, Campanella remained unpersuaded by the Copernicans; their position appeared to him unproved. Beyond a number of specific astronomical issues[248] Campanella held Copernicus at arm's length for several fundamental reasons: his basic Telesianism with its ontological division between the sun's heat and the earth's cold; the descent of the sun toward the earth; and his firmly maintained belief in the world's end or transformation in express opposition to the Aristotelians' stabilizing doctrine of the world's eternity and any new system of presumably enduring, permanent laws. Ultimately his prophetic priorities made a wholehearted acceptance of the helicocentric system impossible. He could be heliolatrous without being heliocentric in astronomical commitment.[249] The very number of systems he will be seen to entertain suggests their equal probability or uncertainty within a basically Telesian framework. Rather than any opting for a Tychonic solution, Tycho Brahe's compromise position, Campanella seems to manifest a measure of "astronomical agnosti-

---

[247] TC-*Op. Lat.*, II, 555–61; Firpo, "Adami," 112–15.

[248] See the impressive study of this problem by Michel-Pierre Lerner, "Le 'Livre vivant' de Dieu: La cosmologie évolutive de Tommaso Campanella," in *Actes de la xe session Internationale d'Étude du Baroque* (Montauban, 1987), 111–29, esp. 124–26, 128: the displacement of the equinoxes, the decrease in the planetary apsides, the diminution of the solar eccentric in the approach of all the planets and in particular the sun to the earth. On the possibility of a brief, early acceptance of heliocentrism, see LF-*Bibl.*, 172/55.

[249] TC-*P*^{1} 216/82, 228/89. On this point, see the pungent thoughts of Antonio Corsano, "Campanella e Copernico," *GCFI* 53 (1974): 438–42.

cism" all in the interests of preserving the world from any fixed order, any permanent, constant laws, and to open it up to his own prophetic, eschatological vision. Thus he can rejoice at his own age's perception of celestial novelties and irregularities and celebrate their reality as evidence of his own prophecy regarding the end of the present, known world or its presumed total transformation. Furthermore he validates a universe wherein God reenters His own creation to work His will, effecting thereby the overthrow of the Aristotelian eternalized world and even Galileo's new laws.[250]

Indeed Campanella's opposition to the idea of the world's eternity lay at the very core of his controversy with the Aristotelians; and it was here in fact that he decisively parted company with his apparent mentor, Telesio, who had maintained the idea by means of his own heterodox devisings.[251] As the prisoner had told Pope Paul V and his cardinals fifteen years earlier: "I was born to oppose the schools of Antichrist, namely Aristotle, who claimed the world to be eternal with the equinoxes, the stars and their motion always to be in the same order, place, and way."[252] In the *City of the Sun* the Solarians may be uncertain as to how the world was created, but that it was created they are certain, and on this point to a man they oppose Aristotle, while awaiting the renewal and perhaps the end of the world.[253] Campanella is able to subscribe to the emerging master image of the mechanical clock, but it is a very different one from that of an assured regularity, defying any need for divine intervention. On the contrary the world is a clock in the hands of God to be accelerated or decelerated according to His will.[254]

Moreover current celestial novelties feed prophecy. In his own *Astrology*, begun after 1613, Campanella at the outset reminds his readers of St. Paul's warning to be alert to the signs, for the day of the Lord will come as a thief in the night. Thus the *mutationes* in the heavens regarding apogees, obliquities, eccentrics, equinoxes require constant attention, for astrology is not something that can be pursued intermittently. What has been marvelously begun by Copernicus has been better pursued by Tycho and still better by Galileo. Yet

---

[250] Indeed Campanella can be most Copernican when able to use Copernicus as evidence in support of the mutability of the heavens (TC-*AP*, 46–47). For the most thorough study of the complex problem of Campanella's anti-Copernicanism, see Lerner, "La cosmologie," esp. 114–29. But for a Tychonic reading of the evidence, see Robert S. Westman, "Magical Reform and Astronomical Reform: The Yates Thesis Reconsidered," in *Hermeticism and the Scientific Revolution*, Clark Library Seminar, March 9, 1974 (Los Angeles, 1977), 5–91, esp. 53–59. Cf. also Germana Ernst, *Religione*, 239–44.

[251] On Telesio's heterodoxy regarding this doctrine, see De Franco, *Telesio*, 118, 236–39. In the *Quaestiones Physiologicae* of 1637 Campanella will here understand Telesio as humbly pursuing philosophy while leaving the matter of the world's creation to the theologians. (TC-*PR/QP*, 7)

[252] TC-*Lett.*, 65.
[253] TC-*CS* (1981), 108–9.
[254] TC-*AP*, 118, 266.

none of them has philosophized regarding the signficance of these signs for future verities. This task has been given to Campanella *in prophetalibus* to pronounce on the prophetic import and explicate as it were the "prophetability" of these celestial changes.[255] Campanella could well remind his stalwart German friend, Tobias Adami, the liberator of his philosophy and its prophecies northward, that if the present order of things, this world, is a great animal, then like all animals, it is not eternal but must die.

• • •

Despite the demise soon suffered by Rosicrucianism following the Battle of the White Mountain with its stunning blow to Protestant interests in central Europe, the Germanies offered a far more congenial environment to the holistic pansensism of the Campanellan gospel being so faithfully purveyed by Tobias Adami. Paracelsism, alchemy, Hermeticism would here long linger on in a context that lacked the intellectual criticism and volatility emerging in France and soon in England. If, however, the empire afforded a positive reception to the philosophical aspect of Campanella's writings, shorn of their anti-Lutheran features, the political aspect of the Neapolitan philosopher was bound to prove negative, indeed most repellent. In a world of intricate confessional division drifting toward civil war, overarched in turn by the rival hegemonies of Spain and the Turks, Campanella's theocratic papalism mixed with quasi-Machiavellian, philohispanism could not help but prove explosive.

The chief protagonist in the assessment and purveying of Campanella's political thought in the empire was that most learned polymath, outstanding jurist, and long-time friend of Kepler, Christoph Besold. His rendering of the *Monarchia di Spagna* into German, appearing in successive editions of 1620 and 1623, would prove of decisive importance for the European reception and perception of Campanella in the seventeenth century. Nevertheless the German learned public had been introduced to the Neapolitan prisoner during the previous decade in ways far more disturbing: first through the mysterious figure of Caesar Branchedaurius, identifying himself simply as a noble from Turin, but one possibly primed by Schoppe; second through the excerpting and reworking of the twenty-seventh chapter of the *Spanish Monarchy*. Branchedaurius's extensive treatise, "Oratio praemonitoria," appeared in 1609 in *Monita politica, ad sacri romani imperii principes, de immensa curiae romanae potentia moderanda*.[256] The title announces the anticurial character of the book's contents. Indeed the work was a vital conduit for placing Guicciardini's most antipapal texts before the German public.[257] While playing his

---

[255] TC-*Astr.*, 4–5.
[256] Frankfurt: Nicolaus Hoffman, impensis Petri Kopf, 5–32.
[257] See Vincent Luciani, *Francesco Guicciardini and his European Reputation* (New York, 1936), 225, 228.

own part in this respect, Branchedaurius included a striking portrait of Campanella, emphasizing his dangerous, even demonic subtlety and his guile in trying to obtain release from imprisonment. Branchedaurius reveals an intimate knowledge of the Dominican friar. In fact he justifiably accuses him of wanting to innovate not only concerning polity but also the papal religion, and he appears to be the first to label the Neapolitan reformer as a simulator.[258] Appearing first in 1609 in the *Monita*, this portrait of Campanella constituted the initial introduction of the world reformer to the German public. The passage from Branchedaurius's oration[259] would figure in the two German translations by Besold of the *Spanish Monarchy* as prefatory material together with its use in the later *Compendium* of 1628.

The second instance proved more upsetting not simply because of its political substance but by its reaching a much wider public. It originated with an unknown Flemish patriot excerpting chapter 27—"Of Flanders and Lower Germany"—from the *Spanish Monarchy* and reworking its Machiavellian features into a Spanish plot for the conquest of this area. Appearing first in Latin, then Flemish, later German, repeatedly reprinted, the tract imparted to its horrified reader the sense that he held within his hands the master plan for the king of Spain's conquest of central Europe.[260]

Thus Besold found the ground well-mined when he brought out his German translation as the first edition of the *Monarchia di Spagna*. If the leading constitutional jurist of the empire believed that by incorporating a fragment of Branchedaurius's oration in the preface, he adequately signaled the reader as to his own skepticism regarding universal monarchy, the catastrophe befalling the Protestant cause at the Battle of the White Mountain in the autumn of the year demonstrated the first edition's inadequacy. As with so many of the fraternity, those who had earlier been protagonists of Rosicrucianism now became its victims. Besold's own withdrawal, which had started earlier, would be hastened by events and further complicated by a growing restlessness and disillusionment with Lutheranism, which by 1635 would land him in the Roman Catholic camp as one of its most celebrated converts. In the course of this trajectory and in an atmosphere that he himself described as one of syllogisms and swords,[261] Besold brought out a second German edition of the *Monarchia di Spagna* but this time with an *Anhang* or appendix that focused on that most contemporaneous problem—monarchy, both universal and particular. There

---

[258] Firpo, *Ricerche*, 208–10; cf. *Compendium librorum Politicorum de Papana & Hispanica Monarchia* (n.p., [1628]), sig. [C^v]. On this last, see Rodolfo de Mattei, "Un Compendium anticampanelliano," in TC-*Misc.*, 159–70.

[259] *Monita*, 21–23.

[260] Firpo, "Adami," 103; cf. also his "Appunti campanelliani, Un opera che Campanella non scrisse-il 'Discorso sui Paesi Bassi,'" *GCFI* 31 (1952): 331–43.

[261] For the best succinct treatment of Besold, see Richard van Dülmen, *Die Utopie einer christlichen Gesellschaft: Johann Valentin Andreae 1586–1654* (Stuttgart/Bad Connstatt, 1978), 59–64.

is something most significant, even momentous, that at what can later be recognized as the dusk of universal empire and the dawn of the territorial sovereign state, one of the most eminent legal minds of the time should formulate as a result of his study of Campanella's work the fateful question: "whether the entire earth, or at least the Christian world, should be ruled by one head or monarch." Here he introduces a much needed clarification in the usage of this word "monarchy"; he observes that while political thinkers and practitioners tend to understand the term to signify any polity ruled by a king and thus admit a plurality of monarchies at any one time, the historians and theologians understand by the term a single, comprehensive, universal world order. The first usage had its model in Aristotle's *Politics* and had recently been reaffirmed by Giovanni Botero in his advocating medium-sized administrable kingdoms; the second had its origins with Eusebius and Hellenistic notions of kingships and had been perpetuated by that associated with the succession-of-four-world-monarchies view of history.[262] Proceeding with his argument, Besold advances only two major reasons for universal empire: the propagation of the faith and effective defense against the Turk. His analysis reveals that Germany's chief justifications for universal empire—the extirpation of the Turk and the propagation of the faith, each having an eschatological import—have implicitly been assumed in the meanwhile by the Spanish monarchy.

Nevertheless in entertaining arguments for political particularism and pluralism, Besold seems to be more at ease.[263] In the first place nature itself has prescribed topographic and linguistic distinctions between peoples that need to be recognized and respected. Indeed it seems grotesque that peoples, different by nature, should be subjected to a single set of customs or to the rule of a dominant people. Given his cabalistic predilections, Besold, in keeping with the age, employs an unmodern argument to achieve a modern goal: he affirms that diverse regions have diverse angels presiding over them. He claims both the authority of natural law and that of Scripture in affirming national distinctions that run counter to universal monarchy. If the origins of the four monarchies are examined, no legal basis can be discovered other than the tyrannical one of subjugation of the weaker by the stronger.

There can be little doubt where Besold stands regarding the question at issue: amidst a still traditional framework, curious affirmation of the emergent national realms and regions of Europe. To be sure, in the 1641 Amsterdam edition of the *Spanish Monarchy*, the publisher, Louis Elzevir, considered it necessary to counter Besold's appendix with a further postscript, drawn from Lipsius's *Admiranda, sive, de magnitudine Romana*, reaffirming the universal

---

[262] For this point and Besold's important distinction regarding the understanding of *monarchia*, see my "Gattinara, Erasmus and the Imperial Configurations of Humanism," *Archiv für Reformationsgeschichte* 71 (1980): 83–84.

[263] The following four paragraphs are taken from the present author's "Ehe Türckisch als Bäpstisch: Lutheran Reflections on the Problem of Empire, 1623–28," *Central European History* 20 (1987): 12–17; cf. also DeMas, *L'attesa*, 157–64, 226–28, 235, 293, 299–302.

import of the Roman imperial tradition and exhorting his distraught age that all the world might be *quasi una civitas*. Yet something closer to Besold's own immediate experience and sensibilities compelled the distinguished jurist to reemphasize his newly won conviction that the final outcome of history is not in our dreams and aspirations but remains with God, unknown to us. Now in concluding, he seeks to draw the lines of significance amidst the current mood of disillusionment by squarely confronting the feeling of disquietude that pervades his time. Many of simple piety, he declaims, are seized today and aspire by sublime and unknown arts to the fatuous belief in an instant universal reformation as declared by that famous fraternity of the Rose Cross. These absurdities delude honest men. So difficult—even slippery—is the interpretation of prophecies that it is intolerable for any person to ascribe this gift to himself. The Münsterite Anabaptists, he continues, arrogated similar gifts to themselves with claims of restitution and renovation that linger to this day. False, absurd prognostications and revelations abound, ensnaring one's neighbor with lies. And one can be deceived by the imagination and persuaded that oneself is the very temple of God, which God not only inhabits but from which oracles even pour forth as if from Delphi. How marvelous and stupendous these vain dreams and delirious imaginings! The intolerable arrogance of their outrageous claims to be able to discern accurately within the ambiguous!

Such vehemence suggests a disillusionment with Rosicrucianism that had only developed after the stormy events of 1620: the triumph of the Catholic League at the Battle of the White Mountain and the subsequent Habsburg overrunning of Bohemia occurred too late in the year to make possible any introduction of an appendix to his first translation of Campanella's *Spanish Monarchy*. Yet Besold's disenchantment at this moment would appear to be nearer home, extending to Lutheranism itself. By 1623, however, the course of events together with his own inner development served to puncture whatever grand schemes and prophetic fantasies that Rosicrucianism had earlier entertained. In thus settling accounts with the fraternity of the Rose Cross, Besold was implicitly attacking the notion of universal monarchy, nourished specifically by apocalyptic prophecies.

In his profound assessment of Campanella's *Spanish Monarchy*, pondered in the aftermath of the Bohemian disaster, Besold charted his own way and that of a later generation out of the prophetic, idealistic morass. Here his efforts amounted to a sophisticated rejection of the Neapolitan prophet's remedies. The weight and extent of that rejection have detained us in that they suggest at least three converging currents brought into focus by Campanella's political advent in the empire at its descent into the holocaust of the Thirty Years' War: (1) the crisis and decay of the notion of universal monarchy; (2) the conscious advancement of the emerging political pluralism of competing, sovereign territorial states; and (3) the collapse of the Rosicrucian bubble. Besold's friends, Kepler among them, registered their own withdrawal from any allurements that imaginary universal orders might have earlier exercised.

In the empire at this time the recession of utopianism pertains to that type nurtured by prophetic, millennial aspirations and specifically to the deflation of the Rosicrucian bubble.[264]

Yet the spirit of the Neapolitan prisoner, released from still another bottle, managed further to torment the distraught empire. This time the *Discorsi ai principi d'Italia* provided the offending material. Without place or date indicated, but actually in 1628 and probably from Stuttgart, there appeared a small octavo printed on execrable paper, entitled *Compendium librorum Politicorum de Papana & Hispanica Monarchia*. Playing to the widespread fear of the specter presented by Spanish-papal involvements in central Europe, the tract sported on its title page the broadly current slogan "Ehe Türckisch als Bäpstisch" ("Better Turkish than Papal") as if to signal to the already sufficiently alarmed reader the import of its contents.

The work takes the form of a translation into German of Campanella's first two *discorsi* and a detailed, learned confutation of each. In the first discourse Campanella argues that Emperor Constantine abandoned Italy and only the pope gave it order and, uniting arms to wealth, can now extend religion to the world. In the second discourse Campanella claims that although all princes, except the Chinese emperor, aspire to world monarchy, only the Ottoman and the Austrian can effectively vie for this prize. In comparing their separate treatments of the nobility, the learned, and the common people, he urges that all should prefer the Austrian and lend their support "alla monarchia d'Austriaci." Against the first of these arguments our author pursues the Lutheran line that the papacy is the *Apostatische* rather than *Apostolische sitz*: it prefers possessions and *Reichthumb* to religion and its clergy is half priest, half cavalier. While not taking issue with Constantine's donation as a historical fact, our author bewails the impact of his openhandedness upon the Church, its riches providing so many windows of iniquity. And in referring to chapter 27 of Campanella's *Spanish Monarchy*, he registers righteous horror and alarm at the linking of weapons with money in the interest of religion; the crusade of this foul monkish soldier seeks to advance religion with fire and sword.

In the second part of the tract our unknown author pursues the theme of "better Turkish than papal." Directed toward a concerned Lutheran readership and relying on the traditional Lutheran ambivalence toward the Turk, the tract prefers in contrast to Campanellan blandishments the relatively tolerant rule of the turban to the harsh oppressiveness of the Austrian-papal-hispanic conglomerate.[265]

---

[264] Cf. DeMas, *L'attesa*, 291–93. For an interesting and relevant example of the continuance of millennial thinking in the later seventeenth century, see Susanne Åkerman, "Queen Christina of Sweden and Messianic Thought," in *Sceptics, Millenarians and Jews*, ed. David Katz and Jonathan I. Israel (Leiden, 1990). For mid-seventeenth-century iconographic evidence of continuity of millennial expectations, see Peter Burke, "*Donec Auferatur Luna*: The Facade of S. Maria della Pace," *JWCI* 44 (1981): 238–39.

[265] Headley, "Ehe Türckisch," 19–28.

After 1628 the impact of Campanella's writings in the empire had apparently spent itself. Their avid reception for more than a decade had depended upon the efflorescence of certain unorthodox features within Lutheran Orthodoxy as well as a political configuration that began to dissolve with the anti-Habsburg policy of the new pope, Urban VIII, after 1623. Then the hammer blows of the Swedish Lion of the North would change everything. In the general disillusionment with grand schemes of reform Campanella produced either ridicule or denunciation. In 1646 Andreae, former translator of his poems, now associated the name of Campanella with Machiavelli and Nostradamus as spirits worthy only of utmost detestation.[266] Among former supporters only the first and foremost, Tobias Adami, remained faithful. Friend of Galileo, reader of Bacon, intimate of Kepler, the prisoner's faithful champion for the publication of his writings somehow missed the emerging configuration of the modern world.[267] And yet for Campanella in 1628, if the Germanies were closing their doors, a new arena of opportunity and influence appeared to be opening up in the France of Richelieu and Mersenne.

An Emerging Philosophy

During the course of 1613 Campanella accomplished his third and decisive redaction of the huge *Metaphysics*. We can thus at this point take a sounding as to his philosophy.

In this most formal and complete statement of his philosophy, of which he entertained an extraordinarily inflated esteem, Campanella significantly begins with individual self-consciousness and moves outward toward the world and God. Although in his second, if earlier, most important philosophical statement, *Del senso delle cose*, the self and the perceived world come dialectically into focus more immediately, and it is difficult to speak of the first without reference to the second, we may proceed by way of his own deliberate division of the *Metaphysics* into three parts: epistemology (*principia sciendi*), ontology (*principia essendi*), and practical philosophy (*principia operandi*).[268] Thus before constructing a metaphysics, Campanella finds it necessary to establish the reality of knowing. He seems to have been the first philosopher to feel the need of explicitly stating the problem of knowledge as an introduction to his philosophy.[269] Previously satisfied through long exposure to Telesio, with the sensing nature of all things including man, by 1604 he is convinced that the mind that God has infused into man not only has sensitive

---

[266] DeMas, *L'attesa*, 277.

[267] Ibid., 293.

[268] *Thomae Campanellae Stylen. ord. Praed. Universalis Philosophiae, seu Metaphysicarum rerum, ivxta propria Dogmata, partes tres, Libri 18* . . . (Paris, 1638), 6.

[269] Bernardino M. Bonansea, *Tommaso Campanella: Renaissance Pioneer of Modern Thought* (Washington, D.C., 1969), 41.

discourse and animal memory but something higher and more divine.[270] He therefore pursues a universal theoretical doubt. That he should repeatedly use both here and elsewhere the image of the cheese and the worms from contemporary folk culture, applying it not ontologically or cosmogonically but cognitively to accent the isolation and limitations of the mind in its normal condition, serves effectively to affirm the priority and centrality of epistemology to metaphysics or ontology. Indeed in his decisive emphasizing of the subject over the object he is more inspired by Augustine than his own much vaunted Aquinas.[271] This subjectification of being will be elaborated in a way that fortifies both Campanella's idea of the correspondences among man, the world, and God, as well as the understanding of man as microcosm (*epilogo*) of the totality.[272]

Emerging from the scholastic responses to his fourteen countervailing arguments, posed as doubts, Campanella entertains the possibility of his own self-deception. Here he has explicit recourse, paraphrasing it at length, to the famous passage in the *City of God*, where Augustine counters the Academic skeptics with his "Si fallor, sum."[273] It is this direct intuition of oneself "that we are, that we know, and that we will" that is now grafted onto the general sensory nature of all things in which the self not only participates but toticipates.[274] From this sustained engagement with Augustine, indeed the very length of the quotation being an attestation of its impression upon his astonishing memory, derives the basis for the later primalities of *Potentia*, *Sapientia*, and *Amor*. Innate knowledge belongs to the very nature of things by reason of this primalitarian structure,[275] the soul itself having just such a structure. Although between 1617 and 1623 Descartes read more of Campanella than he would ever wish to admit—namely, *Prodromus philosophiae instaurandae*, *De sensu rerum et magia*, *Apologia pro Galileo*, and *Realis philosophia epilogistica*[276]—the striking similarities between the Campanellan "Cognoscere est esse" and the Cartesian "Cogito, ergo sum" are more apparent than real. While Descartes creates an emphatic distinction between soul and body, Campanella instead of separating the two substances seeks an identity of being and thought. It is the differences between a philosophy of instinct, sensation, and élan vital as opposed to a philosophy of mathematical certitudes, clear and distinct ideas, and a universal, impersonal reason. The effective identity of Being and Knowing, a panpsychism constituting a

---

[270] TC-*DSCM*, 11.
[271] TC-*Meta.*, I, 30.
[272] TC-*DSCM*, 161–62.
[273] TC-*Meta.*, I, 108. For Augustine, see *De civ. dei* 11.26; *De lib. arb.* 2.3.7.
[274] For *toticipatione*, see TC-*Meta.*, I, 224.
[275] Bonansea, *Campanella*, 47–48.
[276] Léon Blanchet, *Les antécedents historiques du "Je pense, donc je suis"* (Paris, 1920), 267–69.

pantheism, allows consciousness to act as a sort of instinct of conservation for the functioning of body. Campanella's inwardness even more than his empiricism adapted itself to the needs of communicating, if obscurely, between the two quite different substances.[277]

Campanella's construction of a higher level to the intellect's functioning that establishes individual self-consciousness—a construction that dates from 1602 and clearly emerges by the time of the third redaction of the *Metaphysics* in January 1611—constitutes a significant grafting upon his earlier held Telesian sensualism. A consideration of this preceding stage to his epistemology prepares the infrastructure to his ontology. By the term "intellect" Campanella understands two distinct faculties: the *intellectus sensualis*, which is held by man in common with the animals and is capable of grasping particulars but unable to go beyond the senses; and the *intellectus mentalis*, which aspires to invisible and eternal realities.

Here he presents a twofold view of the intellect quite similar to what Telesio offers in the two later editions of his work. Sense commands its own inherent certainty in its apprehension of singulars. Experience denies that for sensing fire one must engage the form of the fire; rather it suffices simply to be slightly burned.[278] Sensation involves a perception of feeling, or passion from outside "to the extent that from the little by which it is affected, it can infer the rest of the power of the object acting upon itself." For Campanella knowledge does not, however, remain at this sensory, Telesian level but comes to involve a process of assimilation: each thing is sensed and known insofar as it is itself a knowing nature, the knowing essence of the thing becoming the object to be known. Proceeding on his principle "cognoscere est esse" he claims that things are known inasmuch as the knower becomes similar to them. The process of identification or assimilation amounts to a transformation of the knower into the object known.[279]

In practical terms Campanella's empiricism manifests a healthy respect for the evidence of direct witness or experience (*testimonia*) over traditional belief based upon some distant authority—hence *opinio*. By effacing the authority of Augustine and Lactantius on the existence of antipodes, the witness of Christopher Columbus represents the best and most repeated example of this distinction. Sense here attests to things as they are, imagination as we believe them to be.[280]

In reaction to Aristotle Campanella presents a Neoplatonizing metaphysics that seeks to be in accord with a Telesian physics. As subtitle to the *Del senso della cose e della magia* we read: "the world is shown to be a living and truly

---

[277] Bernardino M. Bonansea, "Campanella as Forerunner of Descartes," *Franciscan Studies* 16 (1956): 37–59, esp. 52; Blanchet, *Les antécedents*, 209, 226, 283.
[278] TC-*DSCM*, 80.
[279] Bonansea, *Campanella*, 76, 83, 96, 101, 106–7.
[280] TC-*Meta.*, I, 82–84.

conscious image of God and all its parts and details to be endowed with sense perception, some more clearly, some more obscurely, to an extent sufficient for their preservation and that of the entirety in which they share sensation." Being is thus predicated of God, *per se* and *simpliciter*, and of creatures analogically as effects of God, their first cause.[281]

Campanella explicates the nature and structure of Being by means of his original doctrine of the primalities. Campanella's reading of the universe as consisting of power, sense or knowledge, and love seems to be a natural outgrowth both of his pansensism and of his Augustinian base. By 1602, he had come to express through his poetry this participation of all things in these modes of the divine, insofar as all things are imitations of God. Yet certainly in Latin theology these trinitarian principles had been evident since Augustine as *Posse*, *Nosse*, and *Velle* in the trinitarian procession of God. Nearer in time they were available in varying designations in St. Thomas, over the gates of Dante's hell, and at the end of Ficino's commentary on Plato's *Symposium*. Power, Wisdom, and Love, the primalities constituting Campanella's *Monotriad*, provided him with the philosophical base of departure from the central Christian theological doctrine of the Trinity. As metaphysical principles the primalities are so inherent in the very effects they produce that Campanella can speak of their "essentiating" a being and also of their total pervasiveness (*toticipatione*) or coessentiation rather than mere participation in a lesser ontological manifestation.[282]

While the principles of this coessentiation are the same by nature of function, they differ in terms of origin: Love derives from Wisdom and Power, and Wisdom from Power only which stands as the source of the other two. By making being a transcendental composite of Power, Wisdom, and Love, Campanella rejects the Aristotelian distinction of act and potency. An inner act inheres in the *potentia essendi*.[283] The second primality, *Sapientia*, amounts to being the inevitable development of his idea of universal sensation. All things without any clear distinction, whether rational, animal, or material, are endowed with some measure of sense perception imprinted in them by this primal Wisdom. All created beings are thus essentially related to one another and participate primatically in the essence of the infinite being. Love and knowledge, appetite and perception being conjoined, *Amor* as third primality is a manifestation of knowledge. Love involves a process of becoming something else, the subject becoming imperfectly the object loved. By identifying beauty with goodness rather than understanding it in terms of Aristotelian proportion, Campanella once again announces his Platonic derivatives. The operation and functioning of all three primalities presuppose their transcendent unity.[284]

[281] Bonansea, *Campanella*, 144.
[282] Ibid., 146–47.
[283] Ibid., 147, 151.
[284] Ibid., 156–68.

Campanella's philosophy of nature is inspired by Telesio's effort to explain nature through itself. From his first published work he announced an opposition to Aristotle's hylomorphism. He rejects the idea of matter as pure potency actualized by form and attributes to it a measure of reality all its own. Nor does he accept form in its scholastic understanding. Form is the mode or quality of a thing, representing the idea as it is actualized in things outside the mind. The essence of a thing differs from its form, which is not to be identified with its total entirety. Inconsistency in terminology obscures the clarity of his distinction. Scorning the Aristotelian structure of matter, form, and quality, Campanella hoped to build a new edifice on the Telesian ideas of heat and cold as active principles vying for sole mastery of matter as passive substratum. Nevertheless he was by no means completely successful in disentangling himself from the conceptual world nor the terminology of the Aristotelian tradition. He confidently asserted that the senses perceived form directly: body is body in its own right without the complexification of claiming something to be bodily because of its form. Having rejected substantial forms, he substituted the two active informing principles of heat and cold. Form is replaced by *temperamentum*— the arrangement and blending of internal parts—as the structure of matter. In rejecting the scholastic notion of form as a substantial principle of being he also rejects its identification with act.[285] In short, material beings emerge as the product of two active principles (heat and cold) and one passive principle (matter). Form is the heat that derives from the sun, uniting itself to matter— and providing therein matter's external configuration.[286]

From this emanationist cosmology man emerges as a microcosm, a little universe of his own, although Campanella uses for this familiar Renaissance idea the term *epilogo*. Conjoined in the human microcosm are the five "worlds" or orders: archetypal, of ideals; mental; mathematical or universal space, the basis and substratum of all bodies; the material, with its vicissitudes of change; and finally the material or physical world to which time belongs.[287] In the resulting Platonic theory of the world as a most perfect animal with its own body, spirit, and soul, an essentialist view of language, dissolving the distinction between signifier and signified and undermining all individual differentiation and distinctiveness, pervades his perception of reality.[288]

Campanella's debt to Renaissance Platonism is obvious and profound. As a measure of that indebtedness we may leave him at the very end of his *Metaphysics* rummaging now enthusiastically, now skeptically, through that vast attic of Gnostic metaphysical goodies, the *pleroma* of Valentinus.

---

[285] Brian Copenhaver, "The Italian Philosophers of Nature and the Fate of the Occult Philosophy: Tommaso Campanella and the Metaphysical Decay of Magic," unpublished paper read at the Newberry Library, May 6, 1988, kindly made available to me by the author.
[286] Bonansea, *Campanella*, 189–93.
[287] Ibid., 220–21.
[288] On this last point, see Vickers, "Analogy," *passim*.

94   CHAPTER II

THE PRISONER AS REFLECTED IN TWO CONTRASTIVE MIRRORS

Both for the prophet himself and for his prophecies the little bell, his veritable device, continued to tinkle. Whatever the failure of the German Catholic effort to free the prisoner, he himself relentlessly worked to reach out for any possible source of help. Among the admirers of Campanella on the outside was Antonio Querengo, an erudite Paduan prelate, scholar, and poet serving in Rome as secretary to the influential Cardinal Alfonso d'Este. Having heard of the unusual nature of the prisoner, Querengo had expressed esteem, concern, and the hope of proffering a good word for him in high places.[289] On learning of this esteem that saw Campanella as among the miracles of nature, placing him above Pico della Mirandola and inviting correspondence, Campanella, in reaching for the glimmer of liberation, composed one of his more important and revealing letters on July 8, 1607. The favorable comparison with the great Pico, epitome of the high noon of the Italian Renaissance, proved challenging and provocative.

Rising to the occasion, Campanella artfully begins by depicting his sorry condition: a subterranean cell, with walls oozing dampness; a foul, sweaty straw mattress for a bed; himself manacled, sustained on bread and water, seeing no light or day—in fact seeing eternal night except for three hours of semilight in the afternoon, when he manages clandestinely to write and a little more during the day at ten o'clock for reading the office.[290] Thus to be some Pico or above Pico seems far too exalted for him. Pico was noble and rich, and had books and a commodious and tranquil life. Since the age of twenty-five he, Campanella, has been on the run, hounded by the Aristotelians. He has studied all sciences by himself alone and has come to philosophize differently from Pico. Now his notable boast: "I learn more from the anatomy of a plant than from all the books in the world." For he had learned to read the Book of God; by referring to the original Book of Nature, he could correct all the bad human copies.[291] Thus he has been able to read all the authors with facility and keep them in memory. Pico was truly a noble and learned mind, but he philosophzied more upon the words of others than upon nature; very thin on moral and political matters he gave himself to the divinatory and cabalistic sciences and to turning pages. In concluding, Campanella deems him a great man more for what he aspired to do than for what he actually did. Then, in pleading his own inadequacy for expressing himself in a properly courtly fashion to Querengo, Campanella leaves us with a weighty psychological result of his imprisonment which, if exaggerated, still needs to be recognized in

---

[289] LF-*Autobi.*, 217–18.
[290] TC-*Lett.*, 132; LF-*Autobi.*, 220.
[291] *LF-Autobi.*, 222; TC-*Lett.*, 134.

judging his intellectual deportment: "for eight years I have not spoken sensibly in my language or with any person of the world."[292]

Have we here a decisive internal tension, even opposition, within the Renaissance program between the humanistic reception of ancient, authoritative texts and the authority of direct experience? Or does Campanella's much vaunted empiricism dissolve into simply another form of verbalism that actually aligns him more with Pico than he would have liked to admit? In contrast to himself Campanella represents Pico as elegant, accomplished, bookish. Nevertheless they shared a common endowment: the driving precocity of the youthful thirst to know, the gift of prodigious memory, great personal charm, an extraordinary capacity for expression, a sense of wonder, and (fatefully) the aspiration for radical Christian renewal. Yet Pico was more careful to distinguish true knowledge from superstition and pseudoscience. From infancy Campanella had been nourished with the occult, with popular beliefs and fears from his own rustic world so poor and remote from the centers of culture and power.[293] In his first work, the *PSD*, Campanella had managed to adhere to Pico's critical rationality toward astrology as evinced in the latter's *Disputationes*. But soon after this stance would dissolve through his exposure to astrology and the resort to magical modes for a solution to the problem of nature. In the *Astronomy* of 1630 he confutes Pico regarding the astrologers. The issue of astrology would distance the two but without diminishing Campanella's respect for his great predecessor.[294]

In the mirror of a more contemporary eminence Campanella would struggle for self-definition. The transfer to Castel dell'Ovo, where he would remain from 1608 to 1614, afforded him the opportunity to receive visits from admirers and disciples as well as a better ambiance for writing and for expediting the Latin translation of many of his works.[295] The new accessibility would allow for the greater reception of books. It was in this period that he received through the good offices of Adami William Gilbert's *De magnete* and the books of Tycho Brahe from Antonio Persio.[296] It was also in this new context and period that he obtained a copy of the far more momentous *Sidereus Nuncius*.

From his first letter to Galileo, dated January 13, 1611, it is clear that he has not as with Gilbert had to wait over a decade for the reception of the work;

---

[292] LF-*Autobi.*, 225.

[293] Luigi Firpo, "Pico come modello dello scienziato nel Campanella," in *L'Opera e il pensiero di Giovanni Pico della Mirandola nella storia dell' umanesimo*, Convegno internazionale, Mirandola, 15–18 sett., 1963 (Florence, 1965), 2:362–71, esp. 365–66.

[294] Nicola Badaloni, "L'influenza di Giovanni Pico sulla giovanile 'Philosophia sensibus demonstrata' del Campanella," in *L'opera . . . umanesimo*, Convegno . . . Mirandola, 2:373–88, esp. 378, 387.

[295] *DBI*, 17:383.

[296] TC-*DSCM*, 25; TC-*AP*, 300.

rather the substance of this electrifying book has been communicated to him within a year of its publication and in two hours of reading he devoured a copy provided again by his good friend and ardent Telesian, Antonio Persio.[297] Not having learned of Galileo's removal to Florence and recalling his encounter with the distinguished mathematician in Padua in 1593, Campanella addresses him there as mathematician at the university (*gymnasii*). He writes in Latin, which will be dropped for Italian in all later missives. Besides being Campanella's own preference, is the use of Italian encouraged by learning of Galileo's own shift from an university environment dictating the use of Latin to the environment of the court, promotive of the vernacular and seeking a larger public? Whatever the reason Campanella's shift to Italian in dealing with his eminent acquaintance from a former time registers a significant refocusing occurring in the European centers of learning and science.[298]

In his exuberance at the news Campanella's mind soars off on a trajectory of speculation that could only leave his intended correspondent coolly aloof, his wariness affirmed. The prophet's enthusiasm ranges over new worlds and earlier prophecies, the possibility of lunar inhabitants, the reassertion of Italy's cultural leadership, the expectation of a Stoic destruction and renewal of the world. "O! Would that it might be permitted for me to confer with you regarding these matters."[299] While anxiously assessing the distance between Florence and Naples, Galileo could have only rejoiced at every stone, every bar that kept this Calabrian volcano securely immobilized.

In a more positive light, however, Campanella's letter reveals a sensitive, agile mind, anticipating profound issues, some to be amplified soon in the *Apology*. Especially suggestive is his allusion to other populated planets whose inhabitants may be free of original sin unlike our own.[300] Brunian also is the fleeting vision of freely moving and sustained celestial bodies, no longer

[297] TC-*Lett.*, 163; Luigi Firpo, "Campanella e Galileo," *Atti della accademia della scienze Morali* 103 (1960): 49–69, esp. 53.

[298] See on this point the suggestive statements of Bruce T. Moran, "Patronage and Institutions: Courts, Universities, and Academies in Germany; an Overview 1550–1750," in *Patronage and Institutions: Science, Technology and Medicine at the European Court 1500–1750* (Bury St. Edmunds, 1991), 169–83, esp. 169–70, 176–77; cf. also Bernd Moeller, *Imperial Cities and the Reformation*, ed. and trans. H. C. Erik Midelfort and Mark U. Edwards Jr. (Durham, N.C., 1982), 113–15.

[299] TC-*Lett.*, 163–69.

[300] In the subsequent *Apologia*, citing Ephesians 1:[10] and quoting from memory Colossians 1:[20]—"reconcilians in sanguine suo, sive quae in coelis, sive quae in terris, etc."—Campanella caressed the possibility of inhabited stars but cautiously refrained from asserting it (TC-*Apol.*, 51). Indeed other inhabited planets and the salvation of their populations posed problems worthy of Giordano Bruno. Yet two decades later the Anglican bishop, John Wilkins, acting upon Campanella's cue, would assert the probability of an inhabited moon. For a sensitive examination of this interesting issue, see Karl S. Guthke, *The Last Frontier: Imagining Other Worlds, from the Copernican Revolution to Modern Science Fiction*, trans. Helen Atkins (Ithaca/London, 1990), 136–52.

encased in crystalline shells but animated "Origenistically" ("si motus telluris sit ab anima origenica").[301] At the same time the strain upon his own Telesian view of the universe is evident.[302] There also begins to emerge that coupling of the two great navigators, terrestrial and celestial, Columbus and Galileo.[303]

In his third letter (March 8, 1614), the second having been lost, he shows a mind that is already preparing itself, as it had earlier demonstrated in his first exuberance, to invoke patristic authorities in order to gain room for a world system that may be less offensive to Christianity than present Aristotelianism. Having forsaken Latin for Italian, Campanella spares nothing in exhorting and showing respect for one who is uniquely gifted to reveal the true construction of the universe. Anxious to offer astrological aid for Galileo's current infirmity, he expresses surprise to learn that he does not believe in its efficacy. To Galileo's unique offer, advanced through Adami, to send some money for Campanella's maintenance, the proud prisoner refuses. In doing so he significantly refers to an incarceration "to which for the sins of youth God subjects me."[304]

By the spring of 1616 the first stage in what would prove to be the Galileo affair had been reached: the Florentine mathematician-philosopher had been summoned to Rome to appear before Cardinal Bellarmine. There has been considerable doubt as to the validity of Campanella's claim that he was invited by the notably liberal and open-minded Cardinal Caetani to render an opinion on the Copernican issue and Galileo, as well as uncertainty regarding the time in which he wrote the *Apologia pro Galileo*. Exhaustive research has persuasively established, however, that Campanella did not fabricate the cardinal's invitation to write and that he completed the composition in late February, prior to March 7, 1616, the time at which the Congregation of the Index brought down its condemnation of Copernicanism.[305] Once again Campanella's publisher, this time Adami, made the work appear more assertive than actually intended, for the original title was more tentatively *Disputatio ad utramque partem*.[306] Through the assistance of a disciple, P. G. Failla, the book had been expedited by way of Cardinal Caetani. On hearing nothing from Galileo by November, Campanella wrote to him, notifying him of his

---

[301] TC-*Lett.*, 164. Cf. also his earlier statement that he found it inconceivable that God would limit His power to this small ball ("questa picciola palla") and his earlier vision of freely floating planets (TC-*DSCM*, 32–33).

[302] TC-*Lett.*, 167–68; Firpo, "Campanella e Galileo," 54–56.

[303] TC-*Lett.*, 166; on this theme, see the interesting article by Andrea Battistimi, "'Cedat Columbus' e 'Vicisti, Galilaee!': due esploratori a confronto nell'immaginario barocco," *Annali d'Italianistica* 10 (1992): 116–32.

[304] TC-*Lett.*, 176–78. On the different astrologies of each, see Germana Ernst, "Aspetti dell'astrologia e della profezia in Galileo e Campanella," in *Novità Celesti*, 255–66.

[305] See the preface to Salvatore Femiano's edition of the *Apologia per Galileo* (Milan, 1971), 22–30; Antonio Corsano, "Campanella e Galileo," *GCFI* 44 (1965): 313–32, esp. 318–19.

[306] TC-*Meta.*, I, 224.

expectation and conveying to him the import of his own defense: Galileo's mode of philosophizing conformed to Scripture or was at least better than Aristotle in this respect.[307] Galileo preserved his silence and his distance.

The encounter (if one can call it such) between the two men presents a contrast between two cultures, one defined by discrete precision of research, the other by imposing vastness—speculative, prophetic, pulsating with poetic and metaphysical vibrations; two philosophies of nature from which derives a fundamental difference regarding scriptural exegesis—that of Galileo, cautiously negative to assure the autonomy of scientific research, that of Campanella, seeking to devalue the written Codex in order to permit the constant rewriting of the more authentic Codex of Nature. As it has been well expressed, a mechanical/mathematical model here opposes a hypermetric one that puts in question every system of measure in light of the final day.[308]

Besides a philosophic contrast in the different worlds represented, there is also the contrast between the total context, identity, and status of each man. Perhaps there is something of greater significance in Campanella's shift from the apparently more formal Latin to the more familiar Italian vernacular. In fact, however, the rhetorical signals would seem to be reversed. For in his initial choice of Latin, which harked back to the thin camaraderie in the Paduan university context of earlier and better days, Campanella uses the familiar second person. In resorting later to the Italian he remains with the distinctly more formal third person, always addressing Galileo as "Your Lordship." In each instance he adopted the prevailing rhetorical conventions of the respective language: in Latin, the intimate Ciceronian *tu*; in Italian, the dignifying *Vostra Signoria*. Certainly the Italian would be more appropriate for the distinctly courtly, nonacademic environment that distinguished the grand duke of Tuscany's *mathematicus* and *philosophus*, following his shift from Venice to Florence. In contrast with his own negative credentials of prisoner, condemned heretic, and political outcast, Campanella, except for his prophetic claims, could only feel dwarfed by the changed, magnificently enhanced status of his former acquaintance and the increasing eminence he had come to enjoy after 1610.

The Final Decade of Neapolitan Incarceration

Over the years Campanella's detention had assumed a certain pattern, shaped by the ongoing efforts of the Holy Office to get him extradited, the resistance of the viceroy, and occasional shifts in the location and degree of that detention. In his later *Syntagma* dictated to Gabriel Naudé he would present his life in terms of a welter of writings bubbling forth in various degrees of incompleteness, depending upon interruption, confiscation, searches. At any one

---
[307] TC-*Lett.*, 179–80.
[308] Corsano, "Campanella e Galileo," 330–31.

time his creative energies could be deployed on a number of levels—metaphysical, political, poetical, magical, astrological, medical—which to a later age might seem inhuman and impossible, but managed to be quite natural for one of demonic energy inhabiting a pansophic universe, before the compartmentalization or recompartmentalization of knowledge. The year 1609 may serve as illustrative of his industry: for German exposure he translated the *Del senso* (*DSCM*) into Latin, developed from its hitherto political nucleus the physical and ethical dimensions of the *Epilogue magno*, advanced the autonomy of the *Etica*, initiated the vast *Quaestiones physiologicae*, composed *De Gentilismo*, laid out an early version of his *Medicina*, and set on foot in Latin a second version of the *Metaphysica*, while beginning to nurture the missionary idea that would later mature in the *Quod reminiscentur*. Yet against this background of feverish activity, adding a dimension of harsh reality to an otherwise gargantuan cerebral enterprise, were repeated searches, confiscations, and efforts at extradition. Despite frequent interruptions and harassment from the officialdom, the juggernaut of intellectual enterprise rolled on: when in 1610 a search of his cell led to the confiscation of the second version of the *Metaphysics*, the prophet/survivor set to work to compose a third Latin version in thirteen books.[309]

Already evident in the earlier period the patterns of carceral composition and production from conception and drafting to completion, translation, and dissemination persisted into the last decade, which would see among other works the completion of the *QR* by 1616 and the thirty books of the *Theologia* begun in 1613, completed July 20, 1624.[310] This last period began with the prophet/survivor's shift back to San Elmo; the viceroy had come to deplore the excessive bustle of visitors and activities in Campanella's cell. From the fall of 1614 to May 1618 the regime at San Elmo bent every effort, at least officially, to place the utmost constraints on any compositional endeavor by Campanella. Nevertheless among other writings this period saw the radical reworking of the *Medicina* as well as the composition of the *Apologia pro Galileo* and that which he deemed one of his greatest works, the *QR*.[311] As well as being a monumental attestation of human persistence and will, the sheer achievement serves to celebrate the permeability of seventeenth-century European prisons and the enduring corruptibility of humankind.

In June 1616 the count of Lemos left the government of Naples to the new viceroy Pedro Girón, duke of Osuna. Capricious, restless, and irresponsible, Osuna disastrously raised the hopes of Campanella by the apparent personal interest he took in the notorious prisoner. For his own curiosity and amusement Osuna held several interviews with him. Two years into his viceregal

---

[309] *DBI*, 17:384.
[310] TC-*Lett.*, 203; cf. LF-*Bibl.*, 159–61.
[311] *DBI*, 17:386.

stay he had the prisoner transferred to the far more salubrious atmosphere of Castel Nuovo. In one of those long letters of self-advertisement (dated December 22, 1618) to the highest authorities, in this instance Pope Paul V, Campanella, having already offered His Holiness a vast panoply of intellectual goods, presents his most alluring offer: leaving five of his relatives as hostages for twenty months, he would go into Germany to create a school for preaching against all the sects. Then warming to the point that he be brought to Rome, there to flash his wares, Campanella avers that Osuna already says he wants to free him and has repeatedly pronounced him innocent. He goes on to claim that the viceroy had received him with increasing favor and wished to be of use to him. Cannot the papal nuncio confer with the viceroy for his proper liberation?[312]

Baseless hopes, cruelly raised! That most worldly-wise observer, Kaspar Schoppe, reported to Faber from Augsburg at the very beginning of the new viceroy's incumbency that speculation swirled as to whether Osuna would free Campanella. In his own judgment—only words, or if he did it at all, it would simply be for kicks (*per bizzaria*).[313] By autumn Schoppe was still laughing: according to news reports the viceroy has Campanella come into his presence well accompanied.[314] Later, from Mantua, in May 1619 Schoppe entertains the possibility that Osuna might be coming to Rome with Campanella in his train. Then shortly afterwards he drops the enticing rumor in Faber's direction to be leaked, if appropriate to Campanella, that the duke thinks of taking him from both Spain and the pope for himself; the only matter preventing this is his concern and uncertainty regarding his own standing and his affairs in Spain.[315] The bizarre viceroy might well manifest concern, for his freewheeling actions on the chessboard of European politics as well as in the *regno* would land him in the prisons of his master back in Madrid, there to die in 1620.

The transfer to Castel Nuovo in May 1618 would mark the last eight years of Campanella's Neapolitan imprisonment as the least oppressive and offering the most commodious ambiance for his work and for receiving visitors. The summons to repeated colloquies with Osuna led to permission to receive visitors, broadening out to the giving of lectures and casting a few horoscopes, while all the time pushing ahead on a number of manuscripts, principally at this time the *Theologia*.[316] The Neapolitan noble, G. B. Contestabile, mentions having heard Campanella give lectures on physics at this time.[317] Among his visitors Christoph von Forstner, an emerging Tacitus scholar and Württemberg diplomat, visited the prisoner between 1624 and May 1626; he

[312] TC-*Lett.*, 194–96.
[313] Amab., *Doc.*, II, 52/175.
[314] Ibid., 52/176.
[315] Ibid., 54/181, 182.
[316] *DBI*, 17:387.
[317] Firpo, "Appunti campanelliani," *GCFI* 24 (1943): 187.

would later write Campanella in the fall of 1627, congratulating him on his freedom and hailing him as the miracle of the age. Like Forstner some arrived in the cell bringing their albums as was the custom of the age (*de more aevi*) with the intent of obtaining the autograph of the now famous prisoner plus any chance phrase or testimony from the distinguished person.[318] Indeed if nothing else Campanella would appear to be the first celebrity in Western history. Nevertheless the prophet/survivor never enjoyed anything like clear sailing, steering among first the reinstituted prohibition to write, leveled by the Congregation of the Index, then the censures but on balance favorable response of Cardinal Bellarmine to the *QR*, rededicated to the new Ludovisi pope, Gregory XV, and then the Holy Office's denial of authorization to resume the celebration of the Mass.[319]

His tireless pursuit of liberation by every means possible in his constrained circumstances had been remarkable from the very beginning, but during the early 1620s in Castel Nuovo it becomes particularly noticeable. With his peasant instincts did he sense some decisive weakening in the system and culture of his detention? After a quarter century did he imagine in his nostrils the distant scent of freedom? Among surviving letters, for a single day, March 21, 1621, we have three separate appeals—to the Caetani prelates, to Cesi, to Faber—pressing his case and in the last instance trying to regalvanize Schoppe.[320] With the succession of Urban VIII to the Holy See Campanella again updates his rededication of the *QR* to press this gift into the scales for his recognition and release. By June 1624, he has presented his case to Cassiano dal Pozzo—a shrewd choice, as Cassiano was the most prominent figure in the immediate entourage of the Barberini as well as being unique in his self-created role of the most important private art patron in Rome and of his age. Campanella urged his mediation in gaining access to and the attention of Cardinal Borghese and allowing his disciple in theology, Dionigi di Castelvetere, to come to Rome to negotiate his affairs for the appearance of the prisoner himself there.[321] Disappointed with the apparently feeble efforts of his disciple and scribe, Failla, to press his affairs in Rome and for a more direct presentation of his case and even person in Madrid, Campanella also held him accountable for failure to present the recently completed thirty books of *Theology* to Pope Urban and to get the *QR* published. Campanella now looked to his latest disciple, Castelvetere, and to the good offices of Cassiano for effective representation in Rome.[322]

---

[318] Firpo, "Appunti campanelliani," *GCFI* 29 (1950): 86–87: "debes famae tuae, quae te saeculi miraculum atque heroëm potius ac daemonem, quam hominem credit."
[319] *DBI*, 17:388.
[320] TC-*Lett.*, 197–99.
[321] Ibid., 201–2; on the reputation of Cassiano dal Pozzo, see Francis Haskell, *Patrons and Painters: A Study in the Relations between Italian Art and Society in the Age of the Baroque* (New York, 1963), 98–117.
[322] TC-*Lett.*, 202–3, 205–6.

The year 1626 began badly for the importunate prisoner with the Holy Office rejecting for the fourth time his request to celebrate the Mass. Nevertheless the legal/political wheels for Campanella's liberation had been in motion since December 1622. Rather than any intervention on Rome's part it was the favorable attitude of the papal nuncio, Innocenzo de'Massimi, toward the prisoner, his continuous advocacy, and the esteem that he enjoyed with both Olivares and the viceroy that effected the change of mood. Early in 1626 Madrid granted the viceregal government the authority to reach a decision regarding Campanella. On May 15, its Collateral Council approved the release of the notorious inmate but with the understanding that he should remain on a short leash. Eight days later Campanella emerged from his long ordeal. He had survived.[323]

A free man? Now it was Rome's turn with the offender. Barely a month elapsed before the nuncio in Naples had him arrested. In order to avoid Spanish resistance Campanella was disguised as a secular priest, given a false name, and extradited in chains for embarkation to Rome. By July 8 he was safely ensconced behind the walls of the palace of the Inquisition, there to render account before its ecclesiastical tribunal. The Roman phase had begun.

---

[323] *DBI*, 17:389; Gianfranco Formichetti, "Campanella a Roma: I *Commentaria* ai *Poëmata* di Urbano VIII," *Studi Romani* 30 (1982): 325–26.

Chapter III

THE CELEBRITY FADED

Roman Years

The Rome of 1626 was a very different city from that which had been so brutally sacked a century before. The astonishing evidence of a restored confidence and energy that marked the Counter Reformation Church in the course of the later sixteenth century and the revival of the papacy, a pronounced triumphalism, attained in many ways its culmination at this very time with the formal consecration of the new St. Peter's in November of that year. At the threshold of what would prove one of the longest of pontificates Urban VIII would now undertake the decoration of the completed construction's interior.[1]

Yet the new Barberini pope, himself both poet and humanist, inspired hopes of a Maecenas among writers as much as artists.[2] Even today the achievement of the latter accosts the eye and the imagination to proclaim as much the Rome of Bernini as of the Barberini.[3] But for the most immediate, if less apparent, monument of the literary world, gathered in Rome behind the bustle of the artists with their commissions, one must turn to that contemporary profile of litterateurs coming from the pen of a most distinguished Greek scholar, a *scriptor* in the Vatican Library, and later its librarian, Leone Allacci. The famous *Apes urbanae*, as its unwinding title elaborates, amounts to being a discursive bibliography of all the distinguished persons present in Rome between 1630 and 1632 who had published anything; it represents a veritable portrait of the Roman intellectual world, produced in the very same year, 1633, that its celebrated president, the Barberini pope, would deliver a terrible blow to the intellectual life of Europe by way of the condemnation of Galileo. But this event lay beyond Allacci's immediate horizon as he proceeded to celebrate a Roman city and community that nurtured, harbored, inspired, and protected a Republic of Letters, a Lycaeum of the World, a cultural excellence and leadership for Italy, Europe, and the globe at a time when Europe and indeed Italy itself found themselves afflicted with war and pestilence.[4] Among those participating in this single, much vaunted Roman Academy, afforded by

---

[1] On this point, see the unpublished doctoral dissertation of Louise Rice, "The Altars and Altarpieces of New St. Peter's (1621–1653)" (Columbia University, 1992), 162.

[2] Marc Fumaroli, *L'age de l'éloquence: Rhétorique et "res literaria" de la Renaissance au seuil de l'époque classique* (Geneva, 1980), 202–26.

[3] See, for example, Torgil Magnuson, *Rome in the Age of Bernini* (Uppsala, 1992).

[4] Leone Allacci, *Apes urbanae, sive De viris illustribus, qui ab anno MDCXXX, per totum MDCXXXII Romae adfuerunt, ac typis aliquid evulgarunt* (Rome: Ludovicus Grignanus, 1633), sigs. A²–[A³ᵛ], 9–13.

the city under its new pontiff, could now be found the old Calabrian conspirator.[5]

Except for the heady atmosphere of ecclesiastical and theological power, inescapable and pervasive, much of the celebratory mood would have been lost on the Neapolitan captive, who had simply been removed to another form of imprisonment. In the course of the next two years it would be a gradual process of gaining complete freedom of movement and access that began with the Holy Office's directions that he be kept in strict isolation under lock and key in a cell of the palace of the Inquisition, although with full material support and comfort, to ever greater degrees of freedom of movement throughout the building. On July 27, 1628, he was able to remove, again under a system of detention, to Santa Maria sopra Minerva, the official citadel of the Dominican order, where he had all his books restored to him by order of Urban VIII.[6] It was not until January 11 of the following year that he at last won complete freedom and shortly thereafter the removal of his name and books from the Index.[7] Indeed early January 1629 marked the apex of his Roman sojourn. Behind him was a series of censures, examinations, and defenses of his writings, which now with growing papal favor seem to have won approval. Before him for the next four years would emerge a new set of constraints, enemies, and suspicions, which would ultimately compel his departure. With freedom would come not acceptance, fulfillment, affirmation, which might be expected at the dusk of any life and especially one so tormented as that of Campanella, but rather the experience of new constraints, frustrations, and exasperations. The developments in this period can be reduced to three interlocking issues: the ambiguous reception of his works; his rise and fall in papal favor; and the final epistolary encounters with Galileo as the great mathematician descended to his own confinement.

On September 15, 1626, the bishop of Molfetta consigned to the Inquisition manuscript copies of three of Campanella's works: the *QR*, the *AT*, and the *Monarchia messiae*. Together they probably represent better than any other three of the Neapolitan philosopher's writings the range and import of his mind. The *QR*, having a little earlier acquired the favorable opinion of Cardinal Bellarmine despite some censures, would nevertheless resist publication, convulsing as will become evident the last years of Campanella's relations with the papal curia and not seeing print until the twentieth century. The *MM*, derivative from the very early and soon lost *Monarchia Christianorum*, hyperpapal and theocratic, would at last see publication in Jesi in September 1633; after four months on the bookstalls it would be reviewed by Niccolò Riccardi, master of the Sacred Palace since June 1629, and be suppressed on the

---

[5] Ibid., 240–43.
[6] *DBI*, 17:391.
[7] Ibid., 389–91.

grounds of its potential offensiveness to secular rulers.[8] As for the *AT*, its enigmatic, sinister ambiguities would leave the longest trail of censures, questions, and doubts that continue to stretch down to the present. Indeed after sending his disciple, Pietro Giacomo Failla, to Rome charged with the task of obtaining the publication of these same works in 1621, Campanella soon found the *AT* occasioned such censures from the inquisitorial fathers as to require a separate defense. The resulting *Apologeticum* directed to Cardinal Bellarmine raised fundamental issues that would in later controversy distinguish the Pelagianism of Campanella.[9] After enjoying a brief moment of publication in Rome in 1631, the *AT* too would be suppressed and censured, not to reappear until 1636 and then from Paris.

Between November 1627 and February 1628, a special commission was called, presided over by Cardinal Desiderio Scaglia and including among others Campanella's two later powerful enemies, Niccolò Ridolfi, then master of the Sacred Palace, soon general of the Dominican order, and Riccardi, his successor and known for his prodigious memory as "Il Mostro."[10] The commission's task was to pass judgment on a list of 160 *Assertiones* drawn from the *AT*. The results of their lively and less than benevolent discussions prove revealing for the contemporary official interpretation of Campanella's most difficult work. Most of his theological propositions, when not referred to as heretical, are considered impious, dangerous, and erroneous, while the philosophical assertions are seen as false, fatuous, and fantastic. From a more exact theological point of view the commission believed the *AT* to be a recycling of the Pelagian heresy: the equation of Christianity with rationality, the confusion of the law of nature with the law of Christ, the extension of this first law to all men, the effective abolition of Christ and the gospel, and the apparent opening the door of salvation to the Turk. In short, Campanella is faulted as wishing always to exclude grace and exalt nature. Most telling is the recognition that this posturing Solomon leaves a trail of references from Pythagoras to Plato and looking beyond to Origen he begins *ad origenizzare*. Riccardi reminds his associates that Arius also drank from the springs of Plato.[11]

In identifying a Pelagian head to the hydra, had the commission correctly assessed the import and the challenge of Campanella? If Christianity is seen as inevitably possessing an exclusive element, or differently expressed, if Christ is seen in a fair degree as the *scandalon*, ultimately an offense to reason, if there is any meaning to orthodoxy, whatever the Christian ecclesiastical ar-

[8] Ibid., 388, 394; LF-*Bibl.*, 103–4.

[9] "Il ritrovato *Apologeticum* di Campanella al Bellarmino in difesa della religione naturale," ed. Germana Ernst, Teste e Documenti, *RSF* 3 (1992): 565–86.

[10] Germana Ernst, *Religione, ragione e natura* (Milan, 1991), 82.

[11] Ibid., 81–85; idem, "L'edizione dell' *Atheismus Triumphatus* di Tommaso Campanella. Varianti e censure," in *Le edizione dei testi filosofici e scientifici del '500 e del' 600; Problemi di metodo e prospettive* (Milan: Franco Angeli, 1986), 113–22, esp. 116–21.

rangement, then the broad, universalizing tendencies within the thought of the reformer threatened the very identity of early-seventeenth-century Catholicism and Christianity, as traditionally understood. In the persisting challenge the Church faced in finding a balance between the Church's compromise with the world to engage it and lead it more effectively and the Church's withdrawal from the world to preserve its own identity, Campanella's advocacy of the former alternative seemed a compromise leading to the Church's veritable dissolution in the world. The warnings of the commission with respect to the Platonizing forces in the *AT* gain added significance in terms of the Church's deliberate effort since the pontificate of Clement VIII to throttle such tendencies in its theology. And yet within its own theological spectrum Catholicism since Trent, under the influence of the Jesuits, had partly distanced itself from Augustinianism to expand the realm of nature at the expense of that of grace. The assertive voice of the Dominicans on the panel would have been sensitive to even the most modest tendencies in this respect. The commissioners' heavy hand upon their errant friar would now have been far more evident except for the intercession of papal favor. which in the censure simply asked for the correction of bad propositions, or, if necessary, for composing the whole matter anew from the ground up.[12]

In a sense Campanella did a little of both: piecemeal handling of the censures plus the composition of a new and different work, *De praedestinatione*, wherein he tried to enlist St. Thomas against the harsh Spanish predestinarian tendencies within current Dominican theology. Only the first need concern us here. His tinkerings sufficed, especially in light of papal favor toward its author, for its submission to a Roman printer; but by the end of 1630 at the time of expected diffusion, new objections were raised by a censure—fifteen doubts of varying import, which Campanella will call the *postcensura*, requiring the addition of new layers of explanation to an already heavily qualified text, thereby producing new ambiguities and objectionable obscurities. But papal favor had by the end of 1629 run out for Campanella and he would have to wait for a later date and a French context for the actual publication of his work.[13]

In the apparent rehabilitation of Campanella nothing seems so incongruous as his coming into favor and for a brief, intense moment into intimate association with Pope Urban VIII. Again the wayward Dominican of the poorest peasant background had to deal with a most sophisticated and cultured Florentine, this time of humanistic and artistic accomplishment. The ground had already been prepared before the prisoner's extradition to Rome. And, as one might expect, the game to be played on the highest stage of Christendom would be fraught with grave dangers as well as obvious opportunities for the Neapolitan player.

---

[12] See also Ernst, *Religione*, 85; idem, "L'edizione," 116.
[13] Ernst, *Religione*, 85–89.

Among his many accomplishments the new pope possessed more than the ordinary early modern European's intellectual commitment to astrology. He had acquired the habit of casting the horoscopes of some of his cardinals and openly predicting the dates of their deaths, mindless of the possibility that more than one could play the same game. For beginning in 1626 astrologers started to prognosticate Urban's own imminent death, and by 1628 the rumors were flying so thick and fast as to indicate that the situation had gotten out of control. Urban would manage to restore order ultimately by his bull "Inscrutabilis" of April 1631, which ferociously confirmed the earlier bull of Sixtus V of 1586 against judicial astrology but now made it a crime of *lèse-majesté* to predict the deaths of princes and especially of popes and their families.[14] Between 1626 and 1631 Campanella's favor with Urban would rise and decline.

Although Campanella brought the cunning of a peasant to a situation that best invited the *discrezione* and simulation of a courtier, he could hardly be faulted for advancing on too narrow a front. For he sought to engage the favor of the highly cultivated Barberini pope by both stroking His Holiness's poetic talents and feeding his astrological fancies. In 1627 he began composing his bulky, winding, laudatory *Commentaria* on the *Poëmata* (1620) of the humanist pope, ending the first volume in 1629, starting a second in 1631, and continuing until 1632. Beyond the hyperbolic claims for Urban's poetic genius as surpassing that of Dante, Pindar, and Homer, the work has been shown to have no small importance not only for demonstrating some continuities in Campanella's thought but also for disclosing his practice of incorporating himself and his own specific purposes into the work of another: the numerous references in the commentary's preface to the *De Gentilismo* and the *Apology* promote the theme of the restoration of the sciences, now to be affected, however, by the powers of music and poetry. Such a restoration is seen as integral to the world's movement toward a golden age and the unity of the true religion. Campanella represents Urban as the restorer of poetry and thus willy-nilly having a hand with Galileo as protagonists of the New Age; as with Galileo's discoveries, so with Urban's poetry the two are placed in a more comprehensive framework with Campanella as its messianic interpreter.[15]

Regarding the papal astrological fancies Campanella had within three months of his arrival in Rome composed a little work entitled *De fato siderali*

[14] D. P. Walker, *Spiritual and Demonic Magic from Ficino to Campanella* (London, 1958), 205–6; for the larger context and more immediate analysis, see Germana Ernst, "Astrology, Religion and Politics in Counter-Reformation Rome," in *Science, Culture and Popular Belief in Renaissance Europe*, ed. Stephen Pumfrey, Paolo L. Rossi, and Maurice Slawinski (Manchester/New York, 1991), 249–73, and also the same author's *Religione*, 255–79.

[15] For the definitive work on Campanella's *Commentaria*, see Lina Bolzoni, "I 'Commentaria' di Campanella ai 'Poëmata' di Urbano VIII: Un uso infidele del commento umanistico," *Rinascimento* 28 (1988): 113–32; idem, "La restaurazione della poesia nella prefazione dei *Commentaria* e campanelliani," *Annali della scuola normale superiore di Pisa. Classe di lettere e filosofia*, 3, ser. 1 (1971): 307–44, esp. 320–29, 338, 340.

vitando for the ailing pontiff assailed by dark rumors. The work—which, as events would prove, had a long fuse attached—offered an astrological program of propitiatory rites that might be put into practice for greater papal salubrity in the present time of stress.[16] Obviously the manuscript was intended only for papal eyes and managed to draw the prisoner into more than the good graces of a pope embarrassed to find such talent under detainment and investigation by the Inquisition. In the ensuing months the meeting between Campanella and Urban became a major subject of rumor and speculation throughout *caput mundi*. In July 1628 the Tuscan ambassador reported that the pope was most eager to have "a certain Campanella most able and unique in astrology as well as many other talents" to come into his private chamber to counter the other opinions regarding his death in 1630.[17] A month later the Venetian ambassador reported that the pope obtained his relief from care by the study, observations, and exposition of astrology, all of which allows the long-imprisoned Dominican, Campanella, to preside much in favor. While professing the astrology of necromancy, he cunningly adjusts his opinions to ingratiate himself with the pope.[18]

D. P. Walker has brilliantly reconstructed and analyzed the special form of magic contrived by Campanella for the prophylactic needs of the pope in warding off the disease-bearing eclipses and the evil influences of Mars and Saturn. Campanella forsook his earlier primitive magic and had recourse to the more sophisticated practices of Marsilio Ficino's spiritual magic presented in the latter's *De vita coelitus comparanda*, reworked in a more demonic direction in the *De fato siderali vitando*. Campanella's rite called for a sealed room, specially prepared with aromatic substances, decked with silks and branches, lit by two candles and five torches (representing the seven planets), infused with Jovial and Venereal music, and capped with the consumption of astrologically distilled liquors. The contrived room served both as a miniature model of the heavens and the stage for a religious ceremony directed toward planetary angels. Ficino's sources were Neoplatonic and Hermetic, which Campanella tried to fortify with the authority of St. Thomas in order to provide a magic with a demonic dimension sporting under the guise of being natural and spiritual. There was surely enough here to have the ceremony in normal circumstances fall afoul of Sixtus V's bull.[19]

Given Campanella's very special magical and astrological talents in the service of the pope, some during these months of 1628 might see the former conspirator and heretic not only moving gradually toward full liberation but also toward the exercise of that power which his own philosophy so fondly

---

[16] LF-*Bibl.*, 98.
[17] Amab., *Doc*, II, 153/210.
[18] Ibid., 154/216.
[19] Walker, *Magic*, 204–36; cf. also Amab., *Doc*, II, 170–79/242.

adulated. In his astonishing rehabilitation might he not become a cardinal?[20] Even more immediately alarming stood the very real prospect of Campanella obtaining the post of consultor in the Holy Office, which would have allowed considerable influence over the censorship of theological publications. It was at this point that his most distinguished potential enemies, Ridolfi and Riccardi, the general of the Dominican order and the master of the Sacred Palace, may well have moved to bring him down by means of a nasty trick.[21] In 1629 a Lyons printer was publishing Campanella's *Astrologicorum libri VI*. The two high-placed Dominicans together probably with the powerful Cardinal-Nephew Francesco Barberini managed clandestinely to rush *De fato siderali vitando* into print as a supplement that it might appear as the seventh book to the Lyonese publication; while contriving the appearance of a French source, the two conniving Dominicans most probably had it produced in-house by the cameral Roman printer Andrea Brugiotti.[22] By October they could present the pope a copy of this very compromising little treatise with its description of his own astrological antics.[23] Urban was properly furious. Campanella lost that very special, charmed connection with his pontifical friend. Nevertheless he

[20] On Campanella's disappointment here, see TC-*Lett*., 283; cf. *DBI*, 17:392.

[21] The exact nature of this imbroglio leading to the fall of Campanella from papal favor continues to be shrouded in mystery. Certainly the astrologue emerged scarred and forever bitterly opposed to Riccardi and all too prompt to impugn his motives. The persuasive, if not altogether convincing, rehabilitation of Riccardi and Ridolfi by Dominican scholarship leads one to question the complicity especially of Il Mostro in this affair as well as the reliability of Campanella's personal judgments after decades in prison. Riccardi seems to have been of a kindly, all too trusting disposition. His vacillation and change of judgment both in the case of Campanella's *AT* the following year and Galileo's more notorious *Dialogue* the next year (for which the Dominican would suffer and be reprimanded) helps confirm Riccardi's reputation as a cleric open and not unsympathetic to the possibilities of the new science. That he should have given Galileo sufficient leash first to obtain Rome's imprimatur and then seek to have the *Dialogue*'s publication shifted to Florence beyond the master's jurisdiction suggests one who was far too indulgent toward innovative currents to conform to Campanella's picture of Il Mostro as monster rather than prodigy. Indeed that Riccardi could, after further vilification from Campanella, later write the Neapolitan now in Paris a conciliatory, brotherly letter a half year before their almost simultaneous deaths in May 1639 argues for a more temperate view of the man. For one like Campanella, who had no dearth of enemies, it is possible that especially at this time there might be justifiable alarm at his candidacy as consultor. Scholarship has perhaps moved too rapidly to the drum of Luigi Firpo in affixing blame upon Riccardi and Ridolfi at this juncture and not given sufficient weight to the warped judgment of Campanella, soon to be quite manifest in his French connections. On the Dominican rehabilitation of Riccardi, see Ambrogio Eszer, O.P., "Niccolo Riccardi, O.P.—padre Mostro," *Angelicum* 60 (1983): 428–61; on Ridolfi, see the comments of Michele Miele, O.P., "Un opuscolo inedito ritenuto perduto di Tommaso Campanella. Il 'De praecedentia religiosorum,'" *AFP* 52 (1982): 267–323, esp. 275–76.

[22] Gianfranco Formichetti, "Il 'De siderali fato vitando' di Tommaso Campanella," in *Il mago, il cosmo, il teatro degli astri: Saggi sulla letteratura esoterica del Rinascimento*, ed. Gianfranco Formichetti (Rome, 1985), 199–217, esp. 202–4; but cf. Firpo, "Il Campanella astrologo e i suoi persecutori romani," *RF* 30 (1939): 203–15.

[23] Walker, *Magic*, 207–8; LF-*Bibl*., 98–101.

weathered the storm; through occasional letters and the continuation of his labored commentary on Urban's *Poëmata*, he managed to retain a modest measure of favor in papal eyes.

In fact Campanella shortly afterwards managed to further his connections with other members of the Barberini family. He served as the probable author of the program pursued by Andrea Sacchi in the fresco of the *Divine Wisdom* for the ceiling in the north wing of the Palazzo Barberini under the patronage of Taddeo Barberini, nephew of Urban VIII and prefect of the city of Rome. Campanella's contact with Taddeo at the time of Sacchi's creation of the fresco in 1630 can be established by the philosopher-magus's performing of astral rites to counteract an illness of Taddeo's eldest son. Campanella's plan for the fresco incorporated the characteristic primalities and combined biblical with astral imagery. We have here a celebration of the sun's approach to the earth, the great conjunction of Jupiter and Saturn—a veritable cosmic transformation worthy of the Barberini papacy as well as a distillation of the prophet's own proclivities, expectations and aspirations. Here also the created book of God's wisdom affirms the revealed Book of His divine wisdom in Christ.[24]

Earlier, writing to Urban in June 1628, Campanella had in a long letter resumed a theme broached formerly with Paul V: "the tacit conspiracy of scientists in our age, seeking to obscure the evangelic truth." In fact it was the perennial theme as to his own orthodoxy and in this instance, significantly, his astronomical orthodoxy. He represents himself as being against both Ptolemists and Copernicans as well as all those who would eternalize the world, imposing on it a predetermined, rational jacket. In a nice comparison he claims that the "scientists" draw up the account without the innkeeper, disallowing the world's end and its changes with the Incarnation: "there begins imperceptibly this transformation [*mutazione*] with the entire machine of the world consenting and adjusting itself to the innovation and preparation for the humanization of the eternal word, its author, by restoring man and all creatures each according to its capacity as is to be discovered in Romans 8, St. John Chrysostom, and all the better Fathers."[25] Copernicus et al. drew up the ancient account and showed the excesses in heaven but failed to recognize in their rationalization the signs given by Christ.

In an effort to increase the distance between himself and Copernicus, Campanella appeals to the Fathers and to a divinized nature. He is not to be considered in Copernicus's camp, for he has written four books against him. And in his *Apology for Galileo*—originally entitled *Disputatio ad utramque partem*—he had merely argued on both sides of the issues, leaving the ulti-

---

[24] John Beldon Scott, *Images of Nepotism: The Painted Ceilings of Palazzo Barberini* (Princeton, 1991), 88–94.

[25] TC-*Lett.*, 220–21.

mate determination to the Holy Office. Literally true, but in the past decade he seemed to have moved closer to Copernicus. Following the decree of the congregation condemning Copernicanism in 1616, Campanella avers that he had gladly identified the Copernican opinion as heretical. Reverting to his own commentary on Urban's poems, he finds one ode, "Adulatio perniciosa," which the pope had written especially for Galileo in August 1620, surely favoring the opinion of Copernicus already condemned four years earlier. Choosing his words carefully, Campanella observed that according to the Index and His Holiness's orders Copernicus's book can be understood hypothetically when it says that the earth moves, couching this conditionally ("if it were to move"). Thus from this recent glossing of Urban's earlier ode of praise in the codex and the emphasis upon the conditional and hypothetical, Campanella can only deduce that the pope does not favor now this opinion. In keeping with one of his most fundamental epistemological distinctions Campanella recognizes the authority of Copernicus to rest upon his work on the calendar because the Polish astronomer's contribution here relies on sensible evidence and not on opinions, presumably manifest in later "Copernicanism" ("testimonianze vere e potenti dalle sue osservazioni ma non dall' opinioni") By establishing his hypothetical reading, His Holiness has extended his providential care to the Church and to the scientists (*scienziati*) and removed error.[26]

In the dance of shifting perceptions a gradual repositioning of parties is occurring as the third decade in Barberini Rome draws to a close. According to Campanella's assessment of the context the changing mood requires his own distancing from any suspicion of Copernicanism suggested by the defense of his friend a decade earlier. It also requires corrections in the manuscript of his comment on the pope's earlier ode for Galileo, "Adulatio perniciosa," as well as other now potentially incriminating expressions of enthusiasm, which helped explain the opposition of Urban to the publication of the *Commentaria*.[27] But more important it suggests that as the full significance of the condemnation of Copernicus's book began to settle upon the

---

[26] Ibid., 223–24.

[27] Barberini's *Poëmata*, in itself a resounding triumph of literary banality, became one of the outstanding best-sellers of the century, as Giorgio Spini with his characteristic verve has most recently shown. See "Galilaeana Minima," in *Studi in onore di Arnaldo d'Addario*, ed. Luigi Borgia et al. (Lecce: Conte, 1995), 4:1301–15, esp. 1307–15. In all fifteen editions—seven before 1631 and eight more from 1634 to 43, from Galileo's condemnation to the eve of the author's death—"Adulatio perniciosa," praising Galileo for his discovery of Jupiter's satellites and his revealing the blemishes on the sun, managed to survive. Spini argues that the great master poet, sufficiently sustained by egotistical gas, apparently believed that nothing should be omitted or revised in the successive republications, so perfect the precious verse. Its actual presence in the six editions appearing from 1623 to 1631 could have only contributed to Galileo's own misperception of the Barberini pope's attitude toward himself and his scientific enterprise. I want to thank Professor Spini for kindly sending me an offprint of his article.

Roman learned, ecclesiastical community, already by the summer of 1628 there had begun a repositioning of concerned parties regarding the issue of Copernicanism. And along with the comparatively moderate distancing of Campanella from a Copernicus whom he had never effectively accepted, the exquisitely honed sensitivities of the Barberini pope may well have been placing his pontifical self earlier than believed at the head of the pack in the oncoming storm.[28]

During the four years intervening between this early repositioning and the actual appearance of the fateful *Dialogue* in February 1632, Campanella pressed upon both Barberini, the pope, and the all-powerful cardinal secretary, Francesco, his loyalty together with repeated requests to have specific writings published—principally the *QR* as well as the *Commentaria*. Breathing now freely and fully the Rome of the recently established seventeenth Congregation of the Propaganda, Campanella can propose to Cardinal Francesco Barberini the constitution of a Barberini college *de propaganda fide*, founded on the *QR*, its members armed with doctrine, prophecy, and the desire for martyrdom.[29] To Urban he imparts his fears that his pronounced enemies, Brothers Riccardi and Ridolfi, now attempt to poison the mind of Cardinal Francesco against him.[30] He resurrects for himself the identity of Zopir, that faithful but misunderstood servant of King Darius, used earlier with the king of Spain but ever-recycleable according to need: now to Urban, "I am your Zopir, only yours."[31]

It would have been while pursuing his missionary aspirations with the pope that Campanella elicited that remarkable statement reported secondhand by Castelli to Galileo in a letter dated March 16, 1630. According to Cesi's statement to Castelli, Campanella had complained to Urban that his own efforts to draw high-placed Germans to the Catholic faith were being hobbled by the condemnation of Copernicus (1616), a determination that scandalized these potential converts. Urban had responded: "that was never our intention and if it had been up to us, there would never have been such a decree."[32]

By April 1631, Campanella was feeling distinctly forgotten among the friends of Galileo and wrote him to that effect and for not having received a copy of his letters on sunspots.[33] With the publication of the long-awaited *Dialogue on the two Great World Systems* in February 1632, Campanella's shame and frustration in having others preferred to him found petulant expression: ever desirous of sharing in his friend's observations and thoughts he

---

[28] For a more extensive treatment of this issue, see Bolzoni, "Commentaria," 128–30.
[29] TC-*Lett.*, 226–30, 233–35.
[30] Ibid., 230–31.
[31] Ibid., 234; cf. TC-*DPI*, 222.
[32] *Op. GG*, XIV, 88: "non fu mai nostra intenzione; e se fosse toccato a noi, non si sarebbe fatto quel decreto"; Bolzoni "Commentaria," 128–29.
[33] TC-*Lett.*, 232.

complained about never having received a copy of the *Dialogue*, while others had been preferred.[34]

When Campanella next writes to Galileo on August 5, 1632, it is to inform him that he had received in July a copy of the much desired *Dialogue*, advanced through Cardinal Magalotti, and to confess his relish for the three participants in the dialogue. Although many matters astronomic most desired by himself are not treated by Galileo, the letter exudes enthusiastic support. Even if some petty literalist might wish to cause trouble, Campanella claims to defend the book as being not in conflict with the decree of condemnation. Then again the sense of camaraderie, of standing together in the trenches of truth and innovation against obscurantists, a feeling quite unreciprocated, overwhelms him: "I dare say that if we were together in a villa for a year, great things would be settled."[35] Enthusiastically, fully, forcefully Campanella proffers his mite of talent and support in the service of true philosophy and philosophizing.[36]

Then with the reversal of the curial wheels come two weeks later the prohibition and suppression of the *Dialogue*. Immediately to Galileo Campanella registers his disgust coupled with a mounting bewilderment and alarm: although as master of the Sacred Palace, Il Mostro claims to express the mind of the pope, His Holiness is not informed and must think otherwise. Looking around for allies in the forthcoming imbroglio, Campanella lights upon Benedetto Castelli, Galileo's most effective champion. Distinguishing between the rectitude of the decree and its faulty reasoning, he looks to the support of earlier church fathers and to the favorable intervention of the pope.[37] A month later Campanella, now menaced, excluded, angered, presents a darkening scene.[38] In his final letter to Galileo, on October 22, 1632, he imparts a new fear and caution as the case against the new philosophers involving much bluster acquires momentum. He fears that the *apologia*, in which he simply argued on both sides, will be held against him and that he will be implicated. Yet neither he nor Castelli has been called and the curialists wish to keep him uninformed. If his lordship should come and be heard by His Holiness in consistory, Campanella would hope to unburden himself. But then he begs Galileo's understanding for not being more forthright and to excuse his pusillanimity, born of long years of suffering and calumny.[39] If the impending storm of the Galileo affair had imposed the unfamiliar constraints of caution, prudence, and a certain distancing upon the overly generous Calabrian, his eminent Florentine friend, consistently opposed to any year-long tête-à-tête in

---

[34] Ibid., 235–36.
[35] Ibid., 241; cf., 167.
[36] Ibid., 240–42.
[37] Ibid., 242–43.
[38] Ibid., 243–44.
[39] Ibid., 244–45.

a secluded villa, was prudently seeking to assure his own distance and remove. In acquiring a copy of Campanella's *Astrologia*, he now proceeded to mark in the margins all the occasions in which its author appealed to him. Thus he could better assess the possible charge of a dangerous involvement from this direction in the increasingly likely eventuality of a future trial.[40]

Campanella's own final surviving letters to Galileo may inadequately represent a relationship that could have strained toward a new stage when the Holy Office required the Florentine's presence in Rome in February 1633. For Campanella will later claim that he discussed Democritus with Galileo at some time during these weeks when both found themselves in Rome.[41] And on May 10 Gassendi would write to Campanella, asking him to intervene to compose differences between Galileo and Marcus Scheiner.[42] But by this time Galileo certainly had other matters on his mind, and the last thing he needed was closer relations with one who had the solid credentials of Campanella for heterodoxy, if not for heresy. Ever since their encounter at Padua forty years earlier everything dictated to Galileo the prophylactic of distance.

• • •

Given Campanella's sufferings at the hands of the Spanish *monarquía* and his release from its grip since 1626, it is hardly surprising that he would be drawn into the magnetic field of force exercised by the emergent powers of a restored French monarchy effected by the new Bourbon dynasty. In fact with his finely tuned sensitivity to the ongoing confessional strife in these years, he was prompt to hail the fall of the Huguenot redoubt, La Rochelle, to the conquering royal army of Richelieu. Barely had the news arrived in Rome than he composed a celebratory oration apparently delivered by another, since in late November 1628 he was not yet a free man.[43] When four years later Campanella wrote his *Dialogo politico tra un Venetiano, Spagnuolo e Francese*, he allowed his Venetian to have all the winning arguments, favoring Richelieu's policy, France, and that kingdom's approaching ascendancy. A distich in favor of Louis XIII shortly followed.[44]

[40] Luigi Firpo, "Appunti Campanelliani, XXVIII," *GCFI* 41 (1962): 371–72.

[41] On Campanella's recently recovered letter of June 19. 1636, to Peiresc, see chap. 2, n. 7, *supra*: "Galileo in molte cose, massime nei principii, e con Democrito e dal discorrer c'ha fatto meco in Roma" (363).

[42] *Op. GG*, XV, 115, no. 2500.

[43] LF-*Bibl.*, 193/87. De Mattei, correcting both Amabile and Firpo, assigns the earlier date of November 22, 1628. See his "Note sul pensiero politico di T. Campanella (con tre lettere inedite)," in *Campanella e Vico* (Rome, 1968), 93–107, esp. 101.

[44] LF-*Bibl.*, 149–51; *DBI*, 17:394; cf. also a published section of his *Commentaria, De Sancto Ludovico*, ed. Clara Ferri (Rome, 1990), esp. 27–29, wherein Campanella builds up the figure of St. Louis as an occasion to praise France, its origins, customs, and natural defense that Providence has assigned to it.

During the course of the same year he seemed to be drawn increasingly into the orbit of French influence within the city of Rome. In the process of befriending the educational efforts of Calasanzio toward the children of the poor he managed to give a course to ten scholars in an outlying villa where from 1630 to 1632 he stayed as guest of the *scolopi* fathers; there among other lectures he expounded on chapter 11 of St. Paul's Romans at the request of the French ambassador.[45] Through repeated colloquies held during the first half of 1632 Campanella came to be befriended by Gabriel Naudé, librarian to Cardinal de Bagno and later shrewd *érudit* as well as librarian to Richelieu and Mazarin. It is Naudé who draws Campanella's attention to Pierre Gassendi's *Observationes*, which will elicit from the Dominican his first letter to that important French personality and philosopher in May 1632.[46] In the course of this year Campanella will entrust ever more of his work to the French medical doctor and emerging political thinker; at this time he will dictate to Naudé his autobiography, since lost, and the partly autobiographical *Syntagma* of his works, which, after using for his own purpose, Naudé will publish in 1642 after his friend's death.

Taken down by Naudé at the master's dictation, the *Syntagma* affords an interesting conspectus of Campanella's prejudices and emphases at the end of his life. For at one point he will present a sort of list of recommended authors in which Aristotle as the prince of philosophers along with his Greek and Arab expositors looms astonishingly large. Among moderns Bacon is not included, yet Campanella will introduce among his authors the observation that in the shops of artisans "more of real philosophy may be had than in the schools of philosophers," followed by a list of the same.[47] Although familiarity would later lead to contempt, Naudé had apparently had his eye on Campanella for some time. In writing his own warning about the Rosicrucians in 1623, he had highly praised the Calabrian whom he knew through the Frankfurt edition of the *Philosophia realis* and the German *Monarchia di Spagna*, calling him "phoenix of all philosophers and political thinkers." Two years later in his *Apologie pour tous les grands personnages qui ont esté faussement soupconnez de magie* he had situated him honorably among the new philosophers Telesio, Bruno, Vanini (!), and Bacon.[48] His direct literary and intellectual association with Campanella seems to date from the momentous explosion of Vesuvius in December 1631. Campanella studied the phenomenon and delivered his *De conflagratione Vesuvii* as a lecture to the Accademia Capranica early in January. Entrusted to Naudé, but since lost, parts of the lecture possibly showed up in the treatise by that *érudit*, who published his own version the

---

[45] *DBI*, 17:393; Formichetti, "A Roma," 329–30.
[46] TC-*Lett.*, 236.
[47] TC-*Syn.*, 55–56.
[48] LF-*Autobi.*, 271.

same year.[49] In this Roman, first stage of their relationship Naudé appears as the enthusiastic disciple and even generous promoter of the old Neapolitan philosopher.[50]

Not limited to Naudé, Campanella's associations with rising French intellectuals extended to the young Orientalist, Jacques Gaffarel, sent in 1626 to Rome by Richelieu to quarry whatever of exotic interest he could find for that French statesman. In his *Curiositez inouyes*, published in 1629, he tells of a meeting that he and several abbots had with Campanella in his chamber at the palace of the Inquisition, which could only have occurred during this first trip to Rome in 1626. The visitors caught the recently rescued prisoner writing to Cardinal Magalotti but at the same time engaged in a physiognomic effort to transpose his identity—a sort of magical merging of selves by means of focusing on the party through an act of the imagination ("quem [Magalotti] ita imaginando contuetur").[51] Gaffarel's pursuit of the wondrous, the marvelous, would ill-serve him. After a further sojourn in Rome in 1632 he relocated in Venice, bringing with him the Index, updated from 1624, of all the writings of Campanella, organized into ten volumes; he delegated to his more politically minded friend, Naudé, the assemblage of the works of the most important current political writers, as requested by the French resident ambassador to Venice.[52]

Campanella's French connections, which had not yet turned sour, would now serve him well. The viceregal administration in Naples had unearthed a conspiracy led by a former disciple of Campanella, Pignatelli, who proceeded to implicate, unjustifiably, his ostensible master. The nuncio writing from Naples to Cardinal Francesco Barberini on August 30, 1633, reported that the viceroy demanded the extradition of Campanella as an accomplice and as one whose being at large presented a continuing danger to the Crown.[53] By October of the following year the affair had really heated up; reports of seizure mixed with those of the ostensible culprit's imminent flight whisked about Rome.[54] Campanella, drawing closer to the French embassy, finally sought its protection, thereby increasing Spanish fears. Anxious to avoid any jurisdictional imbroglio with Spain, Urban connived with the French ambassador,

---

[49] *DBI*, 17:393; LF-*Bibl.*, 194/90.

[50] Anna Lisa Schino, "Campanella tra magia naturale e scienza nel giudizio di Gabriel Naudé," *Physis* 22 (1980): 393–431.

[51] Jacques Gaffarel, *Curiositez inouyes sur la sculpture talismanique des Persans* (Paris: Hervé du Mesnil, 1629), 266–70; *Correspondance du P. Marin Mersenne, Religieux minime*, ed. Mme Paul Tannery, Cornelis de Waard, and René Pintard (Paris, 1936), 2:170–71. The Latin quotation Gaffarel took from *De sensu rerum*, II, xxxi, TC-*Op. Lat.*, I, 199.

[52] *NBG*, 19:146; see LF-*RC*, 60–63 on the origin of the Index for organizing Campanella's diverse writings; ibid., 56–60, on the work of the Calabrian clerical compatriot, Paolo Gualtieri di Terranova.

[53] Amab., *Doc*, II, 156/219.

[54] Ibid., 154/212.

François de Noailles, to place Campanella beyond Spanish reach. Disguised as a Minim, equipped with a false name, and using the carriage of Noailles, Campanella departed Rome on the night of October 21, 1634, headed for Livorno and from there by ship to Marseilles.[55]

IN THE WORLD OF THE FRENCH SAVANTS[56]

Among the *érudits* and savants outside Italy none mediated so deliberately and effectively between the two foci—French and Italian—of the new intellectual world as did Nicolas-Claude Fabri de Peiresc. Scholar, naturalist, true polymath, one who through extensive correspondence had broad, even global contacts, allowing him to pursue joint astronomical observations on several continents for purposes of establishing a *bureau des longitudes*, Peiresc would later be designated by Pierre Bayle as "Un Procureur Général de la République des Lettres." As a youth of eighteen years he had so impressed G. V. Pinelli in the last year of that great patron and bibliophile's life as to become his spiritual heir in the mission of advancing the arts and sciences.[57] Equally conversant with the salon of the Dupuy and the academy of the Linceans, Peiresc could send the works of Bacon to Dal Pozzo in Rome. His very location at Aix-en-Provence promoted his role as mediator between the *scienziati* of the south and the *savants* of the north in the emerging Republic of Letters. A friend of Galileo, whom he had met at Pinelli's Paduan retreat in better times, Peiresc would in the crisis of that friend's condemnation attempt to intercede twice for the fallen scientist. Apprised by the Genevan, now Paris *parlementaire* Elie Diodati of Galileo's sufferings, he had earlier written to Francesco Barberini that his friend's hard detention could only blemish the splendor and fame of this pontificate. Then more ominously, to be confirmed by history, he wrote to the same party at the end of January 1635, asking that an end be brought to the punishment of Galileo, otherwise it "will run great risk of being interpreted and well compared one day to the persecution of the person and wisdom of Socrates in his country."[58] Such was the gentleman who would serve as Campanella's host and protector in this perforce adopted land during these same years of 1634 and 1635, when Campanella's star would rise and with equal rapidity fall in the community of French intellectuals.

[55] *DBI*, 17:394.
[56] On Campanella in France, historiographically as well as historically, see the definitive study by Michel-Pierre Lerner, *Tommaso Campanella en France au xviie siècle* (Naples, 1995). I wish here to acknowledge the author's generosity in having provided me with a copy at such a time that I could still benefit from some of its finer points.
[57] For a sensitive analysis of Peiresc's system of patronage, see Lisa T. Sarasohn, "Nicolas-Claude Fabri de Peiresc and the Patronage of the New Science in the Seventeenth Century," *Isis* 84 (1993): 70–90, esp. 76–77.
[58] Cecilia Rizza, *Peiresc e l'Italia* (Turin, 1965), 9–43, 102, 189, 211–30.

At least up until 1609 Campanella occupied no apparent place on Peiresc's intellectual horizon. For in that year, the French savant, when preparing for a friend a list of thirty-two notables who must be seen in Italy, did not include the Neapolitan philosopher's name among those of Sarpi, Antonio Persio, and G. B. della Porta.[59] It would not be until May 1624 that he could claim to have received some of Campanella's writings (*les cahiers*). He expressed interest next year in seeing the *Apologia* and it would be as a defender of Galileo that Campanella attracted the support of Peiresc.[60] To Jacques Godefroy in October Peiresc mentioned the availability of Campanella's *Monarchia di Spagna*, published in what he believed to be both German and Latin, but since he, Peiresc, had a manuscript of the Italian, he planned to wait for the price to come down. In 1631, he spoke of having received the *AT* through the agency of Claude Dupuy. Finally on October 4, 1633, Peiresc wrote for the first time to Campanella, conveying the solicitude of a fellow scholar for his kind and a sensitivity that would make all the easier Campanella's passage from Rome to France.[61]

Thus it was hardly surprising that the Roman fugitive on landing at Marseilles on October 29 should dash off a letter to his generous patron, the Aix savant. Having been disguised with the help of the comte de Noailles and Cardinal Barberini, he announced his safe arrival and the need to await the reception of his clothes and writings. He suggested his own regret at the Roman prohibition of Lord Herbert of Cherbury's *De veritate* and would impart his opinion of the book when they met. Here he must cling on account of lack of money spent on mail service and sailors; he opined that once in Paris nothing would be lacking. Continuing in a presumptuous vein, inflated with expectations of his new freedom and land, he looked forward to thriving in Peiresc's company. Ever mindful of that wasted posterior, a fact to which Gaffarel had alerted the French reading public five years earlier in his *Curiositez inouye*, Campanella asked his host to send a carriage or a litter "for age and effort prevent my mounting a horse."[62]

Pierre Gassendi, France's foremost philosopher, on learning of Campanella's sudden advent in the vicinity, hastened to join his eminent friend Peiresc in his commodious hotel in Aix. In his biography of Peiresc Gassendi records the *humanitas* and *laetitia* with which his erudite host entertained the *philosophum celebrem* from Italy.[63] Indeed amidst books, amiable conversation, relaxation, and even astronomical observations, appropriately involving a conjunction of Mercury with the sun, Campanella enjoyed nearly ten days of unique hospitality. Supremely conscious of what the visitor had suffered,

[59] Ibid., 25.
[60] Ibid., 206, 245–46.
[61] Ibid., 246–48; Amab., *Doc*, II, 248–49/313, 272/328.
[62] TC-*Lett.*, 247–48.
[63] Rizza, *Peiresc*, 251.

Peiresc, generous to a fault, wished to wrap him in the support and esteem of his own learned friends. To Naudé he reported how fondly Campanella talked of him[64] and to Bourdelot and the Dupuy his bland, gracious handling of some sensitive questions in conversing with Gassendi.[65] In actual fact there lurked a delayed action bomb already evident in Campanella's earlier correspondence with Gassendi, whose formidable revival of Epicurean atomism alarmed and incensed his Italian counterpart.[66] It is thus all the more surprising that Campanella during these days of reorientation could maintain an uncharacteristic composure and restraint.

Wishing to reach Paris before winter set in, Campanella headed northward by way of Lyons, where he found through the earlier initiative of Gaffarel his *Medicina* in the process of being printed and already half complete. In preparation for an expected encounter with Père Joseph, Bouthillier, and four Sorbonnists visiting the duke at Orléans, he asked Peiresc amidst profuse thanks for still more money: its apparently prompt receipt would allow the donor now to be linked forever in Campanella's mind with his earlier Neapolitan patron, Mario del Tufo, for their extraordinary hospitality and benefactions.[67] His solicitous friend in writing to Naudé anxiously expressed the hope that his recent guest might find a much deserved peace and happiness in Paris.[68] In successive letters in late November, Roberto Galilei, cousin of Galileo, wrote the latter reporting having seen Campanella pass through Lyons in disguise, only making himself known to Roberto on account of the friendship that he held for Galileo. The cousin related soon after that in Paris he was on the crest of the wave.[69]

But waves fall. The initially favorable reception granted Campanella derived from his being seen as a victim of Spain and the Holy Office. There also prevailed at first a general, uncritical admiration of his immense philosophical

---

[64] *Peiresc: Lettres à Naudé 1629–1637*, ed. Philip Wolfe (Paris/Seattle/Tübingen, 1983), 27.
[65] Rizza, *Peiresc*, 251–52.
[66] TC-*Lett.*, 237–39.
[67] Ibid., 254–55. In his *Viri illustris Nicolai Claudij Fabricij de Peiresc, senatoris aquisextiensis Vita* (The Hague: Adrian Vlacq, 1655), 181–82, Pierre Gassendi, immediately after mentioning the celebrated Neapolitan visitor, claims that on the receipt of Peiresc's fifty gold pieces at Lyons, Campanella inserted into his *Philosophia realis*, undergoing final revision, to the already existing statement praising Mario del Tufo as examplar of our age—"haud negem amicos splendida excipendos esse mensa, sed frugaliter & cum opus habent: eumque potius reputabis, qui tibi pecuniam suam, quam qui vitam suam offert"—the following addition: "veluti mirificus Fabricius, Dominus de Perese, Gallorum decus, & Philosophorum, & clarorum virorum Mecaenas, & perennis hospitalarius exemplar est mundo." Indeed whereas the previous 1623 German edition of the TC-*PR* only mentioned Mario del Tufo as "exemplar of our age" for munificent hospitality, along with an assist from Dante (TC-*Op. Lat.*, II, 1078–79; "Oeconomia," 506–7; cf. *Inf.* 29. 128–29), in the final Paris edition of 1637 Campanella comes to associate with his earlier Neapolitan patron, his recent generous host, Peiresc, as exemplar of hospitality for all time (TC-*PR*, 210)
[68] Wolfe, *Peiresc*, 28.
[69] Amab., *Doc.*, II, 215–16/247, 248.

productivity, which could well prove, to say the least, dated once that veritable incandescence of Europe's intellectual life, Paris, had turned its withering beam upon the *opera* and their author. Admired without being known, he would be scorned when once understood.[70] For his part the aged, badly disoriented Neapolitan philosopher would aid and abet this process by his own indiscretions, while devoting his ebbing energies in these final years to the systematic publication of his writings.

According to his own account rendered to Urban VIII, Peiresc, and Cassiano dal Pozzo, arriving in Paris on the first of December, Campanella secluded himself for the next twenty days at the house of François de Noailles' brother, Charles, bishop of St. Fleur. When fully recovered and reclothed, he sallied forth from his kind host's domicile to visit the nuncio Bolognetti, who required that Campanella not publish without his permission. But since some of his writings were in the hands of others, such as the *Medicina* with Gaffarel, there would be ample opportunity for misunderstandings and recriminations. Furthermore, almost immediately taking advantage of the new environment and its apparent remove from curial attentions, he could turn to Richelieu and the Sorbonne for licensing. But it was his reception at court by Louis XIII that most enraptured Campanella. The event occurred on the ninth of February. All were standing, including the king, who with bonnet removed, twice embraced the old Calabrian conspirator, laughing (most uncharacteristically), greeting him several times with "Très bien venu," and manifesting great compassion. Campanella assured his correspondents that to no great personage, whether ecclesiastical or secular prince, had such immense honor been shown. The king granted Campanella a pension, which like most seventeenth-century largesse would be irregularly rendered.[71] For the Crown the event must have provided a special signature to the embarrassment of Spain and the restored confidence of a Bourbon France.

Besides equipping Campanella with money and a carriage, Peiresc had provided his friend with a letter of introduction to M. Pithou, apparently as a means of entry into the charmed circle of the Dupuy, the Puteana, successor to the group established by Jacques-Auguste de Thou and based upon the great historian's library. Campanella speaks of their coming to welcome him almost immediately following his arrival and receiving their caresses: Bourdelot, Moreau, Diodati, Gaffarel, Guise, Bouthillier.[72] Writing to Peiresc, he reports on his favorable reception amidst the assembly of the Sorbonne doctors that left him confident as to the licensing of all his books. Emerging from this happy experience, he met the Dupuy brothers (Signori *Puteani*) bearing Peiresc's letter telling of the safe arrival of his books and writings.[73] Despite growing

[70] Rizza, *Peiresc*, 254.
[71] TC-*Lett.*, 269–75.
[72] Ibid., 261–62.
[73] Ibid., 300.

tensions and misunderstandings at least until mid-July 1635, Campanella inhabited the Dupuy meetings, although his evident relish for and involvement in confessional, polemical matters dealing with the Calvinists certainly struck a sour note in that scholarly circle of savants. That as late as the winter of 1636 he can refer to his activities there, again of a theological, controversial nature, does not prove that he still inhabited their midst.[74] As early as May 19, 1635, Guy Patin, great friend of Naudé and renowned medical doctor of the Faculty at Paris, took out a Saturday afternoon to visit Campanella at his now permanent residence, the Dominican convent of the Jacobins on the Rue St. Honoré. After talking to him for two hours he came to apply to him what Petrarch had applied to Rome: "He owes much of his learning to lies. He knows many things, but superficially." The Parisian intellectuals would poorly conceal their diffidence toward the great Neapolitan magus-philosopher.[75]

To the discomfiture, embarrassment, and mounting anger of Peiresc, who sought during these first months Campanella was in France to orchestrate his friends and connections in the poor unfortunate's favor, the latter worked to contrary purposes. No sooner had he arrived in Paris than he became overly demonstrative and expressive regarding the apparently altogether too long delayed differences he nursed with the manifest atomism of Gassendi. Not only did he belittle Gassendi and make no effort to distinguish between his atomism and that of Epicurus and their different intent but Campanella proceeded to traduce all French savants as being of little weight.[76] For his part Campanella denied having derided Gassendi as empty and deficient. He attested to his esteem for the French philosopher, especially as a mathematician, astronomer, and sharp observer, although he found the Epicurean philosophy of atoms and a vacuum insufficient for explaining the causes of all things.[77] By mid-July Peiresc still received denials from Campanella that he kept on murmuring against Gassendi, nor that he was out of tune with French ways, obdurate in his own beliefs and closed to the information of others.[78] Peiresc had presented his own intellectual deportment and willingness to entertain opposing views. At the same time Diodati could inform Peiresc that he had been counseling Campanella on his conduct, for he deported himself too freely and only to his own harm. Diodati seemed to be alone in crediting him this late with good ideas (*lumières*) and considerable perspicacity of spirit, finding in him great goodness and candor for which he cherished him.[79]

Concurrently, however, another important friendship had soured, turning

---

[74] Ibid., 318, 358.
[75] Rizza, *Peiresc*, 255.
[76] TC-*Lett.*, 237; *Mers.*, 5:165, 172; *Lettres de Peiresc*, ed. Philippe Tamizey de Larroque (Paris, 1893), 4:507.
[77] TC-*Lett.*, 301–3.
[78] Ibid., 316–18.
[79] Amab., *Doc.*, II, 274/331c.

into an ever more virulent wound for Peiresc. Against Naudé Campanella lashed out: he had taken from Campanella's chamber in Rome all the originals of some small treatises, promising to publish them without following through and thereby preventing Campanella from doing so; Naudé had written a panegyric to the pope on the freeing of Campanella without having shown it to the latter; he had used in his own works Campanella's *De libris propriis*, which had judgments of all sorts on writers and sciences.[80] Writing from Rieti to Peiresc in the early autumn of 1635, Naudé expressed anger at his being misrepresented. He found Campanella totally different from the doctrine that he professed; he is awkward, spiteful (*fascheuse, despiteuse*) in the least difficulties, impatient. Naudé claims never to have been so astonished to see a life so little corresponding to the opinion held of him in France and obtained from his published works. A manifest imposture was recognizable in his writings and a simplicity, or better credulity, especially evident in the *Medicina*. Naudé's earlier affection for him had marked the savant as "the Campanellista," which brought great prejudice from the Spanish. Continuing, he affirms that when he returns to the *pays de Liberté* (i.e. France), he will publish two of Campanella's works; but it is not from lack of trying that he has failed to publish in Italy. On the specific matter of the *Syntagma*, only after having smuggled it to Venice did he recognize the truly Augean stable of diction and extravagant judgment and turned to rewriting it. In a fascinating aside regarding Campanella's propensity for claiming that his works have been robbed by others, Naudé claims company with Schoppe. Ask him! Yet his extravagances have not altered his affection for the man. Repeatedly at this time Naudé deemed Campanella to sin more out of simplicity and inadvertence than from malice. He ends by assuring Peiresc that Campanella is *fort subject*.[81] Nine months later, with the apparent continuation of Campanella's calumnies, Naudé departs his earlier calm and rants against what he now sees as a fool, imposter, liar and ingrate. But by the end of the summer he can claim to be satisfied with Campanella's apologies and retractions to Gaffarel and Diodati and consider the matter finished.[82]

In an assessment of this relationship, which witnessed a progressive disappointment, the burden of misunderstanding falls to an aging, querulous Campanella, while the younger, rapidly maturing, earlier disciple shows himself not incapable of some patience and later even considerable generosity. For in the years immediately following Campanella's death Naudé was able in his correspondence, his long-delayed *Panegyricus*, and the published *Syntagma* to hail his old friend with praise and affection.[83]

---

[80] TC-*Lett.*, 324.
[81] Amab., *Doc.*, II, 264–69/327ᵉ.
[82] Ibid., 270–71/327 g and h.
[83] Schino, "Campanella . . . Naudé," 393–431, esp. 424–26.

These two bruising sets of relationships have consumed our attention because they reflect significantly upon the character and the mentality of the liberated hero and celebrated philosopher in the perspective of the most sensitive and advanced learned community in early-seventeenth-century Europe. One must make huge allowances for differences in time, place, and social background of this radicalized cleric of peasant stock, a product of an alien culture, outlook, and concern translated into the most sophisticated intellectual environment of the period. And if Naudé can seek the support of Schoppe's experience, it is because he shares something of that manipulative self-aggrandizement to which the former prisoner had proved so vulnerable. And as a further control one needs to take into account the growing senility of a man who had suffered an unspeakably harsh life, a survivor of the most terrible fortune shaped admittedly by his own outrageous pride. Yet placed under the harsh lens and glaring lights of Paris's intellectual culture, Campanella reveals by his deportment certain undeniable features that helped construct, although they do not entirely define, the measure of the man: the appalling arrogance and bombast of a faded messiah, the presumption and vanity of an authoritarian personality, the impostures of a simulator. The Parisian context had a shredding effect upon both the personality and the reputation of this late Renaissance, displaced philosopher—a shredding effected by the new, emerging philosophical mood upon the assumptions of a passing age. On the continuing theme and problem of Campanella's life and its larger meaning, namely, the relationship of a rampant freedom with an imposed, total order, a small, yet irreducibly true measure of insight derives from the reaction of his now disenchanted friend, Peiresc.

Peiresc was unique in trying to represent Campanella in the best light to the fellow members of the club and to spare him the glare of embarrassment and disapproval. Yet by the end of 1635 he came away truly angered by Campanella's attitude to Gassendi, which had produced a veritable hemorrhaging in Peiresc's ethos of patronage.[84] Indeed more largely he took appropriate alarm at Campanella's lack of respect for another's ideas, for what he understood as intellectual freedom. He feared that liberty of thought would be suffocated by a badly informed principle of authority. He rejected any interference, even religious, in the field of knowledge and associated it with Ultramontane tendencies. Even allowing for his friend's sufferings, Peiresc associated this blind obedience with the frock. Only by freedom of judgment could the truth be sought. His profession of tolerance bore an inevitably relativist conception of knowledge.[85] More immediately a most profound incomprehension divided Peiresc and his friends from Campanella; the former were reorienting them-

---

[84] According to Sarasohn, "Peiresc," 80–81, Campanella had committed a sort of treason—a betrayal of trust and a violation of honor.

[85] Rizza, *Peiresc*, 260–63.

selves toward a knowledge commensurate with the limits of the human intellect and a science positively constructed on the analysis of experienced data that denied the bold speculations and religious, astrological aspirations of Campanella. For Peiresc to be secure knowledge must be direct; the proper fields were the works of man found in history and nature conceived not as something sacred and thus worthy of contemplation but as the result of slow conquest.[86]

But all along, the real decision as to Campanella's acceptance or rejection within the emerging Republic of Letters lay with its chief orchestrator and architect, the recognized secretary of Europe's intellectual life, the formidable Minim, Marin Mersenne. From his cell in the order's monastery near the Place Royale Mersenne presided over a network of approximately two hundred correspondents scattered throughout Europe. To his cell he attracted the leading luminaries of the age. For all his intellectual breadth and tolerance Mersenne pursued a distinct program in the interests of a comprehensive, if eclectic, empiricism directed generally against all forms of animism, Hermeticism, and the occult, and most specifically against the late Renaissance naturalists—Bruno, Telesio, and Campanella. Rosicrucianism had early evoked his opposition. Magic, the occult, and whatever breathed a Stoic pantheism all constituted parts of that animistic universe which to Mersenne represented a monster to be crushed in the interests of a mindless, neutral, mechanistic world of God's creation.[87]

In his solicitude for his Italian visitor and his desire to prepare avenues for his easy acceptance in the learned circles of Paris, Peiresc had good reason to be anxious concerning Mersenne. For in his imposing work, the *Quaestiones in Genesim* published in 1623, Mersenne had in his first public utterance regarding Campanella recommended that his works receive the same treatment as Vanini had most recently experienced from the parlement of Toulouse: being burned. Shortly afterwards, however, Mersenne chanced upon Campanella's *Apologia pro Galileo* of 1622, which gave him reason to consider the Neapolitan philosopher in a kinder light; his book on the plurality of worlds might be read but with care. In fact Mersenne had vainly sent several letters to Campanella proffering aid in the publication of the first part of the fourth redaction of his *Metaphysics*, brought to him from Naples by a mutual admirer, the count de Chateauvillain. Apparently unaware of Mersenne's earlier denunciations, Campanella replied cordially.[88] Yet with further exposure to this naturalistic/magical philosophy Mersenne came away less than enchanted, having identified a clear example of that dangerous naturalism to be

---

[86] This passage amounts to being a free translation from Rizza, *Peiresc*, 270–71, 276–77.
[87] Robert Lenoble, *Mersenne ou la naissance du mécanisme* (Paris, 1943), 83–168, *passim*.
[88] *Mers.*, 1:177–78; cf. 122–23; LF-*Bibl.*, 121.

opposed.[89] Among other menacing features he believed to recognize the old doctrine of the World Soul and its informing participation in an animate universe. Drawing upon Campanella's *De sensu rerum*, where he finds the master idea, "quod terra sentiat, vivat et intelligat," Mersenne counters: "quod res omnes non sentiant neque vivant."[90]

Thus it was with less than enthusiasm that Mersenne could contemplate hastening across the city to meet the great arrival from the south. Despite the mounting requests and importunings from Peiresc, Mersenne could plead throughout the winter of 1635 his distant remove from the Rue St. Honoré, the poor condition of the road, lack of opportunity, inclement weather.[91] For his part Campanella, Achilles-like, nursed his anger. Hence not until sometime in the first week of May did the Minim father sally forth and the repeatedly postponed encounter between the two wary clerics take place. In reporting the meeting of two to three hours with Campanella, Mersenne with heavy irony observed regarding one who had claimed all the minds of France to be as nothing, that he, Mersenne, "le moindre de toute la France," had found that the friar had no basis for such a proposition and that he enjoyed no great ascendancy over all our minds.[92] On seeing him a second time two weeks later Mersenne bearded him on a technical matter pertaining to music, which had lingered in previous efforts at correspondence.[93] With some relish he observed that the great sage from the south, on interrogation, did not appear to know what an octave was. Mersenne concluded: "he has a happy memory and a fertile imagination."[94] Shortly afterwards, in flipping through a copy of the recently published *Medicina* that had come his way, the intellectual secretary of Europe reiterated his former definitive judgment on the poor refugee. And then in case his friend Peiresc had not gotten the gist of his reaction to the visitor, he allowed in a statement, which can only be understood as sarcastic, that if they had been able to entice Galileo to Paris, they would have Italy's two greatest men.[95] When later Mersenne attempted to refer Campanella to Descartes, the *illustris vir* allowed that there was nothing to be hoped from his books. And earlier in March 1638, in writing to Huygens, Descartes delivered himself with breathtaking finality: "j'avois trouvé dés-lors si peu de solidité en ses écrits."[96]

---

[89] Lenoble, *Mersenne*, 40–42; see *Mers.*, 1:63–64, 70, 122, 134, 137; 3:312–13 for Mersenne's earlier attacks on Campanella.

[90] Lenoble, *Mersenne*, 153–55. But on J. B. Doni's efforts to achieve a reconciliation between the two clerics, see *Mers.*, 4:86–87, 384.

[91] *Mers.*, 5:27.

[92] Ibid., 202.

[93] Ibid., 2; cf. 1:604.

[94] Ibid., 5:209.

[95] Ibid., 213–14.

[96] Lenoble, *Mersenne*, 8.

Despite the amends that were made, Campanella had managed by the end of 1635 to become largely excluded from the higher circles of the Republic of Letters in Paris. Lacking magistral degree and being a pronounced anti-Aristotelian, he found the University of Paris for the most part a closed club. His encounter with the young doctor of theology, Jean de Launoy, may have been made through his contact in the Dupuy circle as late as the beginning of 1636.[97] There remained, of course, a number of far less prestigious groups meeting in the great city. In an environment fertile for the development of later academies, the *conférences* of Theophraste Renaudot's *bureau d'adresse* thrived in Paris during the 1630s and early 1640s. However eclectic in its pursuit of science, it enjoyed the active support of Louis XIII and Richelieu. Dilettantes, *virtuosi*, and even some widely recognized scholars such as Jean-Baptiste Morin and Étienne de Claves could be found there. Here Campanella could settle into more congenial surroundings. While such subjects as demonology, astrology, and the occult received attention, an expectably pre-Cartesian skepticism prevailed in their treatment. Nevertheless picking up on long-standing interest in Paris for Ramon Lull and ideas of world unity floated in the previous century by Guillaume Postel, Campanella could and did find here a public platform and outlet for his persisting astrological-political-religious aspirations. The role of the prophet returned. The prophecy remained the same: a reestablished harmony of natural and revealed knowledge but now under the leadership of France. Thus Campanella's presence, evinced both in its sessions and in its weekly *Gazette*, seems to have had a distinct impact upon Renaudot's encyclopedic academy. Renewed interest in Hermeticism and the occult could, however, create more than ripples in an intellectual context being shaped by Marin Mersenne and actually served to exacerbate relations between the incipient academy and the Faculty of Medicine.[98]

• • •

By nature eclectic, agglomerative, and driven by contingency, politics could prove more permeable than thought to Campanellan wiles, especially when the world of thought was that being reshaped in Paris at this time. For their part Louis and Richelieu would not be entirely opposed to a Bourbon France now transformed into a new City of the Sun—within reason. Thus if the doors to Paris's higher intellectual life remained closed to the Neapolitan philosopher, opportunities might well await him in the corridors of power. For if we may return to that moment of heartfelt embrace between the Most Christian

---

[97] See chap. 4, 153–58, *infra*.
[98] Howard M. Solomon, *Public Welfare, Science and Propaganda in Seventeenth-Century France: Innovations of Theophraste Renaudot* (Princeton, 1972), 68, 81, 91–93.

King and the Calabrian conspirator—surely one of the more incongruous events of a career rife with incongruities—even more strained seems the relation of Richelieu, the apostle of discipline, rationality, and exactitude, with our man from the south. Whatever their relationship it was not one that Rome could afford to leave to the two participants themselves or to chance. Two days after Campanella's flight to Marseilles Cardinal Francesco Barberini wrote the papal nuncio to Paris, Bolognetti, alerting him that Campanella was a turbid brain, presuming much with his doctrine, a heresiarch requiring due vigilance.[99] Two weeks later Barberini subjected his nuncio to further coaching: Campanella needs to be watched, particularly in his giving vent to his caprices through the press; he is voluble, inconstant, and not to be trusted, gaining supporters among those liking novelty, extravagance, and impractical things. The cardinal went on to urge that he be discredited with Richelieu but in such a smooth manner as not to excite the press or inadvertently promote some pernicious doctrine.[100] Sounding the alert as if for the approach of the plague, Rome called for vigilance. In fact to ensure such vigilance as well as to assure the express discrediting of the great celebrity the same Barberini cardinal sent the young, alert Giulio Mazzarini as special nuncio. Among his instructions was the strong recommendation that since unstable minds would be naturally attracted to Campanella's doctrinal novelties, it would be best to immobilize him in a convent where a good prior could control those visiting him.[101] In this instance the prior would prove too compliant or not good enough and would suffer for his leniency.[102] Whether Bolognetti's idea of planting what a later age would recognize as a con-man among the Jacobins to gain Campanella's trust and discover his thoughts, especially regarding writing, remains unknown. It would appear, however, that even before Campanella had set foot in Paris the Roman nuncios had primed the savants of the Dupuy circle at the house of De Thou to tear the newcomer apart bit by bit.[103]

In monitoring Campanella's relationship to Richelieu, the pitiless eyes of Bolognetti and of the future Cardinal Mazarin present a burned-out prophet, befuddled, petulant, and ineffective. Before two months had elapsed since Campanella's arrival in Paris, Richelieu is reported as having allowed that he had only seen the man once and that he and his ministers deemed him a person of small judgment.[104] Mazarin went on to opine, still in the first days after Campanella's arrival, that Richelieu does not like his manner and person but

[99] Amab., *Doc.*, II, 218/255.
[100] Ibid., 218–19/256.
[101] Ibid., 223–24/275.
[102] Firpo, "Cinque lettere inedite di Tommaso Campanella," *La Rassegna d'Italia* 3 (1948): 297, n. 3.
[103] Amab., *Doc.*, II, 224–25/276.
[104] Ibid., 220–21/263.

many at court follow the count of Chateauvillain in buying his merchandise, among which is astrology.[105] Shortly thereafter, again writing to the curia, Mazarin reports that Father Joseph registered astonishment that the nuncio would have any dealings at all with one who has spoken so abusively against his patrons; for he had delivered himself both orally and in print against the general of the Dominicans as France's major enemy and against the House of Barberini. Continuing, he assures Cardinal Antonio Barberini that Richelieu has promised not to have anything of Campanella's published without Rome's approval; when in fact Campanella approached him on the publication of a work, Richelieu demurred. In calculating the balance between the French ability to recognize service and the ability to render it, Mazarin comforts himself with the belief that Campanella's judgment does not correspond to his mind.[106] By late April he could report with appropriate satisfaction that despite Campanella's efforts to see Richelieu in order to impart seemingly important matters, the cardinal is in no hurry and puts him off.[107]

Nevertheless Campanella's persistence proved by no means unavailing—a persistence related not just to a vague advancement of himself, but directed toward the publication of his works and the reorientation of his political thought into the service of France. By the end of August 1635 he had acquired the permission of the Keeper of the Seals and the approval of two doctors of the Sorbonne, coupled with the grudging compliance of Rome, to publish the *Philosophia rationalis*, dedicated to the Noailles brothers. The Paris printer Toussaint Dubray received the royal privilege, and the work would appear as volume 1 of the *Opera omnia*.[108] The Sorbonne also granted the license for the publication of three other individually important works: the *AT*, *De Gentilismo non retinendo*, and *De praedestinatione*. With their appearance in 1636 Campanella composed a dedicatory preface to Louis XIII addressing him as "Dextro Messiae brachio." Heretofore the king of Spain had been the arm (*brachium*) of God in the service of the papacy. The shift is completed, with the link being forged between a revived France, victor over the La Rochelle rebels, now restored to Carolingian greatness, and the apostolic principate of Rome.[109]

France and its king could now use any sort of claim, title, or rhetorical appeal and much more besides, for Richelieu and his master had entered the Thirty Years' War against Habsburg Spain. France found itself fighting for its life. The time was 1636, the fateful year of Corbie, when the Spanish army pushed to within thirteen leagues of Paris; even Richelieu's customary composure crumbled. The previous months had seen for Campanella the production

[105] Ibid., 226/277.
[106] Ibid., 227–29/282.
[107] Ibid., 230/288.
[108] Ibid., 231/295; *DBI*, 17:395.
[109] TC-*Lett.*, 339–40.

of a number of political tracts—hortatory, juridically expository—to which Richelieu apparently took an ambivalent stance. On the one hand he appreciated their value sufficiently to allow them to circulate in manuscript, yet not enough to support their publication. In April he could reward the *politico* with a purse of one hundred doubloons.[110] In this same period Campanella enjoyed access to the cardinal's library.[111] Richelieu's support of Campanella in this regard culminated in having the Calabrian prophet deliver a military sermon to members of the court and parlement present at Conflans on June 8, 1636 as the enemy was still advancing.[112] Furthermore given the nature of the source, the Tacitus scholar Christoph von Forstner, a German visitor to Campanella's Neapolitan imprisonment (1624–26) and attendant at the French court as representative of the duke of Württemberg (1635), one may well consider the possibility that Richelieu had been using his visitor as a sort of adviser on Italian matters.[113] By 1636 Richelieu and Louis seemed ready to resort to anything and anyone for possible aid. Indeed the year appears as a bumper one for Campanella in a number of politically active roles. From faroff Rieti in Italy Naudé reacted to rumors drifting down his way that Campanella—ever the Von Tirpitz of the Dominican order—had entered the business of promoting naval armaments with the king. Musing over the apparent incongruity, while summoning up a new, icy rationality with respect to raison d'état, Naudé believed to discover here a confirmation of his long-held theory regarding the excessive subtlety of Italian *politici*: they forever seek metaphysical reasonings in all things and attempt to treat politics as they would poetics and other disciplines, being too ardent in some matters.[114]

Once the crisis had ended and the Spanish Army of Flanders had retreated, matters returned more to normal. By the year's end, while trying to shake some money loose from the pope, Campanella describes to Urban the frustrations of running after Richelieu for payments on his pension: the great minister never stays in any one place more than eight days and by the time Campanella has located a carriage for finding him, the latter has left or is treating with ambassadors; whenever actually cornered, he gives his pursuer caresses enough and commands his subordinates that Campanella be paid, but they fail to perform.[115]

However, for the prophet of fertile imagination opportunity soon beckoned. On September 5, 1638, the queen, Anne of Austria, gave birth to the future

[110] Amab., *Doc.*, II, 281/336c.
[111] TC-*Lett.*, 301.
[112] Ibid., 349.
[113] Firpo, "Appunti campanelliani," *GCFI* 29 (1950): 87: "in Aula Gallica vidi aliquoties, dum apud Cardinal Richelium Ludovicus rex in consilio esset, Thomam Campanellam fama super aethera notum, accitum, deque rebus Italicis sententiam rogatum fuisse."
[114] Amab. *Doc.*, II, 281–82/336e.
[115] TC-*Lett.*, 369, 371.

Louis XIV. Through Richelieu's intervention Campanella was summoned to prepare a natal horoscope; on two occasions he examined the naked child placed on a table before astrologer and minister. The prediction came forth suitably brief, cryptic, and ambiguous: the king's reign would be long and happy, glorious like that of Henry IV, but not without troubles in religion and rule near its end.[116] Then there appeared in print in January 1639 Campanella's Latin Eclogue celebrating the auspicious event. His point of departure had already been made clear to Richelieu in the latest edition (1637) of *De sensu rerum* dedicated to him by its author; after celebrating for Europe and for the world the salvation and unifying of France, *tutum propugnaculum* of the Christian Church, *musarum refugium*, effected by its great minister, Campanella ends by asserting that the City of the Sun, delineated by himself, through Richelieu must be built that it may always shine brightly.[117] Now incorporating that most venerable messianic prophecy, Virgil's Fourth Eclogue of a golden Saturnian reign, he begins: "Muses of Calabria that nursed Virgil, strip me of my old age and renew me, prepare me to sing of great things."[118]

Campanella's task here is twofold: first, to prove by the stars and the prophets that the birth is an auspicious one; second, to explicate, as only he knew how, the shape of the world to be recreated by the newborn. His vision is quite magical, expressive of that late Renaissance animist world so alien to the Parisian savants but apparently not without its place in politics. The chief sources for the Calabrian prophet are less any tradition of Christian prophecy and more the configuration of the stars. His old favorite, the Ferrarese doctor and astrologer Antonio Arquato, again looms large.[119] The inspiration of the sybils and St. Catherine of Siena jostle the observations of Tycho and Galileo. The Eclogue argues that the past century's intensification of celestial anomalies has served to herald the millennium: new stars, comets, and eclipses all suggest great changes; and the conjunction of Saturn in a fiery trigon signifies a return to conditions similar to the age of the apostles and of Charlemagne. In the context of the sun's long-recognized approach to the earth, the birth of the dauphin, *portentose puer*,[120] announces in a magical and astrological way the Sun King. With the passage of world empire's realization from the Habsburgs to the descendants of Pepin, Richelieu as master organizer of empire and Campanella as mobilizer of the muses come to be proclaimed in the same breath.[121] In short all signs beckon Louis, *le Dieudonné*, to construct the City

---

[116] Blanchet, *Campanella*, 64, n. 3.
[117] TC-*Lett.*, 373–74.
[118] TC-P^1, 282.
[119] Ibid., 187; cf. 1354, n. 7.
[120] Ibid., 288/26.
[121] Ibid., 294/67–72; cf. 298/113–300/118.

of the Sun[122] and to preside over the final golden age. Appearing in print less than five months before Campanella's death, this Eclogue celebrating the dauphin's birth represents the Renaissance magician's last effort to comprehend the events of the dawning age. The all-inclusive cosmic framework comprises both a distillation of pagan and Christian magical-philosophical lore and the idiosyncratic view of a man who never lost his sense of messianic calling.[123] What was scientifically being at the very moment demolished by Galileo and Descartes, would, nevertheless, at the same time provide grist for the less discriminating mills of politics.

In his letters from Paris during these final years Campanella manifests an unflagging energy, unfaltering conviction, and attentiveness to a diversity of issues. Admittedly, the many long letters to all three Barberini, pope and papal nephews, are not the most edifying missives in their ever-renewed complaints against Il Mostro, his apparently deliberate withholding of license for the *QR* publication, and Campanella's failure to receive any financial support from Rome.[124] His antagonism toward Riccardi expresses itself more fruitfully, however, regarding a devotional work that the master of the Sacred Palace had composed and that had been published in Genoa in 1626.[125] In fact, once freed from possible apprehension in Rome and safely ensconced in Aix, he will denounce to Urban his chief censor's book as totally pagan, Talmudic, "a burnished burlesque of sacred things and more than ordinary heresies,"[126] or more amusingly later from Paris, "a derision of saints" and "zany burlesques."[127] His unbounded enthusiasm in this regard hardly advanced his cause in the corridors of curial power. Nevertheless, the more he could tie Riccardi, Ridolfi, and Co. to what he saw as the hyperpredestinarian brand of theology promoted by the Spanish Dominicans Alvarez and Bañez within his own order, while countering these tendencies with his own disguised Pelagianism wrapped in the authority of St. Thomas, the better he could represent his own theological proclivities. In attacking this Moorish faith of the *Alvarezisti* and the *Minervisti*, the Dominican hard-liners associated with their headquarters at Rome, Santa Maria sopra Minerva, he can appeal against the present current in his own order to the earlier authority of Cajetan and presently to the Jesuits insofar as they oppose an antecedent predestination.[128] Campanella

---

[122] Ibid., 310/237–38.
[123] I wish to acknowledge here drawing upon an unannotated paper entitled "The Magus and the Monarch: Tommaso Campanella at the Court of Louis XIII" by Richard Wittenberg, whose University of California–Berkeley dissertation remains unpublished.
[124] TC-*Lett.*, 251, 265, 328, 377, 385.
[125] *DBI*, 17:392.
[126] TC-*Lett.*, 249.
[127] Ibid., 258, 267.
[128] Ibid., 369–70.

claims to see in this threat to free will the undercutting of moral responsibility, the fatal disease of Protestant heretics, and worse still the specter of atheism.

This last peril receives even further attention with the final licensing and publication in 1636 of the *AT*. The conjunction of these two developments helps explain perhaps Campanella's increasing preoccupation with the formerly religious but now philosophical problem of the existence of God. Where Campanella had impressively affirmed to Schoppe in the *AT* that one must begin with "I believe in God"[129] when dealing with heretics, now for Campanella the controversy has widened to include not simply recognized heretics, specifically Calvinists, but Il Mostro's *Alvarezisti* and Moslems, who circulate the common argument that God either is or is not. If not, then everything goes and force, sophisms, and hypocrisy reign; if God is, then this omniscient, omnipotent Lord brings man here already judged rather than to be judged. Likewise here also force, sophisms, and sophistry prevail. To this common argument as he calls it, Campanella repeatedly attributes the ruin of the present age and current disobedience to the Church.[130] Although the Neapolitan philosopher would die one year before the eruption of the Jansenist controversy, the idea of a rigid predestinarianism weighed heavily in the theological air from both the revival of Augustinianism of a specifically anti-Pelagian sort and the sputterings of the recent *De auxiliis* controversy, which had consumed itself in pursuit of an evermore precise understanding of the manner in which divine grace operates. Campanella's own Pelagianized, naturalistic theology, whatever its Thomistic wrappings, was bound to conflict with existing theological currents. His persisting emphasis on free will had profound and immediate implications for his political thinking. By linking rigid predestination with atheism and the subversion of political order, Campanella in these final years of polemical proselytizing activity proceeded on a broad front.

Coming out of the later sixteenth century, atheism could mean many things. For Campanella it signifies most immediately an unrewarding, predetermined God, alienating His creatures and thus dissolving society. In the months leading up to the final publication of the *AT* in February 1636 and the subsequent years, there can be no doubt as to how Campanella understands the import of that work or at least how he wishes it to be understood. Exactly a year earlier he can recommend his book as being the most apt (*attissimo*) against atheists.[131] In July he has even changed the title when referring to it as *Contra atheos*.[132] To the king in his prefatory letter it becomes *Adversus atheos*.[133] Then at the end of the month of publication in a letter to Peiresc the title

---

[129] Ibid., 267; cf. TC-*AT* (1631), "Praefatio," [2] (1636).
[130] TC-*Lett.*, 260, 310, 341, 351.
[131] Ibid., 267.
[132] Ibid., 314.
[133] Ibid., 341.

becomes *Contra ateisti*.[134] Finally in his letter to Queen Henrietta Maria, as late as June 1638, he can recommend it in attempting to send her a copy, as there being nothing stronger nor more apt in defense of the faith against those who would make God impious and hateful.[135]

A curious feature in the interpretation of the *AT* obtains from its being understood apparently in its own time as having a libertine and atheistic intent. Yet such a view stands in conflict with the shrewdest late-twentieth-century interpreters like Germana Ernst, Tullio Gregory, and Gianni Paganini who suggest that Campanella like a good merchant displayed all the wares of all religions in the confident belief that religion is something natural to the human race, that Christianity is the most rational, natural, and hence best religion, and that religion being *de iure naturae*, all this is self-evident. Now while the historian usually needs to prefer that reading of the text contemporaneous with the author and not with himself in order to determine the probable intention of its author and the original direction of the work, there is one difficulty here even beyond the clear later claims of the author: except for the six months' currency of the Roman edition of 1631, the *AT* did not appear for European distribution until the Paris edition of 1636, thirty years after the work's composition. Even allowing for intermittent reworkings by Campanella, it represents the product of one cut off from current intellectual developments and a voice from an earlier period. In the Paris of the 1630s it appears in the high tide of libertinism and becomes immediate grist for the libertine mills. As Paganini has shown, the *Theophrastus redivivus* (1659) will give it a most tendentious reading, manipulating the text so that the patristic qualifiers and the context are removed in order to conform to a stridently atheistic end.[136] It would thus appear that Paul Kristeller is again right: we must not understand the philosophy of the late Italian Renaissance in terms of seventeenth-century French libertinism.[137] In leaving this subject we can do no better than refer to the latest analysis of the *AT*. Germana Ernst concludes on the note that Campanella opposes in this polemic all those personal possessions of the truth preoccupied in building walls to set themselves apart, rather than laying out a common project of adherence to the universal school of the *Primò Senno*. In the *Syntagma* Justin Martyr provides a crucial key to the reading of the *AT*: "religion," he claims, "is seeded in the entire human race, although there are some who think it is planted only in their private gardens."[138]

[134] Firpo, "Cinque lettere inedite," 272.
[135] Ibid., 280.
[136] G. Paganini, "La critica della'civiltà' nel *Theophrastus redivivus*," in *Ricerche su letteratura libertina e letteratura clandestina nel Seicento: Atti del convegno di studio di Genova*, 30 ottobre–1 novembre, 1980, ed. T. Gregory et al. (Florence, 1981), 49–82, esp. 56, 75–79.
[137] Paul Oskar Kristeller, "The Myth of Renaissance Atheism and the French Tradition of Free Thought," *The Journal of the History of Philosophy* 6 (1968): 233–43.
[138] Germana Ernst, *Religione*, 104; cf. also TC-*Syn.*, 105.

Campanella's activities during these years extended beyond the theoretical to the practicalities of proselytizing, debate, church property, and Catholic worship; they become part of a larger movement within France at this time as the Counter Reformation gained momentum and developed fronts against both Protestants and libertines. Campanella's six letters to Francesco Ingoli, secretary of the Congregation of the Propaganda and its driving force, attest to his broad activity in the advancement of Catholicism. His commitment to arguing with heretics and unbelievers would carry him throughout the city, into the Dupuy circle and the environs of the English embassy.[139] His converts often are persons of some distinction: a German margrave whose conversion to Catholicism Rome would question;[140] an influential Ethiopian for whom Campanella finds it necessary to deny that he is a heretic;[141] former apostates and ministers of Protestant churches for whom he intercedes to find livings in the Catholic world;[142] the abjurations of thirty persons of French, English, and German origin sent to Cardinal Francesco Barberini, who would surely question their validity.[143] With Ingoli he shared views obtained from the criticism of converts that Catholic priests mutter the Mass and spread idolatry in adoring images. The celebration of the Mass in the vernacular, the use of both kinds, the need for a married clergy come up for review and recommendation. Such missionary work in the "Otras Indias" within Europe itself makes Campanella all the more anxious and frustrated regarding the unpublished *QR*.[144]

Pursuant to his belief that the Catholic religion accorded with nature and was most congruent with God and political society, whereas Protestantism with its harsh predestinationism was undermining and disruptive of politics, Campanella wrote an undelivered letter to Queen Henrietta Maria in January 1637 and again in June 1638. Therein he claimed that all England was ready to revert to the traditional religion but failed to do so out of fear of persecution and the confiscation of properties recently acquired. Just as Luther promoted a popular dimension to politics, so now Calvinism was essentially antimonarchical and would seek to replace the king, her husband, with an aristocratic republic under the control of the Calvinist leaders (*primatibus Calvinistarum*). To her shortly to be beleaguered husband Campanella recommends that he grant liberty of conscience, thereby looking to the vast majority of Catholic

---

[139] TC-*Lett.*, 326, 337, 358, 403.
[140] Ibid., 336, 337, 344, 349.
[141] Ibid., 328.
[142] Ibid., 335–36, 385.
[143] Ibid., 403.
[144] Ibid., 331–32; cf. Blanchet, *Campanella*, 62–63. On the *Otras Indias*, see Adriano Prosperi, "'Otras Indias': Missionari della Controriforma tra contadini e selvaggi," in *Scienze, credenze occulte livelli di cultura*, Convegno internazionale di Studi, Firenze, June 26–30, 1980 (Florence, 1982), 205–34.

insurgents for support and as being ready to accept papal intervention.[145] While such a recipe, needless to observe, would have blown the top off England's volatile situation and accelerated considerably the forces of history, Campanella in his last surviving letter, written ten weeks before his death, shared this advice with Cardinal Francesco Barberini and added that if the king did not grant liberty of conscience he would stand in great peril of losing both his state and his life.[146]

In his final letter to Ingoli dated October 6, 1637, Campanella turns to that issue which looms ever larger in his consideration during the last years of his life—Gallicanism, more generically, regalism or the phenomenon of the territorial (national) state church. He feels grieved, scandalized, and impotent for maintaining the impetus, so poorly sensed, of the universal power of the pope in the face of a threat wherein Lutherans, heretics in general, and even Catholics in the form of the *Alvarezisti* connive with the princes to despoil the clergy and the papacy of estates and temporal goods in the name of reforming the Church, while causing every kingdom and principality to have its own patriarch dependent upon the king. He refers to his *De regno Christi*, little more than a distillation of the earlier *Monarchia messiae* and produced a year before, undoubtedly to stem this hemorrhaging of universal theocracy.[147]

In the attrition suffered by the Huguenot establishment in France after the Edict of Nantes Gallicanism with its vehement anti-Ultramontanism and its reduction of the papacy to a purely pastoral, spiritual role offered an inviting bridge to Calvinists who might wish to convert to Catholicism. Although the former Calvinist elder, Théophile La Milletière, would not actually become Catholic until 1645, he had since 1632 been in the service of Richelieu, arguing for a reunification of Protestant churches to Rome.[148] In the last months of his life Campanella believed to find in La Milletière one inspired by the ideas of the *Alvarezisti* and Protestant heretics that princes ought to take from the clergy all property and jurisdiction. He identifies this man with *la fide minervista*, which claims that to defend the pope is to defend a usurped authority over bishops and princes. Thus the appropriate reform of the clergy becomes the divestment of the Church's temporal property and power over princes and bishops so that every kingdom might in effect have its own pope dependent upon the immediate prince. All this has of course, for Campanella, an original Lutheran root that he proceeds to wrap around the necks of Spanish Dominicans and the theologians of the Oratory. Il Mostro and the Spanish *regenti* have sustained a war against consciences, thereby generating tepidness among converts and the process of conversion and promoting the belief among minis-

[145] Firpo, "Cinque lettere inedite," 280–84; cf. TC-*Lett.*, 355.
[146] TC-*Lett.*, 403.
[147] Ibid., 384–85.
[148] *NBG*, 29:222–23.

ters and bishops that the papist faith and Calvinism are the same. He warns of the pernicious concord preached by La Milletière in his books.[149] Thus in his final letter, in this instance to the Barberini secretary of state, Campanella rings the alarm bell that had been the measure of his entire life.

The last months saw the steady production of his writings into print: the *Philosophia realis* as volume 2 of the *Opera omnia*, brought out by Denis Houssaye in 1637; and as volume 3 the *Philosophia rationalis* by Jean Du Bray in the following year; and eighteen books of the *Metaphysics* as volume 4 printed by Denis Langlois.[150] The letter for a presentation copy of the first of these, *Philosophia realis*, addressed to the grand duke of Tuscany, Ferdinand II de' Medici, possessed a certain finality, touching the major bases of his intellectual career. For according to Campanella the Medici were first responsible for making Plato available in Italy, thus removing the yoke of Aristotle and allowing Campanella to set forth the two Books of God, the republic as evinced in the City of the Sun, and the posing of that fateful question— "Whether a new philosophy ought to be minted?"—as portal to the present work, leading on to the exposition of a Christian philosophy that is truly rational. His mind reverts to Galileo, the bearer of that letter of Ferdinand I de' Medici to Campanella when in Padua in 1593. He admits that the present book shows some discord between himself and the admirable Galileo; but beyond such a discord of intellects shines a concord of wills. Thus in the end the old friar seems to have gotten it right. Yet all too generously he allows that Galileo is such a sincere and perfect man that he will derive more pleasure from Campanella's objections, given in free exchange, than from the approbation of others. Nor is the prophetic dimension lacking here: "The future age will judge us because the present always crucifies its benefactors, but they rise up on the third day or the third age."[151]

However, a happier Campanella comes down to us in these final years, one that had never nor could ever lose his savour for life, one still expressive of youthful spontaneity and fresh emotion. From the pen of the *érudit* Nicolas Chorier, an admirer from Dauphiné, we have the following:

> The man was joyful and light-hearted. When he strolled in the country or in a garden all his actions and speech [worked] to relax the mind and release it from serious matters by means of a happy recreation. He besought the little birds on whose account with his great corpulence he revelled throughout the passage of the seasons. He threw his cap in the air; he directed his entire self to them. Full of spirit and emotional force with satient voice he exclaimed: "Let us inhale! Let us

[149] TC-*Lett.*, 400–406.
[150] LF-*Bibl.*, 93–95, 118–19, 122; TC-*Lett.*, 388–90, 390–94; *DBI*, 17:396–97.
[151] TC-*Lett.*, 388–89.

inhale life from the life of the world." He called air the life of the world which is the soul of nature.[152]

At least at such moments, given his immense residual capacity as a survivor, the youthful poet had mastered the cunning conspirator, the encyclopedic thinker, and now the senile philosopher. A sense of wonder had survived even into an age increasingly marked by the erosive force of an ever more analytic curiosity.

After attempting every possible astronomical and magical prophylactic against death, the old Calabrian magus-philosopher despite all human contriving found himself compelled to pay his debt to nature. He died at the Jacobins on May 21, 1639, amidst the prayers of the Dominican friary. As with so much else the sepulchre would be effaced by the Revolution.

• • •

While in respect to politics and print, Campanella's last years in Paris had not been without some satisfaction, his presence in the emerging capital had encountered serious rebuff. The reasons and significance of that rebuff require further attention and emphasis before concluding.

Let us return to the already quoted reaction of Descartes to Huygens regarding the arrival of the great Italian celebrity: "J'avois trouvé dés-lors si peu de solidité en ses ecrits." What we have here in its affirmation of and quest for *solidité* represents the pungent registering of the distilled import in a mounting sea change in Western attitudes, a revealing flash point in a long process of gradual transmutation, the momentary sign of a shifting of geologic plates in European consciousness. This shift in the perception of reality and in consequent sensibility would occur by means of gradual displacements and accretions as much within the minds of the individual key players as between them.

In the late 1630s events in Paris begin to accelerate this ever-gradual transformation in intellectual sensibility. Expected as an associate of Galileo and the new science, Campanella shortly revealed himself in this uniquely charged context as belonging to the world of Nostradamus. Coming to Paris as a celebrity, he combined in his person the qualities of a Teilhard de Chardin, Nelson Mandela, and Rip Van Winkle: as a Catholic nature philosopher he brought a somewhat suspect orthodoxy, embellished by a number of exotic writings, which now tumbled from the press in increasing numbers; his Mandelan qual-

---

[152] Firpo, "Appunti campanelliani," *GCFI*, 29 (1950): 91: "Vir erat iucundus et festivus. Cum rure aut in hortis spatiaretur, omnia agebat et dicebat, quae relaxare animum laetisque remissionibus a seriis avocarent. Aviculas, quo poterat cursu anni et obesi corporis mole gravis petebat; pileum in aëra iactabat; os vocemque ad eas convertebat; copiose spiritum et animam ducens, contenta voce exclamabat: 'Hauriamus, hauriamus vitam de vita mundi!' aërem vitam mundi vocabat, qui naturae anima est".

ities derive from his having suffered in the Neapolitan dungeons of the Spanish *monarquía* a precisely equal number of years imprisoned, thus conveying to his public the image of a triumphant survivor who had successfully defied an unjust system; as Rip Van Winkle he had been out of touch with Europe's development for over a quarter of a century and what a quarter it had been—Galileo, Kepler, Bacon. Indeed if he had arrived to settle in some Tyrolean village, the gap would have been apparent enough, but to be plummeted into the Paris of Marin Mersenne, the very crucible and dynamo of that change in sensibility and perception now under way, to enter a bin full of intellectual sharks—little wonder that he appeared confused, irritable, and increasingly isolated.

The qualitative, monistic, animistic world of the Renaissance magus, essentially the world of common humanity up to this time, is gradually being displaced by a quantitative, mechanistic, mathematical view of reality: the bright myriad variegated colors of a sensible, qualitative universe of correspondences are slowly giving way to the rationality and bleak one-dimensionality of modernity. While the process of displacement is still working itself out today in a global context, one of the most revealing signs of the coming breakthrough occurred then in Paris during the last few years in the torqued life of a former great Renaissance philosopher, now suddenly turned into a faded celebrity and left in this rarified milieu as some sort of stranded, archaic whale. The increased hemorrhaging of the old intellectual world and the traditional order of things before the cold rationality and quantification of the new age, this shift in philosophical sensibility, this terrible wrench in the perception of reality are all compressed into that splendid, if contemptuous, sniff of René Descartes as he turns away from an invitation to address the mind, the works of the newly arrived Renaissance naturalist philosopher from Italy. No, for the man of the dawning or darkening new age, there was no substance, no *solidité* in Campanella's magical empiricism and ontological exuberances. In the Pythagorean Y of its existence the West was taking a turn from which it could never retreat.

Illustrations

Tommaso Campanella by Francesco Cozza.

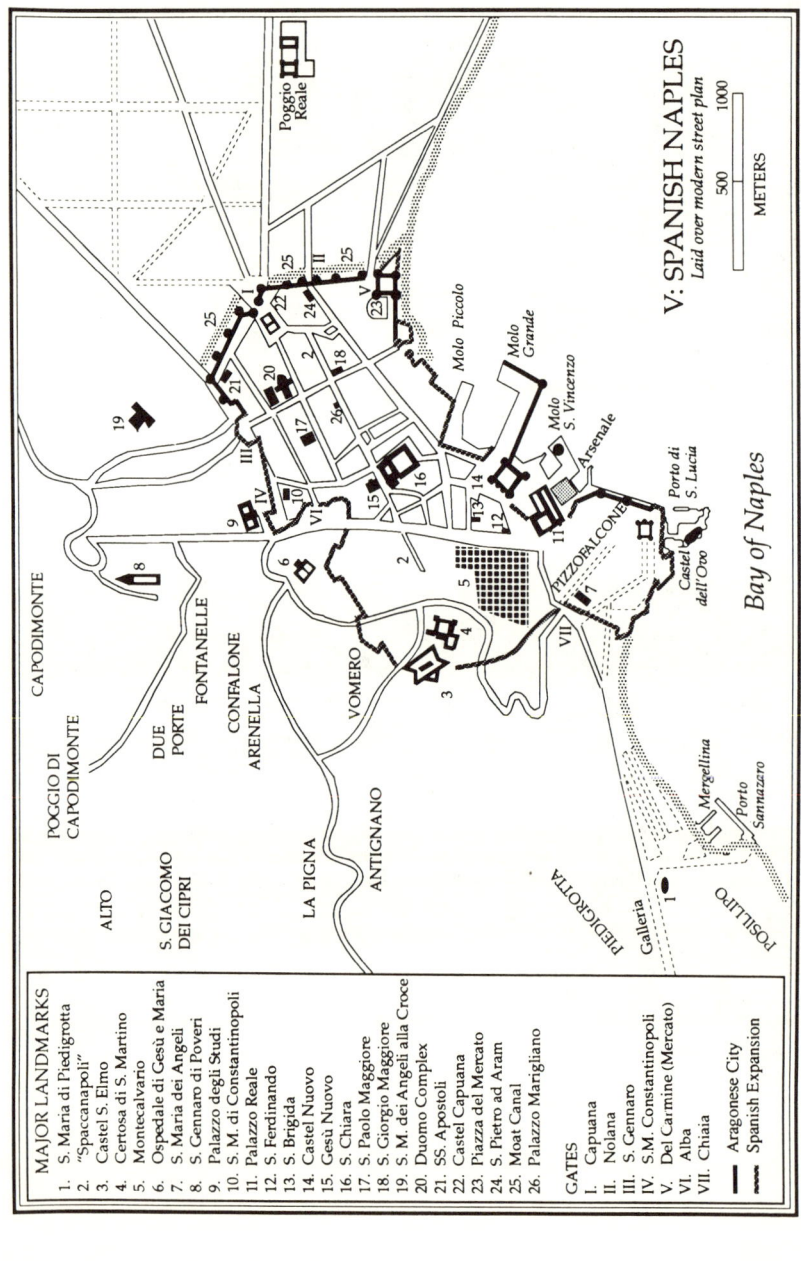

F. THOMAE
CAMPANELLAE
CALABRI DE STYLO,
ORDINIS PRÆDICATORVM PHILOSOPHIA,
SENSIBVS DEMONSTRATA,

In Octo Disputationes distincta,

Aduersus eos, qui proprio arbitratu, non autem sensata duce natura, philosophati sunt.

Vbi errores Aristotelis, & asseclarum ex proprijs dictis, & naturæ decretis conuincuntur; & singulæ imaginationes, pro eo à Peripateticis fictæ prorsus reijciuntur cum vera defensione Bernardini Telesij Consentini, Philosophorum maximi, antiquorum sententijs,quæ hic dilucidantur, & defenduntur,præcipuè Platonicorum confirmata: ac dum pro Aristotele pugnat Iacobus Antonius Marta, contra seipsum, & illum pugnare ostenditur.

Ad Illustrissimum Dominum D. Marium de Tufo.

NEAPOLI, Apud Horatium Saluianum. 1591.

Title Page of Campanella's *Philosophia sensibus demonstrata*.

"Ferrante Imperato's Museum." Frontispiece from Imperato's
Historia naturale, 1672.

Andrea Sacchi's *Divine Wisdom*.

"Plots of Jesuites," 1653.

"A Composite Portrait of Philip IV of Spain." There would appear to be a political statement being made here. For against a Rubensesque background and a late Velázquez-like rendering of Philip IV, the engraver, probably P. de Jode, has situated the distinctive crown of the Holy Roman Empire, thus linking the Spanish monarch with the traditional imperial office.

INTERMEZZO

BEFORE PROCEEDING to examine Campanella's engagement with the major issues of his age, we may well pause to reflect upon the meaning of this life and wish to pose, if not entirely answer, some hard questions. Was there a growth, a development in his personality, or is he all of one piece throughout his career? How sincere was he amidst repeated simulation and dissimulation? Why did he choose to remain within the Church and even more within his own order? In short where may we seize him in order to find him?

Certainly enough has been said here to suggest that a moral development, coupled with an intellectual resolution of sorts, did occur in the aftermath of the abortive conspiracy: the experience of the climactic torture of June 4–5, 1601, while not decisively removing a wreckless pride, began its dislodgement. In the immediately succeeding years up until 1606 he was able to effect an intellectual accommodation with the existing powers and to create a most precarious, constrained space in which to advance a mottled Christianity ever at odds with an alert orthodoxy.

Of simulation and dissimulation in his behavior and writings there was plenty. Indeed by his endurance of forty hours of torture he could have won a doctorate, if not an endowed chair, in simulation. The age that began with Guicciardini in political deportment and Carafa in religious repression had had to reshape and refine the intellectual instruments of dialogue, allegory, and irony to communicate more guardedly. For Campanella's part, whatever his permutations and posturings, he never forsook his prophetic vocation, that inner bell which was his device, nor the monistic vision of his politics and thought.

It would seem that the best point at which we may encounter Campanella is in that supreme moment of his life, when by simulation and the enforcement of sheer will he struggled for his very existence. Dr. Johnson would later claim that nothing so focuses the mind than the recognition that one is going to be hanged the following morning. Yet nothing so focuses the will, the most authentic expression of the self, as the immediacy of the struggle for survival itself. We have already indicated that the experience of defeat, of torture and confinement in the months of late 1599 to mid-June 1601, constituted a watershed in Campanella's existence. He would later reflect upon the significance of his torture for himself and for man in general: most immediately and best known is the passage in the *City of the Sun* (1602), where he mentions one who had determined to endure what amounted to forty hours of torture without revealing his secret. But more extensively and significantly he returned to this event in the "Ethica" of his later *Philosophia realis*. Although published in 1637, the passage in question could date from 1613, possibly a few years earlier, but its later publication in Paris allowed Campanella to review and to affirm it.[1]

The passage begins with his drawing upon his favorite church father, Chrysostom, citing his *Comparatio potentiae, divitiarum et excellentiae regis, cum monacho in verissima et Christiana philosophia vivente*. There the great Antiochene Father and moralist had contrasted the splendid magnificence and glorious power of the king in his *principatum* to the monk's hard-won spiritual coherence and inward presence, of course to the celebration of the latter's own *pristinum principatum*.[2] We are reminded here not only of Campanella's esteem for Chrysostom but also of his more significant esteem for the dignity and power of the monk and the monastic tradition. In pursuing the contrast Campanella emphasizes the war within, the brand borne unseen, the struggle for self-mastery. This battle against diverse passions and thoughts waged by Campanella's ideal monk can only be comprehended by one who has experienced solitude and has had to wage war against the vices: "Indeed I know from experience that nothing is more difficult than to achieve control over one's own flesh, thoughts, and passions. Who attains to this supreme accomplishment is truly lord of all, as I have said in the *Politics*, master legally, internally, although not in actual fact."

Defining injury as a loss of virtue, a blow to one's integrity wherein bodily harm becomes something indifferent, Campanella returns to Chrysostom, this time to his homiletic treatise *Quod nemo laeditur, nisi a seipso* ("That no one is hurt except by himself").[3] What is integral to man is his *virtus*, defined here as his sensing rightly about God and doing good toward his neighbor. For *pietas* alone according to Chrysostom distinguishes us from the brute.

> Man thus is not able to suffer harm unless he consents to depravity. Since consenting is within our power, thus to suffer harm is within our power. The virtuous person does not surrender this power and thus is unable to be harmed. Quite rightly has Horace sung and experience testifies—"The man tenacious of his

---

[1] TC-*PR¹*, 8–9 ("Ethica").

[2] *MPG*, 47:387–93, esp. 391.

[3] *De eo quod nemo laeditur nisi a semetipso* (*MPG*, 52:459–80) is not itself a homily. Nevertheless as a distinct moral treatise it has both in its manuscript and in its typographical tradition been associated with a significant collection of thirty-eight Latin homilies attributed since the seventh century to St. John Chrysostom. The *editio princeps* of the treatise occurs with the Cologne edition of Ulrich Zell before 1470, which in fact preceded the same scholar's *editio princeps* of the thirty-eight homilies published in Urach around 1483–85. Thus Campanella's reference here to the treatise as a homily is itself understandable. On the manuscripts and early imprints of these materials, see André Wilmert, "La collection des 38 homilies latines de St. Jean Chrysostome," *Journal of Theological Studies* 19 (1918): 305–27, esp. 307, 326.

purpose in a righteous cause is, not shaken from his firm resolve" [Odes, III.iii.1–8].[4] I have myself experienced forty hours suspended.

Whereupon he describes the *veglia* with his arms drawn back behind him, alternating his position between the upright with its agonizing pressures upon his chest, arms, and shoulders and the relaxation downward upon a bed of sharp wooden pegs that devoured his buttocks and genitalia.

> Nevertheless from this experience I know that it is in our own power whether we suffer harm or not. For they are neither able to wrench a virtual retraction nor an admission [*verbum*] from [their victims]. But then Aristotle would have called me unfortunate; if I had obeyed him by fleeing death, I would have been conquered, the slave of fear and unworthy of life.

Little wonder that the subsequent book of the "Ethica" is on the freedom of the will. Through a unique combination of prophetic self-assertiveness and simulation, reinforced by sheer will power, he had been able to survive this terrible ordeal.

More prophet than philosopher Campanella conveyed less an intellectual system than a message, a commitment to a vision that for all its vagaries found a response in varying degrees throughout a still late medieval society. Repeated conflicts with the authorities of this world had led him on the one hand to appreciate power and on the other hand to seek its reorientation in keeping with the impending transformation. The Roman Church, distinguished by its hierarchical, comprehensive structures, its long-established claims to universality, and its current triumphalist aspirations to realize globally such claims, provided potentially the most satisfactory framework for promoting and maintaining that transformation. And the Dominican order itself, the Hounds of the Lord, whose preeminence he never tired of advancing, represented the true elite of the Church, the Palace Guard in its occupation of the mastership of the Sacred Palace, its running of the Inquisition and in that long tradition as religious against the infidel as well as the heretic.[5] No matter how apparently intractable, the papal office, ecclesiastical hierarchy, and the religious orders came to be seen principally as instruments of power to be won over to an enterprise of ultimately divine and astral realization. And in his advancing a freshly minted Christian philosophy absent Aristotle, a political program in

---

[4] In what would appear to be a deliberate omission Campanella does not include the second line—"Non civium ardor prava iubentium"—with its reference to the civil sphere of political order.

[5] The principal work here is *De praecedentia praesertim religiosorum*. For the text and critical exposition, see Michele Miele, O.P., "Un opuscolo inedito ritenuto perduto di Tommaso Campanella: Il *De praecedentia religiosorum*," *AFP* 52 (1982): 267–323. See also Luigi Firpo, "Il 'De conceptione Virginis' di Tommaso Campanella," *Sapienza* 22 (1969): 182–248; idem., "Appunti Campanelliani: XVI. Il 'De conceptione Virginis' ritrovato," *GCFI* 29 (1950): 68–77; TC-*AP*, 298–99.

the vein of a theocratic universal *principe sacerdote*, and in almost attaining to the office of a censor in the papal curia, he seemed to his powerful enemies as a quantity to be reckoned with.

In his life, his poetry, and more clearly in his thought, as will become more evident in part 2, two major paradoxes consume Campanella's being: first, the paradox of freedom versus order or less abstractly free thinking in the face of authority; second, the paradox of love/power, which we will argue as being peculiarly enucleated in the image of the monastery with its discipline, regimentation, and fraternal, communal love. It was a paradox less immediately and personally experienced than the first, yet one that inhered to, and imparted itself through, the very nature of that Church which he came to champion. The primalities of Power, Wisdom, and Love represented philosophically the intersection of those two existential abstractions—the mind's freedom versus the imprisoning capacity of authority, the free, creative force of love versus the power of established authority. What appeared conflictive and opposed in the present time would give way in the new time to a mutually reinforcing relationship of an authorized freedom, an empowered love. Operating between two times, across the gap separating two aeons, Campanella experienced the great tension and dilemma of his life in the giant oppositions, freedom/authority, power/love, wherein he strained to achieve a resolution not later as something in heaven but now on earth as it is in heaven.

PART TWO

Engaging the Major Issues of the Emerging Modern World

Chapter IV

THE CONTROVERSY WITH ARISTOTLE

On Minting a New Christian Philosophy

In his first published work, the *Philosophy Explicated according to the Senses* (Naples, 1591), Tommaso Campanella evinced at the outset of his long intellectual career that abiding and most pronounced feature of his entire philosophical position: an opposition to Aristotle. The product of a twenty-one-year-old man, this book conveys a fresh empiricism and is significantly untainted by the impact of astrology, the occultism of G. B. Della Porta, or the later political-religious interests impelled by a personal messianism that would shape his later thought.[1] In combatting the detractors of Telesio against Aristotle, the ardent young Dominican charges the followers of the all highest Stagirite with embracing the sentences of others without bothering to scrutinize the nature of things. Our current affliction, he announces, is to excuse willingly the errors handed down by the ancients, as if bound to them, and to deny our own sensible experience. Chiefly to blame are certain books of dialectic with abstract names and obscure terms that beget great confusion. Their readers have not eyes for reality but only for what they find written in the pages of Aristotle. Without recourse to the country, to the sea, to the mountains, they bathe in the books of Aristotle muttering such words as accidents, potency, act. Science should consider things, not words.[2] Like his English contemporary, Francis Bacon, Campanella will then go on to struggle manfully, if ineffectively, for a method based on sense and experience and at the same time to express the need to find a different philosophical tradition upon which to support his Telesian propensities.[3] Again, like Bacon, considering the West's long engagement with Aristotle as an aberrant deviation, he will turn to the pre-Socratics but also to the revival of Plato that had occurred in Florence in the previous century and most recently in Ferrara with Francesco Patrizi.[4]

---

[1] Luigi Firpo, "Il metodo nuovo," *RF* 40 (1949): 182–205, esp. 182–83. Firpo here provides an effective translation of the preface of the *Philosophia sensibus demonstrata*—a work that has long been almost unobtainable, only nine copies of this edition having survived. Only recently has a new, critical edition been produced by Luigi De Franco, whom I thank for giving me a copy.

[2] Ibid., 184–87.

[3] Ibid., 187–89.

[4] Ibid., 189, 193–97. In a letter of May 18, 1609, to Kaspar Schoppe, Campanella distinguishes between a Thomistic and an Averroistic Aristotle. See TC-*Lett.*, 50. For Campanella's

At this preliminary stage in our inquiry we may well ask whether our youthful friar's quarrel is actually with Aristotle himself or simply with his contemporary practitioners or even with a particular brand of Aristotelianism. For it would be a mistake to treat Aristotelianism simplistically en bloc, particularly at a time of its great efflorescence during the course of the sixteenth century.[5] We may affirm that Campanella's quarrel is from the start against all three: Aristotle himself, his current followers, and that school of heterodoxy or heresy known as Paduan Averroism. Enough has already been said to indicate that he is profoundly disturbed by the way an Aristotelian terminology has penetrated the medieval universities, becoming the very furniture of men's minds, pervading the patterns of thought for all university-trained scholars and corroding the entire intellectual establishment. Furthermore in his first published work, our young Dominican obviously feels it incumbent to defend his very real loyalty to St. Thomas Aquinas. In doing so, he reveals the extent of the front upon which he will seek to engage the enemy. According to Campanella, St. Thomas did not believe in the infallibility of Aristotle. Nevertheless, seeing the world dedicated to the Stagirite from whom it was impossible to disentangle oneself, St. Thomas, in order to avoid further occasion for error as exemplified by Averroes, sought an accommodation. As on later occasions during his life in dealing with this personally disturbing question, Campanella will aver that Aquinas was not a follower of Aristotle but of Christ and sacred theology.[6] Already at this time he adumbrates a view that would shortly be expressed more explicitly in his *Atheism Conquered*, composed in 1605: Christian theology must not be allied with any of the traditional philosophies provided by the ancients and most certainly not by Aristotle; St. Thomas reputes the Stoics, Pythagoras, and Socrates the best, while Augustine in looking to Plato recommends that Aristotle, Epicurus, and Democritus must be kept away from Christian philosophy.[7]

Aristotelian background and the current riveting of Counter Reformation theology to Aristotelian natural philosophy, see Luigi Firpo, "Filosofia italiana e controriforma," *RF* 41 (1950): 150–73.

[5] On the discrimination among types of sixteenth-century Aristotelianism and Renaissance Aristotelianism in general see Charles B. Schmitt, *Aristotle and the Renaissance* (Cambridge, Mass./London, 1983), 10ff. *passim*.

[6] Firpo, "Il metodo nuovo," 196–97; see also Campanella's later "Risposte alle censure dell' Ateismo Triunfato," in *Opuscoli inediti di Tommaso Campanella*, ed. Luigi Firpo (Florence, 1951), 39–41.

[7] *Atheismus Triumphatus seu Reductio ad religionem per scientiarum veritates . . . contra Antichristianismum Achitophellisticum* (Rome: Zannetti, 1631), 13; see also Campanella, "Risposto," 41; *De gentilium philosophia, praesertim peripatetica, non retinenda*, published as *Ludovico justo xiii Regi christianissimo . . . Dedicat Fr. Thomas Campanella . . . tres hosce libellos, videlicet: Atheismus Triumphatus . . . De gentilismo non retinendo . . . De praedestinatione* (Paris: Toussaint Dubray, 1636). The term "Gentilism" deserves more attention than it has apparently received. While Gentiles as pagans or heathen are well enough known in patristic literature, the substantive "Gentilism" or *gentilismus* as broadly synonymous with heathenism seems to be of relatively brief duration. According to the *OED* (4:116) it first appears in English

Although Campanella's polemic against Aristotle and Aristotelianism pervades all his writings, only at one point and in a single work did his attack achieve anything like formal coherence. *On the Gentilism that must not be adhered to* (*De Gentilismo non retinendo*) seems never to have received the attention that it deserves. Written in the less straitened conditions afforded by the Neapolitan prison of Castel dell'Ovo sometime between the end of 1609 and the beginning of 1610, it was originally intended as a preamble to the vast *Quaestiones physiologicae, ethicae et politicae*, completed by 1613.[8] The vicissitudes of imprisonment and shifting publishers prevented its appearance until its author was safely in Paris in 1636. The full title of the manifesto reads "That especially the Peripatetic Philosophy of the Gentiles must not be adhered to: Whether it is expedient to formulate another Philosophy from the Gentiles and if so what."[9] Some of Campanella's Parisian friends apparently deemed it too explosive for publication. As late as October 1635, Jean Bourdelot, the learned humanist and master of requests of Marie de' Medici, writing to Peiresc, observed that he, Bourdelot, had had the manuscript of what he called the *Philosophia ethnica rejicienda* in his possession for a very long time and he believed that Père Campanella would have ample trouble getting it published. Nevertheless, published it was with the license and approval of the Sorbonne.[10] The issue was joined. Campanella's tract seemed a part of a growing tidal wave of opposition to the "Master of those that know," crackling with implications.

According to the most authoritative appraisal of Renaissance Aristotelian currents, *On Gentilism* was probably the closest intellectual heir to the *Examen vanitatis* of Gianfrancesco Pico, written a century earlier in 1520. Charles Schmitt finds in both works the same effort to show the vanity of profane learning and in Campanella's an even more pronounced return to emphasizing the early church fathers.[11] Yet the intentions of the two authors are actually quite different. Forever the optimist, Campanella, transcending

---

in 1577 and crests in the course of the seventeenth century. Of the five major French dictionaries only Godefroy (4:264) cites three cases, one in 1582. The *OED* does not mention Thomas Hobbes' use of it in *Philosophical Rudiments* (London, 1651), 330, where it is distinguished from Judaism, and *Leviathan* 4:45, where it is associated with the nonscriptural traditions distinctive of the Roman Church. In all the encyclopedias and lexicons consulted, it does not appear nor is it mentioned in the articles by Franz Dornseiff, "Der—ismus," in *Sprache und Sprechender*, ed. Jürgen Werner (Leipzig, 1964), 319–29, or by Georg Stadlmüller, "-ismus," *Saeculum* 3 (1952): 341ff.

[8] LF-*Bibl.*, 110; see also 86–87.
[9] Ibid., 110.
[10] Ph. Tamizey de Larroque, "Lettres de Jean et de Pierre Bourdelot à Peiresc," *Revue d'histoire littéraire de la France* 4 (1897): 98–121, esp. 118—dated October 1, 1635. See also TC-*Lett.*, 336, 338.
[11] Charles Schmitt, *Gianfrancesco Pico della Mirandola (1469–1533) and His Critique of Aristotle* (The Hague, 1967), 179.

his own terrible sufferings, partakes of a rising mood of intellectual experimentation and innovation just on that momentous threshold when that "orb the optick glass the Tuscan artist views at evening from the top of Fesole."[12] He does not, however, share Pico's profound sense of the uniqueness of Christianity nor more significantly his skepticism, but has long had ready, made according to a Telesian patterning, a brandnew philosophical suit to replace the old garb worn by Christianity. The new science presented theology with a crisis, but also an opportunity.

A manifesto? And a long-unpublished one at that? Only the singular circumstances of Campanella's existence might allow us to entertain such a possibility. Would that we knew the precise time of the first redaction. It would appear to be a relatively brief, compressed work, heavy in its import, fraught with ideas that had long been maturing in the prisoner's mind and now suddenly released by a singular event—the advent of the *Starry Messenger.* Having enjoyed since 1609 the less straitened confinement of the cell at Castel dell'Ovo, Campanella had been able to write, study and even receive some visitors. Published in early March 1610, Galileo's *Siderius Nuncius* achieved prompt notoriety. During the subsequent months Campanella could well have gathered something of its substance and surmised some implications before actually coming in contact with the book itself. Sometime in the last weeks of that year he received a visit from his old friend, the Telesian philosopher, Antonio Persio, who placed in his hands a copy of the *Sidereus Nuncius,* delivered at the request of Galileo himself. In two hours of reading the prisoner had consumed it.[13] Soon afterwards he would write his exuberant letter of January 13, 1611, to Galileo. And the emerging philosophical epitome now bubbled with Galilean references: "Galileo's new stars," "the recent mathematicians,"[14] and scattered references to the telescope,[15] the name for which was soon to be minted in Prince Cesi's circle of Linceans and would have only at a later date been inserted into the text along with much else during the intervening quarter century.[16] If the major import of *On Gentilism* is the prod-

---

[12] *Paradise Lost,* I, 287–89.

[13] Luigi Firpo, "Tommaso Campanella e Galileo," *Atti della Accademia della scienza di Torino,* Classe di Scienze Morali, 103 (1969): 49–69, esp. 53.

[14] Campanella, 1636:5–6/1637:sig. bij, 19/c^v. Henceforth references to the *De gentilismo* will be given to both the 1636 edition and the 1637 expanded edition, "Disputatio in prologum instauratarum scientiarum ad scholas christianas praesertim parisienses." In *Thomae Campanellae ordinis praedicatorum disputationum in quatuor partes suae philosophiae realis libri quatuor . . .* (Paris: Denis Houssaye, 1637) = TC-PR^1, sigs.b–[eiiii^v] For purposes of contrast, the two successive editions will be designated by their respective dates of publication.

[15] Campanella, 1636:27/1637:[ciij^v]; 1636:42/1637:diiij; 1636:48/1637:e^v; 1636:60/1637: eiiij.

[16] Firpo has noted this practice occurring in a later manuscript of the *Città del sole* datable to 1611. See *La Città del Sole/The City of the Sun,* trans. Daniel J. Donno (Berkeley/Los Angeles, London, 1981), 122–23; 138–39.

uct of an incandescent moment of creativity, the composing of the work had enjoyed the maturing experience both of a release from the worst features of his imprisonment and of a period of enforced, fruitful expectation during the better part of 1610. Among the several innovations that Campanella celebrated, the minting of a new Christian philosophy supportive of the new science was not the least important.

For such an immense undertaking as the dismantling of European Aristotelianism one might expect an authoritative instrument of biblical or Augustinian forging. Yet it is to a church council that Campanella resorts, thereby serving to remind his readers as to the ecclesiastical authority present and at the same time to associate himself with an apparent rejection of humanism and an Aristotelianism that had both emerged contemporaneously with the skepticism of Gianfrancesco Pico. Campanella appeals not only throughout this work but in other works to the eighth session of the Fifth Lateran Council, which affirmed for him that the philosophy and poetry of the pagans had produced for current learning "infected roots" (*radices infectas*): to the prisoner the provenance of the virulent infection was unquestionably Aristotelian. The question as to the precise intention of the framers of this decree, however, prompted conflicting interpretations at the time and has continued to puzzle scholars. The legislation of a philosophical explanation to buttress dogmatically the belief in the soul's immortality seemed to be directed against Paduan Averroistic tendencies, whereas the rulings that those in holy orders could not linger more than five years over the sweets of philosophy or poetry without attending to the study of theology and canon law would suggest a reaction to current paganizing influences. Taken collectively, they appeared as a counterattack by theology and the theologians into the domain of philosophy.[17] Yet the argument has been persuasively made that the inspirers of the decree, Vincenzo Quirini and Tommaso Giustiniani, were reacting more to the Aldine edition of Lucretius, published in 1500, than to Paduan controversies; together they sought to curtail humanism and the immoral overtones of classical poetry.[18]

But Campanella does not share our doubts and hestitations regarding its import: the decree seeks to diminish the authority of the pagans and to increase that of the Christians.[19] It commands readers to condemn Aristotelian dogmas. It identifies an infection that is linked with Aristotle and the entire Aristotelian tradition, including the early Greek commentators, Averroism particularly, and the Renaissance commentators and expositors: Nifo, Pom-

---

[17] John W. O'Malley, *Giles of Viterbo on Church and Reform: A Study in Renaissance Thought* (Leiden, 1968), 42–44.

[18] Felix Gilbert, "Cristianesimo, umanesimo e la bolla 'Apostolici Regiminis,'" *Rivista Storica Italiana* 79 (1967): 976–90. For the best text of the conciliar decree, see *Conciliorum Oecumenicorum Decreta*, ed. Giuseppe Alberigo et al. (Freiburg in Br., 1962), 581–82.

[19] Campanella, 1636:12–13/1637:sig. biiij.

ponazzi, and Jandun, who believe more in the word of Averroes than in Scripture; likewise Zabarella, Cremonini, and other *Averroistae* according to Campanella.[20] Despite the obvious rejection of Paduan Averroism the friar's quarrel is not just with Aristotelians and ostensible Averroists, past and present, but by the explicit listing of un-Christian Aristotelian dogmas, he directs his attack against the Stagirite himself: the eternity of the world, the mortality of souls, and consequently the denial of hell, paradise, purgatory, and the existence of demons and devils; the rejection of Providence; and that God has no knowledge beyond himself.[21] The denial of devils and angels except as motors of spheres and similarly the denial of the divine inspiration of sybils and prophets except by a melancholic spirit would pertain rather to Aristotle's scholastic followers.[22] But Campanella will list the Fathers who impugn Aristotle for the idea that the heavens do not have an elementary matter but are constituted of a quintessence, which Basil and Ambrose consider to conflict with sacred letters. On this last point in the first flush of Galileo's telescopic survey of the heavens, Campanella will thrust that early proponent of nature's uniformity, Empedocles, into the breach for good measure.[23]

To the task of overhauling Christian philosophy Campanella brings two predispositions of quite unequal value: an emotional commitment to innovations and experimentation as an expression not simply of his sensory epistemology but also of his hunger for intellectual freedom; and in the possible relations of science and religion the widely held intellectual metaphor of the two Books, that of Nature and that of Scripture. Allowing even for later interpolations before the 1636 publication, we can understand the Calabrian prisoner's rhapsodizing over innovation and novelty in his *On Gentilism* as a product of that moment when he first hears of and discusses intensely the telescopic discoveries of Galileo, which he soon reports to the Florentine in a letter of January 1611.[24] The discovery of a new world by Columbus, new stars and a new astronomy Copernicus, Tycho Brahe, and now Galileo, a new calendar by the pope, as well as new artillery, the compass, and the windmill all seemed to reinforce the prophecy of Daniel 12:4. As the publisher of Bacon's own *Magna Instauratio* would soon note, in the final time there will be great concourse and agitation with a commensurate increase of knowledge.

In the second instance, given such a context a new philosophy is needed. To resist or do otherwise would be to abbreviate the hand of God in Christianity (*cristianismo*) and remain stuck in the Gentile philosophy. For the truth of philosophical sciences may be had more purely and certainly by Christian genius than by pagan. Deriving from the Fathers the idea of the two quite

[20] 1636:17/1637:sig. [c^v]; 20/cij.
[21] 1636:16–17/1637:sig. c; 46–47/e.
[22] 1636:18–19/1637:sig.[c^v].
[23] 1636:19/1637:sig. [c^v]; 42/diiij.
[24] TC-*Lett.*, 163–69; 1636:88/1637:sig. eiiij.

different but supplementary sources of God's revelation, the Book of Nature and the Book of Scripture, between which, according to Campanella's reading of Lateran V's decree, there is no quarrel,[25] Campanella argued that just as St. Jerome in translating the Bible surpassed the Septuagint, so must we now attend to the Codex of Nature and with an *instaurationem scientiarum* eradicate this former dependence on the pagans.[26]

In a letter of mid-May 1609 to Kaspar Schoppe, contemporaneous with the period of gestation for the composition of *On Gentilism*, Campanella had denounced Aristotelianism as the Antichristic font, the source of Machiavellists, heretics, and atheists because of its heretical dogmas. Proceeding further he asserted that theology is not founded on the philosophy of Aristotle nor Plato nor Pythagoras but on natural philosophy wherever it is recognized.[27] Now in his tract, impelled by the imperative that he believes he found in the decree of Lateran V to cleanse the infected roots of philosophy and banish Aristotelianism forever, he says that the new philosophy should adhere to the interests of theology and canon law, while being guided by reason and utility. After listing the Fathers who condemn Aristotle, Campanella cites Clement of Alexandria in his advice to select whatever has been rightly said by Stoics, Platonists, and Epicureans, as well as Aristotle.[28]

Advocating therefore a broad eclecticism but with notable appeal to patristic theology,[29] he turns in the second part of the tract to the question whether it is permissible to avert, contradict, or diminish Aristotle's authority. After appealing to Lateran V's apparent condemnation of Aristotle's dogmas, Campanella cites Ambrose and Origen's opinion that Aristotle is worse than Epicurus.[30] Patristic authority also supports the belief of contemporary mathematicians regarding the falsity of a quintessence constituting the heavens. Aristotle sits as judge among us, a serpent in our midst and an embarrassment to all the efforts of our missionaries. Must we have Athenians as our teachers?[31] In sum, no philosophy should be set up as teacher of indubitable trustworthiness in Christian schools. Here Campanella stretches again the authority of Lateran V to apply to any total commitment to a Gentile philosophy—to Plato, Parmenides, or Aristotle.[32] Columbus's discovery is used both to invalidate Aristotle totally and all philosophical authorities in general and to revive confidence in a new empiricism.[33] Apparently aware of

---

[25] 1636:10–11/1637:sig. [biij^v].
[26] 1636:4–6/1637:sigs. bij–[bij^v]; 12–13/biiij.
[27] TC-*Lett.*, 149.
[28] 1636:2–3/1637:sig. [b^v].
[29] TC-*Lett.*, 257.
[30] 1636:17/1637:sigs. c–[c^v].
[31] 1636:20–22/1637:sigs. cij–[cij^v]; 6–7/bij^v.
[32] 1636:58/1637:sigs. eiij–[eiij^v].
[33] 1636:4–5/1637:sig. bij; 12–13/biiij; 48–49/e^v.

Quintilian's powerful image of language being a currency like money whose purity can be impaired or possibly alert to Lorenzo Valla's stringent application of this image to the pollution of Christian doctrine, Campanella announces the circulation of a counterfeit coinage of Aristolelian minting whose currency in the West he now proceeds to sketch.[34]

In the very middle of his diatribe against Aristotelian philosophy Campanella offers a brief sketch of the history of Aristotle's presence in the West. He had earlier noted that Aristotle had been in the schools seven hundred years![35] He presents the parallel of Aristotle's introduction into Christian schools with that of Antiochus Epiphanes' opening of the Greek philosophical gymnasia at Jerusalem in order to eliminate the law of God from Jewish minds, an event that would hasten the Maccabean revolt. Campanella depicts "our Roman Jerusalem" to have been the victim of barbarian invasions that laid waste the libraries of the philosophers in Italy, Gaul, Spain, and Africa, St. Ambrose's commentary on the *Timaeus* becoming a notable casualty together with Greek and Plato in general. But then with the victories of Charlemagne schools were reopened; yet by this time the clergy and even the cardinals themselves could hardly read. Here Giovanni Villani testifies that ignorance so prevailed that the later discovery of a mathematics book in the cell of Pope Sylvester and its being mistaken for necromantic activities on the part of the pope, served to queer the pontifical interment. It is in the context of this cultural barbarism that Aristotle, recovered by the Arabs, intrudes himself, the codices of the other philosophers having been lost. Entertaining the current belief that St. Thomas is the author of the entirety of *De regimine principum*, Campanella can have the good scholastic doctor complaining about the absence of Plato in his own time.[36] Only with the Council of Florence does Plato arrive by way of the Greeks. Yet despite the splendid efforts of the Medici princes to whom much is owed for the vindication of Christian spirits, the dominance of Aristotle is not broken, only his authority diminished. The opinion thus thrives that theology might be fallacious and contrary

---

[34] In his specific recourse to the imagery of minting, Campanella used the word *cudere* in the tract's title (see LF-*Bibl.*, 110) and in the text of *On Gentilism* the words *currenti moneta* and *novo aurichalco* (1636:49–50; 1637:sig. e^v); the critical word used by both Quintilian and Valla is *nummus* (*Institutio oratoria* 1.6.3) and *nummos reprobos* (Wolfram Setz, ed., *De falso credita et ementita Constantini donatione* [Tübingen, 1975]; 41:31–33), respectively. It would thus appear that Campanella was essentially familiar with what had become a topos. Here it reinforces his desire to replace a spurious coinage with a new, purified currency, a viable Christian philosophy.

[35] 1636:15/1637:sig. [biiij^v]; see also Campanella's "Commentaria," in *Opere Letterarie di Tommaso Campanella*, ed. Lina Bolzoni (Turin, 1977), 684.

[36] As in so many instances Campanella's attributions are wild; there is no basis in fact for his references to Giovanni Villani and St. Thomas, alias Ptolemy of Lucca. On the rich undergrowth of legend that grew up to obscure the figure of Gerbert of Aurillac, later Sylvester II, see J. J. Döllinger, *Fables Respecting the Popes in the Middle Ages* (New York, 1872), 267–72.

to natural philosophy concerning the eternity of the world, the mortality of the soul, religion, hell, heaven, angels, and demons. It is against such issues that Clement V at Vienne and Leo X at Lateran V have ruled. At this time in the development of his own thinking prior to 1637 Campanella will also include five Parisian synods as well as that at Rheims largely directed against Peter Abelard and Gilbert de la Porrée.[37]

As with many other of his writings Campanella was unable to publish the manuscript of *On Gentilism* until he had fled to Paris in October 1634. No sooner had it appeared in print than its author recognized the need for an expanded version that would do justice to his own rapidly increasing appreciation of the issues he had been treating. For in the learned circles of Paris, probably at the Dupuy and through the Bourdelots, he had encountered a young doctor of theology, Jean de Launoy, who had actually just received his doctorate from the Faculty of Theology at Paris in 1634 and had only recently returned from a visit to Rome; there he had befriended the distinguished scholars of the Vatican Library, Lucas Holstenius and Leone Allacci, and entered into several learned conversations with them. In fact Launoy stood at the threshold of a brilliant career, wherein he would acquire a reputation for courage and responsibility, ever ready to sacrifice piety, especially of an extravagant sort, to truth and would gain for himself the title of *dénicheur de saints*. Gallican, fearless in the pursuit of historical accuracy, and participating in that great surge of French learned scholarship that would culminate toward the end of the century in Mabillon, Du Cange, and Bayle, Launoy would now impart that second piece of evidence, that second authority that would assume its place beside that of Lateran V in Campanella's controversy with Aristotle.[38]

Launoy managed in 1636 to bring Campanella's attention to the fact that Pope Gregory IX in 1231 had ruled explicitly that the arts faculty should desist from reading the *Physics* of Aristotle and implicitly his *Metaphysics* until these books had been corrected.[39] This action had been taken as confirmation of the archbishop of Sens' earlier condemnation of 1210, whereby in

---

[37] 1636:33–34/1637:sig. d; see TC-*Comm.*, 684–86 and TC-*Lett.*, 388.

[38] On Jean de Launoy, see Louis Ellies Du Pin, *Nouvelle Bibliothèque des auteurs ecclésiastiques* (Amsterdam: Pierre Humbert, 1740), 18:34–62, also *BU*, 22:35–37 and *NBG*, 29:912–15. On the probable meeting of the two in the Dupuy circle it can be documented that both attended this important center of learning, although Campanella possibly earlier than Launoy with some overlap during 1636; his chief contact seems to have been the Hellenist Jean Bourdelot, whereas Launoy was more associated with the nephew Pierre Bourdelot. See TC-*Lett.*, 261, 299, 318, 358; and René Pintard, *Le libertinage érudit dans la premiere moitié du xviie siecle* (Paris, 1943), 279–80.

[39] Jean de Launoy, *De varia Aristotelis in Academia Parisiensi fortuna* (Paris: Edmund Martin, 1662), 78–80. See also Hastings Rashdall, *The Universities of Europe in the Middle Ages* (Oxford, 1936), 1:357. It is noteworthy that Rashdall uses Launoy as a source (1:270).

synod with his suffragan bishops he had called upon the schools for the elimination of Aristotle's works as fonts of error and impiety.[40] Campanella seized upon this information, magnifying and treating as permanent its condemnation of Aristotle. Considering this material sufficiently important to require a new version of the *On Gentilism*, he incorporated it into the "Disputatio in prologum instauratarum scientiarum ad scholas christianas." This work appeared as prefatory to his *Philosophia realis*, which he now published at another Paris printing house in 1637. Comparison of the second with the earlier version of the *De Gentilismo* reveals that besides making four substantive additions to the 1636 version[41] along with a number of minor clarifications, Campanella now introduced into his text in nine distinct places the new authority, linking Gregory IX with Lateran V.[42] Thereby he made the Gregorian bull equal in authority with session 8 of the Fifth Lateran Council as supporting evidence for the removal of Aristotle from the intellectual life of Christendom.[43]

[40] Launoy, *De varia*, 6–9, 78–80; Campanella, 1637:sig. [biij^v]; David Knowles, *The Evolution of Medieval Thought* (New York, 1964), 227–28.

[41] Campanella, 1637:sig. biij: "Praeterea Gregorius 9. Jubet ut *satagant fieri theodidacti* [directly quoting from Gregory IX's bull of 1231] non philosophi id est docibiles Dei. ergo in libris divinis Philosophari; secondly sigs. [biiij^v]–c: est Synodus Parisiensis, celebrata anno Domini 1204 [*sic*] ab Henrico Archiepiscopo Senonensis cum omnibus suffraganeis, (ut testatur Joannes Victorinus in memoriali historiarum, quando damnatus est Almericus Carnotensis ab Academia Magistrarum Parisiensis) in qua condemnatur opera Aristotelis & e scholis eliminantur, ut errorum & impietatis fontes, & condemnatio fuit confirmata a Gregorio 9. Hanc mihi nuper relationem Theologus Parisiensis doctissimus & solertissimus tradidit Joannes de Launoy, & typis mandavit totam (cuius ego partem allegaveram in alia editione) sic autem dicit in libello suo. In Rigordo historico . . . vel quocunque modo habere." [See Launoy, 6–7, for this passage. There follows an extensive quotation from Gregory IX's bull, both passages evidently taken from the final section of Launoy's *Syllabus rationum* of 1636. Campanella resumes:] "Ex quibus vides Aristotelis Metaphysicam, & libros naturales à synodo & ab Academia, & a Domino Papa fuisse damnatos, combustos, exsecratos, & ex patribus sicuti nos facimus scientias instaurari oportere, & à Codicibus naturae & scriptura; non à Gentibus ne filii Israel ex parte Iudaice, & ex parte loquantur Azotice, contra quos exclamat Canus, quod gentilizant & habent Aristotelem pro Christo, Averroem pro S. Petro, Alexandro pro S. Paulo & ista Synodus & Decreta & excommunicatio nunquam fuere retracta. Imo propter hoc postea damnaverunt s. Thomam tamquam Decreto inobedientem, quoniam nimius est in allegando Aristotelem in Theologia, sed toleratus est, postquam viderunt zelo fidei Aristotelem exposuisse in meliorem partem, ut infra.

Sed similiter decretum extat nostris temporibus sub Leone X. Concilii Lateranensis ibidem sessionem 8 etc. . . .", sig. [diij^v]. For the text of this third substantive addition, see n. 51, *infra*. The fourth case at sigs. d–d^v does not pertain to the authority derived from Gregory IX but concerns how the opinions of philosophers are to be judged by three rules that Campanella bases on passages from St. Augustine's *De genesi ad litteram*, MPL: 260–62.

[42] Campanella, 1637:sigs. biij/1636:9; biij/10; biiij/14; [biiij^v]/16; [d^v]/34; [dij^v]/37; [diij^v]/41; [diiij^v]/45; and [e^v]/50.

[43] Apparently the additions to the 1637 edition of *On Gentilism*, which serves as the preface to Campanella's *Philosophia realis*, have escaped the otherwise meticulous bibliographical attentions of Luigi Firpo, unless he deemed them too insignificant to note. For according to LF-Bibl.,

Given the fact that the relations between the Paris Dominicans and the university's doctors of theology had been less than cordial since the beginning of the sixteenth century, it was Campanella's good fortune to be able to converse with Launoy. Partly in reaction to Campanella's work and to the second version of *On Gentilism*, the Parisian doctor would be encouraged, if only for setting the record straight, to write seventeen years later his *On the Varying Fortunes of Aristotle at the University of Paris* that would see four editions.[44] It is not therefore from this later work that Campanella derived the new material that will require a second edition of the *On Gentilism* and restore that tract to its commanding position as the propylaeum to his philosophical works. Rather as Campanella tells us in the additional material inserted toward the beginning of article 2, that most learned and intelligent theologian, Launoy, had recently given a report to Campanella and then shortly afterwards committed it to print in a work that proves by Launoy's later statement in the *fortuna* to have been his first publication (1636), the *Syllabus rationum quibus causa Durandi* etc.[45] From this last work, following upon their conversation, therefore Campanella obtained the material for incorporation into his second edition of *On Gentilism*.

In the Dominican's eager and indiscriminate appropriation of Launoy's research regarding Pope Gregory IX's ruling of 1231, we see the collision and contrast of two quite different worlds of learning: that magical, prophetic, syncretic one of what the late Renaissance had become and the historical, critical, philological one of earlier humanism now infused with contemporary currents of skepticism and scientific inquiry. For Robert Lenoble has found in Launoy's relentless pursuit of the historical fact and his examination of the credibility of witnesses a sense of the historically contingent that allows him to claim this theologian to be among the founders of modern history. Amidst the Jansenist turmoil Launoy asked the upsetting question as to whether St. Augustine was an Augustinian and the Church always Augustinian in its theology. In discovering that the Augustinian doctrine of grace appeared in the fourth century as a novelty and not as the traditional doctrine of the Church, Launoy showed how a seeming *sensus communis* could be a historical contingency. Like his two great friends, Mersenne and Gassendi, Launoy followed

---

113, the differences between the two editions of 1636 and 1637 are minor, and since this judgment rendered in 1940, there is nothing in his subsequent articles and publications to modify this view. Indeed when in 1953 Romano Amerio produced his Italian translation of *De gentilismo* he based it silently on the 1636 version and followed in the footsteps of Firpo regarding the two editions. See *Della necessità di una filosofia cristiana* (Turin, 1953), where on p. xv he speaks of "la seconda con lievi ritocchi e piccole aggiunte, pure in Parigi nel 1638 (!)" The 1693 Paris edition of the *De gentilismo* ignores the 1637 version.

[44] *British Library General Catalogue of Printed Books to 1975*, 185:284: Paris, 1653; The Hague, 1656; Paris, 1662; Wittenberg, 1720.

[45] Launoy, *De varia*, 1662:85.

the immanent logic of his discipline.[46] Consequently, it is worthwhile at this juncture to examine briefly Launoy's later work *On the Varying Fortunes of Aristotle at the University of Paris* both for his own account of the reception of Aristotle in the West and for his disagreements in retrospect with Campanella.

In 1653 Edmund Martin published together François Bernier's *Favilla ridiculi muris* and Launoy's *De varia* to defend Gassendi against J. B. Morin and his scholastic adversaries. Again in Launoy's pursuit of establishing a historical fact the ostensibly established orthodoxy of Aristotle's persisting acceptance dissolves before the restitution of historicity. This sense of the historically contingent emerges from the very plurality of fortunes, which do not describe a linear development.[47] Launoy sees eight such shifts or fortunes of Aristotle at Paris. We need only attend to the first four: the beginning of the reception in 1200 that leads to the Parisian synod of 1209 to call for the burning of his books; the general prohibition but the admission of Aristotle's dialectic; Gregory IX's bull, seen as moderating on balance the prohibitions of the provincial council but explicitly forbidding any lecturing on the natural philosophy of Aristotle until the *Physics* is corrected, while remaining silent on the dialectic and the *Metaphysics*; in 1265 Cardinal Legate Simon's renewal of the prohibition until correction occurs, now including specifically the *Metaphysics*.[48] While Launoy's account is hardly a continuous narration or history, it is important to note that although he does indulge in providing a long list of patristic and early medieval opinions about Aristotle, beginning with Justin Martyr and Clement of Alexandria and extending down to St. Bernard, the conscious presence of Aristotle in the West begins sharply and unaccountably in 1200.[49] By forsaking the prevalent belief in the Carolingian origins of the university and Latin Aristotelianism, Launoy distanced himself from a myth that proved to be slower in dying than its dynastic counterpart Pharamond in medieval historiography. In contrast Campanella's wildly inaccurate notion of the seven hundred years of Aristotle in the West at least has the merit, impelled by polemic, of attempting to provide some context and origins.

When seventeen years after his encounter with Campanella Launoy came to compose his account of Aristotle's reception at Paris, Campanella had long since been interred at the Jacobins. It is of some significance, however, that in this work the contemporary with whom the Paris theologian chose to enter into specific controversy and on two distinct matters was Campanella. In the

---

[46] Robert Lenoble, "Histoire et physique: A propos des conseils de Mersenne et de l'intervention de Jean de Launoy dans la querelle gassendiste," *Revue d'histoire des sciences* 6 (1953): 112–34, esp. 121–24.

[47] Ibid., 125–29.

[48] Launoy, *De varia*, 1662:3–6, 69–93.

[49] Ibid., 9–64.

first instance he accuses the Dominican "and others ignorant of these events" of having abusively called Abelard heresiarch when the latter made his peace with the Church and lived piously out his remaining days with Cluniac monks.[50] The second accusation is more complicated, stemming from a problem that Launoy manages to create for himself. For he poses the question of how Albert and Thomas were allowed to make commentaries on the prohibited books of Aristotle. Faced with this apparent lacuna in his evidence and unwilling to admit that truth might be shy and not announce herself, Launoy speculates: perhaps they were not at Paris when they wrote and thus considered themselves immune, or somehow they were simply ignorant of the Gregorian law. Aware that the theologians often sought special permission from Rome, Launoy remained distressed at not finding such a request. And thus he considered that the two princes of theology might in fact have been in violation of Gregory's specific admonition *fieri Theodidacti*. Complaining that Campanella would have it that St. Thomas was not a Peripatetic and that he mangled Launoy's own observation, the Parisian fastens upon the following passage in the revised version of *On Gentilism*, only available as preface to the *Philosophia realis* of 1637:

> Less than a century earlier, Gregory IX had confirmed the condemnation of Aristotle effected by the university and the synod of Paris and had ruled the burning of Aristotle's books and forbade his being lectured upon. But Dr. Thomas was most observant of the authority of the pope and a doctor of the university. Thus in no way must he be considered to have Aristotelized but only to have exposed Aristotle, so that he might oppose what evils had been introduced through Aristotle—and I would believe with the license of the pontiff. Wherefore skillfully yet not sufficiently prudently Dr. Thomas was condemned by certain Parisians as being disobedient to council and to pope, and as being an Aristotelian most willingly.[51]

Obviously indignant at these liberties and embroideries Launoy confesses that he also would gladly believe, if only such a license might appear. But then he opines that "if the blessed doctor were alive now and should be condemned, without doubt he would prefer to be refuted with truth than to be excused with falsehood." Clearly unconvinced yet troubled, the Paris theologian remained open to more plausible explanations.[52]

---

[50] Ibid., 70; see Campanella, 1637:sig. bij/1636:5, [bij^v]/8, [cij^v]/22, ciij/28.

[51] Campanella, 1637:sig. [diij^v]: "Probatur: nam Gregorius 9 paulo ante 100. fere annos confirmaverat damnationem Aristotelis ab Academia Parisiensi, & à synodo factam sub anathemate, & combustionem Librorum Aristotelis ratam habuit, & praecepit ne legeretur. at D. Thomas fuit observantissimus authoritatis Papae, & doctor Parisiensi: ergo nullo pacto putandus est Aristotelizasse: Sed tantum exposuisse Aristotelem, ut occurreret malis per Aristotelem illatis: & crederem, cum licentia Pontificis. Quapropter docte ac non satis prudenter damnatus est D. Thomas a quibusdam Parisiensibus, ut inobediens concilio & Papae & ut Aristotelicus ex animo etc." Cf. Launoy, 1662:85.

[52] Ibid., 83–85.

158   CHAPTER IV

In assessing the exchange that took place between Campanella and Launoy in Paris in 1636, we can say that the credulous, eager friar with generous words for his learned benefactor persisted in his polemical position that St. Thomas was not an Aristotelian. He shows himself prepared to seize upon any historical contingency in order to effect a distancing of his revered St. Thomas from the poisonous Aristotle. For his part the more critical Paris theologian appears somewhat nettled by an encounter that led to the mauling of his evidence. Nevertheless is it possible that Campanella, ever-conscious of his friend Galileo and his recent condemnation in Rome, managed in this instance to deepen Launoy's appreciation of this case and the issues involved? For at the very end of his forthcoming *Syllabus rationum* (1636) Launoy introduced a problem or case of conscience in which, having reported the condemnation of the books of Aristotle by a synod of Paris and Gregory IX and the censure given in Rome on Copernicus and Galileo on the earth's movement, he proposes the following question for resolution: whether the judgment rendered at Rome against the views of Galileo, *which has still not been sent, nor has the University of Paris been notified*, binds more the professors of this university than those that have been borne by the synod of Paris and the bull of Gregory addressed to the doctors of the University of Paris against the books of Aristotle.[53] Perhaps something like an exchange of ideas had occurred in the 1636 encounter between the two clerics.

Fortified with his new evidence and authority Campanella now reinforced

---

[53] Du Pin, *Nouvelle Bibliothèque*, 18: 34–35, describes the content of Launoy's first publication the *Syllabus rationum* (my own italics). I have only been able to confirm Du Pin's statement on the basis of the 1731 Geneva edition of Launoy's *Opera omnia* available to me at the Folger Library: "Rursus ante aliquot annos opinio Nicolai Copernici de motu terrae a Galilaeo renovata & illustrata, Romae damnata est à Pontefice. Sed sententia damnationis ad Magistros Parisienses non est adhuc transmissa. Ex his ergo oritur haec scrupulosa quaestio: Utrum sententia damnationis Galilaei nondum ad Philosophiae professores in Studio Parisiensi directa, magis eosdem liget professores, quam sententia Concilii supra dicti Parisiensis, & Bulla Pontificis Greg. IX. ad eosdem Magistros transmissa. Huic resolutioni penitus se submittent ii praesertim, qui sententiam Copernici, aut Galilaei magis recitando, quam asserendo docuerunt. Praeterea resolutio erit utilis vel ad moderandum eorum studium, qui nimis avide Aristotelem legunt, vel ad pacificandas eorum conscientias, qui forsan eundem nonnisi meticulose docent persuasi, nondum esse jussioni Pontificiae satisfactum" (*Op. omn.* 1.8). It would be too much to suggest that Campanella had alerted Launoy to what had become a cause célèbre ever since July 1633. It would seem to be the greatest bureaucratic snarl of the century that, given the saturation job by Rome to communicate Galileo's condemnation and stem the printing and reading of his works, by apparently concentrating on the mathematicians and astronomers of the universities, the nuncio and his inquisitors never transmitted the sentence to the University of Paris! Thus while Launoy might here express the desire for a definitive resolution, the heavily Gallican Faculty of Theology was officially, and cheerfully, able to play innocent. On this matter, see Armand Beaulieu, "Les réactions des savants français au début du xvii siècle devant l'héliocentrisme de Galilée," in *Novità celesti e crisi del sapere*, Atti del Convegno Internazionale di Studi Galileiani, ed. P. Galluzzi (Florence, 1984), 375. More generally, see the interesting article by Lisa T. Sarasohn, "French Reactions to the Condemnation of Galileo 1632–1642," *CHR* 74 (1988): 34–54.

THE CONTROVERSY WITH ARISTOTLE 159

some of his earlier arguments. Of capital importance is the relationship between the two Books:

> Gregory IX commands that they concentrate on becoming God-taught, not philosophers, that is, teachable by God and thus to practice philosophy only in the divine books. Twofold however is the divine Codex—one, the nature of things and the other Scripture. These are to us the light and whoever bears witness from them is our master in the school of God; whoever has opinions, he is a schoolfellow; but whoever sticks to his own individual fancies, although most honored by many, he must not be accepted but merely heard, as Augustine and other high ecclesiastics, when they deny the existence of the antipodes. Thus because philosophers claim to have accepted sciences from the first Codex, namely that of nature, this first Codex of God does not, however, conflict with the second, for as the eighth session of the Fifth Lateran Council says: "Truths do not contradict each other"; likewise the Apostle: "Has Christ been divided? No, for God is not the God of dissension, but of peace" [1 Cor. 14:33]. They must be examined how they have erred in conflict with the second or whether they might have erred in the first and they must be corrected by those who have accepted the charity of truth from Christ, the wisdom of God, unless we want to condemn all the holy doctors and Columbus and other discoverers of truths.[54]

In both versions of his attack on Aristotle Campanella's repeated recourse to the text of Daniel 12:4 that there will be great concourse and manifold increase of knowledge at the end[55] and now the new emphasis upon *instauratio scientiarum* remind us that the belief in the millennial revival of knowledge together with the emancipation from the stranglehold of traditional Greek metaphysics had by the mid-1630s, especially in Paris, become a pan-European movement no longer limited to the Baconians.[56] Certainly we cannot disallow, and indeed evidence supports, that Campanella despite religious barriers approached during the last years of his life the threshold of English

---

[54] Campanella, 1637:sig. biij; cf. 1636:10: "Greg 9. Iubet vt satagant fieri Theodidacti non Philosophi: id est docibiles Dei. ergo in libris diuinis Philosophari. Duplex autem Dei codex, Rerum natura, (scilicet & Scriptura: hi sunt nobis lumen, & quicunque ex his testatur est noster Magister in Schola Dei; qui autem opinatur, est condiscipulus; qui autem soli propriae phantasiae inhaeret, quamvis laudatissimus a multis, non est accipiendus, sed tantum audiendus, sicut August. & alii P. P. quando negant Antipodas extare: igitur quoniam Philosophi ex primo codice, qui est rerum natura, scientias accepisse profitentur, primus autem Codex Dei non pugnat cum secundo: nam, vt ait Concilium Lateran. sess. 8. verum vero non contradicit: & Apostolus. Nunquid diuisus est Christus? Non est Deus dissensionis sed pacis: Examinandi sunt ex quo errauerint contra secundum, an in primo errauerint: & corrigendi sunt per eos, qui charitatem veritatis à Christo sapientia Dei, acceperunt; nisi velimus condemnare Sanctos DD. omnes & Columbum & alios veritatum inuentores."

[55] 1636:5/1637: sig. bij; 59/sig. eiiij.

[56] In general, see Charles Webster, *The Great Instauration: Science, Medicine and Reform, 1626–1660* (London, 1975), 1–35.

intellectual and religious developments.[57] The burgeoning movement that included such talents as Comenius and Gassendi, Mersenne, and shortly Hobbes made clear enough the object to be attacked—traditionally received Greek metaphysics; the more positive demands of their program, such as the precise contours of the *instauratio* of learning, did not enjoy the same clarity. Yet in varying degrees most critics of the established system shared a buoyant optimism in a new intellectual order distinguished by three characteristics: a diverse, eclectic, preeminently empirical philosophy; a confidence in innovation; and a commitment to expand the new knowledge.[58]

In concluding his second version of *On Gentilism*, Campanella provides us with his clearest statement regarding the much desired revival of knowledge:

> Furthermore it is not useful to the commonweal to confine gifted temperaments to one Book, for thereby a person is dulled and deprived of the discovery of new things and new sciences. For the princes it is even expedient to occupy excellent minds in philosophizing lest their burning of the midnight oil may not prove useful to the government. Multifold study is especially advantageous . . . to the papacy for the confirmation, increase, and enlightenment of its people. . . . Daniel 12:4 says there will be much concourse together with manifold increase of knowledge. . . . As daily experience prompts, the experience of new things indeed daily magnifies and revives the sciences. Multifold study must not be denied; otherwise neither the new hemisphere, nor the new stars, nor the telescope, nor the compass, nor printing, nor the invention of cannon would have been discovered by us, if the inclinations for the entertainment of multiple philosophies had been precluded. . . . A single Codex is useful for the young and for those of mediocre talent, not however for the advanced or for those apt to discover what is higher and better. One must therefore not be committed irrevocably to the words of one doctor. . . . Let the way for discovery be precluded to none. The superfluous especially do not survive the ravages of time.[59]

---

[57] Lord Herbert of Cherbury published the second edition of his *De veritate* in 1633. He gave copies to the Genevan diplomat Elias Diodati, a regular in Paris intellectual circles, through whom they reached Peiresc, Mersenne, Gassendi, and Campanella. According to Peiresc, Herbert, who possessed Campanella's *Astrologia, Atheismus Triumphatus*, and *Metaphysica* (1638), thought highly of the Dominican philosopher. D. P. Walker, *The Ancient Theology: Studies in Christian Platonism from the Fifteenth to the Eighteenth Century* (Ithaca, 1972), 168, 188. For his part Campanella apparently reacted favorably to Herbert's *De veritate* (TC-*Lett.*, 247–48), and in an apparently undelivered letter to Henrietta Maria (ibid., 355, 404), the queen of England, he passed some interesting judgments on the opportunities for a Catholic restoration in England. See chap. 3, n. 145, *supra*.

[58] See also Webster, *Great Instauration*, 513.

[59] Campanella, 1636:59–61/1637:sigs. [eiij^v]–eiiij: "Praepterea [*sic*] vtile non est Reipublicae claudere ingenia sub vno libro; sic enim inuentionibus nouarum rerum, & scientiarum priuatur & hebetatur. Principibus etiam expedit occupare ingenia in philosophando, ne regimini ipsorum vigiles sint non commodi: maxime autem Papatui prodest multiplex studium, vt alibi ostendimus ad sui verificationem, & ampliationem, & illuminationem populi . . . dictur, *Daniel. 12. multi*

Certain points emerge as to the nature of the new Christian philosophy, the first of the two Books or Codices. It is consciously eclectic and diverse in its drawing upon any of the ancients. It is distinguished by a new empiricism, presumably Campanella's but also leaving room for what was believed to be Galileo's. Regarding the relationship between the Books, Lateran V asserts that there can be no quarrel;[60] in fact since Christ as the Primal Reason and Wisdom is the author of both, there can be no conflict. Furthermore philosophy is the catechism to the faith, not the impediment that the insipid Peripatetics have effected.[61] Because theology calls all sciences handmaidens to its cultivation, should there be a conflict, the opposition to faith must be rejected. Yet Campanella is confident that such innovators as Galileo with the telescope will produce no strain. The innovator does not form or reform the sciences contrary to the doctrine of the saints, but from the two Books he erects them from this collapsed condition under the Gentiles.[62]

• • •

When first composed in the course of 1610, Campanella's *De Gentilismo* registered the initial impact of Galileo and his *Starry Messenger* upon an astounded and receptive European audience. During its own tortuous odyssey to print over a quarter of a century later the *De Gentilismo* would anticipate the better known *Apologia for Galileo* of 1616, published at Frankfurt in 1622, wherein culminated the prisoner's intellectual support and tentative commitment to the program of the new science, howsoever misconstrued for his own astrological and apocalyptical purposes.[63] Here he would carry further his efforts to set St. Thomas at odds with Aristotle and to express his own impatience with the excessive overcommitment of current theology to Aristotelian natural philosophy. While Galileo prudently distanced himself from his irrepressibly generous admirer, Campanella, unwearied and never lacking for courage, continued to be frustrated in his efforts to draw closer to him. With that meeting of minds still unrealized and unrealizable at the end of his life, Campanella nevertheless could confidently take that first herald both of his

---

pertransibunt, & multiplex erit scientia. . . . ut quotidiana experientia scientias magnificat, & instaurat, non est negandum studium multiplex: Alioquin nec novum hemispherium nec novae stellae, nec Telescopium, nec magnetis usus, nec Typographia, nec bombardorum inventio, praecluso philosophandi multiplici conatu, nobis comperta essent. . . . Unicus codex adolescentibus, & ingeniis mediocribus prodest, non autem provectis, & invenire aptis altiora, melioraque: propterea non iurandum in verba unius Doctoris. . . . Invenire autem nemini praecluditur via, cum praesertim superflua non transeant saeculi iniuriam: moriuntur enim cum authore suo: nova necessario durabunt semper: non ergo timendum."

[60] 1636:8–10/1637:sig. biij.
[61] 1636:10–11/1637:sig. [biij^v].
[62] 1636:48–50/1637:sig. [e^v].
[63] Léon Blanchet, *Campanella* (New York, 1963), 241–55, 331–55.

own deepest philosophical disposition and of his commitment to the Galilean science and situate it as a portal to his entire thought. At Paris he had obtained not only its approval from the Faculty of Theology but also further important ammunition from a member of that august body. And whatever the differences between himself and Launoy the manifesto of his earlier life had now become sufficiently strengthened to reassume its former intended position as the propylaeum to his total intellectual system and the trumpet call to the necessity for minting a new Christian philosophy.

In Defense of Galileo: Conflicting Empiricisms and the Concept of the Two Books

Heretofore Campanella's controversy with Aristotle assumed the form of an attack upon the pagan's heretical positions on relevant matters of Christian doctrine. In his effort to mint a different Christian philosophy Campanella appealed to scattered authorities in the Church's past, both papal and conciliar, to a St. Thomas Aquinas freed from his presumably false Aristotelian wrappings, and to a patristic tradition that together ostensibly with St. Thomas pressed for an effective alternative to the pagan philosophy of Aristotle. Already evident in the extended trajectory of *On Gentilism*'s development is the further and in many ways more fundamental argument against Aristotle in terms of a late Renaissance empiricism. Beyond the fact that new dimensions and fields of knowledge, ethnographic, geographic, and astronomic, threw into question a natural philosophy commensurate with a closed universe, the understanding of direct personal experience itself raised profound issues as to the nature of the world and of man himself that now must be addressed. Three varieties of empiricism need to be distinguished—Aristotelian, Galilean, Campanellan—at the beginning of the seventeenth century, each with its larger implications for understanding the physical world. And in Campanella's ambivalent intellectual relation to Galileo and the latter's failure to reciprocate, their common opposition to Aristotle will break apart, revealing an ominous rift between this representative natural philosophy of the late Renaissance and something quite new and different, presaging a modern view of reality and of the world.

As a formal philosophy Campanella's has been designated a pansensism. The term suggests at once a living, vibrant, and vital universe, the world as a great animal, breathing, animate, sensitive, a total sensory coherence.[64]

> The world's a living creature, whole and great,
> God's image, praising God whose type it is;
> We are imperfect worms, vile families,
> That in its belly have our low estate.

[64] TC-*DSCM*, 26.

> If we know not its love, its intellect,
>   Neither the worm within my belly seeks
>   To know me, but his petty mischief wreaks:—
> Thus it behooves us to be circumspect.
> Again, the earth is a great animal,
>   Within the greatest; we are like the lice
>   Upon its body, doing harm as they.
> Proud men, lift up your eyes; on you I call:
>   Measure each being's worth; and thence be wise;
>   Learning what part in the great scheme you play![65]

And as an animal, the world, Campanella will remind us, yes, is even mortal;[66] yet he will add significantly that God will reduce it to some other more excellent form.[67] In the pansensist universe language operates differently: words have a conjunctive power, identifying signifier and signified, being and thought, nature and perception; they operate as charms, possessing an incantational capacity when properly charged.[68]

Campanella's pansensism presents a world of likenesses, correspondences, and resemblances open to the manipulation of the magus. The direct accessibility of the divine omnipresence immanent in all things opens the world as well to the sensitivity of the poet. The semiotics of celestial regularities images a world penetrable to the calculated prognostications of the astrologer. To know becomes a matter of reading the divine signs that God has written into nature, God's image, God's Codex. This reading, this understanding, requires an entry of one's own self, one's life into that of which it has altogether been a part. The bonding agent that makes such identification possible is that not incorporeal *spiritus*, conceived hardly in Christian religious terms but rather as belonging to the medical tradition culminating in the Stoic vitalistic principle of *pneuma*. The limits of one's sympathy for nature become the limits of one's knowledge of nature.[69] Campanella's empiricism must work within this understanding of reality.

In a notable letter written in July 1607 to Antonio Querengo Campanella at one point claims to be able to learn more from the anatomy of an ant or a plant than from reading all the books ever written on the subject.[70] This celebration of the world as a book and of the consequent divine induction perhaps attains its culmination in his sonnet *Il mondo e Il libro*:

---

[65] Symonds, *Sonnets*, 121; TC- *P*[1], 16.
[66] TC-*DSCM*, 31.
[67] Ibid., 33–34.
[68] Ibid., 292.
[69] Ernst Cassirer, *The Individual and the Cosmos in Renaissance Philosophy* (New York/Evanston, 1963), 53–54; Michael W. Mönnich, *Tommaso Campanella: Sein Beitrag zur Medizin und Pharmazie der Renaissance* (Stuttgart, 1990), 117–25.
[70] TC-*Lett.*, 134.

>The world's the book where the eternal Sense
> Wrote his own thoughts; the living temple where,
> Painting his very self, with figures fair
> He filled the whole immense circumference.
>Here then should each man read, and gazing find
> Both how to live and govern, and beware
> Of godlessness; and, seeing God all-where,
> Be bold to grasp the universal mind.
>But we tied down to books and temples dead,
> Copied with countless errors from the life—
> These nobler than that school sublime we call.
>O may our senseless souls at length be led
> To truth by pain, grief, anguish, trouble, strife!
> Turn we to read the one original![71]

One may well ask what Campanella precisely sees when he thus studies the ant. It would seem both everything and nothing: on the one hand everything, in that the act of sensuous perception releases a process of drawing analogies that leads to an empathy and community with all being; on the other hand nothing, in that it does not offer any analytical instrument or enterprise. Magic, however, affords the only possibility for a partial mobilization of entities. For Ernst Cassirer Campanella becomes the rational methodologist of magic with an empiricism that leads to the codification rather than refutation of magic. In such a framework "the single 'facts' cluster around each other in colourful abundance but in completely chaotic disorder. The appeal to experience could offer no firm foundation so long as the concept of experience still contained such completely heterogeneous constitutive elements."[72]

Beginning in book 2 of the *Del senso*, Campanella takes issue with the Aristotelian concept of substance as matter and form, the epistemology of substantial forms, and their reference to universals. He seeks to displace the explanation of matter having an appetite for form by substituting instinct for appetite and the Telesian dichotomy of heat/cold through which sense works as a means of displacing the Aristotelian forms.[73] After an application of this scheme to the operation and functions of the human body Campanella turns to a general criticism of the epistemology of forms and their references to universals. Experience denies that for sensing fire it is necessary to engage the form of the fire; rather it suffices simply to be slightly burned.[74] It is a great

---

[71] Symonds, *Sonnets*, 123; TC-*P*¹, 18.

[72] Cassirer, *The Individual and the Cosmos*, 150–52. Nevertheless Brian Copenhaver has here suggestively argued that Campanella's very critique of hylomorphic metaphysics would lead eventually to the metaphysical decay of magic as a serious department of natural philosophy (see chap. 2, n. 285).

[73] TC-*DSCM*, 37–45.

[74] Ibid., 80.

foolishness to believe that knowledge consists in knowing the universal. It is not enough to know Peter to be a man, a rational animal, but to know his specific qualities. Here at issue is the intense reality of direct experience.[75] Campanella attacks the Aristotelian differentiation of intellects and the neglect of an infinite aspiration. He clearly distrusts abstract thought: Aristotelian intellect is sense of the common and of the consimilitude of beings and not of particularity; it is most imperfect knowledge, lacking sense and reason because it is distant and sees only what is in all and not the details.[76] The heavens sense; likewise stones, metals and, according to his Neapolitan instructors Ferrante Imperato and G. B. Della Porta, trees. God Himself, without body, senses.[77] Thus apparently Campanella's pansensist perception of the fundamentally unanalyzed and unanalyzable particular would afford him magical, poetic, and astrological opportunities but would ill-position him for understanding Galileo's empiricism or the import of the Florentine's challenge to the whole grand palace of traditional thought.

In his first letter to Galileo (January 13, 1611), Campanella expresses the euphoria occasioned by his initial encounter with the momentous *Sidereus Nuncius*. In conveying his reactions, he deploys those major themes that will later figure in his own *Apologia pro Galileo*: speculation on new astral worlds, lunar republics, and habitation of the moon; the reaffirmation of Italy's philosophical leadership; the confirmation of biblical prophecy for new heavens and a new world.[78] Given such widely shared current interests and expectations, Campanella shows himself prompt to register the larger implications of Galileo's achievement. But to Galileo himself the propensity of the Neapolitan prophet to veer away from the specifics of the new science would only serve to widen the gulf between the two leading late Renaissance thinkers, despite their common opposition to Aristotle.

In his second surviving letter to Galileo three years later Campanella brings the issue of atomism into focus, an issue that throws into relief their different epistemologies, perceptions of the world, and languages. Campanella had previously invoked Galileo for treating mathematically what heretofore had been metaphysical.[79] Now he seems to confront the bitter fruit of the consequence.

> It grieves me very much, as I wrote you this past summer, that if it is a matter of treating floating bodies etc. you have discovered only atoms, and nothing more to be found than relations and many propositions that you are not able to be assured to say are true and many things that are not able to be maintained so easily, such that you have to [your] enemies given opportunity for denying all the celestial

[75] Ibid., 125.
[76] Ibid., 148–50.
[77] Ibid., 178, 208–15.
[78] TC-*Lett*., 163–69.
[79] Ibid., 164.

matter that Your Lordship indicated to us. . . . Let Your Lordship assume the language of complete mathematics and leave the atoms till afterwards and write at the beginning that this philosophy is from Italy, from Philolaus and Timaeus in part and that Copernicus robbed it from our aforesaid.[80]

In urging Galileo not to generalize, Campanella criticizes not just any capacity for generalization but rather that which has established itself in the atomistic view of things: such a type of generalization reduces the representative potency of the object, declaring that in the object "nothing other than relations are to be found," effecting thus a reduction of its resonances and possible languages. At the same time both too much and too little is being predicated regarding the object, by reducing it to pure relation and local motion. As Biagio di Giovanni has perceptively observed: "the invitation of Campanella to Galileo to remain within his style of perfect mathematics does not at all signify reduction of the universe to an universal calculus but rather the contrary, an invitation not to effect quick deductions, not to generalize in the mechanistic way the absolute language of a knowledge that illumines an aspect of the world."[81]

Thus it would appear that even before the actual composition of the *Apologia pro Galileo* the fault began to emerge in any common ground of opposition to the Aristotelian hegemony: two discordant languages, two different apprehensions of reality. True, it was all a matter of reading the signs. But the signs according to the language and to the perceiver could be read in different ways. To the poetic/magical imagination of Campanella the signs resonated a vibrant, cohering unity, "The world is the image, living temple of God."

> Blessed is he who reads in this book [of Nature] and learns from it what things are, and not from his own fancy; he learns the art and the divine government and thereby is made similar to and at one with God and with Him sees that each thing is good and that evil is mirror and mask of the parts that represent joyous comedy to the Creator and with Him rejoices, admires, proclaims, sings the infinite immortal God—Prima Possanza, Prima Sapienza, e Prima Amore.[82]

As for Galileo, he was by this time rapidly maturing to that position best set forth a decade later in *The Assayer*:

> Philosophy is written in this grand book, the universe, which stands continually open to our gaze. But the book cannot be understood unless one first learns to comprehend the language and read the letters in which it is composed. It is written in the language of mathematics, and its characters are triangles, circles, and

---

[80] Ibid., 176–77; cf. *Op. GG*, IV, 131–34.
[81] Biagio di Giovanni, "Lo spazio della vita Fra G. Bruno e T. Campanella," *Centauro: Rivista di filosofia e teoria politica* 12 (1984): 3–32, esp. 21. I wish to thank Professor Lina Bolzoni of the University of Pisa for providing me with a copy of this article.
[82] TC-*DSCM*, IV, 331; Giovanni, "Spazio," 24.

other geometric figures without which it is humanly impossible to understand a single word of it; without these, one wanders about in a dark labyrinth.[83]

The inexorable geometric language of Galilean empiricism opposed the metaphorical language of Campanellan empiricism.

If beneath the surface conflicting epistemologies and worldviews worked to separate Campanella and Galileo despite their shared anti-Aristotelian stance, more superficially Campanella would begin to cull from Galileo's impact a number of congenial implications to be developed later. In his first two letters to the Florentine *mathematicus* he fulsomely extols Galileo's achievement. Picking up on a theme presented in the preface of his first published work of 1591,[84] he sees that with Galileo the eye of philosophizing has been properly returned to Italy from whence the Greeks had snatched it. Galileo is hailed as the restorer of Italy's proper glory in science. While he is associated with those who in Campanella's belief are Calabrians or Calabrianized—Timaeus, Plato, Pythagoras, Philolaus—the friar neither explicitly identifies the Galilean achievement with Platonic tradition nor recognizes it as the new naturalistic Christian philosophy for the replacement of Aristotle.[85]

Similarly, the same period (from the autumn of 1613 to the spring of 1614) appears to be critical in the Calabrian prisoner's passage over to the new astronomy. According to his second letter to Galileo (March 8, 1614), Campanella, in composing his new theology and presently involved with its fourth book, reveals himself already intent upon showing the agreement between Galileo's discoveries and Scripture, the Fathers and rabbis—a position that would shortly be set forth in the published *Apologia*.[86] Coming from the same period Tobias Adami, Campanella's German Lutheran friend and the chief means for the publication of his works, informs us that initially Campanella had hesitated over accepting the new astronomy; only after Adami had given him shortly after 1613 further evidence based upon subsequent discussions with Galileo, did the Saxon note in his Neapolitan friend a rallying to the Copernican system that will become evident in the *Apologia* of 1616.[87] Yet Campanella will fall short of any full acceptance.

While Campanella wavers, even if all his contemporaries understood him to be supportive of Copernicanism, our real question is the manner in which and for what reasons Campanella accepted Galileo. Well might he express some annoyance in his first letter to Galileo, that he had not read his *Starry Messenger* earlier, for in his writings up until this stage he had opposed the belief in

[83] Stillman Drake, *Discoveries and Opinions of Galileo* (New York, 1957), 237–38.
[84] I here refer to the readily available Italian translation of Luigi Firpo, "Il Metodo Nuovo," *RF* 40 (1949): 182–205, esp. 201–4. See also the recent critical edition of the TC-*PSD*, chap. 1, n. 24, *supra*.
[85] TC-*Lett.*, 165–68, 177.
[86] Ibid., 177.
[87] Blanchet, *Campanella*, 241–42; cf. TC-*RPE*, 18.

the earth's motion. Even beyond this time Campanella seemed to be understandably wedded to his Telesio in attributing all movement to the influence of heat, thus the sun, and all repose to that coldness associated with the earth. Compelled to readjust, Campanella will now confess that the true cause of movement is less the heat but rather the appetite for natural conservation, thus pertaining to the earth and its soul. He begins to free himself from the Telesian notion of the interaction of heat and cold as the source of natural activity. He can recognize a supreme principle that can be identified with that power constituting the first of his three primalities. Behind this admission lurks, however, the dogmatism of a qualitative and dynamic science. Whatever the exchange, astrological priorities prevail over mathematical ones.[88]

In fact Campanella does not look to the new science for a mathematical and rational explanation of astral motions addressing a purely theoretical need but rather for a divination of universal political and religious destinies. Bruno's end is still too raw in men's memories for Campanella to be outspoken on the notion of the infinite number of worlds. Galileo's telescopic discoveries argued massively, however, for the uniformity of nature and thus the collapse of those sublunary walls. An infinite perspective will inevitably begin to unfold. The expanding sense of the infinite plenitude of being is fully at one with the spirit that animates the naturalistic religion of Campanella and provides the principal reason for his adoption of it. Furthermore this astronomy speaks to and provides the sign for an imminent renovation of the world. It is thus hardly surprising that when he came to congratulate Galileo on the *Dialogue* of 1632 on August 5 of that year, all things pleased him indeed, yet the subjects that he desired the most, the astrological and the religious, were not treated. According to Leon Blanchet one senses a cruel finality whereby the emerging specter of the new age brutally ignores, while moving beyond, the searching, yearning, perennial quests of a premodern humanity. And yet for all his astrological naivete and religious expectancy this same man happens to possess a profound sense of the immanence of the laws of nature, the infinity of the universe and its uniformity. If the nature of historical reality is best revealed in the compaction of ambiguities and incongruities impressed into an event, a decision, a man, then there is something forever appropriate that "the most enthusiastic disciple of Copernicus, the most valiant champion of the rights of science against a despotic intolerance routinely exercised and the most combative as well as the boldest of all Galileo's partisans and defenders" would prove to be our Calabrian prophet.[89]

In the period from September 1613 to October 1614 Campanella began drafting his immense *Theologia*, which would run to thirty books and not be

---

[88] Blanchet, *Campanella*, 247–52.
[89] Ibid., 253–55.

completed until 1624.[90] At the very beginning of book 1 he redefines the relationship between the two Codices, thereby pointing toward that principle of accommodation that will soon figure significantly in the *Apologia*:

> The first Codex, whence we obtain sacred knowledge, was the nature of things. But when this did not prove sufficient for us, as we on account of our sins are given over to ignorance and negligence, we required another Codex, more appropriate for us, although not better. For better is that one of nature, inscribed in living letters than that of Scripture written in dead letters, which are only signs, not things, as set forth in the earlier Codex. Nevertheless for the sake of our knowledge at least the Codex of divine Scripture is better because it is easier to understand, for it imparts to us, as to children, what has been concealed concerning God, in a certain human and child-like way comparable to a father speaking to his child in diminutive words and baby talk, as Origen shrewdly reminds us. Wherefore, says Augustine, [those] miracles by which God reveals himself to us in nature are more powerful than those read about in Scripture. For [His] government of the world is greater as is also the growth of much grain from a few seeds than with five loaves and two fishes for satisfying five thousand persons. But men marvel at what is rare, not what is great. I even consider the notion of the most holy Trinity to be more clearly evident in nature, especially intellectually perceived, than in sacred Scripture—in other words in accordance with its very being and not simply as we may happen to apprehend it [secundum se, non tamen secundum nos]. Nor have the angels learned from the preaching of the apostles what was shining in nature, but the counsel of God that had been concealed yet is known better in God's nature than in our Scripture.[91]

In what would appear to be continued juggling of the evidence from the two Codices or Books in order to achieve their conformity or agreement Campanella seems to grant preeminence as well as precedence to the first Book, that of nature. Yet while the new discoveries provided by the first Book would seem to dictate an interpretation of the second that would bring Scripture into conformity with nature, the entire intellectual enterprise is predicated on the underlying assumption and confidence that there can be no disagreement between the faith evoked by the second Book and the findings of the first Book.

In undertaking his *Apologia pro Galileo*, Campanella frames the defense as the response of a sort of theological consultant to Cardinal Caetani, charged to examine the conformity of the new astronomy with Scripture.[92] While ampli-

---

[90] *Tommaso Campanella: Teologia, Libro prima*, ed. Romano Amerio (Milan, 1936), introduzione, xiii–xiv.

[91] Ibid., 17–18.

[92] TC-*Lett.*, 179–80. On the origin of the treatise previously entitled *Apologeticus pro Galileo* and the controversy raised by Salvatore Femiano that it was composed before rather than, as Firpo argues, after the condemnation of March 5, 1616, see Bernardino M. Bonansea, *Campanella's*

fying some of the arguments previously established in his attack upon Aristotle, Campanella's defense does not appear except in one respect to push significantly beyond *On Gentilism*. As his arguments tumble out and are reiterated they come to cluster about three themes: the impelling quest for more knowledge and truth as something peculiarly distinctive of the Christian religion; a mobilization of patristic texts in support of same; and the ongoing organization of knowledge in accordance with the image of the two Books as a further means of promoting the first of these themes—*libertas philosophandi*.

A preliminary sampling of Campanella's argument suggests the interweaving of these themes. To forbid Christians the study of philosophy and the search for knowledge is to forbid them to be Christians, for there is no need to fear what is false.[93] He would appear to extend fearlessly the philosopher's examination by reason and experiment to the dogmas of Christian doctrine. Harmonization of the two Books can also be achieved through a reinterpretation of Scriptures, for Lateran V has said that the works of God do not contradict God.[94] The world as the wisdom of God is a book in which we may read all things. Anaxagoras said that man was made that he might view the heavens.[95] He is endowed with a natural longing, which tells us that more truth may always be discovered.[96] Thus they are mad who believe that Aristotle constructed the true system of the heavens and that further inquiry should not be made.[97] For God has left the world to the disputes of men (Eccl. 3:11) and Christ taught the kingdom of heaven, not natural phenomena.[98] Every law or doctrine that forbids its followers to investigate nature should be suspected of falsehood. Truth does not contradict truth nor the created Book of God's wisdom contradict his revealed Book.[99] It is necessary for the glory of our religion that men may directly observe Christ and the wisdom of God. As stated in his *Atheism Conquered*, the approbation of science by Christianity may prove a great bond, further incorporating men into the Church of God. It

---

Defense of Galileo in Reinterpreting Galileo, in *Studies in Philosophy and the History of Philosophy*, ed. William A. Wallace (Washington, D.C., 1986), 15:205–39, esp. 206–14. I have followed here as before (chap. 2, n. 305, *supra*) Femiano.

[93] The 1622 edition of the *Apologia pro Galileo* has been reprinted under Luigi Firpo's editorship in Campanella's *Opera Latina: Francofurti impressa annis 1617–1630* (Turin, 1975), 1:[475]–532, repaginated as 3–58, here at p. 13. The first English translation of the *Apologia* by Grant McColley, *The Defense of Galileo of Thomas Campanella* (New York, 1937/1976), has proved unreliable in places and most recently been replaced by Richard J. Blackwell's *A Defense of Galileo* (Notre Dame/London, 1994).

[94] TC-*Apol.*, 14. In his reliance on 'Apostolici regiminis' of Lateran V, sess. viii, Campanella leans heavily on its statement "Cumque verum vero minime contradicat," in *COD*, 581.

[95] TC-*Apol.*, 16.
[96] Ibid., 19.
[97] Ibid.
[98] Ibid., 21.
[99] Ibid.,23.

redounds to the glory of the Christian religion to permit the study of finding new sciences and of renewing old ones.[100]

Before further examination of the *Apologia* it would be useful to recognize a remarkable parallelism between the several arguments advanced by Campanella and Galileo's own contemporaneous *Letter to the Grand Duchess Christina*: not only the general appeal to the supporting witness of the Fathers but the sharp, explicit appeal to *libertas philosophandi* and the growing recognition of two distinct areas for human knowledge—the physical world and Scripture—which distinction Campanella will express by resort to the significant image of the two Books.[101] If it were not for the clarity and prominence of these arguments one might well attribute their source to a common intellectual currency at the time, which, except perhaps for the image of the two Books, still somehow has escaped the attention of intellectual historians. A second line of explanation presents itself: the charged atmosphere of the moment generated in the minds of each opponent of Aristotle by a sort of independent, spontaneous combustion a common set of ideas. The final alternative remains that of one borrowing this set of arguments together with its conclusion that the Church stood in imminent danger of catastrophic embarrassment, if it chose to close the door on the new science. In short, who is looking over whose shoulder?

Although the composition of Galileo's famous letter occurs in 1615, thus predating by almost a year Campanella's *Apologia* written in San Elmo, during February 1616, the first does not see print until 1636 at Strassburg; the second appeared through the loving care of Campanella's Lutheran disciple, Tobias Adami, in Frankfurt in 1622.[102] It is impossible to surmise to what extent Campanella in his bubbling enthusiasm might have glutted Galileo with his emerging arguments in that lost letter to the Florentine, written during the summer of 1613 and referred to in his second surviving letter.[103] And of course by way of Cardinal Caetani and Prince Cesi Campanella had had the *Apologia* forwarded to Galileo in September 1616.[104] However, another alternative remains for possible Campanellan sources for the Galilean letter: *On Gentilism* provides some materials for the patristic argument and for elaborations on the theme of the two Books. With its initial composition in 1609–10 and first publication in 1636, meanwhile subject to interpolations and addi-

---

[100] Ibid., 38.

[101] On the image of the two Books, see Ernst Robert Curtius, *European Literature and the Latin Middle Ages*, trans. Willard B. Trask (New York, 1953), 302–47, esp. 319–26; and more specifically for the Renaissance, E. Garin, "La nuova scienza e il simbolo del libro," in his *La cultura filosofica del Rinascimento italiano* (Florence, 1979), 451–65.

[102] Drake, *Discoveries*, 171; Antonio Corsano, "Campanella e Galileo," *GCFI* 44 (1965): 313–32 esp. 318–19; cf. LF-*Bibl.*, 72.

[103] TC-*Lett.*, 176; LF-*Bibl.*, 239, no. 243.

[104] TC-*Lett.*, 179–80; *Op. GG*, XII, 277, 287; cf. Bonansea, n. 92, *supra*.

tions, *On Gentilism* in its published form hardly presents the most certain evidence. Nevertheless, after being with Campanella in Naples for eight months (August 1612 to early April 1613), in order to communicate with Campanella in an exchange of over one hundred letters, Adami had been entrusted with a copy of *On Gentilism*. By mid-May he had entered into familiar discourse with Galileo in Florence.[105] Is it possible that the enthusiasm of Campanella's most loyal disciple might have awakened in Galileo sufficient curiosity to deign its consultation?

If there is any influence and it is in the direction of Campanella to Galileo, it needs to be principally examined in terms of the last two arguments and in light of their shared opposition to Aristotle: the potential link through the patristic argument is too general and could well have been arrived at independently by Galileo. Apart from what might have been communicated earlier by the letter in the summer of 1613 or by cues present in *On Gentilism*, suffice it to indicate that both anti-Aristotelians recognize the diffidence of the Fathers in the extension of the Bible to the physical universe, the flexibility of their exegesis, and of course the principle of accommodation, whereby the words of Scripture are to be understood metaphorically in keeping with the capacity of the vulgar.[106] As we might expect from the author of *On Gentilism* Campanella goes beyond the subtleties of patristic exegesis to enlist the theological positions of the Fathers in support of Galileo and in opposition to Aristotle.

The cause of Copernicanism was rapidly promoting and transforming itself into the even larger issue of the freedom of thought. Expectably this transformation is again more evident with the expansive Calabrian rebel than with the disciplined mathematician. Indeed Campanella has been credited with being probably the first known person to use the phrase *libertas philosophandi*, appearing now in the *Apologia*,[107] the first reasoned argument to be published in support of the freedom of scientific investigation. Here it appears as the more forceful expression of a theme only slightly earlier articulated in the preface to book I of his *Theology*: "sapientia quaerit libertatem animi."[108] Yet earlier cases exist and premonitions evidenced principally and most significantly by Galileo himself, who in his work on floating bodies (1612), will allow "che'l filosofare vuol esser libero," to be repeated in a letter of the following year, and then decisively asserted in the *Letter to the Grand Duchess Christina*, where he deliberately opposed those that block "la strada al libero filosofare circa le cose del mondo e della Natura."[109]

---

[105] LF-*Bibl.*, 110; also his "Tobia Adami e la fortuna del Campanella in Germania," in *Storia e cultura del mezzogiorno: Studi in memoria di Umberto Caldora* (Cosenza, 1978), 77–118, esp. 92–93.

[106] I am here following Drake's translation of Galileo's "Letter" in *Discoveries*, 173–216, esp. 181, 185–87, 198–99, 201, 204; TC-*Apol.*, 22–23.

[107] Ibid., 27.

[108] TC-*T*, I, 10.

[109] R. B. Sutton, "The Phrase *libertas philosophandi*," *JHI* 14 (1953): 310–16, esp. 311,

A more careful examination of the passage and its context reveals that Galileo is here taking conscious issue with Ecclesiastes 3:11, where according to the Vulgate reading "cuncta fecit bona in tempore suo et mundum tradidit disputationi eorum."[110] In keeping with the apparent intent of the entirety of Ecclesiastes, and particularly with this passage, traditional exegetes read the pericope as a dismissal of all human learning about the natural world and the vanity of all knowledge.[111] Galileo's attention would have been drawn to this important, if troublesome, passage by his just having read that astonishing support for the heliocentric view of the universe coming from Naples in the recently published (late winter, 1615) *Letter* of Paolo Antonio Foscarini, a twice appointed provincial of the Carmelite order in Calabria; explosive as the *Letter* proved in leading directly to the Congregation of the Index's condemnation of Copernicanism on March 5, 1616, Foscarini's actual treatment of Ecclesiastes 3:11 remained thoroughly traditional and conservative.[112] In his own *Letter to the Grand Duchess*, which now for good reason would not see publication until 1636 and then in northern Europe, Galileo seems to go out of his way, ostentatiously meeting the passage's admonition head on in order to reject and as if to flout its apparent intent. Is it possible that he was encouraged to do so by the earlier awareness that the passage could be subverted, removed from its moorings, and revolutionized in order to be read not simply as an invitation, but as a trumpet call, to inquiry of the physical world? Admittedly, Galileo was not a person inclined to identify or hearken to trumpet calls, but he had a distant admirer who seemed to be devoting his life not only to identifying trumpet calls but to ringing bells.

---

attributes its first clear use to Campanella, although since the turn of the century the phrase seems to have achieved sudden currency. Hilary Gatti, *The Renaissance Drama of Knowledge* (London/New York, 1989), 34, cites the case of Thomas Harriot writing to Kepler in the first decade of the new century ("I cannot philosophize freely, for here we still stick in the mud") and suggests Giordano Bruno as a likely early candidate. Indeed in his "Oratio valedictoria" to the University of Wittenberg's professors given March 8, 1588, Bruno significantly urges "ut paterimini philosophicam libertatem." *Jordani Bruni Nolani Opera Latine Conscripta* (Stuttgart, 1962) I/1, 23.

[110] Douai-Rheims renders the passage rather tamely: "He hath made all things good in their time and hath delivered the world to their consideration, so that man cannot find out the work which God hath made from the beginning to the end." Galileo himself presents the pericope exactly as in the Vulgate reading (*Op. GG*, V, 320).

[111] *The Interpreter's Bible* (5:21, 46) credits Ecclesiastes 3:11 with being the most difficult passage of the most difficult book of the Old Testament. Much of the difficulty arises from the Vulgate's awkward translation of the very passage at issue—"mundum tradit disputationi eorum"—which is perpetuated by Douai-Rheims translating *disputatio* as "consideration." Here the King James is much nearer to the literal vitality of the original Hebrew: "he hath set the world in their heart"; likewise Luther, for whom God has given the world to man for his use but not for his measuring (*WA*, 20:62–64). For further annotation bearing on the patristic and scholastic exegesis of this pericope, see the present author's forthcoming article in *Bruniana e Campanelliana* 2 (1996): 165–77.

[112] Richard J. Blackwell, *Galileo, Bellarmine, and the Bible*: Including a Translation of Foscarini's *Letter on the Motion of the Earth* (Notre Dame/London, 1991), 87–90, 233.

Whereas Galileo had evidently lifted the verse out of a printed Vulgate, Campanella, who appeals not once but four times to the heart of the passage ("handed over to the disputes of men") has so appropriated its import as to make it—on his own terms, of course—integral to his total intellectual position and a summons to free investigation. Indeed when he first uses this evidence for God's assignment of affairs, he characteristically misattributes it to Ecclesiastes 1 rather than Ecclesiastes 3.[113] Furthermore his own scholastic formation inevitably would have responded positively to the crucial word *disputationi*, understood as serious logical examination and exposition according to long-established university practice and not as idle consideration, vain argumentation, and probable contention as the rhetorical/devotional tradition of exegesis would have it.[114] Hence for Campanella *disputatio*, especially as it is explicated by verbs connoting investigation, can be better read here as "inquiry," although in a scholastic-empiricist rather than in a scientific sense. Despite the internal scholastic and academic developments in the exegesis of the pericope, Campanella's own native boldness now takes the final and fateful step in radicalizing the understanding of the passage.

In the first appearance of "God left the world to the inquiry of men," the passage has been wrested from the grip of the pericope's succeeding statement: "so that man cannot find out the work that God hath made." But the matter does not rest there. Campanella has replaced this negative announcement with the locus classicus for all natural theology in the Christian tradition, Romans 1:20: "so that the invisible things of God may be intellectually perceived through those things He has made."[115] In case we believe our eyes to be deceived, Campanella will repeat the same legerdemain of cropping and

---

[113] TC-*Apol.*, 13. In his critical edition with Italian translation, *Apologia di Galileo* (Turin, 1968), 20, the usually faultless Luigi Firpo follows Campanella in the error of identifying the crucial passage of the Ecclesiastes 3:11 pericope—"mundum tradidit disputationi eorum"—as Ecclesiastes 1:13. It is easy enough to make this mistake as the thought in both passages is the same and the same word *adflictio* is used at Eccl. 1:14 and 3:10 so that the passages bleed into each other: Ecclesiastes 1:14—"vidi quae fiunt cuncta sub sole et ecce universa vanitas et adflictio spiritus"; Ecclesiastes 3:10—"vidi adflictionem quam dedit Deus filiis hominum ut distendantur."

[114] On the centrality of the *disputatio* in the medieval universities, see Hastings Rashdall, *The Universities of Europe in the Middle Ages*, new edition (Oxford, 1951), 1:490–6 *passim*. Like any word *disputatio* is ambiguous, fraught with negative as well as positive connotations. Certainly, however, the Latin oratorical tradition was sensitive to the negative overtones as particularly manifest in Seneca and Quintilian, for which see my forthcoming article in *BeC*. Such examples only begin to suggest the rich rhetorical background to the negative understanding of *disputatio* available to St. Jerome and company in the fourth century.

[115] Romans, 1:19–20—"Deus enim illis manifestavit (20) invisibilia enim ipsius a creatura mundi per ea quae facta sunt intellecta conspiciuntur sempiterna quoque eius virtus et divinitas ut sint inexcusabiles." As TC-*Apol.*, 13 reads "ut invisibilia Dei per ea quae facta sunt, intellecta conspicerent," a slight deviation from the Vulgate, I have been encouraged here not to follow Douai-Rheims.

splinting in the interests of the Book of Nature at the second instance of his use of Ecclesiastes 3:11, although the German printer has failed to catch the passage by italicizing the recently wedded pericopic fragments.[116] What for over a millennium had been a closed door now swings invitingly open. Campanella thus demarcates a realm of human intellectual endeavor different from the spiritual doctrine provided by Moses and Christ but pertaining rather to astronomy and natural philosophy. Such a position figures as a major guideline for his entire argumentation and from the outset serves to define the respective areas of the two Books. The subsequent point regarding the distinctive feature of the Christian being the search for knowledge serves to secure its operation.[117]

The second and third appearances of the passage occur close together and serve to develop the same point:

> In the beginning God left the world to the inquiry of men, so that they might labor and learn of God by the things He had made. He gave us a rational mind so that we might inquire, and as St. Clement interprets the Apostle Peter, he disclosed methods of investigation by the five senses. These are as windows through which man beholds the world, the image of God. As Chrysostom on Psalm 147 and others declare, man then admires what is found in it, and seeks God the artist. . . . It is well known that Moses does not prescribe bounds to human knowledge, and that God did not instruct him in either natural science [*physiologiam*] or astronomy. Solomon says that God left the world to the inquiry of men, and that he himself diligently investigated all things. Nor did he read from the book of Moses but rather from nature. Indeed, when Moses spoke of heaven and earth and of all things in the creation, he described their superficial aspects, and how they serve the lawgiver rather than the natural philosopher [*physiologo*].[118]

With the fourth instance he manages to deliver over to the jurisdiction of the Book of Nature a fair measure of interpretation regarding its counterpart, Scripture:

> Indeed, God left the world, his first Scripture, to the inquiry of men, and within the limits prescribed by the Church, also left to the inquiry of the wise variant meanings of his second Scripture. So Christ, the incarnate wisdom of God (as Origen taught), man himself among the ignorant and the young, prophet among teachers, displayed God to spiritual men. The world is wisdom in material form, and shows us more as we have more capacity.[119]

---

[116] TC-*Apol.*, 21.
[117] Ibid., 13–14.
[118] Ibid., 21–22. The attribution of Ecclesiastes as well as Proverbs and the Canticle to Solomon derives from the patristic tradition and ultimately Origen. See Beryl Smalley, *Medieval Exegesis of Wisdom Literature* (Atlanta, 1986), 40.
[119] TC-*Apol.*, 41. Except for the decisive change of "disputes" to "inquiry" I have chosen to

Campanella's peculiar understanding of the cropped pericope serves to promote both an expansive and a discrete view of man's intellectual destiny but on balance ultimately more expansive than discrete.

The friar's expansive view of human knowledge would make even his contemporary Francis Bacon sweat: knowledge of the heavens and of the earth has not yet been perfected;[120] man's "natural longing, which teaches us more truth always may be discovered. When we inquire concerning celestial things, we inquire of God, for whom we are commanded ever to search. Paul admonishes the Athenians that we are obligated to seek, for we always learn more and thus are made a little more like God";[121] "God always reveals new truths";[122] the Christian has the power to advance in knowledge beyond Plato and any other;[123] "wisdom should be sought in the whole book of God, which is the world, where more truth always may be discovered;"[124] "it is an essential part of the glory of the Christian religion to permit the study of finding new sciences and of renovating the old;"[125] "it is pleasing to God for man to philosophize in his book . . . [nor] in vain to inquire concerning the heavens, but that such inquiry is useful to demonstrate the glory of God and to enlarge both faith in the divinity and the immortality of the human soul."[126]

Such a massive assertion of *libertas philosophandi* in the interests of humankind's expanding knowledge of God and His work draws with it in subordinate function the witness of the Fathers from the Church's beginnings down to St. Bernard and St. Thomas and the discrete apportionment of the intellectual enterprise offered by the image of the two Books.

In short the *Apologia pro Galileo* is not to be read as an affirmation of Copernicanism, something that Campanella never completely accepted: as a scholastic product the book simply examined both sides of the issue and suggested a preference for the new doctrines of Galileo and company as more congruent than Aristotelianism with the Christian tradition. Rather the work is an affirmation of *libertas philosophandi*—an argument promoted by a significantly cropped pericope within the structure of the concept of the two Books. Moreover, it is worth noting that possibly its very first reader, Campanella's disciple, P. G. Failla, immediately grasped the arresting point, therein ad-

---

remain with the McColley translation (pp. 25, 26, 52), barring a few minor changes, rather than shift to the better and most recent Blackwell translation. My purpose in doing so seeks to accent the fact that Blackwell has independently confirmed my interpretation of *disputationi* by translating this word as "investigation" (pp. 65, 66, 97), although he makes nothing of what I consider here to be an important change.

[120] Ibid., 13.
[121] Ibid., 19.
[122] Ibid., 20.
[123] Ibid.
[124] Ibid., 25.
[125] Ibid., 26.
[126] Ibid., 53.

vanced, that to forbid Christians the study of philosophy and the search for knowledge would forbid them to be Christians.[127] Campanella argues that it is more desirable to harmonize one interpretation of Scripture with philosophy and dismiss the discordant interpretation. He applies that relationship between the two Books affirmed in his *Theologia* two years before, that the Book of Scripture enjoys a flexibility of interpretation and thus can give way to the findings in the Book of Nature as possessing superior evidence. And in keeping with his understanding of Lateran V human knowledge does not oppose the divine nor the works of God contradict God.[128] Pursuant to Ecclesiastes 3:11 Solomon recognizes that Moses speaks in accordance with the legislator, pertaining to religion and not for the philosopher. Likewise all the Fathers readily perceive this popular manner of speech and are seen as making allowance for Moses' method of accommodating his books to the capacity of the people.[129] Campanella invokes his readers to seek ever more wisdom in God's great Codex of the world and not the codicils of men that the sacred writers remit to us.[130] Only once does he indicate that the resort to other senses of Scripture in order to achieve harmony between the two Books is not a totally free process, involving endless adjustments on the part of Scripture to ever-new human discoveries in the Book of Nature: rather it remains "intra tamen ecclesiae limites."[131] It is within this apparatus of interpretation and accommodation that Campanella will prefer the new doctrines of Galileo and company as more congruent than Aristotelianism with the Christian tradition.

When compared with Galileo's treatment of the Two books or intellectual jurisdictions (nature and scripture) as presented in the contemporaneous *Letter to the Grand Duchess Christina*, Campanella's handling of the matter certainly appears the more aggressive and ambitious, although within an essentially traditional, conservative, medieval/Renaissance context. Given his characteristic enthusiasm for innovation and the profound dynamic within his own thought that drives toward an all-inclusive monism, both now lent themselves to his argument in a way that threatened the engulfment of Scripture by nature. Little wonder that the *Apologia pro Galileo* was promptly suppressed on arrival in Rome. Galileo's handling of the two types of knowledge is expectably more circumspect, controlled, limited, if only because his implicit challenge to the interpretative authority of the Church proves more immediately explosive. In the *Letter to the Grand Duchess Christina* he draws attention to what had become since the fourth session of the Council of Trent a progressively literalistic interpretation of Scripture: everything mentioned in Scripture was rapidly coming by the first decade of the seventeenth century to be taken as *de*

[127] *Op. GG*, XII, 277.
[128] TC-*Apol.* 14–15.
[129] Ibid., 22–23.
[130] Ibid., 25.
[131] Ibid., 41.

fide, thus creating a disastrous inflexibility in the interpretation of Scripture and an unnecessary heightening of the Church's authority to a maximum vulnerability. How embarrassing that a layman, Galileo, should have to alert churchmen as to their departure from the Church's own Augustinian/patristic tradition of exegesis with the result that Scripture has become overextended into the realm of physical nature where theology does not belong.[132] It thus becomes a matter of clarifying jurisdictions and recognizing what is appropriate to each.[133] Galileo's success lies in the seemingly conservative nature of his aims, his appeal to traditional sources, and his respect for a viable dualism, readjusted. Both violate the current interpretative authority of the church in matters of Scripture but Galileo as layman more outrageously than Campanella. While the contrasts between our two opponents of current Aristotelianism are as usual greater than the similarities, both will clearly warn their clerical readers that ignoring or suppressing the new scientific discoveries could well lead to later embarrassment for the Church.[134]

In concluding his defense Campanella identifies in Galileo's new discoveries the renewal of an ancient and most esteemed philosophy. Advancing the new myth, attributed to Ambrose, that Pythagoras was a Jew and the Hebrew race originated at Samos, Campanella reminds us that the great Calabrian philosopher had fashioned all things by numbers, weight, and measurement,[135] and that he announced to the Gentiles his splendid doctrine of the earth's motion, the centrality of the sun, and a plurality of systems in the heavens. In an apparent effort to launder the sources and harmonize the Books he claims that Galileo and Empedocles got their doctrine from the Jews via the Pythagoreans. With Galileo therefore we now have a reassertion of ancient Pythagorean doctrine but on the basis of valid sensory observation.[136]

In meeting his obligation to present the arguments against Galileo, Campanella finds it necessary to confess that he fails to understand how the destruction of scriptural authority will follow from the doctrine of Galileo.[137] Yet when he put down his pen and addressed the manuscript to the attention of Cardinal Bonifacio Caetani, he knew that the battle was lost. He had already observed that the failure on the part of the Church to act, by diligently seeking to harmonize the new discoveries with the traditional doctrine, would only lead to the immediate embarrassment of Catholicism. From his cell Cam-

---

[132] Blackwell, *Galileo*, 84, 102–5.
[133] Drake, *Discoveries*, "Letter to Grand Duchess Christina," 179–83, 186–87, 200–201. Elsewhere, in another context Galileo will be more forceful in suggesting that Scripture will need to conform to the domain of nature and God's work. See Paolo Rossi, "Galileo Galilei e il libro del salmi," *RF* 69 (1978): 54–71, esp. 63–64.
[134] TC-*Apol.*, 29, 58; Drake, *Discoveries*, "Letter," 206–9.
[135] *Sapientia* (Wisdom) 11:21.
[136] TC-*Apol.*, 56–58.
[137] Ibid., 55.

panella noted that Galileo's hypothesis and the telescope had been avidly accepted by many in Germany, France, England, Poland, Denmark, and Sweden and that the heretics would turn the new philosophy to their own ends.[138] He correctly sensed that some responsible parties within the Church were not doing their homework and that a great misfortune was about to occur.[139] Either oblivious to the crisis or complacent in the weight of their own authority, they pulled ever more closely around them the reassuring cloak of Aristotelianism, unaware that it could turn into a shroud. The ultimate irony emerging from the controversy is that it required the perception of a man already withdrawn from society for fifteen years with a decade more of imprisonment still to suffer, a man literally buried alive in the bottommost pit of Christendom, to sound the alarm as to the catastrophe that would soon befall the Catholic world, affecting it for the next three centuries.

In the more immediate context of Campanella's controversy with Aristotle and his championship of Galileo, he seems further removed from the new science than from the reviled Aristotelianism. For his part Galileo, in opposing all current philosophers and in conscious hostility toward the contemporary pursuit of philosophy, finds himself unable to ally with the only one of the philosophers who hastens now to his defense.[140] As in his preceding letters in the present defense Campanella's explosive mind reads immense implications into Galileo's work, now arguing for a Neopythagoreanism, now pursuing the possibility of new worlds and their inhabitants.[141] But it is their apparent convergence on the concept of the two Books that serves most to distinguish them: not only is there a different apportionment of intellectual jurisdictions but more decisively there is an inevitably different understanding and construction of the Book of Nature, as already evident in their opposing types of empiricism. Within the Campanellan system the two jurisdictions, nature and Scripture, tend toward a monistic comprehensiveness; within the Galilean the future lay with their increasing distinction and removal from each other.

The apparent association of Campanella and Galileo proves deceptive; their differences, fateful and revealing. On the anvil of a common, broadly shared rejection of current Aristotelianism had unwittingly been hammered out the great divide between the late Renaissance magical/astral view of the physical world and the modern empirical/mathematical view. Amidst Campanella's ebullient exhortations, praise, speculations, Galileo for good reason kept his distance.

[138] Ibid., 29–30.
[139] Ibid., 58.
[140] On Galileo and the philosophers with Campanella as the sole, ambiguous exception, see Stillman Drake, *Galileo against the Philosophers* (Los Angeles, 1976), xi–xv, 136.
[141] TC-*Apol.*, 50–52.

Chapter V

THE CONTROVERSY WITH MACHIAVELLI: ON THE REARMING OF HEAVEN

AFTER ARISTOTLE the single greatest intellectual antagonist of Campanella was Niccolò Machiavelli. Although Campanella was born forty years after the author of *The Prince* had died, he experienced a dramatic encounter with some of the immortal remains of his future archenemy. Campanella reports of going to Florence in October 1592 in the hope of some university appointment: Grand Duke Ferdinand I had given him permission to be escorted by the librarian Baccio Valori through the Laurentian, one of the first libraries of Europe, and, to the young Dominican, a treasury of learning that surpassed the much-vaunted library of the Ptolemies in Alexandria. In the course of the tour Valori at one point took the intent visitor back to a secluded treasure chamber, where the most precious codices and manuscripts were kept. There Campanella tells of being shown the books of Machiavelli written in his own hand, and, as the librarian proceeded to regale him with an inaccurate biography of their writer, the already hunted friar stared down upon the manuscript books of the *Florentine History*.[1] During his long life our aspiring world reformer would have cause to reflect upon this encounter.[2]

Whatever the profound differences and opposition distinguishing the relationship between Tommaso Campanella and Niccolò Machiavelli, their strong affinities and even identity of interests most impressed contemporaries. Despite all his disclaimers Campanella only managed further to convince his readers regarding this identity. In his immediately subsequent surviving letters, again to Grand Duke Ferdinand, written two months later, Campanella will recommend himself to the prince as a political expert and one whose special knowledge can only enhance the Tuscan potentate's esteem and power.[3] And in his most expressly anti-Machiavellian work, the notorious *Atheism Conquered*, which announced his antipathy in its original title, Campanella would only confirm the belief of many in his own and subsequent generations that he was himself both Machiavellian and atheist[4]—in fact a

[1] TC-*RC*, 53–54.
[2] Cf. TC-*Lett.*, 4–5; 388–89.
[3] Ibid., 7.
[4] Andrzej Nowicki, "Gli incontri tra Vanini e Campanella," in *Tommaso Campanella (1568–1639): Miscellanea di studi nel 4° centenario della sua nascita* (Naples, 1969), 473–85.

"Second Machiavel" to his second English editor.[5] Yet this very curious relationship to the cunning Florentine seemed to be a disease of the age. Two decades earlier Christopher Marlowe in the *Jew of Malta* had allowed his Machiavel to say: "Admir'd I am of those that hate me most." And Gabriel Naudé, Campanella's friend and advocate, remarks that Machiavelli's doctrines are practiced by those who forbid them to be spread; to distrust all and dissimulate with each as he advises will become the prescription for effective conduct in this Tacitean age.[6] In short the relationship between the two apostles of guile was nothing if not ambiguous and complex.

It seems almost superfluous to rehearse here a subject that has been so beautifully treated by Friedrich Meinecke in one of the more memorable chapters of his classic *Machiavellism*. And yet for all its virtues Meinecke's effort to resolve the apparent enigma of Campanella's lifelong struggle with the idea of *ragion di stato* fails to get to the nub of the matter. Only at one point does his inquiry engage the question of religion as understood by the two combatants but without pursuing it to a possible resolution.[7] And it is upon the issue of religion that we need to focus our attention. In fairness to Meinecke it should be noted that our inquiry is concerned less with the rival uses of *ragion di stato* by the two political thinkers than with the relationship of religion to politics for each.

Italian scholarship on the subject of our present controversy seems nearer the mark when it observes that for Campanella Machiavelli represented not simply a political doctrine but a general conception of the world that has its distant roots in pagan philosophy (designated as Gentilism) and its more recent associations with Renaissance Averroism and libertinism. For when Campanella claims that Machiavellism derives from Aristotelianism, he means far more than what had become a virtual commonplace by 1600; namely, that Machiavelli had modeled his prince upon the tyrant of Aristotle appearing in the *Politics*, book 5. Rather to Campanella Machiavellism meant an all too broad intellectual current, a cultural phenomenon that indeed was taking its toll upon Campanella himself. Machiavelli's beckoning of his generation to the *verità effettuale della cosa* had by the end of the sixteenth century broadened in its implications to involve a sharpened appreciation of the concrete, a tireless scrutiny of political and social phenomena, a *sapientia humana*, all contributing to the new autonomy of politics. Indeed the terrible, haunting vision of an orphaned world continued to obtrude itself, never completely to be suppressed

---

[5] LF-*Bibl.*, 65–66.

[6] See Roman Schnur, *Individualismus und Absolutismus. Zur politischen Theorie vor Thomas Hobbes, 1600–1640* (Berlin, 1963), 53, 77, for these references.

[7] Friedrich Meinecke, *Machiavellism: The Doctrine of Raison d'Etat and Its Place in Modern History* (New Haven, 1957), 98. Besides Meinecke's, other important treatments of this same subject can be found in Rodolfo De Mattei, *La politica di Campanella* (Rome, 1928), 148–66; and the less well known but valuable work of D'Addio, *Scioppio*, 358–80.

or thrust aside. *Atheism Conquered* can be seen as directed against its own author and as assuming the nature of an interior colloquy, thus implicitly making something of Machiavelli integral to Campanella.[8] While incongruities abound, similarities, even correspondences, glare.

Finally, by way of introduction, any effort to achieve a more precise understanding of Campanella's relationship to Machiavelli as well as his very indebtedness to the Florentine must penetrate beyond both the obvious, pronounced points of opposition and also the express points of correspondence and appropriation to the basic assumptions and different frames of reference that motivate the thought of each. Standing in contrast to the crisp, refreshing clarity of Machiavelli's analysis, the ambiguities, obscurities, and tensions characteristic of any baroque thinker suffer an abnormal accentuation in the tortuous existence of the Calabrian prophetic reformer, magus, and prisoner. If his social and political thought seems "to pull apart in opposite directions," if it undergoes an undeniable torquing,[9] there remains nevertheless throughout his work more than sufficient consistency, impelled by his consuming world vision, to warrant an examination of the present problem and its peculiar relevance to the period of the early seventeenth century—this *machiavellisticum saeculum*.[10]

Campanella's acquaintance with Machiavelli's works may well have extended beyond the *Prince* and the *Discourses* but only these are discernible in his own writings. Of course a dispassionate, impartial reading of *The Prince* was no more possible for Campanella's period than that of a comparably explosive work would be for our own: polemic and hearsay shaped his attitude. Campanella's controversy was as much with a Counter Reformation image of Machiavelli as it was with the political thinker himself. According to this image successful politics required freedom from traditional moral and religious principles. To the sixteenth century Machiavelli represented the teacher of evil, a vital commodity, for being evil proved more useful than being good.[11] The positive aspect of Machiavelli, his desire to promote civic virtue and public spirit, was quite lost on the imprisoned friar.

Campanella's formal effort to contend with the threat presented by *ragion*

---

[8] For this passage and the image of an "orphaned world," I am indebted to Giuliano Procacci, *Studi sulla fortuna del Machiavelli* (Rome, 1965), 45–77, 97–98, 106. Cf. also Giorgio Spini, *Ricerca dei libertini* (Florence, 1980).

[9] Joan Kelly-Gadol, "Tommaso Campanella: The Agony of Political Theory in the Counter Reformation," in *Philosophy and Humanism: Renaissance Essays in Honor of Paul Oskar Kristeller*, ed. Edward P. Mahoney (New York, 1976), 164–65.

[10] TC-*AP*, 89. Cf. Cecilia Dentice di Accadia, "Tomismo e Machiavellismo," *GCFI* 6 (1925): 1-16.

[11] Felix Gilbert, "Machiavellism," in *History: Choice and Commitment* (Cambridge, Mass./London, 1977), 158. Cf. TC-*AV*, 128: "La ragion di stato del Machiavello e dei politici consiste in due cose: una, amar solo se stesso e nullo altro al mondo, se non quanto è utile al nostro stato, ed uccidere senza riguardo ad ogni santo ed amico nostro, mentre non va a volontà nostra. L'altra è solo sapere l'istorie de' passati principi, o buoni, o rei, ed acquistar con l'esempio loro, a dritto o a torto, quel che potemo, con simulazioni ingannando gli amici e li nemici."

di stato to religion came in his *Atheism Conquered*. In its fundamental perception of Machiavellism as representing religion not being divinely endowed for all humans, but as a political function of *ragion di stato*, and in its firm attribution of this enormity to Aristotle and Averroes, the *AT* provides the portal for our inquiry into the prisoner's controversy with the notorious secretary.[12] Composed in the dreadful dungeon of San Elmo between April and July 1605, and written in Italian under the more revealing title of *The Philosophical Recognition of the True, Universal Religion against Antichristianism and Machiavellism*, this work first appeared in Rome in 1631 only to be suppressed by the censors.[13] By his melding of Machiavelli with an Averroistic Aristotelianism, which he represented as being diametrically opposed to his own rationalized, naturalistic Christianity, Campanella saw the Florentine to be more than a political menace: indeed he assumed the proportions of a total and most hostile view of reality. In his desperate efforts to get the book approved and republished by meeting the individual censures, Campanella comes forth with some of his most extreme and exaggerated statements against Machiavelli.

These responses to censured passages conduct us beyond Machiavellism and allow us to approach Campanella's Machiavelli. All the evils of the present age in political and religious matters, he argues, derive from Machiavelli's *ragion di stato*, which perceives all faith to be just so many conspiracies and arts of *statisti*.[14] Against the seventh censure Campanella has to explain his statement concerning the duke of Valentinois (Cesare Borgia); he says that he is writing against the *Prince* of Machiavelli who makes religion a craft of state and urges the prince to disregard veracity, oaths, and justice. On the contrary, Campanella wishes to prove that this is not the true art of state because all who have followed such a doctrine have lost *lo stato* and their lives as well. He then proceeds to prove this point with all the historical examples that Machiavelli used, including Valentinois, Cesare Borgia himself, as an example of a prince who lost both the state and his life.[15] Campanella would appear to be arguing, in the same vein as the current anti-Machiavellian moralists, that crime does not pay and that for the statesman honesty is the best policy and advantageous to the state.[16] He now becomes still more vituperative: it is well known how much evil Machiavelli has done to *Cristianità*, legitimating and even prescribing to all princes injustice, treachery, perjury,

---

[12] Tullio Gregory, "Aristotelismo e libertinismo," in *Aristotelismo veneto e scienza moderna* (Padua, 1983), 1:279–96, esp. 292, has here very well encapsulated the heart of the matter and situated it in a larger European context.

[13] LF-*Bibl.*, 101–2.

[14] TC-*RC*, 9.

[15] Ibid., 35.

[16] On the utility of moral virtue and religion for political success and state building, see Robert Bireley, S. J., *The Counter-Reformation Prince: Anti-Machiavellianism or Catholic Statecraft in Early Modern Europe* (Chapel Hill/London, 1990), and idem, "Antimachiavellism, the Baroque and Maximilian of Bavaria," *AHSI* 53 (1984): 139–40.

the killing of parents and of any who are suspected by the *stato politico*, all for purposes of personal self-aggrandizement on the part of the ruler and not in the interest of the community. Machiavelli makes a trifle of religion and claims that Christ, the prophets, and Campanella's fellow Dominican Savonarola preached only to acquire *lo stato* for themselves, as do all tyrants, but that through their ignorance of politics, not knowing how to arm themselves, these unarmed prophets were killed. To which Campanella retorts that the unarmed prophets obtain an empire over the minds of men through their deaths, while the armed prophets, like John of Leyden at Münster, only manage to get themselves and their states destroyed. To the censors the recently freed prisoner explains that he seeks to remove the esteem in which Machiavelli is held by the *politici* and *heretici*—as well as by the unknown author of the *Three Impostors*, earlier ascribed to Campanella himself. Campanella desires to explode the claim that Machiavelli was learned in the sciences and to reveal him as knowledgeable only in human histories and in the practice of perverted politics. On the very same grounds that Machiavelli would be most appreciated by the modern age, namely, his sense of the concrete, the historical, the experiential, and his basing of politics upon human history and experience, Campanella now takes violent issue, for here human cunning becomes *jus politiae*.[17]

In conveying a further, somewhat more specifically political measurement of his enemy, Campanella addresses the issue of the Machiavellian ethos of power as it relates to political performance in his own day and what we have come to associate with the practices of the emerging absolute state. Struck by the increasing omnipresence of the political dimension, Campanella avers: "All the actions of men are directed to the state (*regnum*), as there is nothing that man does not do for its sake, since every prince transgresses religion and virtue, as they say for *ragion di stato*, because domination compensates one for all evils." Thus Machiavelli can praise the wickedness of Cesare Borgia and Agathocles; to which Campanella objects that virtues are in conformity with nature and vices counter to it, and princes who violate religion and nature are ultimately the most unfortunate and condemned before God. Drawing closer to the political events of his own day, Campanella observes that religion, which should direct men to God, is abused for purposes of ruling and that princes change religion in accordance with the greater political utility, as is frequently evinced these days in Germany. Campanella entertains the ideas that the Spaniards occupy the kingdoms of the new hemisphere for political gain, although under the pretext of religion, while a king of France for similar reasons will abjure his sectarian beliefs. Operating within the scholastic framework of the *quaestio*, he soon counters so as to refute these last two

---

[17] TC-*RC*, 38–39, 51–52; on Campanella's perception of the specifically historical in Machiavelli's impact, see TC-*AT*, 85, 162–63.

observations—yet doubts will inevitably remain. To the statesmen and Machiavellists of his day Campanella says: unless at the outset they believe God to exist, to exercise His Providence and to recompense us, by no means are we able to dispute with them. For who will dispute with the insane? Thus religion, however much embattled, is inescapably fundamental to the politics and the political consciousness of Campanella's thought.[18]

At this time the term "religion" was undergoing a number of significant transformations in meaning. Traditionally associated with the life of the monastic orders, the term less prominently referred to a worshipful attitude, a genuine fear or love of God, a personal engagement with God, first defined by Augustine and most recently expressed by some of the Protestant Reformers.[19] With the Reformation, however, had come a confessionalism, a bitter hostility between two religions which by the middle of the sixteenth century had made explicit what had long been threatening: religion becomes pluralized and reified; "a religion" begins to signify an assemblage of practices and beliefs, expressing a complex external reality distinct from its previous definitions. By the early seventeenth century a polemical work has for its title *Calvinismus bestiarum religio*: from a polemical context the age of the "isms" had emerged.[20] Yet within Italy itself such an important transformation in the understanding of the notion did not have to wait for the Reformation. Since the thirteenth century a primitive sociology of religions had been nursed at the University of Padua. There a heterodox form of Artistotelianism understood religion as *lex*, ushered in by an astral cycle, established by a *legifer*, and supported by a suitable allotment of miracles. Indeed Paduan Averroism had come to look upon religions as social and even naturalistic phenomena subject to growth, efflorescence, and decay. Crudely expressed, religion at its best served as necessary social/political cement. From the early fourteenth century with Pietro d'Abano to Pietro Pomponazzi in the early sixteenth century, Padua harbored a distinct tradition that makes more understandable Machiavelli's ability to consider religion as an object of thought and a human phenomenon.[21] Indeed in his political conception of religion Machiavelli repre-

---

[18] While these passages are to be found in Campanella's not readily available *Quaestiones super secunda parte suae Philosophiae realis Quae est ethicorum* (Paris: Denis Houssaye, 1637), 1–2, 11–13, they have been extensively and accurately incorporated into the notes of D'Addio, *Scioppio*, 376–80, who uses them in a somewhat different sense from that presented here. For bibliographical information, see LF-*Bibl.*, 73–97, esp. 86–87, 94–95.

[19] Wilfred Cantwell Smith, *The Meaning and End of Religion* (New York, 1962), 28–44.

[20] Michel Despland, *La religion en Occident: Evolution des idées et du vécu* (Montreal, 1979), 227–30, 178, 292. However, Peter Biller, "Medieval Notions of Religion," *JEH* 36 (1985): 351–69, in criticizing John Bossy, "Some Elementary Forms of Durkheim," *PP* 95 (1982): 3–18 and indirectly Smith and Despland, suggests that the thirteenth century may have had the notion, if not the word, for the diversity of religions and their "reification" as external systems. Of the Paduans only Marsilius, in connection with *lex* and *secta*, is mentioned.

[21] On Averroism in general, see the article by M. M. Gorce in *Dictionnaire d'histoire et de*

sented only one aspect of a much larger development that had been in preparation for over two centuries and would continue to flow from its north Italian headwaters long after he had departed.[22]

Campanella stands among a growing number in the early seventeenth century seeking to redefine religion as something rooted in the rational capacity of all men and therefore natural. Religion is the natural *virtus* with which we are all endowed by God: it is the natural return to God and thus can never be an *arte di stato*.[23] Drawing on Stoic, Platonic, and Hermetic sources, he recognizes a universal rationality in humankind that serves as a preparation and basis for the overgrafting of Christ, who is seen in turn as the Primal Reason.[24] Campanella readily admits the multiplicity of religions, all of which are established by the decree of nature; but, in his view, only Christianity is established by supernature, thereby making that religion uniquely true.[25] In the current reshaping of science Campanella perceived a force which, by reinforcing and informing the Catholic religion, might decisively increase its possibilities for becoming not the religion of a special people but the religion of all.[26] In a certain way, however, he thinks that all peoples are potentially Christian when they profess to want to live according to reason; even not knowing Christ, they seek Him when they seek what is to be found practically (*de facto*) by the sole law of Christ. The world has one natural law in all peoples that no diversity can obliterate. Thomist that he is, Campanella can claim that this natural law is fulfilled and elevated by the supernatural law evident in Christ.[27] In Christianity alone, he concludes, the perfect rationality can be found.

The problem turns upon a controversy over the nature and purpose of religion. According to Campanella, Machiavelli transforms religion into a political art for retaining the people in hope of paradise and fear of hell.[28] It becomes a means of political manipulation, the cunning of friars and clergy

---

géographie ecclésiastiques, 5:1032–92. On Pietro d' Abano's astrology and his relating the rise and fall of religions and kingdoms to the revolution of the eighth sphere of the fixed stars, see Lynn Thorndike, *A History of Magic and Experimental Science* (New York, 1923), 2:882–99; idem, "Franciscus Florentinus, or Paduanus," in *Mélanges Mandonnet* (Paris, 1930), 2:353–69. More recent studies, focusing on method, are of course those of John Herman Randall Jr., *The School of Padua and the Emergence of Modern Science* (Padua, 1961); "Paduan Aristotelianism Reconsidered," in *Philosophy and Humanism: Renaissance Essays in Honor of Paul Oskar Kristeller*, ed. Edward P. Mahoney (New York, 1976), 275–82. On the astral-religious cycle, see Pietro Pomponazzi, *Opera* (Basel: Henricpetrina, 1567), 284–90; and chap. 2, n. 133.

[22] Spini, *Ricerca*, 23–32.
[23] TC-*Lett.*, 103, 192.
[24] TC-*AfP*, 34.
[25] TC-*AT*, 163.
[26] Nicola Badaloni, *Tommaso Campanella* (Milan, 1965), 269.
[27] TC-*AT*, 72–75; TC-*AP*, 135.
[28] TC-*Lett*. 66–69.

being applied to the rulers' domination of the people.[29] Referring to Melchior Cano's *Loci* 10, Campanella claims that the Florentine learned from Aristotle and more specifically from the Paduan Averroists among other prime heresies that religion is instrumental in the art of ruling.[30] Apparently horrified by Machiavelli's total subjection of religion to the principle of utility, the Calabrian prophet, gazing northward, sees that in those kingdoms the *politici* have made religion a suit or hat that can be changed at will. Yet while rejecting this Machiavellian view of politicized religion, Campanella himself affirms religion's political utility, although on a different basis. He insists that no community can last a day without religion;[31] in fact the social necessity of religion is axiomatic for Campanella.[32] As the very soul of the political, religion exercises a natural magic in uniting members of a community.[33] In the *Monarchia di Spagna* we learn that religion, whether true or false (*ò vera ò falsa*), possesses sovereign virtue commanding bodies, swords, and tongues, which are the instruments of empire.[34] Indeed he clearly appreciates the *utilitas* of religion in politics as a power over men's minds, when he observes that no ruler is able to establish and retain *imperium* unless he is truly sent and authorized by God or, at least, is *believed* to be. Religion thus provides the necessary glue binding men to God and subjects to their rulers *in causa imperandi*.[35] With Campanella the political uses of religion seem at times to strain perilously beyond whatever claims religion has to ultimate truth.

On points of detail and tactics he can also agree with Machiavelli:[36] never at a loss for effective resort to cunning acts of political advantage to the state, he can advocate the prompt annihilation of opposition—a measure that would have received the approval of Cesare Borgia.[37] Other Machiavellian moments recur, expressive of political cunning: the lettered, the intelligentsia, should be kept occupied in the study of nature, thereby diverted from such politically troubling matters as the study of theology and philology—a point that would be echoed two generations later by the founders of the Royal Society.[38] Or again so important is it for the papacy to have a well-stocked treasury that the Church would be well advised to raise money *sotto pretesto* of war against the Turk.[39]

[29] Ibid., 102.
[30] TC-*De gent.* (1636), 20; TC-*Lett.*, 66. For this passage in the 1637 version, see TC-*PR*[1], sig. ciii.
[31] TC-*AT*, 167.
[32] Ibid., 26; Badaloni, *Campanella*, 260–65.
[33] TC-*AV*, 74, 109.
[34] TC-*MS*, 28; cf. Machiavelli, *Discourses* 1.12.
[35] TC-*AfP*, {Part II} IX, 1; TC-*MS*, 97, 162.
[36] TC-*AfP*, 99–100; cf. also Dentice, "Tomismo e Machiavellismo," 6–10.
[37] TC-*AfP*, {Part II} XIII, 27.
[38] TC-*MS*, 64–65.
[39] TC-*DUGE*, 508–9; cf. Dentice, "Tomismo e Machiavellismo," 10.

Does Campanella expressly tap those rich springs of political deception deriving from Plato, Averroes, and Padua, wherein the idea of the noble lie and deception as a necessary ingredient of political stability and order had received such important consideration and loving care? In the course of a lengthy treatment of religion that appears in book 16 of the *Metaphysics* Campanella takes up the problem of deceivers as it pertains to a religion. After detailing ten criteria (*notae*) whereby the validity of one claiming to bear a *religio* and *lex* from God might be determined[40]—all reasonable enough tests and for the most part applicable today—he addressed the problem of the deceived as well as the deceiving legislator, sent by demons or devils with God's permission for the sake of a greater good. Among such are Muhammad, the Talmudists, and the gods of the pagans, contrary to nature and to the express prescriptions of God. As one sent by nature while being motivated by reason and love, Lycurgus bore holy laws regarding morals; nevertheless deceived by the authority of the old religion, he established perverse laws on religious rites and doctrines.

> Among the deceivers are also some who are not themselves deceived, since they think that a pernicious deception is something to avoid, but not however one that is promotive of service and utility. Just so did Pythagoras pretend that for two years he had conversed with the gods and Numa meditated laws in a grove and then gave them to the Romans as if received from God. Varro praises this deception and reckons Romulus to have been killed and concealed by the fathers so that it might be believed that he had been taken up by God with the consequence that his laws would be observed as divine; thus Minos is believed to have done, pretending that he was in a grotto speaking with Jove, unless deceived by the devil as was Muhammad from the very beginning. . . . But those who possess all the said marks are immune from suspicion of deception, passive and active. For if God deceives them by presenting a false religion and false dogmas about hell and heaven, so that men may be held to their duties thereby, nothing further must be disputed. For where God wants us to be deceived, we ought to obey. But because this dogma is perverse, that God might be a liar, I judge that religion ought to be embraced which is conferred by God with the ten marks until that religion should come forth having the same signs of God, which have departed from the earlier one. For from this we know the Mosaic law to cease at the disposition of God because the prophets, miracles, martyrdom, and the spiritualization of the believers ceased therein and they passed to Christianity, and the Jews have been given over to a reprobate understanding; they honor Talmudic impieties contrary to Moses, to God, and to nature. But because with Muhammad these gifts of God have not passed from Christianity to Islam, therefore man knows by natural reason that Muhammad has not been sent by God against Christianity but rather by

---

[40] TC-*Meta.*, III, 266–68 (bk.XVI, cap. 7, art. 4); cf. *Teologia*, ed. R. Amerio (Milan, 1936), I, 1.3, where these are later less succinctly set forth.

an impure demon that has not been able to give to him those charisms nor to deprive the Christians of theirs. Among the latter I daily see the saints accomplishing the same miracles, which in their time the apostles accomplished, and are refulgent with the same sanctity of life. If Porphyry might have considered this fact, he would not have preferred paganism to Christianity.[41]

Campanella here appears to go well beyond Machiavelli in the *Discourses* (1.11–12) in accepting the details of Paduan Averroism regarding the political utility and historical course of religions. While recognizing the social need for religious belief and savoring the utility of possible deception in this respect, he dissociates himself from affirming that God might inflict upon man an enduring deception merely for purposes of political order.

Nevertheless on one significant issue the two clearly agree. In the vast heap of Campanella's writings, particularly in the work entitled *Philosophia realis*, it is easy to ignore the *Quaestiones . . . de politicis*, confusedly paginated, which had undergone several redactions since 1609 before appearing for the first time in Paris in 1637. The four questions constitute a criticism of Aristotle's *Politics*, most specifically the second question that focuses on his concept of citizens as narrowed to the warriors and governors. In Campanella's repeated efforts to extend the concept to include artisans, peasants, and in fact all the people, we begin to expect from him an idealization of *il popolo* reminiscent of the heresiarch himself, Machiavelli. In fact that is precisely what we encounter:

> Truly workers constitute a great part of the state. We are not able to do without them. For that reason they must not be excluded from the body of citizens. . . . For if the peasants and workers are not so learned in Aristotle's logic, they are nevertheless learned in the natural and common, public religion. Each artisan is king in his own craft as far as partaking in wisdom, as Solomon said. Justice and temperance, however, are more to be found in the common people than in the nobility, for they believe in the law that is preached daily in the temple and what they hear from their mothers and fathers as well as in daily intercourse, and reverently they obey. The educated, in contrast, reliant on doctrine and agitated by conflicting syllogisms, are not as stalwart in justice, temperance, and fortitude. Even Machiavelli acknowledged this when he noted the people to be more just and trustworthy than princes.[42]

---

[41] TC-*Meta*., III, 270–72 (bk.XVI, 7.4.); cf. TC-*PO*., 264–66.

[42] TC-*PR*³, 92: "Opifices vero sunt magna Reipubl. pars: sine qua esse non possumus. idcirco ex ciuium numero non sunt excludendi, neque enim quia non est oculus idcirco pes non sit de corpore. Argumentum Apostoli validissimum, fundatum in natura: erubescat Arist. Nam & si docti non sunt rustici, & opifices in sua Logica, sunt tamen in naturali & Religione communi. Omnis etiam artifex est Rex in sua arte, quatenus particeps sapientiae, vt dicebat Salomon. Iustitia autem, & temperantia magis inuenitur in plebe, quam in nobilitate: credunt enim legi, quae praedicatur quotidie in templo & a patribus, & matribus audiunt, & a commercio: & reuerenter obtem-

Elsewhere in the same *Quaestio* Campanella can specifically attack Aristotle's portrait of the tyrant that culminates in *Politics* 5.2;[43] he can also linger over a Thomistic understanding of deception that is neither hypocritical nor malign for the good of this same people "because we are still in the world and not yet in paradise."[44] However, here he consciously and admittedly stands on common ground with Machiavelli in idealizing the populace.

If the two political thinkers are so apparently similar, how then does one account for the revulsion that Campanella experiences in confronting the Florentine? If to be Machiavellian means to be capable of resorting occasionally to the amoral, cunning act for purposes of maintaining political community, then Campanella is a Machiavellian. It was in this broad, shallow sense that his age understood Machiavelli and in this same sense that William Prynne, that provocative Puritan bigot, would refer to its author as a "Second Machiavel" in the second English edition of Campanella's *Monarchia di Spagna* (London, 1660).[45] Yet this is hardly a very satisfactory understanding of Machiavelli, sufficient to make him worth our attention. It fails to explain what Meinecke dramatically referred to as a sword, thrust into the flank of the body politic of Western humanity and from which it has been reeling ever since.[46] The nature of that sword thrust has been perceptively defined by Isaiah Berlin in his observation that nothing is so offensive to one brought up in a monistic, religious system than a breach in it. To be confronted by a valid, even necessary, alternative to a hitherto total universal order can only prove devastating to an adherent of that order. For anyone "to attack and inflict lasting damage on a central assumption of an entire civilization is an achievement of the first order."[47] By endowing politics with its own autonomous existence, its own moral and social order, Machiavelli opened the door to another world, another dimension of reality: he shattered the circle, the encyclopedia, the idealized unity of traditional medieval culture and beckoned to the other provinces of life to follow.[48]

Campanella saw this, although not with the precision that later hindsight affords us. Rather he sensed himself struggling with something darkly monstrous, and what he lacked in clarity of perception he made up for in passion of

---

perant: literati vero confisi in doctrina, & syllogismis contrariis agitati, non sunt sic firmi in iustitia, & temperantia, & fortitudine. Hoc etiam Macchiauellus agnouit, vbi iustiorem esse populum, & in faederibus observantiorem, quam principes, notauit." Cf. Machiavelli, *Disc.* 2.58; *Pr.* IX & XX.

[43] TC-*PR*³, 87–92.

[44] Ibid., 94: "Quoniam sumus in Mundo adhuc, nondum in Paradiso."

[45] LF-*Bibl.*, 65–66.

[46] Meinecke, *Machiavellism*, 49.

[47] Isaiah Berlin, "The Originality of Machiavelli," in *Against the Current* (New York, 1982), 76–77.

[48] On the principle of autonomy as a determinant of the Renaissance in general and Machiavelli in particular, see Federico Chabod, *Machiavelli and the Renaissance* (London, 1958), 174–91.

conviction. For him the issues are what we would call pluralism and atheism. At the end of his *Atheism Conquered* he charges Machiavelli with not knowing that encyclopedia whereby all science is for the common use and edification; ethics, politics, the economy of the household are here one cake. When Machiavelli says that probity is good for saving souls but not states, he speaks not only against piety but also, according to the Calabrian, against nature, which through virtue, not through vice, saves all.[49] Having continually referred to Machiavelli as an atheist, for he grants nothing to God but Aristotle's formal initial motion, Campanella will add to the *Atheism Conquered*, composed around 1605, a preface in 1630 asserting that it is necessary to begin not with "I believe in the Holy Church" but "I believe in God," compelling him, Campanella, to demonstrate that God is, that He is one, that man is endowed with an immortal soul, and that God is to be worshiped not fictitiously but by the true religion.[50] For all its confusions *Atheism Conquered* is a powerful document—confessional, apologetic, an inner dialogue. Here the great strands of heterodox Aristotelianism and Neoplatonic syncretism that constitute in large part the complex cultural formation of Campanella's youth compete for ascendancy, only to be resolved by the triumph of the latter. But Paduan Averroism as a somewhat heterodox form of Aristotelianism is never so displaced as not to be able to reassert itself at critical moments.[51]

At this stage in our investigation a closer contrast can prove revealing. Campanella and Machiavelli, each driven by his political demon, differ both with respect to the right interpretation and use of a political Christianity and with respect to the context and frame of reference in which each finds himself. It would be wrong to assume that the autonomy won by Machiavelli for the expression of his political demon is devoid of all religion. On the contrary, religious bonds and habits of mind inhere to the new political enterprise as envisaged by the Florentine; they are for the rulers, however, divorced from any transcendental or metaphysical reference and to be exploited at will. Religion becomes entirely human, a civil matter, and like everything else is mortal. That very notorious passage in which Machiavelli clearly prefers pagan religion to Christianity because of the former's greater capacity to generate public spirit will also include the haunting notion that there is no necessary reason for heaven now to be disarmed; at present, political Christianity suffers to a significant extent from not having the proper leadership and from a false interpretation prompted by indolence.[52] Furthermore in referring to the unitary government

---

[49] TC-*AT*, 174–76.

[50] TC-*AT* (1636), "Praefatio," sig.ciiii; cf. chap. 2, n. 187, *supra*. The second preface is dated from Rome, June 11, 1630.

[51] Cf. Spini, *Ricerca*, 99–104.

[52] Machiavelli, *Disc.* 2.2. Although Mark Hulliung's sufficiently arresting *Citizen Machiavelli* (Princeton, 1983) may be considered an extended meditation on the text of *Disc.* 2.2, the author curiously fails to treat that passage which suggests the possibility of an appropriately militant

presented by the cases of France and Spain, Machiavelli would seem to be condemning the papacy more for its inability to realize its own mastery over Italy than for its geographical location and the consequent political fragmentation of the peninsula into a multitude of jurisdictions. Indeed, Machiavelli would appear to have room for the warrior saints and armed prophets as well as for St. Francis and St. Dominic—those popular leaders of a former age whose austerity, poverty, and sacrifice could move the first beginnings of urban masses in the Western world.[53] Meanwhile he scorns the canon lawyers, the curial administrators, and ecclesiastical lords of his own day. Yet whatever scattered evidence may lurk in the interstices of Machiavelli's writings for his espousal of a militant, crusading Christianity,[54] the weight of his argument falls upon a Church and clergy that need to attend to their properly pastoral function and upon a papacy that he vilifies for its excessive involvement in worldly power.[55] Idealist and more specifically in this respect Marsilian, Machiavelli would reduce the Church to its pastoral role and denounce what his friend Guicciardini referred to as those "wicked priests."[56]

With his far-ranging imagination and aspirations, Campanella on the other hand understands the potentialities of the Church for world rule and thus not only can make his peace with the fact of the ecclesiastical state astride the peninsula, but can see it as the nucleus for a larger state, including the better part of Italy, and thereby serving as an effective base for the exercise of a universal theocracy.[57] More profoundly and astonishingly, early in his career he made the breathtaking observation that Machiavelli, for all his cunning, while admiring papal stability, had failed to see it as a common ground for unity or unified action.[58] Ten years later and almost a full century after the

---

rendering of Christianity: "E benchè paia che si sia effeminato il mondo e disarmato il Cielo, nasce più sanza dubbio dalla viltà degli uomini, che hanno interpretato la nostra religione secondo l'ozio e non secondo la virtù. Perché se considerassono come la ci permette la esaltazione e la difesa della patria, vedrebbono come la vuole che noi l'amiamo ed onoriamo, e prepariamoci a essere tali che noi la possiamo difendere. Fanno adunque queste educazioni e si false interpretazioni." In *Opere*, ed. Maria Bonfantini (Milan/Naples, 1963), 227–28. On some of the Spanish-Italian reactions to Machiavelli's accusation that Christianity has disarmed heaven, see Adriano Prosperi, "La religione, il potere, le élites incontri italo-spagnoli della Controriforma," *Annuario dell'Istituto Storico Italiano per l'età moderna e contemporanea* 29–30 (1977–78): 499–529. I am grateful to its author for giving me a copy of this valuable article.

[53] See the concluding sentences of *Disc.* 1.12. On the mendicant orders, cf. *Disc.* 3.1.

[54] Cf. Timothy J. Lukes, "To Bamboozle with Goodness: The Political Advantages of Christianity in the Thought of Machiavelli," *Renaissance and Reformation* 8 (1984): 266–77, esp. 273–75.

[55] Gilbert, *Machiavellism*, 156–57.

[56] Francesco Guicciardini, *Ricordi*, B14 in *Maxims and Reflections of a Renaissance Statesman*, trans. Mario Domandi (New York/Evanston/London, 1965), 101.

[57] TC-*DUGE*, 476–80, 506–7; TC-*DPI*, 151–54.

[58] TC-*DUGE*, 505–6: "Questo [the political capability of the Papacy working among Chris-

composition of the *Prince*, Campanella, living in the transformed Italy of the high Counter Reformation and the apparently imposing restored papacy, could turn with new eyes to chapter 11, "On Ecclesiastical Principalities": there Machiavelli showed himself to be impressed by Alexander VI's demonstration of how a pope might prevail by recourse to money and force. In the *Antiveneti* Campanella expressly takes issue with the claim made by the master of *ragion di stato* in the next chapter that the pope was the ruin of Italy; Machiavelli's observation pertaining to the Renaissance papacy prior to the *Sacco* seemed to a shrewd observer of the early seventeenth century to be ignorant and unfounded.[59]

Frankly espousing the vigorous exercise of a political Christianity, Campanella counters Machiavelli by preferring the political/administrative responsibilities of prelates to their pastoral function; in contradistinction to a papal pronouncement of March 18, 1624, Campanella recommends that if compelled to make the choice, cardinals who are bishops should remain in Rome to serve in the curia rather than pursue in their dioceses those pastoral functions prescribed by the Council of Trent.[60] Linking *potestas* to *caritas* in the cleansing of the Church itself, Campanella, despite his motley, magical heterodoxy, speaks with an authority and force that neither Guicciardini nor Machiavelli could muster: from the depths of his cell and from his inhuman physical suffering he can invoke not some assortment of armed prophets for purposes of clerical reform but rather God Himself, calling upon Christ to come, but to come armed!

> My life, my sufferings bear Thy stamp and sign,
> If Thou return to earth, come armed; for lo,
> Thy foes prepare fresh crosses for thee, Lord!
> Not Turks, not Jews, but they who call them Thine.[61]

---

tian princes and states] non conobbe l'astutissimo Machiavello, che si ammira della stabilità del papato. . . . Quando il Papa sarà signore d'Italia, sarà anche del mondo; però deve procurar ogni via di arrivar a questo."

[59] TC-*AV*, 89–90; cf. *Disc.* 1.12.

[60] TC-*DUGE*, 515–17. By claiming that Campanella had written a now lost work on this matter "per compiacere qualche porporato mal disposto ad allontanarsi da Roma" Luigi Firpo suggests, without any apparent evidence, that Campanella was not in earnest. In 1940 Firpo dated this work to early 1631, following Amabile (LF-*Bibl.*, 194–95), then in both the 1949 and the 1968 editions of TC-*DUGE* he backdated it to around 1624, when Urban VIII had made a comparable demand, arguing that it would be unlikely for Campanella to have directly contravened a papal bull in the later period because his own status at the curia then hung in the balance. In either instance of papal legislation, 1624 or 1634, Campanella, according to Firpo, was seeking to please some high-placed official, whether pope or cardinal. Given Campanella's commitment to papal theocracy and the apparatus of power, however, one may not have to devise extraneous motives.

[61] "A Cristo, Nostro Signore," sonnet 18 in "Scelta di poesie filosofiche", TC-*P*[1], 33. The translation is that of Symonds, *Sonnets*, 135.

194   CHAPTER V

In what might be taken as an express reply to the implicit challenge presented by Machiavelli in the *Discourses* (2.2), Campanella avers that Christian laws, if not providing marvelous heroes like Caesar and Alexander, will produce a Moses, Peter, and Paul, whose surpassing heroism is adored and resounds throughout the world.[62] Yet Campanella's efforts go beyond trying to give more bite and greater snap to the athletes of the faith. Ever desirous of uniting faith with power, love with force, he occasionally alludes to the Moslem example of an armed high priest. Furthermore he will remain consistent throughout his life in advocating that the supreme pontiff should be armed: indeed the very wealth, magnificence, and power of the papacy secure its position over against all other princes.[63]

Nevertheless it is in distinguishing the respective contexts of the two that we discover the decisive difference. Machiavelli's vision of politics is a product of long exposure to the rampant individuality and political illegitimacy of the Italian Renaissance brought to a pitch by the unhinging event of the French invasion of 1494. Fragmentation and permanent improvisation characterize this world: "And as the observance of divine institutions is the cause of the greatness of republics, so the disregard of them produces their ruin; for where the fear of God is wanting, there the country will come to ruin, unless it be sustained by the fear of the prince, *which may temporarily supply the want of religion.*"[64]

From this observation Machiavelli will go on to argue the greater value of good laws to a mortal prince, while admitting the improbability of ever attaining the relatively solid ground provided by such good laws. If the Florentine knows neither the state nor raison d'état as we today know, or think we know it, he grasps the essential temporality, the harsh necessities, the continuing improvisations that mark the life of that entity which we call the state, both product and attestation of a persisting emergency. On the other hand Campanella, venturing globally among vast imperial conglomerates that dwarf the restricted, intense view of his predecessor, never loses his holistic perspective and remains thoroughly within a single universal order that he aspires to drive to an even greater, more effective realization.

There is yet another perspective from which we can better appreciate the controversy between these two political giants over the issue of religion and its relation to *ragion di stato*. Running throughout the *Discourses* and the *Prince* is a kind of nostalgia for an earlier age when a basic religious fervor

---

[62] Amab., *Doc.*, II, 140/201.

[63] TC-*DUGE*, 471–72, 476, 507 [1593–95]; TC-*AV*, 87–88 [1606]; TC-*DPI*, 151–54 [1607]; TC-*MN*, 301 [1635].

[64] *Disc.* 1.11, Mod. Libr. trans. Christian E. Detmold (my italics): "Perché dové manca il timore di Dio, conviene o che quel regno rovini o che sia sostenuto dal timore d'uno principe che sopperisca a' defetti della religione" (ed. Bonfantini), 124.

infused civil society with greater fear, reverence, and natural discipline, so badly lacking in the Italy that Machiavelli experienced. In the cataclysm marked by the French invasion of Italy, partly explicable by the disappearance of religious customs,[65] the astute Florentine reacted with a sense of loss to an age wherein religious fervor was generally at a low ebb.[66] A century later, however, Campanella stands at the apex of the Catholic Church's revival in the Counter Reformation; thus he belongs to a time that could address more moralistically the problem of the wound in Europe's side. Machiavelli stood at the threshold of a new dimension divorced from religion as an ontological reality but eager to exploit its political utility. Campanella lived in the revival, no matter how inadequate, of Catholicism, and in his own political theory he would incorporate not only religion as a reinforced and expanded catholicity but the state itself into his Church.

Yet whatever Campanella's moralistic ministrations to the wound in Christendom's side, his opposition to Machiavelli differed exponentially from that of the contemporary anti-Machiavellians. The gulf separating the Calabrian prophet both from his own age and specifically from all the other self-proclaimed opponents of Machiavelli can best be appreciated under the category of time. The emergence of the sovereign territorial state posited its own *aevum*. Yet with respect to time conceived as the potentiality for expectation or hope, for liberation or redemption, Campanella, despite all his magical, astrological, naturalistic vagrancies, stood closer to the intrinsically Christian perspective on the future than did his contemporaries. For "an age without apocalypse" had from the beginning of the century come to settle upon Italy and gradually extend itself to the rest of Europe: by 1660 England seemed the last to succumb, following the death of the more florid Puritan dreams. It can well be urged that Europe certainly needed to cool off after the excess of apocalypses experienced during the long sixteenth century. The new age, however, placed worse than a low premium on such a destabilizing factor as eschatology or any tension toward the future. Implicitly the absolutist conception of time sought an obliteration of any challenging comparison or basis for criticism and amounted to a recrudescence of the harsh, mythic cycles of pagan naturalism: "in philosophy supporters and negators of Aristotelianism remain substantially enclosed in the iron circle of natural reality without opportunity for escape or final redemption; in politics Machiavellism, Tacitism, *ragion di stato* likewise constitute expressions of a radical distrust in the possibility of subverting the empirical data of historic actuality; the religion, ecclesiology and piety of the late Counter Reformation lack any suggestion of

---

[65] Cf. Chabod, *Machiavelli*, 46–61, where in treating the phenomenon of the prince as the final expression of Renaissance life, Chabod incisively analyzes the more general malaise.

[66] *Prince*, chap. 11; *Disc.* 1.11.

eschatological tension or criticism of the existent. *Il Seicento italiano* is in large part prisoner of man of the present."[67] On the other hand both Machiavellians and anti-Machiavellians played the game within the constituted, recognized order. Little wonder that *il secolo senza apocalisse* would find it necessary to keep the exceptional, the radically prophetic, securely confined in the bottom of successive Neapolitan prisons for over a quarter of a century.

In concluding let us once more confront the question: in what sense can Campanella be understood to be a Machiavellian? For good reason did Campanella's English readers refer to him as a "second Machiavel" or as "that most politick friar."[68] The actual indebtedness of Campanella to Machiavelli was more than peripheral, exceeding simply the incidental resort to cunning tactics. By profoundly appropriating the idea of religion's social and political utility, originally a product of Paduan Averroism, Campanella joined many political theorists of the Counter Reformation in judging religion by its effects, its utility, while nevertheless maintaining for himself its claims to truth.[69] In their common preoccupation with power and its effective exercise in this world Machiavelli formulated the question and imparted to Campanella what became the central problem of his life: the empowerment of Christianity. The friar attempted to resolve for his own age the question that the secretary had hesitated to address in his own time; in his quest to achieve the predominance of a viable ecclesiastical state in Italy as well as papal theocracy throughout the world, Campanella in effect took up Machiavelli's challenge to realize a politically militant Christianity. That other interpretation of Christianity, to which Machiavelli occasionally alluded, Campanella would spend a lifetime pursuing in order that heaven might truly be rearmed.

Yet in the end Machiavelli and Campanella are light years apart: the Florentine is willing to divorce himself from the traditional system in order to construct a new dimension of reality and to use religion for whatever it can provide: in contrast the Calabrian remains within the old system, using some of the new materials of the age not only to shore up but to universalize most drastically the traditional, monistic order.

[67] On the idea of this new period as lacking the energizing force of apocalypse, see Spini, *Ricerca*, 42–44, here quoted; on *aevum* as a new dimension of time, between eternal and temporal, of sempiternal duration and perduring continuity, see Ernst H. Kantorowicz, *The King's Two Bodies: A Study in Medieval Political Theology* (Princeton, 1957), 275–84.

[68] Henry Stubbe, *Campanella Revived or an Enquiry into the History of the Royal Society* (London, 1670), 3.

[69] Cf. Prosperi, "La religione," 528, n. 53.

Chapter VI

UNIVERSAL MONARCHY: ON IDENTIFYING THE ARM OF GOD

> [A] city greater than any that upon earth the air encompasseth, whose amplitude no eye can measure, whose beauty no imagination can picture, whose praise no voice can sound, who raises a golden head amid the neighbouring stars and with her seven hills imitates the seven regions of heaven, mother of arms and of law, who extends her sway o'er all the earth and was the earliest cradle of justice, this is the city which, sprung from humble beginnings, has stretched to either pole, and from one small place extended its power so as to be co-terminous with the sun's light. . . . 'Tis she alone who has received the conquered into her bosom and like a mother, not an empress, protected the human race with a common name, summoning those whom she has defeated to share her citizenship and drawing together distant races with bonds of affection. To her rule of peace we owe it that the world is our home, that we can live where we please, and that to visit Thule and explore its once dreaded wilds is but a sport; thanks to her all and sundry may drink the waters of the Rhone and quaff Orontes' stream, thanks to her we are all one people.
> —Claudian, *On Stilicho's Consulship* 3.130–40, 150–59 (Loeb ed.); referred to and quoted in part in the postscript of the Elzevir Latin editions of the *Monarchia di Spagna*

IN ORDER TO understand Campanella's political thought with its resort to a global, universal empire it is best to dispense with the idea and present reality of the national or nation-state as well as nationalism, for they properly belong to a later period. Their attendance here only confuses the issue. At best a dim national consciousness lurks beneath the surface of a world organized in terms of privileged orders and estates, of patrons and their clients, of royal authority and its ceremonial. For in the late Renaissance, prior to the emergence of the national state in the nineteenth century, imperial, territorial, and urban polities coexist within a disintegrating feudal-ecclesiastical matrix: imperial, universal, monarchical, national, territorial, urban, and regional motifs abound. The process of sorting out, of integration and consolidation goes on without any clear determination until the middle of the seventeenth century. While the ultimate resolution from a twentieth-century perspective would be along the lines of a national/territorial integration, in the early modern period the universal/imperial set of motifs, characteristics, and institutions long predominate. Nor is this predominance one that stands in polar opposition to the national, territorial consolidation. Rather there will be a Germanic, a Spanish, a French, an English, and always an Italian version of universal empire. Indeed the universal motif seems to generate and promote the national which, outside Rome, is associated with royal authority.

Admittedly, the claim to universality had always fallen far short of practical reality. And in the case of its most obvious bearer, the Holy Roman Empire, its title had acquired in the course of the fifteenth century the delimitation "of the German nation," thereby territorializing the ailing construct. Moreover despite the confessional unrest of the age Europe seemed to be developing in the direction of an assemblage of territorial sovereign states that belied the occasional rhetoric of inflated claims to world empire. Nevertheless at the beginning of the seventeenth century the remarkable recovery of the Counter Reformation papacy, the rapid growth of the Spanish *monarquía* as both a global and a central European power, and the joint imperialisms of the two branches of the House of Habsburg now coalesced to give new dimensions and resonance to the idea of universal monarchy.

In fact even earlier the idea of world empire or universal monarchy had managed to enjoy a fateful revival at the beginning of the sixteenth century in circles near to Charles V and his Habsburg successors.[1] Its substance was sufficient to persist and even to preoccupy the political calculations of the age. At the end of this development, in the opening decades of the seventeenth century, the Spanish refashioning of this idea, involving a necessary displacement of German preeminence and the increasingly ominous presence of Spain in central Europe, caused growing alarm among Lutheran circles. The famous tract of the Netherlandish publicist Philippe de Marnix that had warned his own generation in 1581 regarding the threat of tyranny posed by Spanish universal monarchy allied with the papacy now suffered successive reprintings in 1619, 1625, and 1626.[2] By 1629, at the end of the period here under consideration, a mood of despondency and helplessness prevailed among Lu-

---

[1] There is a considerable literature on this subject; for example, see my own "Gattinara, Erasmus, and the Imperial Configurations of Humanism," *Archiv für Reformationsgeschichte* 71 (1980): 64–98, esp. 82–83. The subsequent prefatory paragraphs are taken from my article "Ehe Türckisch als Bäpstisch': Lutheran Reflections on the Problem of Empire, 1623–28," *Central European History* 20 (1987): 3–28, esp. 4–8, which may be consulted for fuller citations.

[2] See Franz Bosbach, "Die Habsburger und die Enststehung des Dreissigjährigen Krieges: Die 'Monarchia Universalis," in *Krieg und Politik, 1618–1648: Europäische Probleme und Perspektiven,* ed. Konrad Repgen (Munich, 1986), 151–68, esp. 159–61. I wish to thank the author for very kindly sending me proofs of his article.

therans according to a German who had emigrated to the Netherlands: among high and low it was generally held that nothing availed to resist the hispanicized imperial or imperial hispanicized power.[3] In short preceding the territorial or even protonational resolution to Europe's political ordering, the reality of a Habsburg-papal recrudescence of universal dominion and the fear that it engendered warrant more attention than they have received from historians.

Within a context of vibrant apocalyptical and eschatological prophesying, the experience of Habsburg dynasticism under Charles V had revived the idea of universal monarchy in the early modern period. Indeed the twin eschatological signs provided by the discovery of America and the Antichristic presence of the Turk had promoted a resurgence of the idea of world empire, haunting some of the leading minds of Europe and suffusing much of the political thought of the age at least until 1640. Furthermore the traditional understanding of world history in terms of four successive monarchies, of which the present Roman one was a late, final, and most tenuous extension, provided the essential categories for conceptualizing past and present events. Admittedly the territorialization of the Holy Roman Empire made that venerable construct a not altogether convincing champion of universalist claims. Certainly Jean Bodin had recently given its title, whether to a monarchical or universal form, some rough handling. In fact as early as 1566 the French jurist, while noting the rapid rise of Spain to effective global power, had seen that monarchy as far surpassing in territorial extensiveness the absurdity of empire claimed by the Germans. In 1623 another most prominent European jurist, Christoph Besold, would also consider the Iberian kingdoms, especially with their colonial empires, a far better candidate for universal monarchy than the Holy Roman Empire.[4]

Yet whatever the younger branch of the House of Habsburg lacked in the latter part of the sixteenth century, the senior, Spanish branch endeavored to realize. Pursuant to the negotiations over the Caroline succession that almost destroyed the accord within the Habsburg family at midcentury, Antoine de Granvelle, bishop of Arras, drawing upon the experience of Charles V's entire reign, delivered himself on the subject. In a memorandum he recommended that the succession for the empire pass to Philip because the imperial idea could not be embodied unless the occupant of the office could draw on forces outside the *Reich*.[5] In the last years of Philip's reign and in the reign of his

---

[3] Diethelm Bottcher, "Propaganda und öffentliche Meinung im protestantischen Deutschland, 1628–1636," in *Der Dreissigjährige Krieg: Perspektiven und Strukturen*, ed. Hans Ulrich Rudolf (Darmstadt, 1977), 325–67, esp. 326–28.

[4] John Bodin, *Method for the Easy Comprehension of History*, trans. Beatrice Reynolds (New York, 1945), 266, 292–93. On Besold, see DeMas, *L'attesa*, 161.

[5] Peter Rassow, *Forschungen zur Reichs-Idee im 16. and 17. Jahrhundert* (Cologne, 1955), 12–13.

son, Philip III, the notion of a new and different sort of world empire, reflecting the realities of Spanish global power, began to come into focus. Juan de Garnica, doctor in theology and law at Salamanca as well as at Naples and Rome, composed in 1595 a tract entitled *De hispanorum Monarchia ab Adam*, which he dedicated to the future Philip III. An "Epistola ad Hispanos," constituting the preface, exalted Spain's task as protector of the Church. More significantly Garnica dismissed empire as being vacuous and denied that Philip II was emperor. Thereupon he proceeded to contrast empire and universal monarchy—the latter truly corresponding to the papal jurisdiction as counterpart to the spiritual and indicative of Spain's preeminence in not admitting any superior in temporal matters.[6] At the end of our period J. J. Chifflet in his *Vindiciae hispanicae*, apparently seeking to benefit from the implications of both terms, addressed Philip IV as king of kings, archking of the Old World and emperor of the New.[7]

Yet certainly the realities of political power in the first decades of the seventeenth century seemed to argue mightily for the world as well as for the European supremacy of the Spanish king. In his effort to brief the newly arrived Spanish ambassador to the curia, the political counselor and publicist Girolamo Frachetta noted: "It now appears that in place of Caesar has succeeded the king of Spain who does not have to be elected and confirmed but stands as *il maggior prencipe (sic) della cristianità*." By his multiple possessions and interests in Italy he cannot afford to have an ill-disposed pope.[8] Indeed for Traiano Boccalini the Spanish presence in Italy was all too evident, serving to inspire his bitter, brilliant satire *De' ragguagli di Parnaso*; in one instance he represents the Spanish monarchy as suddenly having grown so large that all princes must don a jacket of mail, for this power is young and may attain to universal monarchy.[9] In the first half of the seventeenth century other texts might be adduced to the same effect from Virgilio Malvezzi or Juan de Salazar.[10] But the striking feature about this great surge of imperialist theory

[6] J. Beneyto Perez, *España y el problema de Europa* (Madrid, 1942), 327–28.

[7] Ibid., 346. J. J. Chifflet, *Vindiciae hispanicae* (Antwerp: Balthasar Moretus, 1647), 154.

[8] A. Enzo Baldini, *Puntigli spagnoleschi e intrighi politici nella Roma di Clemente VIII: Girolamo Frachetta e la sua relazione del 1603 sui cardinali* (Milan, 1981), 50, 98–99.

[9] Traiano Boccalini, *The New-found Politicke* [De'Ragguagli di Parnaso, Venezia, 1612] (London, 1626), 70.

[10] Virgilio Malvezzi on "La riduzione del mondo all'uno e la monarchia universale," *Pensieri politici e morale XLVI* or Juan de Salazar's *Politica española* of 1619.The symbiotic relationship between the Spanish *monarquía* and the papacy, represented in the political literature at this time, as well as Spain's claim to preeminence among all other temporal kingdoms, is clearly evinced by the titles of the following works: Fr. Juan de la Puente, *De la conveniencia de las dos Monarquías Católicas: la Espiritual de la Iglesia Romana y la temporal de España y Defensa de la precedencia de los Reyes Católicos de España a todos los Reyes del mundo* (Madrid, 1612); Gregorio López Madera, *Excelencias de la Monarchia y Reino de España* (Valladolid, 1597); Camillo

is that it stood in direct contrast to the main tradition of Spanish political thought, which emphasized political pluralism and naturally opposed any universal imperial claims coming from outside. Here the school of the Dominican moral theologians is particularly explicit: Domingo de Soto forcefully registered opposition to the statement of Baldus and Bartolus that it was a sacrilege not to recognize the emperor as *dominus mundi*.[11]

By the decade following Philip II's death, the notion of the Spanish ruler had emerged not just as another king but as a *monarca*, a king of kings, and the Spanish *monarquía* as a universal, political reality that now vied to displace the traditional Holy Roman Empire. Indeed that imperial publicist of gargantuan productivity, the premier archival miner and assembler of political texts, Melchior Goldast, registered more than passing anxiety regarding the Spanish preponderance displacing a Germanic preeminence. In his *Politica imperialia* of 1614 he devoted an entire section to "consiliis et machinationibus Hispanicis pro nova Monarchia." The idea of shifting the European *monarchia* to the king of Spain in order to avoid an otherwise impending Turkish engulfment proved emotionally disturbing to Goldast.[12] Nevertheless whatever the distribution of theoretical, universalist claims between the two branches of the House of Habsburg, together they would soon emerge in the course of the seventeenth century as the *Augustissima Casa de Austria* or simply *Austriacismo*—a match for the rest of Europe.[13]

"The glorious Spanish Monarchy which encompasseth the whole earth"

From the perspective of the twentieth century we poorly appreciate the general perception of Spanish power throughout the first half of the seventeenth century. Here we are ill-served by Gloriana and Anglo-Saxon mythology. For after all did not the defeat of the Grand Armada hopelessly doom the Spanish monarchy? Yet according to the latest judicious tally 72.44 percent of Medina Sidonia's fleet returned to port.[14] And for the next two generations until 1639

Borrell, *De regis catholici praestantia* (Milan, 1611). On this last, written by a Neapolitan jurist, see especially Pablo Fernández Albaladejo, "*De Regis Catholici Praestantia*: Una propuesta de 'Rey Católico' desde il reino napoletano en 1611," in *Nel sistema imperiale l'Italia spagnola*, ed. Aurelio Musi (Naples, 1994), 93–111.

[11] *De iustitia et iure* 4.4.2.

[12] *Politica imperialia sive discursus politici: Acta publica et tractatus generales*, ed. Melchior Goldast (Frankfurt: Johannes Bringer, 1614), 1143–92. This section (xxvi) includes five treatises, of which the fourth (1346–69) is most pertinent here.

[13] José Maria Jover, *1635: Historia de una polemica y semblenza de una generación* (Madrid, 1949), 166–68.

[14] M. J. Rodriguez-Salgado, "The Spanish Story of the 1588 Armada Reassessed," *Historical Journal* 33 (1990): 461–78, esp. 474. See also the same author's article, "Pilots, Navigation and

Spain would manifest a wondrous capacity to mount new armadas.[15] Moreover the assassination of Henry IV in the following year, 1610, afforded Spain a respite in Europe that contributed to allowing the generation of 1635 in Castile to look back upon the reign of Philip III as a golden age of Spanish greatness—great by discoveries, conquests, and propagation of the faith.[16] And if the opening of a Thirty Years' War would cast the perception or illusion of Spanish power into the hazard, the smashing victory of 1620 in central Europe, redounding to the advantage of the Habsburgs, was only made possible by Spain's contributions, which constituted half of the army of the Catholic League.[17] Thus in our haste to telescope the historical development and read the nation-state back into an earlier period, we must refrain from pulling the curtain too early on the fact of the Spanish *monarquía* and the world of relics and realities, uncertainties and complexities that it embraced.

For all its exaggerations and eccentricities the *Monarchia di Spagna* of Tommaso Campanella provides a conspectus of the resources, problems, and opportunities presented to the vast, far-flung Spanish monarchy in the first decade of the seventeenth century. It belongs to the literature of counsel, which seeks to recommend both the author and the policy of that author. Opportunism, fortified and fed by a sincerity amounting to an enduring, passionate conviction, comes to advance at this time a global policy commensurate with its author's vision of universal theocracy. The *brachium*, arm or actual promoter and maintainer of that universal order, would change with time according to the estimate, correct as events would prove, attained by that most politic friar, the author of the tract. But the commitment to a universal order in which church and empire were as one and the resulting global perspectives would persist in his thought. Finally it bespeaks the fear and fascination exercised by Spanish power over the emerging European polity and upon the imaginations of Europeans that the readership of the treatise should crest in the 1640–1660 period immediately subsequent to the recession of Spanish power.

Strategy in the Gran Armada," in *England, Spain and the Gran Armada 1585–1604: Essays from the Anglo-Spanish Conferences, London and Madrid, 1988* (Savage, Md., 1991), 134–72, where at p. 161 she gives eighty-seven as the number of ships that returned. In the same collection see also J. L. Casado Soto, "Atlantic Shipping in Sixteenth-Century Spain and the 1588 Armada" (pp. 95–133), which represents the distortions in the traditional historiography to the obscuring of Castile's superior navigation and shipbuilding for the better part of the century (pp. 95–98). But cf. Lawrence A. Clayton, "Ships and Empire: The Case of Spain," *Mariner's Mirror* 62 (1976): 235–48, which argues for a decline of uniformity, quality, and innovativeness in the face of the Dutch and the English beginning in the last quarter of the sixteenth century.

[15] J. H. Elliott, *The Count-Duke of Olivares* (New Haven/London, 1986), *passim*.

[16] Jover, *1635*, 205–7.

[17] Geoffrey Parker, *The Thirty Years' War* (London/Boston/Melbourne/Henley, 1984), 50–61.

Campanella's hispanophilism is not limited to this treatise but imparts itself in specific tracts from this same period and in scattered statements in many of his writings until 1628. At the end of his life he will define for us the canon of his pro-Spanish works: writing to the cardinal-nephew, Francesco Barberini December 4, 1634 he says: "I do not know what shocking things I have done to make me so odious to the Spaniards. I wrote *Della Monarchia di Spagna* for them, the *Panegirico ai principi d'Italia* for that monarchy, and the *Articoli profetali*; and they have these and use them in Spain."[18] The *Panegirico* or *Discorsi* and the *Articuli prophetales* are writings that both mature during the 1606–7 period in Campanella's prison cell. Other than in a scribe's garbled redaction to be read in 1624 by Cardinal Trejo y Paniagua,[19] no evidence has yet come to light that the last of these was known and read in Spain. Regarding the *Discorsi ai principi d'Italia* the presence of manuscripts, reported by Luigi Firpo, are as widely scattered as London and Leningrad, but he cites nothing for the entire Iberian peninsula.[20] However, John Elliott, struck by the similarity of some of Olivares' and the Dominican's ideas, has found the *Discorsi* included in the catalogue of the count-duke's library.[21] It would have to have been a manuscript book, since the entire *Discorsi* first appeared in print only in 1848.[22] Presumably now for that in the Biblioteca de la Real Academia de la Historia, inspection reveals a fairly faithful translation into Castilian by a humanist cursive hand of the period.[23] Would that we might know more of its provenance and the reasons for the translation of this work into Castilian. Yet its very existence belies the regnant view, redolent with irony, if true, that Campanella was not read in Spain. What of Campanella's principal work in this respect, and that best known of all his writings to seventeenth-century Europe? What of the *Monarchia di Spagna* itself, its reception and readership in Spain? Here the more comprehensive and recent analysis provided by Kristeller's *Iter Italicum* suggests a more extensive Spanish readership specifically of the *Monarchia di Spagna* and of Campanella in general. Except for the materials sent to the Cardinal de Trejo all

---

[18] Quoted from Anthony Pagden, *Spanish Imperialism and the Political Imagination* (New Haven/London, 1990), 160, n. 154, who cannot here be faulted for not knowing of the evidence that makes Campanella's claim justifiable; cf. TC-*Lett.*, 259.

[19] Cardinal Trejo's letter of January 1, 1625, replying to Campanella can be found in Luigi Firpo, "Appunti Campanelliani," *GCFI* 41 (1962): 381–86, esp. 381.

[20] LF-*Bibl.*, 132–33.

[21] J. H. Elliott, *The Revolt of the Catalans* (Cambridge, 1963) 198; idem, *Olivares*, 199.

[22] LF-*Bibl.*, 133.

[23] In a letter of May 18, 1987, Professor Elliott kindly distinguished between that at the Real Academia de la Historia and one attributed to the Vatican, which he had not been able to locate. He expressed his frustration in trying to find evidence of a real link between this Campanella manuscript and Olivares.

these writings, although in some instances fragmentary or epitomes, are emphatically of a political nature.[24]

While pressing and important for our study, the question of Campanella's Spanish readership implicates the much larger and more significant matter of the *Monarchia*'s reception, its transformations and deformations in the larger, European context. The immense philological and textual difficulties associated with this work surpass in complexity those of any other of Campanella's recovered writings and help explain the absence of a critical edition of the *Monarchia di Spagna* up to this time. We can only hope here to make a few hitherto neglected clarifications. In order to appreciate them we will need to remind ourselves of the largely silent circulation of manuscripts and that at least until the middle of the century the age was probably as much scribal as typographical in its intellectual culture.

In the myriad complexities surrounding the *Monarchia di Spagna* the dating of its genesis has been contested as being either immediately before Campanella's first year of imprisonment (in the course of 1598) or during the first year of his confinement (after April 1600). Until most recently (1989), one could say with the authority of Luigi Firpo that the treatise derived from the latter part of 1600. However, a critical analysis of five similar, closely corresponding copies of the manuscript, three of which are not present in Firpo's *Bibliografia*, reveals the strong possibility of a "first youthful draft" sometime between June 1593 and September 1595, almost coincident therefore with the lost *De monarchia Christianorum*.[25] Like so much else that was preserved in

[24] Kristeller's *Iter Italicum IV* (London/Leiden, 1989) reveals the following conspectus of Campanella manuscripts in Spain. (All page references in the right-hand column refer to *Iter IV*.)

MS	Bibl. Nac. (Madrid)	522a
	Bibl. Central (Barcelona)	490b
	Archivo y Bibl. capitolares (Toledo)	642b
	"	644b
	"	645a
DPI	Real Acad. Hist (Madrid)	514a
	Bibl. Nac. (Madrid)	564b
	Arch. y Bibl. Cap. (Toledo)	642b
AP	Bibl. Nac. (Madrid)	524a
AfP	"	539b
	"	577a
ApG	"	524a
AV	Arch. y Bibl. Cap. (Toledo)	642b
CS	Bibl. Nac. (Madrid)	524a
DUGE	Arch. y Bibl. Cap. (Toledo)	642b
MM & DNH	Arch. y Bibl. Cap. (Toledo)	642b
	Bibl. Nac. (Madrid)	522b

Cf. also Rodolfo De Mattei, *Studi Campanelliani* (Florence, 1934), 75–76.

[25] *La Monarchia di Spagna: Prima stesura giovanile*, ed. Germana Ernst (Naples, 1989), 7–17, 79–82. I am indebted to Dr. Ernst for kindly sending me a copy.

the prodigious memory of the man, Campanella carried in his head into his prison cell the organization and in most places the phrasing of the work so that what he wrote under his new constrained circumstances coincides with the earlier draft except for expansion, opportunistic adjustments, and elaborations. Since some of the manuscripts explicitly provide the date of 1598 and Campanella himself would later in several instances refer to that time, the composition of the work occurs before his extended imprisonment. The prior deployment of the basic arguments for the providential imperialism of Spain would serve to reduce the aura of opportunism and simulation that has hung over the interpretation of the work. In short this new, earlier edition of the troublesome *Monarchia di Spagna* reinforces the sense of Campanella's more enduring and basic commitment.

Reconstituted probably in the latter half of 1598, the *Monarchia di Spagna* only began to receive attention in Campanella's correspondence six years later, when he was forging his connections with German princes through the efforts of his then ostensible friend Kaspar Schoppe.[26] Schoppe was most likely responsible for conveying the manuscript from the dungeons of Naples. It remains uncertain whether he or Johann Faber, chancellor of the Academy of the Linceans at Rome, was responsible for what followed.[27] Beginning in the late nineteenth century scholars began to note that the printed text of the work included interpolations from the works of Giovanni Botero. The investigation of this matter culminated in 1927 with Rodolfo De Mattei, who found so many Boteran interpolations beginning with chapter 9 and increasingly littering the rest of the text that he drew the impossible conclusion that Campanella took with him into his cell at least Botero's *Ragion di Stato*.[28] The physical unlikelihood of his having any of Botero at the time of composition is further confirmed by the existence of some uninterpolated manuscripts of the work. The actual interpolation occurred at the hands of Schoppe and/or Faber in the latter's Roman workshop, which seemed to be generally engaged in the transcription and multiplication of Campanella's writings.[29] Schoppe bore at least one of the interpolated versions into the German context that would be first receptive and supportive of Campanella's ideas.[30] From here the noted

---

[26] On the recent redating of the work's second redaction, see again Germana Ernst's "Introduzione" to her definitive edition of the text to be published soon. I want to thank Dr. Ernst for allowing me to consult the typescript. On Firpo's dating, see LF-*RC*, 198ff. In the course of 1603, following further tinkering, the manuscript was left with the Neapolitan *Reggente* Marthos Gorostiola, who in 1611 said that it had been in his hands nine years. See also Luigi Firpo, "Un memoriale inedito e un indice delle opere di Tommaso Campanella," *RF* 38 (1947): 213–29, esp. 227.

[27] On the house of Faber as the Roman center for the possible diffusion of Campanella's manuscripts, however, see TC-*AfP*, 24. On Schoppe, see TC-*Lett.*, 101; LF-*RC*, 39–41, 203–6. Here I am following the argument of Dr. Ernst in her "Introduzione."

[28] Rodolfo De Mattei, *La politica di Campanella* (Rome, 1928), 22–69.

[29] TC-*AfP*, 24.

[30] D'Addio, *Scioppio*, 62.

Tübingen jurist Christoph Besold made a German translation of the work that first appeared in print in 1620. Another followed in 1623, the same Besold translation that Campanella would mistake for a Latin edition; included was an important appendix. For the remainder of Campanella's life typographical neglect settled upon the work. Only beginning in the year after his death succeeded five Latin editions, two in 1640, two more in 1641, and one in 1653. Then in 1654 Edmund Chilmead's English translation appeared, later to be reproduced in 1660 with a preface by William Prynne.[31] Although this account does not complete the representation of the treatise's editions appearing in the later seventeenth century, it provides all the context necessary for beginning to assess the work's European reception.

First to be noted is that Campanella's original composition was never printed; rather it is the interpolated tradition that has come to prevail in all printed versions. Thus one needs to keep in mind a twofold Campanellan treatise: the original, smaller work more nearly representing the author's intention; and the interpolated version known to a much later reading public. The incongruity of the latter increases when one considers that materials belonging to Giovanni Botero, who represented essentially in his *Reason of State* a pluralist view of a comity of consolidated, administrable, territorial states, are being taken over into a universalist, monistic context of thought. Interestingly enough, however, Botero can include at this time the extended, far-flung Spanish monarchy among such compact polities on account of its superior navigation and the new navigability of the oceans.[32] Perhaps the most obvious common denominator between the two types is the capacity of each author for global meditation.

Returning to the sixty-year span of the work's tortuous odyssey, we may divide this period into three equal segments. The first, 1600 to 1620, defines the pretypographical, scribal period, when transcriptions, interpolations, and multiplications of the manuscript occurred. Although not all ascribable to this period, nevertheless the number of recovered manuscript copies has grown from sixty in 1940 to presently a hundred.[33] Beyond a few disconnected glimmers we know exasperatingly little about this most interesting period of the treatise's existence, when before it saw typographical day, manuscripts of the *Monarchia* circulated, undergoing sometimes chameleon-like changes and by their very circulation attesting to how the European political imagination remained mesmerized, transfixed, by Spain's presence and power.

The most notorious and combustible as well as chameleon-like of all these glimmers is the *Discorso sui Paesi Bassi*, which first appeared in print in Leyden in 1617, followed by other elaborated Flemish, Latin, and German

---

[31] LF-*Bibl.*, 56–67.
[32] Giovanni Botero, *Reason of State*, trans. P. J. and D. P. Waley, (New Haven, 1956), 1:7.
[33] Ernst, "Introduzione," at the beginning of the "Nota filologica."

editions in 1618, 1626, 1630 (*Spanisch Angelhacken*), and 1632.[34] Despite its brevity, no other work so spread the name and reputation of Campanella as a guileful, bellicose Machiavellian as this slight tract. Protestants, in reading it, believed they held within their hands the king of Spain's master plan for the conquest of northern Europe.[35] The tract represents a reworking of chapter 27 of the *Monarchia di Spagna* by an anonymous Fleming who had availed himself of one of the manuscripts in circulation. His omissions were guided by patriotic pride and zeal for Calvinism. His own additions are slight.[36]

Evidence deriving from this preprint period allows us to return to the earlier question regarding the apparent silence from Spain. The presence in Firpo's list of surviving manuscripts of one existing at Barcelona and another at Madrid, more recently increased by the *Iter Italicum*'s three at Toledo, makes us suspicious about the seeming Spanish ignorance of Campanella and specifically of this major treatise. Beyond the strong possibility of one momentous Spanish reader of Campanella in the count-duke of Olivares, we surely have a pronounced reader of his *Monarchia* in Juan de Salazar, whose *La Politica española* follows Campanella verbatim in significant places. The fact that Salazar's work appeared in Logroño in 1619 signifies that he had to have tapped into the manuscript tradition; his presence in Rome in 1606 would have allowed him to have recourse to this tradition at its headwaters.[37]

The third instance of apparent activity within the manuscript tradition takes us to England, where Firpo found in the library of Basil Feilding, second earl of Denbigh, evidence leading him to believe that Campanella's *Monarchia* was being read in English after 1607. Edmund Chilmead published his translation in 1654, the year of his death, but an English translation had been prepared possibly forty years earlier in this first, pretypographical period.[38]

Our second period, which brings us clearly into the stage of print, is marked by the two Besold German editions. Taken together with the translation of the first two *Discorsi* into German, these German editions of the *Spanish Monarchy* registered the Lutheran alarm at the looming Spanish presence in central Europe during the first years of the Thirty Years' War.[39] Furthermore it was part of a broader reception of Campanella's philosophy largely engineered by the Dominican's loyal promoter and friend, Tobias Adami, together

---

[34] Ibid., 32–35.
[35] TC-*DPI*, 52–53; cf. also LF-*Bibl.*, 32–34.
[36] Luigi Firpo, "Un opera che Campanella non scrisse," *GCFI* 31 (1952): 331–43. Firpo vacillated, believing Campanella never claimed it but Ernst at n. 36 avers that much later, in the *Dialogo tra un veneziano etc*, he did indeed claim it. See Amab., *Doc.*, II, 212/244.
[37] Henry Méchoulan, "Juan de Salazar lecteur de *La Monarchie Espagnole* de T. Campanella dans *La Politique Espagnole*," *Ethno-Psychologie* 28 (1973): 103–21. On the possibility of a Roman workshop, associated with Johan Faber, chancellor of the Lincean Academy, engaged in the transcription and multiplication of Campanella's writings, see TC-*AfP*, 24.
[38] Luigi Firpo, "Appunti Campanelliani," *GCFI* 24 (1943): 284–92; cf. LF-*RC*, 194, n. 20.
[39] See the present author's previously cited article, "*Ehe Türckisch*."

with his contacts at the University of Tübingen; radical Catholicism and third-generation Lutheranism momentarily shared a common, exotic ground of concern—prophetic and astrological, naturalistic and neo-Gnostic.[40] Yet by the 1630s specific interest in the text of the *Spanish Monarchy* had apparently waned; silence reigned.

Thus becomes all the more astonishing the burst of editions in our third period with the Elzevir Latin Leyden edition of 1640 from which derive or relate all the later Latin editions for the rest of the century as well as the two English editions. Ignoring for the moment Elzevir's prefatory letter, we learn from the advertisement that the book was presented to the public of Benevolent Readers as providing a lens, a *speculum politicum*, wherein the current political phenomena of Europe might be viewed. The utility of this glass and the celebrity of its author recommend the work. Its instructive character receives particular attention in the preface to the first English edition, which treats the Catholic foreigner with sympathy, curiosity, and respect. Six years later, on the eve of the Stuart monarchy's reestablishment, the brilliant polemicist William Prynne will devise a new preface for another edition in which he reveals Campanella as an arrant Machiavellian and his stratagems for destroying England as a warning to avoid parliamentary discord and espouse monarchical unity.[41]

Whatever the claims of the later Latin editions to being *novissima, aucta,* and *emendata*, at least the first five until 1653, if not the subsequent three from Frankfurt on the Oder of 1685, 1686, and 1709, would include the prefatory letter of Louis Elzevir to the accomplished Hessian diplomat, Jacques Wicquefort, which figures in the 1640 Leyden edition.[42] The letter's wistful

---

[40] See Luigi Firpo, "Tobia Adami e la fortuna del Campanella in Germania," *Storia e cultura del mezzogiorno: studi in memoria di Umberto Caldora* (Cosenza, 1978), 77–118, esp. 97–114. On the intellectual life at Tübingen during this period, see *Theologen und Theologie an der Universität Tübingen*, ed. Martin Brecht (Tübingen, 1977), esp. 141–46, 277–92. Cf. also Robin Bruce Barnes, *Prophecy and Gnosis* (Stanford, 1988), for the astrological, prophetic, neo-Gnostic proclivities in third-generation German Lutherans.

[41] Rodolfo de Mattei, "Le edizioni inglesi della *Monarchia di Spagna* di Tommaso Campanella," *GCFI* 23 (1969): 194–205.

[42] LF-*Bibl.*, 64–66 claims that the three later Frankfurt editions simply follow Elzevir faithfully and include the letter. However, an examination of the Library of Congress's 1686 copy reveals the absence of the Elzevir letter. While I have not had a chance to inspect copies of the 1685 and 1709 editions, the fact that the latter represents itself as *Editio tertia* would suggest that all three are unchanged and represent a separate tradition in the editing of the manuscript. For the German editors take to task the corruptions and general *depravationem* stemming from the first Latin edition of 1640 to the extent that their own, ostensibly corrected according to manuscript evidence, is not to be considered the fourth edition, plodding after the previous three, but rather as *rectrix, moderatrix & magistra* (p. 6). In his study of publishing in northern Europe, principally the empire, Maclean ("Market," 23) notes that the licensing of books depended upon an edition being new or improved; thus publishers were obliged to claim and be able to prove that their publication was *nova* or *recognita* or *locupletior*.

bemusement and condescension toward Campanella and the rising tide of confidence in the Dutch accomplishment come at that very moment when the Spanish monarchy is reeling under the blows of its many enemies. It bespeaks the mood of a new order that will only begin to become apparent at the end of this third period in 1660.

> Recently my company of partisans desired for your benefit that this book be reprinted . . . [something] that recommends itself only on account of rare antiquity or the novelty of the argument that might delight the reader. Of this sort is the present work, which is grand and illustrious with its title of Spanish Monarchy. True it declares that the king of Spain might not be so all powerful as he by his own design or that of others might or would have ever wished. Lest this monarchy ever is or may be achieved, the kings of the British and French zealously will take alarm, likewise that Estates General, which all tax the Spanish treasury in expensive wars, with glittering successes snatching away the best lands in Belgium as well as in both Indies. The monarchy that this Dominican ascribes to Philip seems to me to be more a Platonic Republic than a real and stable empire. He constructs empires on God, prudence, and opportunity. But as matters now stand, it is not yet in the order of things for one Spain to rule all peoples. If the Catholic king strives for this with a prudent contrivance, he has not yet obtained what he intends because of the contravening counsels of so many prudent princes. Not only one opportune moment has in the past presented itself for the Spanish monarchy, but because she has failed to seize a full-haired opportunity by the forelock, now she is vainly left scrambling and sweating [to seize] the later slippery baldness of affairs. Campanella does not always prescribe bad laws for the kings of Spain, but he treats less happily those means that he provides for the monarchy, because he himself simply did not know. For these matters are beyond the cowl and the order of preaching. Since he has grasped many subjects with his genius, so this most learned man has held forth more freely and audaciously, than reliably, regarding philosophical matters and the complex affairs of princes. . . . But this man must be forgiven for admiring his own rather than another, the new rather than the old. It is not for me, most excellent Sir, to pass judgment on Campanella. But I set forth the opinion of others who have read more thoroughly the writings of this man of the greatest and more lofty genius. I recommend this book to you not because you love monarchy and Spanish power but because you rejoice with me that this power has been shaken off from our necks and shoulders. Farewell . . . 26 July, 1640.[43]

---

[43] TC-*MS* (1653), 2*–3*: "Nuper tuo beneficio meus factus jam typis excusus tuus iterum esse desiderat. Soles quippe, praeter eas curas, quas optimis maximisque Principibus commodas, etiam literarum & elegantiorum studiorum meminisse; & eorum nobis copiam facere, quae vel ab antiquitate precium habent, vel argumenti rarioris novitate lectorem delectant. Huius generis est opusculum praesens, titulo Monarchiae Hispanicae grande & illustre. Verum non tam quid sit potentissimus Hispaniarum Rex, quam quid vel sua vel aliorum destinatione esse optet, aut opta-

The Spanish preponderance, so real in fact and so terribly menacing to European perception at the beginning of the century, would seem less awesome, although still considerable, at midcentury. Even as late as the period of Louis XIV's last two great wars Campanella's treatment of the Spanish monarchy and the world scene in general had not lost its fascination at least for German audiences; the utility of the book and the celebrity of its author still manage to impel his late-seventeenth-century German editors.[44] Nevertheless the man and the book that had hailed the august power of Spain in 1600 would both by the century's end be well en route to becoming curiosities.

Yet in 1600 the exotic air that Campanella breathed even in Naples' darkest dungeons possessed the exhilarating and restorative qualities of Iberian expansiveness and impending global unity. It is not that the Castilian kingdom, which served as the motor for the vast aggregate, the Spanish *monarquía*, did not suffer grave dislocations and incoherencies at this time. Rather there coexisted along with the alarm increasingly being sounded by the *arbitristas* and quite apart from the supporting additive of biblical and astrological prophecy, a very real confidence in the awesome momentum of the *monarquía*, its past glories and future discoveries. For some prophetic statesmen all things militated to the Spanish king's realization of being *señor del mundo todo*.[45]

---

verit aliquando, declarat. Ne Monarchiae sit, aut fiat unquam, sedulo cavebunt Galliarum & Britanniarum Reges, cavebunt sedulo Foederati Ordines. quorum illi magnis subinde & sumptuosissimu bellis aeraria Hispanica accidunt; hi praeter Belgii validissimas terras, Indiam utramque illi claris successibus ereptum eunt. Quam hic Monarchiam Philippis adscribit sacri ordinis autor, Platonicae mihi Reipublicae similior videtur, quam vero stabilique Imperio. A Deo, Prudentia & Occasione imperia suspendit. Sed, ut se res dant, nondum in fatis est, unum omnibus populis Hispanum imperare. Si prudenti machinatione eo contendit Rex Catholicus, tot prudentum Principum contrariis consiliis nondum adeptus est, quod intendit. Militavit olim pro Monarchia Hispanica non una occasio sed quia fronte capillatam prehenderc neglexit, jam frustra circa post calvam sudat & luctatur. Leges non ubique malas Hispaniarum Regibus praescribit Campanella. Sed quibus modis Monarchiam sibi comparare possit, infelicius tratat, quia ignoravit ipse. Sunt enim haec supra cucullum & praedicatorum ordinem. Vir doctissimus uti multae ingenii complexus fuit, ita liberius audaciusque quam solidius de rebus Philosophicis & Principum arcanis pronunciat. . . . Sed condonandum hoc viro sua potius, quam aliena; nova, quam vetera, admiranti. Non est meum, Vir praestantissime, de Campanella judicium ferre. Sed aliorum sententiam, qui scripta viri maximi & erectioris ingenii Monachi, attentius legerunt, expono. Tibi autem libellum hunc inscribo, non quod Monarchiam & potentiam Hispanicam ames, sed quia eam humeris & cervicibus nostris decussam mecum gaudes. Vale."

[44] TC-*MS* (1686), 5: "Fuit hic monachus Dominicanus, ut ex scriptis eius liquet, vir perspicacis ingenii, magni studii, plurimae cognitionis & experientiae . . . , 6–6ᵛ."

[45] On Spanish providentialism, imperialist confidence, and aspirations, especially with respect to *Terra Australis Incognita*, see the present author's "Spain's Asian Presence, 1565–1590: Structures and Aspirations," *Hispanic American Historical Review* 75 (1995): 623–46, esp. 625–26, and idem, "The Sixteenth-Century Venetian Celebration of the Earth's Total Habitability," *Journal of World History* 8 (1997): 1–27, esp. 19–24. For further evidence of the Spanish enterprise in global imperialism at the end of the sixteenth century, see the fundamental articles of Geoffrey Parker, "David or Goliath: Philip II and the World in the 1580s," in *Spain, Europe and the Atlantic*

In turning to an examination of the first and by all means most important of Campanella's hispanophile works, the *Monarchia di Spagna*, we may use Giovanni Botero's *Ragion di Stato*, given the intricate interrelationship between the two works, as affording a point of departure. What is the substantive relation of the former to the latter? Certainly what Campanella wrote, the uninterpolated manuscript, shows a knowledge of Botero's *Reason of State* as well as his *Greatness of the Cities*: the prisoner has absorbed the former Jesuit's appreciation of the importance of population and men as the wealth of a kingdom and can agree that a multinationed army is superior to one constituted by a single people, for each nation will or at least should vie to surpass the other;[46] but Campanella can also disagree with Botero regarding the latter's preference for medium-sized states, and he will join the Alfred Thayer Mahans of his age whom Botero abuses for believing that the mastery of the sea leads to mastery of the land.[47] With respect to the distinction between Campanella's original work evident in the unpublished manuscript tradition and the published interpolated editions, Botero is undeniably present in the former by means of Campanella's appropriation of several ideas.

Regarding, however, the published versions, what did Schoppe or the editors in the presumably Roman workshop have in mind when stuffing the prisoner's manuscript with Boteran matter? In the first place the additions do not substantively change Campanella's intention but usually provide more learned and extensive examples. Nevertheless a careful reading of the German, Latin, and English titles, prefaces, and advertisements suggest that an assumption has early been made, possibly, because of the general currency and influence of Botero's work as a best-seller, possibly, because of the general preoccupation of contemporary rulers and their counselors with *ratio status*: Campanella must be doing the same thing as Botero. But if the *Monarchia* provides the *speculum politicum* claimed by its Latin and later English advertisements, it accomplishes this end in a very different way from that of Botero. For Botero's work is a general manual on statecraft, a how-to book that bulges with learned examples drawn from both classical and recent history on how to maintain and expand the state. Lacking direction and focus other than that provided by the general demands of the state, any states in their broad variety but above all medium-size states like Sparta and Venice, the work offers a

---

World: Essays in Honour of John H. Elliott, ed. Richard L. Kagan and Geoffrey Parker (Cambridge, 1995), 245–66, and the same author's "Hacia el primer imperio en que no se ponia el sol: Felipe II y el tratado de Tordesillas," *El Tratado de Tordesillas y su época*, Congreso Internacional de Historia, June 3–7, 1994 (Madrid, 1995), 3:1417–31. I want to thank Professor Parker for kindly sending me an offprint of this last one.

[46] Botero, *Reason*, 11.13, 7.11–12; cf. Bireley, *The Counter-Reformation Prince*, 66–67.

[47] El, 105; EC, 80; cf. Botero, *Reason*, 10.7. Henceforth in designating the various editions of the TC-*MS*, the following abbreviations will be observed: El–Elzevir's 1653 edition of the *De monarchia hispanica*; EC-Chilmead's English edition of 1654.

quarry of maxims and precepts for a maxim-ridden age. And while not lacking in insights, which Campanella sometimes appropriates, the work has sometimes been characterized as being the Polonius of political literature.[48] What it lacks and what Campanella's work precisely possesses is the temporal dimension. Although Botero can discuss *opportunità*, the subject, as with his entire work itself, lies outside time and apart from *kairos*. For while Botero can leisurely review all the possibilities of political life, Campanella cannot afford the luxury of minting abstract rules and general precepts. Impelled, it is true, by the necessities of his own dreadful condition, by opportunism, but also by the scriptural, prophetic, astrological evidence as he understands it, the prisoner recaptures something of the urgency of Machiavelli.

From Besold to Chilmead Campanella's editors and translators have tried to blunt this powerful sense of temporal urgency by absorbing the work into a Boteran framework and stuffing it with Boteran examples. In this respect only William Prynne, as evinced in his extended title to the 1660 English edition and his new preface, does justice to this sense of immediacy, while ruthlessly distorting the work for his own ends. With Campanella *occasione* no longer remains a scholastic definition but comes to inform his work; nor are all states and polities given equal time under the so-called political glass of his editors; rather polities other than Spain are considered only in so far as they bear upon, might aid, or resist the Spanish juggernaut. For the Spanish monarchy in 1598 is his subject and the Spanish king, not the benevolent reader of a European public, his audience. In short the Boteran framework and interpolations could well have contributed to a misreading of Campanella's tract in its several published forms—a misreading only challenged by the ruthless distortions of Prynne and earlier by the anonymous Flemish editor of chapter 27.

In his preface the author alerts his reader to the method of presentation adopted: proceeding in a consciously political way he will first treat the subject generally and then descend to specifics.[49] A consideration of Campanella's titles to his chapters supports this approach with a break or shift being effected by chapter 8 that deploys the specific subjects for later examination. Thus in the seven opening chapters Campanella rapidly lays out the basic features distinguishing the special power and destiny of the Spanish monarchy: the astrological, astronomical, and prophetic evidence pointing to Spain's realization of the Fifth Monarchy;[50] the fact of its global presence, military, naval, and political; the opportunity for a coup in Germany; Spain's respectful subordinate role to the papacy in advancing an ecclesiasticization of offices; the coinherence of God, prudence, and *occasione* for the realization of

---

[48] Botero, *Reason*, p. viii. For Botero's later gravitation toward the Spanish *monarquía* as the necessary answer to universalism, see Richard Tuck, *Philosophy and Government, 1572–1651* (Cambridge, 1993), 67.

[49] EI, 1–2; EC [A4ᵛ].

[50] EI, 19; EC, 12.

Spain's universal monarchy. Amidst a number of epicyclic secondary subjects such as the danger presented by the Turk and the difference between prudence and a Machiavellian *astutia*, two of Campanella's major and more basic points demand attention: the necessity of the king of Spain's subordination to the papacy and the need for Spain's aggressive intervention in the Holy Roman Empire.

Regarding the former Campanella warns that none can be *monarcha* unless he is delegated by and dependent upon the pope. Fundamental is his conviction of the social and political power as only mobilized by religion; whether true or false, as long as it is believed, religion thus effectively commands bodies, swords, and tongues, the veritable instruments of empire. It would prove ruinously divisive for the king to reduce the pope to the role of chaplain. In fact the king of Spain's role of deferential respect and subordination to the papacy leads on to Campanella's demand for a clericalization of offices whereby cardinals and bishops will assume governorships and the preaching orders—Jesuits, Dominicans, and Franciscans—penetrate the councils of the monarchy. The legal justification for such an ecclesiastical assumption of temporal power rests upon the Constitution of Constantine, the notorious Donation.[51] While the nature and extent of ecclesiastical power need not detain us here, its fundamental presence, established at the outset of the work, will impart itself to the whole Spanish world enterprise, the interlocking of the temporal and spiritual, and all future references to religion.

On the other hand, in the symbiotic relationship between Spain and the papacy at the beginning of the seventeenth century Campanella's predilections and the needs of his argument give a preeminence to the latter that did not conform to the political realities of the time. Beyond the obvious fact of Spain's preponderance in Europe and specifically in Italy and its role as the preeminent political power of the Counter Reformation, the most authoritative analysis of papal finances for the period reveals that the pope was more the client than the patron of Spain. For the Spanish-held Italian territories figured as the most important for the financial sustenance of the Roman curia, which derived a large part of its income from benefices provided by Naples and Milan. Furthermore major sums in pensions and ecclesiastical spoils poured into Rome from the Iberian peninsula. In contrast French and German lands counted much less significantly.[52]

Campanella's pursuit of *occasione*, opportunity, as it pertains to the German scene reinforces the sharp temporal reference of the treatise. For we are on the eve of the conflagration about to beset central Europe for thirty years. Convinced of Spain's need to master the empire, Campanella urges that its

[51] EI, 27–42; EC, 19–28.

[52] For this assessment, see Wolfgang Reinhard, "Papal Power and Family Strategy in the Sixteenth and Seventeenth Centuries," in *Princes, Patronage and the Nobility: The Court at the Beginning of the Modern Age*, ed. Ronald G. Asch and Adolf M. Birke (Oxford, 1991), 354–55.

king appear on the scene in force with an international army mobilized under papal authority in order to suppress the heretics, muzzle the free cities, and dislodge the three Protestant electors from their posts.[53] Fantastic as such a Spanish abruption in central Europe would appear, it had its Habsburg precedents and possessed the stuff of which Protestant princes and divines had nightmares during these first years of the century. And regarding the friar's further recommendation that the king of Spain get himself elected emperor there was nothing at all fanciful in this proposal.[54] For Philip as grandson of Maximillian II held more direct claims to the crowns of Bohemia and of Hungary than did Ferdinand of Styria and only by the Oñate agreement of 1617 did Philip step aside, clearing the way for his nephew's coronations in Prague and Pressburg. Philip's abandonment of offices that might better promote his candidacy to the empire did not, however, go unrewarded. What Spain received in return only served to reduce the fancifulness of Campanella's recommendation: imperial territories in Alsace securing Spain's ability to intervene in central Europe.

Having established the most elemental features of the Spanish monarchy in contexts astrological and prophetic, European and global, Campanella proceeds after his list of institutions provided in chapter 8 to examine each in turn. But the tract manages to escape a review of what might otherwise be unrelated parts by being driven by a single, consuming, powerful idea: hispanization. While pervading the entire treatise, the principle of hispanization informs and dominates the more analytical part of the work, chapters 9 through 20. The idea recurs as a refrain: to acquire the whole world the king of Spain must *spagnolare* all peoples, that is, make them Spanish, allowing them to participate in both the government and the army, as did the Romans and as do the Turks;[55] intermarriage will be promoted among Spanish, Italians, and Flemings *per Spagnuolar il mondo* and dominate it more securely;[56] Italy as the seat of empire is to be particularly favored by Spain's presence there so that Italian institutions and customs provide a model and reflect a felicity that will draw the other nations to enjoy such hispanization—"afin che godano le altre nazioni di spagnolarsi."[57]

Campanella elaborates this concept, hispanization, more as a desired result than as an ongoing process in order to achieve the maximum possible degree

[53] El, 35–36; EC, 23–24.

[54] El, 19, 35–36; EC, 12, 23–24.

[55] El, 71; EC, 53. The Italian passages quoted here and in the following two cases in order to establish this issue of hispanization were initially culled from the flawed St. Geneviève ms. 3343 fols. 57, 62ᵛ, and 76 but have now been checked and confirmed against Dr. Ernst's typescript as belonging to the uninterpolated version of the manuscript, this specific case being found in the third paragraph of chap. 12.

[56] El, 90; EC, 73; cf. TC-*MS*¹, 54 and 77 and in Ernst's typescript in the middle of chap. 15 and middle of chap. 32.

[57] El, 162; EC, 126; cf. the second paragraph of Ernst typescript, chap. 20.

of political coherence and military power for the disjointed Spanish monarchy. Here hispanization conforms roughly to the modern concept of acculturation except that the donor nation in extending its culture and system to recipient peoples is emphatically concerned with the production of military power. A modern application of the concept of acculturation to the Spanish monarchy might examine such topics as religion, law, language, education, the army, accessibility of higher offices and rewards, policy toward local elites. In the subsequent chapters Campanella examines some of these; king and kingship (9); a new imperial philosophy (10); Laws and language (11); Government personnel (12–13); the nobility (14); the army, its recruitment and education (15); the popular mood and its control (17–19); application at home base in Spain itself (20); the navy, its recruitment and education (31). Reassembled, the last four topics might be grouped under Campanella's major idea informing his program of hispanization: the seminary as the basic institution for eugenics and education.

In his treatment of the king's education and character there is nothing exceptionable until Campanella directs his fertile imagination to the issue of royal breeding in its eugenic sense. The modern reader will doubtless stumble over the thought that the quality of the king's semen should be a matter of international concern and will further find arresting, if not alarming, that the king's copulation with the queen should be conducted under the most astrologically propitious planetary signs. Nevertheless one's agitation can be mercifully contained by the realization that the approved medical theory and practice of the day had recourse to astrology to help understand the mystery of human conception. This alliance with astrology would continue in such a medical faculty as that at Paris until the end of the seventeenth century.[58] Important for appreciating Campanella's social application of eugenics both in the present work and two years later in his *Città del sole* is his possibly Lycurgan but very suggestive remark that men devote more attention to developing a fine breed of horse than to the improvement of their own breeding of humans.[59] Apparently that summer of 1591, spent on the estate of his Neapolitan Maecenas, Mario del Tufo, where he had noted the marquis' stock breeding of horses, left on the Dominican a distinct impression, which, when associated later with Platonic and Neoplatonic themes, would have mind-boggling results.

Regarding the institution of an "imperial philosophy," the term is our own, not Campanella's; nevertheless it captures the sense of his idea that all the great monarchies of the past have renewed the sciences and with them religion. One might expect here a restatement of that Paduan tradition whereby

[58] Jacques Roger, *Les sciences de la vie dans la pensée française du xviiie siècle* (Paris, 1963), 67–68.

[59] El, 45–46; EC, 33; for the possible source or reinforcement of this idea in Lycurgus, see *Plutarch's Lives*, Loeb ed., vol. 1, trans. Bernadette Perrin (Cambridge, 1939), 253.

with each astrological revolution a new legislator will bring forth new *lex*, a new order and religion. But Campanella is obviously not prepared to get rid of Christianity and is content to devise major changes within the Christian tradition. In the great French effort at world empire, represented for Campanella by Charlemagne, the Frankish emperor is credited with opening up the Aristotelian schools in the West, presumably the great scholastic mills, the medieval universities. In the new order, schools for Platonism, Stoicism and especially the Telesian philosophy should be opened to displace an Aristotle who holds the soul to be mortal and denies divine Providence. Campanella urges a concentration of public attention on the natural sciences less in the interest of truth and more for political reasons to distract intellectuals from otherwise unsettling and trouble-making ideas, thereby avoiding the questions of theology pursued by the northern schools. Likewise, apparently constraining the new currents of European humanism and biblical scholarship, he urges the abandonment of the schools of Greek and Hebrew, which can only promote heresy; instead true to the interests of his order he would replace these with the teaching of Arabic to oppose the Moslem, thus reviving not simply the interests of Raymond Lull and the Council of Vienne but, more immediately, current Iberian educational practices all too inadequately applied. Furthermore schools for mathematics (= astrology) together with cosmographers and talented astrologers are to be imported to the New World. Ever conscious of the political implications of learning and the preeminence of political stability as the ruling criterion for organizing knowledge, Campanella advances a notion that will become axiomatic in the latter half of the seventeenth century and in fact written into the guiding principles constituting the Royal Society: letters are to be eschewed for the more politically neutral and utilitarian natural sciences. In this respect Henry Stubbe in 1670 would specifically identify this feature of the Royal Society with the influence of Campanella.[60]

The world reformer carries a few steps further his plans for the political mobilization of learning. Remotely inspired perhaps by a passage from book 9 of the *Ragion di Stato* in which Botero takes to task the Castilians for their failure, especially when compared with the Portuguese, to celebrate and publicize their achievements—a passage that the presumed and presumptuous Roman editors would stuff into the final chapter of the *Monarchia*[61]— Campanella requires that books be written to note and praise Columbus, Magellan, Vespucci, Cortés, Pizarro, and other great captains. Then, resorting to magical and astrological influences as a means of providing at once a pervasive propaganda and the invocation of beneficent influences, Campanella

---

[60] Henry Stubbe, *Campanella Revived or an Enquiry into the History of the Royal Society* (London, 1670), 3.
[61] De Mattei, *Politica*, 62–63.

urges that statues of Charles V and other princes of the Habsburg dynasty be placed about the Antarctic pole.[62]

Campanella's treatment of laws proves disappointing. Given his pronounced commitment to hispanization, one is surprised to discover an apparently missed opportunity to achieve greater coherence and equivalence among the parts. Yet when he cautions against new laws, he suggests an uncharacteristic prudence and higher wisdom that respect the existing anomalies. Such conservatism does not prevent him from advocating legislation that would have wide popular support and not simply represent the will of the prince. Alva's actions in the Netherlands represent the best example of what to avoid. The tongue is to be preferred to the sword. Notable in Campanella's brief consideration is his linking of law with language, reflecting the humanist Nebrija's well-known statement, appearing in the preface of his grammar of 1492, that with conquest Castile's new subjects must accept its laws and with them its language. Insofar as such laws and language are held in common to allow "commerce" among the monarchy's many peoples, Campanella can applaud it, but he remains mindful of the competition Castilian faces with the Latin of the Church and of learning. Also notable and relevant to hispanization is the reformer's advocacy of mixing and shifting peoples—more specifically, sending proven Italians to places where Spaniards have become hateful.[63]

With chapter 12 ("Of Counsel") the theme of hispanization comes into focus. In Chilmead's English translation, for the Spanish king to be lord of the world "it must be his care to draw on all Nations to comply with Spanish Manners and Customs; that is make them all Spanish." Yet again Campanella seems strangely alert to and respectful of the differences, while ready to use those different talents for advancing the Spanish monarchy: the Portuguese and Genoese for navigation; the Germans for technical and mechanical matters; the Italians for government, diplomacy, and religion. Notable for the overhauling of the monarchy's myriad councils are their penetration by prelates and the religious orders, each council being more representative of and responsive to its respective territory.[64] In actual fact the territorial councils of the Spanish monarchy in Europe did recognize the need to include two natives from their respective regions.[65]

The subsequent chapter on justice carries further the question of personnel and staffing of government offices by diverse local elites. Campanella's analysis seems quite innocent of the terrible barrier presented by the racial laws bearing on *limpieza de sangre* and remains virtually oblivious to the increas-

---

[62] El, 62–66; EC, 45–49.
[63] El, 67–70; EC, 50–52.
[64] El, 72–74; EC, 52–57.
[65] J. H. Elliott, *Imperial Spain, 1469–1716* (London, 1963), 166–67.

ing venality of offices, if aware of favoritism and creeping corruption. Campanella is not unmindful of the need for accountability to the people.

A recent treatment of hispanization, at least as perceived by the Neapolitan intellectuals of the eighteenth century, seems suggestive but proves on the whole misleading: "The strategy of the crown had been, unknowingly perhaps, to follow precisely the advice that Campanella from his Neapolitan cell had offered it, to Hispanize its foreign subjects, to persuade them to exchange their old cultural habits (*ordini e costumi*) for those of their alien rulers. As we shall see, in the terms of Doria's vocabulary, this meant the replacement of a society based upon trust for one based upon honour."[66] It is not made clear that what is being taken for reality is Paolo Mattia Doria's perception of reality and that what Doria attributes to a deliberate policy on the part of Spain to effect the corruption of the Neapolitan nobility derives much earlier from the unsettlement of Neapolitan affairs during the Angevin period in the fourteenth century. Spanish viceroys inherited an aggressive, feudal nobility and simply built upon it, alliance with local elites being the line of least resistance. Finally in Pagden's subsequent, all too sharp contrast between civic participation (Ciceronian *negotium*) and private indolence (*otium*) Campanella's scathing criticism of the Neapolitan baronage hardly serves to advance the cause of the latter and their lifestyle.

In treating the role of the nobility and the monarch's policy toward them, Campanella neither seeks to dissolve this estate into an egalitarian condition of the people nor to exalt unduly its members. Rather he remains ever mindful of the king's continuing need for good men. The most likely pool of such serviceable talent could expectably be found among the nobility, if the original meaning of a noble as one distingushed by *virtù* still prevailed. Unfortunately it does not, and a gap has developed between the ideal and the actual. Recognition of this fact drives Campanella to lash out at the Neapolitan baronage as the most advanced example of a corrupt nobility promotive of much evil and disorder. He paints a picture of their cyclic motion from the extortions they inflict upon their estates to the luxurious buffoonery that they indulge in at court, only to return to their estates, when their resources are exhausted, there to distinguish themselves by new methods of robbing the people. Inheritance perpetuates such luxury and arrogance. We are reminded that the friar's rebellion of 1599 was most immediately directed against this baronage and thus possessed a populist dimension. Campanella can momentarily commend the great Turk for the elimination of an hereditary nobility. But despite his admiration for the Turkish *devshirme* and its resulting institutions he distances himself from such a radical measure and ends his consideration of the nobility in the Spanish monarchy by affirming the second estate as the pillar of the

[66] Pagden, *Imperialism*, 70.

monarch, while trying to make it both more serviceable to the monarch and more accountable to the people.[67]

The case has been persuasively made for the radical populism and egalitarianism of Campanella, especially as expressed in his indictment of both the Neapolitan baronage and the policy of the monarch. Earlier in 1594–95 Campanella had held these barons to be unproductive parasites and the worst excrement that lingers in the body of the commonwealth. Together with merchants and usurers they help manipulate prices to the detriment of the people, especially the small farmers, day laborers, artisans, peasants, and domestic servants.[68] Admittedly, Campanella is remarkably sensitive to the exploitation of the *popolo minuto* by the acquisitive baronage of his day; nevertheless he is by no means arguing for an egalitarian society. Rather he prefers to cleanse the old system by ways that seek to reduce the nobility to service, to responsibility and in short keep them cabined, cribbed, and confined. Their incomes are to be reduced, their political attendance on the monarch increased, and their habits, manners, and garb hispanicized by Spanish tutors. If such measures add up to a cultivation of honor for Campanella, at least such honor expresses itself in political responsibility, service, and care for the people—in short a translation of civic responsibility into the conditions of seventeenth-century Europe.[69]

With chapter 15 on the military the demographic problem comes glaringly into focus, entangling the issue of hispanization—glaringly, because aspects of Campanella's solution can only appear raw and brutal. This focus on the problem of population and especially as it relates to Spain Campanella probably obtained from Botero[70] rather than from contact with any writings of the earliest *arbitristas*. Demography, the increase of population, and the mixing and intermarriage of the various peoples of the *monarchia* will dominate the next five chapters at the very heart of his treatise and will return in the final two chapters, all to reinforce itself as the most significant means for advancing the central issue—hispanization, wherein the seminary serves as the main instrument for eugenics and education.

Except for the notorious chapter 27, separately published as the *Discorso sui paesi Bassi*, the present chapter on the military is the longest one in the work. It begins with a characteristic observation and lament: the observation that Spanish women are less fruitful than northern women; the lament that because a largely Protestant north rules against publicly regulated brothels, an alarming waste of sperm occurs. Herein Campanella manifests a Catholic ex-

---

[67] El, 80–86; EC, 60–65.

[68] Bock, *Campanella*, 101–10; 227–29. On the nobility in general as social excrement, if idle, see TC-*T*, X/1, 104–7.

[69] See my article "On the Reconstruction of the Citizenry: Campanella's Criticism of Aristotle's *Politics*," *IPP* 24 (1991): 28–41.

[70] Botero, *Reason*. 8.11–12; 8.5.

clusive concern for procreation of the species. And already in 1598 the mental wheels are in motion that four years later will produce the program of eugenics that distinguishes the *City of the Sun*. At this stage, however, despite numerous scattered appeals to Plato throughout the work, Campanella will not find his solution in the father of philosophy but nearer at hand with the Turk and the system associated with the *devshirme*: the seraglio, cloister, or seminary productive of civil servants as well as soldiers. It is into these seminaries that the sultan has drawn the best youth from his conquests where, removed from parents, they are brought up in sole devotion to their new father whom they will serve, some with pen, others with arms.[71]

Pursuant to his convictions that men not metal constitute the king's wealth, Campanella, guided implicitly by Telesian notions of hot and cold, urges a steady program of enforced intermarriage: the Spanish with the Flemings and with the Italians. In this respect he finds especially vexatious the fact that the Spaniards in Naples marry not the local Italian women but their own kind. Intermarriage will promote hispanization and also spread the Catholic faith of the male. Campanella even encourages the Spanish soldiery in rapine, seizing their women in war and siege, later to marry them but always to beget children whose ultimate support falls to the king. Thus becomes apparent the need for a system of seminaries providing the receptacles and nurseries for children of the poor as well as the natural offspring for purposes of a military education. The recruitment of these seminaries even extends itself to including children of heretics and of Moslems taken in war. It is not at all clear how the female population directly relates to these nurseries for soldiers; while no explicit provision is made for there being places of insemination, the presence of women, presumably in some form of workhouses, would appear to be for more than making shirts and the accoutrements of war.[72] And if there prevails the Turkish model with these cloistered cells for indoctrination and training, its Roman and more recently Tridentine parallel reinforces the centrality of this institution.[73] Such colleges existed according to Campanella from apostolic times and now through the pope those of the Marionites, Franciscans, and Dominicans are nothing else but seminaries for apostolic soldiers. In relating the two emerging types of seminaries, Campanella observes that the Church is all too frequently burdened with useless *religiosi*, who lack the

[71] El, 89–90; EC, 68.

[72] The implied workhouses for women are curiously reminiscent of the *gynaecea* that David Herlihy describes, where in many instances the cloth works apparently doubled as brothels. Herlihy goes on to observe significantly that this institution, principally for weaving and the production of clothing, constitutes one of the very few bridges spanning the gulf between the classical world and the Middle Ages, references to the *gynaeceum* persisting from the fifth to the thirteenth centuries. See Herlihy, *Opera muliebria: Women and Work in Medieval Europe* (Philadelphia, 1990), 18–19, 20, 84.

[73] Concilium Tridentinum, sess. xxiii, canon XVIII, *COD*, 726–29.

vocation, yet seek this life for security, comfort, and scandal, thus depriving the king of vassals, tribute, and soldiers. The new military seminary would correct this sad state of affairs, extending to all peoples a system for constituting their hispanicity.[74]

The seminary system, whatever its utopian or dystopian overtones, figures significantly in countering the inequalities and injustices of current Mediterranean societies. In emphasizing the necessity for mutual love (*lamore scambiole*) as the virtual cement of society, Campanella finds such unity seriously undermined by Europe's exploitation of America. For the gold of the New World, by generating avarice, has to a significant extent ruined the Old World. It has created great inequalities, driving a wedge between very rich and an excessive number of very poor. By raising the price of basic commodities, it has led many to penury, others to banditry, begetting disorder, rapacity, and pride against which Plato warned. Instead of the saving balm of equality and love, present society allows a few of inordinate wealth to use their riches in support of a lifestyle marked by dogs, horses, and jesters, gold trappings, prostitutes, and display, resulting in the intimidation of justice and the arrogant swagger of arbitrary abuse—a picture that Campanella appears to draw from his Neapolitan observations. Among his recommendations to the king for bridging the gap and constraining the rich looms prominently the program of international mixing of populations by intermarriage and the military seminaries, both seeking to redress the general hatred felt for the Spaniard. Through the seminaries especially soldiers from diverse nations will be mutually nurtured and sustained.[75]

Because of the bewildering richness of Campanella's fertile imagination as it spills itself out through repetitions and circumlocutions of the *Monarchia di Spagna* one can easily lose sight of his main argument, particularly when provided with Boteran lenses. It becomes all the more important to insist upon the centrality of hispanization as preeminently expressed in a program of eugenics and recruitment involving intermarriage of populations and a system of seminaries. Furthermore, although stated principally in the middle of the work, the theme persists in the later chapters. Indeed our presumed Roman editors of Campanella's manuscript did not miss the point but among the Boteran materials included a passage from book 5 in which the ex-Jesuit observes that the kings of Portugal have founded in India colleges and seminaries in which great numbers of youths from all nations submit to the splendid discipline of the Jesuits, who have produced marvelous results with their seminaries both in Germany against the heretic and in the New World with the infidel.[76]

---

[74] El, 90–97; EC, 68–79; cf. also TC-*T*, XXIII, 170–95.
[75] El, 113, 123–26; EC, 86–87, 94–97.
[76] De Mattei, *Politica*, 33–34; El, 148–49; EC, 114–15.

On his own part Campanella in his chapter on Spain distinguishes two types of educational practice to be pursued in the seminaries: for his foreign subject the new Austrian order—to be established as the king's preachers[77]—will impart arts and languages; for those within Spain proper such fare is subordinated to the necessity of military sciences and the exercise of arms. Throughout the provinces of Spain by means of intermarriage and a common set of seminaries the old customs gradually give way to Castilian gravity. Yet the very fact that such a process is to be tempered by Italian influence and that even in Spain itself Italians are to bear offices along with the Spaniards suggests that hispanization is not a one-way street: Campanella seeks the best from other peoples to effect the universality of the Spanish monarchy. Within the Iberian peninsula itself, given its first unification since the Visigoths, hispanization assumes the fateful form of a mixing and sharing of offices, the implicit breakup of the Castilian monopoly to preferment that now must be extended to Portuguese and Aragonese as well as to the remotest peoples of the peninsula—Asturians, Valencians, Biscayans—so that the disparate, disseveral parts of Spain might enjoy a common familiarity. A quarter century later a possible reader of this passage would express more pungently the same idea in a proposal to his sovereign master for a Union of Arms: that the parts might come to know themselves as one and His Majesty become truly king of Spain.[78]

In treating Sicily and Sardinia, Campanella looks to the seminaries for the training of soldiers whose mothers have been taken from the Turks and Moors; navigation figures significantly and an emphasis upon instruction in Arabic would appear to link these seminaries with the convents of the friars.[79] Furthermore the Turkish threat gives added importance to matrimonial exchange and the seminaries as the chief means for Spain to build up its population and train its soldiers.[80]

Given these priorities, Campanella's argument, when it addresses the New World, proves hardly surprising. In accordance with his previous statements, he insists that the true wealth of the Indies is not bullion at all but men. Although he can readily recommend that a gifted Indian convert can be educated as a priest and serve in converting his own people or that a converted Indian chieftain be rewarded with a Spanish barony as a means of engaging his affections, the entire native population of America becomes a vast quarry for resolving the problem of labor in Spain's global empire. Apparently innocent of the ghastly loss of population suffered by the Indians through disease during the course of the sixteenth century and equally innocent of their unsuitability for hard labor, Campanella will recommend that the unconverted

---

[77] El, 147–48; EC, 113.
[78] Elliott, *Catalans*, 199–200; El, 164–71; EC, 125–28.
[79] El, 177–78; EC, 136–38.
[80] El, 259–60; EC, 201.

serve as a pool of recruitment for use in the galleys and the converted participate in a global resettlement and repopulation. Transported to the shores of Africa, Asia, and Spain, they will establish colonies and be trained in agriculture, artisanry, manufacture. In being hispanicized, some may become soldiers and even *religiosi* but the main point would be to relieve the Spaniard of labor and free him for concentrating upon soldiery. In each province of the New World an Austrian seminary is to be established for training young soldiers who, according to the Turkish model of the Janissaries, would know no father other than the king. A seminary for women and another for mariners would supplement the military seminary of the new Austrian religious order.[81]

Would that we might know more about the women's seminary and its relation to the military and naval seminaries. Other than suggesting that it constitutes a workshop for poor women, Campanella leaves the reader's imagination unmoored. Regarding the marinal or naval seminaries he is somewhat more informative: in the final chapter on navigation he calls for the establishment of such seminaries from Sicily to the Canaries, Hispaniola and on to the Philippines, girdling the globe and back to the shores of Spain—seminaries where youths may learn how to build ships, to know the stars, and to learn the use of the compass, marinal tables, and charts.[82]

In the final third of the *Monarchia di Spagna* Campanella treats Spain's relations to other lands, peoples, and polities throughout the world. There is no need to follow his effervescent political imagination through the wealth of idealistic proposals, cunning designs, and arresting insights. No matter how seemingly preposterous, he needs, however, to be taken seriously: for example, the idea of a Spanish naval mobilization in the Baltic based on Danzig would in fact assume the form of a Spanish-German trading association with naval/military implications for Poland against Sweden in the 1626–28 period.[83] The prisoner's political imagination, shaped by European developments of the final decade of the sixteenth century, conveys a growing anxiety in the face of England's mounting marinal enterprise. Indeed the magic of Magellan's achievement has been capped by Drake.[84] Beyond the thematic undercurrent of hispanization persisting in these final chapters Campanella's recommendations for Spain's global policy in 1600 are largely shaped by his perception of *occasione* enunciated earlier in chapter 8: Spain's opportunity consists in the religious/political discord of its enemies and the present miraculous navigation of Spaniards. Thus he will advocate for the king of

---

[81] El, 284–85; EC, 218–19.

[82] El, 289–90; EC, 223. It should be noted, however, that this final chapter of definitive redaction is significantly shorter than that of the published, interpolated editions.

[83] On the specter of a Spanish Baltic presence from a Protestant perspective, see Michael Roberts, *Gustavus Adolphus: A History of Sweden, 1611–1632* (London/New York/Toronto, 1958), 2:281–82, 315–18, 349–50.

[84] El, 201–2; EC, 155–56.

Spain a policy of *divide et impera*: in the British Isles England should be set against Scotland, Parliament's republicanism developed against the Crown, the sectarianism of Calvinism promoted; in France, if the heretics do not succeed in dividing the kingdom, work to make the kingship elective; to the Turk export the current philosophies and grammatologies in order to convey every possible ounce of discord. Our second Machiavel speaks the current political language of dissimulation, force, and *ratio status*.

Although the Spanish monarchy sorely lacks that territorial consolidation evident with the Turk, through superior naval power (a Boteran note) the disjointed parts are held together. Little wonder that the final chapter of the work deals with navigation. As earlier noted, it is by superior seamanship, marvelous navigation, that Spain has overcome its greatest problem of distance and the division of its own kingdoms, thus enabling it to maintain and augment such an empire. Warming to his subject in the penultimate chapter on the New World's discovery by Spain, Campanella observes that whereas Solomon took three years to reach Goa and Ceylon, Spain now makes the journey in three months, girdling the globe and shrinking by marinal skill those very distances that would otherwise weaken this empire.[85] Campanella calls for a navy of a thousand ships and new cities lining the shores of Spain's possessions that the English threat might be withstood and commerce among the disparate parts developed. The newly established marinal seminaries will train the young in using the stars, the compass, and maps for navigating. Just as the Flemings and Germans are to have their mathematical and scientific skills employed in the New World, so the Portuguese and Genoese are to have their marinal talents tapped. Arsenals and shipyards are to cover the globe, Columbus's seminal desire to know the world advanced—all in order that the entire earth may become hispanized ("e cosi si spagnolarebbe il mondo").[86] Hispanized indeed under Italian leadership! Here as elsewhere, Campanella's very conceptualization of manifold provisions for a global, oceanic navy allows him to qualify as the veritable Von Tirpitz of the Dominican order

Campanella's words help remind us of the naval and navigational superiority achieved by Spain during the sixteenth century: Spanish ships course throughout all oceans; Spanish technical works on navigation are disseminated and read in all western European languages; Spanish shipyards along the Biscayan coast are among the most productive in Europe. Indeed only by naval prowess might the Spanish *monarquía* transcend its invertebrate nature. In a sense throughout the discourse Campanella represents the Spanish monarchy as an oceanic power—at the very least the first Atlantic power. This naval superiority seems to have crested in the early 1580s just before the

---

[85] EI, 271; EC, 212.

[86] EI, 293–94; EC, 224–27. The Italian can be found in the middle of chap. 32 of the definitive, uninterpolated original. See also n. 55, *supra*.

Grand Armada, at a time when its ostensible commander, the experienced Admiral Alvaro de Bazan, marquis of Santa Cruz, still supervised naval matters, a time when the governor of the Philippines could write the Great King that a force of eight thousand Spaniards and a fleet of twelve or thirteen galleons would suffice to bring the Chinese Empire to its knees, a time when Philip himself pondered turning the entire Pacific into a Spanish lake by establishing controlling fortresses at the Straits of Magellan and at Malacca in the Moluccas.[87] Yet by the last quarter of the century the productivity of Spanish naval yards began to falter, experiencing a growing lack of resources.[88] Worse still, after 1588, along with the difficulty of obtaining resources, a dearth of trained personnel became evident. To check this decline of the navy, which continued into the next reign, Philip III, acting on the recommendations of a naval commission, will provide for the establishment of two marinal seminaries in November 1607.[89] Against such a background Campanella's sense of the English challenge to Spain's traditional naval superiority appears all the more fateful.

The closing passages of the final chapter, celebrating this "glorious Spanish monarchy which encompasseth the whole earth,"[90] possess special weight and dramatic force as events would prove. From the beginning Campanella had been quick to write France off, ever since the Carolingian failure, as an imperial power and rival to Spain; imprisonment after 1599 prevented his fully assessing at this time France's new, energetic king, Henry of Navarre. England, however, presented a very different case. Although lacking imperial pretensions, according to Campanella, England's naval enterprise and increasing omnipresence and depredations along the shores of a Spanish world cast a deepening shadow over Campanella's assessment of the universal monarchy's opportunities and danger. His long imprisonment, beginning in 1599, managed to spare him knowledge of the even greater naval and colonial challenge presented by the Dutch, now turned against the Spanish global empire rather than against England, as Campanella would have liked. With the reality of Spain's empire in the balance both in fact and in the friar's mind at the time of

---

[87] Irving Leonard, *Books of the Brave* (Cambridge, Mass., 1949), 236–38, 220. The global imperialism of both papal Rome with its *Romanitas* and Gothic Spain is well attested by the two sonnets appearing at the beginning of Fray Juan González de Mendoza's *Historia de las cosas mas notables, ritos, y costumbres del gran Reyno dela China* (Rome: Barth. Grassi [sic], 1586), [8]–[8ᵛ]. See the present author's "Spain's Asian Presence," 623–46. See also the fundamental articles of Geoffrey Parker cited in n. 45, *supra*.

[88] Lawrence A. Clayton, "Ships and Empire: The Case of Spain," *Mariner's Mirror* 62 (1976): 235–48.

[89] Jesús Varela Marcos, "El seminario de marinos: Un intento de formacion de los marineros para las armadas y flotas de Indias," *Revista de historia de America* 87 (1979): 9–36.

[90] El, 253–54; EC, 196. The English rendering is that of Chilmead, who in his translation or interpretation has shifted the emphasis from the navy's global presence to that of the Spanish empire.

his second redaction at the end of 1598, the gathering crisis required a wise mariner to adjust the tiller, a prudent pilot to grasp the rudder. Well might he call in his concluding appendix for *un saggio timoniero*. Given the current regime of the duke of Lerma, Spain would have to wait for the subsequent reign before a statesman advanced to the demanding challenge of grasping that tiller. Of the several qualities that the count-duke of Olivares shared with the Neapolitan prisoner a flair for the grand design, for policy of global dimensions, appeared prominent.

We have devoted apparently inordinate attention to the *Monarchia di Spagna* not only because of its import for the subject of universal monarchy but also because it was the most widely read of all Campanella's works during the early modern period. In places amazingly perceptive and shrewd the prisoner with comparable frequency overshot the mark. As Louis Elzevir would observe, Campanella's legal prescriptions were often sound enough but the means of implementing these recommendations were lacking, for he simply did not know. His adherence to Spain as the appropriate vehicle for universal monarchy would continue until 1628 not out of any love for the hispanic but principally out of respect for its apparent power. In fact as late as the *Monarchia messiae* of 1633 we can catch stray remains of that Spain which is *brachium Dei*.[91] Two years of relative freedom after his release from Neapolitan dungeons in 1626 sufficed to attenuate that awe for Spanish power and begin the process of shifting his hopes to France, but not before he had restated his basic position toward Spain's imperial destiny in works deriving from the earlier period of his Neapolitan captivity. All those works belonging to the hispanophile canon, to which should be added parts of the *Aforismi Politici* dating from 1601, crowd the first years of his imprisonment. By 1609–10 Campanella will desist from the effort to liberate himself by means of fervent loyalty to Spain.[92]

In the *Aforismi politici* Campanella elaborates some already established points. On Spain's use of language for empire Campanella has reason to assert that "qui non hispanizat non catholice christianizat" and that the New World was gained more by use of language than arms, in referring to the achievement of the religious orders. When he remarks that Charles V's empire was composed more by language than by arms, we must assume that he intends the American not the European one. Speculating on population, he places the French at twenty million and the Spanish at three million; although the latter prevail by use of language, still with an earlier population of eleven million (!) the Spanish have sent so many to America and throughout Europe that Spain's position becomes precarious and hardly rectified by the fact that they fail to

[91] TC-*MM*, 71.
[92] TC-*DPI*, 17; cf. TC-*AfP*, 12.

hispanize their allies and subjects, as did the Romans.[93] Here Campanella exaggerates a note struck by Botero concerning the demographic drain of American conquest and settlement upon both Spain and Portugal.[94] Nevertheless he can still cast Spain in the role of gathering together the world at the disposal of God to achieve the prophesied unity and conversion to the golden age of innocence.[95]

In the *Discorsi ai principi d'Italia* among the now familiar themes bearing on Spain a new one pertaining to its presence in the Italian peninsula emerges. Spain receives both praise and blame: since the creation of the world there has never been such a great and admirable empire as that of Spain, founded more by the secret Providence of God than by human ingenuity; yet along with the Columban achievement of carrying Caesar and Christ to a new hemisphere, Spain suffers from lack of population on account of the sterility of its women, the loss by warfare, the practices of primogeniture, the number of clergy, and above all the failure to adopt the remedy "con insertar i semi o con spagnolizzar l'altre nazioni" so that the world might be united under one religion and one happy principate in which all might live as in the golden age.[96] From an Italian perspective, however, in the first decade of the century the Spanish enjoy preference; if any foreigners are to be suffered, the Spanish are the least offensive. Insofar as they seek to realize the providential one sheepfold and one shepherd (John 10:26), the Spanish are not to be excluded but are to receive support. Moreover since they already have a great part of Italy, it is best that they remain and like the former Lombards be Italianized, rather than inviting in new peoples to Italy's ruin.[97] Campanella would here make Italy and Italians the beneficiaries of Spain's providential mission of conquest, which has its sole justification in the propagation of religion. Indeed the king of Spain should be welcomed even to the extent of his coming to Italy, there to make his seat of empire.[98]

Like so many of Campanella's writings the most consistently prophetic and apocalyptic, the *Articuli prophetales*, had a long gestation beginning from the earliest moments of Neapolitan imprisonment and culminating in 1607. Insofar as Spain figures in this work its expectably prophetic role remains uppermost. With a messianic sword the Spanish will prevail in the New World and then the golden age will break in.[99] More than any other nation, Spain by its achievements conforms to the prophecies of Scripture, especially those in

[93] TC-*AfP*, 17/6–8.
[94] Botero, *Reason* 8.5.
[95] TC-*AfP*, pt. 2, X, 21–22.
[96] TC-*DPI*, 115–28 (V).
[97] TC-*DPI*, 145–48 (VIII).
[98] TC-*DPI*, 157–58 (X).
[99] TC-*AP*, 131.

228 CHAPTER VI

Isaiah where the unique and final *brachium* of God (Isa. 51:5) can only be the ultimate monarchy of the Spanish king.[100] Had not the Gallic kingdom expended its imperial effort at the time of Charlemagne against the Moslems? Reiterated is the expectation of the Spanish king's election to the empire.[101] Prophecy, astrology, the course of the sun as it approaches the earth, all attest to the fact that no other universal monarchy can be expected than that of Spain.[102] Its navigators press on to the Arctic and Antarctic poles; a Spanish/Jesuit takeover is expected in Japan.[103] Thus Campanella believed in the first decade of his imprisonment. Twenty years of mounting personal frustration, Spain's own faltering performance in Europe, and the more decisive actions of its Gallic rival would shake that confidence in Spain and redirect it.

UNIVERSAL MONARCHY RECONSIDERED: BOURBON FRANCE EMERGENT

Campanella's political writings, which figure so significantly in his total oeuvre, derive from two periods in his life: those from the first decade of his imprisonment purveying an hispanophile aura; and those from the last decade of his life, when he turned to France as the instrument for the realization of his persisting vision—the realization of universal monarchy. Within diversity exists consistency. And the shift from Spain to France not only conformed to the development of his own personal interests but also to the realities of European political events. In the new articulation of his basically consistent political vision one element will appear to have suffered displacement: traditional title to empire, the election to Holy Roman Emperor, no longer figures as apparently indispensable to that kingdom seeking world hegemony.

The advance of the Spanish Army of Flanders into France in 1636, its Polish cavalry marauding to within thirteen leagues of Paris, may well have been a feint on the part of the cardinal-infant,[104] but to Richelieu and Louis XIII it seemed horribly real. Corbie, where the Spanish thrust ultimately stayed, would give its name to that dreadful moment. And before *l'année de Corbie* had run its course Paris would be in an uproar, Richelieu would be reduced to convulsive, inarticulate sobs, and something like a *levée en masse* would be attempted.[105] At the beginning of the campaign the likelihood of such events must have seemed remote. Then, Richelieu was relaxing in the last days of May at Conflans-l'Archevêque, the splendid chateau expanded

[100] Ibid., 171–79.
[101] Ibid., 241.
[102] Ibid., 283.
[103] Ibid., 289–90, 78.
[104] J. I. Israel, "A Conflict of Empires: Spain and the Netherlands, 1618–1648," *PP* 76 (August 1977): 70; on the presence of Polish cavalry in the Army of Flanders see R. A. Stradling, *Spain's Struggle for Europe, 1598–1668* (London/Rio Grande, 1994), 260–61.
[105] Carl J. Burckhardt, *Richelieu and his Age: Power Politics and the Cardinal's Death*, trans. Bernard Hay (New York, 1965), 3:174–75.

and embellished by Villeroy in the preceding century. The cardinal would have wandered in the gardens formerly dignified by Ronsard and gazed upon the distant confluence of the Marne with the Seine. With the court residing at Fontainebleau he even found time to arrange for a royal preacher.[106] Yet for himself and his own entourage he seemed to have ready at hand for the occasion a more exotic cleric.

The emerging crisis clearly called for a rallying cry, an affirmation of purpose, an assertion not just of the endurance of the French realm but of its essential greatness, its strength, and even its impending triumph. While these tense months were to see no lack of propaganda from both the Spanish and the French sides and the present moment certainly required an exhilarating, stiffening statement, the presence and work of one major figure have been ignored by most treatments of the subject.[107] Ever since his flight from Rome in October 1634, Tommaso Campanella had been well received in France, at least up to this time, lionized at court and in the circles of the Dupuy. Campanella bore the celebrity of a man who had sought to overthrow the Spanish viceroyalty in Naples, had suffered twenty-seven years of continuous imprisonment, had written prodigiously on all subjects, and now to the detriment of France's great enemy had renounced his long-held conviction of the Spanish monarchy as the instrument of universal order and turned instead to his host country, France, as the vehicle for the realization of his persisting vision. Before the charm wore off and the celebrity faded, France could only delight in its own acquisition and the discomfiture of its rival. How best could he be used in the present crisis?

In a letter of July 15, 1636, to the cardinal-nephew Francesco Barberini in Rome Campanella reports in a postscript of having delivered in the presence of Richelieu himself, together with assembled bishops, *parlementaires*, and titled nobility, a sermon at the express request of the cardinal-duke on June 8 at Conflans entitled "On the Authority of the Pontiff for Establishing or Shifting Empire."[108] The sermon has not survived. We are left with two passing statements of an otherwise lost event. If, however, we are to credit Cam-

---

[106] Gabriel Hanotaux, *Histoire du Cardinal de Richelieu* (Paris, 1944), 5:152; *Lettres, instructions diplomatiques et papiers d'état du cardinal de Richelieu*, ed. M. Avenel (Paris, 1863), 5:476. Richelieu's letters signed from Conflans begin on May 26 and run at least through June 22, 1636; by the thirtieth Richelieu was back in Paris (5:472–95).

[107] For Campanella's absence, see such notable treatments of the subject as William F. Church, *Richelieu and Reason of State* (Princeton, 1972), and José Maria Jover, *1635: Historia de una polémica y semblenza de una generación* (Madrid, 1949).

[108] TC-*Lett.*, 349: "All'8 di giugno ho fatto un sermone De auctoritate pontificis supra imperio instituendo, mutando etc., in presenza del cardinal duca che me l'ha comandato, e di vescovi e consiglieri del parlamento e titulati in Conflan[s]. Altrice lo dirá." Campanella's earlier letter to Peiresc, dated June 19, 1636, most recently recovered by Germana Ernst and Eugenio Conone (cf. chap. 2, n. 7, *supra*), further confirms the event, in this manner: "io facessi un discorso politico sopra li presenti affari" (362).

panella's postscript, two points emerge. First that the announced theme of the sermon, at least as represented by Campanella to the papal curia, was the pope's right to shift the title and thus the reality of empire from one dynasty to another. While it was prudent of him to represent to Cardinal Barberini the event of the sermon under the rubric of advancing papal authority, we can be sure that such a theme served as but one among several selected issues entangled in the network of a larger context, a political program that he had been devising in the previous months. His earlier representation of the event as having given "a political discourse on present affairs" may be nearer the mark. Despite the characteristic indiscretion of its author, even Campanella would not expect to hold the attention of a largely Gallican audience for long by celebrating the virtues of papal authority. Second, it is worth noting that according to Campanella Richelieu had commanded the sermon. The cardinal seemed to know his man for the occasion. Both points direct our attention to the fact that for the past eighteen months Campanella had been engaged in making a number of political statements, often of a fragmentary, piecemeal sort, none of which was published during his own lifetime and would only begin to be published in the late nineteenth century, continuing up to the present. At this moment of invasion it appeared that there would be no harm and perhaps even some good in committing the friar's words to the air.

Other than attempting to reconstruct the needs, priorities, and preoccupations of the moment, how does one recover the content of a lost sermon? Fortunately, the 1635–36 period constitutes a watershed in Campanella's political thinking and the second great period of productivity in his political writings, the earlier having occurred during the first ten years of his imprisonment (1600–1610). It can be argued that the opportunity to deliver his sermon defined a moment that crystallized his political program and dramatized his own effective shift from Spain to France as the appropriate vehicle for realizing universal monarchy. Thus all the available writings from this period might be freely exploited. Indeed there is a remarkable consistency among the political ideas of Campanella during this period: the same themes, refashioned in the course of 1635, recur repeatedly, later enjoying an occasional elaboration. A more cautious approach would be to limit oneself scrupulously to those surviving fragments that clearly precede the event of the sermon. Such an approach, however, would truncate the momentum in the development of Campanella's thought and the potential impact of the opportunity to address the French government. Despite the fact that the most illuminating and extensive work of this period and in many ways of Campanella's entire political development—*The Monarchies of the Nations*—has been variously dated as having been completed either before or after the sermon but within this same two-year period, all the major themes had been enunciated and deployed in these works written in the course of 1635, especially the *Documents for the French People* and what amount to being drafts of the later *Monarchies of the*

Nations.[109] Consequently we propose to reconstruct the sermon in terms of the themes elaborated in the earlier works—principally the *Documents*, the draft "Whether the Monarchy of Spain is growing, remaining stable or faltering," and the *Political Aphorisms for the Present Necessity of France in 1635*. We will only have recourse to the possibly subsequent works, completed in the second half of 1636, insofar as they clarify or elaborate the formulation of a position. Coming as it did in the wake of Campanella's reconstruction of his political priorities in accordance with the new philogallic orientation, the military sermon represented the culmination of his political thinking in the final period of his life and his ultimate program for attaining that goal enunciated from the very beginning of his career—universal monarchy.

Of all the tracts, orations, and discourses making up the pastiche of Campanella's piecemeal pamphleteering during this period, certainly the most interesting, judged by its various titles and its literary form, is the *Documenta*. Like so much else in the reconstitution of the Campanellan corpus the tract was identified and published by the late Luigi Firpo. Its subtitles provide suggestive background and motivation for its composition. The first reads: "Response to the murmurings and clandestine books spread throughout Paris against the Most Christian King and the Cardinal Duke, the King's Achates and the realm's Joseph, in the year 1635 and the means for overthrowing Hispanism. Charlemagne to the French." A variant title, more succinct, offers the following: "Charlemagne, 1635. *Documents for the French*. Defense of the King and of the Regime and chief ministers and Indication of the way for

---

[109] Firpo has here resolved many of the tangled threads involving *Le Monarchie*. In LF-*Bibl.*, 197, he first identified one of its parts, *An Monarchia hispanorum sit in augmento vel in statu, vel in decremento*, as philogallic and deriving from the 1628–32 period. Later in his *Opuscoli inediti*, 169–70, he identified it as TC-*CA*, written in 1635. Still later, in 1961 (TC-*US*, 775–76), Firpo, having acquired new manuscript sources, identified this title with the first part of *Le Monarchie*, dating it late 1636 rather than Amabile's estimate of the end of 1635. Firpo also hazarded that the Conflans sermon probably corresponded to a hitherto unidentified title appearing in the 1638 index, volume 10 of Campanella's works as "Utrum imperium Romanum hoc tempore mutari debeat, et possit, et a quo." A later part of *Le Monarchie* is represented by the *Comparsa regia*, which Amabile had designated as "un disegno di appello del Re di Francia, al Papa, contro Spagna, perchè il Papa nominasse motu proprio il Re dei Romani e transferisse," and which Firpo believed to be absorbed into the larger Italian work in 1635 but not before July 31 (LF-*Bibl.*, 151–52). By 1969 on the basis of the new evidence (TC-*OC*, 304–10), Firpo seemed to be ready to accept Amabile's earlier dating of that composite Italian work *Le Monarchie* as being toward the end of 1635 (cf. TC-*DMI*, 213, n. 3) Much of this bibliographical tangle stems from the fact that the titles to fragments of *Le Monarchie* are shifting and do not correspond precisely to anything in the later index. In her forthcoming "Introduzione," Professor Ernst, while decisively and dramatically reentitling the work *Monarchia di Francia*, correctly emphasizes that it is a work in a state of becoming where the materials have not been systematically assembled. It would thus appear to be fruitless to try to affix a specific date to its completion in the 1635–36 period. It should also be clear that even if by a remote chance Campanella finished with *Le Monarchie* in the latter half of 1636, the ideas and issues defining his new philogallic position had been established by the time of the Conflans sermon.

the overthrow of Hispanism."[110] Artfully Campanella places the entire discourse in the mouth of Charlemagne, who now is made to address his people. While the presentation is scholastic and wooden, the intention is clear enough. Beyond simply adding authority to his thoughts, Charlemagne occupied a particular place in the understanding, or better misunderstanding, of the Dominican friar. Almost a decade previously he had grouped Constantine the Great, Theodosius, and Charlemagne together as three magi in a common effort to advance universal empire under the aegis and authority of the papacy.[111] In his continuing quest for the empowerment of Christianity Campanella, by constantly representing Charlemagne as the loyal, effective champion of the Church, sets the context of his argument and reminds us of his priorities. Fed by current imperial aspirations from the years of Henry IV, the contemporary resort to the name of the Carolingian ruler made Campanella's appeal to Charlemagne thoroughly appropriate.[112]

In his casting about during this period of transition for an effective polemical form of exposition, Campanella had attempted using the dialogue in what amounted to being his earliest express support for the policies of Richelieu. This "Political Dialogue among a Venetian, a Spaniard, and a Frenchman," ostensibly dating from 1633, Campanella composed shortly before his flight to France.[113] Campanella seems to have abandoned this form and espoused instead a more discursive style, evinced in the *Political Aphorisms* of 1635 and the draft of what would develop into the *Monarchies of the Nations*. All these polemical writings conform in their essential thematic content: after a more or less rambling comparison of the relative strength of Spain and France that invites the denunciation of the former and the acclaim of the latter, the author addresses the substantive issues of the legitimate use of heretics to advance one's political ends, the invitation for the pope to intervene in the election of the king of the Romans, the consequent release of France for intervention in Italy and Germany, the liberation of the Italian peninsula for Italians, and the destiny of France as the instrument of universal empire. Given this imposing Campanellan panoply of issues, the occasion at Conflans allowed for their

---

[110] TC-*DG*, 57.

[111] Campanella, *Theologia* (La Prima e la seconda resurrezione), ed. Romano Amerio (Rome, 1955), 27:108.

[112] On the Charlemagne theme, see Corrado Vivanti, "Henry IV, the Gallic Hercules," *JWCI* 30 (1967): 176–82; and on the expressly imperial aspiration, see Gaston Zeller, "Les rois de France candidats à l'empire," *Revue historique* 173 (1934): 518–21, as well as Rudolf von Albertini, *Das politische Denken in Frankreich zur Zeit Richelieus* (Marburg, 1951), 146–59, for some contemporary claims to empire and *Monarchie universelle*, reminiscent at times of Pierre Dubois, at others even of Campanellan infection. On France's imperial aspirations during the first third of the seventeenth century, Duchhardt (n. 128, *infra*), 158–59, in considering the contrasting views of Hermann Weber and Fritz Dickmann, observed in 1977 that the final word had not been spoken.

[113] LF-*Bibl.*, 149–51.

exposition. In our effort to reconstruct the sermon we will pursue some of them here.

Before proceeding, however, we need to consider the unique value of one other document, which, although subsequent to Conflans, proves revealing and useful. A memorial of Campanella to Louis XIII, written but three months later and only made available to scholarship since 1986, reveals something nearer to the probable themes and organization of the military sermon and, consequently even more important, the impact of its presentation upon the thinking of the author. The memorial's greater clarity, succinctness, and force, when compared to the other efforts of Campanella in this period, suggest something of that distillation possibly evoked by the opportunity afforded at Conflans. Indeed this memorial to the king, who apparently did not attend the sermon itself, compresses all the themes and issues represented here and possesses an oratorical ring that has undoubtedly been shaped by the experience of the earlier, now lost sermon.

It is reasonable to expect that in keeping with his previous polemical activities Campanella led off with a heavily weighted comparison of the two great powers: certainly both the need to establish context and to encourage the leading members of the Richelieu ministry at its moment of extreme crisis invited a contrast favorable to France. In weighing the superiority of France to Spain in terms of food production, armor, population (always a paramount concern of Campanella), finances, and soldiers, he affirms that God has empowered Louis as His *brachium*—a fateful term taken from Isaiah (51:5) betokening for Campanella the secular champion of the imminent universal theocratic order—to oppose those, he continues, whom now we fear with a false fear. Then after reviewing the sterility of Spanish lands and population, the expulsion of the Jews and Moors, the depletion of its manhood, its soldiery, its bullion, he asks, "Quare ergo timemus?"[114] Campanella appears to have compressed therein all his political revisionism of the past three years in a way that may well have been anticipated by the opportunity of the sermon three months earlier. Let us examine more carefully his specific ideas on the basis of writings prior to June 1636.

In his ruminations of 1635 on the increase or decrease of the Spanish monarchy Campanella framed his argument from the outset in terms of the following question: what must be done at the present time with the Germans and Italians for completing the overthrow of hispanism? He begins by depicting a besieged and failing Spain that can be easily conquered: the Dutch rebellion has compelled the Spanish to yield license to navigate in the New World, where the Dutch obtain acquisitions in Brazil; in Europe they lose Flanders; in Germany, the empire; in Italy they incur a dreadful reputation and encounter the resistance of Savoy. Turning to the relationship of food to population,

[114] TC-*DMI*, 212–21, esp. 216.

Campanella claims that while formerly unable to feed a population, presumably projected for the entire peninsula, of twelve million, now Spain is even unable to feed a reduced population of three million. The Dominican will be somewhat more accurate in his contrasting figure for the current French population—twenty million.[115] Returning to possibly his most fundamental principle concerning the Spanish monarchy, Campanella cites its failure to hispanicize its various peoples as the Romans managed to romanize theirs: what had been an admonition and an exhortation a third of a century earlier during his hispanophile period now becomes a flail to whip his opponent. And another earlier perception is turned against the failing giant. The Spanish power has been sustained by foreign officers—Parma, Spinola, Colonna, Wallenstein, Columbus.[116] In the concurrent composition of the *Monarchies of the Nations* he will condemn Spain for its dependence upon foreign technology—the compass, the printing press, the arquebus derived from Germans and Italians.[117] Compared with the relative consolidation of the French realm and the essential coherence of its people, a point clearly stated in the memorial to Louis XIII,[118] Campanella presents a famous image of the Spanish monarchy as a global monster far more monstrous than Pufendorf's later characterization of the Holy Roman Empire: the Spanish monster is three-headed (triceps), with its essence in Germany, its existence in Spain, its worth in Naples, *monstrose quidem*, its members dissociated from an absent body.[119] In the concurrent *Monarchies* America becomes almost a fourth head to this great, global serpent.[120] Such is the vulnerability of history's greatest world empire piled together since 1520, while the French realm has matured by way of consolidation over the past 1,200 years.[121]

Central to Campanella's indictment of Spain is what he claims to be its cynical use of religion. Thus he perceives the dreadful specter of his lifelong enemy Machiavellism, that erosive political, secularizing current of the age which now encourages him to associate with the cardinal-duke's ongoing propaganda of the *Bon Français* party. Beyond his general accusation of Spain's manipulation and misuse of religion, the soul and life of any kingdom, the specific issue becomes the legitimate political use of heretics. Although this issue appears in all the friar's political writings of this period, it proves of

---

[115] These various figures appear in the two memorials Campanella published in TC-*DMI*, 208 and 214, the first addressed to an unknown French gentleman in the spring of 1636; the other, to Louis XIII in the autumn of the same year (205).
[116] TC-*CA*, 109–10; cf. TC-*MN*, 316.
[117] TC-*MN*, 317–18.
[118] TC-*DMI*, 216–18.
[119] TC-*CA*, 111.
[120] TC-*MN*, 312–13.
[121] TC-*MN*, 322; cf. also 302, 304.

some significance that it should receive the fullest attention in the *Documenta*. He places his entire argument in the mouth of Charlemagne, who for Campanella represents along with Constantine the Great the correct service of the secular power to the clerical and theocratic.[122] The mythology that Campanella brings to fruition around the figure of Charlemagne during these months had seeds scattered in his thought. It now served to endow the Frankish emperor with a special aura of *religiosità* measured in terms of obedient service to and championship of the papacy. On account of its falling away from this vital principle following the death of Charlemagne, the first French Empire deteriorated and succumbed to heresy.[123] This lapse into heresy remains unexplained. Yet in three successive letters to Urban VIII Campanella credits himself with preaching and conversions by which the French will be returned to the faith, the obedience, and the piety of Charlemagne[124] without which France will not recover its former imperial splendor. This idea of the renewal of empire for France as an event associated with the figure of Charlemagne our Dominican reiterates in the *Monarchies*.[125] In April 1636 in a dedicatory letter to Louis XIII for the Paris edition of *Atheism Conquered* he worked to commit the French king to this supposed Carolingian tradition.[126] Little wonder that in his subsequent memorial to Louis in September he should exhort the monarch to read the life of Charlemagne even while eating![127]

Hence in addressing the *Documenta* we need to hearken to this Campanellan Charlemagne as he explains the political use of heretics. He avers that those who would use heretics for the sake of advancing heretical interests sin absolutely, but whoever uses a heretic *per accidens* and not for heretical purposes does not sin. Just as God can employ the bad and the unjust to chastise Jerusalem, why may He not permit King Louis to use heretics against heretics and pseudo-Christians? Campanella has Charlemagne claiming that heretics can be used against the usurpers and betrayers of the empire, which indeed justifies the horrid medicine represented by the Swedes in being directed against the tyranny of the Habsburgs. Campanella is here heaping blame upon Charles V and Philip II for creating an oppressive, hostile hispanism. Charlemagne calls for the liberation of the electors and empire from this

---

[122] TC-*DG*, 89–91.
[123] TC-*MN*, 301. On earlier references to Charlemagne in Campanella's thought, see TC-*MS*, 93–94, for Charlemagne's fulfilling the protective role for the Church in the past; and TC-*AP*, 171, for the idea that the Gallic kingdom had exhausted itself under Charlemagne in the supreme effort to achieve universal monarchy.
[124] TC-*Lett.*, 352, 362, 375.
[125] TC-*MN*, 320, 342.
[126] TC-*Lett.*, 339–40.
[127] TC-*DMI*, 218, line 96.

tyranny to restore it to its former Carolingian brilliance. Providing Charlemagne with one of his stock notions, the Dominican has him claim that it was not Luther who made the Dutch, the German princes, and the imperial cities heretical but rather Charles V, by allowing Luther to preach and establish his own rite all as a means of keeping the papacy in bondage. Campanella finds the Lutherans in a curious twilight position with respect to the empire. For Luther taught them that the empire of the Germans was the head of the Beast killed in the Apocalypse but resuscitated by the pope. Now as heretics or because of Spanish power or both, the Lutherans are excluded from competing for elections to the imperial office and for participation in the life of the empire. Apparently unaware of the real danger of a Protestant succession to the empire during the period after 1555 and the generally equitable provisions of the Peace of Augsburg for the Lutherans, Campanella urges a restoration of something like normalcy, by the Lutherans returning to the Catholic fold with all admitting the sure true religion as the soul of the republic. He attacks a situation in which all vassals hold to the religion of the prince and with the prince changing they change: thus today it is as if religion were a suit or hat to be changed at will and not maintained as the common cult and way to God. Blaming now the Habsburgs for this confusion, sedition, and the prevalence of sects that deny Providence, the immortality of the soul, and free will, Campanella can claim that Louis XIII the Just fights for faith, the Church, and empire when he opposes the Habsburgs. He uses heretics not as such but as so many hacks or auxiliaries (*caballis*) to achieve a greater end. With the *dévot* party implicitly in mind Campanella asks: is there any among you who would object (*murmuret*) to such action? You may be instructed that it is better for hacks rather than men to perish by war and better heretics than Catholics for effecting liberty and empire in the interest of Catholics.[128]

Earlier in his *Political Dialogue between a Venetian, a Frenchman, and a Spaniard*, Campanella had educed some interesting contemporary cases for the political use of heretics or those of contrary religious belief: the king of France and the Turk, Charles V and his Lutheran sack of Rome, and Cortés' use of the Tlaxcalans against Montezuma. In the dialogue's exchanges the Venetian expresses Campanella's own views. And he allows the prudence of his spokesman gradually to win over the Frenchman, a person of apparently *dévot* inclinations, to Richelieu's policy of exiling the queen mother and Gaston d'Orléans after 1631. Regarding the legitimacy of using heretics the Venetian now speaks:

---

[128] TC-*DG*, 81–84. On the reference to Luther's statement on the empire of the Germans, see WA, 54:282, *Wider das Papsttum zu Rom, vom Teufel gestiftet*, which would have been encountered by Campanella through its Latin edition of 1545 from Wittenberg or Strassburg. On the danger of a Protestant succession to the empire, see the excellent work of Heinz Duchhardt, *Protestantisches Kaisertum und Altes Reich* (Wiesbaden, 1977).

History is full of such coalitions; and the Venetians have a saying, that as we make use of horses, and elephants, and war ships, and like instruments of our will, there is no reason why we should not make use of unbelieving men, or even of devils, in our great necessities. Of such God Himself made use against Egypt, against Sennacherib, against sinful nations. Without accepting their law or sharing their wickedness and their false opinions, we merely use them as instruments, evil instruments for our good; and this rather because we have no commandment of God expressly forbidding us to do so. But leaving this point to the theologians, let us talk as politicians; and so speaking, I say that Richelieu, in all that he has done, has acted most prudently.[129]

Campanella's specific interest in French political developments predates the composition of this dialogue. He appears to have become an intent observer of Richelieu's activities shortly after his release from Neapolitan confinement. For in the first half of December 1628, the news scarcely having arrived in Rome, Campanella devised an oration, now lost, celebrating the fall of La Rochelle.[130] Although the oration seems to have been requested and even delivered by someone else, we can conveniently date from this time the Dominican's increasing attraction to France and to Richelieu.

The problem of the just use of heretics did not limit itself to Richelieu's foreign policy. The siege of La Rochelle in 1628 had raised for Spain the issue of the legitimacy of using heretics to achieve the raison d'etat of Catholic Christian powers. Campanella expectably argues here like a *bon français* but within a broader European ambiance. While somewhat uncomfortable with the peace of Alais and its religious recognition of the Protestants, he can afterwards take heart that such able Huguenot warriors as Rohan, La Force, and Gassion serve well their king.[131] Nevertheless in arguing for the legitimate use of heretics Campanella comes perilously close to that cynical exploitation of raison d'état of which he accused the much abhorred *machiavellistae*. Only his ostensibly higher aims of Catholic empire and papal theocracy might save him from this charge.

Campanella's long-standing controversy with Charles V for having not burned Luther at Worms broadens out now, following the French entry into the war, to a general assault upon the Habsburg dynasty and its apparently private possession (*peculium*) of the imperial office. Indeed Charlemagne reminds us that both the papal and the imperial offices were elective, not heredi-

---

[129] I am here using the English translation provided by Thomas Hodgkin, "Richelieu and His Policy: A Contemporary Dialogue," *English Historical Review* 17 (1902): 20–49, esp. 43. The original is available in Amab., *Doc.*, II, 185–214/244.

[130] LF-*Bibl.*, 193.

[131] TC-*DMI*, 216:80. On the awkward nature of the debates within the councils of Olivares over which side to relieve at La Rochelle, see J. H. Elliott, *The Count-Duke of Olivares* (New Haven/London, 1986), 327–30.

tary. Yet matters recently have degenerated so as to allow the Habsburgs to obtain control not for the good of church or empire but in the interest of Spanish domination. The most recent and calamitous example is Ferdinand II's sending forty thousand troops in 1629 to fight in Italy against Catholics, opposing Catholics to Catholics, leaving Germany open to the Swedes and the Protestants. Here the Habsburgs are clearly not fighting for the faith or the Church but to satiate Spanish ambitions in Mantua. But such Habsburg violations and depredations go back to Charles V, to the sack of Rome, and to his failure to kill Luther as Sigismund had Hus, or at least imprison or exile him.[132] In effect Charles gave Luther license to preach and as a consequence of the Augsburg Interim, one might choose between Luther and the pope. Because Luther, according to Campanella, preached that the clergy ought not to have temporal dominion, Charles presumed to take Rome and the ecclesiastical state, leaving to the pope only the spiritual authority with dependence on him, as the Moslem Mufti depends on the Great Turk. In his espousal and effective nurturing of the Lutherans and his appropriation of the ecclesiastical, Charles V comes to be compared with Henry VIII of England. Little wonder that Pope Paul IV prayed in consistory against this emperor who usurped another's jurisdiction, judged in matters of faith, and filled Christendom with heresies. But Campanella presents an even more sinister feature regarding the Habsburg conniving with heretics in reference to the empire: by retaining the German princes in heresy, Charles had effectively excluded them as competitors for the imperial office.[133] At this juncture, assuming that Campanella included this point in his harangue, some *maîtres des requêtes* and parlementary counselors might well have registered impatience, if not alarm, at Campanella's misunderstanding of the empire's constitution and operation after 1555. For the specter of a Protestant emperor hovered over these decades. And although Bodin's interpretation of the Holy Roman Empire as an aristocratic regime certainly prevailed among French officialdom at this time, Campanella's own concerns suggest a new concentration on the power of the emperor's office, which in the French perception of the Holy Roman Empire would enjoy some recognition during the seventeenth century.[134]

Given the apparent usurpation and abuse of the imperial office by the Habsburgs, Campanella could well argue for effective intervention to translate the office to another dynasty or at least unfasten the Habsburg hold over its pos-

---

[132] TC-*DG*, 74–77. Campanella's perception of Charles V as a sort of crypto-Lutheran occurs as early as 1595 in one of his first tracts, *Dialogo politico contro Luterani, Calvinisti ed altri eretici* (Lanciano: Carabba, 1911), 152, where the emperor is represented as having used the heresiarch in order to advance raison d'état against the papacy.

[133] TC-*MN*, 310, 324–25. See also TC-*Lett.*, 391, 404.

[134] Klaus Malettke, "La presentation du saint empire Romain Germanique dans la France de Louis XIII et Louis XIV," *Francia* 14 (1986): 209–28, esp. 227; but cf. also Duchhardt, *Kaisertum*, 159–61, and n. 153, *infra*.

session. According to Campanella's own representation of his sermon at Conflans to Urban VIII the appeal to papal intervention in the affairs of Europe constituted the sermon's centerpiece. In the previous year he had caused "Charlemagne" to allude to it:

> Thus Louis the Just fights not against piety and faith, which the Habsburgs profess with words, yet negate with their deeds, but against the property of the Spanish monarchy and truly as it is called, the workshop of impiety and against the secret ruin of Christendom by [ostensible] Christianity. I marvel that the great pontiff Urban VIII does not select by *motu proprio* the king of the Romans, which often in difficult situations popes have done, as history, the canons, St. Thomas and other doctors testify; . . . so that by this selection according to papal authority he might abolish bitter wars that rage so long over the issue of selecting a king of the Romans and that they [the Habsburgs] might not continue to possess by heredity the sanctuary of God. For regarding this possession both heresies and wars have been spawned and increased.[135]

In the drafts for the later *Monarchies of the Nations*, completed shortly before the sermon, Campanella enunciated the idea of the French king's appealing to the pope to nominate *motu proprio* the king of the Romans and transfer this dignity from the House of Austria to another dynasty.[136] As reiterated in the *Monarchies* itself, *translatio imperii* to another family becomes the means for ending heresy, tyranny, war, and the exaltation of hispanism over the princes and clergy.[137] For Campanella the pope is so empowered to appoint such a king according to ancient custom and laws.

To those who would claim that the French will never grant that the pope has temporal dominion over kings, Campanella assures his audience that history attests to this power of transfer; Constantine, Charlemagne, and others confess it. Papal intervention does not derogate from the king of France. With the Habsburgs acting not for the good of the Church or the empire but rather for the advantage of the Spanish monarchy, the situation required what would have appeared to his listeners as an embarrassing resort to some defunct theoretical machinery.[138] The best way to bring down the Spanish monarchy is to work through the pope.[139]

Assembling his authorities to justify papal intervention, he cites St. Thomas and Bartolus in providing two reasons (heresy and tyranny) for shifting the empire from the Germans to another nation. This empire has been so long in

---

[135] TC-*DG*, 79–80.
[136] Ibid., n. 1.
[137] TC-*MN*, 328–32.
[138] Ibid., 333. On the last theoretical statements of *translatio imperii*, see Werner Goez, *Translatio imperii* (Tübingen, 1958), 322–29.
[139] Campanella's "Aforismi politici per le presenti necessità di Francia nel 1635" is only available in Amab., *Doc.*, II, 291–97/344, esp. 292–93.

the House of Habsburg as to become hereditary, not elective, thus producing wars and the growth of heresies. As manifest in Charles V's Interim decree, permitting heresy and his having become hispanicized, the empire has been rendered into the private property of the House of Austria and the Spanish monarchy.[140]

Earlier, in drafts of the *Monarchies*, Campanella advanced the appropriateness of a French Empire for the Germans, urging that French and Germans are consanguine and similar, while the Spanish in customs, physiognomy, and blood had nothing in common with the French. He appealed to their mutually shared Carolingian tradition and then seemed to veer away from pressing the idea of a specifically French candidate for the empire; instead he returned to the notion that France would restore to the Germans the power of election that the House of Austria had seized for establishing hispanism over all German princes. He invokes the Germans to elect one from their midst and even suggests the duke of Bavaria or the duke of Neuburg.[141] In terms of confessional orthodoxy and traditional French interest in the empire both the elector and the Count Palatine were reasonable recommendations.[142]

All these drafts of 1635–36, as well as the *Monarchies* tract in which they culminate, draw to their conclusion by means of nationalist-imperialist exhortation. It is reasonable to assume that the sermon likewise ended on this hortatory note. The French have not combatted Spain in order to make for themselves an empire more cruel, absolute, and despotic than that of the Habsburgs but in order to liberate the Church and the princes of both Germany and Italy from the hispanicized Austrian tyranny.[143] Not only as a liberator in the empire but also in the Italian peninsula Campanella would have France intervene. His elaborate plans for realizing an Italy for Italians already evident in this material, yet culminating after June 1636 in the individual addresses to Venice, Genoa, and Savoy, probably did not figure significantly in the sermon and need not detain us. Enough to say that according to Campanella's assessment, France does not want a foot of Italian soil, but for expelling Spain with the cooperation of Venice and the papacy and its benign, remote police service, France would be rewarded with the state of Avignon. For Campanella understands France's interest to be one of internal consolidation and unification; indeed his reading of Botero and his criticism of the Spanish global monster would promote this view. France as the vastest, richest, and most populous of kingdoms would now displace Spain as the *brachium* of the Church and what had heretofore pertained to the supreme secular power in Europe as champion of papal universality now applies to France as *padrona*

---

[140] Ibid., 297.
[141] TC-*CA*, 117–18.
[142] On this point, see Zeller, "Les rois," 522; and Duchhardt, *Kaisertum*, 158–59.
[143] TC-*MN*, 327.

d'Europa.¹⁴⁴ Repeatedly, despite Gaston Zeller, Campanella had enjoined Louis to assume France's proper possessions between the Pyrenees and the Rhine, including Flanders and Burgundy, to achieve its natural frontiers "fines naturales, limites tibi a natura datos" from which consolidated position it could as *padrona d'Europa* comfortably preside with the papacy over Christendom.¹⁴⁵

Campanella may well have concluded his sermon by imparting his powerful sense of *kairos, occasio*, the opportune moment. This preparation for the renewal of empire for the French becomes elsewhere largely a matter of propaganda, of winning men's minds. In contrasting the mentalities of the two nations, he finds the Spanish far more politically adept than the French, who tend to be impulsive and fickle, relying on deeds and personal bravery. The Spanish on the other hand, if faulted for possible timidity, are more astute and pursue the enterprise of empire with negotiations and words.¹⁴⁶ With tongue and pen and the expertise of the intellectual community (*scientiati*) the French cause must be advanced—at Rome among the prelates, among the various offices, congregations, and religious orders. Here particularly and specifically in the Dominican order, given the inroads of Spanish predestinarian theology into the universities of Germany and Italy, the Spanish doctors and their teachings must be replaced. Those sciences that embellish the state must be promoted so that the world turns anew to learn at Paris, as was true during France's first empire, presumably for Campanella at the time of Charlemagne. To hammer home the interlocking nature of the political and the cultural, Campanella cites, as he had on other occasions, the patronage of Cosimo de'Medici in securing his lordship over Florence.¹⁴⁷

For France the moment of *monarchia* has struck. That moment required a

---

[144] Ibid., 335–36, 338, 341; cf. also Franz Bosbach, "Die Habsburger und die Entstehung des Dreissigjährigen Krieges. Die 'Monarchia Universalis.'" in *Krieg und Politik 1618–1648: Europäische Probleme und Perspektiven*, ed. Konrad Repgen (Munich, 1988), 167, in which such a shrewd political mind as Saavedra Fajardo will claim in 1645 that France now pursues universal monarchy, which has been the issue from the beginning.

[145] TC-*DG*, 97; TC-*CA*, 119; TC-*MN*, 346. In the autumn 1636 memorial to Louis XIII Campanella will again identify these *proprios limites* (TC-*DMI*, 208:49–52). In arguing against the contemporary understanding of natural frontiers, Gaston Zeller, "La Monarchie d' Ancien Regime et les frontières naturelles," *Revue d'histoire moderne* 8 (1933): 305–33, does allow (331) that in a period of about three centuries one can come up with a handful of publicists "sans mandat ni responsibilité" who have pronounced for the Rhine frontier as "limites naturelles." More recently Fernand Braudel, *The Identity of France* (London, 1988), 1:321, in considering such statements as "pebbles by the roadside," refers to the apocryphal will of Richelieu, written probably by someone in his entourage, which reads: "the aim of my ministry has been to restore to France the boundaries that nature allotted it. . . . to make Gaul coincide with France and wherever the ancient Gaul existed to restore the new." Braudel avers that before 1642 "one does not find any comparable text anywhere" and that afterwards one must wait until the Revolution.

[146] Jover, *1635*, 322.

[147] TC-*AfP*, XV, 10.

panegyric similar to what Campanella had earlier wrought for Spain, proving that it is more useful for the nations of Europe to yield and subject themselves to France than to Spain, which he would seek to have driven out of the Old World to concentrate its hitherto scattered efforts in the New. He calls for mobilizing the preaching of the clergy in order to remove a current image of the French as heretics and to represent them now as liberators. Capitalizing on French courage and brilliance Campanella urges celerity on the military-political as well as on the cultural levels. He importunes the French to include with their army a philosopher to explain their defects, for he is convinced of the French capacity to acquire but not to conserve. To maintain their fighting élan Campanella would have preachers and poets in the army recounting heroic enterprises, glory, and the Catholic faith.[148] Military as well as cultural discipline constituted part of a larger social disciplining.

If Campanella delivered himself at Conflans, June 8, 1636, of the sermon that he claimed, it would have included, given the audience, the occasion, and the one stated subject of papal intervention, that vast tangle of political ideas he had been devolving during the previous months of 1635 and 1636. While this same period had witnessed a deterioration of his relations to the court and even to Richelieu, his contacts were not so frayed as to prevent him from being consulted on critical occasions up until the end of his life.[149] For once, this Renaissance magus's sense of *occasio* happened to correspond with what appeared to be a fateful shift in European political preponderance. Beyond the papal theocratic universal reference and the preoccupation with Italian politics, there lurked in his thought Boteran notions of territorial consolidation, demographic coherence, and administrability together with Lipsian sensitivity to military and social discipline, all of which made Campanella's counsel very much a product of the period. Most notable is the congruence between the thinking of Campanella and Richelieu in their assessment of defects in the French character, the contrasting Spanish astuteness, and the need for discipline. While none of these ideas is unique or lacking contemporary expression elsewhere, the prominence and vehemence with which both the cardinal and the friar maintained them are striking. Indeed was it possible that the only influential aspect of Campanella's program proved to be the mobilization of the cultural, intellectual life of France for purposes of greater political integration? From the beginning of his political career and reinforced by the commitment endemic to Dominican preaching, he had insisted that by words rather than by arms peoples are led and held together. Their minds must be captured and held by the propaganda of words, yes, and even by pictures and music. If this solarian mobilization of culture for political ends was hardly lost upon the great cardinal at what had been represented to him as the supreme opportunity

[148] TC-*MN*, 342–46.
[149] Blanchet, *Campanella*, 63.

of the French nation, Campanella's perception would capture three centuries later the imagination and performance of V. I. Lenin in another apparently critical moment of history.[150]

In conclusion three issues, stemming from the impact of the Reformation and reflected in Campanella's sermon, need concern us briefly: (1) the papacy's capacity to intervene for shifting the imperial office from one house to another; (2) the extremely hostile Catholic perception of Charles V as a promoter of the Lutheran heresies; and (3) the legitimate use of heretics for political ends. Regarding the first issue, certainly by the time of Pope Paul IV's abortive challenge to the legality of Ferdinand I's assumption of the imperial office, the effectiveness of papal intervention appeared chimerical and part of a past age.[151] Yet at the end of the century both Cardinals Bellarmine and Baronius could champion the idea, and more recently in 1625 the work of P. Santarelli, *De haeresi, schismate, apostasia . . . et de potestate Romani Pontificis in his delictis puniendis*, had incurred the censure of the Faculty of Theology at Paris for asserting the papal right to deprive princes of their crowns.[152] Given Campanella's own commitment to universal papal theocracy, the Dominican friar's espousal of this idea is hardly surprising. But beyond the theorizing and nearer to the political realities of any attempt to shift the succession of the imperial office, the central role of Bavaria with the presence of France looming in the background recurs repeatedly through the entire seventeenth century. Again Campanella seemed to be aware of current political attitudes manifest in the intermittent imperial aspirations of France and its long-standing affinity for Bavaria as potential ally or as alternative candidate. Furthermore if Campanella's resort to papal intervention appeared somewhat archaic, at least he had come to focus upon one of the hottest political issues confronting Europe at the time, namely, the Habsburg virtual possession of the imperial office: indeed two years later the duc de Rohan in his *De l'interest des princes et estats de la chrestienté* would call for the displacement of this dynasty; and in 1640 Boguslaw Philipp von Chemnitz would even advocate the *exstirpatio* of the Habsburgs and the dismantling of the imperial office.[153]

Similarly with respect to his hostility toward Charles V Campanella draws upon a long-standing tradition of interpretation that goes back to the time of

[150] Mikhail Heller and Aleksandr M. Nekrich, *Utopia in Power* (New York, 1985), 53.

[151] On this matter of apparent contemporary irrelevance, see the countervailing argument of Franz Bosbach, "Papsttum und Universalmonarchie im Zeitalter der Reformation," *Historisches Jahrbuch* 107 (1987): 44–76.

[152] On Bellarmine and Baronius, see Goez, *Translatio imperii*; on Santarelli, see André Tuilier, "Richelieu theologien et la Sorbonne," in *Richelieu et le monde de l'esprit*, Sorbonne, November 1985 (Paris, 1985), 285–86.

[153] Cf. Zeller, "Les rois," 516–29, and n. 133, *supra*. On contemporary plans for the removal of the Habsburg dynasty from the imperial office, see the references in Duchhardt, *Kaisertum*, 160–62.

the League of Cognac and the first papal brief (June 23, 1526) to the emperor.[154] The idea of Charles as a sort of crypto-Lutheran was to be sustained in this early period by the Venetian humanist and diplomat Andrea Navagero, but to receive its full efflorescence and stamp at the hands of Gianpietro Carafa, later Paul IV. The Neapolitan prelate's soaring hatred of the Habsburgs constituted the iron theme running throughout his entire career. With increasing indignation he had watched the numerous encroachments of the emperor upon the Church, which Carafa interpreted as the acts of one who sought to use the Protestant agitation as a means of destroying the temporal power of the papacy and of ruling alone in Italy. As fellow Neapolitans, Carafa and Campanella from different periods could agree that the Kingdom of Naples needed closer integration with the papal states. And it was the Carafa pope who would fix upon the Augsburg Interim of 1548, passed without the consent of the Holy See, as the source for establishing two religions. Thus at the inception of his pontificate Paul began proceedings against Charles and Prince Philip in the Roman Inquisition, claiming that the Augsburg decrees proved the emperor to be a schismatic and an abettor of heresy.[155]

Curiously enough what we might call the Carafan interpretation of Charles V and his relation to the Protestant heretics survived and served to reinforce our early-seventeenth-century champions for the legitimate use of and alliance with heretics. In defending the current regime from its Jesuit and *dévot* accusers and in representing the Habsburgs as the earliest friends of heretics, Richelieu's publicist François de Fancan (1627) sought to strip Charles V of any sanctity and religious aura by turning him into a conniving *politique*. In fact he specifically cites the Interim of 1548 whereby Charles becomes the father of schism that has divided Christendom and the promoter of a political relativism toward the religious. One year earlier in another tract Fancan specifically drew upon Campanella's *Monarchia di Spagna* to claim that the House of Habsburg pursues a policy of promoting jealousies and divisions among the German princes in order to advance its own domination and the Spanish penetration of the empire.[156]

---

[154] On the clash between Charles V and Clement VII in 1526 and the propaganda campaign involving the *Pro divo Carolo*, see the present author's *The Emperor and His Chancellor* (Cambridge, 1983), 86–113.

[155] L. von Pastor, *History of the Popes* (London, 1924), 14:76–77, 348–55; on Paul IV's initiation of proceedings against the Habsburgs, see Royall Tyler, *The Emperor Charles the Fifth* (Fair Lawn, N.J., 1956), 110.

[156] Cf. TC-*MS*, 182–86, for the passage used by Fancan. I have had to rely here largely on extensive quotations from Fancan's tracts present in Léon Geley, *Fancan et la politique de Richelieu de 1617 à 1627* (Paris, 1884), 239–57. François de Langlois, Sieur de Fancan, was no ordinary pamphleteer but a stridently anti-Spanish *politique* and at the center of Richelieu's pamphleteers during the early years of his ministry. See William F. Church, *Richelieu and Reason of State* (Princeton, 1972), 98–100, 110–11, 116–20 *passim*. Albertini, *Das politische Denken*, 141, virtually ignores Fancan, rather surprisingly, and does not include his writings in his bibliography (cf. 214, 217).

A decade later in the great contest of rival propaganda campaigns in 1635, the French position distinguished the autonomy of the political realm from the theological and moral, whereas the Spanish publicists advanced the one overriding idea of the subordination of the political to the religious as the basis of the *monarquía católica*. In defending his master's alliances with heretics, the preemient French publicist Jeremy Ferrier asserted that by using Lutheran soldiers against France, Charles V had long ago made licit the employment of heretics. If Charles could claim to use them as subjects (*subditos*) and not *infideles*, likewise the king of France can ally with the Turks not as infidels but as allies. While Ferrier urged balance rather than a single hegemony as the appropriate condition for European political life, his fellow publicist Besian Arroy invoked the image of Charlemagne as the prototype for France's monarchy of the West. For the king of France has more authority than any other monarch of the world. Rejecting the legality of any subsequent alienation from the realm of Charlemagne, Arroy calls upon Louis the Just to rule over all this kingdom, including Spanish, Italian, and German appendages. And Arroy affirms that outside their doctrinal errors heretics are able to effect some good and just actions. Hence it becomes permissible to ally with them, yet without partaking of their errors.[157]

Thus again it would appear that Campanella reflects many of the currents of his age. If he dreams, he dreams with considerable shrewdness the dreams and aspirations of that age. For he had managed to imbibe deeply from the political currents present at this time in Richelieu's France. All the major elements including that of universal monarchy were real enough and part of the political atmosphere in 1636.

Campanella's own shift from Spain to France as the vehicle for realizing his persisting vision of a future universal, theocratic order seems here to have been remarkably smooth. True, the identification of the current hegemonic power with the traditional office of Holy Roman Emperor in 1636 did not appear necessary, or as necessary as it had at the beginning of the century. But the definitive territorialization of that empire and the contemporary French efforts to forge an independent imperial cum universal tradition made understandable such a tentative uncoupling on Campanella's part. If Campanella seems to tilt the cause of empire ever so slightly in the direction of the territorial state, it is not to abandon his lifetime commitment to universal monarchy.[158] In fact, whatever tensions and ambivalence seen in this last stage of his political thought, are the tensions and ambivalence of this age, caught

---

[157] Jover, *1635*, 43–68.
[158] Despite its brilliance and subtlety I cannot agree with the argument of Joan Kelly Gadol, "Tommaso Campanella: The Agony of Political Thought in the Counter-Reformation," in *Philosophy and Humanism: Renaissance Essays in Honor of Paul Oskar Kristeller*, ed. Edward P. Mahoney (New York, 1976), 164–89, insofar as it represents the main features and contours of that thought. For it seems to misconstrue the consistency and continuity in Campanella's political thought and not give proper attention to its final French phase.

between the decay of universal monarchy and the emergence of a new system, providing an uneasy balance of power. The thought of the grand statesman of the age itself moves between *une juste balance* and *l'Arbitre de la Chrestienté* for France, reflecting therewith the age's forces at play.[159]

One logical discrepancy, however, did manage to protrude in the Campanellan transference: the French dualism or distinction between the new, autonomous order of politics and the old order of a Christian, Augustinian justice. In this respect the *monarquía católica* of the Spanish polemicists offered a more consistent and coherent scheme for any champion of Christian universalism. Yet whatever the inconsistencies and logical incoherences, the Machiavellian ambiguities of our most politic friar would be able to contend with this challenge.

As for the sermon at Conflans and its audience in the late spring of 1636, if ever delivered to such an ostensible audience in anything like the substance and proportions that we have suggested, it would have incorporated large doses of prophetic and astrological evidence in support of the speaker's ideas. We need not follow him down this line of argument except to observe that appeal to the conjunctions of the stars would hardly have caused the crisp silks of the cardinal-duke to rustle impatiently. Indeed Richelieu will shortly avail himself of the service of Campanella to cast the horoscope of the recently born dauphin. There, gazing upon the naked flanks of the future Louis XIV, the old Calabrian conspirator would impute to this Sun King and Grand Monarch of history the realization of the City of the Sun and the long-sought universal monarchy.[160]

[159] Albertini, *Denken*, 141–61.
[160] Blanchet, *Camp.*, 64–65.

Chapter VII

UNIVERSAL THEOCRACY AND THE ECCLESIASTICAL STATE: THE FIGURE OF MELCHISEDECH

Pasce oves meas: Pastoral and Imperial Motifs in the Counter Reformation Church

When Jesus the Christ turned to Peter and said, "If you love me, feed my sheep," did he imagine at that time the traditions of later inquiry and debate, of learned controversy and tragic division consequent to this crucial passage (John 21:17)? For the theology that the West developed over the next millennium and a half would be based upon such key scriptural texts or pericopes explicated and fortified by reason and law. And in the imposing majesty of the resulting intellectual structures no other text so forcefully brings into focus the problem of church and world as *pasce oves meas*, "feed my sheep." That vast commission, raising questions of authority, ministration, and scope, best constitutes the portal to a study of Campanella's political theology. For by the operations of the Church in the world the fundamental realities of love and power would find expression in the myriad relations of that compelling yet enigmatic issue, forever being reanswered in the life of the Church. In the ongoing tradition of mutually adjusting power and love, of squaring the circle, the exegetical interpretation of John 21:17 remains closely associated with and reflects currents in the contemporary Church at any one time. We seek to examine that interrelationship of exegetical, moral, and jurisdictional currents first briefly in its medieval development but then with greater attention following the advent of Luther, culminating in the early seventeenth century with the triumphalist Counter Reformation Church and the curiously contrasting, yet similar, responses of Thomas Hobbes and Tommaso Campanella.

We do not intend to prejudge this continuing task of mutual adjustment as an absurd undertaking. Quite on the contrary, such an effort would seem to be one of the most fundamental and meaningful pursuits of the human enterprise, although one that Penelope-like must forever fall short of effective realization. The very series of failures in this most noble endeavor constitutes much of the history of the Christian Church. But more simply and immediately it needs to be noted that power and love, if ultimately doomed to intractability and incoherence, are not necessarily always polar opposites: love itself possesses power, a spiritual power; power, if it is to be exercised responsibly, must ever crave to be clothed in that social guise of love, namely, justice. Power is not forever condemned to express itself as naked force. Yet essentially the opposition between the two is profound. Love seeks association or union through mutuality; power, through the unilateral imposition of force. A father exercises various degrees of absolute power over his son, but all such efforts are powerless in themselves to beget love. Indeed they may well beget the very reasons for the son's estrangement. The paradoxical nature of the love/power relationship would seem to be built into the human condition itself. One does not have to be a Christian to admit the supreme meaningfulness of an omnipotent God, who chooses to divest Himself of His power, and, impelled by a sacrificial love, comes to man in the form of human frailty and suffers the fate of a common thief. Again whether for the believer, the atheist, or the agnostic the *scandalon*, the stumbling block that is Jesus the Christ, serves to address that grand enigma, irresolvable from man's side.

The patristic exegesis of our pericope usually skirts the pastoral and imperial motifs, not laying bare the moral and jurisdictional strains present in Christ's command. Augustine recognized that feeding the sheep included both teaching and governing, but he also claimed that the pastoral office required a love of Christ in contradistinction to any self-love. With Augustine's Eastern contemporary St. John Chrysostom, that Father most favored and quoted by Campanella, a special role consciously claimed for Peter becomes more pronounced: Chrysostom sees Jesus as entrusting Peter with preeminent authority in the Church.[1]

Two dynamic tensions and ambiguities in Augustine's thought command our attention, for their unilateral resolution by the ongoing Church would promote a sharper, harder exegesis of our pericope. In his dealings with the Donatists Augustine came to reverse his former position, which had rejected compelling schismatics into communion. Religious coercion now becomes a distinct mode of the pastoral function and justified as a sort of medicine administered to an unwilling patient for his own benefit. It is thus to be understood as a true work of God, for God scourges those whom he loves. From such justification of coercion emerges the important notion of *disciplina*, which becomes an integral part of the pastoral function, enhancing the specifically jurisdictional understanding of *pasce oves meas*.[2] As corrective punish-

---

[1] For the patristic, Renaissance, and some of the Reformation exegesis of this pericope I am drawing liberally from an unpublished paper by Professor John McManamon, "'Feed My Sheep': Reformation Interpretations of John 21 and the History of Exegesis."

[2] On Augustine and religious coercion, see the perceptive exposition of R. A. Markus, *Saeculum: History and Society in the Theology of the St. Augustine* (Cambridge, 1970), 138–43. Regarding the Church's charitable application of force, Karl F. Morrison, *The Mimetic Tradition of Reform in the West* (Princeton, 1982), can speak of Augustine's "Tactics of Terror" and "the corrective mimetic strategies" to restore disbelievers to wholeness (83–92) as well as Gregory the Great's applying "the medicine of correction to the insane minds" of those very Donatists who

ment discipline provides the appropriate medicine for that great invalid which is humankind.[3] Yet if in his sermon on Christian discipline Augustine understands the Church as a house of discipline or better perhaps a school of discipline (*domum disciplinae, disciplinae scholam*), it is an openness to the gospel, begetting love of one's neighbor and fulfillment of the law, which still constitutes part of such discipline at this early stage.[4]

The second Augustinian tension that suffers dislocation and unilateral resolution pertains to the important issue of time and the Church's movement in history. If apocalyptic is a device for drawing God back into time[5] to effect some specific political good, eschatology may be understood as an affirmation of the divine initiative. By maintaining the eschatological edge whereby the Church must await its realization in another time, Augustine preserved the dynamic tension and ambiguity between Church and City of God, between the Church Militant and the Church Triumphant. This dynamic tension disappears to a large extent over the course of the Middle Ages to reveal the divine institution of the Church, ontological, static, a timeless reality.[6] The jurisdictional/administrative reality of the medieval Church will begin to be consolidated in the interest of Rome and the papacy by the Gregorian reformers at the end of the eleventh century.

In the next century St. Bernard, as the great conscience of the West, expresses his concern to keep Spirit and Structure together, to affirm the emerging administrative order but also nourish charisma.[7] In *De consideratione*, his treatise of counsel addressed to Pope Eugenius III, Bernard's argument culminates in his treatment of *pasce oves meas*. He had earlier identified the pope as being of the order of Melchisedech and in a single statement he had united Matthew 16:19 and John 21:17 as the twin pillars of papal preeminence: "You are the one to whom the keys have been given, to whom the sheep have been entrusted." Neglecting the first pericope he had pursued the other, explicating the unity and universality of the Petrine community in terms of all sheep having been entrusted to that single apostle.[8] But beginning in book 4, chapter

---

had so exercised his predecessor in these North African matters (109). On St. Augustine and the Donatists, see Peter Iver Kaufman, *Redeeming Politics* (Princeton, 1990), 138–47.

[3] Peter Brown, *Augustine of Hippo* (Berkeley/Los Angeles, 1967), 236–40.

[4] *Corpus Christianorum. Series Latina* 46.207ff.

[5] On this nice point see J. G. A. Pocock, "Time, History and Eschatology in the Thought of Thomas Hobbes," in *The Diversity of History: Essays in Honor of Sir Herbert Butterfield*, ed. J. H. Elliott and H. G. Koenigsberger (Ithaca, N.Y., 1970), 192.

[6] John Tonkin, *The Church and the Secular Order in Reformation Thought* (New York/London, 1971), 7–8, 160–70.

[7] On this and related issues regarding St. Bernard's major work, see Elizabeth Kennan, "The 'De consideratione' of St. Bernard of Clairvaux . . . and the Papacy, in the Mid-Twelfth Century: A Review of Scholarship," *Traditio* 23 (1967): 73–116.

[8] St. Bernard, *De consideratione*, trans. and ed. Elizabeth Kennan and John D. Anderson (Kalamazoo, Mich., 1976), 66–67.

3, Bernard mounts his great criticism of the current Church: in place of a caring ministry of earlier times with an episcopate distinguished by sacrificial love, the new acquisitive ecclesiastical bureaucrats prove themselves ravenous, even vulpine in their self-seeking.[9]

> Loving no one, no one loves them. . . . You, the shepherd go forth adorned with gold and surrounded by colorful array. . . . This is Peter, who is known never to have gone in procession adorned with either jewels or silks, covered with gold, carried on a white horse [an imperial motif], attended by a knight or surrounded by clamoring servants. But without these trappings, he believed it was enough to be able to fulfill the Lord's command, "If you love me, feed my sheep." In this finery, you are the successor not of Peter but of Constantine. . . . You are the heir of the Shepherd and even if you are arrayed in purple and gold, there is no reason for you to abhor your pastoral responsibilities: there is no reason for you to be ashamed of the Gospel. . . . To preach the Gospel is to feed. Do the work of an evangelist and you have fulfilled the office of the shepherd.[10]

Evangelizare pascere est.[11] Little wonder that the heresiarch Luther would later treasure St. Bernard. The moral, charismal, indeed evangelical glares, blares through the jurisdictional/political structure.

With Christian humanism and the Reformers the issues once more come into focus. Capitalizing on the philological breakthrough of Lorenzo Valla, Erasmus confronts the hard realities of the Greek verbs used in the crucial text—*boske* and *poimaine*. The first suggests feed or nourish (*ale*) while the second clearly suggests rule ("ut pastor regit gregem"). Yet while admitting the jurisdictional import of the text, Erasmus sees the whole passage (John 21:15ff.) dominated by the warning that only the one who loves Christ can undertake the pastoral task.[12] In his *Response to Luther* of 1523 Thomas More fastens upon Erasmus's affirmation of the jurisdictional, but again, if less incisively, at least consciously he seeks to preserve the moral/spiritual mode to the pastoral function: "Jurisdiction and the function of charity are not altogether the same, even if it is true that there is no Christian jurisdiction which has not been instituted out of charity."[13]

Despite the violence of its tone and language More's *Response* lacks any sense of clerical triumphalism. More the layman presents a sinning, erring Church that requires correction; in an image possessing deep-seated popular

---

[9] Ibid., 113–17.
[10] Ibid., 114–17.
[11] For the Latin text, see *MPL*, 182:176.
[12] *Responsio ad Lutherum*, ed. John M. Headley, trans. Sister Scholastica Mandeville, *The Complete Works of St. Thomas More* (New Haven/London, 1969), 5:904–5; cf. McManamon, unpub. art., 13.
[13] *Responsio*, 766.

dimensions he represents God as a loving mother whipping her child, His vicar, but then wiping away the tears and tossing the switch into the fire.[14] God as the ultimate pastor here applies to His Church the appropriate *medicina* and *disciplina* of the pastoral office in what today's world would understand as an act of tough love.

To appreciate the suggestive overtones of More's position on this question it is worthwhile to consider the way in which John Fisher deals with the same question in article 25 of his *Confutatio*. Fisher's treatment of papal primacy in this article was sufficiently important to enjoy several independent reprintings during the course of the century. Fisher adduced Jerome to support the common understanding of *pascere* as "to rule"; according to the Greek, it certainly means that the papacy is *praesidis & superioris*. He then turns to Luther's claim that pope and papacy depend for their validity upon their capacity to love Christ. He allows that Peter exceeded all others in his love of Christ but asserts that the papal primacy and love are different realities and need to be separated. The primacy remains, even if love is lacking. Thus the pope does not give up the primacy, if he does not love Christ. Fisher rejects Luther's suggestion that the papacy was instituted by the text *Simon amas me*: "And for the last time it is false that without love this power is unable to exist. For just as the power of absolving and of baptizing and even of consecrating the Eucharist remains, with love having been removed by sin, so also this power remains, although love shall have for the moment been lost."[15] Thus did the bishop of Rochester weigh in heavily to emphasize the uniqueness and totality of the commission to Peter as well as its clear implication: feeding means ruling.

Martin Luther stands as both product and producer of this scurrying for a more relevant understanding of the scriptural notion of the pastoral office. More immediately and meaningfully than the posting of the 95 Theses, *Luther's Explanation to Proposition Thirteen on the Power of the Pope*, the veritable substance of the Leipzig debate (June–July 1519), represents the opening shot to the Reformation. In his handling of the two pillars of papal preeminence (Matthew 16:18 and John 21:16ff.) Luther attacks the special role of Peter and claims each pericope pertains to all the churches. *Pasce oves meas* pertains to all the apostles. Here Christ has made love a prerequisite for pastoral office. The task of feeding means loving and teaching, which to Luther's satisfaction reveals that there has not been a pastor in the Roman

---

[14] Ibid., 142–43, 896.

[15] Ibid., 766–77: "Falsum est & postremum, quod sine amore nequeat haec potestas esse. Nam sicut manet absolvendi potestas, & baptizandi, atque etiam consecrandi eucharistiam, amore per peccatum sublato: ita manet & haec potestas, quanquam ad tempus deperierit amor." John Fisher, *Opera quae hactenus inveniri potuerunt omnia* . . . (Würzburg: Georg Fleischmann, 1597), 571.

Church since Gregory the Great.[16] In the following year he identified the feeding of the pastoral office with loving, *weyden* with *lieben*.[17] Never far removed from the pastoral issue evident in John 21:17ff., Luther at the end of his life claimed in his most savage attack upon the papacy that the pope and his jurists were at odds regarding the establishment of the papacy. Whereas the former based it on Matthew 16:18, Luther gloated with reference to the decretal *Significasti* that the jurists located its foundation in the Johannine pericope.[18]

Nevertheless it would be wrong to represent the exegesis of the pastoral pericope by members of the old Church as having quite forsaken the moral/spiritual mode of love. Such was never the case. It amounted to a matter of emphasis. And while Catholic controversialists might press the decisive text for all it was worth in order that it might emit a convincingly jurisdictional shriek, affirming Rome's unique and universal preeminence, the love motif could also be brought to the fore. The most authoritative opponent of Luther, the Dominican Cardinal Cajetan, required love of Christ as the sine qua non for the right exercise of any ministry. Indeed Luther could observe that his former opponent had almost become Lutheran late in life.[19] Yet no matter how apparent at times the verbal and emotional agreement, the essentially hostile exegetical traditions, Protestant and Catholic, were now unfolding within their respective confessional camps, whose opposing doctrinal and ecclesial positions reinforced their mutual hostility and made the gulf between them all too real. We need to address the total ecclesial position of the Roman papacy at the end of the sixteenth century in its European context and significance.

Our task requires that we come to understand some of the implications of that greatest of amphibians, the papacy, operating both as a territorial, yes, ecclesiastical state and as a universal spiritual authority. The twofold character of the papacy almost from the very beginning of its endowment, the patrimony of Peter, has been such an obvious phenomenon of European history that it has virtually escaped serious consideration. In his extraordinary study, *Il sovrano pontefice*, Paolo Prodi takes seriously the fact of the late medieval Church as a forerunner of the modern state and of the pope as prince-pastor, the *papa-re*; he analyzes both the interrelations of the papal monarchy's two aspects and the meaning of that interrelationship as a process of integral importance occurring between 1450 and 1650. Culminating in the pontificate of Urban VIII (1623–44), this process of state formation was transforming the pope and papacy so that they were no longer conceivable in medieval terms. The process permeates the institution of the Church and transforms it even in its most

[16] *WA*, 2:194–97.
[17] Ibid., 6:316–21.
[18] Ibid., 54:241.
[19] McManamon art., 17–19.

impermeable core, the papacy itself, and in turn is profoundly affected by that institution. For the papacy is the leader in this process of modern state formation and its realization. From the Reformation to the close of the Counter Reformation we see the fusion and interpenetration of the two aspects, the religious and the political, hitherto considered separate. In the increasing reduction of religion to politics noted by so many in the early seventeenth century, a greater clericalization of the papal state apparatus assumes the form of almost a second ecclesiastical structure superimposed over the first. The resulting imbalance between the political and the recognizably religious derives from a deep-seated logic, an inner dynamic relentlessly rationalizing and politicizing the papacy. One misses the point of Prodi's analysis if the territorial preoccupations of this early modern papacy are seen as being opposed to its universalist pretensions; rather papal state building represents not an alternative to the exercise of universalism but an effort to make this universalism survive in new historical circumstances.[20]

In a mood of growing triumphalism this amalgamation of the modern sovereign territorial state as the necessary base to an universal pastorate now moved toward its apparent completion. In the last decade of the sixteenth century during the pontificate of the Aldobrandini pope, Clement VIII, the new confidence of a revived Rome and its clergy found its preeminent expositors in three ecclesiastics: Cesare Baronio, Roberto Bellarmino, and (to a lesser degree) Giovanni Botero. Writing at the turn of the decade (1588–91), Botero provided the broad, political context for the other two by representing Roman Catholicism as the preeminent, stabilizing force; he argued that Catholicism could contribute more to the strength and order of a state than any other religion and that the best recipe for worldly greatness was obedience to the pope.[21] In these last years of the century all events from a Roman perspective seemed to conspire to accent the universal authority of the pontiff. The global outreach of Rome's religious orders into heathen lands mocked the losses to Protestantism in the backwoods of northern Europe. Architecturally, symbolically, intellectually the stones announcing this universal authority appeared to be drawn into place. During the previous pontificate of Sixtus V ancient obelisks had been erected, now Christianized by appropriate inscriptions, and the statues of Peter and Paul emerged atop the triumphal columns of Trajan and Marcus Aurelius. More than any other event at this time, that marking the elevation of Baronius to the cardinalatial dignity conveyed most emphatically the restored mood of confidence. For Baronius had chosen as his title church that of St^s. Nereus and Achilleus and the formal transfer of the saints' remains to their church on May 11, 1597, afforded the opportunity for a

[20] Paolo Prodi, *Il sovrano pontefice* (Bologna, 1982). See my review in *The Journal of Religion* 69 (1989): 407–10.
[21] William J. Bouwsma, *Venice and the Defense of Republican Liberty* (Berkeley/Los Angeles, 1968), 302, 335.

Christian triumph. The procession of the relics conveyed to the crowds, attendant in order to receive a plenary indulgence, that the new Rome had triumphed over the old, the martyrs over the emperors in such a way as to integrate the Roman and the Christian, Roman Empire and Christian Empire in a distinctively Roman Christianity.[22] From this triumphalist context would appear, as both product of and reinforcement to that confident mood, the bulky volumes of Baronius's *Annales ecclesiastici*.

Beyond being the confessor and theological adviser to the pope, whereby his opinions would carry considerable political weight as the Spaniards ruefully learned, Baronius assumes major importance as the preeminent historian of the Catholic Church. The problem of time needed to be addressed and mastered. For the Reformers had driven an eschatological wedge between the historical Church and the Kingdom of God that now must be plastered over to effect something nearer to a merging of the institutional Church with the future kingdom in a sort of realized eschatology. Baronius achieves these high, if not very historicist goals, by reading the present back into the past to convey the sense of an overwhelming, unchanging reality, the sheer narration of whose history had a self-authenticating quality. Historical truth narrowed to what was systematically and doctrinally necessary; what had actually happened at best possessed but incidental relevance. In the words of a modern authority the work sought "to reveal not so much the history of the church as . . . its constant superiority to history . . . [serving] as an extended celebration of the [Church's] triumph over time."[23]

Baronius's politics could be flexible, as evinced in his promoting the absolution of Henry IV of France by Clement VIII. But for the most part they reflected an almost Augustinian intransigence. He played a prominent role in the Venetian affair (1606–7), urging the papacy to take a strong stand. At the time of the Interdict Baronius proclaimed in full consistory that Peter's mission was to feed and to kill, and he called upon the new pope Paul V to execute the latter office. Resorting to those Old Testament figures that confirmed the Levitical and Aaronic background to the Roman priesthood, he called upon the pope to strike hard. Taken together with his treatise that undermined the validity of the *Monarchia Sicula*, Spain's claim to total authority, ecclesiastical as well as secular in the Kingdom of Naples, Baronius's politics along with his politically inspired history amounted to a massive affirmation of the institutional Church.[24]

A close collaborator of Baronius was his fellow Oratorian Tommaso Bozio.

---

[22] Richard Krautheimer, "A Christian Triumph in 1597," *Essays . . . presented to Rudolph Wittkower*, ed. Douglas Fraser, Howard Hibbard, and Milton J. Lewine (London, 1967), 74–78.

[23] Bouwsma, *Venice*, 309, 323.

[24] Cyriac K. Pullapilly, *Caesar Baronius* (Notre Dame/London, 1985), 118, 132–34; see also the comprehensive treatment by Agostino Borromeo, "Il Cardinale Cesare Baronio e la corona spagnole," in *Baronio Storico e la Controriforma* (Sora, 1982), 57–166.

In the third of several polemics against Machiavelli (*De antiquo et novo Italiae Statu* [1595]) Bozio had urged that Italy had never been so happy as under papal authority; wherefore Machiavelli's inciting to rebellion represented the source of great calamities. He claimed for the pope "directam potestatem in regna," that tithes are owed to the clergy by divine law, that ecclesiastical power extends itself to all. Such a close collaboration helped confirm Baronius's assertion that since all power came from Christ to His vicar, there could be no derivation of the Church's apparently secular powers from the Roman emperors; in subscribing to a tradition that went back to the minting of the Donation of Constantine in the eighth century, the cardinal stated that Constantine had given nothing but simply ceded what properly belonged to the Church.[25] The immense, all-inclusive power of the emerging "clerocracy" begins to assume Leviathan-like proportions with Bozio's rendering of Job 41:24: There exists on earth no power that may be compared to the Church.[26] The same passage would later dignify a more famous rendering of this figure.

The claims of Baronius and Bozio moved in step with the curialists' disposition to seek their authorities in the Old Testament rather than the New. And in this alignment, even fusion, of the spiritual and temporal powers as something reasonable and natural, the figure of Melchisedech looms through the argumentation as the type, the epitome, the primordial authority for the priest-king, the *papa-re*, the supreme ruler who is at once prince and pastor.[27]

From 1605 to 1607 a papal interdict cast its long shadow over Venice, whose legislation had limited the acquisition of real property by the Church. The Venetian Interdict brought many of the larger political and spiritual interests of the age into focus for testing and review. In a Europe that was crystallizing into relatively discrete units of territorial sovereignty the papal claim to a right of intervention in the political life of another state in order to defend ecclesiastical interests provided a certain guarantee for future trouble. That the defense of this papal right should principally fall to a moderate, arguing merely for an indirect rather than a direct power, only reveals more clearly the explosive nature of this issue. To the evident disgruntlement of the hard-line curialists and the pope himself, Robert Bellarmine had nicely defined this indirect power in his monumental *Controversies*, in book 5, "On the Supreme Pontiff," all of which had emerged from a German press in 1590. With a clattering of their regalist wings all the crows came home to roost at the beginning of the next century: the Venetian dispute over clerical exemption (1606–7); the royal absolutism of James I of England (1607–9); and the sim-

---

[25] On the shift from donation to cession, see Charles T. Davis, "Ptolemy of Lucca and the Roman Republic," *Proceedings of the American Philosophical Society* 118 (1974): 30–50, esp. 43–47 and the sources cited therein.

[26] Salvo Mastellone, "Tommaso Bozio, teorico dell'ordine ecclesiastico," *IPP* 13 (1980): 186–94, esp. 188.

[27] Prodi, *Il sovrano*, 61.

ilarly absolutist as well as Gallican positions of William Barclay and Roger Widdrington.[28] In each Bellarmine figured significantly. Of the three the first, the Venetian, had the most immediate European reverberations and before it had run its course Venice would see fit to republish St. Bernard's *De consideratione ad Eugenium III P.M.* In the formidable issues drawn between a Church that was dangerously defining itself as a system of clerical control and discipline and the secular state alert to new responsibilities and opportunities Venice's great defender, Paolo Sarpi, provides some revealing remarks: "the famous and august name of Church appears to be ever more restricted to signifying solely the clergy"; and then the soothing advice addressed to both laity and clergy under Venetian rule, to calm their minds and consciences in pursuing godly service "sotto la protezione del Prencipe."[29]

With Bellarmine we resume that exegetical trail leading to the definition of the pastoral office. At the turn of the new century the perennial questions seem to await a new sort of response: Who is the pastor? How extensive is his office? What specifically is meant by "feeding"? Bellarmine will provide traditional answers, elegantly and comprehensively rendered. In his *Controversies* he opens the matter by taking issue with Luther's definition of *pascere* that omits the jurisdictional motif of supreme administration and instead urges the offering of food and ministering. Bellarmine avers ease in demonstrating that *summam potestatem* is here being attributed to the pontiff: "The pastoral act is not so much one of offering food but rather of leading, rescuing, guarding, superintending, ruling, punishing. Why? Do the pastors of sheep offer only food to their charges? Do they not also rule and direct with the staff so that [the sheep] may be obedient?"[30] *Pascere* elicits the familiar coinage of argumentation—*poimaine* and *praeesse*. Bellarmine confidently asserts that *oves meas* pertains to all Christians everywhere. The singleness of the sheepfold is anchored in John 10:16: "There will be one sheepfold and one shepherd." Thus Christ has committed His universal flock to Peter and from him as if from their head and emperor (*imperatore*) do they depend.[31]

Similarly on the pope having temporal power *indirecte*, to be exercised only when spiritual (= ecclesiastical) interests are jeopardized, Bellarmine's arguments culminate in a consideration of *pasce oves meas*. The future cardinal understands the passage as giving all faculties necessary for a pastor to guard

---

[28] John Courtney Murray, "Bellarmine on the Indirect Power," *Theological Studies* 9 (1948): 491–535, esp. 494–95.

[29] *Paolo Sarpi. Pensieri*, ed. Gaetano e Luisa Cozzi (Turin, 1976), liii, lix–lxi.

[30] *Disputationes Roberti Bellarmini . . . De controversiis Christianae fidei* (Ingolstadt: D. Sartorius, 1590), I.V.xx.666C: "Porro actus pastoralis non est tantum praebere cibum, sed etiam ducere, reducere, tueri, praeesse, regere, castigare. Quid? Pastores ovium num solum pabulum illis praebent? nonne etiam regunt, & baculo cogunt ut pareant?"

[31] Ibid., I.V.xx.666A–671B.

his flock. This capacity is threefold: against wolves or heretics who waste the church; against furious rams or those disobedient Catholic princes who disrupt the sheepfold; as pastor to feed or teach the faithful so that they convene together. Such a pastor ought to be able to command all Christians and compel them to serve God, each according to his estate.[32]

While the relative moderation of Bellarmine's claims for the papacy encountered more than enough criticism in their own time from both within and outside the sheepfold, the most severe criticism and total reconception of the pastoral office had to await the midcentury. In Thomas Hobbes we are confronted with a peculiarly secular rendering of that virtual integration of the temporal and spiritual and a consequently secular definition of the pastoral office. For once having created his Mortal God in the dimension of reason and nature evident in the first two books of *Leviathan*, Hobbes had to turn to explain how that great figure of sovereign authority appearing in the frontispiece, overarched by the fearful words of Job 41:24, might brandish so confidently the pastoral staff as well as the temporal sword.

For Hobbes two quite different quiddities required mastery and control—time and words. A secular time needed to be created, free from spiritual harassment of any sort. Surveying the unrest of his own age, Hobbes was persuaded that it could well dispense with the harassment of the preachers, impelled by the spirit, whether holy or not. Accordingly, he defines and reiterates his definition of three worlds that are to be understood as *saecula*, three aeons or periods of time on this earth: the first world, from the creation to the flood; the second, this present world from the flood to the day of judgment; and the third, the world to come, from the judgment forward, everlasting, as promised by Christ.[33] More specifically Hobbes has the present world begin with the end of that Kingdom of God evident in the old Hebraic order, "wherein God was king and the high priest was to be, after the death of Moses, his sole viceroy or lieutenant." This theocratic order comes to an end in 1 Samuel 8:7, when the elders demanded a king, thereby initiating not only a new polity and a new order, but a new world in the sense of aeon.[34] Hence this present world. And hence the hope and prayer for a future world or kingdom, otherwise it would be superfluous that we pray "Thy kingdom come" unless there is intended the restoration by Christ of that Kingdom of God interrupted through the election of Saul.[35] Hobbes cannot here be faulted for not taking his Protestantism seriously. For if Protestantism is a religion of the word, of faith in God's promise, and of prophecy, Hobbes emerges as an apostle of all three,

[32] Ibid., I.V.vi.1064A; vii.1066C–1069B.
[33] Thomas Hobbes, *Leviathan*, ed. Michael Oakeshott (Oxford, 1960), 303, 318–19, 354, 380, 398–99, 413.
[34] Ibid., 268.
[35] Ibid., 268–70. Pocock, "Hobbes," 171–72, to which I am greatly indebted here.

yet using them to declericalize the present world and effect the secularization of the present aeon.[36]

Hobbes marshals his nominalism and his materialism to bring words under control all in the same effort to choke out the Spirit or any pretensions to spiritual outpouring or inflations. For Hobbes suffered acutely from those of scholastic temperament who endowed God with timeless attributes and essences, apparently subject to rational perception, and also from the saints of enthusiastic temperament, crying up a world of spirit within time. Hobbes' God, however, is not to be known through the operation of the Spirit upon our spirits but only through His words. Philosophical and spiritual attributions give way to historical statements, for knowledge of these words is historical knowledge. Experience of God thus is possible only in the past and in the future, the two times or worlds in which God's civil kingdom exists. In the present world we live in hope and faith in His promise. The Church thus becomes truly a community of the faithful awaiting the future act of a God perceived as power, present in history, not mediated by a structure of essences.[37]

Having plugged every hole through which spirit might be injected into the present world and its distinctly secular order, Hobbes can now turn to deal specifically with Bellarmine and the papacy, which he recognized as "the kingdom of the fairies," constructed on nonexistent essences.[38] Predictably the paramount abuse of Scripture and source of all other abuses lies in identifying the Kingdom of God with the present Church. In countering Bellarmine point by point on the matter of papal power and specifically on the hotly contested issue of the pope having temporal power *indirecte*, Hobbes twice covers the ground defined by *pasce oves meas*.[39] It is no more than a commission to teach, properly belonging to the several Christian sovereigns. Since he had earlier demonstrated that sovereigns are supreme teachers by the nature of their office, the sovereign deftly assimilates the supreme pastoral charge, complete with whatever coercive power adhering. By the time that Hobbes has come to contest Bellarmine on wolves, rams, and the pastoral function of teaching, it has become clear that one of Protestantism's distinctive doctrines has been jettisoned: namely, that the pope is the Antichrist. For the pope neither denies Christ nor claims to be Christ.[40] Furthermore while Hobbes can dismiss the pope's universal pastorate and evaporate the papacy and the Catholic Church into the kingdom of the fairies or at best "a confederacy of deceivers,"[41] he nevertheless grants the pope the same role as pastor that any

[36] Pocock, "Hobbes," 178–82.
[37] Ibid., 182–94.
[38] *Leviathan*, 361ff.
[39] Ibid., 366–67, 383–84.
[40] Ibid., 364–65.
[41] Ibid., 397.

other secular prince possesses: "For every Christian Prince . . . is no less supreme Pastor of his own subjects than the Pope of his. . . . This is true; for Christian kings are no more but Christ's subjects, but they may, for all that, be the Pope's fellows; for they are supreme pastors of their own subjects, and the Pope is no more but king and pastor, even in Rome itself."[42] Thus the papal prince and the ecclesiastical state over which he rules receive recognition in the new emerging order as one among a number of territorial sovereign states. Thus while the pope's secular authority has been confirmed, he has been summarily stripped of his mystical, apocalyptic dignity as the Antichrist.

In conclusion we may note that the kingdom of the fairies continued to enjoy a resilience and substantiality that belied the English philosopher's extended witticism. In the preceding generations it had come to aspire to global authority in a Roman pale that had expanded beyond Europe. The heterodox Dominican Tommaso Campanella reflects this updated universalism, and for all his peculiarities he shares as much common as opposing ground with Hobbes. Both conceived of God in terms of power. Both saw political life in terms of an unitive power wielded by the pastor-prince, although for Hobbes this integration of power was more total and expressed by a number of territorial rulers rather than by a single universal ruler; in a sense Hobbes pluralized the priest-king of the Counter Reformation Church. Both Hobbes and Campanella gave crucial historical significance to 1 Samuel 8:7 as creating a new age, but while Hobbes could thrive on the secularization of time and power, Campanella reviles the general dissolution, occurring with Saul, of what he saw as a healthy union of powers according to the order of Melchisedech; he read the text as expressive of God's displeasure with the secular kingdom's displacing the sacerdotal power—an imbalance that he will later seek to redress according to the order of Melchisedech.[43] Both could essentially agree on the intermediate nature of the present aeon, but whereas Campanella breathlessly awaited, if not anticipated, the breakthrough of the Kingdom of God, Hobbes, with a philosophic patience, could cheerfully accept its indefinite postponement; indeed for him the kingdom's advent could only be welcomed as a distinct inconvenience. Each worked within this present world—Campanella feverishly to clericalize its leadership at every level; Hobbes to declericalize. Both represent extreme products of their respective religions, reacting to the general development of European political life during the first half of the seventeenth century.

Finally *pasce oves meas* assumes paramount significance for Campanella. He reads the text as the preeminent authorization for universal community under sacerdotal power as well as the superiority of the clergy over the laity. Superior love warrants superior jurisdiction. What pastor is unarmed against

[42] Ibid., 382; cf. Prodi, *Il sovrano*, 41.
[43] TC-*MM*, 13, 55, 82.

260   CHAPTER VII

wolves and disobedient sheep? Expressly anti-Marsilian, Campanella claims
for the pastoral office the use of coercive power together with a directive
power.[44]

> As St. Augustine says on this Johannine text regarding Christ, a great doctor has
> come from heaven because a great sickness was spreading on earth. And Plato
> calls the legislator a doctor of souls. Consequently the Church in the virtue of its
> Christ uses iron and fire against heretics and schismatics, not out of vengeance as
> lay princes once did, but as a medicament against extreme and incurable diseases,
> when the spiritual sword and admonitions do not work. Thus the holy doctors
> must be interpreted, when they deny the use of the sword out of pride . . . or for
> compelling by force infidels not yet converted to the gospel, for faith must be
> persuaded, not commanded, as Bernard says. But none of the saints denies the use
> of the sword *pro medicina* after faith has been accepted. May the unhappy
> Erasmus fall silent.[45]

To the Dominican Campanella the opportunity for universal, spiritual empire, evinced by scriptural and astrological prophecy as well as by the current global outreach of Rome through its missionaries, seemed too obvious to dispute, too imperative to ignore. And in Rome's soterial quest to realize unity and community on a universal, global scale, that love, which Bernard and Cajetan among others had made fundamental to the exercise of the pastoral office, now appeared to be dangerously obscured by power. The predominant rendering of Mother Church as *Machtkirche* would in the seventeenth-century European context be challenged, enhanced, and moderated by the emerging territorial states, those Mortal Gods of the new order.

THE ECCLESIASTICAL STATE AND HIEROCRATIC UNIVERSALITY

For any study of Campanella's concept of the Church, the ecclesiastical state, and the papacy his *Monarchia messiae* must figure significantly as the veritable centerpiece. First written in Italian in 1605 and known to have reached the hands of Cardinal Aldobrandini (San Giorgio) by the beginning of 1607, nevertheless not until 1633 at Jesi did it see the light of typographical day, almost immediately, however, to be suppressed. Only a few copies of the original

---

[44] Ibid., 36, 59–62; TC-*AV*, 58–59.

[45] TC-*MM*, 36: "ut ait S. Aug. Super Ioan. de Christo: Magnus de caelo venit medicus, quia magnus in terra iacebat Aegrotus. Et Plato legislatorem vocat medicum animorum. Idcirco ecclesia in virtute Christi sui, utitur ferro, & igne contra Haereticos, & scysmaticos, non ad vindictam, ut Principes layci olim sed pro medicamine contra morbos extremos, & incurabiles: ubi gladius spiritualis, & monitiones non prosunt, & sic interpraetandi sunt Doctores sancti, ubi negant usum gladij, hoc est ad superbiam, & vindictam, & avaritiam, & ambitionem dilatandam, vel ad cogendum infideles nondum conversos ad Evangelium per vim: nam fides est his suadenda, non imperanda, teste Bern.: sed nemo sanctorum negat usum gladij pro medicina post acceptam fidem. Taceat infaelix Erasmus."

publication survive; the *De regno Christi* among his last composed works is but an abstract of his fuller and most complete statement on the Church. Supplementing this important work and stemming from the same seminal period, the first decade of his long incarceration, is the *Antiveneti* of which we first hear from a letter he sent to Paul V, August 13, 1606. By June of the following year the finished work had been entrusted to Kaspar Schoppe, who, unwisely passing through Venice, suffered its confiscation. Only in 1945 would the fragments of the three books constituting the work be reassembled by the ever-attentive Luigi Firpo.[46]

Yet preceding this period of activity (1605–7) is Campanella's earlier incarceration at Padua in the prisons of the Holy Office, September–December 1593, when he composed his *De monarchia Christianorum* and the *De regimine ecclesiae* (= *Del governo ecclesiastico*). The loss of the former wherein he laid out those fundamental principles of ecclesiastical polity that would apparently persist throughout his career represents one of the most serious misfortunes for Campanella research. The other work, of a more practical nature, managed to survive in some form the imprisonment and the later conspiracy of 1599, to be redrafted and reconstituted in 1631.[47] To this last may be added the *Aforismi Politici* as a supplement to the practical features of the contemporary Church. The work had a more than usually complicated provenance, stemming first from the last months of 1601 and going through three phases of redaction (1601–13), two more (1614–19), and three further elaborations, cresting in 1633–34.[48]

Consequently, within the broader ambiance of Campanella's oeuvre we wish to focus on this nucleus of his writing and proceed first with a consideration of the pope, papal authority, and the resulting universalism; the relation of the Church, so conceived, to the state, to Italy, and to the ecclesiastical state; the College of Cardinals and the hierarchy; and conclude with an examination of monasticism and the religious orders. Beyond the remarkable consistency of this material a few issues recur: the vision of papal theocracy, first devised in an ecclesiastical prison, then reinforced and developed during a much longer imprisonment, again under the shadow of the Holy Office, inevitably raises the issue of opportunism and dissimulation; second, the facts of monarchy and hierarchy, overwhelming and persistent as they are, do not prove so oppressive as to obscure Campanella's sensitivity to community, whether that of a free city or a monastic order. Regarding the first issue, provisionally we may continue to affirm that although the matter of simulation can never entirely be discounted, the passionate, enduring commitment to a comprehensive unity and order in the Dominican's thought displaces, dis-

[46] LF-*Bibl.*, 103–5, 142–47; TC-*AV*, 178–89.
[47] LF-*Bibl.*, 177, 139–42.
[48] TC-*AfP*, 12, 45–46.

solves, amalgamates whatever appearances of simulation or dissimulation. Regarding the second issue, any analysis of Campanella's ecclesiastical polity must give due weight to his Dominican predecessor, Ptolemy of Lucca, at once high papalist and fierce republican.

The appropriate point of entry to our problem would appear to be that provided by Campanella himself, when he first turned to this matter in the Paduan prison of the Holy Office in late 1593. For he places at the very beginning of his disquisition on ecclesiastical government a list of twenty-four texts that, as further developments made clear, he would spend a good part of his life explicating. Of the twenty-four, all of considerable hierocratic resonance, twenty-two are scriptural—usually brief and pungent. Here we encounter the weighty affirmation of Psalm 109:4 regarding that priest forever according to the order of Melchisidech; the one sheepfold and one shepherd of John 10:16; that dominion from sea to sea of Psalm 71:8–11; the imperious *reminiscentur* of Psalm 21:28; the expectable *pasce oves meas* of John 21:17, preceded and fortified by Ezechiel's (34:23) claim that all are to be fed by one pastor; culminating with the inevitable granting of the keys in Matthew 16:19.[49]

The two nonscriptural texts belonging to the list possess considerable importance. At the head of the entire list stands a passage from St. Bernard's *De consideratione* (2.15), previously mentioned, where the formidable abbot predicates of the pope every office, dignity, and power appropriate to Abel, Noah, Abraham, Melchisidech, Aaron, Moses, Samuel, Peter, and Christ. Concluding the list is a passage ostensibly drawn from 3.10 of St. Thomas Aquinas's *De regimine principum*. But later scholarship has come to recognize that the Angelic Doctor's own work does not go beyond 2.4 and the very significant and extensive remainder of the treatise can be attributed to his student, Ptolemy of Lucca. Campanella here partakes of a misunderstanding that generally pervaded the Renaissance. In this instance the misattribution would allow the prisoner to endow the high papalism as well as lurking republicanism of this Tuscan Dominican with Thomistic and even according to the company, quasi-scriptural authority.

Depending upon two manuscripts, one at the Vatican and the other in the Berlin Staatsbibliothek, the *Governo ecclesiastico*, insofar as it may serve as an entry into Campanella's earliest thinking about the Church, suffers from the redaction of 1631, but two years before the publication of the *Monarchia messiae*.[50] In fact the work is replete with references to at least five of his later political writings, culminating in the *QR* of 1616–18. Furthermore references to the pontificate of Gregory XV and to the assimilation of Urbino in 1624 into the papal states push the work further into the 1620s. This treatise on the

[49] TC-*DUGE*, 467–69.
[50] LF-*Bibl.*, 139–42.

Church and its reform, begun in the 1593–95 period, inevitably comes to impart itself as a product of a period at least three decades later.

Despite the obvious later interpolations by the author himself *Del governo ecclesiastico* betrays one feature that is nowhere so evident in his other works: a contrast, or better a paralleling, of the apparent concentration of power in the monarchy of the pope—a point with which the work begins by means of the twenty-four texts, to be clinched by the proposition that the pope is father, priest, and king[51]—and images that reflect the broad community of humankind to be brought imminently under the most perfect law of Jesus God to whom it is prayed "Thy kingdom come."[52] This notion of a truly just *republica* alone secured to a basically rational humanity in Christ, *Ragion Prima*, and His Vicar involves a gathering of all nations and a conversion of all peoples[53] wherein the tongue precedes the sword, which only confirms the conquest affected by the expansive, preached word.[54]

To concentrate on this peculiar mix of monarchy, hierarchy, and community we need to consider the now lost but more theoretical sister to that which managed to survive the experiences of prison, namely, *De monarchia Christianorum*. The title provides an interesting clue that the content of the work is not the monarchy of the papacy but the monarchy *of Christians*. We can collect further confirming notions of the work's content and argument from Campanella's later statements regarding the lost treatise. At the end of his Roman period in the autobiographical *Syntagma* he claims to have shown in this work "by what means the Christian [public] order (*res*) has grown, will grow, how diminished and how recovered, politically speaking, and I presented the parallel between the kingdom and the kings of the Hebrews, and the kingdom and kings and emperors of the Christians." And in letters of 1607 and 1618, respectively, he affirms to have demonstrated in the *Monarchia* as "no philosopher before has been able to depict, the commonwealth (*rem publicam*) as instituted by the apostles at Rome" or in a book "to the lord pope and all the nations regarding their jurisdictions and grades and their fraternity (*fratellanza*) according to Scripture and nature; and the ruin of Christians is born from neglect of what this book contains."[55]

For the present it is enough to have adduced this peculiar conjunction of monarchic/hierocratic with communitarian notions of ecclesiastical polity—pseudo-Thomist, "Ptolemaic," and potentially Dominican in origin—that may well have received its most forceful theoretical expression in this early lost

---

[51] TC-*DUGE*, 472.

[52] Ibid., 469.

[53] Ibid., 474.

[54] Ibid., 469.

[55] See LF-*Bibl.*, 177–78, for references to the individual passages examined. On explication of the important point that previous philosophers had failed to present the true political order, state, republic (*rempublican*) because it required an *ecclesiastical* rendering, see TC-*AT*, 84.

work, *De monarchia Christianorum*. If so, it would suggest that the "republican" base to Campanella's view of ecclesiastical polity appeared most stridently in his early career before the long imprisonment. Its immortalization in a fictive form would occur with his composition of the *City of the Sun*, written in the darkest shadow of defeat and earliest imprisonment. As he had apparently done in the abortive conspiracy,[56] in the earliest years of his longest imprisonment he takes most seriously the communal implications of Plato's *Republic*, *Laws*, and *Alcibiades* 2, which he incorporates into his own vision of a final righteous commonwealth, the promised kingdom, and the restored age of innocence. In darkest dungeon this bright afterglow of what had been probably constitutive of the white hope of 1599 will never completely disappear from his larger political vision; this Platonically reinforced conviction receives expression, even apotheosis, in his monastic, Dominican, Joachimite understanding of the Church, its past and its future. We need to be prepared for the continuing importance of the communitarian ingredient to papal monarchy, when we later encounter such terms as *felicissima respublica monarchica* in 1607,[57] *republica dell' Apocalissi*[58] in late 1611, and *aristocratiam monarchicam*[59] in 1623.[60] Never disappearing, a necessary constitutive force and element in his ecclesiastical/apocalyptical vision, it suffers, however, during his Neapolitan imprisonment an inevitable displacement by the better known and more conspicuous papal, hierocratic, and expressly monarchical element in his thinking, which now needs to be addressed.

Campanella lays the foundations of his hieratic monarchy by affirming a number of dogmatic propositions: more natural for man to be ruled by one than many; better the prince be elective than hereditary; better this prince have both temporal and spiritual power.[61] The first proposition as argument is circular and relies upon analogy. "Natural" refers apparently here to that which is prevalent in the practice of bees and presumably other creatures according to Homer and St. Ambrose and discovers its ultimate analogical support in God's rule of the universe. Less traditional and at first possibly surprising is the next proposition, advocating the elective over the hereditary ruler. Here one may find Campanella's healthy prejudice against the Neapolitan nobility but also more significantly his awareness of the constitutional practices of the Church and specifically of a collegiate body such as the Dominican order, as well as the more obvious instance of the Sacred College in its deliberations. In this last instance especially, given his confidence in a process of discovering the

---

[56] Pagden, *Spanish Imperialism*, 42.
[57] TC-*AP*, 80.
[58] Luigi Firpo, "Un memoriale inedito e un indice delle opere di Tommaso Campanella," *RF* 38 (1947): 218.
[59] TC-*T*, XXVI, 126.
[60] LF-*Bibl.*, 160.
[61] TC-*MM*, 9–10.

best, the canvassing for the right prince should be general and not limited to one's own nation; he should be from the elder and more experienced, and be celibate rather than distracted by the entanglements of matrimony.[62]

With the third proposition—the fusion of the two powers—reappears that final authority in the list from the partly contemporaneous *Del governo ecclesiastico*. Apparently from the *De regimine principum* (3.10 or 3.18–19) of Ptolemy of Lucca, alias St. Thomas Aquinas, the exact words are not to be found in the text and would seem to be some later editor's distillation of the sense of these chapters, as either a heading or a marginal note.[63] Given Campanella's overriding axiom that religion is the soul of any political body (*respublica*), the priestly and the royal best convene in the supreme prince in whom the people recognize their intercessor before God and more willingly obey his laws. When armed, such a religious ruler commands invincible respect unless challenged by another religion, better armed and presumably better equipped with charisms. Campanella insists upon this political ingredient to the properly ecclesiastical as an essential reinforcement. For almost all great princes have been at once kings and priests, as evinced in the priest-king Melchisedech up through the Caesars to Constantine, who Campanella claims ceded rather than gave the empire to Pope Sylvester.[64] Since the secular granting of empire to the papacy would implicitly deny such an hieratic fusion of the two powers, the sense of donation must be transformed. Whereas earlier in the *Antiveneti* Campanella seemed to observe the plain sense of a donation of the empire in the West by Constantine to the papacy, now in the later period and with ample access to Roman libraries he can insist on Ptolemy's meaning of *cessit*,[65] whereby he partakes of the earlier Dominican's contention that the Donation was not a grant but a restitution of what had been hitherto unlawfully held by pagan emperors.[66] While having picked up his cue from Ptolemy, Campanella pursues a more theological and legal rather than historical bent: "since all power is from Christ, whatever princely donors give to the Church belonged previously to Christ, from whom they accepted [it]. Thus they do not give but place in common what they held individually. . . . they give the practical use to the pope himself, not the authority according to Right."[67] As a further reinforcement for the merging of *regnum* and *sacer-*

[62] Ibid., 10.

[63] An examination of the Folger Library copy of the Italian translation of the *De reg. prin.*, *Trattato del governo de principi / di San Tommaso d'Aquino/Angelico Dottore al Re di Cipri* (Florence: Giorgio Marescotti, 1577), does not resolve the problem. Campanella would here appear to be abstracting the issue.

[64] TC-*MM*, 11–12.

[65] *De reg. prin.* 3.10. The text is available in *Sancti Thomae Aquinatis . . . Opera omnia* (Parma, 1852–73; New York, 1950 repr.), 16:225–91, esp. 259.

[66] Charles T. Davis, "Roman Patriotism and Republican Propaganda: Ptolemy of Lucca and Pope Nicholas III," *Speculum* 50 (1975): 410–33, esp. 423.

[67] TC-*MM*, 37: "Sed hic notandum, quidquid Principes dant Ecclesiae, prius fuisse Christi, a

dotium in a single ruler Plato's letter to the Syracusans and his *Politicus* are cited.

With 1 Samuel 8 the ideal of the prince-priest falls apart. Reluctantly God condescends to a lay kingdom from which follow the controversies between prophets and priests on the one hand and kings and lay princes on the other, perpetuated in Christendom by the discord between Guelphs and Ghibellines with successive permutations. While musing on the Melchisedechian roots of his ideal order, Campanella affirms significantly that the highest priest, unarmed and without temporal dominion, is contemptible.[68] Love requires enforcement. Only through the coming of the Messiah in Christ will God reunite once again priesthood and kingdom and thus introduce the happy age of a recovered innocence and an absence of wars.[69] Relaxing his imagination, Campanella allows that with a comprehensive world monarchy the resulting abundance of knowledge and observations, especially in such fields as astronomy, astrology, physics, and politics, would through greater commerce and communications advance the sciences and serve to dissolve present human fragmentation as worms in a cheese.[70]

In a revealing manner Campanella takes issue with Aristotle on the possibility of a universal principate. He sees the preparations for such a polity in the wars of Cyrus, Alexander, and Caesar and also, interestingly enough, in so many Israelite migrations spreading the knowledge of the one true God throughout the world. For through unity of faith a single comprehensive order becomes not only possible but imperative. Aristotle erred in not believing that one can rule the entire world; it is possible through vicars stationed in the provinces. Furthermore Aristotle never lived to see the empire of Augustus and the subsequent emergence of religion as the very soul of the commonwealth (*republica*), informing its members with the same articles of faith, the same fear and love of God. On the contrary Aristotle knew only servile fear, not the spiritual fervor of the friars (*religionis vires*), unless as political astuteness in the fashion of Machiavelli. Indeed if Augustus had had a solid, unitive religion and not one divided and idolatrous, he would easily have been able to expand, unite, and conserve universal empire. Our Dominican concludes this Paduan, relativist assessment of religions with the present case of Spain, whose king rules vast spaces scattered over the surface of the globe; he has his viceroys and their officialdom, but it is chiefly religion that collects them into one. Likewise the pope has his patriarchs, archbishops, and synods. And if that Aristotelian addict, De Soto, a member of Campanella's own order, im-

---

quo acceperunt. Ergo non dant, sed ponunt in communi, quod habebant in particulari. Qui enim dat, privat se data re: At omnes donatores possunt esse clerici, & re data frui. Ergo dant usum de facto ipsi Papae; & non auctoritatem de iure." Cf. also 12, 53, 63.

[68] Ibid., 13.
[69] Ibid., 13-14.
[70] Ibid., 15. See chap. 8, n. 54, *infra*, for the Latin text of this interesting passage.

prudently asserts that the governance of the entire world under one prince is impossible and contrary to nature, his fellow Dominican critic now observes that it is nevertheless the custom of the Aristotelians to call whatever does not please Aristotle as being contrary to nature. Indeed if De Soto can accept the universal dominion of the pope in spiritual matters, why not the same dominion in temporal matters?[71]

In specifically arguing for the temporal power of the pope Campanella enters into the treacherous crosscurrents of theological debate. Here John 21:17 serves as his sheet anchor. Confident that *pascere* is the same as *regere* in Greek, he can pair the two in his quoting of the text.[72] He cites Plato as believing that only the priest near to God is able to be prince of the entire human race and allows that Aristotle has well demonstrated that no layman is able to be universal king.[73] Included now in Campanella's rogues' gallery of heretics along with Wyclif, Huss, Peter Waldo, Lutherans, and Calvinists but most closely associated with Marsilius of Padua is his old acquaintance of 1593, Paolo Sarpi, whom he never mentions by name but refers to as "a certain theologian"[74] or as in the earlier *Antiveneti* a "hired (*venduto*) theologian" and proceeds to list the Venetian Servite's seventeen opposing arguments ending with Dante.[75] Campanella admits that Catholics are here divided, the majority arguing for an indirect power in temporal matters for correcting and directing polities into conformity with religion. He cites Bellarmine and Torquemada for this position, De Soto in a much more limited sense, and Covarrubias not at all. Claiming that the better theologians as well as the bulk of the canonists advocate the pope to be lord of all the world *in spiritualibus et temporalibus*, Campanella clutches for his favorite individual authority, the pseudo-Thomistic completion of *De regimine principum* by Ptolemy of Lucca. For once he hesitates in claiming that St. Thomas himself in "*Republica*" (3.18–20) makes the pope universal lord in temporal and spiritual matters: "Although this book does not seem to be by Dr. Thomas because of a certain inserted story occurring after his death . . . the book seems to be by a learned man not unequal to Dr. Thomas, if nevertheless not his own. That this [statement], however, can be taken as his opinion is demonstrated by the *Sentences*, distinction 44, where he asserts the same."[76]

Ultimately Campanella's argumentation must come back to its fundamental

---

[71] Ibid., 15–17.
[72] Ibid., 20; cf. 33.
[73] Ibid., 20.
[74] Cf. TC-*MM*, 64.
[75] Ibid., 22; cf. also TC-*AV*, 36.
[76] TC-*MM*, 24: "Et quamuis liber ille non videatur esse D. Thomae, propter quandam Historiam insertam, que post mortem eius contigit. . . . Sed liber ille videtur esse viri docti, D. Thomae non inaequalis, si tamen non est eius. At hanc esse eius opinio prebatur ex Sent. d. 44 lib. ubi idem asserit."

principle: Christ is the Primal, Essential, Eternal Reason and all dominion is based upon reason. Thus all depends on Him and He has left both powers, spiritual and temporal, to His Church. Moreover the priesthood of Christ is not according to the order of Aaron but has superseded that Levitical Aaronic one and has been instituted according to Melchisedech, the notable difference being that to Melchisedech is annexed royal power, which prefigures the future monarch, universal king, and priest. Rather than there being visibly a thousand-year rule of Christ on earth after His death, temporal dominion is exercised through vicars, the papal kingdom being the messianic kingdom. All the better theologians assert that Christ came to restore perfectly the state of the natural law. All tend to a realization of the figure of Melchisedech in the restored *saeculum* of the first natural law.[77]

The Church's *principatus* over all the earth began under Constantine, when all persecutions ended and the Church sensed itself as teacher and ruler of the world. All peoples were now to be subjected to Christ. Campanella cites scriptural support, especially the Psalms, lest any think that the kingdom is only spiritual, in preaching, and not in power, for constraining the faithful. Thus the sword of Constantine, of Charlemagne, and of the Spaniards constrains the enemies of the Church. And if kings are called pastors of their respective peoples by Homer and others, the name of pastor applies better to the spiritual dominion as evinced in John's *pasce oves meas*. Encouraged by his reading of Plato's *Laws*, the friar firmly grasps the sword of iron for the medicinal, ministerial use on the Church's flock.[78] The monarchical and the pastoral come to reinforce each other. The term "monarchical" cannot be applied appropriately to secular rulers, but as the noblest form of polity, especially representing the unity of God, it pertains properly to Peter, the head of the universal Church as instituted by Christ. Then shifting from Matthew 16:18 to John 21:17 Campanella claims that because Peter loved more than the other apostles, he obtains the imperium over them and the laity. Love and power coinhere, love serving as the justification for power and power as a function of love.[79]

In establishing the preeminence and lordship of the pope and the priestly in temporal as well as spiritual matters, Campanella goes well beyond Bellarmine's tentative argument for the pope's indirect power. Amidst repeated scuffles with De Soto and Covarrubias the friar shapes his hieratic position by the application of a few sources used as authorities and pushed to their extreme: the effective working out of the implications of the figure of Melchisedech; the mutual reinforcement of love and power in the pastoral imperative of John 21:17; and then, of course, the apparently Thomistic texts provided by 3.18–20 of the *De regimine principum*. He now effectively grasps

---

[77] Ibid., 27–30.
[78] Ibid., 30–36.
[79] Ibid., 39, 46, 48.

Ptolemy of Lucca's notion that the emperor does not grant, for he cannot give empire to the pope, but cedes it.[80] He even appropriates Ptolemy's erroneous notion that Gregory V had founded the German college of the seven imperial electors in 1030; the emperor whom they nominated had to be confirmed and crowned by the pope before he could function outside Germany.[81] Thus with the same legerdemain with which Pope Hadrian (!) translates empire to Charlemagne, Gregory V translates it to the Germans.[82] For further defending his claim to papal power in both temporal and spiritual *directe,* he calls upon a genuine St. Thomas Aquinas in his *Commentary on the Sentences,* where he claims that only the pope as *conditor juris* is able to remit punishments determined by practical law.[83]

Another favorite source joining Ptolemy and John the Evangelist as an authority is John Chrysostom. He is claimed never to have obeyed lay princes and to have proved in *Babilam* that the dominion of the world pertains more to priests than to imperial agents; here as elsewhere he shows not only bishops but also monks to be better than kings by natural law.[84] The ultimate direction of Campanella's thinking suddenly obtrudes itself when he seeks to counter the argument that when Christ said, "Who has set me as judge over you?" (Luke 12:14) in responding to the request that he divide an inheritance among his brethren, he was deliberately renouncing judgment in temporal matters. Campanella's response is electrifying: "Christ came not to divide properties but to make all common, as appears in His Republic, constituted in a community similar to Socrates' as St. Clement, Philo, and St. Luke bear witness. Division, however, has been made among Christians in order to accommodate to imperfections. But community has remained in the clergy and with the monks and perfection among the professing friars."[85] And then on to the subsequent argument.

Given Campanella's proclivity for rooting out and inflating spurious texts, one cannot help but be suspicious when he advances for his hierocratic argument the concluding speech of Emperor Basil I at Constantinople IV, the eighth ecumenical council. Indeed in the final quarter of the *Monarchia messiae* he has recourse to it four times.[86] Nevertheless the text as part of the documentation surviving the council and coming to the Latin West is genuine.

[80] Ibid., 53; cf. 12, 63.
[81] Davis, "Roman Patriotism," 418: *De reg. prin.,* 266.
[82] TC-*MM,* 56. In mistaking Leo III for Hadrian Campanella is simply following Ptolemy faithfully. See III.10, p. 259.
[83] TC-*MM,* 63; cf. Aquinas, *Opera omnia,* VII/11, 846 (4 Sent., d. 20, Q. 3, a.2).
[84] TC-*MM,* 58–59.
[85] Ibid., 59: "Nam christus venerat non dividere substantias fortunae, sed facere omnia communia, sicut apparet in sua Reip. constituta in communitate simili Socratice, teste S. Clemente, & Philone, & S. Luca. Divisio autem facta est inter Christianos condescendendo imperfectis: sed remansit Communitas in Clero & monachis, & perfectionem profitentibus fratribus."
[86] Ibid., 61, 72, 79, 82.

In his rendering of the passage Campanella stretches the generous statement of the emperor from an expression of respect for the integrity of the Church, its agents, and its operation to an admission of absolute subordination of the imperial and secular to the papal and clerical: "We are not able to equal the priest anymore than the sheep the shepherd;"[87] or, "If the pope is pastor and every emperor a sheep, it follows necessarily that the sheep is able to do nothing against the pastor unless according to the law imposed by the pastor."[88] In these citations Campanella draws the text nearer to the intention of his most likely source, Baronius's *Annales*.[89] As the eleventh volume of this history including the years 843 to 1008 did not emerge from the press until 1602,[90] Campanella could not have had access to it along with a good deal else that he takes from Baronius until after 1626, when he was in Rome. The fact that this text had had relatively little currency throughout the intervening period would argue for its Roman origin and availability to first Baronius and then Campanella.[91]

As Campanella's argument for an all-inclusive papal plentitude of power or what he calls at one point *Pontifex Christianus Melchisidecheus*[92] rolls along on wheels of authorities either curious or spurious, he faces around to deal with Dante. The Florentine's arguments for the bifurcation of power represented especially by the symbol of the two suns scandalized Campanella. Such division between temporal and spiritual overthrows for him the entire Bible and all polity. As he had previously noted, Dante erred by far when he failed to give temporal dominion to the pope, associating him with the Levitical inheritance rather than with that of Melchisedech. Now toward the end of his work Campanella sees Dante as ruthlessly tearing apart the hierarchy of the Church from its earthly copy.[93] In the end Campanella has Emperor Basil, Isaiah with his prediction of the New World, St. Bridget, Ezechiel, even

---

[87] Ibid., 61: "Nos, ait, non possumus aequari Sacerdoti: sicut nec Ovis Pastori unquam."

[88] Ibid., 72: "Si Papa est Pastor, & omni Imperator est ovis, necessario sequitur, nil posse ovem contra Pastorem, neque plus; nisi secundum legem a Pastore i[m]positam."

[89] *Caesaris Baronii. Annales Ecclesiastici*, ed. Augustinus Theiner (Bar-Le Duc, 1868), 15:161–62.

[90] Pullapilly, *Baronius*, 100.

[91] For the materials from the eighth general council barely survived transmission across the Adriatic (Daniel Stiernon, *Konstantinopel IV* [Mainz, 1975], 57–58; 182–83; 194–96); Anastasius Bibliothecarius had translated it in the late ninth century along with the other materials (*MPL*, 129:173CD–174A); and in the protracted polemics concerning *Regnum* and *Sacerdotium* following Gregory VII we find recourse to the speech of Emperor Basil I only occurring twice, first with Cardinal Deusdedit in 1097–1100 and then again almost a century later. (Monumenta Germaniae Historica, *Libri de lite*, II, 307–8, 316; III, 151). On Tridentine recourse to the Greek originals, see *CT*, I, 195, 226; X, 67–68.

[92] TC-*MM*, 74.

[93] Ibid., 71; cf. 29.

Bellarmine marching to the single drum of Rome's preeminent jurisdiction and universal pastorate.[94]

Despite the extreme intensity of the papal hierocratic argument in the *Monarchia messiae* Campanella is capable in another context and a broader perspective of placing clear limits on papal power. In combatting the Lutheran charge that the papal Antichrist will make himself universal lord, the Dominican friar responds:

> I deny that the pope makes himself lord in spiritual and temporal matters, but only minister, steward (*oeconomus*), dispenser, and vicar, constituted over his immediate entourage (*familia*) and universal pastor over the sheep of Christ, as we have declared. Nor is the pope able to change the law divine or natural, nor the sacraments, the Scriptures of God, nor the laws divine. He is nevertheless universal bishop, because he is pastor of the entire Church, since he is successor of him to whom it was said: *Pasce oves meas, et pasce agnos meas*, not these, nor those, but all, and when even the bishops may be sheep, even they pertain to the care of the pope. Nor did the pope ever call himself lord, but servant of the servants of God and bishops of the catholic Church.[95]

The *Monarchia messiae* nevertheless represents the most extreme statement of Campanella's papalism and hierocratic clericalism, so extreme that it apparently embarrassed contemporary curialists, who compelled its withdrawal from publication. In the work the Dominican had gone considerably beyond the tense, balanced position of Bellarmine, who for his moderation on the pope's indirect power in temporal matters was rewarded with abuse and censure in the inner corridors of the curia. As evinced perhaps most obviously in his repeated recourse to Emperor Basil at Constantinople IV, Campanella came to fasten on the issue of church–state relations and what he saw as the proper absolute subordination of the secular within a hierarchically papal monism. It is against this basic position, extremely affirmed in 1633 but essentially a constant in his thinking, that we wish to consider two different cases of the relation of secular power to the Campanellan papacy. A consideration of Venice and of Spain in this perspective will reveal significant implications for the papal role both in Italy and in Europe as well as suggesting the complexities of this Dominican, even "Ptolemaic" political thinker.

Campanella wrote the *Antiveneti* in the autumn of 1606 specifically to advance the papal cause in its conflict over the Interdict and Venice, but more personally to recommend himself and his inhuman sufferings in the dreadful dungeon of San Elmo to the favor and relief of Paul V. As in so many of his other writings Campanella's obvious opportunism, rather than vitiating the

[94] Ibid., 72–83.
[95] TC-*T*, XXVI, 138.

import of the work, enhances and reinforces it. For the prisoner could well have written a shrilly polemical, abusive tract as a better means of leveraging himself out from the present, cruel confinement. Instead with the first of the three books he adopts the mode of lamentations, as he would later explain to Gabriel Naudé in 1632 in the *Syntagma*, Lamentations "instar threnorum Jeremiae."[96] Thus the tone of an ultimately loving mother for her wayward child is adopted and in the two succeeding books the lamentations give way to discourses whereby this disobedient child may be reasoned with and admonished. Campanella's care and respect for Venice and its noble republicanism shine through the work. Political, yes, but more than political the *Antiveneti* according to its distinguished editor, Luigi Firpo, is vintage Campanella, "now ingenious, now ingenuous, candid and malicious, tortuous and inspired," an intensely human document.[97]

By allying himself with the cause of the papal interdict, Campanella entered upon a conflict that clearly opposed two camps, two polities, two worldviews: the hierarchical authority of the Counter Reformation as opposed to the Renaissance republicanism of the city-state. At the very outset Campanella claims that liberty consists in living according to the Eternal Reason and that Venice by its apostasy has fallen into unreason and bondage. Indeed the Roman religion alone defends free will today and alone maintains men free in a world wherein so many peoples have apostasized, like England, to become slaves to tyrants. Except for the papacy "we are all asleep in the dark night of this age." He represents the papacy as the glory of Italy without which all Italian states would be slaves to foreigners like so many of its other members. Venice's role comes to be placed in a sort of domino theory, whereby, if it continues in its apostasy, Venice forsakes its true glory, abandons its proper obedience, undermines the glory and safety of Italy evinced in papal power, unravelling thereby other obediences, and by following in the ways of northern Europe exposes Italy to become a bordello for foreign nations, as Dante had warned.[98]

True, Campanella concedes little to Venice. The Republic of St. Mark would scarcely be heartened to learn that its true glory was in recognizing the pope as *Deus deorum*.[99] And in fact the liberty propounded by the Dominican differed *toto caelo* from that more expressly political liberty advanced by Venice and its Servite defender.[100] Yet while Campanella's theological liberty lay in an adherence to an hierarchical order, that *principato assoluto* equipped with both swords is not without its compensating political assurances.[101] For

[96] TC-*AV*, 175, 181.
[97] Ibid., 189.
[98] Ibid., 16, 26–28; 33–35; cf. Dante, *Purg.* 6.78.
[99] TC-*AV*, 18.
[100] Bouwsma, *Venice*, 423–27.
[101] TC-*AV*, 57.

he wishes to establish the Catholic Church as the veritable guardian of free will against the predestinarian heresies of the north that would otherwise undo Venice.[102] Similarly it is to the benefit of Venice and all of Italy that the pope saves both, by holding the balance between Spain and France. Here a *religione disarmata* would be useless. In this respect Campanella cites as an ignorant assertion Machiavelli's remark that the pope is the ruin of Italy.[103] Campanella manages to wrap Venice's welfare and the greatness of Italy in the broad surplice of papal hegemony: you ought not to be obstinate and stand apart because the Roman Church will lose authority in the countries of other princes and will not be able to harmonize them to the needs of Christendom, especially against the Turk—a fact that would hurt you first; and the majesty of Italy that rules in all the world *per sacerdotale imperio* would be diminished together with your own honor.[104]

While arguing for the papacy as that which is peculiarly common to Italians and thus to the larger, appropriate interests of Venice, Campanella touches upon the specific issues dividing the two combatants. He sees a hired theologian, Sarpi never named, advancing Venice's claims to the income of churches and their spiritual and temporal jurisdictions.[105] To subject the clergy to the laity is to subvert the divine and the natural orders.[106] Nevertheless the prevailing theme throughout remains the integrity of the papacy and the Roman religion as the necessary basis for free will and all order. When in the third book Campanella comes to indulge in the major intellectual pursuit of the late Renaissance, the alignment of astrological prediction to scriptural prophecy, he avers that free will cannot be forced by the stars any more than by forty hours of torture, alluding to his own experience.[107] Then darkly he will add for the benefit of Venice that for the past two hundred years the stars have been inimical to republics; with its progressive approach to the earth the sun turns from republics to monarchies, as evinced in the New World, in old Saxony, throughout southern Asia, and, as he hazards in 1607, with the Spaniards in Antarctica.[108]

If Campanella enters the lists in clear support of the papacy and its necessary role in Italy and in Europe, which now threatens to be unstrung, his intention is never to annihilate Venice but rather to call it back to what he deems its proper role. Is this respect for Venice consistent with his other statements rendered on other occasions regarding the great republic of the

---

[102] Ibid., 26–28, 77–81.
[103] Ibid., 87–89.
[104] Ibid., 100.
[105] Ibid., 36.
[106] Ibid., 58.
[107] Ibid., 131.
[108] Ibid., 132–42; on the contemporary Spanish aspirations in Antarctica, see my article "Habitability," *Journal of World History* 8 (1997): 1-27, esp. 19–24.

Adriatic? We find that with slight retouching he will introduce into book 1 a most laudatory sonnet to Venice, first composed shortly before August 1601, wherein the city is represented as an ark of salvation against the onrush of barbarian hordes.[109]

> Thou wonder of the world, Rome's loyal heir,
> Thou pride and strong support of Italy,
> Dial of princes, school of all things wise!
> Thou like Arcturus steadfast in the skies,
> With tardy sense guidest thy kingdom fair,
> Bearing alone the load of liberty.

If six years earlier he could be so respectful, even worshipful of Venetian grandeur, six years after the *Antiveneti*, in the first composition of his *Quaestiones . . . de politicis* to be further developed and finally published in Paris in 1637, he appears equally admirative. In rebuking Plato and Aristotle for constructing the laws of their polities in the interest of enhancing their respective military capacity, he reminds his readers that the end of the republic is the felicitous conservation in life ordained to God, and war does not conserve. Here Venice is exemplary in its slight regard for arms, happier by far and longer-lasting than Sparta, Crete, or Rome. Admittedly Venice experienced trouble with mercenaries but its polity was so well tempered that her inhabitants seem to have enjoyed felicity both in the present and in the past.[110] Then shortly afterwards Campanella returns to the case of Venice when he considers the mistrust of Plato and Aristotle for locating a city by the sea. Sicily provided a nest of tyrannies and Naples was never free. Campanella sees only Venice as immune to such evils on account of the best laws, its inaccessibility, and its nautical arts. Its navy and marine exercised by its nobles make Venice the guardian of the entire Adriatic. Then allowing that of course Aristotle was hopelessly ignorant of marinal matters, Campanella veers away, plunging into another consideration.[111]

In short a basic consistency prevails in the friar's respect for the Republic of Venice; in advancing the claims of a universal hierocratic order, he could nevertheless adjust this republic, so venerable and viable, to fit into what he conceived as the papal order in Italy and Europe. Returning to the same period as the composition of the *Antiveneti*, in the *Articuli prophetales* of the following year, we find a statement more reminiscent of the republicanism of Leonardo Bruni than that of Ptolemy of Lucca. Regarding the transformation of a bad event to good ends, Campanella cites the example of the Venetians, who did not rebel from the empire, but rather seeing Aquileia attacked by Attila, they betook themselves to the lagoons and constituted there a new and

[109] TC-*AV*, 32–33; Symonds, *Sonnets*, 147.
[110] TC-*PR*³, 80.
[111] Ibid., 96.

free republic from the empire to which they had formerly been subjects, thereby turning bad even into good.[112] Thus in the context of the friar's persisting respect for the city of the lagoons, the composition of the *Antiveneti* becomes a more complex achievement without ever being an act of consummate simulation.

In returning to the *Monarchia messiae* of 1633 and now the case of Spain, we find that apparently for the last time, only a year before his shift to France, Campanella could understand Spain and the Spanish monarchy as the *brachium* of God.[113] Isaiah's image of God's arm, connoting here that service and subordination of the secular to the papal, needs no further elucidation except insofar as Spain's position at Naples impinged upon Campanella's conception of the papal ordering of the Italian peninsula. Nothing could so easily enflame relations between Rome and Madrid as to raise the issue of just precisely how the king of Spain held Naples, the Kingdom of the Two Sicilies, and whether the *Monarchia Sicula* fairly abrogated any dependence of that realm upon the papacy. In fact since the publication of Baronius's volume 11 in 1605 the cardinal's questioning of Spain's right to Naples through the notorious *Monarchia Sicula* had continued to ravage hispano-papal relations.[114] Later freed and with infinitely easier access to Baronius's *Annales*, Campanella could note that the *Monarchia Sicula* had become such a burning issue that copies of the good cardinal's work, where he preferred doubts as to the propriety of Spain's possession of Naples, were being delivered by Spaniards to the flames.[115]

In order to appreciate the December–January 1624–25 exchange that occurred between Campanella and the distinguished Spanish prelate, Cardinal Gabriel de Trejo y Paniagua, the prisoner's own position on Naples needs to be reviewed. In the *Aforismi Politici* Campanella had dwelt repeatedly on the necessity of the *papato armato* that combines both swords.[116] Beyond the clearly emerging figure of the priest-king, buttressed both by scriptural authority and ostensibly by wise election, this work also floats another idea, later to be developed when the liberated Dominican was in France: that Naples served only as a dreadful apple of discord between France and Spain, weakening Europe before the Turk and gravely endangering Italy. The solution: let the pope remove from both parties the apple or they themselves yield it into his hands.[117] Actually the idea had an earlier genesis, dating from the period of the conspiracy, when Campanella had apparently advocated that Naples as the apple of discord must be plucked back to the pope.[118] In 1636 he would

[112] TC-*AP*, 297.
[113] TC-*MM*, 71.
[114] Borromeo, "Baronio," 111ff.
[115] TC-*MN*, 311–12, 330.
[116] TC-*AfP*, 38, 70, 89–90; VIII, 7; X, 16.
[117] Ibid., XII, 2; TC-*DUGE*, 507.
[118] Amab., *Doc.*, II, 169–70/241.

reiterate this idea that the contention of the two great powers over the Kingdom of Naples only served to ruin Christendom and play into the hands of the Turk.[119]

Holding high office in both the curia and the monarchy, Trejo was a cardinal of no small account. Formerly professor at Salamanca and prior of Calatrava, Franciscan tertiary, and fervent supporter of the Franciscan teaching on the Immaculate Conception of the Virgin Mary, Trejo had received the purple in December 1615 and become archbishop of Salerno in June 1625.[120] In the conclave of 1621 he had obtained fifteen votes.[121] Campanella had learned of the benevolent interest of the cardinal in his case. Quick to cultivate a possible liberator, the prisoner had approached him in a letter (now lost) which he had entrusted to a Spanish cleric, Cipriano Martinez, a friend and associate of the Piarist School. The letter and a list of his writings never reached Trejo. Also in 1623 he had addressed the dedicatory letter of his treatise, ostensibly supporting the doctrine of the Immaculate Conception, to Cardinal Trejo.[122] Apparently curious, even concerned about the notorious Neapolitan prisoner, Trejo had written to the viceroy, Alvarez de Toledo, who informed his charge about the cardinal's request for a letter and a list of his books.[123] Eager to accommodate a potential patron Campanella replied in a second letter expressing appreciation for his interest. He used the opportunity to draw the cardinal's attention to *The Spanish Monarchy*, *The Panegyric to the Princes of Italy*, and what proves to be the *QR*. Referring to the earlier letter, the lists of published and manuscript works, and the production of materials to be forwarded to the cardinal, Campanella went on to lament the difficulty, even impossibility of producing manuscript copies under the conditions presented by his confinement.[124]

The cardinal replied promptly in a letter dated January 1, 1625. Despite its greater extent in the letter, the spiritual consolation, humane and deeply felt, does not concern us here, but rather the early, political part that deals with his reaction to Campanella's writings. While admitting his general satisfaction and interest in them, Trejo complains that he has only been able to encounter a few and these all in manuscript and all too frequently redacted most wretchedly; of these he knows only the *Prophetic Articles*, the *Political Aphorisms*, the *City of the Sun*, and the *Apology for Galileo*. He has seen but not read *On the Sense of Things*. He continues:

[119] TC-*MN*, 319, 337.
[120] Luigi Firpo, "Appunti Campanelliani XXX," *GCFI* 41 (1962): 375–80.
[121] José López de Toro, "Repuesta del Cardenal Trejo a una carta de Tomas Campanella," *Revista de Estudios Politicos* 122 (1962): 161–78, esp. 161–62.
[122] Toro, "Trejo," 166; Firpo, "Appunti XXX," 375–76.
[123] Toro, "Trejo," 167; TC-*Lett.*, 212.
[124] TC-*Lett.*, 213; Toro, "Trejo," 168.

From those that I have read many things please me indeed, some displease, but these few in number and then most slight. . . . Only one matter do I wish not to pass over, which, because it pertains to your welfare, I believe now to be the right moment to speak. . . .

More than once I have observed in the *Politics* that you desire a king who in governing possesses both swords and is able to exercise both sovereign powers, temporal and spiritual, kingdom and priesthood at the same time. What pertains to the political substance of this desired prince and whether it is entirely appropriate for the political order I do not care, but on this I shall ever maintain: that if you speak about the ultimate ruler whose empire will terminate with the life of the world, then I agree; but if you speak about him whose succession is necessary with the extinction of his life and the continuance of time, it is necessary that the successor be legitimate or elective. The first is not permitted to the priest-king; the second offends all political precepts according to which now it seems more probable that kingdoms by hereditary succession are more lasting than elective ones, and less vulnerable to tyranny. But now comes the point that concerns me, or rather you: namely, that because the Neapolitan kingdom pertains by direct right to the Apostolic See and is governed by our Spanish king according to the secular concession by the same See, a certain suspicion always hangs over Neapolitans, especially those oppressed by adverse circumstances, that they would take delight in a revolution, as if in the alteration and instability of things they might constitute the anchor of their own hopes; what then if with things having changed, the public matters of this kingdom should by right be recalled to the sacred hand of the pope, not undeservedly could the argument of that man generate a suspicion of the desired change—the man who not only states that it is useful to have a leader, who is at once both king and priest, but who also presents before the eyes of the multitude this unfamiliar rationale for governing, once again in an ambiguous fashion. For if the leaders of the Neapolitan kingdom and the people may be persuaded to this end, easily they may rebel against the Catholic king and, having forsaken that loyalty which they ought to manifest to the prince constituted by the Roman See, they now take refuge in that very pontiff who, at once king and priest, would satisfy both your and their judgment. Whence my counsel to you, lest you incite further those who once hated you and might with the multitude attribute to you new cause of suspicion, that what pertains to this article, you either delete or explain in a way that should not offend the mind and the ears of the ministers of a king who is neither, nor is able to be, a priest in order that they may still [not] hold you in suspicion. And because by no means are kingdoms today better able to be stabilized and confirmed than by legitimate succession, which right of blood is totally excluded in the case of pontiffs, it is necessary to remove this theory that advances a priest-king. . . .

Finally, Jesus, true king and priest, did not want to exercise the kingship; armed with the two swords, which He pronounced sufficient, He reproved Peter for the use of the [former sword] that he wanted to belong to the secular power, and in the exercise He distinguished clearly between kingdom and priesthood. And although afterwards kingdoms have been offered to the popes, with few being retained and these being judged suitable to the honor and majesty of the Apostolic See, the rest have been commended to secular princes, lest having been oppressed with temporal matters, the papal power might lose the spiritual matters which, as they are of greater weight, need greater care and ought to be treated by that prince in whom by Christ's promise the Spirit of God is present. The office of the pope is to lead souls to heaven; the task of the king, to lead soldiers to war. But let these words suffice, not with the intention of disputing but rather of counseling that this type of opinion might not injure you and you not be believed by others to be most hostile to the king and desire with the removal of kings that the kingdom devolve upon the Roman See.[125]

[125] Luigi Firpo has published the Latin text of this letter in "Appunti Campanelliani XXX," *GCFI* 41 (1962): 381–86, 381–83 here translated: "Placent quidem ex his quae legi multa, displicent nonnulla, eaque pauca et levissima. . . . Solum unum nollem reticere, quod, quoniam ad tuam pertinet utilitatem, nunc dicere credo opportunum. . . . Animadverti non semel in *Politicis*, te desiderare regem, qui utrumque actu possideat gladium et utrumque exercere possit imperium, temporale et spirituale, regnum simul et sacerdotium; et quod attinet ad politicam huius desiderati principis substantiam, et an sit reipublicae omnino conveniens, non curo, sed adhuc subsisto; nam, si de ultimo principe loqueris, cuius imperium simul cum orbis vita terminetur, placet; at si de eo loqueris, cuius successio sit necessaria, vita eius labente et perseverante seculo, necesse est ut successor sit legitimus, vel electivus; ille sacerdoti regi non conceditur, iste omnibus politicis praeceptis repugnat, quibus iam est probabilior sententia successiva regna diuturniora electivis, minusque obnoxia tyrannidi. Sed haec nunc missa facio; quod ad me pertinet, vel potius ad te, illud est, quod cum Neapolitanum regnum directo iure ad Sedem Apostolicam pertineat, et a rege nostro Hispano seculari eadem Sede concedente gubernetur, semper suspicio quaedam imminet Neapolitanis, maxime tamen illis qui rebus adversis opprimuntur, rerum mutatione delectari, ac si in vicissitudine et instabilitate earum anchoram spei suae constituissent; et cum, mutatis rebus, ad pontificis sacram manum res publicae illius regni essent de jure revocandae, suspicionem desideratae mutationis generare non immerito posset iuditium illius, qui non solum expediens iudicat eum habere principem, qui simul rex sit et sacerdos, sed insolitam istam gubernandi rationem ante oculos vulgi proponit semel et iterum duplicata narratione; nam, si regni Neapolitani proceres et populus hoc sibi suaderent, facile a Rege Catholico deficerent et, negata illi fide, quam ut principi a Sede Romana constituto debent exhibere, ad ipsum pontificem confugerent, qui, simul rex et sacerdos, tuo et illorum iuditio satisfaceret. Unde tibi consulere (ne ulterius progredi qui te iam semel odio habuere possint, novamque cum vulgo causam suspicionis adversus te causari incipiant), ut quod ad istum articulum pertinet, vel e [loco] deleres, vel saltim explicares, eo sensu quo regis, qui nec est nec esse potest sacerdos, a[nimus] suorumque ministrorum aures offenderentur, ne te adhuc suspectum haberen[t]. Et cum regna nulla ratione hodie melius stabiliri et firmari possint quam legitima successione, quae in pontificibus jure sanguinis omnino improbatur, necesse est eam obliterare sententiam, quae regem sacerdotem insinuat. . . . Denique Iesus, verus rex et sacerdos, regnum exercere noluit et, duplici armatus gladio (quem satis esse dixit), exercitium illius in Petro reprehendit), quem ad secularem potestatem pertinere voluit, distinctumque in actu reliquit regnum et sacerdotium. Et licet postea pontificibus oblata sint regna, paucis sibi retentis, quae ad decorem et maiestatem Sedis Apostolicae expedire judicarunt, secularibus principibus commendarunt relique, ne, temporalibus negotiis oppressa, pontificia potestas evacuaret spiritualia, quae, ut maioris sunt ponderis, ita et maiori indigent cura, et

The cardinal might just as well have asked the Ethiopian to change his color or the leopard his spots, so central to Campanella's whole political thought was the very point that Trejo sought to disclose. As the perceptive reaction of a high-placed contemporary as well as being an integral part of a jewel-like letter of counsel, surely among the best that the Promethean prisoner could ever expect to receive, the cardinal's criticism carries particular weight. It goes to the very heart of Campanellan polity, the centrality of the priest-king from whom all authority would seem hierarchically to descend, yet places this issue in probably the most vexed contemporary context: Naples and the *Monarchia Sicula*. The elective character of this exalted office further enhanced its peculiarity in the merging age of absolutist theory wherein hereditary succession and the blood kinship buttressed sacrosanct kingship. Although the cardinal's letter correctly claimed that the monarchs of Europe were secular rulers and not priests, he failed to observe that on the threshold of regalist doctrine they were becoming the effective pastors of their respective peoples. In the case of Campanella it would be superfluous to emphasize his commitment to the idea of the priest-king that effectively incorporates the religious dimension so essential to his understanding of politics. But his preference for elective office as a means of including the best needs emphasis and further attention. Since 1613 he had noted that only Poland, for which the deluge still remained in the future, and the papacy represented elective states, thus escaping tyranny.[126] No matter how remote these grand theories and speculations may seem, the Spanish cardinal's sensitive analysis of a potentially combustible situation, bringing into focus the fact of the elective *papa-rex*, priest-king, in the Neapolitan context of the Spanish viceroyalty and the disputed *Monarchia Sicula*, casts a possibly clarifying, if lurid, light over the intentions and thinking of our Dominican friar and Calabrian conspirator of 1599.

That direct temporal power, which Campanella so strenuously claimed for his papacy, served not only to enhance the proper dignity of the Church but also to exercise the proper ecclesiastical superintendence in Italy and even in Europe. Writing at the high tide of Rome's recovery and the Counter Reformation, the friar presented a view of the papacy at the beginning of the new century that was not far removed from the political realities of southern Europe. Apparently quite early, in his *Del governo ecclesiastico*, he articulated that idea from which he never wavered: that very papal stability, so admired by the astute Machiavelli, provided in fact the sole common ground for unity and unified action among the disparate princes and republics of Christen-

---

apud eum principem debent tractari, cui ex Christi promisione adest Spiritus Dei. Ducere hominum animam in Coelum pontificium munus est, ducere milites ad bellum regius labor. Sed haec sufficiant, non animo disputandi dicta, sed consulendi, ne huiusmodi sententia tibi officiat et ab aliis Regi exosus credaris, desiderareque ut regnum ad Sedem Romanam, eiectis regibus, devolvatur."

[126] TC-*PR*³, 88.

dom.[127] Aspiring to universal monarchy, the pope should always divide and balance one prince against another, France and Spain, in such a way that one cannot move without the pope. In not calling foreigners to Italy, in accumulating new territories for the papal states in Italy, the pope will become lord there and hence lord of the world. Indeed among the three cities that Campanella expected to be incorporated into the papal states—Ferrara, Urbino, and Parma—Ferrara passed to the pontiff in 1598 and Urbino in 1624.[128] Here Campanella alluded to a tradition of secular bequests to the Church evinced by Countess Matilda, Edward the Confessor, and Charlemagne.[129] Little wonder his impatience with and expectation of the Neapolitan apple of discord. In Naples, Urbino, and Ferrara wise cardinal legates, acting at the time of cession, should by means of friars and priests move the people in the Church's favor. Neither religion alone nor diplomatic ingenuity (*arti*) will suffice but a certain amount of military constraint, applied by the pope upon princes, will be required.[130]

Campanella adumbrates here a program of reforms that would make the ecclesiastical state a pilot and laboratory for the reform of others. All sciences and arts ought to come into the hands of the religious. Let theology only be in Latin, the other sciences in the vernacular. Because Plato and Aristotle have done more harm than good, let them be displaced by Telesio and his concord with theology. The science of the stars would come into the hands of the religious, and mathematics, by which he intends something closer to plain arithmetic, would be made common to all. To meet the influx of laity into the schools, the Jesuits would need support. In order to engage the affections of the people law and medicine would be provided gratis by the religious. Canon law would displace Roman law and a simplified compend of canon law afforded to the people. The resulting ecclesiasticalization of society offers interesting comparison with that shortly to be presented in *The City of the Sun*. While Campanella could hope that such reforms at least be introduced into the ecclesiastical state so that all peoples of other princes might desire to be under the Church, the harsh realities of existing practice made him recognize differently.[131]

Despite Campanella's relative insensitivity to the modernizing developments in the Church he has grasped the essential point that it is a state, but if so, this ecclesiastical state should be exemplary not only as a model to others but also to command their adherence and obedience. In a letter of this same period (September 1606) written to Pope Paul V he says:

---

[127] TC-*DUGE*, 505.
[128] Ibid., 480.
[129] Ibid., 479.
[130] Ibid., 506–7.
[131] Ibid., 484–86.

In order to make in fact her enemies lose their impudence and the people disbelieve in the theologians, who are hired Jezebelite prophets, it is necessary to govern the ecclesiastical state in a way that all other people might envy and desire to stand under the Church. For what is the difference between ecclesiastical peoples and others? The punishments, tributes, imprisonments, tortures, and oppression are the same for all. Therefore we all walk down one road; and thus the princes believe that the papacy is the same as their rule, and obey it to make use of it, and not to serve it; and this happens because we use God and do not serve God. And in so doing faith is lost.[132]

In actual fact the pope does not have the West (*l'Occidente*) in his grip, not even Italy for that matter. Indeed the ecclesiastical state is governed worse than the secular ones because "that virtue and religion upon which the papacy was founded, have been internally sapped by the world and externally the clergy are terrorized by injustice, avarice, and penury without being able to criticize in a way that they might not be interrogated as heretics or enemies of the Church. This condition only produces heresy and confirms them in it."[133] While Campanella can go on to attack the luxury of cardinals and prelates upon which heretics can lavish their rhetoric, he has here struck a personal note in an Erasmian framework despite himself. For smarting under the abjuration compelled at the Minerva in mid-May 1595, he can urge a policy of persuasion and dissuasion rather than force: the more things prohibited, the more heretics born. How much worse to pronounce *de fide* what is not clearly *de fide*, a practice that only makes heretics.[134] Much as he distrusted Erasmus, Campanella had by force of circumstances come around to the great humanist's policy of minimalism or limited liability in fixing on doctrines as so many points of contention and perceived error.

Almost a decade later Campanella returned to the issue of an empowered papacy as the means of public order in Italy and Europe. Beginning with the sixth discourse of the *Discorsi ai principi d'Italia* Campanella reiterates the now well known theme of the papacy as the glory of Italy along with the newer effort to represent to the Italian princes Spain's presence and peninsular domination as the least bad of any possible European power; furthermore the cooperation between Spain and the papacy in the advancement of the faith provides unity to the new hemisphere, Old World and New, that would otherwise fall apart.[135] While to abase Spain would only leave Italian princes preys for heretics or the Turk, the presence of the highest priest endowed with both temporal and spiritual arms prevents any Christian prince from arriving at the monarchy of Christendom. The aggrandizement and exaltation of the papacy

---

[132] TC-*Lett.*, 44; for partial quotation, see Prodi, *Il sovrano*, 165.
[133] TC-*DUGE*, 519.
[134] Ibid., 494–97.
[135] TC-*DPI*, 105, 140–43, 145–48; TC-*AfP*, X, 16, 21–22.

provide the true means for the conservation of Italy and its princes against falling prey to its enemies. Campanella sees the pope as moderator and arbiter among princes; by appealing to the historical instance of the successful papal mobilization of powers against the Hohenstaufen attempt at *monarchia*, he reveals himself to be operating more in a medieval frame of reference than in that of a complex of territorial quasi-sovereign states of which the papacy was one.[136] If the pope were disarmed and poor, he would lack such authority to arbitrate and balance forces. The security of states against internal and external control requires that the papacy be rich, magnificent, and powerful. Because the papacy is so important as the stabilizing factor especially in Italy, Campanella can recommend to Italian princes that they make the Catholic Church the heir to their states, when legitimate succession fails. In turn republics ought to devise a law preferring devolution to the papacy than to a tyrant. Thereby the papacy might acquire in time Italian monarchy and its ancient glory.[137] It was in this same system of reference that he could represent the disastrous nature of Venice's disobedience in his *Antiveneti* of the previous year.[138]

Looking beyond the immediacies of Italy, Campanella gives his blessing to the world aggrandizement of Spain so long as it understands its only justification to be the propagation of religion. Indeed the king of Spain should be welcomed, even to the extent of his coming to Italy, to make there his seat of empire.[139] For in the nuptial diplomacy of the Habsburgs and the imbalance of forces within that dynasty such a shift of the imperial title to the senior branch of the family seemed a reasonable expectation to some in the first decades of the seventeenth century.

In his final discourse addressed to the Italian princes Campanella calls for a common senate of all Catholic princes meeting at Rome under the presidency of the pope. Each prince would have a voice through his agents and each might have at least one cardinal protector. All matters pertaining to public utility ought to be decided by majority vote, the pope or his legate breaking any tie. Such a body might move effectively against any delinquent member.[140]

With the cardinals, the princes of the Church, our inquiry can be redirected to the internal administration of the Church. The establishment of the congregations by Sixtus V in 1588 had marked the culmination of a process by which the papal sovereign had removed those ecclesiastical princes from their more

---

[136] TC-*DPI*, 151–54; TC-*AfP*, 88–90. On misunderstandings of the papacy in the new era by contemporaries, see Franz Bosbach, "Papsttum und Universalmonarchie im Zeitalter der Reformation," *Historisches Jahrbuch* 107 (1987): 44–76 and, of course, Prodi, *Il sovrano*, esp. chaps. 5 and 6.
[137] TC-*DPI*, 155–56.
[138] TC-*AV*, 114.
[139] TC-*DPI*, 157–59.
[140] Ibid., 160–61; cf. also TC-*DUGE*, 497.

congenial habitat of power and influence in the consistory and reduced them effectively to papal agents, operating for the most part in the new ministries or departments of state afforded by the congregations.[141] Campanella misses this fact of modernization, this clear subjection to the papal sovereign. Again he tends to project into the present a more medieval pattern of papal universalism and grandeur, enhanced by close cooperation with the senators of the Church. Since his very early *Political Dialogue against Lutherans and Calvinists* he had represented the Church in its pontificate and its senate of cardinals as being the best constituted of states.[142] While there is no question that the pope is legislator,[143] Campanella believes that the senate of cardinals rules together with the pope.[144] Again in considering the highest power as that of the sword, he affirms that capital punishment, which in the Roman Republic belonged to the people and with the Venetians to the doge and the nobles, in ecclesiastical government belongs to one power "although the senate of cardinals rules with the pope at the same time."[145] And later at one point in his *Theologia* he provides in passing an abbreviated taxonomy of governments: in some, one dominates as the king of Spain; in others, many as the patriciate in Venice; in others, all as with the Swiss; in still others a mixture of the three as in Sparta, or of two as in ancient Rome with the senate and people, or now with the pope and the cardinals.[146]

Since the cardinalate figured significantly in Campanella's understanding of the Church's well-being, it is not surprising that he gave some thought to its constituents and their performance in conclave. Modeling his thoughts on a constitution of Pope Gregory XV for the election of pontiffs, Campanella argued that the secrecy of the vote be preserved; that whoever is elected ought to be Italian rather than of another nation; from another state than that of the Church; a friar rather than a priest; steady rather than brilliant; and the cardinals themselves poor rather than rich so as better to be able to address the public good.[147] This last point was profoundly out of keeping with current expectations and requirements associated with the cardinalatial dignity throughout the period.[148]

For the conclave following the death of Gregory XV on July 8, 1623, and which would lead to the election of Urban VIII on August 6, Campanella boldly applied himself in the latter part of July to devise an admonition, spe-

[141] Prodi, *Il sovrano*, 174–85.
[142] TC-*DPLC*, 162.
[143] TC-*AfP*, 70.
[144] Ibid., 16.
[145] Ibid., III, 7.
[146] TC-*T*, X/3, 30.
[147] TC-*DUGE*, 510.
[148] On the expectation of a magnificent style of life by Counter Reformation cardinals, see, for example, A. V. Antonovics, "Counter-Reformation Cardinals: 1534–90," *European Studies Review* 2 (1972): 301–28.

cifically advising the two leading protagonists, Cardinals Borghese and Ludovisi, of the forthcoming conclave. These former cardinal-nephews could have hardly appreciated the prisoner's analysis of the workings and effect of the system of nepotism. The admonition singled them out especially as the obvious potential leaders of rival factions in the conclave. Campanella laid bare a system whereby those raised to the purple were distinguished not by personal talent but by grace of being papal nephews; where the thirst for self-advancement and the supreme exaltation of the papal office had to contend with the prevailing mood of servility; where once elected, the new pope threw off the ingratiating mask and now deliberately disfavored those who had earlier supported him; where concern for exalting the fortune of one's nephews and one's family dominated. Such being the situation, Campanella's recommendation, individual and moral, fell short of an effective solution: to advance to the pontifical office the most learned and upright candidate, even if he were not a cardinal, in order that the pope might be the best man in the world.[149] Given human nature and existing practices, however, it appeared unlikely that the system could produce such a person without more radical measures.

Campanella participated in that common effort of the Counter Reformation to distinguish clergy from laity and exalt ecclesiastics over commoners at every point. When that luminous mind, the Roman intellectual and aristocrat, Virginio Cesarini, asked the friar to write a treatise on titles, Campanella obliged with a report that had as its main point the condemnation of the promiscuous application of titles. Certain titles for cardinals and bishops, for emperors and dukes, would seem to be unalterable, signifying the dignity; yet they suffer change from usage and the canons of fashion. It is important that ecclesiastical titles are not shared with the laity: *sanctissimo* befits a pope, but to apply indiscriminately *illustrissimo* to cardinals, bishops, barons, and chamberlains of the pope is a practice to be avoided. The titles that signify princes should not be given to cardinals and bishops.[150] In the very last years of his life Campanella became aware of another development far more insidious for the distinctive preeminence of the clergy than the confusion in conferring titles: a reform that despoiled clergy and papacy of all properly temporal goods and jurisdiction, reducing them purely to a ministerial, pastoral function and promoting within each principality or kingdom a local pope or patriarch

---

[149] Luigi Firpo, "Un opuscolo del Campanella sul conclave," *IPP* 6 (1973): 235–41. For a more accurate appraisal of the practice of nepotism, see the sobering analysis by Wolfgang Reinhard, "Nepotismus. Der Funktionswandel einer papstgeschichtlichen Konstanten," *Zeitschrift für Kirchengeschichte* 86 (1975): 145–85. And by the same author, on the networking in conclave, "Papal Power and Family Strategy in the Sixteenth and Seventeenth Centuries," in *Princes, Patronage and the Nobility: The Court at the Beginning of the Modern Age*, ed. Ronald G. Asch and Adolf M. Birke (Oxford, 1991), 351–53.

[150] TC-*Lett.* 216–18. On Virginio Cesarini, see Pietro Redondi, *Galileo Heretic*, trans. Raymond Rosenthal (Princeton, 1987), 90–96 *passim*.

dependent upon the prince.[151] Not altogether dispassionately did Campanella blame the Spanish Dominicans and their influence at the Minerva in Rome for what can be recognized as an early form of regalism.

The issue of pastoral residence for a cardinal with episcopal responsibilities throws into relief Campanella's own preference for administrative over pastoral needs. The issue emerges in the context of two papal pronouncements, the first March 18, 1624, and the second December 12, 1634, calling upon cardinal-bishops to respect the Council of Trent's requirements on residence. In conflict with these measures Campanella wrote a now lost tract at an undetermined time, not necessarily in this decade. While the title itself manifests his own countervailing view, the import of this writing becomes apparent in what he chose to include in his reworking of *Del governo ecclesiastico*. In this treatise while admitting that a cardinal-bishop, if not employed in a congregation, should reside in his bishopric, Campanella goes on to prefer the assistance rendered by the cardinal at the center and head of government; presence at Rome comes to be seen as essential, displacing residence as secondary.[152] The friar's own misperception of the cardinalate's effective power better explains the hard choice here than does any personal response to a particular cardinal's favor.

Campanella, however, does not underestimate the importance of the bishop in his specifically pastoral function. The neglect of preaching and teaching and visiting for the pursuit of private gain in various forms of avarice and extortion lay the clergy open to the accusation of Machiavelli that religion is simply a craft for domination, or better, Dante's picture of the greedy shepherd in *Purgatorio* 16.101–3, whose evil leadership contaminates the laity. It is notable that Campanella should repeatedly quote this passage, pronounced more forcefully than anywhere else in the entire *Comedia* by the same Marco Lombardo, who moments later will present that very Dantesque bifurcation of power that the friar deplores.[153] Undeniable as is the pastoral function of the bishop, his administrative function would still seem to prevail. In conjunction with Spain in both hemispheres, archbishops are seen as collaborating with dukes in provinces to advance the universal empire.[154] The papacy is uniquely blessed in being able to grant from an almost bottomless cornucopia of benefices the necessary rewards to its staff who have no family or heirs.[155] Throughout the world, we are told, the papacy is served by bishops and by monks, dispersed as so many prefects everywhere.[156]

With the monks and the monastic tradition Campanella's understanding

---

[151] TC-*Lett.*, 384–85, 401, 404.
[152] TC-*DUGE*, 516–17. See also chap. 5, n. 60, *supra*.
[153] Ibid., 517; TC-*Lett.*, 44.
[154] TC-*AfP*, X, 22.
[155] TC-*MM-Disc*, I, 33.
[156] TC-*AfP*, XIII, 13.

of the Church's destiny—its past glories, present struggles, and future fulfillment—becomes discernible. With the monks and specifically the friars papal obedience and republican, more precisely, communal commitment are brought into focus. Of the constituent elements promoting this belief in the Church's progress through time three stand out: the communalism to be offered by Plato and Socrates; the collective contribution and role of the Dominican order; and the pervasive influence of Campanella's compatriot, his fellow Calabrian, Abbot Joachim of Fiore.

As a good scholastic Campanella can debate the relative value of virginity as a virtue and of monasticism as an institution. With respect to virginity Campanella, in presenting his objections, can argue that it is harmful to a commonwealth because with the more excellent professing virginity, namely, the monks, friars, and clergy in general, not only fewer but the less well endowed will be procreating. It would appear that what is good for religion is not so for secular polity.[157] He considers chastity as appropriately controlling the venereal instinct, which itself is to be used only for the conservation of the species. Sterility, as evinced by the Manichees or in the aborted conception of Onanism, is seen as a grave sin. Although virginity certainly appears a virtue in accordance with its end, yet if plague or some other such general disaster should strike, virginity would cease to be a good, given the need for propagation. He goes on to cite Augustine as preferring virginity to matrimony, while the heretics Jovinian and Vigilantius are seen as equalizing them. Campanella can both commend and abuse Luther: the heresiarch justly attacks unchaste monks, who violate their vows by incontinence, but in wanting that they keep their vows for as long as it is pleasing to them, Luther would make a travesty out of the religious orders. Coitus becomes a crime where it lacks the intention for begetting children and particularly so in cases of sodomy, with animals, not to mention demons. The scholastic argumentation allows him to entertain a measure of relativism that does not dismiss a practice or an idea out of hand: Luther and Wyclif err when they say that all monks are hypocrites, yet some in fact are, who take the habit not for becoming holy but for feigning holiness.[158]

On monasticism and the religious orders as a whole Campanella will again be concerned with virginity but also poverty and obedience. In assembling against this institution those arguments that will later be successfully rejected, Campanella shows himself alert to some of the best contemporary criticism of the religious orders. Moreover in the very entertainment of these ideas he cannot entirely be divorced from a sediment of their weight. Only the better arguments warrant our attention here: virginity, if more generally followed, would allow Christendom to be swamped by Jews, Turks, and heathen. Here with a breathtaking confidence that would leave a modern demographer en-

---
[157] TC-*T*, X/1, 14–15.
[158] Ibid., X/2, 14, 18, 20, 34, 78.

vious, Campanella argues that Italy under the Romans had twenty-five million people, but now scarcely ten million; Spain formerly had thirty and now hardly has eight million. Polygamy as formerly practiced in Judea and now observed by the Moslems is advanced as a means of reducing nunneries and meeting the danger of depopulation. Because the clergy do not individually pay taxes, in Spain, where they are inordinately numerous, the burden falls heavily on the laborers. Peoples such as the Swiss and the Dutch who have overthrown monasticism are represented as thriving and in the latter case they have stymied the king of Spain after sixty years of war. By overthrowing monasticism the northern peoples benefit economically. Moreover bequests to the clergy defraud the fisc and impoverish the kingdom as is especially true in Naples. The clergy and the religious orders specifically afford an escape hatch for criminals and make a mockery of public order. Machiavelli and Luther would appear to be vindicated.[159]

With the familiar scholastic *At in contrarium* Campanella drops anchor, ends the drift of objections, and begins his defense by deploying countervailing arguments. In the first place the counsels of continence, poverty, and obedience are not to be pursued by all of society. Here the Anabaptists err in universalizing as common precepts those counsels intended for a few. In emphasizing the necessity for a society maintaining a plurality of functions, Campanella refers to his favorite Father, St. John Chrysostom, who could affirm the possibility of a society of workers but not one entirely made up of contemplatives. Significantly Campanella faults the Genevans along with the Anabaptists for the monocular view that all citizens must labor with their hands.[160]

While admitting the sins of the clergy generally and its failure to serve the people, Campanella denies that virginity was the cause for the loss of so many kingdoms to the Ottoman onrush but rather the improbity of the clergy as a whole. Similarly to combat the argument that there is some necessary connection between the overthrow of monasticism and the political economic success of the Dutch, Swiss, and Germans, Campanella claims that the issue here is that of the *libertas* of free cities; likewise the Venetians and Genoese preserved their liberty most gloriously for many centuries, while maintaining celibacy and monasticism. According to Campanella the issue is not the breaking of the monastic grip but rather an advanced commerce and civil prudence that explain the flourishing condition of these citizenries.[161]

In considering the ratio of clergy to laity in Christendom, Campanella estimates an average 10 percent, a gross exaggeration, 15 percent appearing to him unlikely. Continuing, he believes the clerks regular, monks, friars, and

---

[159] Ibid., XXIII, 170–76.
[160] Ibid., 176–80.
[161] Ibid., 190–92.

mendicants to constitute 8 percent of the entire population. He rejects the accusation that the mendicants burden the condition of the laity who have more than enough of their own drones. For in Naples a scandalous nobility, criminous, idle, vicious, constitutes with their retainers a third of the city. Thus laziness and corruption come from the laity itself. Admittedly in dire public necessity the Church must surrender its wealth, but until then princes must learn to live more soberly. In considering further the clergy's excessive accumulation of wealth, Campanella faults the Jesuits and recommends the Capuchins as a possible alternative for pious instruction. The charge of their being a dangerous drain on the increase of population would not exist if only those religious, living sincerely through alms and their own labor, were admitted to an order. And in Spain, if half the wealth belongs to the Church, consider how much it renders the monarch through *cruzadas* and ecclesiastical taxes. In keeping with the conviction that his own Dominican order is the true elite of the Church, he can urge that those noted for intellectual or contemplative gifts should either be transferred to the Domincans or Carthusians, or be freed from manual labor in their present order. For monasticism constitutes the very eyes and brain of the Church and thus the folly of heretics who would seek to abolish it.[162]

The affirmation of community breaks through: "if all Christians gradually gave their goods to religion, a condition would be reached in which nothing would be left to laymen and all would live in community just as St. John Chrysostom and Clement of Rome sought while praising the republic of the Platonists, in which everything was common, even wives, as Clement says to have existed under the apostles, as Luke, Acts 4 (34–35) attests, although regarding wives, as Tertullian bears witness, only as far as obedience and not with reference to the bed. As to the many advantages thereby accruing to this republic we have already taught by having written about the City of the Sun."[163] Again citing St. Clement, and referring to his own *Political Questions* to be considered shortly, Campanella explains that division of goods only prevailed by the law of nations on account of human iniquity, with the resulting competition and inequality of possessions. For all ought not to live in common and community unless voluntarily, as formerly in the case of the apostles.

> I hope nevertheless that it will come about that all the cities of Christians may revert to their life. Pontiffs may consider whether they wish for the goods of all Christians to be held in common, and through the prudence of the religious, all to be drawn to the Church, or whether to remain there in proprietary division. The first system promotes those religious orders living on the basis of common property; the second will welcome those living by the labor of their own hands.[164]

---

[162] Ibid., 180–88.
[163] Ibid., 190.
[164] Ibid.

The precise import of Campanella's effort to align the community of early monasticism with the naturalistic rational community of Plato's *Republic* need not concern us here and can be deferred. Enough, however, to observe that it is not a stray statement but recurs in the *Theologia*[165] and elsewhere, figuring as more than just another authoritative source. Its importance will need to be weighed later.

In the present passage quoted it is curious, however, both at this juncture and shortly afterwards Campanella can advocate that where there is a surplus of religious[166] or where others have become rich and spiritually blinded[167] they are to be sent to the New World for preaching the gospel and in the second instance for tempering their avarice in evangelical service. Such an attitude was not that of Emperor Charles V, when he made his admirable choice of Bishop Zumárraga or with Cortés' Twelve Apostles, but then these were all Franciscans!

In his hastening to the defense of the new Piarist schools and the work of Giuseppe Calasanzio among the poor, Campanella conveyed an implicit criticism of some of the more established religious orders in their educational practices. The essential difference between the Jesuits and Calasanzio early became evident when the latter tried to enlist the aid of the Jesuit father general in establishing a school for the illiterate poor: Jesuit policy dictated that acceptance depended upon the boy having already mastered the rudiments of Latin.[168] Once freed and in Rome, writing in 1631–32, Campanella brought his generous trust in the expansion of knowledge and a concomitant expansion of the citizenry to focus on this issue. In his tract supporting the Piarist efforts, he finds ample room for their work in the towns and villages among the humble because the Jesuits are only to be found in the great cities, teaching the nobles.[169] The two orders are thus complementary. He can afford by means of his scholastic objections to float the idea of the Jesuits as linked to wealth in keeping with Aristotle's dictum: "First one must get rich, then one can study philosophy."[170] Essentially respectful, however, of the Jesuits, Campanella is here arguing that there is ample room for both groups, but whereas care for poor children is only accidental with the Jesuits, it is central to the purposes of the Piarists.[171] Campanella was probably ill-advised to press the Piarist curriculum into the higher faculties of learning for its students—an aspiration

---

[165] Cf. also ibid., XVIII, 92–93; XXVII, 62.
[166] Ibid., XXIII, 190.
[167] Ibid., 192.
[168] Paul F. Grendler, *Schooling in Renaissance Italy: Literacy and Learning, 1300–1600* (Baltimore/London, 1989), 382.
[169] "Liber apologeticus contra impugnantes institutum scholarum piarum," ed. K. Jensen and A. K. Liebreich, *Archivum Scholarum Piarum* 8 (1984): 29–76, esp. 46–47, Latin; 63–64, English.
[170] TC-*LASP*, 49, 66.
[171] Ibid., 52–53, 70–71.

that might well bring their schools into real friction with the Jesuits. Treading with uncharacteristic care, Campanella, while noting the great service of the Jesuits and the Franciscans, contrasts unfavorably their willingness to accept estates and possessions, following the Aristotelian dictum, with the poverty of the Piarists.[172]

The question of the religious orders and the special role that will be given the Dominicans raises a much larger issue. Implicit in Campanella the Dominican is a papal/monastic view of the Church, its nature and destiny, which continues to break through occasionally but is always present, always current. The apparent incongruity of the hierarchical with the republican, or more accurately the collegiate, becomes more understandable when one considers the source of part of its inspiration in Ptolemy of Lucca, alias Thomas Aquinas. But the matter requires further explication. Originally the mendicant orders had emerged at a time when the Church faced the challenge presented by the new urban communities and their populations. Born aloft in the surge of enthusiasm for the *vita apostolica* or *evangelica*, the mendicants, Franciscans as well as Dominicans, committed themselves to a fresh interpretation and representation of this ideal. Their warrant came from no local bishop but from the bishop of Rome. Freed necessarily from Gratian's linking of office to benefice, the tie that binds, the mendicants, possessing some of the qualities of Troeltsch's sect-type, found their inspiration not in the Pastoral Epistles but in the Synoptic Gospels and the egalitarian principles of Acts (4:32–37). This New Testament source imparted the ideal of the apostolic life, signifying not only a life of apostolate but a lifestyle defined by that of the early disciples. In contrast with the developing monarchy of the pope and the bishops, the mendicants revealed a brand of egalitarianism manifest in a respect for a variety of spiritual gifts or talents and immediate personal fellowship organized into a system of capitular government, where the superiors were elected for a term of office rather than the offices held for life by bishops and abbots. Removed by papal license from the local supervision of the bishop, as with the apostles, so the friars transcended local boundaries. A new face or arm of the Church had emerged, more mobile and flexible in the mendicant instrument of mission and ministry.

With the sixteenth century come the Protestant Reformation, the encounter with a New World, and an enormous intensification and expansion in the scope of pastoral practice. To meet the challenge of heathen and heretic an episcopally limited Church would have been helpless. It is only with the expansion of the missionary model provided by the friars into new religious orders and especially the Jesuits that new worlds may be won. For it is the Jesuits who will popularize the word "mission" and its implications. In fact two traditions reveal themselves as operating unevenly and with different vo-

---

[172] Ibid., 55, 73.

cabularies in the life of the Church: in one the model of the Church as sacrament, in the other as herald; in the first the agency of the priest, in the second that of the prophet and charismatic layman; in the former diocesan stability contrasts with the journey, the pilgrimage, the mission of the evangelist which distinguish the latter.[173]

Whether the Troeltschian distinction between church-type and sect-type successfully ensnares the meaning of this reality in the Catholic Church is immaterial. The fact of its being throws into relief the special pressures and aspirations operative in the thinking of Tommaso Campanella as Dominican. For we need to take seriously the Dominican context and tradition of our prisoner, since it constitutes a significant part of a larger dynamic that sees the Church as herald and missionary instrument rather than as sacrament or stable, faithful flock. Such a perspective helps explain the use of the bell as symbol to his life's intent, that bell reinforced by John 10:16, which appears on so many of his works. Likewise it illuminates his preference for John 21:17 to Matthew 16:18, the emphasis falling upon infinite expansion rather than a fixed, divine institution. Indeed it makes more understandable why the popular metaphor of the wormed cheese must be transformed from a cosmogonic to an epistemological meaning in which the billionfold compartmentalizations dividing human awareness, the cellular isolation of human perception might dissolve in a universal recognition. For the Dominican prisoner—all word, language, communication—the cruel incongruities of his own tragic experience thus might be resolved, sublimated, transformed in the apocalyptic realization of the Church's proper destiny.

Strongly elitist in his understanding of the institutional church, Campanella identifies his own order as the vanguard of the clergy and thus of all Christian society. For whatever his populism and egalitarianism that pertained to aspirations in the present political order and realizations in the future theonomous order, Campanella observed a hierarchical ranking for the Church itself in the present course of time. In asserting the superiority of the clergy to the laity, he was merely affirming a good Counter Reformation attitude.[174] But Campanella would go beyond this position to seek a clericalization of society. Within the clergy itself the monks, the monastic, and the regular clergy enjoyed clear preference. Quoting Wisdom 6:26, "For in the multitude of the wise resides the health of the world," Campanella can explain that the philosophers and monks unite and through their prayer and more divine life they maintain society (*rem publicam*) in the fear of God without which fear, disor-

---

[173] John W. O'Malley, S.J., *Tradition and Transition: Historical Perspectives on Vatican II* (Wilmington, Del., 1989), 137–50, 169–70.

[174] On this point, see Adriano Prosperi, "Clerics and Laymen in the Work of Carlo Borromeo," in *San Carlo Borromeo: Catholic Reform and Ecclesiastical Politics in the Second Half of the Sixteenth Century*, ed. John M. Headley and John B. Tomaro (Washington/London/Toronto, 1988), 112–38, esp. 123–24.

der, and calamity would follow. For those who seem more leisured are more fruitful.[175] And within the regular clergy itself the Dominicans have precedence.

The strongest expression of the commanding role, carved out for the Hounds of the Lord, occurs at the culmination of his *Articuli prophetales*, dating from 1607:

> The friars of St. Dominic are expected to preach that long-awaited universal commonwealth with the Church singing: "Calling the world to the nuptials of the Lamb, the time of communion, the Father chooses for this sublime partaking of fellowship St. Dominic as herald." Regarding these nuptials and the golden age we have spoken throughout the Articles and the Dominican St. Vincent Ferrer was this great herald of the new age, sent by God, and in his *Response* he speaks about us. "These draw the car of the gospel as strong, mottled horses." St. Catherine, a Dominican, teaches the same, her sons, our brothers, in the Epistles; clearly we ourselves shall bear the olive branch of peace to the Turks. In Revelation appears the white army against the Antichristians, and granted whatever proclaimer is signified on the white horse, according to Bede, nevertheless the Dominican is preferred by title because we have been called the Order of Preachers by the divine oracle of the pope. Thus no religious order has celebrated this doctrine of the future age and world as much as the Dominican: St. Vincent, St. Catherine, Savonarola, Frater Rusticianus, Master Catharinus, blessed Raymond of Capua, and others to whom we safely subscribe. And the Apostle says: "Covet earnestly the better gifts, but rather that ye may prophesy, for ye may all prophesy one by one."[1 Cor. 12:31; 14:1, 13]. Therefore we ought to seek out and prepare for this office, because God does not deny grace to those properly prepared, for indeed how much less grace was given to Balaam and to the Sibyls.[176]

In 1625, while still campaigning for the favor and support of Cardinal Trejo, Campanella composed his treatise *De conceptione Virginis* in a similar vein. The apparent purpose of the exercise was to lend support to the doctrine of the Immaculate Conception advanced by the Franciscans and fervently promoted by the cardinal. However, Campanella's own subscription to the hotly debated Franciscan teaching proves less than wildly enthusiastic. In fact the exercise thinly disguises an opportunity seized to advance the dignity and preeminence of the Dominican order. Addressing the charge that the Dominicans fail to demonstrate proper devotion to the Blessed Virgin, Campanella claims that the order and St. Thomas in particular are second to none in honoring her. The Order of Preachers constitutes the veritable elite of humankind, if it is true that the clergy is superior to the laity, the regular better than the secular clergy, the friar more learned than the monk, and so on. With un-

---

[175] TC-*T*, X/1, 106.
[176] TC-*AP*, 298.

characteristic respect for aristocratic values he argues the inferiority of the Franciscans to the Dominicans because of the formers' use of the title, Minor, and because Francis was the son of a merchant and ignorant of all knowledge, while Dominic was nobly born, holy, and learned from infancy. Campanella has the temerity to indulge in a number of invidious comparisons between individual theologians of the two orders, leaving no doubt as to who walks off with the palm.[177] The import of the work hardly suffered from the opportunism present in its original inspiration: if its author revealed "an odd mixture of political cunning and ingenuous rashness,"[178] the latter had certainly scored again. And with its triumph the Dominican prisoner's cell door could expect to remain locked.

This Dominican preeminence is but part of a more comprehensive monastic/mendicant/missionary perspective that Campanella brings to his understanding of the Church, its past, and its destiny. Beyond the fact that they were both from Calabria, Tommaso Campanella and Joachim of Fiore, "our compatriot" (*conterraneus noster*),[179] they shared a common view of the Church's nature and future. In respect to ecclesiology and history Campanella can be seen in some respects as affecting an *aggiornamento* of Abbot Joachim and a reapplication to his own age of a vision that necessarily lacked the benefits of a knowledge of the New World, the dangers of widespread northern heresies, the new science, and the apparent confirmations of late Renaissance astrology. Although occasionally mentioned in the body of Campanella's writings, only in the *Articuli prophetales* and a late volume (1623) of the *Theology* does his great Calabrian predecessor emerge. While it lacks the distinctively trinitarian organization of history, Campanella's view shares the Joachite idea of the imbrication of successive historical periods, the clerical meaning to the historical development, and the monastic fulfillment of the final age.

Campanella adopts the more traditional and conventional hexameral scheme of periodization to which Joachim has recourse as a subordinate temporal pattern. Ideally one thousand years are allotted to each of the six periods, but as events crowd toward the end, the temporal apportionment does not quite work out that way. If the eighth age is the posttemporal and posthistorical age of paradise, the seventh serves as a sort of a sabbath of fulfillment, a golden age identified with the Second Coming. In the understanding of the six periods only the last two need concern us, as their character provides the identification for Campanella's own age. Possibly because of the very involvement of one period in another and out of another Campanella will appear to vacillate as to whether he is at the end of the fifth or the beginning of the sixth period. For example, it is not definitive when early in the *Articles* he claims

[177] Luigi Firpo, "Il *De conceptione Virginis* ritrovato," *GCFI* 29 (1950): 68–76, esp. 70–73.
[178] For this happy characterization of Campanella, see D. P. Walker, *Spiritual and Demonic Magic from Ficino to Campanella* (London, 1958), 214.
[179] TC-*AP*, 113.

Columbus as bearing Christ to the New World in the sixth millennium. Following a revelation of St. Bridget that always figures significantly in Campanella's prophecies, the Church will flee and find shelter in the New World. In the sixth state of the Church a New Jerusalem will descend from heaven bringing in the golden age and paradise on earth. With the seventh millennium the translation of the Church into the heavenly paradise occurs. At least to his own satisfaction Campanella here affirms that his exposition seems to be similar to Abbot Joachim's.[180]

Nevertheless the apportionment of events to the troublesome fifth, sixth, and seventh periods will undergo a change within the same work. Campanella understands himself to be in agreement with St. Bernard and Abbot Joachim in maintaining that the golden age comes immediately after the fall of the Antichrist. Standing in the sixth millennium, the Dominican friar expects the imminent breakthrough of the golden age. Extrapolating from the authority of St. Bernard, Campanella affirms a *respublica aurea* under one prince and one law, apparently constituting a seventh millennium.[181] Shortly, however, he manifests difference from Joachim in a reluctance to believe that the sixth age has begun.[182]

Only toward the end of his *Articles* does he speak with somewhat greater certainty, confirming the most basic features to this perception of history but not without some vacillating on his own age. We are at the end of the fifth age, seal, horn. In this fifth age after Luther, as the ultimate precursor of the Antichrist, comes the Antichrist itself for the sixth. After the conventional three and a half years the newly cleansed Church will appear and the golden age begin. The seventh age is the sabbath. Supported by Cardano, who believed the breakthrough of universal monarchy and a transformation of laws following 1583, Campanella, appealing to great astral conjunctions and astrological evidence, affirms that the sixth age began in 1583. Settling into this identification with the sixth age and the heightened devastation produced by heretics, he believes himself to be in agreement with St. Bridget and Abbot Joachim.[183]

The Prophecy of Christ, which Campanella wrote in 1623, represents his most sustained treatment of periodization in the Church's history and the passage of the Church into the millennium; not even that other historical book of the *Theology, On the Antichrist*, can compete, for its focus remains on the Roman Empire and the role of the Turk. From Campanella's own admission that some of the writings of Abbot Joachim were made available to him after

---

[180] Ibid., 38–44. On St. Brigida the best contemporary source would have been the *Onus Mundi*, of which that used here is the Vatican Library copy (Rome: Eucharius Silber, 1485): on the special role of the Dominicans, 9, 15; on her special relation to Naples, 10ᵛ; on Abbot Joachim, 23ᵛ; on Brigida as *nova apostola Christi*, 59.

[181] TC-*AP*, 96–106.

[182] Ibid., 114.

[183] Ibid., 243–51, 285.

his second sojourn in the dreadful subterranean dungeon of San Elmo, it would appear that the twelfth-century Calabrian abbot is partly responsible for the attention given to this subject. It is his inspiration that prevails.

The work commences with Campanella sloshing around in a welter of diverse chronologies, contending heroically with their discrepancies. In reconciling the astronomical evidence of Ptolemy, Copernicus, and Albategnius with the prophetic evidence in order to indicate the brevity of time remaining, Campanella includes the Hindu Brahmans and other peoples to his own satisfaction but excludes the Moslems from his argument regarding the world's six thousand years' duration. Conventionally enough he affirms the seven ages of the world, of the Church, and of man.[184] Citing the support of Abbot Joachim, he asserts that Christ will return to assume the kingdom of all the world; just because 1,623 years have passed does not vitiate this certainty.[185] Because Christ will reign after the fall of the Antichrist in the golden age for a thousand years, according to Revelation 20 and the collective import of the Fathers, we need to add a seventh millennium to the life of the world; with the eighth the Church is transferred to heaven.[186]

On the opening of the seven seals, Campanella reports on Joachim's disclosure: the first is opened under Zachariah, the father of John the Baptist; the second in the Resurrection of Christ; the third with Constantine; the fifth (!) under Charlemagne; the sixth with Joachim himself when shortly will begin the Order of Preachers, namely, the Dominicans and the friars minor, the Franciscans at whose end is expected the seventh seal and rest with the devil, bound for a thousand years, followed by the eighth period, the translation of the Church into heaven.[187] Campanella's own exposition generally adheres to Joachim's but with some interesting variations and elaborations. In the second state of the Church God appears in the blood of the martyrs.[188] Nicaea marks the third state at which time Constantine declares the pope and bishops to be over all kings of the earth and he accepts his power from the pope ("et ab eo accipit potestatem").[189] The fourth state of the Church is that of the monks.[190] With Charlemagne the empire is divided between a Greek and a Gallic part.[191]

The sixth millennium begins with St. Bernard, but the fifth state includes the emergence of what Campanella claims to be the five major orders—the Dominicans, Franciscans, Carmelites, Augustinians, and Minims.[192] Together

---

[184] TC-*T*, XXV, 32–34.
[185] Ibid., 50.
[186] Ibid., 62–64.
[187] Ibid., 150.
[188] Ibid., 84.
[189] Ibid., 92.
[190] Ibid., 102.
[191] Ibid., 110.
[192] Ibid., 114.

with the Jesuits these constitute that chariot of Zechariah, whose preaching runs through the New World to create a new Christ, a new Adam, and a new, dove-like Church (*Columbam Ecclesiam*). Through Castilian and Portuguese navigation Americans and for that matter Indians throughout the circuit of the earth now take Christian names in baptism in what amounts to being a Christianzation of the globe.[193] Thus if the sixth state of the Church saw all the depredations and agonies involved with the Protestant heresies[194] the sixth seal or state of the Church sees a preparation of the Church for the golden age.[195] Attributing to Joachim the spirit of prophetic intelligence, Campanella claims his authority for believing that we are presently under the sixth seal, awaiting the revelation of the Antichrist.[196] Like Luther, whom Campanella considers as the great precursor of Antichrist, but not Antichrist itself, the friar comes to consider the Antichrist as something other than a person.[197]

An interesting disagreement inevitably develops between Joachim and Campanella over the critical issue of the beginning of the sixth seal: inevitable because the friar stands four hundred years later in the course of the Church's progress; critical because of the imminence of the millennial kingdom. The passage is worth extended presentation:

> In his time, with the mystery of the fifth seal still not having been completed, Joachim reckons the opening of the sixth to have begun to which he attributes two times in his exposition of [Rev.] 9:12 and he warns that in the fifth, one contends with the heralds or precursors of the Antichrist. He predicts this struggle to occur in chapter 16 through the order of the clerks regular and conventuals against the enemies of the faith. Now however we see the conventuals to be the Dominicans, Franciscans, Carmelites, and other mendicants; on the other hand the clerks regular are the Jesuits and Oratorians (*Phillippinos*) from whom stem Bellarmine and Baronius, the crucifers (*crucillarios*) and other new orders of clerks regular. Nevertheless we have written that the order of friars began in the fifth seal wherein the Church truly combats the heathen in the new hemisphere as well as Africa and Asia, and against the Jews and Lutherans in our own and the battle still rages. And God almost forcefully moved me to write the book entitled *Quod reminiscentur et convertentur ad Dominum universi fines terrae*, addressed to the four

---

[193] Ibid., 126.
[194] Ibid., 118.
[195] Ibid., 132.
[196] Ibid., 148.
[197] Here striking similarities exist between Campanella and his fellow Dominican Thomas Malvenda on the advent of the Antichrist and the millennial kingdom. See the latter's *De Antichristo liber undecim* (Rome: Carolum Vulliettum, 1604), X, 479–510, where Luther is among the precursors of the Antichrist; the kingdom follows the death of the Antichrist and precedes the second Resurrection. That Campanella can directly refer to him at one point (TC-*T*, XXVII, 24) suggests that he had read Malvenda. It would appear that within the Dominican order at this time chiliasm had wider currency than just the case of Campanella.

great peoples of the world, the Christian, the heathen, the Jewish, and the Moslem, in which I dispute against each sect and about recognition of the true religion through spiritual warfare, not to mention a military and philological one, seeking the conversion of the nations contrary to what Joachim considered to be contended in the sixth seal. I had not read [these matters] in Joachim, when I wrote these books, God requiring that I be imprisoned in a subterranean dungeon. These books will pertain to the sixth state which I reckon not yet to have begun unless perhaps impacted in [*commixtam*] the fifth. . . . Thus the beginnings of one state are confused in the ends of the preceding state as Joachim himself teaches.[198]

Thus across the watershed of four hundred years of ecclesiastical development the two Calabrians argue over the allotment of historical periods.

While it is unnecessary to follow Campanella in his intricate astrological calculations as well as his refutations of Galileo in order to safeguard his own doctrine of the sun's descent upon the earth, it is important to note their place in any consideration of the imminent breakthrough of the millennium—a millennial kingdom that he here describes as so often elsewhere to be a restoration of the original state of innocence and a restitution of natural law. It needs to be emphasized that prophetic and astrological evidence cohere marvelously for this radical Dominican.[199]

Regarding the special fate of Rome and the papacy in the onrush of the seventh age, Campanella had earlier in the *Articles* followed St. Bridget in presenting the desolation of Rome after the Antichrist and the Turk with the migration of the Church to the New World.[200] Campanella's condemnation fell on Rome and Roman Christianity, upon which destruction would be visited.[201] Nevertheless not all of the Church would be exterminated. If the Turk would waste all of Italy, after the conventional three and a half years of the final Antichrist, whose specific nature Campanella will never identify, the newly cleansed Church would emerge in the golden age.[202] At the end of his later work, reflecting his more conscious appreciation of the abbot, Campanella sees Rome's fate through the lens of the Joachite image of Rome being at once Babylon and Jerusalem. Citing a list of authorities culminating in Dante and Petrarch, who sing of the ruin of the Roman curia followed by the renewal of the Church, Campanella seeks to distinguish between the city and the Roman curia extended through all the world, wherever the Latin language and the Roman imperial laws are observed, as one reality and on the other the Roman Church itself. According to Joachim the former is called Babylon, the latter Jerusalem. Insofar as it is the Church of God the Roman Church is not

---

[198] TC-*T*, XXV, 150–52.
[199] Ibid., 174, 180; cf. TC-*AP*, 80.
[200] TC-*AP*, 142.
[201] Ibid., 188–89.
[202] Ibid., 238, 243.

able to fail. Campanella even concedes that Rome will be destroyed and plowed under, but the Church does not fail. He concedes that the papacy will be struck not only in its members but in its head, and here he speculates that there will be some evil pontiff for whose sins the Church will be afflicted as at the time of Boniface VIII. The fate of Greek Christianity hovers in his thoughts. Again he resorts to Joachim's image of Rome as Babylon within which Jerusalem peregrinates, unable to be discerned until the end. Under the very Antichrist that will exterminate the papacy Rome will resume its former pride and idolatry as at the time of Nero or again with Cola di Rienzo. Campanella finds the sack of Rome in 1527 inadequate for fulfilling the revelation in store. Still apparently clinging to the great abbot, he hesitates over the issue of a *papa angelicus* as preceding or succeeding these terrible events. Certainly all saints, spiritually minded persons, and literate expect some restoration of the collapsed commonwealth. As Joachim believed, the Roman Jerusalem will be trampled upon but not possessed as was the Greek Samaria.[203] It would appear that something like the Joachite passage from the second stage, (*ordo clericorum*) to the final stage (*ordo monachorum*) will have occurred.

Ever given to excess, the speculations of Tommaso Campanella appear to have gone beyond the usual limits of prophecy to ponder since the earliest moments of his imprisonment and perhaps even prior to that event the nature of what the impending seventh state might be like. Here he left Abbot Joachim aside. From a Calabrian perspective, always nearer, both historically and geographically, than the rest of Italy and the West to those Eastern and earliest forms of Christianity, he would achieve that amalgamation of specifically Platonic, patristic, even Gnostic elements to substantiate the vision that haunted him. What would appear to later ages as simply another utopia could never be such to its author. For it lacked the playfulness of a Thomas More's and with it the author's ability to escape the constraints of his own creation. A consuming vision, it would persist to the end. Shaped in the monastic perspective of Christian history, the *City of the Sun* presents an artistic rendering of a persisting vision as to the ultimate stage of the Church and the human condition.

THE CITY OF THE SUN: PLATO AND THE MONASTIC CONCEPTION OF THE CHURCH'S DESTINY

While to the scholar of literature Tommaso Campanella's *The City of the Sun* provides almost endless possibilities for delightful interpretation, to the historian attempting to understand Campanella's work and career within the context of his age it presents a number of distracting problems. For this ostensible utopia is a total anachronism creating a rupture with current European cul-

[203] TC-*T*, XXV, 204–16.

ture.[204] Worse still we are presented with the anomaly of a friar standing directly in the monastic tradition, advocating a community of women for a state-run program of eugenics. Would that this utopia might be ignored as a *jeu d'esprit*, a passing fancy that never recurred later in his writings. But it does recur, he does mean it, and we know that he means it by his repeated affirmations, culminating in the last work he ever wrote, a month before his death: in a Latin Eclogue for the birth of the dauphin, the future Louis XIV, the Sun King is called upon to realize now the City of the Sun.[205] Since Campanella surely meant it, what did he mean?

A distinguished historian has recently argued that a text is often best attacked at its most enigmatic point: "By picking at the document where it is most opaque, we may be able to unravel an alien system of meaning. The thread might even lead into a strange and wonderful world view."[206] Indeed there may be a real virtue in concentrating attention upon the feature, if not perhaps the most "opaque" in the text, yet certainly the most objectionable and embarrassing to long-established Western mores—so objectionable that editions of the work in the late Victorian period would find it necessary to omit the offending passage entirely. Surely the matter of a state-run system of procreation, advanced by a renegade friar, is sufficiently problematic as to warrant the test of opacity as a means of unlocking the import of the text and the intention of the author. Only postmodernists might be outraged by the naive arrogance of such an undertaking.

Firmly grasping the nettle, let us therefore address this awkward question of a community of women and the resulting elimination of the family. To understand the issue of eugenics and how it is both feasible and viable for a priestly governed society, we need to review briefly the Platonic background and Campanella's application of it in his *City of the Sun*. Early in book 5 of the *Republic* Plato introduces the matter of wives and children of the guardians being held in common. Socrates has persuaded Glaucon that men and women, possessing equal abilities, have the same duties and thus the same training. Such being the

---

[204] Luigi Firpo, "La cité idéale de Campanella et le culte du soleil," in *Le Soleil à la Renaissance. Science et Mythes*, Colloque Internationale, 1963 (Brussels/Paris, 1965), 325–40, esp. 328.

[205] Amab., *Doc.*, II, 347–55/347: "Et quam in vanum Rex cupit aedificare Suecus/Admirandam urbem, solis de nomine dictam,/Me signasse tibi puer alto corde resigno" (351).

[206] Robert Darnton, *The Great Cat Massacre and Other Episodes in French Cultural History* (New York, 1984), 5; cf. 78. On the bowdlerized editions of the *City of the Sun*, see *Ideal Commonwealths*, ed. Henry Morley (New York, 1901), who on p. vi says of this English translation that there are "one or two omissions of detail which can well be spared." The chief omission (p. 155) is of course that pertaining to the matter of procreation included in the authoritative Daniel J. Donno translation (see n. 218, *infra*) from mid-page 52 to mid-page 56. Likewise *Ideal Empires and Republics*, ed. M. Walter Dunne (Washington/London, 1901), silently uses the same translation as Morley, the omission here occurring on p. 290.

case the women of the guardians can expect to pursue their exercises nude along with the men, for will not virtue be their robe? Having gotten Glaucon to accept this feature without it sticking too much in his craw, Socrates—in a passage that can only seem somewhat amusing to the modern reader—warns in effect that if Glaucon had trouble in accepting the last, just try this one on for size: the community of wives. At the outset of the ensuing discussion Socrates carefully distinguishes the utility of the measure from its possibility, relegating the latter issue to another occasion never realized by Plato. In order to promote the best of the species, the braver and better youths are given the better opportunities for procreation. Parents are to be in the prime of life: women ideally twenty but continuing to forty, men beginning at thirty and lasting to fifty-five. Pairing apparently occurs at state religious festivals. Those participating above or below that age have transgressed and even those within the prescribed age, if they form unions without state certification they are raising up bastards to the state. One's children will be all those born to the state in the seven- to ten-month period following conception and those in that group will be brothers and sisters. Thus the guardians are to have their children as well as their wives in common.[207] At this point some of us can sympathize with the Italian humanist Leonardo Bruni, who, on encountering the passage on women, found his passion for translating the *Republic* to be waning and rapidly engendered a preference for the cooler *Politics* of Aristotle.[208]

With Bruni's slightly younger contemporary, Pier Candido Decembrio, we encounter a notable effort to master the difficulties posed by *Republic* 5 for a Christian society. By means of the most sophisticated hermeneutical legerdemain Decembrio manages to emasculate the worst features of the passages referring to community of wives and liaisons that amount to free love, all in order to make these passages acceptable to the Christian West, while at the same time allowing Plato's image to emerge with enhanced prestige. For beyond the enormity of marital communism Plato's calm disposal of such issues as casual liaisons and the consequent abortions and infanticides could only prove abhorrent to a Christian society and sufficient cause for deliberate mistranslation, obfuscation, and omission. When then in 9.619B Glaucon avers that the much discussed city is in fact an ideal one, nowhere to be found on earth, Socrates will rejoin: "Well, perhaps it is laid up in the heavens as a pattern for anyone who wants to see it, and seeing it, to found it in himself. It makes no difference whether it exists anywhere or ever will exist. It is the only

---

[207] Plato, *Rep.* 454–63, esp. 458d.
[208] *The Humanism of Leonardo Bruni: Selected Texts, Translations and Introductions,* ed. Gordon Griffiths, James Hankins, and David Thompson (Binghamton, N.Y., 1987), 261. Indeed a century earlier Ptolemy of Lucca, in learning indirectly of Plato's community of wives through his study of Aristotle's *Politics*, had registered consternation and disbelief. Cf. *De regimine principum* IV.4, in *Sancti Thomae Aquinatis Doctoris Angelici Ordinis Praedicatorum Opera Omnia* (Parma, 1865/New York, 1950), 16:273.

city in whose affairs he can take part." At this point Decembrio will derive the title "Celestial Polity" for his rendering of Plato's Republic. And he continues: "So help me God, I do think Plato wanted to set out in words not a human but a divine and celestial polity, to be sought not in fact but in prayer."[209]

Celestis politia indeed. Decembrio soon found it necessary to defend his translation and interpretation before a circle of learned Milanese during 1438. He argued that Plato's material and marital communism pertained only to the guardians and these amounted to being a few senators. Significantly, however, he goes on to compare the communism of goods to that of the early Church and to St. Francis's prohibition of private property; removal of the causes of dissension would only serve to promote mutual love and devotion to the common good "as Franciscan friars love each other and their order the more by being separated from their families and from worldly cares."[210]

Subsequently in the mid-quattrocento mistranslation and distortion of the offending Platonic passages would reverse their course all in a conscious, extensive effort to undermine the West's growing love affair with the holy, wise, and pious Plato. The career of George of Trebizond represents a sustained effort to defame Plato. In the interstices of George's arguments, however, there are occasional points of agreement that provide us with *loci* for understanding how bridges might be effected between the most awkward, indigestible passages of Plato and the Christian tradition: that Plato intended his laws for a celestial polity of unfallen men;[211] that limitation of parents to a procreative period of ten years seemed reminiscent of how the Fathers understood the behavior of unfallen man who obeyed natural reason.[212] If placed within the structures and operation of Christian apocalypse and the thirst for a primal innocence, the regeneration of fallen man might be realized, a lost innocence and rationality recovered, and Glaucon's *nusquam* be transformed into an ideal, even celestial city.

Between Decembrio in the early fifteenth century and Campanella at the beginning of the seventeenth century the intervening period is not lacking in eugenic programs that most likely shaped or at least encouraged the entertainment of this matter in the utopian city of the Solarians. One of the mid-sixteenth-century critics of the late Renaissance and Italian world, Anton Francesco Doni, advanced for his own utopia the community of women as a means of freeing society from all the envy, litigation, and disturbance associated with marriage and the family. We know that Campanella read it.[213] Al-

---

[209] James Hankins, *Plato in the Italian Renaissance* (Leiden/New York, 1990), 1:126–43, esp. 142–43.
[210] Ibid., 151–52.
[211] Ibid., 181.
[212] Ibid., 182.
[213] Paul F. Grendler, *Critics of the Italian World 1530–1560* (Madison, Wis./London, 1969), 173–74, 196–98.

though we cannot be certain that he also read the *Examen de Ingenios* of the Spanish medical doctor Huarte de San Juan, first published in Spanish in 1575 and by 1600 having run to five Italian editions, it is perhaps more important that the emerging European intellectual community had come to be exposed, through the multiple translations and editions of the work,[214] to its frankly physiological and naturalistic understanding of the differentiation of intelligence, associated with the Galenic temperaments, and its attention to secondary causes. While concerned principally with psychology, Huarte in a concluding chapter addresses the eugenic questions of proper mating of prospective parents in order to avoid sterility, to procreate boys instead of girls, and to procreate talented sons. We find Plato's friendly state supervisors of copulation welcomed back to the scene. As a medical doctor he is admittedly much more concerned with the physiological than the social and political implications. Nevertheless, Huarte specifically recommends the intervention of public officials in the mating of parents as well as in the supervision of domestic health conditions.[215] The book ends with a short section on hygienics and the temper of Christ's brain, which, according to one historian, the Spanish Inquisition found "most uncouth."[216]

Before examining the *City of the Sun* we need to admit two other unlikely, if influential, eugenicists that figure in Campanella's less than modest proposal. The first is the obscure Pythagorean-Platonic Greek writer Ocellus Lucanus, who affirms the magical dimension of Neoplatonic natural philosophy. The Latin translation of Ocellus's only surviving work, *De universi natura*, or what has been attributed to him, dates about 150 B.C. and would have been readily available to Campanella in the 1559 Venice edition or through the annotations of Ludovico Nogarola. Ocellus's name recurs occasionally in the writings of Campanella, never entirely disappearing from sight but enjoying extended consideration in *Del senso delle case et della magia*. There Campanella makes clear his indebtedness to Ocellus for recommending that before copulation the pair gaze deeply upon the statues or pictures of illustrious men so that by a magical transference of the force of images the future progeny may be enhanced. Ocellan also would appear to be the source of the recommendations for the best pairing of potential parents for the best results *sub felicibus astris*.[217] On the other hand the contribution of the Second Isaiah,

---

[214] M. de Iriarte, *El Doctor Huarte de San Juan y su Examen de Ingenios. Contribución a la historia de la psicología diferencial* (Madrid, 1948), 85.

[215] Juan Huarte, *Examen de Ingegnios para las sciencias* (Antwerp: Francisco Rafelengio, 1593), 228–29.

[216] Carlos G. Noreña, "Juan Huarte's Naturalistic Humanism," *Journal of the History of Philosophy* 10 (1972): 71–76.

[217] See TC-*DSCM*, 305–6. On Ocellus, see *Paulys Real-Encyclopädie der classischen Altertumswissenschaft*, Neue Bearbeitung begonnen von Georg Wissowa (Stuttgart, 1937), 17:2361–80. Michael J. B. Allen kindly called my attention to what he somewhat facetiously, if appro-

while less technical and extensive, proves more important: the prophetic—eschatological dimension itself coupled with the expectation that in the new dispensation women will be able to give birth without pain (Isa. 65:23).

In turning now to Campanella's *City of the Sun*, we are only concerned with the matter of eugenics as it operates in Solarian society. Nevertheless this matter is for Campanella integrally related to philosophical and ecclesiastical dimensions of a communal society that he is advocating against Aristotle. Regarding the practical mechanics of this society, enough to know that the *City of the Sun* is ruled by the high priest Hoh, also named Metaphysic, who has three princes serving under him—Power, Wisdom, and Love—the last being responsible for food and sex, reproduction in all forms. We must now address the administration of Love and his subordinate officialdom, yet be prepared to recognize the philosophical and ecclesiastical implications of its practices for a utopian communist society.

Except for the fact that the act of procreation is treated more religiously, ritualistically, and even magically in the *City of the Sun* than in Plato's *Republic*, we witness here the return of the by now more familiar Platonic features of common gymnastics in the nude, official identification of the best pairs, and all the attentions that one might ever want from matrons, magistrates, and medical men. There is, however, one additional feature, characteristically Campanellan, that manages to bring all this bustle into the seventeenth century and give it an appropriately scientific stamp. The most auspicious moment for procreation is determined by the best astrologers.[218] If at this point the apparent naivete of Campanella should allow us to experience a patronising smile, we may well wish to repress it, for the best medical knowledge of the day available in the Faculty of Medicine at the University of Paris advocated the recourse to astrology for such practical guidance. Among both Aristotelians and Galenists for the better part of the century astral and planetary influences were admitted and entertained in trying to understand the problem of biological and specifically human conception.[219]

---

priately, refers to as "the bio-math" that Plato emits in the *Republic* 8:546–47. Here Plato returns to the question of eugenics and in a brief passage that perplexed Proclus and Iamblicus and later convulsed nineteenth-century German scholarship, he indulges in a geometricization of numbers to provide the guardians with that law of births and copulations, which, if unobserved, will make impossible good or fortunate offspring. In 1566, a Venetian noble, Baroccius, perhaps guided by the recent publication of Ocellus, dilated to his own satisfaction, on the meaning of the passage. Cf. *The Works of Plato* (London, 1876), 2:430–31. Most recently Professor Allen has elaborated his findings in an intense study of Ficino's overlooked commentary of 1496 on Plato's fatal geometric number, *Rep.* 8:546A1–D3, with obscure, resonating implications for eugenics, astrology, politics, and history conjoined. See *Nuptial Arithmetic: Marsilio Ficino's Commentary on the Fatal Number in Book VIII of Plato's Republic* (Berkeley/Los Angeles/London, 1994).

[218] Tommaso Campanella, '*La Città del Sole: Dialogo Poetico/The City of the Sun: A Poetical Dialogue*, trans. Daniel J. Dunno (Berkeley/Los Angeles/London, 1981), 54–57.

[219] Jacques Roger, *Les sciences de la vie dans la pensée française du xviiie siècle. La généra-

Composed originally in Italian in 1602, *The City of the Sun* first appeared from Frankfurt in Latin in 1623. But beginning in 1609 and reworking it in 1613, Campanella was bringing to fruition a criticism of Aristotle's *Politics*, presented in the form of four scholastic *quaestiones* with their articles, objections, and counterobjections. The fourth and last of these was expressly conceived as a colophon to be added to his utopian dialogue, defending and explicating the principles of this ideal society.[220] Thus beyond Campanella's formal championing of Plato over Aristotle on the thorny matters of community of property and community of women, we may catch in this fourth *quaestio*, in the very matrices of its scholastic argumentation, a better understanding of Campanella's intention regarding his earlier masterpiece. The issue requiring defense and urging Campanella to compose the articles of this *quaestio* is specifically the communist ideal and that ideal as it applies to women, eugenics, and the elimination of the family. Community of property, while treated, receives less attention in the defense represented by the *quaestio* under review.

In the political *Quaestiones* published a quarter of a century later along with the second edition of the *City of the Sun* Campanella in the fourth and final question, conceived as a colophonic addition and defense of his "utopian" dialogue, immediately engages Aristotle's condemnation of Plato's community of goods and of women. The defense of community and specifically community of women will unfold in terms of its theological, philosophical, and ecclesiastical implications. In short the issues of community and eugenics coinhere. Through an exchange of argument and objections in the first article Campanella manages to situate his utopia in both Christian theology and the Church's history. By a practice that recurs repeatedly in his thought, he will align grace to nature, revelation to reason in such a way as to absorb the former into the latter. While theologians protest that Plato's Republic cannot be realized except in the state of innocence, Campanella, resorting to a favorite idea, avers that Christ recalls us to that very state.[221] Admitting that laws are to be observed only to the best of one's ability Campanella continues:

> Christ has taught a most wondrous commonwealth without sins that the apostles themselves barely managed to serve uprightly; thence it withdrew from the

---

tion des animaux de Descartes à L' Encyclopédie (Paris, 1963), 67–68. See chap. 6, n. 58, *supra*.

[220] TC-*PR*³, 100–112. Quaestio IV reads: "Epil[o]gistica, in Appendicem de Rep . . . De optima Rep.; and the first article: Utrum recte, & utiliter post doctrinam Politicam, de Rep. dialogum addiderimus pro Colophone."

[221] "Plato ideam Reip. descripsit, quae licet in totum observari non possit sub natura corrupta, ut dicunt Theologi recentiores, tamen in statu innocentiae optime servari poterat. Christus autem nos ad statum innocentiae revocavit." (TC-*PR*³, 101). Cf. also *Articuli prophetales*, ed. Germania Ernst (Florence, 1977), 80–81; *Atheismus Triumphatus seu Reductio ad religionem per scientiarum veritates . . . contra Antichristianismum Achitophellisticum* (Rome: Zannetti, 1631), 74–79.

people into the clergy, and thereupon into the monks alone. And in these now it has persisted; in others you may find it manifest among precious few beyond the religious. Thus we present our own republic not as if given by God but as a philosophical discovery pertaining to human reason for demonstrating that the truth of the gospel conforms to nature. But if on some matters we deviate from the gospel *or would seem to deviate*, it ought not to be ascribed to impiety but to human weakness that considers many things appropriate prior to [Christ's] revelation that afterwards would not be maintained, as we will say of the community of wives. Therefore we situate in paganism this republic that awaits the revelation of a better life for whose grace it worthily strives to realize ["ac meretur de congruo ipsam habere"], while according to the dictates of natural reason it observes the order of life. Thus [the Solarians] are as if in the catechism to the Christian life, just as Cyril says in his book against Julian, that philosophy was given to the pagans, as a catechism to the evangelical faith. Thus we teach Gentiles to live rightly, if they wish not to be neglected by God, and we persuade Christians that the life of Christ is according to nature and thus His example has been taken as in the case of St. Clement of Rome from the Socratic Republic and similarly by Chrysostom and Ambrose etc.[222]

The passage is of considerable interest and requires analysis, for it is replete with tensions and contradictions. Beyond the fact that it serves to deflect accusations from Campanella on the issue of the community of women, he charts a history of the Church, where an almost impossible charge has rapidly gravitated to the monks and their culmination in the religious orders, and while conforming to the traditional patristic notion of classical civilization serving as a propaedeutic in preparation for Christ, he seems to look forward to a future wherein the Christian will have regained a lost innocence and live a life, if only through Christ as the Primal Reason, that conforms more to pagan rationalism than to apostolic Christianity. While Campanella is necessarily ambiguous, and seeks to merge a naturalistic, rational social order with his

---

[222] TC-*PR*[3], 101: "Remp. Christus mirificentissimam docuit sine peccatis, quam vix Apostoli integre servaverunt deinde ex populis in clerum seccesit, mox in Monaches solos. Et in his nunc perseverat: in aliis vera per pauca illius vides instituta praeter Relig. Nos autem fingimus illam non tamquam a Deo datam sed Philosophicis syllogismis inventam. & quantum potest humana ratio, ut hinc elucescat veritas Evangelii esse naturae conformis. Quod si aliquibus ab Evangelio deviamus, vel videamur deviare, hoc non impietati adscribendum, sed imbecillitati humanae, quae multa putat recte fieri ante revelationem, quae postmodum haud sic se habent, ut dicemus de communitate coniugum. proptereaque fingimus hanc Rempub. in gentilismo, quae expectat revelationem melioris vitae, ac meretur de congruo ipsam habere, dum quod naturalis dictat ratio observat vitae institutum. Unde sunt quasi in Catechismo ad vitam Christianam, veluti Cyrillus dicit in lib,. contra Iulianum, datam esse gentilibus Philosophiam, tanquam Catechismus ad fidem Evangelicam. Nos ergo Gentiles docemus, ut recte vivant, si a Deo velint non negligi, & Christianis suademus vitam Christi esse secundum naturam, hinc sumpto exemplo, sicut S. Clemens Romanus ex Rep. Socratica, itidem Chrys. & Ambr."

own conception of the apostolic life, he has weighted the scales in favor of classical culture.

There is one other matter that need detain us in this first article: the role of the monks and monasticism in Campanella's understanding of church history. Here the first and eighth objections and their responses are instructive. To the claim that a Platonic society of living together in common and without sins is impossible to realize, Campanella counters that something like it was achieved at the beginning of the Church when under the apostles. He appeals to St. Clement of Rome (presumably his fourth epistle) to Luke, and to the type of living observed under St. Mark at Alexandria according to Philo and St. Jerome. Likewise the life of the secular clergy until Urban I reinforces his confidence in its possibility. And just as he finds St. John Chrysostom desiring the monastic life as a possibility for the entire state, Campanella expects its realization in the imminent future after the ruin of the Antichrist, as prophesied. Regarding that former condition of innocence which our Aristotelians would claim to be forever lost, Campanella argues that the Fathers have made it salvageable and Christ comes to restore it. This rationalization of the Atonement combined with an apocalyptical twist, whereby Christ is understood as guaranteeing the realization of a future society of innocence in another dimension of time—all this is vintage Campanella and can be found reiterated in several of his other works.[223] Monks and even to a degree the Anabaptists prove the reality of this ostensibly utopian life. Indeed Campanella entertains a persisting fascination and respect for the Anabaptists and radicals of the Protestant Reformation; here he presses their case as an effective example of the realization of God's Kingdom, a holy community on earth as well as in heaven:

> just as it is more in accordance with nature to live by reason than by sensual affections and to live more virtuously than viciously, as Chrysostom and in fact monks demonstrate and now the Anabaptists living in common, who, if they held

[223] Ibid., 102. Important confirmation of Campanella's proclivity evident in the *Quaestiones* to coalesce the community of early monasticism with a naturalistic rational community best evinced in Plato's *Republic* comes from reading the later and very extensive *Theologia*, composed during 1614–24, whose several volumes are in the process of being edited by Romano Amerio. In the *Cristologia, Theologia* (Rome, 1958), 18:92–93 we read: "Quanta fuerit caritas inter Apostolos et inter sequaces eorum mutua ita ut, sicut Christus pro omnibus mortuus est, cuperent mori pro altero alter, non modo historiae testantur, quoniam erat eis cor unum et anima una, et non dicebat quis *meum* et *tuum*, sed erant illis omni communia, ut Lucas et Philo testantur, et clericorum et monachorum communitas usque in hodiernum diem, *quod Socrates et Plato in sua desideravit republica*, sed etiam ipsa docet ratio abundanter." Curiously here the accompanying Italian translation has omitted the crucial passage that associates this Christian monastic communism with the import of Plato's *Republic*. Did the editor nod or flinch? Most probably the former, for Plato and Socrates do reappear to take responsibility in the Italian translation of a further confirming passage. See n. 240, *infra*.

the right dogmas of the faith they would in this matter make greater progress. Would that they were not heretics and were serving righteousness, as we say, for they could provide an example of this truth. However by some folly they reject what is better.[224]

Moreover it would appear to be no typographical error but rather quite deliberate that Thomas More's *Utopia* is referred to as his Eutopia—Good Place rather than Nowhere—recommending itself to Campanella by its naturalistic rationality.[225]

Having emphasized the role of monasticism in church history and the coming supreme drama, Campanella now confronts his own eighth and last objection, which reads:

> It is natural for man to investigate the works of God, to travel about the world, to acquire everywhere the sciences and to experience all things. Living however in such a republic they are as monks who study only their own books, and when they hear what is not written in them they are scandalized and disturbed as now scarcely do they believe the observations of Galileo, just as formerly they did not believe Columbus, the discoverer of a new hemisphere, because St. Augustine had denied it.[226]

Writing less than four years after Galileo's condemnation, the bold Dominican pillories the action taken by Rome, but goes on to defend and promote the religious orders. For in his response to this objection he claims that as with the monks and friars so also with his Solarians in their legations, embassies, and peregrinations, they have sought to achieve great collections of observations, experience, and sciences from all lands. You will not find more done in any place for learning and the preservation of the sciences, he tells us, than in the orders of the monks and friars. In his *Quod reminiscentur*, composed in the 1613–18 period, Campanella makes even more emphatic the aspiration of the regular clergy to an intellectual leadership and preeminence over the laity with specific reference to the sciences. Campanella concludes here that mo-

---

[224] Ibid., 103: "sicut magis secundum naturam est vivere ratione, quam sensuali affecto, & virtuose quam vitiose, teste Chrys. & quidem Monachi id probant, & nunc Anabaptistae in communi viventes, qui si dogmata Fidei recta [h]aberent, in hoc magis proficerent: utinam haeretici non esseri[n]t, & iustitiam ministrarent, uti nos dicimus: nam exemplum facerent huius veritatis: sed nescio qua stultitia quod melius est respuunt." Although he denounces John of Leyden and Fra Dolcino, Campanella will adopt their doctrine of the community of property and of women. Cf. *Aforismi Politici con Sommari*, ed. Luigi Firpo (Turin, 1941), 64.

[225] TC-*PR*³, 101: "Remp. Eutopie fictitiam."

[226] Ibid., 101: "Naturale est homini inquirere opera Dei, peregrinari per Mundum, scientias undique acquirere, omniaque experiri. Viventes autem in tali Rep. sunt sicut Monachi, qui libris solis student. & cum audiunt, quod in eis non legerunt, scandalizantur, & conturbantur. Unde nunc vix credunt observationibus Galilei, sicut pridem, nec Columbo inventori novi Emispheri, quod S. Augustinus negarat."

nasticism has been instituted for the sake of increasing holiness and wisdom, not for enhancing submissiveness.[227]

Although the second article bears almost totally upon the issue of community of property, it does provide further insight into the centrality of the monastic tradition for Campanella. Our reformer leads off with a text, apocryphal and of disputed interpretation, although present in Gratian's *Decretum*,[228] which represents his chief authority for all things being held in common: St. Clement of Rome's fourth epistle (actually of ninth-century Pseudo-Isidorean confection), which states that all things ought to be held in common—even the women. Tertullian and Epiphanius had earlier moved in to tidy up this last point by distancing the Church from any suggestion of a community of wives. Yet for Campanella according to a string of church fathers—St. Luke, Clement, Tertullian, Chrysostom, Ambrose, Augustine, Philo, and Origen—the apostles and earliest Christians maintained this ideal of communality at least insofar as it pertained to property; this ideal was then reduced to the clergy championing it with a new and shorter string (Jerome, Prosper, and Pope Urban I); then with Pope Simplicius around 470 a distribution of goods occurs whereby the bishop, the fabric of the Church, the clergy, and the poor each received a share. Yet prior to this event he perceives Chrysostom as even trying to extend and apply the monastic life to all—a measure that recommends him greatly to Campanella. For among all the fathers Campanella

---

[227] Ibid., 103–4: "Monachatus ad augendam sanctitatem & sapientiam est institutus: non ad gravandam subiectibilitatem, ut hypocritae conantur." Cf. TC-*QR*, 1:59: "Et medicina et mathematica et scientiae omnes floreant in monasteriis et conventibus, et seculares indigeant religiosis in omni re."

[228] C. XII.Q.1.c.2. On the Pseudo-Isidorean and early-sixteenth-century involvement in the tradition of this apocryphal text, see Norman Cohn, *The Pursuit of the Millennium* (London, 1957), 203–5. The canon's critical words "in omnibus autem sunt sine dubio et coniuges" are lacking from the original in the more recent printed editions and from several of the manuscripts such as those of the Vatican and of San Marco, Florence. According to Clement of Alexandria (*Stromata* 3.2) and St. Epiphanius (*Panarion* 31), the Carpocratians, a radical Gnostic sect, used the passage (n. 207, *supra*) in Plato's *Republic* 5 to sanction a community of wives for their own libidinous practices. For his part Tertullian denounced such an extension of the idea and specified that all things were to be held in common except women: "omnia indiscreta sunt apud nos, praeter uxores." Unwilling to leave the matter at that, Tertullian, obviously relishing the opportunity, continued: "in isto loco consortium solvimus, in quo solo caeteri homines consortium exercent, qui non amicorum solummodo matrimonia usurpant, sed et sua amicis patientissime subministrant ex illa, credo, majorum et sapientissimorum disciplina, Graeci Socratis et Romani Catonis, qui uxores suas amicis communicaverunt, quas in matrimonium duxerant liberorum causa et alibi creandorum, nescio quidem an invitas; quid enim de castitate curarent, quam mariti tam facile donaverant? O sapientiae Atticae, O Romanae gravitatis exemplum! Leno est philosophus et censor" (*Apologeticus adversus Gentes* 471–73, *MPL*, 1:535–36). In general, on the Greek philosophical tradition of utopian communism culminating in the Carpocratians, see Doyne Dawson, *Cities of the Gods: Communist Utopias in Greek Thought* (New York/Oxford, 1992), esp. 28, 39–40, 89, 191, 231–33, 264–87.

appeals most frequently to John Chrysostom as the image of the effective bishop. Familiar with the great preacher and later patriarch's homilies and his *De sacerdotio* Campanella presents Chrysostom as denouncing all mine and thine as lies and teaching the people of Antioch that nobody is lord of his own goods but that each must be a dispenser of his ostensible property like the bishop in his church; indeed whatever layman abuses his goods is to be punished and not allowed to communicate. Moreover St. Augustine did not want to ordain clerics unless they placed all things in common. Claiming to follow Cajetan and De Soto on the superiority of community of property that is supported by natural law, Campanella sees this natural law being undermined by *jus gentium*, the law of the peoples, for nature does not teach division. Campanella avers that the Church came to permit departures from the communal ideal based on natural law, such as the institution of property, without ever having advocated such changes. Throughout this presentation of the Church's gradual acceptance of private property, wherein the reader is jerked around amidst sundry patristic authorities, our Dominican manages to associate the monastic tradition with the apostles and the purposes of natural law.[229] All three affirm the communal order of society and for Campanella the monks are the bearers of that order.

In the third and final article Campanella returns to his saving text, the Clementine epistle, and applies it in a way that reveals his entire position: according to the doctrine of the apostles, wives ought to be held in common. But in our present Christian context to guard against offending Christian honor the gloss afforded by canon law is to be applied: community pertains to the routine responsibilities of society, not to the bed. Campanella dutifully hastens to condemn the ancient heresy of the Nicolaites and some Gnostics that would advocate community of women for sexual gratification. By community Campanella seems to mean the equality of women with men in all matters including warfare but not in government or politics. Repeatedly, however, he returns to the point that community of women for purposes of procreation of the species conforms to natural law, and it is only divine law together with positive ecclesiastical law that forbids it and makes it sinful—in short, Christianity, Christian practices, and current ecclesiastical canons. In other words the present Christian dispensation displaces such use and understanding of the community of women. Yet Campanella will not let the matter drop: returning to the attack he dwells once more upon the merits of a society ruled by natural law in which the best and the strongest are produced under the careful direction of doctors and matrons at the appropriate times for generation, as determined by the science of astrology. The system would reduce infertility, sterility, and debilitations, while obviating deformed offspring. In a selective

[229] TC-*PR*³, 104–7.

application of historicity and a sense of anachronism Campanella says that such a naturalistic practice prior to the teaching of Christian laws does not warrant our condemnation any more than one might want to condemn Socrates for drinking the poison in accordance with Athenian law, when evangelical law against suicide was still unknown. Thus the Solarian community of women in its full implications is not opposed to natural law but actually conforms to it.[230] The aberrant canon of St. Clement has become a loose cannon.

To the charge that such an arrangement would exclude human love, Campanella argues the superior virtue of the natural love evinced by the collectivity of fathers toward that certain age group of offspring for which they are generally responsible. This is all very reminiscent of Plato's Republic. Contrary to the belief that such a common love becomes attenuated and meaningless, Campanella appeals to three significant cases in the past when a common love effectively prevailed: the monastery; the Roman Republic, when private citizens were poor and the public interest rich; and the apostles. Where division rules, man loves his own children and spurns those of others more than is fitting.[231] With publicly controlled procreation there is no adultery and its related crimes. The avarice associated with the family is undercut. Carried away by his responses to his own objections, Campanella appeals to the natural community among animals and to the polygamy of the patriarchs in the Bible. The heresy of the Nicolaites lies in a promiscuity that is contrary to natural law and impedes proper reproduction of the human species.[232]

It would appear that the patriarchal experience of the earliest Church and nature itself conspire in presenting a communitarian ideal that challenges the adulterous and avaricious implications of the individual family. In order to emphasize his basic distinction between a dispensation based on natural law and the present one determined by God's law made evident in the New Testament and by church ordinance Campanella concludes his inquiry with a stunning query: when one considers that the Jews and the Romans permitted divorce, that the philosophers swapped wives, and that Plato and Socrates taught the community of women (*id*), "how, therefore, is the Solarian of our republic able to know according to purely natural lights that only the form of our [present Christian] matrimony is not a sin?"[233] No other statement throws so sharply into relief the uniqueness of the present Christian dispensation for Campanella with its specific rulings on marriage and sex whereby that com-

---

[230] Ibid., 108–9.
[231] Ibid., 110.
[232] Ibid., 111.
[233] Ibid., 112: "Hortens. seu Cato vir sapientissimus & doctissimus mutuo concessit uxorem suam Bruto ut prolem susciperet ex ea, quas ex natura iudicans ille rigidus Stoicus id fieri secundum Charitatem naturalem. Quomodo igitur potest Resp. solaris ex puris naturalibus scire, quod sola matrimonii nostri forma non est peccatum, quando Iudei, & Romani divortia habuere & Philos. per mutationes & Plato, & Socrates id docuerunt?"

munity of women justifiable by natural law becomes a heresy, criminal and entirely inappropriate now according to divine law and ecclesiastical ruling.

What then are we to believe about Campanella and what does he want us to believe? In the first place we need to recall the original purpose of all this cerebration: to defend and explicate an imaginary society as a philosophical discovery devised by reason to demonstrate that the truth of the gospel conforms to nature. Such may be the case theologically, if we can accept the notion that Christ is simply to be understood as the Primal Reason. However, on specific matters the coincidence of the naturalistic and Christian orders is less than perfect. For Campanella has made monasticism both the vehicle for the new naturalistic order and the connecting link between the respective dispensations. In doing so he has implicitly associated himself with a view of church history, originating in the early Middle Ages and maturing in the course of the High Middle Ages, which identifies the true original form of the Church with the monastic, initially made evident in the church of Jerusalem, and comes to equate *vita apostolica* with *vita communis*.[234] The basic authoritative text is Acts 4:32–37 together with John Cassian (Inst. 2.5), who advanced two versions for the apostolic origins of monasticism, one the church at Jerusalem, which would receive currency in the West, and the other, the community under the evangelist St. Mark at Alexandria. Cassian also promoted the idea that the spread and success of Christianity seriously impaired the purity of the original apostolic/monastic practices. Rupert of Deutz's *De vita vere apostolica* and Peter of Celle's *Disciplina claustralis* present two significant medieval expressions of this Western tradition whereby the monastic *regula* becomes actually the *regula apostolica*, and the apostles having been monks, therefore the monks become the true successors to the apostles. And indeed the political reality of the controversy between secular and regular clergy had persisted into Campanella's own day. It is the powerful sense of community with its absorption of the individual into a higher public good that allows Campanella to see monasticism as the bearer of the Christian mission in time and identifiable with the communalism of a future naturalistic society. Yet the nasty question lingers: what of the monk's asceticism, and for that matter what of Christian asceticism?

Here we are left with a twofold ambiguity, the first integral to Campanella's entire experience, the other endemic to Christianity itself. Let us dispose rapidly of the first. In the new order of the Solarians according to his earlier *City of the Sun* monks are absent and for that matter clerical celibacy as well.

---

[234] See Glenn Olsen, "The Idea of the *Ecclesia Primitiva* in the Writings of the Twelfth-Century Canonists," *Traditio* 25 (1969): 61–86, esp. 65–70. On the term *apostolica vita* referring to a mode of life and not to a function or office (i.c., preaching), see M-D. Chenu, *Nature, Man, and Society in the Twelfth Century* (Chicago/London, 1968), 202–38, esp. 204–7. On the penetration of monasticism and asceticism into the early Church, see R. A. Markus, *The End of Ancient Christianity* (Cambridge, 1990), 165, and esp. chaps. 11–13.

Indeed it would appear that because the priestly officials, as intellectuals, can be assumed to be probably deficient in the appropriate animal spirits, in order to compensate eugenically and pursuant to a most exquisite programming, Campanella would have them matched with the most vivacious women. For as we are reminded, the aim should be "to improve natural endowments not to provide dowries or false titles of nobility."[235] Of monasticism's basic features—regimentation, communality, asceticism—the last, at least in its most strident form, has become a casualty. Furthermore because this utopia is far less the daydream of a detached philosopher but probably something like the plan for a republic that Campanella expected to effect during those mad days of revolt in 1599 against the Spanish viceroyalty, our question becomes less abstract. And in fact it becomes painfully concrete when we attempt to assess the conflicting evidence regarding Campanella's own sexual deportment at this time. Are we to trust the extravagant accusations directed against him during his trial by some of his former collaborators?[236] One remains in doubt. A personal, existential element to the problem persists.

Regarding Christianity, as a conclusion, we must be brief. Christianity was born in a sea of Gnosticism and in the desperate effort to define its existence, it took on some of the features of that prevalent disease plaguing late antiquity. The distinctive feature of Gnosticism was the mastering sense of the radical evil of and alienation from this world. While the Protestant Reformation would later glorify marriage as the ideal state between the sexes, and churches since the Reformation would say nice things about marriage, at its inception Christianity considered marriage a second best and a poor one at that. In this respect the weight of Jesus' preaching is to commend "eunuchs for the sake of the kingdom of heaven" (Matt. 19:12) and to exhort those that are worthy of the next life neither to "marry nor give in marriage neither can they die any longer—they are equal to the angels and are children of God" (Luke 20:35–36) Chastity and virginity become the great consuming ideals, as well as abstinence even within marriage. Through the practice of virginity one might recover a former childlike simplicity and innocence.[237]

Monasticism answered this need for perfection, for the recovery of almost a lost innocence. And shortly thereafter the secular clergy adopted it—even less

---

[235] TC-*CS*, 56–59. Campanella the eugenicist can become painfully explicit. See his *De homine, Thelogia*, IV/2, 176–79, and his *Del senso*, 305–6. In the former instance he will revert to one of his favorite texts, Isaiah 65:23, to remind us that the prophet teaches that in the golden age copulation and generation will be without perturbation from libidinous passions and irrationalities.

[236] Amab., *Cong.*, I, 113, 165, 218–19; Amab., *Doc.*, I, 262/311, 378–79/371, 434/393.

[237] Robin Lane Fox, *Pagans and Christians* (New York, 1987), 362–63, 366. Cf. also Elaine H. Pagels, "Adam and Eve, Christ and the Church: A Survey of Second-Century Controversies concerning Marriage," in *The New Testament and Gnosis: Essays in Honor of Robert McL. Wilson* (Edinburgh, 1983), 146–75, which distinguishes the highly ascetic, negative position of Jesus and Paul from the more positive and accommodating position of the deutero-Pauline pastoral materials.

perfectly than the regular clergy. This early Christian "living like angels" echoes the restored innocence of Campanella's naturalistic society. Tinged with Gnosticism that we know historically in practice vacillated between extreme asceticism and promiscuity,[238] Campanella would now impose a Platonic order of eugenic policing upon his Solarians.

Therefore in assessing and balancing off the tensions and ambiguities of Campanella's position on eugenics, the community of women, and his utopian society at the end of his life, we find that he still remains true to an apocalyptic expectation of the new society; in the present interim of historical Christianity he has literally glossed over the community of women and its future realization by his claim that "because of human weakness many things were considered appropriate prior to Christ's coming that afterwards were not sustainable."[239] Still this statement would seem to pertain to the present Christian envelope of time and not to the future glorious realization wherein Campanella has identified Christ as Primal Reason affirming the natural order and has persisted in reiterating and remaining faithful to his community of women as conforming to nature. Elsewhere, in his *Theologia*, in charting Isaiah's new heaven and new earth, he would prove more forthright, thereby affirming that complex eugenic program he had first presented in *The City of the Sun* and had reiterated with varying modulations throughout his life.[240]

In the long trail of criticism directed against *Republic* 5, running from Aris-

---

[238] See Peter Brown, *The Body and Society: Men, Women and Sexual Renunciation in Early Christianity* (New York, 1988), 61, where with Epiphanes, the Carpocratians, and the Nicolaitans in mind the author asserts that we cannot discount the real possibility of esoteric Christian groups that had turned to free love. The contemporary claim that their initiates had turned promiscuously to explore the nature of "true communion" may well not have been just the idle fancy of a polemicist's imagination.

[239] See n. 222, *supra*.

[240] TC-*T*., XXVII, *La prima e la seconda Resurrezione* (Roma, 1955), 62, 70: "Praeterea philosophi hunc statum desiderantes descriperunt sub nomine de optima republica, ut Socrates, Pythagoras, Plato, qui in fine libri addit vel Deos vel filios Deorum vivere aut victuros esse in sic descripta republica. Christus autem nos omnes filios Dei fieri satagit. Et in lib. de Sanctitate et de Voto, et de Legibus, expectat Socrates et Plato instauratorem divini cultus et legum. Hanc rempublicam in communitate tenuerunt a principio Apostoli, teste S. Clemente Romano in Epist. 4 ad Iacobum fratrem Domini et citatur Gratiano cap. dilectissimi 12, q. 1. ubi omnia communia, etiam coniuges, ponit. Sed Tertullianus exceptuat uxores, quoad thorum, non quoad obsequium. . . .

Et sic nos in Civitate Solis descripsimus generationem sub felicibus astris et dispositionibus parentum bonis, scelere purgatorum. Et quoniam generatio et mors puerorum centenariorum non erit in caelo, nisi in paradiso machometico, consequens est ut Isaias loquatur historice, non anagogice, nisi forte, quia paulo ante loquitur de caelo novo et terra nova, sit simul historicus et anagogicus, ut utramque felicitatem amplectatur, alteram in terra, sicut praeludium, alteram in caelo, sicut perfectionem finalem: sicut angelus simul de septimanis Zorobabel, ut praeludiis, et de septimanis Christi, ut complementis, loquebatur.

Sed dicent aliqui quod sub caelo novo et terra nova erit generatio et mors et saeculum terrestre apud Isaiam: ergo solum spiritualiter intelligendus est. Respondetur quod Ecclesiae renovatio in animabus et corporibus vocatur caelum novum et terra nova historice et anagogice, et utrumque fit a Messia."

totle through the Fathers and the Middle Ages and culminating in the Italian Renaissance, *The City of the Sun*, as Campanella's prevailing idea of Christian polity, occupies a unique place. His work represents the frankest and most complete acceptance of these unlikely Christian practices ever dared and with such an acceptance a momentous intellectual affirmation of Plato in the tangled history of that author's appropriation by the West. We have tried to suggest here the intellectual strands that bridged the gulf between Plato's utopia and the monastic/apocalyptical community of a radical Christianity: the recovery of a lost innocence for a fallen humanity; the apocalyptical restoration of unfallen nature and thus a restored innocence; the correlation bordering on identification of natural reason and divine grace in a Christian rationality.

In short Plato's idea of the community of wives continued to haunt Campanella both for its providing an orderly method of reproducing the species and for its suppressing the particularist interests of the family that would otherwise undermine community. But while Plato limited his communist practices to the guardians, Campanella would extend them to all his Solarians. Moreover, convinced by appropriate astrological and apocalyptical indicators, Campanella now awaited with breathless expectation the realization of his Solarian city and of that community whose possible accomplishment Plato two millennia earlier had failed to pursue.

Chapter VIII

NATURALISTIC RELIGION, AMERICA, AND WORLD EVANGELIZATION

IN SEVERAL major respects the sixteenth century emerges as the most revolutionary in the Western experience. The increasing impact of printing, Copernicanism as a delayed action bomb, and the discovery of America, together with the encompassing of the globe, all introduced a new instability as well as opportunity. More immediately and narrowly within the European encampment the Protestant Reformation had shattered the medieval catholic unity of the Church, creating in its wake in Lambeth Palace, Wittenberg, Geneva, and numerous state churches a polycentric ecclesiastical landscape. Nevertheless the general persistence of that arrangement, inherited from Emperor Theodosius and the late Roman Empire, whereby the single true religion is axiomatic for political unity and the sole basis for social order and ethical conduct, now had the effect of maximizing hostility between differing dogmatic/political constructs and throttling dissent within these same polities. With the crystallization of dogmatic positions and confessional camps the last half of the sixteenth century saw a destabilized, polycentric Europe thrusting into the poorly perceived, yet tantalizing other worlds present on a suddenly expanded, if slowly shrinking planet.

Any assessment of the intellectual context at the end of the century needs to take into account the currents stemming from the Italian Renaissance. As a preeminently cultural and intellectual movement promoted by a new elite, the Renaissance would in its later stage now take its revenge upon that essentially religious, popular movement of the Reformation that it had done so much earlier to sire. For both revived Stoicism and Florentine Platonism would have the effect of dissolving the rigidities and sharp edges of confessional positions and the exclusiveness of dogmatic Christianity into a more comprehensive and general rationalism or naturalism. For its part the Stoic current advanced ideas of a rational, natural law that provided a potential basis of equality and community not simply for Europeans but for all humans insofar as they were rational creatures. On the other hand Renaissance Platonism, multiform and hybrid, diffuse and all too often turbid, would nevertheless advance the notion of a universal theism, a *prisca theologia* that emphasized the fundamental unity of all religions whatever their different guises. The frequent resort to the legendary figure of Hermes Trismegistus as an authority reminds us of the importance of astrology, magic, and the occult as the science of the day, in the universalizing process. In the course of the later sixteenth century the Hermetic influence leaves its trail in the work of the great French Orientalist, Guillaume Postel, of the Protestant apologist and friend of Henry of Navarre, Philippe de Mornay, and of the Platonist Francesco Patrizi, whose works were condemned by Rome.[1]

Projecting forward into the seventeenth century we can assess the fruit of these forces in Lord Herbert of Cherbury's *On Truth* (*De veritate*), first published in 1625. In his reductive theology Lord Herbert claimed the reality of five common notions regarding religion that were natural and thus accessible to all men. Significantly, he almost never mentions Christ, and the doctrinal importance of the Incarnation and the Crucifixion is virtually ignored. The Christian God as Creator, insofar as it is Christian at all, is thus easily reinterpreted in terms of the Platonist One. Herbert is unable to subscribe to a literal need for redemption through a special act of grace. Considered by some the forerunner of deism, Herbert remains broadly indebted to Ficino and specifically to the Florentine philosopher's *De Christiana religione* 1.4, which posits a single universal religion in a diversity of rites and forms.[2] It is noteworthy that when this statement of easy optimism regarding a universal access to the Creator God was republished in 1633, Herbert, who possessed some of Campanella's works and apparently admired him, arranged to have the Dominican receive a copy of *De veritate*. Although we cannot be sure of the reaction, it seems to have been favorable.[3]

Given the exuberant speculation in prophecy evinced by Lutheranism, English Puritanism, and even the radical edges of mendicant Catholicism, it is hardly surprising that early-seventeeth-century theologies should seek to enlist the current sciences of astrology and magic for calculating the universal end as well as renovation of all things. Contemporary cosmologies reveal a further important ingredient constituting the intellectual background to the age: the sense that the present planetary system was not likely to persist and would shortly come to an end.[4] Indeed Campanella had melded prophecy and magic with an astronomy proclaiming the sun's approach to the earth. Those apocalyptic as well as astronomical predictions for the year 1600 had proved disastrously false for Campanella and his followers. But failure and long imprisonment did not prevent him from continuing to celebrate new comets, new stars, new continents as heralding Isaiah's new world.[5]

---

[1] On this last point, see R. D. Bedford, *The Defense of Truth: Herbert of Cherbury and the Seventeenth Century* (Manchester, 1979), 218–24.

[2] Ibid., 177, 218.

[3] D. P. Walker, *The Ancient Theology: Studies in Christian Platonism from the Fifteenth to the Eighteenth Century* (Ithaca, 1972), 168, 188.

[4] Charles Webster, *From Paracelsus to Newton: Magic and the Making of Modern Science* (Cambridge, 1982), 48.

[5] For example, see his letter to Galileo, August 5, 1632, TC-*Lett.*, 241.

Turning from the intellectual to the institutional base for world evangelization we need first to remind ourselves of those traditional mendicant religious orders (the Augustinians, Franciscans, and Dominicans), which had been in the business of missionary endeavor and conversion of the infidel in North Africa and China since the thirteenth century. Acquisitive of the new techniques of argumentation provided by the universities and precocious in learning the necessary Asian and Oriental languages, the friars served as the happy combatants in extending the faith.[6] With a flair for publicity the Jesuits, the best known of the new religious orders produced by the Counter Reformation, would appear to outstrip their rivals in energy and effectiveness. Operating within that arrangement known as the Patronato Real, whereby the organization and directives for the Church in Spain's American holdings came not from Rome but from the Spanish king and his Council of the Indies, the Jesuits notwithstanding experienced no inner tension or division; they believed that the best interests of Roman Catholicism and the Spanish Empire coalesced and that in good conscience they could act as agents of both the faith and its temporal champion.[7] The collective achievement of Catholic religious orders in promoting missions, learning the native languages, developing grammars, and laying out new dioceses presents a stunning contrast to the contemporary quiescence of Protestantism in this respect. Admittedly, the Catholic world continued to nurse a universal outlook and dynamic that now allowed it to mount a global effort to convert all peoples of the earth. Perhaps most awesome in this enterprise was the immense and ultimately impossible task of seeking to Christianize the most sophisticated and oldest civilization on earth—that of China.[8]

Because of the tight control of state churches over their colonial empires, Rome appeared slow to create an administrative arm that might preside over the task of universal conversion. Indeed in the reorganization of the papal curia by Sixtus V in 1588 a Congregation for Missions was not to be found among the fifteen established at this time. Not until Gregory XV in June 1622 did the papacy take the fateful step with the creation of the *Congregatio de Propaganda Fide*, constituting a panel of thirteen cardinals charged as much with the task of regaining the heretic in Europe as winning the infidel beyond Europe. The universal outreach of Rome in these decades, the vision of the commitment to a vast enterprise of global evangelization, the winning of new

---

[6] Berthold Altaner, "Sprachstudien und Sprachkenntnisse im Dienste der Mission des 13. und 14. Jahrhunderts," *Zeitschrift für Missionswissenschaft* 21 (1931): 113–36.

[7] Peggy K. Liss, "Jesuit Contributions to the Ideology of Spanish Empire in Mexico," *The Americas* 29 (1973): 322–23.

[8] See the extensive, illuminating introduction of J. S. Cummins to his edition of *The Travels and Controversies of Friar Domingo de Navarrete, 1618–1686* (Cambridge, 1962), vol. 1; also the same author's "Two Missionary Methods in China: Mendicants and Jesuits," *Archivo Ibero-Americano* 38 (1978): 33–108.

peoples and cultures to the faith can best be measured by the fact that the printing office of the congregation had at its command fifteen different fonts for the various scripts, and by 1643, twenty-three different languages.[9]

The driving force in the newly established congregation was its talented, high-minded secretary, Francesco Ingoli. Largely to him fell the task of defining the nature and effectiveness of this new administrative arm of the papacy. A contemporary described him as the head, the body, and the feet of the new congregation. Blocked from entering into the Patronato Real of the Catholic king, Ingoli, insofar as the Portuguese patronal system allowed, promoted a Roman presidency over efforts to implement a native clergy and a locally organized system of examination for the missionaries.[10] From Paris, Campanella would address five letters to him in the last years of the Dominican's life (1635–37), in one of which he felt free to urge that the mumbled Mass must be spoken in the vernacular and that the clergy might be married and the laity allowed to communicate in both kinds.[11]

Campanella's own commitment to global missionary endeavor was deeply rooted in his being and integral to his total thought. The Dominican partook generously of the heady intellectual atmosphere of the late Renaissance and fervently espoused the current magical and astronomical pursuits that seemed to lend support to the universal realization of biblical prophecy and apocalypticism. Although his passionate concern for evangelization penetrated all his works, the most specific dealing with this issue remained his *Quod reminiscentur et convertentur* (Ps. 21: 28),[12] composed largely in the first months of 1618, if conceived two years before. Campanella always considered it along with the *Metaphysics* as one of his two most important works and in fact spent

---

[9] Willi Henkel, "The Polyglot Printing-Office of the Congregation," *Sacrae Congregationis de Propaganda Fide Memoria Rerum. 350 anni a servizio delle Missioni* (Rome, 1972), 335–50; esp. 337, 343.

[10] On the important figure of Francesco Ingoli, see Josef Metzler, "Päpstlicher Primat als pastorale Verantwortung und missionarischer Auftrag in frühen Dokumenten der Progaganda-Kongregation," in *Konzil und Papst: Historische Beiträge zur Frage der höchsten Gewalt in der Kirche*, Festgabe für Hermann Tüchle, ed. Georg Schwaiger (Munich/Paderborn/Vienna, 1975), 373–86, esp. 375–78; and also by the same author the several articles on the Propaganda and Ingoli appearing in *Sacrae Congregationis de Propaganda Fide memoria rerum*, I/1; Jean Beckmann, "La Congrégation de la Propagation de la Foi face à la politique internationale," *NWfMW* 19 (1963): 241–71, esp. 245–51; P. Nicola Kowalsky, "Il testamento di Mons. Ingoli, primo segretario della Sacra Congregatione 'de Propaganda Fide,'" *NZfMW* 19 (1963): 272–83; Josef Grisar, "Francesco Ingoli über die Aufgaben des kommenden Papstes nach dem tode Urban VIII.(1644)," *Archivum Historiae Pontificiae* 5 (1967): 289–324.

[11] TC-*Lett.*, 326.

[12] All biblical references will be to the Vulgate—*Biblia Sacra iuxta vulgatam versionem*, ed. Robert Weber (Stuttgart, 1969)—and in this particular instance to the Gallican version of the Psalms. Their English equivalents follow Douai-Rheims: "All the ends of the earth shall remember, and shall be converted to the Lord and all the kindreds of the Gentiles shall adore in his sight."

the last years of his life in Paris vainly trying to obtain Rome's permission for its publication. In the ecumenical impulses and missionary enthusiasm that constitute the genesis of the *QR* and become evident in the larger enterprise of his *Theologia* (1614–24) there is a climate that anticipates the founding of the Propaganda.[13]

In the development of a theology that sought to be accessible to all peoples and promotive of the efforts of missionaries Campanella avails himself of those same currents of Stoicism and Florentine Platonism that were shaping the discourse of his contemporary Lord Herbert. Yet while the latter manifested no clear commitment to Christianity, Campanella did not part company from the Christian tradition. His position is certainly ambiguous and much more complicated than that of his English contemporary. As one who wished to use the power and universal structure of the Church as an instrument for an ecumenical religion, he could only benefit from identifying with the papacy. As an ardent Dominican and admirer of St. Thomas Aquinas he loudly claimed to adhere to the Angelic Doctor's teachings. And in fact some modern interpreters, in emphasizing his formal theology, will urge its orthodoxy.[14] Yet in his reshaping of Christianity into a missionary doctrine to engage the varied populations of an abruptly enlarged jurisdiction, Campanella inevitably responds to the possibilities afforded by astrology and magic, Stoicism and Platonism in order to dissolve the more exclusive features of the Christian faith and open it up to the community of humankind. In a sense Nicola Badaloni is right when he suggests that, like Grotius for Protestantism, Campanella sought to develop the *communitas* of Christianity while dismantling the traditional concept of God in order to make way for science and human power.[15]

In his construction of a natural theology that perilously presents the features of a naturalistic religion, Campanella affirms the universality of the religious instinct.[16] Man's mind is itself a divine remembrance (*Dei memoriale*) and in the image of God.[17] With the scriptural support of Ecclesiasticus 1:16 he asserts that in the womb has been created the fear of the Lord which constitutes religion.[18] But the major springboard for his universal religious naturalism derives from specific recourse to the stock text provided by Ficino in *De Christiana religione* 1.4 that peoples do not disagree in religion but *in ritu* and in the notion of the divine.[19] Beginning with the definition of religion in

---

[13] Luigi Firpo, "A proposito del *Quod Reminiscentur* di T. Campanella," *GCFI* 21 (1940): 271–75. See also LF-*Bibl.*, 153–57.
[14] See "Preface," n. 1, *supra*.
[15] Nicola Badaloni, *Tommaso Campanella* (Milan, 1965), 284.
[16] TC-*Meta.*, III, 110.
[17] TC-*QR*, 8.
[18] TC-*Meta.*, III, 184.
[19] Ibid., 112.

Ecclesiasticus 1:16 and ascending through the Fathers to St. Thomas, Campanella comes to rest with Ficino (*Theologia platonica* 14.9): "I understand religion to be itself an instinct common and natural to all people whereby everywhere and always a certain providential ruling of the world is recognized and honored that first we know by natural sagacity, then by philosophical reasons, and finally by prophetic words and miracles."[20] From here it is a short Stoic step to claiming that one natural law in the hearts of all defies whatever diversity.[21]

Central and decisive to any form of Christianity is its understanding of Christ—the aspects and features it chooses to emphasize, and those it seeks to minimize or suppress. Such is certainly the case with Campanella. Again in his formal theological statements he can appear quite orthodox, but peeping out from the interstices of his writings, especially those of an "aphoristic" sort, a number of dissident themes present a distinctively less orthodox picture of Christ. In short he espoused the Christ in glory prominent in early medieval Christianity; the Christ of the Passion and Crucifixion left him uneasy, even upset.[22] One of Campanella's more moving sonnets, deriving from the period of his early imprisonment, explicitly challenges a piety that makes so much of Christ's six hours on the cross and yet fails to do justice to Christ in glory, *Christus triumphans*, ruling heaven in splendor and soon to bring His glory to earth.[23] Here we find a conscious rejection of that late medieval piety persisting into the Counter Reformation that emphasizes Christ's agony to the neglect of His lordship and rule. Faced with a need similar to that of Lord Herbert to provide a blander Christianity to a more universal public, Campanella emotionally shuns the very Cross that gives distinctive force to Christian thought and piety. In order to appreciate the curious affinities and tensions in his position we may recall Blaise Pascal's Fifth Letter, where it is claimed that a Dominican, a member of Campanella's own order, will complain to Rome and to the Propaganda that the Jesuits in China specifically suppress the offense of the Cross and preach only a glorious and not a suffering Christ.[24] While notable, the congruence of the Dominican Campanella with the Jesuits on properly confessional matters, excepting education, is hardly surprising.[25]

---

[20] Ibid., 212.

[21] TC-*AT*, 109.

[22] On Campanella's understanding of Christ, see chap. 2, nn. 132–34, *supra*.

[23] TC-*P*¹, 37, sonnet 22, "Nella resurrezione di Cristo."

[24] Blaise Pascal, *Les provinciales* (Cinquième Lettre), in *Oeuvres complètes*, ed. Jacques Chevalier (Paris: Gallimard, 1954), 705–6. See also Cummins, *Navarrete*, lxi, for the Jesuit reluctance to press the Cross in their catechizing. And yet in America the great José de Acosta, S.J., will urge the teaching of the mystery of Christ first and foremost—Christ and *hunc crucifixum*. See *De procuranda indorum salute libri sex* (Cologne: Birckmann, 1596), 451.

[25] Noteworthy is the measure of agreement shared by the Dominican Campanella with the Jesuits on many theological matters and on missionary practices. See Giovanni di Napoli, "Ecumenismo e missionarismo in Tommaso Campanella," *Euntes docete* 22 (1969): 265–308, esp.

Less emotional and more philosophical is Campanella's emphasis upon Christ as the Primal Reason to which all men as rational beings give their assent.[26] Early in his imprisonment he had identified Christ as the purest expression of the law of nature to which Christianity had simply added sacraments, thereby distinguishing Christ and the Christian.[27] In *Atheism Conquered* (*Atheismus Triumphatus*), composed first in Italian in 1605, then in Latin 1607 but not published until 1631, then to be immediately sequestered, censured, revised, and only finally republished in Paris in 1636, Campanella defined more explicitly the identification of Christ as Reason: all peoples recognize Christ as the Primal Reason (*Deum primam Rationem*), and all peoples are Christian when they live according to reason even though they may not even know Christ. In Christianity alone is perfect rationality as the early church fathers had urged. Christ is the head of all rational creatures. While supportive of a comprehensive natural law, Christ also manages to embody a supernatural *magiam* imparted through the sacraments.[28] In the more formal treatment of this issue provided by his *Theologia*, Campanella will recognize the need to keep in balance Christ as Redeemer and Christ as Legislator, yet he will associate Protestantism with a single-minded plumping for the former, while he himself gravitates toward Christ as King, as Doctor, but preeminently as Legislator.[29]

The thorny issue of predestination and free will reveals the direction and intent of Campanella's theologizing. Once again formally orthodox and apparently Thomistic he will nevertheless build up a sediment of preference in his recourse to authorities that will weight the scales in favor of the general rationality of the early Greek Fathers, especially the Alexandrian School and John Chrysostom, and away from Augustine, particularly the later Augustine. He contrasts the Augustinian tradition whereby predestination seems to follow from an invincible decree with that of the Greek Fathers—Origen, Chrysostom, Theophylact, Athanasius, Basil, Cyril, Cassian, and Justin Martyr—which he claims takes into account a divine foreknowledge of human merits.[30] Campanella presses a distinction between God's antecedent will (whereby all are saved) and His consequent will (whereby divine predestina-

---

271–72, 283; TC-*AV*, 118–19; TC-*MS*, 148–49; TC-*QR*, 55; and the citations of N. Bobbio in his edition of the *Città del sole*, 113. On their most significant disagreement regarding education, where Campanella finds the Jesuit program too "elitist," see chap. 7, n. 169, *supra*.

[26] TC-*Lett.*, 93–95.

[27] Ibid., 63.

[28] TC-*AT*, 72–75, 109, 126; TC-*Meta.*, III, 296.

[29] TC-*T*, XVIII, 168; cf. TC-*T*, XXI, 10, 14, 32, 38.

[30] TC-*Meta.*, III, 356, 358. Campanella continues to attribute to Justin Martyr the spurious *Confutatio dogmatum quorundam Aristotelicorum* (*MPL*, 6:1491–1564), wrongly attributed to San Giustina da Fozio but possibly the work of Diodorus of Tarsus. See TC-*Op. in.*, 41, n. 4. For another example of Campanella's specific opting for the Fathers prior to St. Augustine, see TC-*MS*, 236.

tion and reprobation follow according to the most secret foreknowledge of our merits and demerits).[31] Campanella continues to take as his basic premise and guide 1 Timothy 2:4 (God wants all to be saved). Thus among several reasons for his continuous recourse and reference to Origen is the great Alexandrian's doctrine of the total restoration of all things (*apokatastasis panton*) whereby ultimately the whole of God's creation, including Satan and the fallen angels, will be taken up into a universal reconciliation with God.[32] Nevertheless he seeks to distance himself from Origen's most distinguished modern promoter, Erasmus, as too Pelagian, while claiming for his own position a Catholic middle way defined by the Councils of Orange (529) and Trent.[33] For his broad, generous view of the soterial process, Campanella has frequent recourse to his favorite church father, St. John Chrysostom. God is not an accounter of persons but to all has He wanted to offer and does offer grace.[34]

Throughout his life Campanella remained profoundly troubled on the one hand by the multitude of peoples on the earth and on the other hand the limited number of the saved even within the Christian camp. The magnitude of this problem—namely, the number of peoples, populations, and cultures that remain in idolatry and ignorance, removed from a European Christ and His salvation—can be found in his *Theologia* of the 1614–24 period.[35] Earlier in his *Atheismus Triumphatus* he had expressed the belief that it is absurd to think that only Christians, a small part of humanity comparable to a finger on the entire human body, will be saved. Here he had asked the question how God can be a good father of all men and yet neglect the Tartars, the Japanese, the Chinese, and the Arctic and Antarctic peoples.[36] In the review of the work by the Roman censors, the new master of the Sacred Palace, Niccolò Riccardi, had apparently first not objected and indeed a Dominican consultor, attached to the Holy Office, deemed the study "surely a golden work . . . worthy . . . to be brought to light for the benefit of the entire Christian community." The book duly appeared from a Roman press in 1631. Shortly, however, the shine began to wear off; doubts beset Il Mostro, and he managed a reversal of the decision, to be repeated more momentously the following year in the case of Galileo's *Dialogue*.[37] Riccardi would rapidly become in the eyes of Campanella the most bitter, deceitful, and dangerous of his enemies. For our purposes here Campanella had to meet the doubts of the master of the Sacred Palace with specific replies as well as by recasting the *AT* in a more patristic

---

[31] TC-*T*, XVIII, 106, 108; I, 357–59.
[32] TC-*Meta.*, III, 346; but cf. TC-*T*, XXX, 238, for a more orthodox statement.
[33] TC-*T*, XIII, 42, 44, 50, 58, 64, 70, 74.
[34] Ibid., I, 364–66.
[35] Ibid., XVIII, 30; XXVII, 16, 48, 50, 52, 110.
[36] TC-*AT*, 9–10; TC-*RC*, 12.
[37] TC-*RC*, 9–11, nn. therein: "opus certe aureum . . . dignum . . . quod ad totius reipublicae Christianae utilitatem in lucem prodeat."

mold. In the process he revealed his all too liberal propensities regarding salvation as well as his further indebtedness to Chrysostom and an open world far more sensitive to engaging and winning the Jew or uncommitted Gentile, pagan or infidel. Thus we encounter the following positions: none is damned to hell to suffer physical punishments there except for one's own sins, not for original sin; all children are spared;[38] although baptism is necessary, some may be saved by recommending themselves to God;[39] according to our native endowment ("facere quod in se est") and 1 Timothy 2:4 God wants all to be saved; in defending his own words, "Salvabitur ad regnum" (he will be saved for the kingdom) Campanella seeks to include the unbaptized so long as they serve the natural law.[40] And in Paris Campanella's last years would be convulsed by the ongoing *De auxiliis* controversy between the Jesuits and his fellow Dominicans over the operation of divine grace. In this conflict regarding the perennial and now obsessive issue of predestination and salvation it is noteworthy that Campanella aligned his own position and sympathies perilously close to the Jesuits and granted a greater role to human merits and effort in the process of salvation than the hard-liners, his own Dominicans, would allow.[41]

The problem of how to adjust a Eurocentric Christianity to a global arena made all the more pressing the definition and recognition of a universalized religion. In the explicit task of missionary endeavor, quite apart from the thorny debates back home in Europe on predestination, Campanella as a Dominican participated in a rich and most influential tradition. Almost a century earlier Francisco de Vitoria and the Spanish natural law school of theologians had revamped Stoic notions of rationality and natural law in a revival of Thomism that would make a parochially hardened Christianity more supple and accessible. When Vitoria came to examine the reasons and justification for the Spanish presence in the New World, he found none except for a narrow, tenuous, but ultimately most vital one, derivative from natural law: the right of peoples to communicate. This right of commerce among peoples most immediately provided the justification for Christian missionaries to have free access to possible converts and also the right of all races to move freely from one community to another. The impelling right and need for communication, the power of the word and of the tongue, and the triumph of Spanish navigation in encircling the globe are all of capital importance to Campanella's program and total vision. From his Dominican as well as magical perspective, the new devices of printing press, compass, and arquebus possess an almost sacral quality in affirming this right of communication.[42]

[38] Ibid., 16.
[39] Ibid., 20.
[40] Ibid., 31.
[41] "Compendium," in TC-*Op. in.*, 128–30.
[42] On Vitoria and the "titulus naturalis societatis et communicationis," see Anthony Pagden,

324   CHAPTER VIII

Nevertheless for our Dominican it is always language, the tongue, the preached word that enjoys ascendancy. This right, indeed imperative, to communicate achieves its best expression in one of the *legationes* or commissions serving as chapters to the later sections of Campanella's formidable presentation of Rome's current apostolate, the *Quod reminiscentur*. Acting upon the commonly held European attitude, recently reaffirmed by Botero, that Ming China had arrogantly turned away from all external associations and looked inward upon itself, Campanella abjures its emperor in an unsent letter to the monarch of the Chinese. He resorts to the image of the cheese and the worms, which was broadly current in his own time and has been recently made familiar to a modern audience by Carlo Ginzburg. But here, as elsewhere in the Dominican's writings, he uses it for cognitive and political purposes rather than in the cosmogonic sense of Menocchio. Campanella admonishes the emperor:

> Those men [your subjects] are lacking in aspiration; they seem not men but like worms born inside a cheese, who reckon nothing more nor better there to be in the world beyond their own cheese from which they are nourished, sustained, hidden, or as worms born in man's stomach who know nothing of man, nor his mind, but cocooned away, complacent, not wanting to be disturbed, jealous of their remove. So, O king, you seem to be to us. . . . Stick your head out beyond your cheese, beyond the stomach of your land.[43]

Laced now with Western *curiositas*, the passage distills much of that immense Christian dynamic, experienced so deeply by the imprisoned friar.

Against such an intellectual and institutional background can now be examined the operation of Campanella's thought on a world and specifically American, hemispheric scale.

• • •

If Campanella's thought possessed a single informing figure it was probably that of Christopher Columbus. Columbus's name appears in the majority of Campanella's works, for he never tires of showing how the actual experience of encountering another hemisphere brought to naught the traditional authority of respected church fathers asserting that no antipodes could exist. In the

---

"The School of Salamanca and the 'Affair of the Indies,'" *History of Universities* 1 (1981): 71–112, esp. 85; also the same author's "Dispossessing the Barbarian," in *The Languages of Political Theory in Early Modern Europe* (Cambridge, 1987), 79–98, esp. 81, 86–87, which shows how this capacity for communication, rooted in natural law, provides both *jus peregrinandi* and *jus praedicandi*.

[43] TC-*QR*, 221, and also TC-*MM*, 15; LF-*Tutte*, 1228. See TC-*Meta.*, I, 144; and TC-*T*, XXIX, 89, for the philosophy of Aristotle as the proverbial worm in the stomach of man. Cf. also TC-*Lett.*, 100. For a permutation of this important and recurring image, conveying a sense of the human condition as one of isolation and noncommunication, see TC-*P*[1], sonnet 4, 16.

preface to his immense *Metaphysics* he leads off with Christopher Columbus as providing the supreme evidence for experience over authorities, for empirical testimony over opinions. For this world as the codex of God, the Book of Nature, we learn to read through the external senses. And where we cannot directly read all of it ourselves we must credit the testimony of others. But not all men are to be credited, for too many falsely transcribe their own books from the divine codex and represent their books as the original autograph and not as copy. Whereas *opinio* becomes the reading from our own self-devised books, *testimonium* is the direct reading from God's book. Thus what better confutation of the authoritative opinions of Lactantius and Augustine in their negation of antipodes than Columbus's testifying by his own navigation into another hemisphere?[44] Direct experience displaces venerable opinion.

Early in his Neapolitan imprisonment (1603) Campanella had identified Columbus as providing the bridge between Christ and Caesar. He had hailed this "audacious genius" and prior to the notoriety of Galileo he had included Columbus with two other Italians, Vespucci and Telesio, as having exceeded in action and performance what the Greeks could only fabulate.[45] In his earlier Italian *Poetics*, composed in 1596, and in the later Latin *Poetics* Campanella pursued his lonely war against the poetry of fables—Homer, the Greeks in general, and now the currently fashionable Ariosto, Boiardo, and Tasso—all in the interest of advancing a poetry of power and utility. Throughout he insists on the majesty and import of Columbus's achievement as being the very stuff of great epic, although his own age had failed to accept this challenge. For what is suitable to Jason is not so to Columbus or Caesar: not all wars or grand enterprises are just and marvelous, "only those that bring great utility to posterity and give laws to the conquered . . . thereby producing a change of empire and religion, itself the soul of empire, and the innovation of a new age."[46] In the later Latin *Poetics* of 1613 Campanella includes among the truly marvelous, suitable for serious poetic celebration, "the new discoveries such as that of the New World, of artillery, of a new heaven and new planets by my friend Galileo, the astronomic hypothesis of Copernicus, of Timaeus and Philolaus, and of all that is not ordinary." Human actions ushering in a new epoch of the world commend themselves to epical exposition: for example, the arrival of Aeneas in Italy, Joshua's entry into Palestine, the land-

---

[44] TC-*Meta.*, I, 78–84. Geoffrey Atkinson, *Les nouveaux horizons de la Renaissance française* (Paris, 1935), 255–61, quotes twenty-four separate European authors from the sixteenth century who cite the confirmation of antipodes but largely to celebrate the superiority of moderns to ancients or superior navigation. While there is a trace of the epistemological importance in N. Le Huen and Acosta only Jacques Cartier in his *Brief Récit et succinte narration* (1545) specifically makes the point: "experientia est rerum magistra." None apparently refer to Columbus and none sustain this appeal to experience and to Columbus as does Campanella in too many instances to cite.

[45] TC-*P*[1] 100–101.

[46] TC-*P*[2], 353, 358.

ing of the Spaniards in America, with Columbus beggaring all other human enterprises.[47] Whoever will write this long-overdue epic of Columbus "will record what happened to him in the voyage with respect to his crew, what he experienced from the sea, from the weather, from monsters, and from the inhabitants of the new continent and whatever served to retard or hasten the occupation of the New World."[48]

Yet other than an epistemological significance, Columbus has a cultural, moral, and ultimately religious significance. Never unmindful of the apocalyptic dimensions to America's discovery, Campanella sees Columbus not only as bearing Christ to the New World but as establishing the Columbian Church (*Columbam Ecclesiam*).[49] For good reason Campanella had begun his huge *Theologia* by asserting the principal causes impelling his work; the first three were the heresies associated with the Protestant movement, the discovery of the New World with its unknown and unknowing people, and the discovery of new stars and a new construction of the world, requiring incorporation into a new theology.[50] He would go on to observe that Luther and Columbus have shaken philosophers and theologians from a sleep of ignorance and negligence.[51] If the impact of Luther would impel Rome to a closing of ranks and a definition of doctrine, in short to clarification and defensiveness, that of Columbus drove Rome toward meeting the challenge and the opportunities of a globe without walls and to the true realization of its univeralism. What before had seemed unnatural, Columbus had now made natural. And in his wake Spain had girdled this globe with its navigation, introducing religion and polity where there had been only barbarism.[52] In short Columbus creates for Campanella—and for succeeding European generations—a more ample and comprehensive vision of the physical, moral, and religious world.

The discovery of new stars and a new understanding of the universe, of course, brings Galileo into focus. Both Christopher Columbus and Galileo Galilei release two distinct cognitive, conceptual processes of immense, transforming influence for Campanella as well as for his age. Here the Dominican seems to have maintained a more balanced comparison than will later develop largely at the hands of Galileo's Tuscan admirers, who, in comparing the Genoese admiral to the Florentine astronomer, will exalt the latter as produc-

[47] TC-*P*³, 1036–38.
[48] Ibid., 1128.
[49] TC-*MM*, 87.
[50] TC-*T*, I, 3.
[51] Quoted in Romano Amerio, *Il sistema teologico di Tommaso Campanella* (Milan/Naples, 1972), 140: "in artibus humanis et scientiis fiunt quotidie homines sapientiores ob inventionem novarum rerum, unde excitamur in studiis ad profectus maiores. Profecto Lutherus et Columbus excitarunt philosophos et theologos de somno ignorantiae et negligentiae."
[52] TC-*T*, XXVII, 90, 92.

ing accomplishments more intellectual and celestial.[53] Although for Campanella the Galilean issue came into focus only after 1611, he engaged most meaningfully but in different ways during the rest of his life the implications of both men's accomplishments. And in this ongoing interpretation of each, profound as well as revealing, Galileo never displaces Columbus in the friar's estimation.

This child of Galileo, Vitoria, and yes, Machiavelli but always with a Dominican voice, Campanella has drawn the essential conclusion from the event of Christopher Columbus: the construction of the greatest empire in history and the achievements of Spanish navigation had created not simply an American theater but a global context. In the *Monarchia Messiae*, we read:

> If all the world were ruled by one, knowledge would be increased on account of all the land and sea traffic, the trade and by communication of subjects known in individual nations with those better observed and known in other nations—especially astronomy, astrology, physics, and politics, which require much observation—and what one does not know, the other knows. But the devil, envying us such opportunity, would want that we all remain within our own boundaries, as worms within a cheese, so that he may render us all ignorant and deceive us. Likewise he desires that we do not communicate with one another what we observe and know, nor journey to investigate the works of God in foreign regions, nor that we might get to know and see one another but rather that we be separated by language and religion, so that, with no common knowledge, the nurturer of mutual love among us, we would enter into contacts between regions only through wars and death in continuous fear, without charity in God our Father and in our all being sons of the same. But in order that the necessary commerce and communications of this type may be accomplished God permits wars, famines, plagues whereby . . . we might be compelled by His flails to set forth and seek the sciences and contemplate the world, its parts and the works of God, seeking remedies for our evils and entreating the favor of God who brings forth all wealth. . . . Thus we may transport religion and polity, so that the seeds are planted in the warm southern parts of the world or the frigid northern parts or elsewhere. . . . The discovery of the new hemisphere has produced marvelous sciences among us; indeed we may surpass the ancient philosophers, unless mutual envy buries us.[54]

[53] On the contemporary comparison of Columbus with Galileo, see the interesting article by Andrea Battistini, "'Cedat Columbus' e 'Vicisti, Galilaee!': due esploratori a confronto nell'immaginario barocco," *Annali d'Italianistica* 10 (1992): 116–32.

[54] TC-*MM*, 15: "[S]i totus mundus regeretur ab uno, multiplicaretur scientia, ob tutas navigationes, & itinera, & mercaturas, & communicationes rerum, quae sciuntur, in singulis nationibus, cum his, quae sciuntur in alijs; & melius observantur: praesertim Astronomia, Astrologia, Physica, & Polytica, quae multis observationibus indigent, multisque observatoribus; & quod alius ignorat, alius scit. Sed diabolus invidens nobis tantum bonum, vellet, ut omnes maneremus intra

The possibilities for a new world order, a Spanish/papal amalgam, afford commercial, cognitive, and scientific opportunities.

Campanella's universalism is inevitably and unashamedly Eurocentric: he does not hesitate to exploit ostensible American resources but always for maintaining the larger universalizing purposes of Spain. In *Monarchia di Spagna* Campanella had early indicated his sensitivity to problems of demography. He considered the decline of Spain's population to be its greatest problem. To correct this matter he sought to convince Philip II that his greatest riches from America should be men, not gold. He then proceeded to urge the transporting of Indians to Spain for training in agriculture, artisanry, and other pursuits. He would even go so far as to coopt the more intelligent for bishoprics, abbacies, and baronies. Campanella recommends that a gifted Indian convert can be educated as a priest and serve in converting his own people or that a converted Indian chieftain be rewarded with a Spanish barony as a means of engaging his affections. In actual fact, however, the entire native population of America becomes a vast quarry for resolving the problem of labor in Spain's global empire. Apparently ignorant of the ghastly loss of population suffered by the Indians through disease during the course of the sixteenth century and unaware of their increasingly evident unsuitability for hard labor, Campanella urges, as noted earlier, that the unconverted serve as a pool of recruits for use in the galleys and the converted participate in a global resettlement and repopulation. Transported to the shores of Africa, Asia, and Spain, they will establish colonies and be trained in agriculture, artisanry, manufacture. In being hispanicized, some may become soldiers and even members of religious orders (*religiosi*) but the main point would be to relieve the Spaniard of labor and free him for concentrating upon soldiery.[55] Weird as this suggestion appears and impossible as it would have proved in contending with existing social prejudices and the social structure, it was part of a much larger concept for the resuscitation of Spain: as with the Romans in the process of romanizing their subject peoples during the empire, the Spanish must

---

terminos quilibet regionis suae, sicut vermes intra caseum, ut nos reddat ignorantes, & decipiat. Item cupit ut non communicaremus invicem, quae observamus, & scimus; nec peregrinaremur ad investiganda opera Dei in regiones exteras; nec nos invicem cognosceremus, neque videremus: sed ut Lingua, & Religione diversificaremur, ita quod ammissa mutua cognitione, matre mutuae dilectionis inter nos, commercia iniremus de regione in Regionem, tantummodo per bella, & mortes, in continuo metu, absque charitate in Deum Patrem nostrum, & in nos omnes eiusdem filios. Sed Deus . . . permittit bella, fames, pestes; quibus nos, qui nimirum omisimus studium divinarum rerum, & mirabilium effectuum eius, ijs flagellis cogeremur ad peregrinandum, & quaerendum scientias, & contemplandum mundum, & partes eius, & opera Dei; quaerentes remedia malis nostris, & rogantes Deum, qui opem ferat. . . . Item quo Religionem, & Polytiam transportaremus, & semina insererentur Australia calida, frigidis Borealibus, & e contra. . . . Inventio novi Haemisphaeri, mirabiles peperit inter nos scientias, & superaremus priscos phylosophos, nisi invidia mutua nos deprimeret."

[55] TC-*MS*, 279–80.

learn to hispanize their diverse populations and thereby make them a living, functional part of their empire.[56] In urging this solution, Campanella struck a vital chord for the survival of any polity or system. Here he seems to have preceded the swelling chorus of alarm spread by the *arbitristas* and the later fatal, remedial action undertaken by Philip IV's great minister Olivares to de-Castilianize the Spanish *monarquía*.[57]

Equally unsettling to traditional European parochialism appears his plan for the relocating of the Holy City that would be Jerusalem, not Rome. Again in the *Monarchia di Spagna* he broaches this idea as something occurring after the fall of the Antichrist and involving the establishment of his ideal state, presumably of a thousand years' duration.[58] Following a revelation of St. Bridget and the prophecies of Isaiah and Zechariah, he seeks to reconstitute a sacred center of space where Jews, Moslems, and Christians may commune as one; he prophesies that in the first Resurrection the Roman Church will migrate to the New World, first being in Spain, later in Peru, afterwards in Japan, circling the earth from our Occident again into the Orient and from Japan along the shores of Asia coming into the Red Sea and finally to the Jews who will be converted.[59] Presumably Campanella was fully aware of the canonical maxim—"ubi papa, ibi ecclesia Romana" (wherever the pope, there the Roman Church)—for from Jerusalem the king of Spain and the pope would rule the divine empire.

Columbus and the new technology evinced by Spanish navigation have changed everything, opening up the world and requiring mental adjustments and relocations of every sort. Among possibly the oddest to the twentieth-century imagination, but real enough to Campanella's contemporaries, is one appearing in the immense lumber yard of his *Theologia*: Columbus and subsequent Spanish navigation have proved that purgatory, paradise, and even the Elysian Fields are no longer to be located in that other hemisphere. In the process of their relocation Campanella follows Augustine in reassigning hell to the center of the earth.[60] Yet as he ponders, the friar is aware that the Spanish thalassocracy has by no means penetrated all shores. Writing in 1606, he is correct in his belief that Spanish navigators are pressing on to the Antarctic, if not Arctic pole.[61]

[56] Ibid.

[57] Perhaps J. H. Elliott's most succinct statement on these matters can be found in his *Revolt of the Catalans* (Cambridge, 1963), 179–87, 249–51.

[58] TC-*MS*, 271; cf. also TC-*AP*, 40–41, 144, 232; TC-*T*, XXVII, 128.

[59] TC-*T*, XXVII, 118–28. For the transfer of the Roman Church to the New World and several other ideas that seem to parallel as well as anticipate Campanella, see Marcel Bataillon, "La herejía de Fray Francisco de la Cruz y la reacion antilascasiana," in *Études sur Bartolomé de Las Casas* (Paris, 1965), 309–24.

[60] TC-*T*, XXIX, 52. Cf. also TC-*T*, IV/2, 186–88; and on the location of Abraham's bosom, see TC-*T*, XXI, 8, 44.

[61] TC-*AP*, 289–90. Given the fact that Pedro Fernández de Quirós was at this very time

Only rarely does Campanella provide any specific recommendations regarding the tactics of his missionaries. Of the possible missionary methods outlined by José de Acosta in his *De Procuranda Indorum Salute* (How the salvation of the Indians is to be achieved)—the apostolic, with no military force even for protection; the missionaries, preceded by a military force, as advocated by Sepúlveda; the missionaries evangelizing under military protection—Campanella could agree with Acosta in adopting the last for America.[62] Yet Campanella will credit the contemporary missionary with a special gift. After reading the histories of present evangelizers in Japan and China, he claims them to be specially endowed with the same miracles as those of the apostles, the saints, and the martyrs. He can even provide a principle for the availability of miracles: where Catholics are *in possessione*, no miracles occur; but with heathen or heretic, whether it be St. Francis preaching to Moslems in Egypt, or Dominic being tested in Toulouse, or Campanella, as he imagines himself at Wittenberg, challenging the Lutherans to the ordeal by fire, miracles are forthcoming according to need.[63]

Following St. Bernard as well as Vitoria he urges that evangelization be by persuasion, not by force: Christ sent His apostles as sheep among wolves; He did not equip them with bombards.[64] While the realities of the American context would compel him more frequently to violate the limits of persuasion and find justification for the use of force, in his more formal, systematic work, the *Theologia*, he could promote a broader, more comprehensive, and more inclusive set of practices. On the critical matter of baptism, and specifically the baptism of infant children, heretic or infidel, he considers the option of relying upon the authority of the Church in possible opposition to the will of the parents, only to reject it. Instead he adheres to St. Thomas in requiring that the law of nature be observed and that sons be recognized as being under the will and power of their parents. If the son is an adult and proves willing and well instructed, baptism is enjoined, for in returning to his parents, he may

---

pursuing abortive efforts to define and claim *Terra Incognita Australis* for Spanish Catholicism (see following n. 62), Campanella was almost uncannily au courant.

[62] *De Procuranda Indorum Salute* (Salamanca: Guillelmu[s] Foquel, 1589), bk. 2, chap. 8, pp. 235–36. See also *La Australia del Espíritu Santo: The Journal of Fray Martin de Munilla O.F.M. and Other Documents relating to the Voyage of Pedro Fernández de Quirós to the South Sea (1605–06) and the Franciscan Missionary Plan*, ed. and trans. Celsus Kelly, O.F.M. (Cambridge, 1966), 1:17–18.

[63] TC-*QR*, 130, 179. The continuance and even more specifically the resumption of miracles in a missionary context find confirmation in the contemporary Catholic theology of Bellarmine and his associates, who consciously point to the contrasting evangelical quiescence of the Protestants, sitting by the fireside or lying in their warm beds "whilest the Jesuits go into barbarous countries to worke miracles." See D. P. Walker, "The Cessation of Miracles," in *Hermeticism and the Renaissance*, ed. Ingrid Merkel and Allen G. Debus (London/Toronto, 1988), 111–24, esp. 117–18.

[64] TC-*T*, X/3, 58.

convert them.⁶⁵ As early as his *Monarchia di Spagna* (1598) Campanella had manifested dissatisfaction and impatience with what he understood to be the prevailing practices of missionaries: catechisms should be in the native language and brief histories are to be composed after the fashion of the early fathers who converted the gentiles, and not the verbose stuff of our moderns. He even advocates the nurturing of a native clergy whose preachers might be sent into the less accessible mountainous areas to convert their brethren.⁶⁶

Of all the works of Campanella his *Quod reminiscentur et convertentur*, invoking the summons of Psalm 21:28 to conversion, stands among those most esteemed by the Dominican. Long-contemplated and planned, but not composed until the 1616–18 period during his return engagement to the dreadful dungeon of San Elmo,⁶⁷ the work captures that sense of Rome's universal pastoral outreach that would shortly find institutional expression in Gregory XV's establishment of the *Congregatio de propaganda fide*. Dedicated in turn to Popes Paul V, Gregory XV, and Urban VIII, the work, much to his disappointment in Campanella's last years, would never see publication until the mid-twentieth century. The very word *reminiscentia*, recollection, suggests the Platonic assumption that knowledge is simply the conscious recovery of something already latent in the mind. As a promise to conversion *reminiscentia* represents a powerful invocation to a universal response. Indeed the time for this intellectual/spiritual recovery (*tempus huius reminiscentiae*) had now arrived for the realization of that one universal sheepfold under one pastor according to John 10:16.⁶⁸

In his memorial of December 22, 1618, to Paul V Campanella presented a distillation of the total work, providing the pattern and plan of a fourfold composition.⁶⁹ Although the tract would be divided into four books—the first being directed to the Catholic European rulers, schismatics, and Protestant heretics; the second to the outer world of heathenism stretching over the

---

⁶⁵ TC-*T*, XXIV/1, 200–204. On such evangelical tactics, see Richard Trexler, "From the Mouths of Babes: Christianization by Children in sixteenth-century New Spain," in *Religious Organization and Religious Experience*, ed. J. Davis (London/New York, 1982), 115–35.

⁶⁶ TC-*MS*, 282.

⁶⁷ N. 13, *supra*.

⁶⁸ TC-*QR*, 8–9, 14–15; A. J. Marquis, "Le traité missionaire 'Quod Reminiscentur' de Tommaso Campanella," *NZfMW* (Supplementa) 17 (1971): 331–60. It is interesting to note that in his scholastically constructed *Theologia* he can take these same texts, John 10:16 and Psalm 21:28, and present a darker, more realistic appraisal of the world scene for missionaries as a scholastic objection to be eschatologically demolished: the greater part of the globe remains in ignorance of God and in idolatry; the same Hebrews continue to be apostate; the foul Moslems lord it over thirty kingdoms; the interiors of Asia, Africa, and all of America walk in darkness; if the Church has acquired much power over secular princes since its victory over the Roman Empire, still that power is not so great that it is able to subject without resistance all the realms of the earth. TC-*T*, XXVII, 16.

⁶⁹ TC-*Lett.*, 191–92; Luigi Firpo, "Un memoriale inedito e un indice delle opere di Tommaso Campanella," *RF* 38 (1947): 213–29.

greater part of the globe in Asia, Africa, and America; the third to the Jews; and the fourth to the Moslems—like the Propaganda itself no essential distinction was made between the apostolate to the heretic and that to the Indians, both Western and Eastern. The breathtaking scope of the work captures the dynamic of Rome at this time as well as the irrepressible energy and confidence of the Dominican friar. Notable in the general program of world evangelization is the calling of an assembly to Rome that would include all peoples and rulers—Persian, African, Jew, Christian, Moslem, pagan—whereby their legates and learned might be engaged in persuasive *disputatio*.[70] Campanella experiences the temporal crunch: on the one hand why has a benevolent God withheld His remedies and doctrine from the better part of the world for so long, referring thereby to the peoples of Africa, the Far East, and southern Asia, the supposedly innumerable peoples of the Arctic and Antarctic, as well as the inhabitants of the New World?[71] On the other hand the calculations of both prophecy and astrologic time would announce that the moment for the convoking of all peoples had struck.

In such a vast global enterprise it is still somewhat startling that the problem of the conversion of the American Indian occupies less than 20 percent of the space devoted to the gentiles in book 2 and only about one percent of the total work. Nevertheless the passage presenting the American legation is more compressed, intense, and less rambling than many of Campanella's other treatments. While aware of the ethnological question as it bears upon the prevailing theory of the general diffusion of humankind from a single Noachian source, Campanella refuses to be much troubled by the problem that was coming to convulse some of the best minds of the age.[72] Regarding the spatial problem of transmigration Campanella answers those who would ask how people in another hemisphere are able to migrate from our parents in Phoenicia to a place so remote without memory or method (*ratio*), by urging that from the Chinese coast to Japan is but a hop and from Japan to the American mainland (*Quiviram*) in the other hemisphere seems equally simple; and likewise simple the same sort of stepping stones from European islands in the Atlantic to the latent American shore.[73] Temporally, apart from his earlier

---

[70] TC-*QR*, 30; cf. also TC-*Lett.*, 15–17; TC-*AP*, 284–85. Emeric Crucé, in his *Le nouveau Cynée* (Paris, 1623), 73, has been recognized as recommending a Society of Nations seated at Venice, convoking all monarchs of the earth, including the Great Turk. Campanella would seem to have anticipated Crucé in such a notion.

[71] TC-*QR*, 37.

[72] On this issue, see Margaret T. Hodgen, *Early Anthropology in the Sixteenth and Seventeenth Centuries* (Philadelphia, 1964), 218ff. Robert Brerewood, in his *Enquiries touching the diversity of languages and religions* (1614), observes the same quatripartite division of world religions as does Campanella. For the most recent comprehensive study of the theological implications, see Giuliano Gliozzi, *Adamo e il Nuovo Mondo* (Florence, 1977).

[73] TC-*QR*, 202–3. For *Quivira*, see Botero's *Le relatione universali*, which presents America under two headings—"Peninsula septentrional" and "Peninsula Austral" (fols. 217, 223, 238).

rhetorical question, he will observe that it has been 2,300 years since the prophet Isaiah predicted the coming of Christ and that in several ages after His advent His doctrine would come to Japan. Now 1,600 years have passed since its arrival for the instruction of Europeans by word and example in the ways of God, who has sent those Europeans to bear witness to that truth throughout the entire world before He returns to judge humankind.[74]

Campanella subscribes to that early anthropological notion perhaps best evident in his fellow Dominican Las Casas but also voiced by other European minds of the sixteenth and the seventeenth centuries that in the beginning all peoples were barbarians—except apparently for Campanella the Greeks and the Hebrews with a special assist from his native Calabrians:

> As when Greece flourished almost two thousand years ago, refined by wisdom and the arts, all peoples that did not share in her polity and philosophy were called barbarians, as if beasts living without human virtue. Then when the domination of the Latins had been diffused through the world, Greece having been conquered, the Romans as partakers of virtue were no longer called barbarians. Truly the Romans themselves did not consider all Italians, nor Greeks as barbarians. For from the Greeks, they accepted laws and philosophy, nor had the Greeks yet been conquered in war. And in Italy that province now called Calabria was then called Magna Graecia and the Greeks recognized it [as the source of their] philosophy and religious rites. . . . According to Diogenes Laertius, therefore the Greeks and Italians mutually communicated. Likewise the Hebrews perhaps by a higher law labeled all peoples non-Judaic as Gentiles, as being like a multitude, an untaught race, and good for nothing as we know from Isaiah and Esdras. . . . For barbarian and Gentile signify him who is ignorant of divine wisdom, not taught by God, as a son is, but alienated as a slave, enemy, or brute is. And thus we have all been Gentiles and barbarians. . . . God, however, rich in mercy, . . . dissolving the walls separating us from each other, has incorporated us into one family, visiting us and calling us into His school and inheritance; and He has adopted us as sons by means of legates, sent throughout the world, who by a certain divine wisdom, attested by miracles, virtues, and the deification of man, have led us back to the one God.[75]

With the former Botero claims that Francisco Coronado (1579) in his northernmost explorations penetrated *El reyno de Quivira*, which would be identified broadly with the Midwest of the United States today. He describes this area as being not as populated and united as others (fols. 234ᵛ–235ᵛ). None of the Italian editions being available to me earlier, I used a Spanish rendition: *Descripcion de todas las provincias y reynos del mundo* (Gerona: Caspar Garrich, 1622). Yet with later access to the Vatican Library copy of *Le relationi universali* (Venice: Agostino Angelieri, 1608) Quivira appears on the map of America between p. 192 and p. 193 as being southern California.

[74] TC-*QR*, 217–18.

[75] TC-*QR*, 199–200. On the Lascasian parallel, see J. H. Elliott, *The Old World and the New 1492–1650* (Cambridge, 1970), 48–50.

334   CHAPTER VIII

Thus Campanella explains at the outset of book 2 the twin labels of barbarian and Gentile, distinguishing the great mass of humanity and the twofold process of Greeks and Hebrews in bringing this latent dross of humanity to God.

Once outside Catholic Europe Campanella organizes his great work on missions in terms of a series of *legationes* or commissions. On the issue of cannibalism presumably present in central Africa, the Dominican moves easily from his sole heathen African legation to that single legation directed to the American continent.[76] Here his known sources for treating America will be Las Casas, Girolamo Benzoli, and Botero.[77] He begins the legation by reminding his Indian audience of the gospel delivered to them almost 130 years ago, a gospel from which they had withdrawn "just as we and almost the entire human race with the exception of a few from the stock of Noah" survived the flood "as our histories and your traditions in Mexico, Peru, and China attest." His wording is almost intentionally ambiguous in including the American Indian in the original Noachian dispensation and as with many contemporary ethnographers in exhibiting the presumed similarities betraying the desired common origin.[78] In his *Theologia* he confidently affirms that there was circumcision in Yucatan as there had been in Egypt, Africa, and with the Hebrews. He goes on to speculate that possibly by force of the winds ships have been driven from Africa to the New World, where memory of the event came to be lost for lack of writing.[79] Indeed whatever his heterodox hesitations, Campanella's Christian universalism and program of world evangelization dictate adherence to the monogenetic-biblical derivation for the *Americani*. The single-source Adamic origin of humankind necessarily serves to reinforce the universal order envisaged.[80] Quite uncharacteristically for his own more compromising, Jesuit-like approach to the problem of converting the Indian but quite in keeping with the hard-sell tactics of his own fellow Dominicans, Campanella pitches his evangelizing to lead off with the Incarnation, Passion, Resurrection of Jesus Christ—in other words he does not hesitate to present the true *scandalon* for both rational and illiterate men.[81]

It is of course the Genoese Italian, Christopher Columbus, who as a *columba* has brought the Christian faith to the shores of the New World. Yet

---

[76] TC-*QR*, 256.

[77] In his "Documenta ad Gallorum Nationum" (1635), TC-*Op. in.*, 95, Campanella specifically recommends the writings of Las Casas and Benzoni in order to appreciate the reduction of a people to ashes. Cf. also TC-*MN*, 311–12. For evidence of his knowledge of Botero's *Relationi universali*, which he would have read before his long imprisonment, see TC-*CS*, 129, n. 2, and 139, n. 72.

[78] TC-*QR*, 256. On presumed similarities among peoples, see Hodgen, *Early Anthropology*, 297–337.

[79] TC-*T*, IV/1, 16.

[80] Gliozzi, *Adamo*, 356–67, esp. 361–63.

[81] TC-*QR*, 256–57; on the tougher evangelizing practices of the Dominicans, see Cummins' article cited n. 8, *supra*.

while celebrating the wondrous achievements of Spanish navigation and Spanish arms, Campanella can give voice to the conquered and subjected Indians, articulating their alienation and suffering:

> Our leaders have reckoned you Spanish to be the sons of God descending from the clouds in ships and with thundering cannon, as God Himself, fighting atop animals, as if centaurs, and immortal beings. . . . But now we are aware that you are as mortal as we, avid for gold and silver, having killed our kings against your own pledged word; and we know that the art of artillery, the clock, of letters, and horsemanship to be human inventions, not divine and that you exterminate us natives cruelly or hold us in servitude. We understand fully you Spanish to be men, rapacious, cunning, ambitious, who under the false pretext of proclaiming the gospel have subjected and pillaged the kingdoms of others. Wherefore we do not reckon your religious practices (*religiones*) to be better than ours, which we now find similar in many things, in many preferable. Nor has God abandoned us for so long a time, caring nothing for us, if He is the one God of all, if many [gods, then] each cultivates his own.[82]

Thus Campanella, despite his preoccupations with power and order, assumes a position in the Lascasian tradition of protest in defense of the American Indian. And among the very last words that he wrote at the end of his life, in notes explicating his Eclogue to the dauphin, shortly Louis XIV, he will remember the Indians in their sufferings and sing of a new world in which they are liberated from their crucifixion in the mines for which the Americans, justly, hate the Christians.[83]

Yet expectably the grand purpose of evangelization will justify all such base actions. As he had written a decade earlier, Spain's only justification for being in the New World was evangelization.[84] Whatever the presumed common origin and perceived parallels and connections between Indian and Christian religions, he can dismiss the former as being arrogantly sunk in deviltry, depravity, and the tyranny of false gods.[85] For the devil is able to move all bodies locally[86] and has introduced sodomy, whereby semen is misspent, polygamy, whereby love is dissipated, and cannibalism, whereby murder prevails and safety evaporates.[87] Given such depravity, only by the great mercy of God have the Spanish liberators been sent to them. Indeed liberation from idolatry by means of the gospel and introduction to sciences and arts will

---

[82] TC-*QR*, 258.
[83] TC-*P*¹ 308.
[84] TC-*DPI*, 158.
[85] TC-*QR*, 258–60.
[86] TC-*QR*, IV, 132.
[87] TC-*QR*, 260–61. On the devil as responsible for messing up the biblical monogenetic scheme in America especially and most of Africa, see TC-*T*, XXVII, 48–52. For reiterations of this explanation by Robert Burton and José de Acosta, see Hodgen, *Early Anthropology*, 219, 267, 302.

ultimately justify for Campanella the enormities of the Spanish presence in the newfound hemisphere.[88] In short it is the American Indian's violation of the natural law by sodomy and cannibalism, idolatry and cultivation of the diabolic that warrants and even justifies the harsh action of the Spanish conquest. The desperate nature of the situation required the shift from persuasion to force: "we were compelled to resort to iron as a doctor in desperately mortal cases."[89]

Actually elsewhere in his *Theologia* and in a sermon constituting the appendix to his *Monarchia messiae*, both stemming from this same period of 1618, Campanella presented his argument in conscious opposition to the great Thomists of the previous century. Cajetan, De Soto, and Vitoria were wrong in claiming that Christian rulers have no right to use force, even if their missionaries are attacked. Indeed insofar as possible one should proceed by persuasion and not by force. If first received, then attacked, the preachers should be able to expect armed defense. The blatant violation of natural law by cannibalism, idolatry, and sodomy demands that the pope send not only doctors of the gospel but also soldiers to exterminate the crime and punish the criminals. Campanella cites as example Alexander the Great, who founded his empire on this law: he subjected the barbarians and introduced civilization. For his preceptor Aristotle taught that those violating the laws of nature ought to be subjugated like so many beasts. And if De Soto believes the king of Spain hardly to be a competent judge for such very different peoples, Campanella refers to the pope and invokes the power of the keys.[90] More specifically in the *Theologia* he argues that the pope may have the material sword and is able, when persuasion proves ineffective, to constrain the entire human race to rationality. The Americans had dishonored humankind and merited being subjected as beasts and compelled to humanity ("cogi ad humanitatem").[91] If a harsher justification of force by a churchman can hardly be found, the majesty of the cause summoned. As an apparent product of third-generation missionary attitudes regarding the Amerindian, Campanella here reflects the prevailing mood of pessimism and ethnic prejudice that had come to settle on the Spanish colonial bureaucracies both secular and ecclesiastic in contrast to the

[88] TC-*QR*, 262.
[89] TC-*QR*, 263; cf. also TC-*MM*, 36.
[90] TC-*MM*, 84–87.
[91] TC-*T*, X/3, 58. Germana Ernst has recently republished this passage based, however, on Bibliotheque Mazarine, MS. 1077—*De furto et rapina cuiuiscumque rei et de iuribus Hispan. in Novum orbem*—along with the original Italian redaction of the Latin discourse appended to TC-*MM*, wherein she finds Campanella's position, in urging Bernardine persuasion rather than force and in its emphatic denial of any right of the king of Spain to divest the Indians of their property or possessions, to be more cautious and qualified. See her "Monarchia di Cristo e nuovo mondo," in *Studi Politici in onore di Luigi Firpo*, ed. Silvia Rota Ghibaudi and Franco Barcia (Milan, 1990), 11–36.

earlier Franciscan optimism.[92] When aligned with the *conpelle intrare* (Luke 14:23) of an earlier Church, the imperative of the apostolate in his own age would suggest that the sheepfold of salvation must be transformed and expanded to apply to a comprehensive, global assemblage, distinguished by European principles of humanity and rationality.

• • •

In conclusion it can be said that Campanella deeply partook of the principles driving that great preaching order, the Hounds of the Lord, of which he was a member. He shared that immense momentum of the age stemming from Rome and from the mendicant tradition—the natural theology of St. Thomas and his *Summa contra Gentiles* to convert. But Campanella brought his own peculiarly torqued and radical perspective that would abandon the dominant Aristotelianism of the day, capture the prophetic and eschatological, and seek to enlist the new, the innovative, the expansive, promoted by the terrestrial and celestial discoveries of his age. He strains to mobilize the innovations implicit in the work of Columbus and Galileo in order to reinforce the interests of a universal papal theocracy, Eurocentric essentially, but capable of making huge compromises and dilutions in current orthodoxy that it might extend to the pagan, the heretic, and the infidel an often unrecognizable Christianity in the form of a naturalistic religion, presided over by papal Rome.

What finally then does America signify for Campanella? In the first place America possesses epistemological as well as cognitive significance, for its very discovery by the Europeans attests to the authority of direct experience and thus the displacement of long-esteemed authors, venerable *auctoritates*. Second, America had immense eschatological significance for Campanella, who shared the prevalent conviction most deeply experienced by the religious orders themselves, that only when the evangel had been preached to all men would the end occur. In the light of Matthew 24:14 and comparable texts the fact of America and its peoples provided enormous stimulus to missionary activity. Intimately associated with the sense of the end's imminence looms the impressive intellectual activity and achievements of his own age—achievements that a later period would identify with the rapidly maturing Scientific Revolution. Indeed Daniel 12:4 had prophesied that there would be great concourse and increase of knowledge, and the ship that passes through the pillars of Hercules in the frontispiece of Bacon's *Magna Instauratio* reminds us of this contemporary reality.

[92] On the harder mood at the end of the sixteenth century, see C. R. Boxer, *The Church Militant and Iberian Expansion 1440–1770* (Baltimore/London, 1978), 18. See also J. H. Elliott, "Renaissance Europe and America: A Blunted Impact?" in *First Images of America: The Impact of the New World on the Old*, ed. Fredi Chiappelli, 2 vols. (Berkeley, 1976), 1:15–16.

Still there remains a third level of significance, less clear and evident, nevertheless ultimately perhaps more important and distinctively Campanellan. America serves as a summons to world community, calling us forth from the parochial to the global, the universal, envisaging a world without walls, a global order nurtured by unhampered commerce, communication, and intellectual exchange.[93] In short America impels toward a growing sense of global interconnectedness. Just as in the previous generation Giordano Bruno had grasped the meaning of Copernicus by positing the reality of an infinite universe, so Campanella now struggled to adumbrate for his own generation the meaning of Columbus by dimly discerning a truly global world order.

Yet we must not exaggerate. Such a suggestion of global interconnectedness would seem to fall short of a true transformation of consciousness or even a transposition of perspectives directly attributable to the impact of America. Like other Europeans Campanella was unable to accept or understand America on its own terms; rather America comes to serve and to confirm existing needs, perceptions, and aspirations. Campanella does not escape an inevitable Eurocentrism, but it is one opened up, extended, and universalized to realize now a global enterprise.

Nevertheless such a world order can only be of God's making and not of man's. For the figure of Columbus ultimately possesses apocalyptic and broadly eschatological significance. And whatever the global scope of evangelization it can only be properly seen as one among several signs confirming this world's oncoming end and then the Church's renewal in the thousand years of a golden age, constituting its seventh state. For our Dominican the narrow shoal of present time dwindles before the fulfillment of all the prophesied signs. Not in the current temporal course but only in a new aeon will the brotherhood of a cleansed humanity and Christianity be realized.

[93] TC-*MM*, 15.

Epilogue

CAMPANELLA AND THE END OF THE RENAISSANCE

FIVE CRISES or major issues involving early-seventeenth-century Europe have been examined here as they impinge upon and affect Campanella's thought. In presenting this symbiotic contextualization we have by means of such an analysis not argued for any specific progression in Campanella's intellectual development but rather have sought to reveal his very peculiar total involvement, by the mind's thrust, in these issues despite his own physical remove. Undeniably, however, he experienced in the last years of his life, in Paris, his own intellectual isolation in the face of a new intellectual movement, new culture, and new age being mobilized by the philosophic interpreters of the Galilean model of reality and the new criterion of truth: Mersenne's associates—Hobbes, Gassendi, Descartes. As a means of resituating him in the historical development of his century and in a final effort to understand him in the broad currents of his age, we wish to use Campanella as a terminal figure of the late Renaissance.

We may begin by taking issue with the title itself—End of the Renaissance. Do historical periods, or better yet, historical movements have an end, a definitive termination? It is hardly necessary to observe that historical periods exist in historians' heads as means of defining the past; such periods can only begin to have substantive meaning insofar as they may be informed by a movement sufficiently self-conscious and coherent as to achieve contemporary identity over a succession of years, thereby demarcating a fairly distinct period, a historical period to the later historian. Rather than as a period the Renaissance can better be understood preeminently as a cultural movement, affecting and redefining the aristocracy during the years 1300 to 1600. Although the ambiguity of the term "Renaissance" as both a movement and a period in history remains, and in doing so serves a useful function, it is largely as a historical movement that we wish to consider the Renaissance.

Thus to return to the question: is there an end to that cultural movement that we call the Renaissance, and if so how and when? Obviously, we may note at the outset that while there is an end, historical movements do not end as do railroad tracks or a football game. For as an historical agent the movement itself has throughout been undergoing transformation or transmutation. In fact transmutation is certainly a more accurate term, for it preserves the historical texture of continuity, while committing us to a chemical rather than mechanical imagery, whereby the fluidity and polyvalent character of a historical movement can be better understood. The notion of terminus or end as used here in the title only serves as an exhortation to clearer definition of the various elements constituting this cultural movement and at what point they become dissociated and transmuted, undermining the essential characteristics and integral features of that movement, while realigning themselves with different, even alien contemporary developments. Furthermore it would appear that historians have spent more time reflecting on the origins than on the ends of movements. Therefore the task of trying to conceptualize the termination of anything so complex as the Renaissance would seem to be, if ludicrously dangerous, at least marginally useful.

A further venture into intellectual alchemy encourages the merging of the Renaissance with the medieval context in such a way that their confluence and contemporaneity may be entertained without dismissing the recognizable features of each. For the Renaissance as a lay, urban, patrician movement, evincing a more practical Christianity, assumes form and develops within the comprehensive medieval context of a preeminently clerical-ecclesiastical civilization from which had also developed a chivalric—military culture. In Braudel's long sixteenth century that extends well into the seventeenth we are reminded on the one hand by Marcel Bataillon that "the sixteenth century [is the] culmination of the Middle Ages in so many matters"[1] and on the other hand by Marjorie Reeves that only when the educated ceased to take prophecy seriously and the sense of involvement in the divine purposes of history disappeared did the Middle Ages truly end.[2] Examples of what normally appear to be characteristics of different ages and their cultures coexist and can be readily recognized in such cases as the Dominican prophet and popular preacher Savonarola in his humanist, Florentine context; or the conservative nature of the Renaissance in Spain that under Cisneros would clip the wings of whatever might endanger church or monarchy; or the vigorous, late medieval piety and religious consciousness of *Utopia's* author, Thomas More. In the same time span we need to accustom our gaze to apparently conflicting features and motifs coexisting in the same person and the same context.

Precariously situated and dangerously vulnerable, we are now driven to ask what the integral elements, the essential characteristics that constitute the cultural movement we call the Renaissance are. Three suggest themselves, all of which are sufficiently evident in Petrarch: first, the conscious adoption of a perspective on the past, as passed, and the quest to appeal initially to the aesthetic and later moral and philosophic norms in that past, identified as that

---

[1] Marcel Bataillon, "La herejía de Fray Francisco de la Cruz y la reación antilascasiana," *Études sur Bartolomé de Las Casas* (Paris, 1965), 309–24: "estamos en el siglo xvi, culminación de la edad media en muchos materias" (312).

[2] Marjorie Reeves, *The Influence of Prophecy in the Later Middle Ages: A Study in Joachimism* (Oxford, 1969), 508.

of ancient Rome, all in order to evoke these norms as models or forms to effect potential reform in the present; second, an affirmation of the primacy of the humanist/rhetorical tradition in contrast to the contemporary devotion to dialectic and to the emerging protoscientific interests evident in the arts and medical faculty at Padua; third, the assertion of the authority of the direct experience of the individual, best evident in Leonardo da Vinci, the verification pursued by the Paracelsians and perhaps most pungently evinced by Sagredo's countering of Aristotle's authority with sensible experience, as presented at the beginning of the "Second Day" of Galileo's *Dialogue Concerning the Two Chief World Systems*.[3] In all three elements the priority of will needs to be noted along with the enhanced integrity, autonomy, and authority of individual experience. We are reminded of Petrarch's claim in *On his own Ignorance* that he would prefer "to will the good than to know the truth." Likewise rhetoric, ever conscious of its audience, seeks to capture and convince the total self, emotional as well as purely intellectual; the will and the affections become the proper object of eloquence.[4] Similarly with both Pico and Ficino man relies primarily on himself and the right orientation of his will for salvation. Regarding the autonomy of man and its implications for the validity of individual experience, nominalism as well as some forms of mysticism of the late Middle Ages has given new depth, force, and definition to human individuality.[5] A final point at this stage might be made: if principally evident during the first half of the Renaissance, these three characteristics— intellectual perspective, the rhetorical mode, the authority of direct experience —persist throughout the movement with varying modifications, attaining in the case of experience, as evinced in Galileo, a decisive and momentous formulation conjoined with his mathematics.

In advancing the Dominican friar Tommaso Campanella as some sort of terminal figure to what we understand the Renaissance to be, we are not suggesting any causal relationship of the former upon our movement. Nor are we arguing that there is something typical about him. Rather the encyclopedic, far-ranging mind of this Italian philosopher, prophet, and reformer affords a useful sort of lens whereby one may better apprise some of the complexities in the late, attenuated Renaissance as it encounters new currents at the beginning of the seventeenth century. For Campanella stands athwart that decisive trans-

---

[3] Galileo Galilei, *Dialogue Concerning the Two Chief World Systems—Ptolemaic and Copernican*, trans. Stillman Drake (Berkeley/Los Angeles, 1962), 106–8.

[4] Cf. Hanna H. Gray, "Renaissance Humanism: The Pursuit of Eloquence," *JHI* 24 (1963): 500–502.

[5] Cf. Heiko A. Oberman, "Some Notes on the Theology of Nominalism, with Attention to Its Relation to the Renaissance," *Harvard Theological Review* 53 (1960): 60–65, 70–74; also the same author's *The Harvest of Medieval Theology* (Cambridge, Mass., 1962), 327–33, where the coinherence of nominalism with a voluntarist type of mysticism we have here attempted to carry a step further.

formation of learning occurring in the first third of the seventeenth century. His own intellectual formation derives essentially from the last third of the preceding century, yet is by no means impervious to the changes registered by the emerging new science. However, despite his peculiar appropriations of Galileo and Machiavelli, the constant, the centerpiece of his entire thought is a universal, hieratic order, a single monistic system. In fact Campanella compels us to contend with the reassertion of medieval features—a sort of revenge of the medieval evident in the prophetic, the universal, the imperial, the monastic, and the encyclopedic working to snuff out the discrete, the critical, the republican—long since departed—the rhetorically exuberant, and the classically normative. He asserts a medieval monastic-apostolic Christianity permeating and penetrating the late Renaissance, curiously associable and associated with some of the latest currents of thought and intellectual endeavor.

In a quick assessment of Campanella against the present laundry list of Renaissance characteristics, turning to the first, the intellectual perspective of resort to the classical past for revival in the present, the very principle of renascence or renewal itself, one finds the Calabrian reformer standing in striking contrast: his prophetic-apocalyptic expectancy and his almost childlike delight and trust in the new, the innovative, affect his orientation toward the future. Indeed his truly emotional commitment to innovation and experimentation derives as much from this hunger for intellectual freedom as from his sensory epistemology. Here may be recalled his massive effort to mint a new philosophy that might replace the Aristotelianism of his day; or listen to his reaction to the appearance of Galileo's great Dialogue in 1632: "these innovations (*novità*) according to ancient truth, of new worlds, new stars, new systems, new peoples etc. are the beginning of a new age."[6] Encouraged by Stoic and Origenistic themes, as well as by Ficino's resurrection of Plato, Campanella looks forward to a renovation of all things. He is a real modern in preferring recent deeds to those of Alexander the Great, Pyrrhus, and Jason.[7]

If his departure from any sort of conscious Renaissance appeal to the past is abrupt, no less decisive is his abandonment of the humanist/rhetorical tradition. In the *City of the Sun* the Solarians pursue an education in the mathematical, physical, and astrological sciences whose mastery is necessary for anyone to be considered for public office. It is true that a basic familiarity with the mechanical arts, we are told, and the history of all peoples, their ceremonies,

---

[6] TC-*Lett.*, 241; cf. Lynn Thorndike, "Newness and Craving for Novelty in Seventeenth-Century Science and Medicine," *JHI* 12 (1951): 584–98, which is largely guided by the titles of contemporary publications and thus overlooks Campanella's important contribution to this vein of thought.

[7] Tommaso Campanella, *Commentaria*, in *Opere Letterarie di Tommaso Campanella*, ed. Lina Bolzoni (Turin, 1977), 886. On the prophetic, almost apocalyptic, in Ficino's Platonism see Allen, *Nuptial Arithmetic*, 83–88, 100, although Campanella would not have had to have been conversant with *De numero fatali* for these Ficinian propensities.

rites, and governments together with the inventors of all the arts and laws is required. But history and the mechanical arts can each be learned in two days because both are clearly set forth graphically on the walls and are practiced. The Solarians deliberately eschew an Aristotelian sort of learning or for that matter traditional literary authors as a "knowledge which requires only servile memory and which deprives the mind of vitality because it meditates upon books instead of things."[8] Indeed Campanella seems to express here an Americanism worthy of Henry Ford.

Likewise in clearly preferring the study of the natural sciences to all other intellectual pursuits, Campanella appears to be driven not only by their utility but also by their diverting minds from dangerous philosophical speculation and literary pursuits that beget social and political unrest. So real is the danger presented by such studies to political stability that he recommends importing a juggernaut of philosophers and philologists to destabilize the Ottoman Empire.[9] This theme pervades Campanella's works, especially his *Monarchia di Spagna*, which saw English editions in 1654 and 1660; thus in 1670 Henry Stubbe can believe to find a case of "Campanella Revived" in the new Royal Society's conscious pursuit of a politically safe concentration upon the investigation of nature.[10] Indeed the retreat from a high-flown rhetoric would become general to Europe after 1660, but Campanella's own controversy with rhetoric at the beginning of the century proves instructive. As early as 1596 and again at the end of his life in 1634 Campanella lashes out at Ariosto and Tasso, who pursue the fabulous taste of the crowd. Preferring moral weight and religious depth to fashionable aesthetics, he celebrates Dante and his transcending of the conventional.[11] In seeking to define the proper subject for the poet, Campanella radically opposes the resort to classical mythology and expresses a contempt for the fables of Greece. The poet should honor true, public heroes, especially contemporaries: if someone might describe the seamanship of Columbus with that of Magellan, Cortés' conquest of Mexico, or Drake's circumnavigation of the globe interposed as subordinate episodes, thereby imparting the marvelous novelty of the lands, customs, and new peoples, the great ardor and the generous thoughts of the leader, there would be no need to imagine new fables such as the Greeks in describing Jason.[12] Thus Campanella. One need only recall his own rough-hewn sonnets, massive in their moral and religious import, their political and social indignation, to perceive this refreshing anomaly in an age of fashionable, prettified poetry. It

---

[8] Tommaso Campanella, *The City of the Sun: A Poetical Dialogue*, ed. Daniel J. Donno (Berkeley/Los Angeles/London, 1981), 45.

[9] TC-*MS*, 64–65.

[10] Henry Stubbe, *Campanella Revived or an Enquiry into the History of the Royal Society* (London, 1670), 3.

[11] TC-*Po*, 33–38.

[12] Ibid., 82–83.

is true that Campanella here appears not to be taking issue with Renaissance aesthetics but with what they had become in mannerism and the baroque. Nevertheless in his rupture with contemporary practices and the humanistic tradition he asserts a political view of poetry, namely, that it is an instrument of doctrinal and moral management in the hands of the wise legislator.[13] Clearly we are far removed from Renaissance aesthetics. We discover a deliberate turning away from the humanist/rhetorical tradition because it is either frivolous or politically disruptive.

If Campanella divorces himself from our first two characteristics for understanding the Renaissance, he is an ardent champion of our third characteristic —the authority of direct experience. His own empiricism dictates such a position: he affirms that he learns more by examining the anatomy of an ant or a plant than by reading all the books in the world.[14] What exactly does his raw vision reveal? When turned toward the external world of physical reality, this direct experience, glorying in the variety of nature for the entirety of the sixteenth century, misses any method of controllable, repeatable experiment that might provide a rigorous systematic ordering and a productive instrument for new knowledge. Such external sense experience amounts to being visual, autoptic, proving raw and inadequate.[15]

Nevertheless direct experience has a more comprehensive, pervasive significance. For more than anything else it is the epistemological implications of a single event that most impress Campanella. Recurring repeatedly throughout virtually all his works is the reference to Christopher Columbus. That the Genoan proved by his own achievement that the antipodes did exist, despite the claims of St. Augustine and Lactantius to the contrary, establishes definitively for our Calabrian the superiority of direct experience to the books and asseverations of the most august *auctoritates*: the testimony of the senses and of direct experience is to be preferred to the venerable opinions of past sages.[16] The fundamental reality of the individual's experience seems to have survived the vicissitudes of the Renaissance and awaits the disciplining and

---

[13] Ibid., 35.

[14] TC-*Lett.*, 134.

[15] On the cognitive inadequacies of the autoptic experience, see the pungent observations of Frank Lestringant, "L'expérience d'André Thevet: empire de la cosmographie et refus de l'alchimie" and also Michel-Pierre Lerner, "Campanella et Paracelse," both in *Alchimie et philosophie à la Renaissance*, Actes du colloque international de Tours (December 4–7, 1991), ed. Jean-Claude Margolin and Sylvain Matton (Paris, 1993), 289–306, 379–93, esp. 303–4, 287–93. See also more generally Anthony Pagden, *European Encounters with the New World: From Renaissance to Romanticism* (New Haven/London, 1993), chap. 2, esp. 83–85.

[16] For the most reflective statement of this oft-repeated issue, see *Thomae Campanellae Philosophiae Universalis seu metaphysicorum Dogmatum Pars Prima*, I, Proemium (Paris, 1638), fol. 3: "Ecce enim S. Augustinus & Lactantius negant extare Antipodas, & sunt sapientes sancti. Christophorus Columbus navigans in alterum hemispherum testatur extare Antipodas, utri credendum est? . . . profecto peccatum est anteponere opiniones testimoniis."

refinement of the new age. With respect to the naive enthusiasm of their empiricism, Campanella and Bacon share a common horizon.

The immensity of the implications stemming from the authority of direct experience, if it possibly provides a clue to the central import of the Renaissance, must not be allowed to deflect our present enterprise. Nevertheless, if we may indulge momentarily in the fateful practice of the late-sixteenth-century Paduans, the intermediate *negotiatio*, a reflection upon the subjective, inner experience is in order, before passing on.[17] The new identity, singularity, and autonomy afforded to man by nominalism and the resulting implicit authority of the individual's experience promote an overarching reality that inheres to the Renaissance, making it, despite Troeltsch, the true threshold of modernity: the integrity of an inner experience forged from the displacement occasioned by a new perspective and the emerging capacity to appropriate the intellectual attributes from that changed relationship. This perspectival consciousness manifests itself most pungently and dramatically in Copernicus. While displacing the world from its central location in the universe, he nevertheless affirms an anthropocentric consciousness, whereby man can now achieve his ideal goal enunciated earlier by Anaxagoras: to become *contemplator caeli,* the contemplator of an universe that God has constructed according to Copernicus on our account, *for us* (*propter nos*). Thus anthropocentrism becomes detached from physical location, from geocentrism, and finds its proper home in the newly excavated depths of man's thought with its idealization of the world's center. The senses, not reason, have lost their paradise.[18] Perhaps this deepened consciousness is what Burckhardt intended when he spoke of man's subjectivity asserting itself so that he now becomes an intellectual/spiritual individual (*geistiges Individuum*) and recognizes himself as such.[19]

Our argument here is historical and not just apparently logical, not resting merely upon the scattered witnesses of Pico and Ficino or even Giordano Bruno. Consider the following texts from Campanella's great contemporary, Johann Kepler:

> Thus it is apparent that it was not proper for man, the inhabitant of this universe and its destined observer, to live in its inwards as though he were in a sealed room. Under those conditions he would never have succeeded in contemplating

---

[17] Cf. John Herman Randall Jr., "The Development of Scientific Method in the School of Padua," *JHI* 1 (1940): 200–201.

[18] I am here extensively dependent upon Hans Blumenberg, *The Legitimacy of the Modern Age*, trans. Robert M. Wallace (Cambridge, Mass./London, 1983), and by the same author and translator more specifically, *The Genesis of the Copernican World* (Cambridge, Mass./London, 1987), esp. xii, 124–25, 172–75, 188–89, 200–203, 224–25, 319, and the review of the same book by Karsten Harries, "Copernican Reflections," *Inquiry* 23 (1980): 253–69.

[19] Cf. Jacob Burckhardt, *Die Kultur der Renaissance in Italien: Ein Versuch*, 9th ed. (Leipzig, 1904), 1:141.

the heavenly bodies, which are so remote. On the contrary, by the annual revolution of the earth, his homestead, he is whirled about and transported in this most ample edifice, so that he can examine and with utmost accuracy measure the individual members of the house.[20] . . . Moreover, as I said in the "Optics," in the interests of that contemplation for which man was created, and adorned and equipped with eyes, he could not remain at rest in the center. On the contrary, he must make an annual journey on this boat, which is our earth, to perform his observations. So surveyors, in measuring inaccessible objects, move from place to place for the purpose of obtaining from the distance between their positions an accurate base line for the triangulation.[21]

Thus man the observer, the measurer, the surveyor of God's creation. And similarly there comes from the depths of a Neapolitan dungeon the ringing affirmation of our Calabrian prisoner: "Man's knowledge concerns this earth which, admittedly, is a point, if compared to the universe; nevertheless our knowledge pertains to this point, which *for us* is not a point."[22] Through the subjective experience of displacement and enforced perspective the perceiving self is challenged to comprehend and reconstruct the universe imaginatively within his own consciousness. The emerging perspectival consciousness comprises that sense of distance and separation from the classical past which Panofsky defined as being comparable to the fixed distance between the eye and the object in focused perspective; at the same time this new depth to the self posits the need to master and control that other space.[23]

When we arrive at the beginning of the seventeenth century our Renaissance has become an attenuated and fragmented movement, its front broken up by a number of emerging forces: the territorial state, the advance of confessionalism, the increasing preoccupation with matters of natural philosophy. In southern Europe at least the contextual framework remains—the medieval hierarchical/clerical order of power—to be sure, more certain in Campanella's head than on the chessboard of European affairs.

---

[20] Kepler, *Astronomiae Pars Optica*, ed. Franz Hammer, *Gesammelte Werke* (Munich, 1939), 2:277, 21–29, quoted from Edward Rosen, *Kepler's Conversation with Galileo's Sidereal Messenger* (New York/London, 1965), 148, n. 399.

[21] Quoted from ibid., 45 (Both Rosen's translations).

[22] Tommaso Campanella, *Universalis Philosophia*, Monumenta Politica et Philosophica Rariora, ed. L. Firpo, series 1, no. 3 (Turin, 1960), 17 AB; cited in Blumenberg, *Legitimacy*, 515, 655, n. 48, but here my own translation: "scientia hominis est de rebus, quae nobis circumstant; quae licet ad caelum sint quasi punctum, tamen scientia nostra de hoc puncto est, qui nobis non est punctum." Campanella may be here consciously exalting what Seneca had earlier demeaned: "Hoc est illud punctum quod inter tot gentes ferro et igne dividitur? O quam ridiculi sunt mortalium termini!" (*Naturales Quaestiones*, I, Pref. 8–10, trans. Thomas H. Corcoran, Loeb Classical Library 7 [Cambridge, Mass./London, 1971], 6–9).

[23] Erwin Panofsky, *Renaissance and Renascences in Western Art* (Stockholm, 1960), 108; cf. Louis Green, *Chronicle into History* (Cambridge, 1972), 6.

At this point let us attempt to posit three prevailing characteristic features of the late Renaissance, similarly to what we earlier attempted for the Renaissance as a whole but especially for its earlier development. In doing so, we recognize that these principles are even more debatable than those of the first group, for they lack any boundary-maintaining controls and the cluster lacks the earlier internal coherence; because of their very permeability they suggest a transition from the late Renaissance toward a new ordering of reality. If the term did not itself connote a certain linear definition, we would recognize these most arguable features of the late Renaissance as being marginal to its original dynamic, extrinsic rather than intrinsic, more the result of external forces upon the movement than forces inherent in the movement itself. The three together constitute a filter through which European culture is passing at the extreme attenuation of the Renaissance. We deliberately take up an advanced position in our movement as it disintegrates into mannerism, the baroque, and classicism.

First there is a return to speculation and metaphysics—a signal departure from the practical orientation of early humanism despite the very real affiliations of this new development with the original humanism. The conjunction of Medici rule and the abrupt importation of Platonic or more precisely Neoplatonic interests coalesce in the capital of the Renaissance by the midquattrocento to make the concerns of a citizen in an urban republic less relevant in the changed context than the aspirations of a courtier. As evinced in the oration of Pico, there had turned out to be more than one past—in fact a bewildering number together with their sources. Once having turned to the past for its own sake the Renaissance would press on to come up with more than Cicero and Plato but now Epicurus, Archimedes, cabala, Christ (!), and the dark wealth of Hellenistic demonic cosmology that Alexandria inflicts ever anew upon Athens.[24] The ontological extravagancies of Florentine Platonism would produce such intoxicating and exuberant derivatives as Hermeticism, Paracelsism, and the taste for cabala. Speculation and metaphysics, mystery and the occult together with a reinforced astrology predominate.

Subsequently there emerges as our second chief characteristic a delight in the singular, the arcane, the emblematic, the curious. This delight of the virtuoso in his collecting of rarities manifests a direct experience that has allowed perception and curiosity to run riot and to seed in a chance assemblage of curiosities. The oncoming mastery of nature will not lie in this direction. Thus notable, even fateful, is an observation of Francis Bacon in the *New Organon*.

---

[24] On this last point, see of course the classic study of Aby Warburg, "Heidnisch-Antike Weissagung in Wort und Bild zu Luthers Zeiten," *Gesammelte Schriften* (Leipzig/Berlin, 1932), 2:487–558, esp. 534. Admittedly, the present characterization of Alexandria as the source of a kind of spook literature hardly does justice to the mathematical tradition that culminates in the cartography and astronomy of Ptolemy. For its impact on an earlier stage of the Renaissance, see Samuel Y. Edgerton Jr., *The Renaissance Rediscovery of Linear Perspective* (New York, 1975).

Here he abjures those who forsake the ordinary and the common to investigate the less frequent and familiar. In contrast, Bacon's natural history would incorporate an examination of the common: "But I, who am well aware that no judgment can be passed on uncommon or remarkable things, much less anything new brought to light, unless the causes of common things, and the causes of those causes, be first duly examined and found out, am of necessity compelled to admit the commonest things into my history."[25] The statement is all the more striking in that Bacon will shortly afterwards call for the compilation of all monsters and prodigies of nature, whatever rare and unusual.[26] Although we are still a long way from Hume's belief that the passion for the marvelous was the hallmark of the ignorant, distingushing the vulgar from the learned, nevertheless the lord chancellor's exhortation can be taken as the opening wedge of a movement that would ultimately reduce the preternatural and the supernatural to the one natural order.[27]

Finally our third feature that has emerged by the end of the sixteenth century is the discovery and impact of America. We may ask at this point whether the dimension of space must figure into our understanding of the Renaissance. Certainly the temporal dimension with its distinctive perspective upon the past is essential to any understanding of the Renaissance. But what of the spatial dimension? Whatever the actual parochialism of Christianity and of European culture at this stage of their development, there is nothing about the Renaissance, once extended beyond its northern Italian foundations, that must limit it to the European "stockade." Indeed, if any credence is to be given to Michelet's Renaissance as the discovery of the world and of man, then America is the veritable fulfillment of that destiny. Had not Burckhardt begun his "Fourth Part" with Columbus? Yet it would seem that just as the Renaissance's creation of a perspective upon the past would lead to a profusion of pasts that would obscure and confuse the ostensible clarity in perceiving the original norms and models of the movement, threatening to subvert its definition, so now in the very global outreach of the West, the models of classical greatness would be surpassed, producing a liberation from ancient example and thus a further dissolution of this great cultural movement.[28]

---

[25] *The New Organon and Related Writings*, ed. Fulton H. Anderson, trans. James Spedding (Indianapolis/New York, 1960), bk. 1, aph. cxix, p. 109.

[26] Ibid., bk. 2, xx.

[27] Cf. Katherine Park and Lorraine J. Daston, "Unnatural Conceptions: The Study of Monsters in Sixteenth and Seventeenth-Century France and England," *PP* 92 (1981): 20–54, which in fact emphasizes quite properly Bacon's vagrant curiosity rather than his focusing on the common, the ordinary.

[28] The first to broach this problem of the spatial dimension to humanism is, to my knowledge, Alphonse Dupront, "Espace et humanisme," *Bibliothèque d'Humanisme et Renaissance* 8 (1946): 7–104, although differently treated from what is presented here. The image of the stockade for Europe's traditonal mental boundaries obtains from J. H. Elliott's *The Old World and the New* (Cambridge, 1970), 29. On Burckhardt's own failure, however, to incorporate America effectively

Our third feature, the discovery and impact of America, promotes the growing recognition of a global unity and the community of humankind. The revival of Stoicism especially in the hands of the Spanish moral theologians would make intellectual sense out of this immense and unique experience. But more profoundly at the end of the sixteenth century the self-experience and perception of Michel de Montaigne would articulate the universal reality of the common, human stamp. This late product of the Renaissance, if such it may be considered, the aspiration to world community, goes beyond that more benign and certainly nobler aspect of Western society, the passion to communicate and specifically to evangelize. For in its time an appalling amount of intellectual as well as material energy will be mobilized to express that darker aspect inhering therein—the Western passion to exploit, to conquer, to master.[29]

Before allowing our Dominican friar to venture into the murky and increasingly agitated currents of this late Renaissance complex of forces, we need to attend to the challenging statement made forty years ago by the great historian of science, Alexandre Koyré:

> The epoch of the Renaissance was one of the periods least endowed with critical spirit that the world has known. It is the epoch of the grossest and most profound superstition, an epoch where the belief in magic and in witchcraft enjoyed a prodigious expansion and was infinitely more widespread than in the Middle Ages.... [A]strology plays in this epoch a far greater role than astronomy.... And if we consider the literary production of this epoch, it is evident that the beautiful volumes of translations from the classics coming from the Venetian presses do not constitute the great success of the book trade, but rather the works on demonology and magic; it is Cardano and later Della Porta who are the great authors universally read.[30]

In the context of the present issues Koyré's arresting statement proves illuminating with respect both to its insights and to its oversight. The preeminent source of such credulity is Florentine Platonism that produces the great watershed in the development of this cultural movement. Revived Neoplatonism is the culprit. Admittedly, the witch craze cannot be directly attributed to this revival but, if to anything, the bull *Summis desiderantes affectibus* of Innocent VIII (1484) and the publication of the *Mallus maleficarum* (1486). Nevertheless the recovery of Alexandrine thought provided the mental climate and supporting view of nature that helped launch Europe on two centuries of fer-

---

into his understanding of the Renaissance, see the arresting essay of Kenneth R. Bartlett, "Burckhardt's Myopia" (forthcoming).

[29] See Montaigne, "Of Coaches" 3.6 and of course "Of Repentance" 3.2. Cf. also the extraordinary work of Tzvetan Todorov, *The Conquest of America* (New York, 1984).

[30] Alexandre Koyré, "L'apport scientifique de la Renaissance," in *Études d'histoire de la pensée scientifique* (Paris, 1966), 38–47, esp. 38–39.

vid witchhunting. Renaissance Platonism's syncretistic, universalizing tendencies and the neglect of distinction and differentiation reflect a single comprehensive system in which all things are resemblances of one indwelling reality. Nevertheless Koyré has taken a part of the Renaissance, perhaps the most influential part, for the whole. Despite its merits his statement overlooks the fact that before Renaissance Platonism there had been earlier developments within humanism that had possessed a sense of the discrete and had in Lorenzo Valla and shortly thereafter in Poliziano and a wealth of great textual scholars developed the critical, textual techniques associated with the emerging discipline of philology. Not only was the Renaissance at least in one of its major aspects not lacking in critical force, but it would ultimately be this very critical talent of philology which in the person of Isaac Casaubon would puncture the inflated figure of Hermes Trismegistus and its accompanying myths.

For charting and assessing the course of the late Renaissance Koyré's statement has considerable value, despite its exaggerations and prejudices.[31] It suggests a break or serious deflection in this cultural movement occurring in the later Quattrocento. Beyond the immense impact of the Platonic reception at the capital of the Renaissance, beyond the purely intellectual elements in this complex of forces, other developments contribute to the creation of this watershed: the advent of printing at the midpoint of this cultural movement; and the beginning of that shift from the Renaissance urban, republican environment to the court, a harbinger of the later princely baroque culture.[32] Two further points emerge from Koyré's understanding of the Renaissance: first, while proceeding to note a boundless curiosity as a sort of obverse of the medal of Renaissance credulity, he goes on to posit as the prevailing formula for the Renaissance *tout est possible*, which, to the extent that it is true at this stage in the movement, can only hasten the attenuation and incoherence of the Renaissance as a cultural reality; second, there occurs at another level a maturing of a disciplined, controlled experience culminating in the specifically designed and mathematically expressed *experimentum* of Galileo.

Briefly then how does Tommaso Campanella relate to these later trends? To the first, the speculative, quite substantially. Neither a Paracelsian nor a cabalist, Campanella does, however, manifest some interest in Hermetic themes strengthened by his own affinity for Origen and for what would appear to be

[31] For a less sympathetic, more critical consideration of this same passage of Koyré that specifically resurrects Pomponazzi, see Brian P. Copenhaver, "Did Science Have a Renaissance?" *Isis* 83 (1992): 387–407, esp. 390–92.

[32] In his effort to define the baroque apart from the Renaissance, Sergio Bertelli, *Ribelli, libertini e ortodossi nella storiografia barocca* (Florence, 1973), xi–xvii, identifies the latter with the political, ideological, and cultural world of the citizen—the civil, republican, urban. On the advent of printing at the midpoint of the Renaissance time span see Elizabeth Eisenstein, *The Printing Press as an Agent of Change* (Cambridge, 1979), 1:170–80, 296–302.

neo-Gnostic influences. His long years in prison permitted him ample opportunity to give vent to his speculative instincts especially evident in his *Metaphysics* and *Theology*. And his pronounced involvement in astrology and magic remains patent.[33] The concept of man as microcosm, trumpeted by Pico and adhering to so much of the Hermetic as well as Paracelsian literature, does not, however, significantly penetrate Campanella's thought.[34]

In contrast Campanella did not share the age's developing interest in the obscure, the rare. It would seem only in one instance, with respect to the subjects appropriate to true poetry, does he border on a baroque enthusiasm for the marvelous. In his *Poetica* of 1634/1638 Campanella urges that the poem as a magic instrument must be marvelous. The admirable or wondrous as evinced in nature such as the sun, the stars, monsters, or according to recent human ingenuity, such as bombards or the discovery of the New World, or the new heavens and planets by Galileo, Copernicus's construction of the world all lend themselves immediately to the poet: as we have seen, whatever is rare—Joshua's entry into Palestine, the beginning of the Roman Empire, the Spanish entry into America, or above all the achievement of Columbus— offers itself. For whenever the marvelous is lacking, fables take over. Nor would Campanella limit his consideration to the West but is prepared to advance the religious rites and the deeds of the Japanese and the Chinese as suitable subjects, for the good poet ought to speak of all the world.[35] Yet the total import and direction of Campanella's thought with its emphasis upon communication and the creation of a single coherent world order militate against any private lingering over the obscure for its own sake. The man who would reduce all human learning to graphics and depict them on the walls of his city would have neither the patience nor the place for any private enjoyment of rarities.[36] Here indeed Campanella decisively undermines what has been identified as one of the definitive characteristics of the magician's art— the private, secret pursuit of knowledge for a private, individual benefit.[37]

With respect to our third characteristic it is more accurate to speak of Campanella's identification rather than relationship, for his commitment to the

---

[33] See Walker, *Spiritual and Demonic Magic*, 203–36, for the best treatment of Campanella's astrology.

[34] Apparently while perfectly aware of the term *microcosmos* Campanella does not apply it directly to man but prefers the virtually synonymous term *epilogus* in the sense of *compendio* or *ammiratore* of the universe: cf. TC-*DSCM*, 161–62; 331. Indeed avoiding the actual Greek term he will refer to *picciolo mondo* or in TC-*T*, IV/1, (*De homine*), 18, to *parvus mundus*. But cf. also TC-*Meta.*, III, 158–59.

[35] TC-*P*[3], 1040: "pro mirificis canemus peregrina quoque et nova, ut Iaponensium et Chinarum mores et gesta et ritus. Nam bonus pöeta, praesertim epicus, totum mundum introducet." Cf. also chap. 8, n. 47, *supra*.

[36] TC-*CS*, 33–37, 43–45.

[37] On the distinctive feature of magic as the privatization of knowledge, see Vickers, "On the Goals of the Occult Sciences," 68.

unity of humankind at least in the perspective of world evangelization is total and fundamental. As a Dominican he belonged to a tradition of aggressive preaching and proselytizing. As part of the generation associated with and promotive of the *Congregatio de propaganda fide*, and perhaps personally influential in its founding in 1622, he shared in that vast momentum experienced by the Counter Reformation Church to win over the recently discovered populations of the earth. Both his apocalyptic vision and his naturalistic form of Christianity called for the salvation of all men and their incorporation into a single world order. His preoccupation with the realities of global unity is evident in many ways and in most of his works, although in none so specifically as his *Quod reminiscentur* of 1615–18. Here in the second part he fastens upon the issue of the right to communicate with all peoples. To appreciate his exhortation to the emperor of China—to emerge from the cheese of his cocooned isolation—we need only recall how profoundly and distinctively Western this notion is, rooted in Aristotle and impelled by Christian universalism, yet at the same time how intimately Dominican and evangelical. For the great Dominican Francisco de Vitoria in his *De Indis* (3.1.230) had affirmed that whatever meager claims Spain had for being in the New World derived only from the natural right to society and to communication.[38] And yet Campanella's total experience of the impending world unity is not limited to the spiritual and intellectual dimensions; it embraces the material and the very instruments of power. In *The City of the Sun* he speaks of compass, printing press, and arquebus as *segni* of the imminent union of the world.[39] He clearly celebrates a technological as well as a spiritual unification of the world.

In conclusion as we look over our score card, what then is the score? Professor Trevor-Roper has suggested and Professor Lewis Spitz has concurred that the Renaissance had spent itself by 1620.[40] Such agreement among historians, reinforced by the recently noted downturn, both abrupt and lasting, in the number of Latin humanistic books advertised at the Frankfurt Fair after 1630,[41] encourages us to seize a narrow ledge of time on which to construct our answer. We can hazard some conclusions regarding that generation coming to maturity in the first decades of the seventeenth century. Campanella's own creative activity peaked during the first decade itself. We have tried to use his mind as a sort of lens to perceive the kaleidoscopic issues fanning out from one movement, while penetrating and dissolving or being reconstituted into another. If Campanella's mind does not always offer the most accurate and

---

[38] See chap. 8, nn. 42 and 43, *supra*.
[39] TC-*CS*, 121.
[40] Lewis W. Spitz, "The Course of German Humanism," in *Itinerarium Italicum: The Profile of the Italian Renaissance in the Mirror of Its European Tranformations*, ed. H. A. Oberman and T. A. Brady Jr. (Leiden, 1975), 380–81.
[41] Maclean, "Market," 18.

representative of lenses, it is intense and profound in its eccentricity, yet comprehensive in its sweep, revealing some often neglected, deep-seated forces.

Although in its undercurrents and indirect influences no historical movement is entirely obliterated but rather leaves a sediment of human experience for later inspiration, nevertheless as a conscious, coherent movement the Renaissance by the early seventeenth century was being overwhelmed both fore and aft first by the quest for the new, by innovation with or without America, and second by the earlier forces of prophecy, apocalyptic, and confessionalism. The first casualty of these developments was the deliberate appeal to past norms for evocation in the present. While affirming a classical order, the age of growing absolutism presented a hostile face to any potential challenge offered by past models; the American experience and the forward orientation of the moderns further reduced the impact of such norms. Moreover the development of philology, beyond our present survey, would serve to indicate both the inaccessibility as well as the inapplicability of the past and freeze the classical authors in achievements of breathless scholarship.[42] With respect to the humanistic/rhetorical tradition, it would persist, fragmented and attenuated, its individual members bowdlerized, slowly, ever so slowly, giving ground to a new preoccupation and confidence working in its midst. This new sort of learning would later define itself as the scientific and technological tradition, broadly perceived and hailed, if misunderstood, by Campanella. The validity of direct experience did survive, even flourish, and would be developed and refined to become associated with a mathematics of which Campanella was quite innocent. At the same time that more profound, introspective experience of the anthropocentric, perspectival consciousness, already evinced in the high and late Renaissance, would shortly receive its baroque expression in the dreadful grandeur and terrible exaltation manifest in the awareness of that Cartesian *manqué*, Blaise Pascal, as he ponders the eternal silence of those infinite spaces. As for the unity of humankind, its spiritual realization, unachieved by our Calabrian and his age, would continue to elude Western efforts, although the technological unity was in process of realization during Campanella's lifetime. We are reminded of the three primalities, amounting to the modes of God, a veritable Trinity that inspired Campanella's philosophy—Power, Wisdom, and Love, these three. But for Campanella— and here at least so expressive of the Western experience—the greatest of these is Power.

Finally the undercurrents of the prophetic, astrological, and apocalyptic working through the medieval-Renaissance matrix would have their ultimate

---

[42] Discussed by Kenneth C. Schellhase, *Tacitus in Renaissance Political Thought* (Chicago/London, 1976), 136–49; but cf. also Anthony Grafton and Lisa Jardine, *From Humanism to the Humanities* (London, 1986), 160–70, 188–99.

resurgence at midcentury in the course of the English civil war, shortly thereafter to suffer Hobbesian curtailment. But two decades earlier, in Paris, to which Campanella had removed as a final asylum, a new order was beginning to emerge. We catch a fleeting glint of its nature in the correspondence of the newly appointed nuncio extraordinary to the court of Louis XIII, Giulio Mazzarini, soon to be known as Cardinal Mazarin. Having been sent to Paris with the express purpose, among others, of casting a cold eye upon the warm reception given to Campanella and of reporting on the doings of the Calabrian celebrity, Mazzarini would work to contain and reduce the influence of the prophet at court. At one point in the correspondence with his chief at Rome, the secretary of state, and cardinal-nephew, Francesco Barberini, the rising Roman ecclesiastic calculatingly observes in a December 3, 1634 statement portentous of the future: "I am persuaded, however, that the king will not be counseled to tie himself to any resolution based on good constellations and that he will consult what may be most advantageous for him with his prudence and effective powers rather than with those of celestial influence."[43]

At least for some in circles in Paris and also in Rome and shortly to follow in London it may be said that what we understand as the Renaissance together with its medieval undertow, perceived as a composite of cultural forces, was being displaced, transmuted, decisively transformed. For in the chemistry of history can there ever be a terminus to a great movement?

[43] Amab., *Doc.*, II, 226/276.

SELECT BIBLIOGRAPHY

PRIMARY SOURCES

Publisher's names are provided only for imprints prior to 1800.

Acosta, José de. *De procuranda, De natura Novi orbis, libri duo, et de promulgatione evangelii, apud barbaros, sive De procuranda Indorum salute, libri sex.* Salamanca: Guillelmus Foquel, 1589.
Allatii, Leonis. *Apes Urbanae, siue de viris illustribus.* Rome: Ludouicus Grignanus, 1633.
Amabile, Luigi. *Fra T. Campanella: Documenti*, I–II. Naples: Murano, 1882, 1887.
Athanasius, Rhetor. *D. Athanasii rhetoris, presbytere Byzantini, antipatellarces . . . Anticampanella in compendium redactus.* Paris: J. Jacquin, 1655.
Baronius, Caesar. *Annales ecclesiastici.* Bar Le Duc, 1868.
Bellarmine, Robert. *Disputationes Roberti Bellarmini. De controversiis christianae fidei.* Ingolstadt: D. Sartorius, 1590.
Bernard of Clairvaux. *Five Books on Consideration.* Ed. John D. Anderson and Elizabeth T. Kennan. Kalamazoo, Mich., 1976.
Berte, Domenico, ed. *Nuovi documenti su Tommaso Campanella: tratti dal carteggio di Giovanni Fabri per cura di Domenico Berte.* Rome, 1881.
Birgitta, Santa. *Revelationes, olim a Card. Turrecremata recognitae et approbatae et a Consalvo Duranto . . . notis illustratae.* Cologne: Bernard Walter, 1628.
Boecler, Johann Heinrich. *Bibliographia historico-politico philologica curiosa.* Frankfurt: Hamm & Schrey, 1677.
Botero, Giovanni. *Reason of State.* Trans. P. J. and D. P. Waley. New Haven, 1956.
Bruno, Giordano. *Jordani Bruni Nolani Opera Latine Conscripta.* Stuttgart/Bad Connstatt, 1962.
Calancha, Antonio de la. *Coronica moralizada del orden de S. Agustin.* Barcelona/Lima: Prado Pastor, 1638–39.
Cardano, Girolamo. *Opera omnia.* Lyons: A. Ravaud, 1663.
Collectanea S. Congregationis de Propaganda Fide, 1622–1906. Rome, 1907.
Conciliorum oecumenicorum decreta. Ed. Giuseppe Alberigo. Freiburg, 1962.
Costo, Tommaso. *La apologia istorica del regno di Napoli.* Naples: Giovanni Domenico Roncagliolo, 1613.
Crispo, Giovanni Battista. *De ethnicis philosophis caute legendis disputationum ex propriis cuiusque principiis quinarius primus.* Rome: Alois Zannetti, 1594.
Crucé, Emeric. *Le nouveau Cynée ou le discours d'Estat représenté les occasions et les moyens d'Etablir une paix générale et la liberté de commerce par tout le monde.* Paris: Jacques Villery, 1623.
Cyprian, Ern. Sal. "Vita Th. Campanellae." Utrecht: Steph. Neaulinus, 1741.
De Silva, Fray Juan. *Advertencias importantes acerca del buen govierno, y administracion de las indias.* Madrid: Francisco Correa Montenegro, 1621.
Della Porta, Giovanni Battista. *Magiae naturalis libri viginti.* Frankfurt: Andr. Wecheli heredes, 1597.

———. *De humana physiognomonia*. Frankfurt: Jacob Fischer, 1618.
Ferro, Giovanni. *Teatro d'imprese di Giovanni Ferro*. Venice: Giacomo Sarzina, 1623.
Ficino, Marsilio. *Three Books on Life: A Critical Edition and Translation with Introduction and Notes*. Ed. and Trans. Carol V. Kaske and John R. Clark. Binghamton, N.Y., 1989.
Friedberg, Emil, ed. *Corpus iuris canonici: Pars prior Decretum Magistri Gratiani*. 2nd Leipzig ed. Graz, 1955.
Gaffarel, Jacques. *Curiositez inouyes sur la sculpture talismanique des Persanes, horoscope des Patriarches et lecture des estoilles*. Paris: Hervé Du Mesnil, 1629.
———. *Unheard of Curiosities*. Trans. Edmund Chilmead. London: G. D. for H. Moseley, 1650.
Garcia, Gregorio. *Origen de los Indios de el Nuevo Mundo e Indias occidentales*. Valencia: P. P. Mey, 1607.
Hinschius, Paulus, ed. *Decretales Pseudo-Isidorianae et capitula angilramni*. Leipzig, 1863/Aalen, 1963.
Imperato, Ferrante. *Dell'historia naturale libri XXVIII*. Naples: Vitale, 1599.
Kopff, P., ed. *Monita politica ad Sacri Romani Imperii Principes de immensa Curiae Romanae potentia moderanda*. Frankfurt: N. Hoffmann, 1609.
Launoy, Jean de. *De varia Aristotelis in Academia Parisiensi fortuna*. Paris: Edmund Martin, 1662.
———. *Opera omnia*. Vol. 1. Geneva: Fabri & Barrillot, 1731.
Libelli de lite imperatorum et pontificum. Monumenta Germaniae Historica. Vol. 2, Hannover, 1892; vol. 3, Hannover, 1897.
Loys le Roy dict, Regius. *Les politiques d'Aristote*. Paris: Michel de Vas Cosan, 1576.
Luther, Martin. *Werke*. Weimar, 1883– .
Mabillon, Jean. "Réflexions sur les prisons des ordres religieux." In *Ouvrages posthumes de D. Jean Mabillon et de D. Thierri Ruinart, Benedictins de la Congregation de Saint Maur*. Vol 2. Paris: Fr. Babaty et al., 1724. 321–35.
Malvenda, Thomas, O. P. *De Antichristo libri undecim*. Rome: Carolus Vulliettus, 1604.
Mersenne, Marin. *Correspondance du P. Marin Mersenne, religieux minime*. Vols. 1–5. Ed. Cornelius de Waard. Paris, 1932–59.
Motolinía, Toribio de. *Carta al Emperador*. Ed. José Brano Ugarte. Mexico, 1949.
Naigeon, J. A. "Campanella." *Encyclopedie Methodique: Philosophie ancienne et moderne*. Paris: Panckoucke, 1791. 596–608.
Naudé, Gabriel. *Instruction à la France sur la verité de l'histoire des Frères de la Rose-Croix*. Paris: P. Julliot, 1623.
———. *The History of Magic by Way of Apology to All the Wise Men, etc.* Trans. J. Davies. London: John Streater, 1657.
———. *Lettres de Gabriel Naudé à Jacques Dupuy (1632–1652)*. Ed. Phillip Wolfe. Edmonton, Alberta, Canada, 1982.
Patrizi, Francesco. *Nova de universis philosophia*. Ferrara: Benedictus Mammarellus, 1591.
Paulmier de Courtonne, Jean. *Memoires touchant l'etablissement d'une mission chrestienne dans le troisieme monde autrement appelle la terre australe, meridionale, antartique, et inconnuë. Presentez à nostre S. Pere le Pape Alexandre VII par un Ecclesiastique originaire de cette mesme terre*. Paris: Claude Cramoisy, 1663.

Peiresc, Nicolas-Claude Fabri de. *Lettres de Peiresc, 1626–1637*. Vol. 4. Ed. Philippe Tamizey de Larroque. Paris, 1893.
———. *Lettres à Cassiano dal Pozzo, 1626–1637*. Ed. Jean-François Lhote and Danielle Joyal. Clermont-Ferrand, 1989.
Politi, Ambrogio Caterino. *Vita di Santa Caterina*. Trans. Raymundus de Vineis. Siena: Michel Angelo di Bartolomeo, 1524.
Pomponatius, Petrus. *De naturalium effectuum causis sive de Incantationibus*. Hildesheim/New York, 1970; repr. from *Opera*, Basel, 1567.
Postel, Guillaume. *De orbis terrae concordia*. Basel: Oporinus, 1544.
Ptolemy of Lucca. *Trattato del governo de principi di San Tommaso d'Aquino Angelico Dottore al Re di Cipri. Tradotto di Latino in volgare per il Reverendo Don Valentino Averoni Monaco di Vall'Ombrosa, e Moderno Abate di Santa Trinita*. Florence: Giorgio Marescotti, 1577.
Reszka, Stanislaw. *De atheismis et phalerismis evangelicorum libri duo quorum prior de fide posterior tractat de operibus eorum*. Naples: I. I. Carlinus and A. Pacem, 1596.
Sandys, Edwin. *Europae Speculum or a View or Survey of the State of Religion in the Western Parts of the World*. The Hague, 1629.
Sandys, George. *A Relation of a Journey Begun A.D. 1610*. London: W. Barrett, 1615.
Stubbe, Henry. *Campanella Revived or an Inquiry into the History of the Royal Society*. London: The Author, 1670.
Telesio, Bernardino. *De rerum natura iuxta propria principia, libri IX*. Naples: Horatius Salvianus, 1586.

Works of Tommaso Campanella

Aforismi politici con sommari. Ed. Luigi Firpo. Turin, 1941.
Antiveneti. Ed. Luigi Firpo. Florence, 1945.
Apologia pro Galileo. Frankfurt: Godefried Tampach, 1622. In *Opera Latina*, I.
Articuli prophetales. Ed. Germana Ernst. Florence, 1977.
Astrologicorum libri VII (1630). In *Opera Latina*, II.
Atheismus triumphatus. Paris, 1636. (See *Ludovico justo xiii* below.)
Atheismus Triumphatus seu Reductio ad religionem per scientiarum veritates . . . contra Antichristianismum Achitophellisticum. Rome: Zannetti, 1631.
"Cinque lettere inedite di Tommaso Campanella." Ed. Luigi Firpo. *La Rassegna d'Italia* 3 (1948): 271–97.
La città del sole: testo italiano e testo latino. Ed. Norberto Bobbio. Turin, 1941.
La Città del Sole/The City of the Sun. Ed. Daniel J. Donno. Berkeley/Los Angeles/London, 1981.
De civitate Solis (1623). In *Opera Latina*, II.
"Commentaria." In *Opere letterarie di Tommaso Campanella*. Ed. Lina Bolzoni. Turin, 1977.
De Gentilismo non retinendo. Paris, 1636. (See *Ludovico justo xiii* below.)
A Defense of Galileo, the Mathematician from Florence. Trans. Richard Blackwell. Notre Dame/London, 1994.
Della necessità di una filosofia cristiana. Trans. Romano Amerio. Turin, 1953.
Discorsi ai principi d'Italia. Ed. Luigi Firpo. Turin, 1945.

Discorsi universali del governo ecclesiastico per far una gregge e un pastor in *Scritti Scelti di Giordano Bruno e di Tommaso Campanella*. Ed. Luigi Firpo. Turin, 1968.
"Disputatio in prologum instauratarum scientiarum ad scholas christianas praesertim parisienses." In *Thomae Campanellae ordinis praedicatorum disputationum in quatuor partes suae philosophiae realis libri quatuor* . . . Paris: Denis Houssaye, 1637.
La filosofia che i sensi ci additano. Ed. and Trans. Luigi de Franco. Naples, 1974.
Lettere. Ed. Vincenzo Spampanato. Bari, 1927.
Ludovico justo xiii Regi christianissimo . . . *Dedicat Fr. Tommaso Campanella* . . . *tres hosce libello, videlicet: Atheismus Triumphatus*. . . . *De gentilismo non retinendo*. . . . *De praedestinatione*. Paris: Toussaint Dubray, 1636.
Metafisica. Ed. Giovanni di Napoli. 3 vols. Bologna, 1967.
De monarchia hispanica. Amsterdam: L. Elzevir, 1653.
La monarchia di Spagna: Prima stesura giovanile. Ed. Germana Ernst. Naples, 1989.
Monarchia Messiae. Jesi: Gregorio Arnazzino, 1633. (Repr. Ed. Luigi Firpo. Turin, 1960.)
"Le monarchie delle nationi . . ." In *Fra Tommaso Campanella ne' Castelli*. Vol. 2. Ed. Luigi Amabile. Naples, 1887. 299–347.
Philosophia sensibus demonstrata. Naples: Horatius Salvianus, 1591.
Philosophia sensibus demonstrata. Ed. Luigi de Franco. Naples, 1992.
"Poesie." In *Tutte le opere di Tommaso Campanella*. Ed. Luigi Firpo. Verona, 1954.
Poetica. Ed. Luigi Firpo. Rome, 1944.
"Quaestiones super tertia parte suae philosophiae realis, quae est De politicis." In *Disputationum in quatuor partes suae Philosophiae realis libri quatuor*. Paris: Denis Houssaye, 1637.
Quod reminiscentur et convertentur ad dominum universi fines terrae (Psal. xxi). Libri I & II. Ed. Romano Amerio. Padua, 1939. III; *Per la conversione degli Ebreii*. Florence, 1955. IV; *Legazioni ai Maomettani*. Florence, 1960.
"Risposte alle censure dell'Ateismo Triunfato." In *Opuscoli inediti di Tommaso Campanella*. Ed. Luigi Firpo. Florence, 1951.
Del Senso delle cose e della magia. Ed. Antonia Bruers. Bari, 1925.
De sensu rerum et magia (1620). In *Opera Latina*, I.
Teologia. Vol. 1. Ed. Romano Amerio. Milan, 1936. Vols. 2–30. Rome, 1955–80.
Tutte le opere di Tommaso Campanella. Ed. Luigi Firpo. Verona, 1954.

SECONDARY SOURCES

Äkerman, Susanna. "Queen Christina of Sweden and Messianic Thought." In *Sceptics, Millenarians, and Jews*. Ed. David Katz and Jonathan Israel. Leiden, 1990.
Albertoni, Ettore. "Impero e Spagna nel pensiero politico italiano dal XVI al XVII secolo." *IPP* 22 (1989): 20–37.
Allen, Michael J. B. *Nuptial Arithmetic: Marsilio Ficino's Commentary on the Fatal Number in Book VIII of Plato's Republic*. Berkeley/Los Angeles/London, 1994.
Altaner, Berthold. "Sprachstudien und Sprachkenntnisse im Dienste der Mission des 13. und 14. Jahrhunderts." *Zeitschrift für Missionswissenschaft* 21 (1931): 113–36.
Amabile, Luigi. *Fra Tommaso Campanella. La sua congiura, i suoi processi, e la sua pazzia, narrazione con molti documenti inediti politici e giudiziarii* . . . 3 vols. [including *Documenti* I = Doc. I]. Naples, 1882.

―――. *Fra Tommaso Campanella, ne' Castelli di Napoli, in Roma ed in Parigi; Narrazione con molti documenti* . . . 2 vols. [including *Documenti* II = Doc. II]. Naples, 1887.
Amerio, Romano. "L'opera teologico-missionaria di Tommaso Campanella nei primordi di Propaganda Fide." *AFP* 5 (1935): 174–93.
―――. "Tommaso Campanella, Mathematica." *AFP* 5 (1935): 194–240.
―――. "Circa il significato delle variazioni redazionali nell'elaborazione del 'Reminiscentur' di Fra Tommaso Campanella." *Sophia: Rivista internazionale di filosofia e storia della filosofia* 7 (1939): 419–53.
―――. "L'ultima forma del mito solare nella teologia politica di Fra Tommaso Campanella." *Jahrbuch der schweizerischen philosophischen Gesellschaft* 4 (1944): 28–59.
―――. *Introduzione alla teologia di Tommaso Campanella.* Turin, 1948.
―――. "Un'altra confessione dell'incredulità giovanile del Campanella." *RFNs* 45 (1953): 75–77.
―――. "Sulla redazione primitiva dell'*Atheismus Triumphatus* del Campanella." *RFNs* 47 (1955): 154–64.
―――. "L'enciclopedia della scienze nel pensiero di Tommaso Campanella." *Filosofia* 17 (1966): 157–80.
―――. *Il sistema teologico di Tommaso Campanella.* Milan/Naples, 1972.
Armas Medina, Fernando de. *Cristianizacion del Peru (1532–1600).* Seville, 1953.
Arnold, Paul. *La Rose-Croix et ses rapports avec la Franc-Maçonnerie: Esprit de synthèse historique.* Paris, 1970.
Arquillière, H. X. "Sur la formation de la 'Théocratie' Pontificale." In *Mélanges d'histoire du Moyen Age offerts à M. Ferdinand Lot.* Paris, 1925. 1–25.
Ashworth, William B., Jr. "Catholicism and Early Modern Science." In *God and Nature.* Ed. David C. Lindberg and Ronald L. Numbers. Berkeley, 1986.
Astarita, Tommaso. *The Continuity of Feudal Power: The Caracciolo di Brienza in Spanish Naples.* Cambridge, 1992.
Aston, Margaret E. "The Fiery Trigon Conjunction: An Elizabethan Astrological Prediction." *Isis* 61 (1970): 159–87.
Atkinson, Geoffrey. *Les nouveaux horizons de la Renaissance française.* Paris, 1935.
Bacco, Enrico, Cesare D'Engenio Caracciolo, et al. *Naples: An Early Guide.* Ed. and trans. Eileen Gardiner. New York, 1991.
Badaloni, Nicola. "I fratelli Della Porta e la cultura magica e astrologica a Napoli nel '500." *SS* 1 (1959–60): 677–715.
―――. "L'influenza di Giovanni Pico sulla giovanile 'Philosophia sensibus demonstrata' del Campanella." In *L'opera e il pensiero di Giovanni Pico della Mirandola nella storia dell'umanesimo: Convegno internazionale*: Mirandola, 15–18 Settembre, 1963. Vol. 2. Florence, 1965. 373–88.
―――. *Tommaso Campanella.* Milan, 1965.
―――. "Il programma scientifico di un bruniano: Colantonio Stelliola," *SS* 26 (1985): 161–75.
Baldini, A. Enzo. *Puntigli spagnoleschi e intrighi politici nella Roma di Clemente VIII: Girolamo Frachetta e la sua relazione del 1603 sui cardinali.* Milan: Franco Angeli, 1981.
Barnes, Robin Bruce. *Prophecy and Gnosis: Apocalypticism in the Wake of the Lutheran Reformation.* Stanford, 1988.

Bataillon, Marcel. "Novo Mundo e fim do Mundo." *Revista de Historia* 8 (1954): 343–51.

———. "La herejía de Fray Francisco de la Cruz y la reacción antilascasiana." *Études sur Bartholomé de Las Casas*. Paris, 1965. 309–24.

Battistini, Andrea. "'Cedat Columbus' e 'Vicisti, Galilaee!': due esplorati a confronto nell'imaginario barocco." *Annali d'Italianistica* 10 (1992): 116–32.

Baumgartner, Frederick. "Galileo's French Correspondents." *Annals of Science* 45 (1988): 169–82.

Beaulieu, Armand. "Les réactions des savants français au début du XVIIe siècle devant l'heliocentrisme de Galilée." In *Novità celesti e crisi del sapere: Atti del convegno di studi Galileiani*. Ed. P. Galluzzi. Florence, 1984. 373–82.

Beckman, Jean. "La congrégation de la Propagation de la foi face à la politique internationale." *NZfMW* 19/4 (1963): 241–71.

Bedford, R. D. *The Defense of Truth: Herbert of Cherbury and the Seventeenth Century*. Manchester, 1979.

Berte, Domenico, ed. *Nuovi documenti su Tommaso Campanella: tratti dal carteggio di Giovanni Fabri per cura di Domenico Berte*. Rome, 1881.

Bertelli, Sergio. "Presentazione." In *Il libertinismo in Europa*. Milan/Naples, 1980. 3–24.

Biagioli, Mario. "Galileo's System of Patronage." *History of Science* 28 (1990): 1–62.

———. *Galileo, Courtier: The Practice of Science in the Culture of Absolutism*. Chicago/London, 1993.

Bianchi, Luca. "*La Apologia pro Galileo* e la condonna di Tommaso d'Aquino." *Intersezione: Rivista di storia delle idee* 2 (1982): 179–90.

———. *L'inizio dei tempi: Antichità e novità del mondo da Bonaventura a Newton*. Florence, 1987.

Bireley, Robert, S.J. *The Counter-Reformation Prince: Anti-Machiavellianism or Catholic Statecraft in Early Modern Europe*. Chapel Hill/London, 1990.

Black, Christopher. "Perugia and Post-Tridentine Church Reform." *Journal of Ecclesiastical History* 35 (1984): 429–51.

Blackwell, Richard J. *Galileo, Bellarmine and the Bible*. Notre Dame/London, 1991.

Blanchet, Léon. *Les antécedents historiques du 'Je pense, donc je suis.'* Paris, 1920.

———. *Campanella*. New York/Paris, 1920.

Blet, Pierre, S.J. "Richelieu et les débuts de Mazarin." *Revue d'histoire moderne et contemporaine* 6 (1959): 241–68.

Bleznick, Donald W. "Spanish Reaction to Machiavelli in the Sixteenth and Seventeenth Centuries." *JHI* 19 (1958): 542–50.

Blumenberg, Hans. *The Legitimacy of the Modern Age*. Trans. Robert M. Wallace. Cambridge, Mass./London, 1983.

———. *The Genesis of the Copernican World*. Cambridge, Mass./London, 1987.

Blunt, Anthony. *Nicholas Poussin*. New York, 1967.

Bock, Gisela. "Bemerkungen zur neueren Campanella-Forschungen." *Quellen und Forschungen aus Italienischen Archiven und Bibliotheken* 51 (1971): 390–421.

———. *Thomas Campanella: Politisches Interesse und philosophische Spekulation*. Tübingen, 1974.

Bolzoni, Lina. "La restaurazione della poesia nella prefazione dei 'Commentaria' campanelliani." *Annali della scuola normale superiore di Pisa: Classe di lettere e filosophia*, 3rd ser., 1 (1971): 307–44.

———. "La poetica latina di Tommaso Campanella." *GSLI* 149 (1972): 481–521.

———. "I 'Commentaria' di Campanella ai 'Poëmata' di Urbano VIII." *Rinascimento* 28 (1988): 113–32.

———. "Tommaso Campanella e le donne: fascino e negazione della differenza." *Annali d'Italianistica* 7 (1989): 193–216.

Bonansea, Bernardino M. "Campanella as a Forerunner of Descartes." *Franciscan Studies* 16 (1956): 37–59.

———. *Tommaso Campanella: Renaissance Pioneer of Modern Thought*. Washington, D.C., 1969.

———. "Campanella's Defense of Galileo." In *Reinterpreting Galileo: Studies in Philosophy and the History of Philosophy*. Vol. 15. Ed. William A. Wallace. Washington, D.C., 1986. 205–39.

Bosbach, Franz. "Monarchia universalis: Ein politischer Leitbegriff der frühen Neuzeit." *Schriftenreihe der Historischer Kommission bei der bayerischer Akademie der Wissenschaft*, 32. Bonn, 1986.

Bouwsma, William J. *Concordia Mundi: The Career and Thought of Guillaume Postel (1510–1581)*. Cambridge, Mass., 1957.

———. *Venice and the Defense of Republican Liberty: Renaissance Values in the Age of the Counter Reformation*. Berkeley/Los Angeles, 1968.

Boxer, C. R., and J. S. Cummins. "The Dominican Mission in Japan (1602–1622) and Lope de Vega." *AFP* 30 (1963): 5–88.

Brackett, John K. *Criminal Justice and Crime in Late Renaissance Florence, 1537–1609*. Cambridge, 1992.

Brading, D. A. *The First America*. Cambridge, 1990.

Bradner, Leicester. "Columbus in Sixteenth-Century Poetry." In *Essays Honoring Lawrence C. Wroth*. Portland, Maine, 1951. 15–30.

Braudel, Fernand. *The Mediterranean and the Mediterranean World in the Age of Phillip II*. Vol. 1. New York, 1972.

Brockliss, L. W. B. "Aristotle, Descartes and the New Science: Natural Philosophy at the University of Paris, 1600–1740." *Annals of Science* 38 (1981): 33–69.

———. "Philosophy Teaching in France, 1600–1740." *History of Universities*, 1 (1981): 131–68.

Brotóns, Victor Navarro, and José M. López-Piñero. "Galileo in Spain." In *Firenze e la Toscana dei Medici nell'Europa del '500*. Vol. 2. Florence, 1983. 763–76.

Buck, August. "Traiano Boccalini (1556–1613) als Zeitkritiker." In *Das Ende der Renaissance: Europäische Kultur um 1600*. Ed. August Buck and Tibor Klaniczey. Wiesbaden, 1987. 37–48.

———. "Introduction." In *Die okkulten Wissenschaften in der Renaissance*. Ed. August Buck. Wiesbaden, 1992.

Buhler, Stephen M. "Marsilio Ficino's 'De stella magorum' and Renaissance Views of the Magi." *RQ* 43/2 (1990): 348–71.

Burckhardt, Carl J. *Richelieu and His Age*, vol. 3, *Power, Politics and the Cardinal's Death*. Trans. Bernard Hay. New York, 1965.

Burke, Peter. "Donec Aufertur Luna: The Facade of S. Maria della Pace." *JWCI* 44 (1981): 238–39.

———. "Southern Italy in the 1590s: Hard Times or Crisis?" In *The European Crisis of the 1590s: Essays in Comparative History*. Ed. Peter Clark. London, 1985. 177–90.

Büttner, M. "The Significance of the Reformation for the Reorientation of Geography in Lutheran Germany." *History of Science* 17 (1979): 151–69.

Calabria, Antonio. *The Cost of Empire: The Finances of the Kingdom of Naples in the Time of Spanish Rule*. Cambridge, 1991.

Calabria, Antonio, and John A. Marino, eds. *Good Government in Spanish Naples*. New York, 1990.

Capp, Bernard. *Astrology and the Popular Press, 1500–1800*. London/Boston, 1979.

Caprariis, Vittorio de. "Libertinage e libertinismo." *Letterature Moderne*, 2 (1951): 241–61.

Caraman, Philip. *The Lost Paradise: An Account of the Jesuits in Paraguay, 1607–1768*. London, 1975.

Carusi, Enrico. "Nuovi Documenti sui processi di Tommaso Campanella." *GCFI* 8 (1927): 321–59.

Casado Soto, José Luis. "Atlantic Shipping in Sixteenth-Century Spain and the 1588 Armada." In *England, Spain and the Gran Armada, 1585–1604: Essays from the Anglo-Spanish Conferences, London and Madrid, 1988*. Ed. M. J. Rodríguez-Salgado and Simon Adams. Savage, Md., 1991. 95–133.

Causa, Raffaelo. *L'arte nella Certosa di San Martino a Napoli*. Naples, 1973.

Chabod, Federico. *Scritti sul Rinascimento*. Turin, 1967.

Clark, Elizabeth A. "The Virginal Politeia and Plato's *Republic*: John Chrysostom on Women and the Sexual Relation." In *Jerome, Chrysostom and Friends: Essays and Translations*. New York/Toronto, 1979. 1–34.

Clarke, Angus G. "Metoposcopy: An Art to Find the Mind's Construction in the Forehead." In *Astrology, Science and Society: Historical Essays*. Ed. Patrick Curry. Bury St. Edmunds, Suffolk, 1987. 171–95.

Clayton, Lawrence A. "Ships and Empire: The Case of Spain." *Mariner's Mirror* 62 (1976): 235–48.

Clubb, Louise George. *Giambattista Della Porta, Dramatist*. Princeton, 1965.

Cochrane, Eric. "The End of the Renaissance in Florence." *BHR* 27 (1965): 1–29.

Cohn, Norman. "Medieval Millenarism: Its Bearing on the Comparative Study of Millenarian Movements." In *Millennial Dreams in Action*. Ed. Sylvia L. Thupp. The Hague, 1962. 31–43.

Copenhaver, Brian P. "Iamblichus, Synesius and the Chaldean Oracles in Marsilio Ficino's *De vita libri tres*: Hermetic Magic or Neo-Platonic Magic?" In *Supplementum Festivum: Studies in Honor of Paul Oskar Kristeller*. Ed. James Hankins, John Monfasani, and Frederick Purnell Jr. Binghamton, N.Y., 1987. 441–55.

———. "The Italian Philosophers of Nature and the Fate of the Occult Philosophy: Tommaso Campanella and the Metaphysical Decay of Magic." Unpublished paper, May 6, 1988.

———. "Did Science Have a Renaissance?" *Isis* 83 (1992): 387–407.

Copenhaver, Brian P., and Charles B. Schmitt. *A History of Renaissance Philosophy*, vol. 3, *Renaissance Philosophy*. Oxford, 1992.

Corbett, Theodore G. "The Cult of Lipsius." *JHI* 36 (1975): 139–52.
Corsano, Antonio. "Per la storia del pensiero del tardo Rinascimento: G.B. della Porta." *GCFI* 38 (1959): 76–97.
———. "Campanella e Galileo." *GCFI* 44 (1965): 313–32.
———. "Campanella e Copernico." *GCFI* 53 (1974): 438–42.
Costa, Dennis. "Poetry and Gnosticism: The *Poetica* of Tommaso Campanella." *Viator* 15 (1984): 405–18.
Courtenay, William. "Bellarmine on the Indirect Power." *Theological Studies* 8 (1948): 491–535.
Cozzi, Gaetano. *Paolo Sarpi tra Venezia e l'Europa*. Turin, 1979.
Cozzi, Gaetano and Luisa, eds. *Paolo Sarpi, Pensieri*. Turin, 1976.
Crahay, Roland. *D'Erasme à Campanella*. Brussels, 1985.
Creytens, Raymond, O. P. "Les constitutions des Frères Prêcheurs dans la rédaction de S. Raymond de Peñafort (1241)." *AFP* 18 (1948): 5–68.
Cro, Stelio. "Storia, letteratura e scienza nella 'Città del Sole' di Tommaso Campanella." In *Letteratura e scienza nella storia della cultura italiana: Atti del IX congresso dell'associazione internazionale per gli studi di lingua e letteratura italiana*. Palermo, 1978. 511–18.
———. *Tommaso Campanella e i prodormi della civiltà moderna*. Hamilton, 1979.
———. *The American Foundations of the Hispanic Utopia*. 2 vols. Tallahassee, Fla., 1994.
Crombie, Alistair C. "Experimental Science and the Rational Artist." *Daedalus* 115/3 (1986): 49–74.
Cummins, J. S. "Palafox, China and the China Rites Controversy." *Revista de Historia de América* 52 (1961): 395–427.
———. *Travels and Controversies of Friar Domingo Navarrete (1618–1686)*. Cambridge, 1961.
———. "The Dominican Mission in Japan (1602–1622) and Lope de Vega." *AFP* 33 (1963): 5–88.
———. "Two Missionary Methods in China: Mendicants and the Jesuits." *Archivo Ibero-Americano* 38 (1978): 33–108.
Curtius, Ernst Robert. *European Literature and the Latin Middle Ages*. Trans. Willard R. Trask. New York, 1953.
D'Addio, Mario. *Il pensiero politico di Gaspare Scioppio e il Machiavellismo dei Seicento*. Milan, 1962.
———. "Considerazioni sui processi a Galileo." *Rivista di Storia della Chiesa in Italia* 38 (1984): 47–114.
Dagens, Jean. "Hermétisme et Cabale en France de Lefèvre d'Étaples à Bossuet." *Revue de Litterature Comparée* 35/1 (1961): 5–16.
Dainville, François, de., S.J. *La géographie des humanistes*. Paris, 1940.
Damiani, Rolando. "Rassegna campanelliana." *Lettere italiane* 30 (1978): 546–65.
Daniel, E. Randolph. *The Franciscan Concept of Mission in the High Middle Ages*. Lexington, Ky., 1975.
Daston, Lorraine J., and Katherine Park. "Unnatural Conceptions: The Study of Monsters in Sixteenth and Seventeenth-Century France and England." *PP* 92 (1981): 20–54.
Davidson, Georgiana. "Caesar Baronius and the Catholic Renewal: History and Piety

in the Post-Tridentine Era." Unpublished Ph.D. diss., University of California–Berkeley, 1981.
Davidson, Nicholas. "Unbelief and Atheism in Italy, 1500–1700." In *Atheism from the Reformation to the Enlightenment*. Ed. Michael Hunter and David Wootton. Oxford, 1992.
Davis, Charles T. "Ptolemy of Lucca and the Roman Republic." *Proceedings of the American Philosophical Society* 118 (1974): 30–50.
———. "Roman Patriotism and Republican Propaganda: Ptolemy of Lucca and Pope Nicholas III." *Speculum* 50 (1975): 410–33.
De Armas, Frederick A. *The Return of Astraea: An Astral Imperial Myth in Calderon*. Lexington, Ky., 1986.
De Franco, Luigi. *Introduzione a Bernardino Telesio*. Messina, 1995.
De Giovanni, Biagio. "Lo spazio della vita fra Giordano Bruno e Tommaso Campanella." *Centauro: Rivista di filosofia e teoria politica* 11–12 (1984): 3–32.
De Grazia, Margreta. "The Secularization of Language in the Seventeenth Century." *JHI* 41 (1980): 319–29.
De Mas, Enrico. "Antilia e Macaria: due progetti di società cristiana nel Seicento." *IPP* 9 (1976): 339–64.
———. *L'attesa del secolo aureo (1603–1625)*. Florence, 1982.
De Mattei, Rodolfo. "La 'Monarchia di Spagna' di Campanella e la 'Ragione di Stato' di Botero." *Rendiconti della Accademia nationale dei Lincei: Classe di scienze, morali storiche e filologiche*, ser. 6 (1927): 432–85.
———. *La Politica di Campanella*. Rome, 1928.
———. "Contenuto ed origini dell'ideale universalista nel Seicento." *Rivista internazionale di filosofia del diritto* 10 (1930): 391–401.
———. "Manipolazioni, falsificazioni, plagi nel Seicento." *Accademie e biblioteche d'Italia* 5 (1931): 75–78.
———. "Nuove richerche sui codici della 'Monarchia di Spagna" di Tommaso Campanella." *GCFI* 14 (1933): 456–65.
———. "Polemiche secentesche italiane sulla 'Monarchia universale,'" *ASI* 110 (1953): 145–65.
———. "Il mito della Monarchia Universale nel pensiero politico italiano del Seicento." *Rivista di studi politici internazionali* 32 (1965): 531–50.
———. "Le edizioni inglesi della *Monarchia di Spagna* di Tommaso Campanella." *GCFI* 23 (1969): 194–205.
———. *Studi Campanelliani*. Florence, 1934.
———. "Nota sul pensiero politico di T. Campanella (con tre lettere inedite)." In *Campanella e Vico: Atti del convegno internazionale*. Rome, 1969. 67–108.
Dentice di Accadia, Cecilia. "Tomismo e Machiavellismo nella concezione politica di Tommaso Campanella." *GCFI* 6 (1925): 1–16.
Despland, Michel. *La Religion en Occident. Evolution des idées et du vécu*. Montreal, 1979.
Diez del Corral, Luis. "Campanella entre la monarquía española y la francesa." In *Campanella e Vico: Atti del convegno internazionale sul tema, Roma, 12–15 maggio, 1968*. Rome, 1969.
———. *La monarquía hispánica en el pensamiento político europeo: De Maquiavelo a Humboldt*. Madrid, 1975.

Dillenberger, John. *Protestant Thought and Natural Science*. New York, 1960.
Dolcini, Carlo. "'Eger cui lenia' (1245/46): Innocent IV, Tolomeo da Lucca, Guglielmo d'Ockham." *Rivista di storia della chiesa in Italia* 29 (1975): 127–48.
Donnelly, John Patrick, S.J. "Antonio Possevino's Plan for World Evangelization." *CHR* 74 (1988): 179–98.
Dooley, Brendan. "Social Control and the Italian Universities: From Renaissance to Illuminismo." *The Journal of Modern History* 61 (1989): 205–39.
Dornseiff, Franz. "Der-ismus." In *Sprache und Sprechender*. Ed. Jürgen Werner. Leipzig, 1964. 319–29.
Duchhardt, Heinz. *Protestantisches Kaisertum und altes Reich: Die Diskussion über die Konfession des Kaisers in Politik, Publizistik und Staatsrecht*. Wiesbaden, 1977.
Ducros, François. *Tommaso Campanella, Poète*. Paris, 1969.
Dülmen, Richard van. *Die Utopie einer christlichen Gesellschaft. Johann Valentin Andreae (1586–1654)*. Vol. 1. Stuttgart/Bad Connstatt, 1978.
Dupront, Alphonse. "De la Chretienté à l'Europe: La passion westphalienne du nonce Fabio Chigi." In *Forschungen und Studien zur Geschichte des Westfälischen Friedens*. Ed. Max Braubach. Münster, 1965. 49–84.
———. "Croisade et Eschatologie." In *Umanesimo et Esoterismo*. Padua, 1960. 175–98.
Dvornik, Francis. *The Photian Schism: History and Legend*. Cambridge, 1948.
Eamon, William. "Technology as Magic in the Late Middle Ages and the Renaissance." *Janus* 70 (1983): 171–212.
———. "Arcana Disclosed: The Advent of Printing, the Books of Secrets, Tradition and the Development of Experimental Science in the Sixteenth Century." *History of Science* 22 (1984): 111–50.
———. "Court, Academy and Printing House: Patronage and Scientific Careers in Later Renaissance Italy." In *Patronage and Institutions: Science, Technology and Medicine at the European Court, 1500–1750*. Ed. Bruce T. Moran. Suffolk, 1991.
———. *Science and the Secrets of Nature: Books of Secrets in Medieval and Early Modern Culture*. Princeton, 1994.
———. "Natural Magic and Utopia in the Cinquecento: Campanella, the Della Porta Circle, and the Revolt of Calabria." Forthcoming.
Eamon, William, and Françoise Paheau. "The Accademia Segreta of Girolamo Ruscelli: A Sixteenth-Century Italian Scientific Society." *Isis* 75 (1984): 327–42.
Edelstein, Ludwig. "The Function of the Myth in Plato's Philosophy." *JHI* 10/4 (1949): 463–81.
Eliav-Feldon, Miriam. *Realistic Utopias: The Ideal Imaginary Societies of the Renaissance, 1516–1630*. Oxford, 1982.
———. "Universal Peace for the Benefit of Trade: The Vision of Émeric Crucé." In *Religion, Ideology and Nationalism in Europe and America: Essays Presented in Honor of Yehoshua Arieli*. Jerusalem, 1986. 29–44.
Eliav-Feldon, Miriam, and Élie Barnavé. *Le périple de Francesco Pucci: Utopie, hérésie et verité religieuse dans la Renaissance tardive*. Saint-Amant-Montrond Cher, 1988.
Elliott, J. H. "The Discovery of America and the Discovery of Man." *Proceedings of the British Academy* 58 (1972): 101–25.

Ernst, Germana. "Aspetti dell'astrologia e della profezia in Galileo and Campanella." In *Novità celesti e crisi del sapere: Atti del convegno di studi Galileiani*. Ed. P. Galluzzi. Florence, 1984.

———. "Campanella e il *De tribus impostoribus*." *Nouvelles de la Republique des Lettres* 6/2 (1986): 143–70.

———. "L'edizione dell' 'Atheismus Triumphatus' di Tommaso Campanella. Varianti e censure." In *Le edizione dei testi filosofici e scientifici del '500 e del '600: problemi di metodo e prospettive*. Milan, 1986. 113–22.

———. "From the Watery Trigon to the Fiery Trigon: Celestial Signs, Prophecies and History." In *'Astrologi Hallucinati': The Stars and the End of the World in Luther's Time*. Ed. Paola Zambelli. Berlin/New York, 1986.

———. "La Ruse et la nature; Remarques sur le rapport Campanella/Machiavel en marge de la *Monarchie d'Espagne*." *Revue des sciences, philosophiques et theologiques* 72 (1988): 252–62.

———. "Monarchia di Cristo e nuovo mondo. Il 'Discorso delle ragione che ha il re cattolico sopra il nuovo emisfero' di Tommaso Campanella." In *Studi politici in onore di Luigi Firpo*. Vol. 2. Ed. Silvia Roti Ghibaudi and Franco Barcia. Milan, 1990. 11–36.

———. "Astrology, Religion and Politics in Counter-Reformation Rome." In *Science, Culture and Popular Belief in Renaissance Europe*. Ed. Stephen Pumfrey, Paolo L. Rossi, and Maurice Slawinski. Manchester/New York, 1991. 249–73.

———. *Religione, ragione e natura: Ricerche su Tommaso Campanella e il tardo Rinascimento*. Milan, 1991.

———. "Il Ritrovato 'Apologeticum' di Campanella al Bellarmino in difesa della religione naturale." *RSF* 47/3 (1992): 565–86.

Ernst, Germana, and Eugenio Canone, eds. "Una lettera ritrovata: Campanella a Peiresc, 19 giugno 1636." *RSF* 49/2 (1994): 353–66.

Eszer, Ambrogio, O.P. "Niccolo Riccardi, O.P.—padre Mostro." *Angelicum* 60 (1983): 428–61.

Feingold, Mordechai, ed. *The Jesuits and the Scientific Revolution*. Princeton, 1994.

Femiano, S. "L'Antiaristotelismo essenziale di Tommaso Campanella." *Sapienza* 22 (1969): 137–59.

Fernandez Alvarez, Manuel. *Politica mundial de Carlos V y Felipe II*. Madrid, 1966.

Ferrone, Vincenzo. "Galileo tra Paolo Sarpi e Federico Cesi. Premesse per una ricerca." In *Novità celesti e crisi del sapere: Atti del convegno di studi Galileiani*. Ed. P. Galluzzi. Florence, 1984. 239–54.

Field, J. V. "Cosmology in the Work of Galileo and Kepler." In *Novità celesti e crisi del sapere: Atti del convegno di studi Galileiani*. Ed. P. Galluzzi. Florence, 1984. 207–16.

———. "A Lutheran Astrologer: Johannes Kepler." *Archive for History of Exact Sciences* 31 (1984): 189–272.

———. "Astrology in Kepler's Cosmology." In *Astrology, Science and Society: Historical Essays*. Ed. Patrick Curry. Bury St. Edmunds, Suffolk, 1987. 143–70.

Findlen, Paula. *Possessing Nature: Museums, Collecting, and Scientific Culture in Early Modern Italy*. Berkeley/Los Angeles/London, 1994.

Firpo, Luigi. "Il Campanella astrologo e i suoi persecutori romani." *RF* 30 (1939): 200–215.

———."Il Campanella scrittore di cose militari e un inedito discorso giovanile." *GCFI* 20 (1939): 472–80.

———. "I primi processi campanelliani in una ricostruzione unitaria." *GCFI* 20 (1939): 5–43.

———. "A proposito del *Quod Reminiscentur* di Tommaso Campanella." *GCFI* 21 (1940): 268–79.

———. "Appunti campanelliani: due documenti sul processo del 1594." *GCFI* 21 (1940): 431–51.

———. "Una autoapologia del Campanella." *RF* 32 (1941): 96–110.

———. "Appunti campanelliani." *GCFI* 24 (1943): 180–92.

———. "L'opera omnia di Tommaso Campanella nei programmi dell'autore." *RCSF* 2 (1947): 38–59.

———. "Un memoriale inedito e un indice delle opere di Tommaso Campanella." *RF* 38 (1947): 213–29.

———. *Ricerche Campanelliane, con undici tavole fuori testo*. Florence, 1947.

———. "Il processo di Giordano Bruno." *RSI* 60 (1948): 542–97; 61 (1949): 5–59.

———. "Cinque lettere inedite di Tommaso Campanella." *La Rassegna d'Italia* 3 (1948): 271–96.

———. "Processo e morte di Francesco Pucci." *RF* 40 (1949): 371–405.

———. "Appunti campanelliani." *GCFI* 29 (1950): 68–95.

———. "Il '*De conceptione Virginis*' ritrovato: Appunti campanelliani." *GCFI* 29 (1950): 68–76.

———. "Filosofia Italiana e Controriforma." *RF* 41 (1950): 150–73, 390–401.

———. "Appunti campanelliani." *GCFI* 30 (1951): 509–24.

———. "Appunti campanelliani." *GCFI* 31 (1952): 331–43.

———. "Appunti campanelliani, XXII: Un opere che Campanella non scrisse: Il 'Discorso sui Paese Bassi." *GCFI* 31 (1952): 331–43.

———. "Il fior fiore della cultura italiana secondo un diplomatico inglese del primo Seicento." *GSLI* 129 (1952): 108–11.

———. "Appunti campanelliani: Un memoriale inedito dalla fossa di Castel S. Elmo." *GCFI* 32 (1953): 474–87.

———. "Campanella nel Settecento." *Rinascimento* 4 (1953): 105–54.

———. "Cinquant'anni di studio sul Campanella (1901–1950)." *Rinascimento* 6 (1955): 209–348.

———. "Appunti campanelliani." *GCFI* 35 (1956): 541–49.

———. "Un decennio di studi sul Campanella (1951–1960)." *Studi secenteschi* 1 (1960): 125–64.

———. "Appunti e documenti: Gli ultimi scritti politici di Tommaso Campanella." *RSI* 73 (1961): 772–801.

———. "Appunti campanelliani." *GCFI* 41 (1962): 364–404.

———. "La cité idéale de Campanella et le culte du soleil." *Le Soleil à la Renaissance: Science et Mythos Colloque Internationale, 1963*. Brussels/Paris, 1965. 325–40.

———. "Pico come modello dello scienziato nel Campanella." In *L'opera e il pensiero di Giovanni Pico della Mirandola nella storia dell'umanesimo: Convegno internazionale: Mirandola 15–18 settembre, 1963*. Vol. 2. Florence, 1965. 362–67.

———. "Nuove ricerche su Francesco Pucci." *RSI* 79 (1967): 1053–74.

Firpo, Luigi. "Tommaso Campanella e i Colonnesi." *IPP* 1 (1968): 93–116.

———. "Campanella e Galileo." *Atti dell'Accademia di scienze morali. Classe scienze morali, storiche e filologiche* 103 (1969): 49–69.

———. "Un opuscolo del Campanella sul conclave." *IPP* 6 (1973): 235–41.

———. "Campanella, Tommaso." *DBI*. Vol. 17. Rome, 1974. 372–401.

———. "Versioni poetiche campanelliane." *GSLI* 153 (1976): 230–42.

———. "Tobia Adami e la fortuna del Campanella in Germania." In *Storia e cultura del mezzogiorno: Studi in memoria di Umberto Caldora*. Cosenza, 1978. 77–118.

———. "Campanella contro Aristotele in difesa della 'Città del Sole.'" *IPP* 15 (1982): 375–89.

———. *Il supplizio di Tommaso Campanella: Narrazioni, documenti, verbali delle torture*. Rome, 1985.

———. "Idee politiche di Tommaso Campanella nel 1636: due memoriali inedite." *IPP* 19 (1986): 197–221.

Firth, Katherine. *The Apocalyptic Tradition in Reformation Britain, 1530–1645*. Oxford, 1979.

Fisch, Max. "The Academy of the Investigators." In *Science, Medicine and History: Essays in Honor of Charles Singer*. Vol. 1. Oxford, 1953. 521–63.

Flint, Valerie J. "Monsters and the Antipodes in the Early Middle Ages and Enlightenment." *Viator* 15 (1984): 65–80.

Force, James E. "Secularization, the Language of God and the Royal Society at the Turn of the Seventeenth Century." *History of European Ideas* 2 (1981): 221–35.

Formichetti, Gianfranco. "Campanella a Roma: I 'Commentaria' ai 'Poëmata' di Urban VIII." *Studi Romani* 30 (1982): 325–39.

———. "Il 'De siderali fato vitando' di Tommaso Campanella." In *Il mago, il cosmo, il teatro degli astri: Saggi sulla letteratura esoterica del Rinascimento*. Ed. Gianfranco Formichetti. Rome, 1985. 199–217.

Franchini, Raffaello. "Campanella Teorico della storiografia." In *Tommaso Campanella (1568–1639), Miscellanea di studi nel 4° centenario della sua nascita*. Naples, 1969. 339–49.

Fumaroli, Marc. *L'Age de l'éloquence: Rhétorique et 'res literaria' de la Renaissance au seuil de l'époque classique*. Geneva, 1980.

Funkenstein, Amos. "Dialectical Preparation for Scientific Revolutions." In *The Copernican Achievement*. Ed. Robert S. Westman. Berkeley/Los Angeles/London, 1975. 165–203.

Gabrieli, Giuseppe. "Tommaso Campanella e i Lincei della prima Accademia." Rendiconti della Reale Accademia Nazionale dei Lincei, Rome. *Classe di Scienze, Morali Storiche e Filologiche, Rendiconti Roma*, ser. 6, 4 (1928): 250–67.

———. "Bibliografia Lincea IV: Scritti di Giovanni Faber Linceo." Accademia Nazionale dei Lincei, Rome. *Classe di Scienze, Morali Storiche e Filologiche, Rendiconti Roma*, ser. 6, 9 (1933): 276–334.

———. *Contributi alla storia della Accademia dei Lincei*. Vol. 1. Rome, 1989.

Garin, Eugenio. *Italian Humanism: Philosophy and Civic Life in the Renaissance*. Trans. Peter Munz. New York, 1965.

———. *Galileo the Philosopher: Science and Civic Life in the Italian Renaissance*. Trans. Peter Munz. New York, 1969.

———. "La nuova scienza e il simbolo del libro." In *La cultura filosofica del Rinascimento italiano*. Florence, 1979. 451–65.

———. *Astrology in the Renaissance: The Zodiac of Life*. London, 1983.

Garin, Eugenio, ed. "Schede: La nuova scienza e il simbolo del 'libro.'" *RCSF* 29 (1974): 328–34.

Gatti, Hilary. *The Renaissance Drama of Knowledge*. London/New York, 1989.

Geley, Léon. *Le Fancan et la politique de Richelieu de 1617 à 1627*. Paris, 1884.

Gilbert, Felix. "Cristianesimo, umanesimo e la bolla 'Apostolici Regiminis.'" *RSI* 79 (1967): 976–90.

———. "Machiavellism." In *History, Choice and Commitment*. Cambridge, Mass./London, 1977. 155–76.

Gilson, Étienne. "Le raisonement par analogie chez Tommaso Campanella." In *Études de philosophie médiévale*. Strasbourg, 1921. 125–45.

———. *Les métamorphoses de la Cité de Dieu*. Paris, 1952.

Ginzburg, Carlo. *Clues, Myths and the Historical Method*. Trans. John and Anne C. Tedeschi. Baltimore, 1989.

Gliozzi, Giuliano. *Adamo e il nuovo mondo. La nascita della antropologia come ideologia coloniale: dalle genealogie bibliche alle teorie razziali (1500–1700)*. Florence, 1977.

———. "The Apostles in the New World: Monotheism and Idolatry between Revelation and Fetishism." *History and Anthropology* 3 (1987): 123–48.

Gordon, Michael. "The Science of Politics in Seventeenth-Century Spanish Theory." *IPP* 7 (1974): 379–94.

———. "Morality, Reform and Empire in Seventeenth-Century Spain." *IPP* 11 (1978): 3–19.

Gosselin, Edward A. "Fra Giordano Bruno's Catholic Passion." In *Supplementum Festivum: Studies in Honor of Paul Oskar Kristeller*. Binghamton, N.Y., 1987. 537–61.

Gosselin, Edward A., and Lawrence S. Lerner. "Galileo and the Long Shadow of Bruno." *Archives Internationales d'histoire des sciences* 25 (1975): 222–46.

Gregory, Tullio. *Theophrastus redivivus: Erudizione e ateismo nel Seicento*. Naples, 1979.

———. "Aristotelismo e libertinismo." In *Aristotelismo veneto e scienza moderna*. Vol. 1. Padua, 1983. 279–96.

———. "Temps astrologique et temps chrétien." In *Colloques internationaux du CNRS. Le temps chrétien de la fin de l'Antiquité au Moyen Age-IIIe–XIIIe siècles*. Paris, 1984. 557–73.

Grendler, Marcella. "A Greek Collection in Padua: The Library of Gian Vincenzo Pinelli (1535–1601)." *RQ* 33/3 (1980): 386–416.

Grendler, Paul F. *Critics of the Italian World, 1530–1560*. Madison, Wis./London, 1969.

Grillo, Francesco. "Motivi Campanelliani." In *Tommaso Campanella, 1568–1639: Miscellanea di studi nel 4° centenario della sua nascita*. Naples, 1969. 395–423.

Grimm, Jürgen. "Campanella en France." In *La France et l'Italie au temps de Mazarin*. Ed. Jean Serroy. Grenoble, 1986. 79–86.

Grisar, J., S.J. "Francesco Ingoli über die Aufgaben des kommenden Papstes nach dem Tode Urbans VIII (1644)." *Archivum Historiae Pontificiae* 5 (1967): 289–324.

Guillén, Diego Gracia. "Judaism, Medicine and the Inquisitorial Mind in Sixteenth-Century Spain." In *The Spanish Inquisition and the Inquisitorial Mind*. Ed. Angel Alcalá. Boulder, Colo., 1987. 375–400.
Gurevich, Aron. *Medieval Popular Culture: Problems of Belief and Perception*. Cambridge, 1988.
Guthke, Karl S. *The Last Frontier: Imagining other Worlds, from the Copernican Revolution to Modern Science Fiction*. Trans. Helen Atkins. Ithaca/London, 1990.
Hankins, James. *Plato in the Italian Renaissance*. 2 vols. Leiden/New York/Copenhaven/Cologne, 1990.
Hanotaux, Gabriel. *Histoire du Cardinal de Richelieu*. Vol. 5. Paris, 1984.
Harries, Karsten. "Copernican Reflections." *Inquiry* 23 (1980): 253–69.
Haskell, Francis. *Patrons and Painters: A Study in the Relations between Italian Art and Society in the Age of the Baroque*. New York, 1963.
Headley, John M. "Gattinara, Erasmus, and the Imperial Configurations of Humanism." *Archiv für Reformationsgeschichte* 71 (1980): 64–98.
―――. " 'Ehe Türckisch als Bäpstisch': Lutheran Reflections on the Problem of Empire, 1623–28." *Central European History* 20 (1987): 3–28.
―――. "On Reconstructing the Citizenry: Campanella's Criticism of Aristotle's *Politics*." *IPP* 24 (1991): 28–41.
―――. "Spain's Asian Presence, 1565–1590: Structures and Aspirations." *Hispanic American Historical Review* 75 (1995): 623–46.
―――. "The Sixteenth-Century Venetian Celebration of the Earth's Total Habitability." *Journal of World History* 8 (1997): 1–27.
Henkel, Willi. "The Polyglot Printing Office of the Congregation." In *Sacra Congregatio de propaganda fide. Memoria rerum*. Vol. 1. Rome, 1972. 335–50.
Herde, Peter. "Ein Pamphlet der päpstlichen Kurie gegen Kaiser Friedrich II, von 1245/46 (Eger cui lenia)." *Deutsches Archiv für Erforschung des Mittelalters* 23 (1967): 468–538.
Hillgarth, J. N. *Ramon Lull and Lullism in Fourteenth-Century France*. Oxford, 1971.
Hodgen, Margaret T. *Early Anthropology in the Sixteenth and Seventeenth Centuries*. Philadelphia, 1964.
Hyde, J. K. *Padua in the Age of Dante*. Manchester, 1966.
Ingegno, Alfonso. "Galileo, Bruno e Campanella." In *Galileo a Napoli: Atti del convegno Galileo a Napoli, Napoli, 12–14 aprile*. Ed. Fabrizio Lomonaco e Maurizio Torsini. Naples, 1987. 123–39.
Iriarte, Mauricio de. *El Doctor Huarte de San Jaun y su Examen de Ingenios. Contribucion a la historia de la psicologia diferencial*. Madrid, 1948.
Jacquot, Jean. "Harriot, Hill, Warner and the New Philosophy." In *Thomas Harriot: Renaissance Scientist*. Ed. John W. Shirley. Oxford, 1974.
Jemolo, Arturo Carlo. *Stato e chiesa negli scrittori politici italiani del Seicento e del Settecento*. Naples, 1972.
Jensen, K., and A. K. Liebreich. "Liber apologeticus contra impugnantes institutum scholarum piarum." *Archivum scholarum piarum* 8 (1984): 29–76.
Jorgensen, Johannes. *St. Bridget of Sweden*. London, 1954.
Jover, José Maria. *1635: Historia de una polémica y semblanza de una generación*. Madrid, 1949.

———. "Sobre los conceptos de monarquía y nación en el pensamiento politico español del XVII." *Cuadernos de Historia de España* 13 (1950): 101–50.
Jungkuntz, Richard P. "Christian Approval of Epicureanism." *Church History* 31 (1962): 279–93.
Jurgens, W. A., ed. *The Priesthood of St. John Chrysostom*. New York, 1955.
Kagan, Richard L. *Lucrezia's Dreams: Politics and Prophecy in Sixteenth-Century Spain*. Berkeley/Los Angeles/London, 1990.
Kantorowicz, Ernst H. *The King's Two Bodies: A Study in Medieval Political Theology*. Princeton, 1957.
Kirsanov, Vladamir S. "Galileo and Kepler: Two Paths, Two Traditions." In *Novità celesti e crisi del sapere: Atti del convegno di studi Galileiani*. Ed. P. Galluzzi. Florence, 1984. 201–6.
Knowles, David. *The Evolution of Medieval Thought*. New York, 1964.
Kors, Alan Charles. "Theology and Atheism in Early Modern France." In *The Transmission of Culture in Early Modern Europe*. Ed. Anthony Grafton and Ann Blair. Philadelphia, 1990. 238–75.
Kowalsky, P. Nicola. "Inventario dell'Archivio storico della Sacra Congregazione 'de Propaganda fide.'" *NZfMW* 17/1 (1961): 9–15.
———. "Inventario dell'Archivio storico della Sacra Congregazione 'de Propaganda fide': parte II." *NZfMW* 17/2 (1961): 109–13.
———. "Il testamento di Mons. Ingoli, primo segretario della Sacra Congregatione 'de Propaganda fide.'" *NZfMW* 19/4 (1963): 272–83.
Koyré, Alexandre. "L'Apport scientifique de la Renaissance." In *Études d'histoire de la pensée scientifique*. Paris, 1966. 38–47.
Kraus, Andreas. *Das päpstliche Staatssekretariat unter Urban VIII, 1623–1644*. Rome, 1964.
Krautheimer, Richard. "A Christian Triumph." In *Essays in the History of Art Presented to Rudolf Wittkower*. London, 1967. 174–78.
Kristeller, Paul Oskar. "Paduan Averroism and Alexandrism in the Light of Recent Studies." In *Aristotelismo padovano e filosofia aristotelica: Atti del XII Congresso Internzaionale di Filosofia*. Florence, 1960. 147–55.
———. *Eight Philosophers of the Italian Renaissance*. Stanford, 1964.
———. "The Myth of Renaissance Atheism and the French Tradition of Free Thought." *The Journal of the History of Philosophy* 6 (1968): 233–43.
———. "Between the Italian Renaissance and the French Enlightenment: Gabriel Naudé as an Editor." *RQ* 32 (1979): 41–72.
Kuttner, Stephen. "Cardinalis: The History of a Canonical Concept." *Traditio* 3 (1945): 129–214.
Kvačala, J. "Thomas Campanella und Ferdinand II." *Sitzungsberichte der Philosophisch-Historischen Klasse der kaiserlichen Akademie der Wissenschaften* 159/5/1 (1908): 1–48.
———. *Thomas Campanella. Ein Reformer der ausgehenden Renaissance*. Berlin, 1909.
La Rocca, John J. "'Who Can't Pray with me, Can't Love Me': Toleration and the Early Jacobean Recusancy Policy." *The Journal of British Studies* 23 (1984): 22–36.
Larner, John. "Foreword." *Renaissance Studies* 6 (1992): 247–48.

Lauro, Agostino. "Baronio, De Luca e il potere temporale della chiesa." In *Baronio storico e la Controriforma*. Ed. Romeo de Maio, Luigi Gulia, and Aldo Mazzacone. Sora, 1982. 361–418.

Lechner, G. S. "Tommaso Campanella and Andrea Sacchi's Fresco of 'Divina Sapienza' in the Palazzo Barberini." *Art Bulletin* 58 (1976): 97–108; 59 (1977): 307–9.

Lemay, Richard. "The Teaching of Astronomy in Medieval Universities, principally at Paris in the Fourteenth Century." *Manuscripta* 20/3 (1976): 197–217.

Lenoble, Robert. *Mersenne ou la naissance du mécanisme*. Paris, 1943.

——. "Histoire et Physique: A propos des conseils de Mersenne et de l'intervention de Jean de Launoy dans la querelle gassendiste." *Revue d'histoire des sciences* 6 (1953): 112–34.

Lerner, Michel-Pierre. *Tommaso Campanella en France au XVIIe Siècle*. Naples, 1995.

——. "Campanelle, juge d'Aristote." In *XVI Colloque international de Tours. Platon et Aristote à la Renaissance*. Paris, 1976. 335–57.

——. "Le protestantisme vu par Tommaso Campanella, O.P. (1568–1639)." *Revue d' histoire et de philosophie religieuses* 58 (1978): 163–91.

——. "Le 'livre vivant' de Dieu: La cosmologie évolutive de Tommaso Campanella." In *Le discours scientifique du Baroque: Actes de la Xe session internationale d'étude du Baroque, Montauban, 1983*. Montauban, 1987. 111–29.

Lerner, Robert E. "Refreshment of the Saints: The Time after Antichrist as a Station for Earthly Progress in Medieval Thought." *Traditio* 32 (1976): 97–144.

Lesnick, Daniel R. "Civic Preaching in the Early Renaissance: Giovanni Dominici's Florentine Sermons." In *Christianity and the Renaissance: Image and Religious Imagination in the Quattrocento*. Ed. Timothy Verdon and John Henderson. Syracuse, N.Y., 1990.

Lestringant, Frank. "Cosmologie et mirabilia à la Renaissance: L'exemple de Guillaume Postel." *The Journal of Medieval and Renaissance Studies* 16 (1986): 253–79.

Lindon, Stanton J. "Alchemy and Eschatology in Seventeenth-Century Poetry." *Ambix* 31 (1984): 102–24.

Liss, Peggy R. "Jesuit Contributions to the Ideology of Spanish Empire in Mexico, I and II." *The Americas* 19 (1973): 314–33, 449–70.

Lopez de Toro, José. "Repuesta del Cardenal Trejo a una carta de Tomas Campanella." *Revista de Estudios Politicos* 122 (1962): 161–78.

Lubac, Henri, S.J. *La posterité spirituelle de Joachim de Fiore. I De Joachim à Schelling*. Paris/Namur, 1979.

Luciani, Vincent. *Francesco Guicciardini and His European Reputation*. New York, 1936.

Lukes, Timothy J. "To Bamboozle with Goodness: The Political Advantages of Christianity in the Thought of Machiavelli." *Renaissance and Reformation* 8 (1984): 266–77.

Lutz, Georg. *Rom und Europa während des Pontifikats Urban VIII in Rom*. Ed. R. Elze. Vienna/Rome, 1976.

MacClintock, Stuart. "Heresy and Epithet: An Approach to the Problem of Latin Averroism." *The Review of Metaphysics* 8 (1954–55): 176–99, 342–56, 526–45.

Maclean, Ian. "The Market for Scholarly Books and Conceptions of Genre in Northern

Europe, 1570–1630." In *Die Renaissance im Blick der Nationen Europas*. Ed. Georg Kauffmann. Wiesbaden, 1991. 17–31.
McManamon, John M., S.J. " 'Feed My Sheep': Reformation Interpretations of John 21 and the History of Exegesis." Unpublished paper.
Magnuson, Torgil. *Rome in the Age of Bernini*. Uppsala, 1982.
Malettke, Klaus. "La présentation du saint empire Romain Germanique dans France de Louis XIII et Louis XIV." *Francia* 14 (1986): 209–28.
Manuel, Frank E., and P. Fritze. *Utopian Thought in the Western World*. Cambridge, Mass., 1979.
Manzi, Pietro. *Annali della Stamperia Stigliola a Porta Reale in Napoli, 1593–1606*. Biblioteca de bibliografia italiana, 53. Florence, 1968.
———. *La tipografia napoletana nel '500. Annali di Orazio Salviani (1566–1594)*. Florence, 1974.
Maravall, José Antonio. "La utopia politico-religiosa de los franciscanos en Nueva España." *Estudios Americanos*, 1/2 (1949): 199–227.
Margolin, Jean Claude. "Jérome Cardan, Christophe Colomb et Aristote." *Bulletin d'humanisme et Renaissance* 27 (1965): 655–68.
Marino, John A. "I meccanismi della crisi nella Dogana di Foggia nel XVII secolo." In *Problemi di storia delle campagne meridionali nell' età moderna e contemporanea*. Ed. Angelo Massafra. Bari, 1981.
———. "Economic Idylls and Pastoral Realities: The 'Trickster Economy' in the Kingdom of Naples." *Comparative Studies in Society and History* 24 (1982): 211–34.
———. " 'Professazione voluntaria' e 'pecore in aerea.' Ragione economica e meccanismi di mercato nella dogana di Foggia nel secolo sedicesimo." *RSI* 94 (1982): 5–43.
———. *Pastoral Economics in the Kingdom of Naples*. Baltimore/London, 1988.
Markus, R. A. *Saeculum: History and Society in the Theology of St. Augustine*. Cambridge, 1970.
Marquis, A. J. "Le traité missionaire 'Quod Reminiscentur' de Tommaso Campanella." *NZfMW* 27 (1971): 331–60.
Martin, Henri-Jean. *Livre, Pouvoirs et Societé à Paris au XVIIe siècle (1598–1701)*. Vol. 1. Geneva, 1969.
———. "La vie intellectuelle au temps de Richelieu." In *Richelieu et le monde de l'esprit*. Paris, 1985. 183–92.
Mastellone, Salvo. "Tommaso Bozio, teorico dell'Ordine Ecclesiastico." *IPP* 13 (1980): 186–94.
Mazzeo, Joseph. "Universal Analogy and the Culture of the Renaissance." *JHI* 15 (1954): 299–304.
McCuaig, William. *Carlo Sigonio: The Changing World of the Late Renaissance*. Princeton, 1989.
McKittrick, Rosamond. "The Study of Frankish History in France and Germany in the Sixteenth and Seventeenth Centuries." *Francia* 8 (1980): 556–72.
Méchoulan, Henry. "Juan de Salazar lecteur de *La Monarchie Espagnole* de Tommaso Campanella dans *La Politique Espagnole*." *Ethno-Psychologie* 28 (1973): 103–21.

―――. "La critique de l'Espagne par Campanella à partir d'une réfutation manuscrite en français de sa *Monarchie Espagnole: La Monarchie des Nations*." In *L'Age d'Or de l'Influence Espagnole: La France et l'Espagne à l'époque d'Anne d'Autriche, 1615–1666; Actes du 20e Colloque du C.M.R. 17. placé sous le patronage de la Société d'Étude du XVIIe siècle et de l'Université de Bordeaux III. Bordeaux, 25–28 janvier, 1990*. Mont-de-Marsan, 1991. 125–35.

Mendizábal, Alfredo. "On Everlasting Values of the Spanish School of Natural Law (Francisco de Vitoria)." In *Interpretations of Modern Legal Philosophies: Essays in Honor of Roscoe Pound*. Ed. Paul Sayre. Oxford/New York, 1947. 498–520.

Metzler, J. "Päpstlicher Primat als pastorale Verantwortung und missionarischer Auftrag in frühen Dokumenten der Propaganda Kongregation." In *Konzil und Papst: Festgabe für Herman Tüchle*. Ed. Georg Schwaiger. Paderborn, 1975. 373–86

Miele, Michele. "Un opuscolo inedito ritenuto perduto di Tommaso Campanella: Il 'De praecedentia religiosorum.'" *AFP* 52 (1982): 267–323.

Milhou, Alain. *Colon y su mentalidad mesianica en el ambiente franciscanista español*. Valladolid, 1983.

Mönnich, Michael. *Tommaso Campanella: Sein Beitrag zur Medizin und Pharmazie in der Renaissance*. Stuttgart, 1990.

Mönnich, Michael, and Wolf-Dieter Müller-Jahncke. "Medicine and Magic between Tradition and Progress in Tommaso Campanella." In *Medicina e biologia nella rivoluzione scientifica*. Ed. Lino Conti. Perugia, n.d. 15–33.

Montgomery, John Warwick. *Cross and Crucible: Johann Valentin Andreae (1586–1654), Phoenix of the Theologians*. The Hague, 1973.

Moss, Jean Dietz. *Novelties in the Heavens: Rhetoric and Science in the Copernican Controversy*. Chicago/London, 1993.

Muldoon, James. *Popes, Lawyers and Infidels*. Philadelphia, 1979.

Murphy, James J. *Rhetoric in the Middle Ages: A History of Rhetorical Theory from St. Augustine to the Renaissance*. Berkeley/Los Angeles/London, 1974.

Murray, Alexander. "The Epicureans." In *Intellectuals and Writers in Fourteenth-Century Europe*. Ed. Piero Boitani and Anna Torti. Cambridge/Tübingen, 1986. 138–63.

Murray, John Courtney, S.J. "St. Robert Bellarmine on the Indirect Power." *Theological Studies* 9 (1948): 491–535.

Namer, Emile. "L'univers de Giordano Bruno et la destinée humaine." In *L'univers à la Renaissance: Microcosme et Macrocosme: Colloque international tenu en Octobre, 1968*. Brussels/Paris, 1970. 89–120.

Napoli, Giovanni di. *Tommaso Campanella, filosofo della restaurazione cattolica*. Padua, 1947.

―――. "Ecumenismo e missionarismo in Tommaso Campanella." *Euntes docete* 22 (1969): 265–308.

―――. "L'eresia e i processi campanelliani." In *Tommaso Camapanella, 1568–1639. Miscellanea di studi nel 4 centenario della sua nascita*.Naples, 1969. 169–258.

Nellen, Henk J. M., and Philippe J. Wolfe, eds. "Un echange epistolaire de la 'Republique des Muses': Onze lettres de Gabriel Naudé à Ismael Boilliau (1639–1646)." *LIAS* 13/2 (1986): 235–84.

Noreña, Carlos G. "Juan Huarte's Naturalistic Humanism." *The Journal of the History of Philosophy* 10 (1972): 71–76.

Nussdorfer, Laurie. "Vacant See: Ritual and Protest in Early Modern Rome." *SCJ* 18 (1987): 173–89.
Nys, E. "Thomas Campanella. Sa Vie et ses théories politiques." In *Études de Droit international et de Droit politique*. Brussels/Paris, 1901. 206–39.
O'Malley, John W., S.J. *Giles of Viterbo on Church and Reform*. Leiden, 1968.
———. *Tradition and Transition: Historical Perspectives on Vatican II*. Wilmington, Del., 1988.
Oreglia, Giacomo. "Campanella in Svezia." In *Studi politici in onore di Luigi Firpo*. Vol. 2. Ed. Silvia Roti Ghibaudi and Franco Barcia. Milan, 1990. 55–91.
Padley, G. A. *Grammatical Theory in Western Europe: The Latin Tradition*. Cambridge, 1976.
Paganini, G. "La critica della 'civiltà' nel *Theophrastus redivivus*." In *Ricerche su letteratura libertina e letteratura clandestina nel Seicento: Atti del convegno di studio di Genova, 30 ottobre–1 novembre, 1980*. Ed. T. Gregory et al. Florence, 1981. 49–82.
———. "Thèmes et problèmes pomponaciens dans le *Theophrastus redivivus*." *Dix-Septième Siècle* 37 (1985): 349–77.
Pagden, Anthony. "The 'School of Salamanca' and the 'Affair of the Indies,' " *The History of Universities* 1 (1981): 71–112.
———. "The Preservation of Order. The School of Salamanca and the 'Ius Naturae.' " In *Medieval and Renaissance Studies on Spain and Portugal in Honor of P. E. Russell*. Oxford, 1981. 155–66.
———. "The Impact of the New World on the Old: The History of an Idea." *Renaissance and Modern Studies* 30 (1986): 1–11.
———. *Spanish Imperialism and the Political Imagination: Studies in European and Spanish American Social and Political Theory, 1513–1830*. New Haven/London, 1990.
Pagel, Walter. *The Smiling Spleen: Paracelsianism in Storm and Stress*. Basel/New York, 1984.
———. "The Reaction to Aristotle in Seventeenth-Century Biological Thought: Campanella, van Helmont, Glanvill, Charleton, Harvey, Glisson, Descartes." In *From Paracelsus to Van Helmont: Studies in Renaissance Medicine and Science*. Ed. Marianne Winder. London, 1986. 489–509.
Pagels, Elaine H. "Adam and Eve, Christ and the Church: A Survey of Second-Century Controversies Concerning Marriage." In *The New Testament and Gnosis: Essays in Honor of Robert M. Wilson*. Edinburgh, 1983. 146–75.
Pastine, Dino. "Baronio e il Molinismo." In *Baronio storico e la Controriforma. Atti del convegno internazionale di studi Sora, 6–10 ottobre, 1979*. Ed. Romeo de Maio, Luigi Gulia, and Aldo Mazzacone. Sora, 1982. 233–51.
Pastor, Ludwig von. *The History of the Popes*. Vol. 14. London, 1924.
Pasztor, Edith. "La repubblica cristiana di Ottavio Pallavicino." *Rivista di studi politici internazionali* 18 (1951): 67–84.
Pecchiai, Pio. *Roma nel Cinquecento*. Bologna, 1948.
Pelikan, Jaroslav, ed. "Introduction." In *The Preaching of Chrysostom*. Philadelphia, 1967. 1–36.
Perez, Joseph. "Moines frondeurs et sermons subversifs en Castille pendant le premier séjour de Charles Quint en Espagne." *Bulletin hispanique* 65 (1963): 238–83; 67 (1965): 5–24.

Phillips, J. R. S. *The Medieval Expansion of Europe*. Oxford, 1988.
Pintard, René. *Le libertinage érudit dans la première moitié du XVIIe siècle*. Paris, 1943.
Pocock, J. G. A. "Time, History and Eschatology in the Thought of Thomas Hobbes." In *The Diversity of History: Essays in Honor of Sir Herbert Butterfield*. Ed. J. H. Elliott and H. G. Koenigsberger. Ithaca, 1970. 149–98.
Post, Barbara St. Clare. "Tommaso Campanella: The Theory and Practice of Metaphor in Selected Poems." M.A. thesis, Brown University, 1979.
Preus, J. Samuel. "Machiavelli's Functional Analysis of Religion: Context and Object." *JHI* 40 (1979): 171–90.
Procacci, Giuliano. *Studi sulla fortuna del Machiavelli*. Rome, 1965.
Prosperi, Adriano. "'Otras Indias': Missionari della Controriforma tra contadini e selvaggi." In *Scienze, credenze occulte livelli di cultura. Convegno Internazionale di Studi, Firenze, 26–30 Giugno, 1980*. Florence, 1982. 205–34.
Pullapilly, Cyriac K. *Caesar Baronius: Counter Reformation Historian*. Notre Dame/London, 1975.
Rassow, Peter. *Forschungen zur Reichs-Idee im 16. und 17. Jahrhundert*. Cologne/Opladen, 1955.
Redondi, Pietro. *Galileo, Heretic*. Trans. Raymond Rosenthal. Princeton, 1987.
Reinhard, Wolfgang. "Nepotismus: Der Funktionswandel einer papstgeschichtlichen Konstanten." *Zeitschrift fur Kirchengeschichte* 86 (1975): 145–85.
——. "Sprachbeherrschung und Weltherrschaft: Sprache und Sprachwissenschaft in der europaïschen Expansion." In *Humanismus und Neue Welt*. Ed. Wolfgang Reinhard. Weinheim, 1987. 1–36.
——. "Papal Power and Family Strategy in the Sixteenth and Seventeenth Centuries." In *Princes, Patronage and the Nobility: The Court at the Beginning of the Modern Age*. Ed. Ronald G. Asch and Adolf M. Birke. Oxford, 1991.
Rizza, Cecilia. *Peiresc e l'Italia*. Turin, 1965.
——. "Rapports franco-italiens dans la recherche érudite et scientifique: Cassiano dal Pozzo." In *Le XVIIe siècle et la recherche (Actes du 6 Colloque de Marseille, Janvier, 1976)*. Marseille, 1976. 91–102.
Robertson, John. "Andrew Fletcher's Vision of Union." In *Scotland and England, 1286–1815*. Ed. Roger A. Mason. Edinburgh, 1984. 203–25.
Rodríguez-Salgado, M. J. "The Spanish Story of the 1588 Armada Reassessed." *Historical Journal* 33 (1990): 461–78.
——. "Pilots, Navigation and Strategy in the Gran Armada." In *England, Spain and the Gran Armada, 1585–1604: Essays from the Anglo-Spanish Conferences, London and Madrid, 1988*. Ed. M. J. Rodríguez-Salgado and Simon Adams. Savage, Md., 1991. 134–72.
Roger, Jacques. *Les sciences de la vie dans la pensée française du XVIIIe siècle. La génération des animaux de Descartes à l'Encyclopedie*. Paris, 1963.
Romeo, Rosario. "Le scoperte americane nella coscienza italiana del Cinquecento." *RSI* 65 (1953): 326–79.
——. "The Jesuit Sources and the Italian Political Utopia in the Second Half of the Sixteenth Century." In *First Images of America*. Vol. 1. Ed. Fredi Chiappelli. Berkeley/Los Angeles/London, 1976. 165–84.

Roper, Lyndal. "Sexual Utopianism in the German Reformation." *The Journal of Ecclesiastical History* 42 (1991): 394–418.
Rosa, A. Asor. "Intellettuali." *Enciclopedia.* Turin, 1979. 801–27.
Rosen, Edward. *Kepler's Conversation with Galileo's Sidereal Messenger.* New York/London, 1965.
Rossi, Paolo. "Nobility of Man and Plurality of Worlds." In *Science, Medicine and Society in the Renaissance: Essays to Honor Walter Pagel.* Vol. 2. Ed. Allen G. Debus. New York, 1972. 131–62.
———. "Galileo Galilei e il libro del salmi." *RF* 69 (1978): 54–71.
———. "Francesco Patrizi: Heavenly Spheres and Flocks of Cranes." In *Italian Studies in the Philosophy of Science.* Ed. M. L. Dalla Chiara. Dordrecht, 1981. 363–88.
Rotondò, Antonio. "Cultura umanistica e difficoltà di censori. Censura ecclesiastica e discussioni cinquecentesche sul Platonismo." In *Le pouvoir et la plume: Incitation, contrôle et répression dans l'Italie du XVIe siècle.* C.I.R.R.I. Paris, 1982. 15–50.
Rubinstein, Nicolai. "The History of the Word 'Politicus' in Early Modern Europe." In *The Language of Political Theory in Early Modern Europe.* Ed. Anthony Pagden. Cambridge, 1987. 41–56.
Russo, F. "Gioachinismo e Francescanismo." *Miscellanea Francescanea* 41 (1941): 71–3.
Sarasohn, Lisa T. "French Reaction to the Condemnation of Galileo." *CHR* 74 (1988): 34–54.
———. "Nicolas-Claude Fabri de Peiresc and the Patronage of the New Science in the Seventeenth Century." *Isis* 84 (1993): 70–90.
Saunders, Jason Lewis. *Justus Lipsius: The Philosophy of Renaissance Stoicism.* New York, 1955.
Scalzo, Joseph. "Campanella, Foucault and Madness in Late-Sixteenth Century Italy." *SCJ* 21 (1990): 359–72.
Scammell, G. V. "The New Worlds and Europe in the Sixteenth Century." *The Historical Journal* 12 (1969): 389–412.
Schaffer, Simon. "Newton's Comets and the Transformation of Astrology." In *Astrology, Science and Society.* Ed. Patrick Curry. Bury St. Edmunds, Suffolk, 1987. 219–42.
Schino, Anna Lisa. "Campanella tra magia naturale e scienza nel giudizio di Gabriel Naudé." *Physis* 22 (1980): 393–431.
Schmitt, Charles B. "The Faculty of Arts at Pisa in the Time of Galileo." *Physis* 14 (1972): 243–72.
———. "Galilei and the Seventeenth-Century Text Book Tradition." In *Novità celesti e crisi del sapere: Atti del convegno di studi Galileiani.* Ed. P. Galluzzi. Florence, 1984. 217–28.
Schnur, Roman. *Individualismus und Absolutismus. Zur Politischen Theorie von Thomas Hobbes, (1600–1640).* Berlin, 1963.
Scott, Alan. *Origen and the Life of the Stars: A History of an Idea.* Oxford, 1991.
Scott, John Beldon. *Images of Nepotism: The Painted Ceilings of the Palazzo Barberini.* Princeton, 1991.

Scrimieri, Giorgio. "Sulla magia in Campanella." In *Studi in onore di Antonio Corsano*. Mandaria, 1970. 709–46.
Seibt, F. "Liber figurarum XII and the Classical Ideal of Utopia." In *Prophecy and Millenarianism: Essays in Honor of Marjorie Reeves*. Ed. Ann Williams. Essex, 1980. 259–66.
Shea, William R. "Melchior Inchofer's 'Tractatus Syllepticus': A Consultor of the Holy Office Answers Galileo." In *Novità celesti e crisi del sapere: Atti del Convegno internazionale di studi Galileiani*. Ed. P. Galluzzi. Florence, 1984. 283–92.
Shils, Edward. "The Intellectuals and the Powers: Some Perspectives for Comparative Analysis." *Comparative Studies in Society and History* 1 (1958): 5–22.
Shirley, John William. "The Scientific Experiments of Sir Walter Raleigh, the Wizard Earl, and the Three Magi in the Tower." *Ambix* 4 (1949): 52–66.
Smalley, Beryl. *Medieval Exegesis of Wisdom Literature*. Atlanta, 1986.
Smith, A. Mark. "Knowing Things Inside Out: The Scientific Revolution from a Medieval Perspective." *The American Historical Review* 95/3 (1990): 726–44.
Smith, Wilfred Cantwell. *The Meaning and End of Religion*. New York, 1962.
Solomon, Howard M. *Public Welfare, Science and Propaganda in Seventeenth-Century France: Innovations of Theophraste Renaudot*. Princeton, 1972.
Spierenburg, Peter. *The Prison Experience: Disciplinary Institutions and Their Inmates in Early Modern Europe*. New Brunswick/London, 1991.
Spini, Giorgio. *Ricerca dei libertini*. Florence, 1950.
———. '*De Atheismis et Phalarismis Evangelicorum* di Stanislaw Reszka e *Atheismus Triumphatus* di Tommaso Campanella." In *Storia e cultura del mezzogiorno. Studi in memoria di Umberto Caldora*. Cosenza, 1978. 51–76.
———. *Ricerca dei libertini*. Florence, 1980.
———. "Ritratto del protestante come libertino." In *Ricerche su letteratura libertina e letteratura clandestina nel Seicento: Atti del convegno di studi di Genova, 30 ottobre–1 novembre, 1980*. Ed. T. Gregory et al. Florence, 1981. 177–88.
———. "Christianopolitanae nugae." In *Studi politici in onore di Luigi Firpo*. Vol. 2. Ed. Silvia Rota Ghibaudi and Franco Barcia. Milan, 1990. 37–53.
———. "Ricordo di Luigi Firpo." *RSI* 102/1 (1990): 195–203.
———. "Galilaeana Minima" in *Studi in onore di Arnaldo d' Addario*, Vol. 4. Ed. Luigi Borgia et al. Lecce, 1995. 1299–1325.
Spitzer, Leo. *Classical and Christian Ideas of World Harmony: Prolegomena to an Interpretation of the Word "Stimmung."* Baltimore, 1963.
Stankiewicz, W. J. *Politics and Religion in Seventeenth-Century France*. Berkeley/Los Angeles, 1960.
Stiernon, Daniel. *Konstantinopel IV*. Mainz, 1975.
Stolleis, Michael, ed. *Hermann Conring (1606–1681) Beiträge zu Leben und Werk*. Berlin, 1983.
Stradling, R. A. *The Armada of Flanders: Spanish Maritime Policy and European Wars, 1568–1668*. Cambridge, 1992.
Sutton, R. B. "The Phrase *libertas philosophandi*." *JHI* 14 (1953): 310–16.
Sweet, Leonard J. "Christopher Columbus and the Millennial Vision." *CHR* 72 (1986): 369–82.
Sypher, G. Wylie. "Similarities between the Scientific and the Historical Revolutions at the End of the Renaissance." *JHI* 26 (1965): 353–68.

Tamizey de Larroque, Philip. "Lettres de Jean et Pierre Bourdelot à Peiresc." *Revue d'histoire et littérature de la France* 4 (1897): 98–121.
Tedeschi, John. *The Prosecution of Heresy: Collected Studies on the Inquisition in Early Modern Italy*. Binghamton, N.Y., 1991.
Tenenti, Albert. "Libertinisme et hérésie." *AESC* 18 (1963): 1–19.
Thorndike, Lynn. "Newness and Craving for Novelty in Seventeenth-Century Science and Medicine." *JHI* 12 (1951): 584–98.
Thomas, Keith. "The Utopian Impulse in Seventeenth-Century England." In *Between Dream and Nature: Essays on Utopia and Dystopia*. Ed. Dominic Baker-Smith and C. C. Barfoot. Amsterdam, 1987. 20–46.
Tocco, Vittorio di. "Un progetto di confederazione italiana nella seconda metà del cinquecento." *ASI*, ser. 7, 1 (1924): 161–97.
Tomlinson, Gary. *Music in Renaissance Magic: Toward a Historiography of Others*. Chicago/London, 1993.
Tonkin, John. *The Church and the Secular Order in Reformation Thought*. New York/London, 1971.
Torrini, Maurizio. "Giovanni Ciampoli filosofo." In *Novità celesti e crisi del sapere: Atti del convegno internazionale di studi Galileiani*. Ed. P. Galluzzi. Florence, 1984. 267–76.
Treves, Paolo. "Idee ed ipotesi sulla questione dei plagi: Campanella-Botero." *RF* 20 (1929): 152–58.
———. "The Title of Campanella's *City of the Sun*." *JWCI* 3 (1939–40): 248–51.
Trinkaus, Charles. *In Our Image and Likeness: Humanity and Divinity in Italian Humanist Thought*. London, 1970.
Truyol y Serra, Antonio. "Utopia y realismo politico en Tommaso Campanella." *Anuario de filosofia del derecho* 3 (1955): 137–69.
Tuck, Richard. *Philosophy and Government 1572–1651*. Cambridge, 1993.
Tuilier, André. "Richelieu théologien et la Sorbonne." In *Richelieu et le monde de l'esprit*. Paris, 1985. 277–92.
Turnbull, G. H. "Johann Valentin Andreaes Societas Christiana." *Zeitschrift für deutsche Philologie* 73 (1954): 406–32.
Tuscano, Pasquale. "La prosa scientifica dell'Epilogo Magno' e del 'del Senso delle cose e della magia' di Tommaso Campanella." *Letteratura e scienza nella storia della cultura italiana: Atti del IX congresso dell'associazione internazionale per gli studi di lingua e letteratura italiana*. Palermo, 1978. 497–510.
Tyler, Royall. *The Emperor Charles the Fifth*. Fair Lawn, N.J., 1956.
Vaccaro, Emerinziona. *Le marchi dei tipografi ed editori italiani del secolo XVI nella Biblioteca Angelica di Roma*. Florence, 1983.
Van den Broek, R. "The Present State of Gnostic Studies." *Vigiliae Christianae* 37 (1983): 41–71.
Varela Marcos, Jesús. "El Seminario de marinos: Un intento de formacion de los marineros para las armadas y flotas de Indias." *Revista de historia de America* 87 (1979): 9–36.
Vasoli, Cesare. "Colomb et le voyage 'prophetique.'" In *Voyager à la Renaissance: Actes du colloque de Tours, 1983*. Ed. Jean Céard and Jean Claude Margolin. Paris, 1987.
———. "Francesco Patrizi da Cherso e il 'modello' della città dei sacerdoti-sapienti."

In *Modelle nella storia del pensiero politico*. Ed. V. J. Comparato. Città di Castello, 1987. 123–44.
Verzera, Antonino. *La poesia di Tommaso Campanella*. Naples, 1968.
Vickers, Brian, ed. *Occult and Scientific Mentalities in the Renaissance*. Cambridge, 1984.
———. "On the Goal of the Occult Sciences in the Renaissance." In *Die Renaissance im Blick der Nationen Europas*. Ed. Georg Kauffmann. Wiesbaden, 1991. 51–93.
Villari, Rosario. "Naples: The Insurrection in Naples of 1585." In *The Late Italian Renaissance, 1525–1630*. Ed. Eric Cochrane. New York, 1970. 305–30.
———. *La rivolta antispagnoli a Naples. Le origini (1585–1647)*. 2nd ed. Bari, 1973.
———. *Rebeldes y reformadores del siglo XVI al XVII*. Barcelona, 1981.
———. *The Revolt of Naples*. Trans. James Nowell. Oxford/Cambridge, 1993.
Virnich, Maria. *Die Erkenntnistheorie Campanellas und Francis Bacons*. Bonn, 1920.
Vivanti, Corrado. "Henry IV, the Gallic Hercules." *JWCI* 30 (1967): 176–97.
Walker, D. P. *Spiritual and Demonic Magic from Ficino to Campanella*. London, 1958.
———. "Origène en France au début de XVIe siècle." In *Courants Religieux et Humanisme*. Paris, 1959. 101–19.
———. *The Ancient Theology: Studies in Christian Platonism from the Fifteenth to the Eighteenth Century*. Ithaca, N.Y., 1972.
Warnke, Frank J. *Versions of Baroque. European Literature in the Seventeenth Century*. New Haven, Conn./London, 1972.
Webster, Charles. *From Paracelsus to Newton: Magic and the Making of Modern Science*. Cambridge, 1982.
West, Delno C. "Christopher Columbus, Lost Biblical Sites, and the Last Crusade." *CHR* 78 (1992): 518–41.
Westfall, Richard S. "Isaac Newton's *Theologiae Gentilis Origines Philosophicae*." In *The Secular Mind*. Ed. W. Warren Wagar. New York/London, 1982. 15–34.
———. "Galileo and the Accademia dei Lincei." In *Novità celesti e crisi del sapere: Atti del convegno di studi Galileiani*. Ed. P. Galluzzi. Florence, 1984. 189–200.
Westmann, Robert S. "Magical Reform and Astronomical Reform: The Yates Thesis Reconsidered." In *Hermeticism and the Scientific Revolution: Clark Library Seminar, March 9, 1974*. Los Angeles, 1977. 5–91.
———. "The Reception of Galileo's 'Dialogue.' A Partial World Census of Extant Copies." In *Novità celesti e crisi del sapere: Atti del convegno di studi Galileiani*. Ed. P. Galluzzi. Florence, 1984. 329–72.
———. "The Copernicans and the Churches." In *God and Nature*. Ed. D. C. Lindberg and R. L. Numbers. Berkeley, 1986. 76–113.
Wilmott, M. J. "Aristotle's exotericus, acroamaticus, mysticus: Two Interpretations of the Typological Classification of the Corpus Aristotelicum by Francesco Patrizi da Cherso." *Nouvelles de la République des Lettres* [5] (1985): 67–96.
Wittenberg, Richard Charles. "Tommaso Campanella: Political Universalism in the Later Renaissance." Unpublished Ph.D. diss., University of California–Berkeley, 1974.
Woelfflin, Heinrich. *The Renaissance and Baroque*. Ithaca, N.Y., 1964.
Wolfe, Phillip, ed. *Peiresc: Lettres à Naudé, 1629–1637*. Paris/Seattle/Tübingen, 1983.
Wootton, David. *Paolo Sarpi between Renaissance and Enlightenment*. Cambridge, 1983.

———. "Lucien Febvre and the Problem of Unbelief in the Early Modern Period." *The Journal of Modern History* 60 (1988): 695–730.
———. "Unbelief in Early Modern Europe." *History Workshop Journal* 20 (1985): 82–100.
Wright, A. D. "The Venetian View of Church and State: Catholic Erastianism." *Studi Secenteschi* 19 (1978): 75–106.
Yates, Frances A. *Giordano Bruno and the Hermetic Tradition*. Chicago, 1964.
———. *The Rosicrucian Enlightenment*. London/Boston, 1972.
———. "Bruno and Campanella on the French Monarchy." In *Renaissance and Reform: The Italian Contribution: Collected Essays*. Vol. 2. London, 1983.
Zambelli, Paola. "Rinnovamento umanistico, progresso tecnologico e teorie filosofiche alle origini della rivoluzione scientifica." *SS* 6 (1965): 507–46.
———. "Il Problema della magia naturale nel Rinascimento." *RCSF* 28 (1973): 271–96.
———. "Platone. Ficino e la magia." In *Studia Humanitatis. Ernesto Grassi zum 70 Geburtstag*. Munich, 1973. 121–42.
———. "Le problème de la magie naturelle à la Renaissance." In *Magia, astrologia e religione nel Rinascimento: Convegno polacco-italiano, Varsavia, 1972*. Wroclaw/ Warsaw/Krakow/ Danzig, 1974. 48–82.
———. "Fine del mondo o inizio della propaganda." In *Scienze, credenze occulte, livelli di cultura*. Florence, 1982. 291–368.
Zeller, Gaston. "La monarchie d'Ancien Regime et les frontières naturelles." *Revue d'histoire moderne* 8 (1933): 305–33.
———. "Les rois de France candidats à l'empire: Essai sur l'idéologie impériale en France." *Revue historique* 173 (1934): 273–311, 497–534.
Zika, Charles. "Reuchlin's *De verbo mirifico* and the Magic Debate of the Late Fifteenth Century." *JWCI* 39 (1976): 104–38.

INDEX

Abano, Pietro d', 185, 186n
Abelard, Peter, 153, 157
Abraham (rabbi), 18–19, 65
Abraham's bosom, 329n
absolutism, 256, 279, 353; English, 255
Accademia dei Segreti (Naples), 22–23, 24
Acosta, José de, 320n, 325n, 330, 335n
Adami, Tobias, 76, 77, 89, 95; on Bacon, 81; communication with Campanella, 78–79; and Galileo, 82, 172; publication of Campanella's works, 78–82, 84, 167, 171, 207; sonnets to, 56; stay in Naples, 79
Africa: mendicant orders in, 317
Albategnius (= al-Battānī, Abū 'Abd Allah Muhammad), 295
Albertus Magnus, 18; on Aristotle, 157; on astrology, 66
Albumasr (= Abū Ma'shar Al-Balkhī, Ja'far Ibn Muhammad), 66
Aldobrandini, Cardinal, 260
Aldobrandini, Jacopo, 20, 21, 46
Alexander VI (pope), 193
Alexander the Great, 336
Alexandria: occult literature of, 347, 349–50
Allacci, Leone, 103, 153
Altomonte (convent), 17, 18–19
Alvarez de Toledo, Pedro (viceroy), 10, 12, 276
Alvarezisti, 131, 132, 135
Amabile, Luigi, xxiii
Ambrose, Saint, 151
Ambrosian Library, 76
America. *See* New World
Amerindians: Campanella on, 328, 332, 336; exploitation of, 222–23; hispanization of, 223, 328–29; missionary attitude towards, 336. *See also* evangelization, global; salvation, Christian
Amerio, Romano, xvii n, 155n, 306n
Anabaptists, 30, 287; Münsterite, 87; utopianism of, 306
Anaxagoras, 53, 170, 345
Andreae, Johann Valentin, 77, 80, 89
Angevins: in Italy, 9, 218
Anne of Austria, 129–30
anthropocentrism, 345, 353
Antichrist, 296, 329; and destruction of Italy, 297; precursors of, 75, 294
anti-Machiavellism, xix, 195, 196, 255; in *Atheismus Triumphatus*, 180, 183–84, 191
antipodes: existence of, 324, 325n, 344
antiquity: in Renaissance culture, 341; universal monarchy in, 266
aphoristic literature, xviii n, xix, 320
apocalypse, 196n, 316; and discovery of New World, 326, 338; literature of, 40; in Renaissance culture, 353; of sixteenth century, 195. *See also* millenarianism
arbitristas, 210, 219, 329
Ariosto, Lodovico, 343
Aristotelianism: Campanella's opposition to, 15, 17–18, 72, 83, 126, 145–50, 162, 172, 342; Catholic Church's commitment to, 4, 24, 26, 179; dissent from, xix, xx, 16, 17; Latin, 156; at Padua, 185; of Thomas Aquinas, 17, 75, 146, 157–58; types of, 146
Aristotle: in Christian schools, 152; Church fathers on, 150, 151, 156; dialectic works of, 17, 145; Gregory IX on, 54, 153; natural philosophy of, 16; as precursor of Antichrist, 75; reception of, in the West, 156; on universal monarchy, 266, 267. Works: *Metaphysics*, 153, 156, 157; *Physics*, 153, 156, 157; *Politics*, 86, 181, 189, 190, 300, 304
Armada, Spanish, 225; defeat of, 201
Arndt, Johann, 77
Arquato, Antonio, 35, 130
Arroy, Besian, 245
asceticism, Christian, 311, 313
astrology: Arab, 66; Campanella's use of, xx, 19, 35, 36, 64, 65, 95, 100, 108, 124, 316, 319; in *La Città del Sole*, 68–69, 303; in *Discorsi universali del governo ecclesiastico*, 280; of Ficino, 66, 67; and free will, 273; French interest in, 126; in millenarianism, 316; in *La Monarchia di Spagna*, 216–17; in Renaissance culture,

astrology (cont.)
  67–68, 315, 349, 353; Richelieu's use of, 246; and Spanish universal monarchy, 228; at University of Paris, 215, 303; Urban VIII on, 107–8
astronomy: conformity to scripture, 169–70; Galilean, 167, 175; Ptolemaic, 347n; in Renaissance culture, 179; in *Theologia*, 326. See also Copernicanism; Galileo
atheism, 132, 133. See also Campanella, Tommaso: *Atheismus Triumphatus*
atomism: Campanella on, 165, 166; of Gassendi, 119, 121
Augsburg Interim of 1548, 240, 244
Augustine, Saint: Campanella's use of, 17, 90, 92, 146; community in, 309; *Confessions*, 62; and definition of religion, 185; on pastoral office, 260; on predestination, 321; on religious coercion, 248–49; on virginity, 286, 287
Augustinians: global evangelization of, 317
Augustus Caesar, 266
autonomy: human, 341, 343; in politics, 190, 191
Averroism: Paduan, 146, 149–50, 185, 187, 189, 196, 345; Renaissance, 181

Bacco, Enrico, 10
Bacon, Francis, 117, 145, 176, 345; *Magna Instauratio*, 150, 337; *Novum organum*, 81, 347–48
Badaloni, Nicola, 319
Baltic: Spanish presence in, 223
baptism, 47
Barberini, Antonio (cardinal), 128
Barberini, Francesco (cardinal), 109, 112, 134, 354; Campanella's correspondence with, 203, 229, 230
Barberini, Taddeo, 110, 112
Barclay, William, 256
Baronio, Cesare (cardinal), 243, 253, 255; *Annales*, 69, 254, 270, 275
baroque culture, 350
Bartolus, 239
Basil I (Byzantine emperor), 269, 270–71
Bataillon, Marcel, 340
Battle of the White Mountain, 87
Bavaria: alliance of, with France, 243
Bayle, Pierre, 117
Bazan, Alvaro de (admiral), 225

Bellarmino, Roberto (cardinal), 271; and aid to Campanella, 53; and Galileo, 97; Hobbes on, 258; on papal authority, 243, 258, 267, 271; on pastoral office, 255, 256–57; on *Quod reminiscentur*, 101, 104; on universal theocracy, 253
Benzoli, Girolamo, 334
Berillari, Don Basilio, 62
Berlin, Isaiah, 190
Bernard of Clairvaux, Saint, 249–50, 260; *De consideratione*, 256, 262; on evangelization, 330; on *saecula*, 294
Bernier, François, 156
Besold, Christoph, 80; his rejection of Campanella, 87; on Spanish monarchy, 199; his translations of Campanella, 77, 84, 85–86; on universal empire, 86–87
Bireley, Robert, xxiii
Blanchet, Leon, 168
Boccalini, Traiano, 200
body/soul dichotomy, 90–91; of Plato, 60–61
Bohemia: Habsburg domination of, 87
Bologna: Campanella at, 27
Bolognetti, Giorgio (nuncio), 127
Bolzoni, Lina, xxiv
Bonelli, Michele (cardinal), 29
Bon Français party, 234, 237
Borghese, Scipione (cardinal), 284
Borgia, Cesare, 183, 184, 187
Borromeo, Federigo (archbishop), 76
Botero, Giovanni, 334; on China, 324; on Coronado, 333n; *Ragion di Stato*, 205, 206, 211–12, 216; on universal monarchy, 212n, 240; on universal theocracy, 253
Bourbon dynasty, French, 114; intervention of, in Italy, 240; in *Le Monarchie delle natione*, 241–42; papal intervention in, 242; as universal monarchy, xix, 228–46
Bourdelot, Jean, 147, 153n
Bourdelot, Pierre, 153n
Bozio, Tommaso, 254–55
Brahe, Tycho, 82, 95, 150
Branchedaurius, Caesar, 84–85
Braudel, Fernand, 10, 340
Brerewood, Robert, 332n
Bridget, Saint, 64, 270, 294, 329; on destruction of Rome, 297
Bruni, Leonardo, 274, 300
Bruno, Giordano, 4, 20, 173n, 338, 345; burning of, 4, 48, 69, 168; imprisonment of, 29

Bünau, Henry von, 80
Bünau, Rudolf von, 56, 76, 77, 78, 80
Burckhardt, Jacob, 345, 348
Burton, Robert, 335n

cabala: Campanella's study of, 18; of late Renaissance, 347
Caetani, Bonifacio (cardinal), 336; anti-Lutheranism of, 252; and Campanella's *Apologia,* 171, 178; on community of property, 309; on Copernicanism, 97; on pastoral office, 260
Calabria: banditry in, 9, 32–33; intellectual life of, 13; philosophers of, 3, 17, 30, 167, 333; silk industry of, 9, 11; Spanish domination of, 3–4, 9; travelers' accounts of, 11
Calabrian revolt (1599), 32, 218; Campanella in, xx, 3, 36–41, 46, 312; Spanish view of, 46; supporters of, 36
Calasanzio, Giuseppe, 115, 289
calendar, Gregorian, 150
Calvinism, 132; antimonarchical sentiment of, 134; Campanella on, 135–36
Calvinismus bestiarum religio, 185
Campanella, Giovan Domenico. *See* Campanella, Tommaso
Campanella, Tommaso: abjuration of, 29, 32; agreement of, with Jesuits, 320n, 323; at Altomonte, 17, 18–19; anti-Aristotelianism of, 15, 17–18, 72, 83, 126, 145–50, 162, 172, 342; anti-Copernicanism of, 82–83, 110–13, 167–68, 297; aphoristic literature of, xviii, xix, 320; appeals from prison, 51–52, 54–55, 69, 94–95, 99, 101; appeals to German Catholics, 69; arrest of (1594), 29; arrest of (1599), 37–38; autobiography of, 115; and Barberini family, 110; and Bellarmino, 101, 104, 105; biography of, xxii–xxiii; birth of, 13; in Calabria, 33–34; in Calabrian revolt, xx, 3, 36–41, 46, 312; at Castel dell'Ovo, 53, 78, 148; at Castel Nuovo, 47–48, 53, 55, 56, 59; charges against (1592), 26; charges against (1594), 29; charges against (1599), 43–44, 46; charges against (1601), 44, 47, 54; childhood of, 14; on church governance, 283–85; confiscation of works, 28–29; conversion of, xvii n, xx, 60, 63; correspondence with Barberini, 203, 229, 230; correspondence with Galileo, 41, 95–98, 104, 112–14, 148, 165–66, 167; correspondence with Ingoli, 317; correspondence with Paul V, 51–53, 100, 110, 261, 280–81, 331; correspondence with Philip III, 52; correspondence with Schoppe, 72, 151; correspondence with Trejo, 276–79; at Cosenza, 15, 18; death of, 137; demonic evocations of, 62, 65; departure of, for France, 116–17, 229; *De tribus impostoribus* attributed to, 29; dissimulation by, xvii, xxiii, 30, 85, 123, 139, 261–62; dramas of, 33–34; enemies of, among Dominicans, 26; escape attempts by, 65, 70; Eurocentrism of, 328–29, 337, 338; extradition of, by Holy Office, 98, 99, 102, 106; at Florence, 27; French connections of, 114–17, 120–26, 134, 153, 229; in French politics, 129; on Galileo, 64, 167, 326–27; German interest in, 69–77, 78, 84–89; on global evangelization, 319, 323, 328–37, 352; hispanophilism of, 57–58, 63, 84, 203, 211, 226; illnesses of, 14, 19, 30; imprisonment of (1592), 26–27; imprisonment of (1594–98), 30, 56; imprisonment of (1599), xx, 37-38; imprisonment of (1601–18), 5, 49, 51–55, 138, 230, 351; imprudence of, xviii; intellectual isolation of, 339; Italian scholarship on, xxiii; as *lapsus,* 32; and Launoy, 153, 158, 162; lost works of, 193n; and Louis XIV, 130, 246, 299, 335; medical knowledge of, 14, 28; and memorials to Louis XIII, 233, 234n, 235, 241n; and Mersenne, 124–25; messianism of, 31, 39–40, 41, 42, 43, 54, 123, 131; millenarianism of, 63, 293–98, 316, 337; at Naples, 19–25, 32; natural philosophy of, xvii, xxi, xxiii, 25, 93, 151, 162, 168, 319–20, 343; novitiate of, 14–15; opportunism of, xxi, 202, 262; orthodoxy of, xvii; pansophism of, xxi; in Paris, 119–37, 354; patronage by Barberini, 110, 112; patronage by Della Porta, 24–25; patronage by del Tufo, 21–22; patronage by Peiresc, 118–25; Pelagianism of, 105, 131, 132; philogallicism of, 231n; philosophical studies of, 15, 17–18, 20; poetry of, xxiii, 55–64, 80, 142, 320, 325, 343; political philosophy of, 28, 33n, 63, 182, 247; as preacher, 35–36, 37; prison reading of, 53, 95; prison writings of, 5, 53–66, 99; as prophet, 31, 34, 39–40, 45, 54–55, 61, 139; readership in England,

Campanella, Tommaso (*cont.*)
207; reform of Christian philosophy, 145–61; relationship to his age, xix, 341–42; relationship with Galileo, 27, 97, 161–62, 171–72, 179; release from prison, 102, 114; removal from Index, 104; on revolution, 34–35; and Richelieu, 126, 127–30, 229, 230, 232, 242–43; on sacraments, 42, 44, 47; at San Elmo, 53, 56, 59, 60, 74, 99, 271, 295, 331; as "second Machiavel," 24, 190, 196; self-identity of, 40, 69, 95, 346; self-mastery of, 140, 141; senility of, 123, 137; sensism of, 29, 81, 84, 89–90, 145; sentencing of (1601), 48–49; sermon of, at Conflans, 229–33, 239–43, 246; on sexual freedom, 42, 43, 44, 47, 300; his simulation of madness, 3, 30, 39, 54, 56, 139, 141; socioeconomic thought of, xx, xxi; Telesianism of, 15, 26–27, 29, 89, 145; as terminal Renaissance figure, 341–42; textual practices of, 18; on theological liberty, 272–73; his theory of poetry, 64, 325, 344; torture of (1594), 29; torture of (1600), 38, 45, 139–40; torture of (1601), 3, 47–48; translation of his works into German, 71, 72, 78, 80, 84, 85–86; trial of (1591–92), 19, 26–27, 61; trial of (1599–1601), 37–49; and Urban VIII, 104, 106–10, 112, 131, 193n, 235, 239; and use of Italian vernacular, 96, 97, 98; usefulness of, to Habsburgs, 74; visitors of, in prison, 100–101.

Campanella, Tommaso. Works: *Aforismi Politici*, xviii n, 231, 232; —, ecclesiastical state in, 261; —, priest-rulers in, 275, 277; —, Schoppe's use of, 73; —, Spanish universal monarchy in, 226–27; "Al carcere," 31; "Al Sole," 60; *Antilutheran Epistle*, 79; *Antiveneti*, 261, 267, 271–74, 282; —, lamentation in, 272; —, Machiavelli in, 193; —, Schoppe's acquisition of, 70, 71, 73, 261; *Apologia pro Galileo*, 81, 96, 107, 110–11, 113, 165, 276; —, composition of, 99, 166, 171; —, Descartes's reading of, 90; —, freedom of scientific investigation in, 82-83, 172–77; —, knowledge in, 175–77; —, Mersenne on, 124; —, nature in, 175, 176; —, publication of, 161; —, scripture in, 169–70, 175, 176; —, suppression of, 177; *Apologia pro philosophis Magnae Graeciae*, 30; *Appendix ad amicum pro apologia*, 45; *Articuli prophetales*, xxiv, 39, 74, 203, 276; —, Dominicans in, 292; —, millenarianism in, 293–94; —, republicanism in, 274; —, Schoppe's conveyance of, 71; —, Spanish universal monarchy in, 227–28; —, trigons in, 68; *Astrologicorum libri VI*, 109, 114; *Astronomiae libri VII*, 81–82, 95; *Atheismus Triumphatus*, 42, 79, 109n; —, anti-Machiavellism in, 180, 183–84, 191; —, Aristotelianism in, 146, 191; —, Christ in, 321; —, composition of, 62; —, French edition of, 235; —, Inquisition on, 104–5; —, libertinism in, 133, 134; —, Platonism in, 106; —, publication of, 128, 132, 321; —, religion and state in, 182, 183; —, salvation in, 322–23; —, Schoppe's use of, 71–72; —, science in, 170–71; —, suppression of, 53, 183; —, titles of, 132–33; *Cantica*, 79; "Canzone a Berillo," 62; *La Città del Sole*, 276, 298–314; —, astrology in, 68–69, 303; 298–99; —, bowdlerizing of, 299; —, Christ in, 59; —, community in, 264, 310; —, creation in, 83; —, ecclesiastical society in, 280; —, education in, 342–43; —, eugenics in, 215, 220, 299–301, 303, 312, 313; —, primalities in, 303; —, procreation in, 22, 299–300; —, publication of, 81, 304; —, scholarship on, xvii; —, sexual liberty in, 43, 44, 300; —, torture in, 139; —, as utopia, 298–99;—, world unity in, 352; "Commentaria," xxiv, 107, 111, 112; *De conceptione Virginis*, 292; *De conflagratione Vesuvii*, 115; *De fato siderali vitando*, 107–8, 109; *De Gentilismo non retinendo*, 99, 107; —, anti-Aristotelianism in, 147–50, 162; —, composition of, 151; —, Galileo in, 161; —, Italian translation of, 155n; —, publication of, 128, 153; —, revision of, 154, 155, 160; —, Thomas Aquinas in, 157, 162; —, two Books imagery in, 159, 160, 171–72; *De investigatione rerum*, 15; "Della Prima Possanza," 57, 58; *Del senso della cose e della magia*, 24, 64–66, 89, 91–92; —, matter and form in, 164; —, Ocellus Lucanus in, 302; —, translation of, into Latin, 99; *De praecedentia praesertim religiosorum*, 141n; *De praedestinatione*, 106, 128; *De regno Christi*, 135,

261; *De regno ecclesiae,* 71, 73; *De sensu rerum,* 79, 80, 90; —, dedication of, 130; —, Mersenne on, 125; *Dialogo politico contro Luterani e Calvinisti,* 29–30, 238n; —, ecclesiastical state in, 283; *Dialogo politico tra un Venetiano, Spagnuolo e Francese,* 114, 232; —, heretics in, 236–37; *Dichiarazione,* 34–35; *Discorsi ai principi d'Italia,* 28, 88, 227, 281–82; —, manuscripts of, 203; —, Schoppe's conveyance of, 71, 73; *Discorsi universali del governo ecclesiastico,* 28, 193n, 261, 265; —, astrology in, 280; —, reworking of, 285; —, universal theocracy in, 262–63, 279–80; *Discorso sui Paesi Bassi,* 206–7, 219; "Dispregio della morte," 61; *Documenta ad Gallorum nationem,* 230, 231–32; —, Charlemagne in, 235, 237–39; —, heretics in, 235–39; *Epilogo magno,* 32, 71, 99; *Etica,* 99; Latin Eclogue, 130, 299, 335; *Medicinalium iuxta propria principia libri septem,* 99, 120, 122; *Monarchia Christianorum,* 33, 104, 261; —, community in, 263–64; *La Monarchia di Spagna,* xxiv, 58, 118, 244, 276; —, Amsterdam edition of, 86; —, astrology in, 216–17; —, composition of, 34, 39, 45; —, English edition of, 190, 206, 207, 208, 212, 217, 343; —, global policy in, 223–24; —, imperial philosophy in, 215–16; —, influence of, 226; —, interpolations in, 204–5, 211; —, kingship in, 215; —, Latin editions of, 206, 208; —, manuscripts of, 204n, 206, 207; —, military in, 215, 219; —, missionary practices in, 331, 336; —, New World in, 221, 328; —, nobility in, 218–19; —, procreation in, 220; —, and *Ragion di Stato,* 211–12; —, religion in, 187; —, role of women in, 220, 223; —, Schoppe's conveyance of, 71, 73, 205; —, second redaction of, 205n, 226; —, translation into German, 78, 84, 85–86, 87, 207, 208n, 210; —, universal monarchy in, 202, 212–26; *Monarchia messiae,* 71, 73, 135; —, ecclesiastical state in, 260–61, 269–71; —, Inquisition on, 104–5; —, Spain in, 226, 275; —, suppression of, 271; —, universal monarchy in, 327; *Le Monarchie delle natione,* 230–32; —, Charlemagne in, 235; —, French monarchy in, 241–42; —, Germany in, 240;

—, papacy in, 239; *Il mondo e Il libro,* 163–64; *Monotriad,* 92; "My Campanella," 58; *Opera omnia,* 128, 136; "Oratio pro Deo," 63; *Panegyric to the Princes of Italy,* 276; *Philosophia rationalis,* 128, 136; *Philosophia realis libri quatuor,* 32, 59n, 119n, 154; —, Adami's use of, 79; —, Descartes's reading of, 90; —, publication of, 81, 115, 136; —, torture in, 140–41; *Philosophia sensibus demonstrata,* 17–18, 145; —, astrology in, 95; —, dedication of, 21; —, publication of, 26–27; *Poetica,* 30, 325, 351; *Prima-Secondo delineatio defensionum,* 38–40; *Prodromus,* 78, 90; *Il prognostico astrologico,* 71; *The Prophecy of Christ,* 294–95; *Quaestiones physiologicae,* 24, 83n, 99, 147; *Quaestiones super secunda parte suae Philosophiae realis, quae est De politicis,* 185n, 189–90, 274; —, Christ in, 304–6; —, community of women in, 304–5; —, eugenics in, 309–10; —, property in, 288; *Quod reminiscentur et convertentur ad dominum universi fines terrae,* 79, 99, 276, 296–97, 324; —, Bellarmino on, 101, 104; —, clergy in, 307; —, dedication of, 331; —, evangelization in, 318–19, 331–35; —, Inquisition on, 104–5; —, publication of, 112, 131; *Scelta d'alcune poesie filosofiche,* 79; *Syntagma de libris propriis et recta ratione studendi,* 21, 133, 263, 272; —, composition of, 56; —, dedication of, 98; —, Naudé on, 122; —, publication of, 115, 122; *Theologia,* xviii, 99, 100, 101, 319, 351; —, Antichrist in, 294, 296; —, Columbus in, 329; —, composition of, 35, 168–69; —, eugenics in, 313; —, evangelism in, 330; —, government in, 283; —, heresy in, 326; —, monasticism in, 306n; —, papacy in, 336; —, salvation in, 322; —, two Books imagery in, 177; "Three Psalmodic Metaphysical Prayers," 63; *Universalis philosophiae, seu Metaphysicarum rerum,* xviii, 24, 63, 74, 76, 318, 351; —, Adami's use of, 79; —, Columbus in, 325; —, deception in, 188–89; —, publication of, 136; —, redactions of, 89, 91, 99, 124; scholarship on, xvii; *Vita Christi,* 40
cannibalism, 334
Cano, Melchior, 187

388 INDEX

Capuchins, 288
Carafa, Gianpietro. *See* Paul IV (pope)
Cardano, Girolamo, 67, 294, 349; *De subtilitate,* 18
Carpocratians, 308n, 313n
Carthusians, 288
Cartier, Jacques, 325n
Casaubon, Isaac, 350
Cassian, John, 311
Cassirer, Ernst, 164
Castel dell'Ovo (Naples), 10; Campanella in, 53, 78, 148
Castelli, Benedetto, 113
Castel Nuovo (Naples), 10; Campanella at, 47–48, 53, 55, 56, 59
Castel San Elmo (Naples), 10; Campanella at, 53, 56, 59, 60, 74, 99, 271, 295, 331
Castelvetere, Dionigi, 101
Castile, navigational skills of, 202n
Catherine of Siena, Saint, 64
Catholic Church: and acceptance of new science, 178–79; Augustinianism of, 155, 178; commitment of, to Aristotelianism, 4, 24, 26, 179; conclaves of, 283–84; constitutional practices of, 264–65; engagement with world, 105, 192, 247–60; establishment of congregations in, 282–83; exemption from taxation, 13; free will in, 273; Gallicanism in, 256; governance of, 283–85; medieval, 252; migration of, to New World, 297, 329; Thomas More on, 250–51; pastoral role of, 247–60; radicalism in, 208; renewal of, 28; rulings on natural philosophy, 152–53; secular bequests to, 280; on study of poetry, 149; and treatment of heresy, 29n, 43; triumphalism of, 249, 253–55; universality of, 59, 141, 142. *See also* congregations; evangelization, global; Holy Office; Inquisition; papacy; universal theocracy
Catholic League, 87, 202
Catholics, German: and aid to Campanella, 69
cavalry, Polish, 228
celibacy, clerical, 43, 311
Cesarini, Virginio, 284
Cesi, Federico (prince), 171
charisma, 249
Charlemagne, 216; bequests of, to Church, 280; Campanella on, 232, 235–37; in *Documenta ad Gallorum nationem,* 235, 237–39
Charles I (king of Naples and Sicily), 10
Charles V (Holy Roman emperor): Campanella on, 243–44; and Clement VIII, 244n; Lutheran policy of, 236, 237–38, 243–45; universal monarchy under, 199, 235
Chateauvillain, count of, 128
cheese and worms metaphor, 90, 266, 291, 324, 327, 328n
Chemnitz, Boguslaw Philipp von, 243
Cherbury, Lord Herbert of, 118, 160n, 316, 319, 320
Chifflet, Jean Jacques, 200
Chilmead, Edmund, 206, 207, 217, 225n
China: Campanella on, 324, 352; Jesuits in, 320; mendicant orders in, 317; miracles in, 330
Chorier, Nicolas, 136–37
Christ: Campanella on, 58–59, 62, 63; horoscope of, 66; as *legifer,* 59, 185, 321; missionaries' teachings on, 320; as priest-king, 276; as Primal Reason, 42, 263, 268, 305, 311, 313, 321; in *Quaestiones . . . De politicis,* 304–6; as *scandalon,* 105, 248, 334
Christianity: and astrology, 66–67; and Book of Nature, 161; commonwealth of, 31; and disarming of heaven, 191, 192n; empowerment of, 196; Eurocentric, 323, 337; Greek, 298; Machiavelli's effect on, 183–84; marriage in, 312; militant, 193–94, 196; as missionary doctrine, 319; parochialism of, 348; political, 191, 193–94; rationality of, 133, 186, 314, 315, 321, 323; revitalization of, xix; role of Aristotle in, 152–54; salvation in, 42, 44, 105; and science, 170–71, 174–75. *See also* evangelization, global; salvation, Christian; universal theocracy
Church fathers: on Aristotle, 150, 151, 156; Campanella's use of, 147, 150, 151, 162, 170, 171, 172; on community, 308; Greek, 321; on predestination, 321
Cisneros, Francisco Jiménez de (archbishop of Toledo), 340
Clario, Giambattista, 29
Claves, Étienne de, 126
Clement VII (pope), 244n

Clement VIII (pope), 253, 254
Clement of Alexandria, 151, 156, 308n
Clement of Rome, Saint, 288, 306, 310; on community of property, 308, 309
clergy: celibacy of, 43, 311; of Counter Reformation, 283n, 284–85; luxury of, 281, 288; mendicant, 288, 290, 296; in *Quod reminiscentur,* 307; secular, 306, 312; superiority of, to laity, 291, 307
coessentiation, 92
Columbus: Campanella on, 64, 97, 150, 151, 216, 224, 324–27, 329, 344; in Campanella's poetry, 351; as Christ-bearer, 294, 334–35; comparison with Galileo, 326, 327n; and empiricism, 91, 151, 324; eschatological significance of, 338
community: Augustine on, 309; in Campanella's works, 261, 263, 269, 286–89; and love, 310; in Plato, 286, 289; of women, 44, 299–301, 304–5, 308–11, 313–14
Compendium librorum Politicorum de Papana & Hispanica Monarchia (1628), 85, 88
Confessio fraternitatis, 77
Congregatio de Propaganda Fide, 112, 331, 332; Campanella's influence on, 352; establishment of, 317–18, 319; Ingoli in, 134
Congregation for Missions, 317
Congregation of the Index, 101, 104; on Campanella's works, 28–29; and condemnation of Copernicanism, 97, 173
Constantine, Donation of, 88, 213, 255, 265, 268
Constantinople IV (ecumenical council), 269–71
Contestabile, Giulio, 36–37, 100
Copernicanism, 315; anthropocentrism of, 345; Campanella's opposition to, 82–83, 110–12, 167–68, 297; condemnation of, by Church, 97, 111–12, 158, 173
Copernicus, 82, 112, 150, 325; in Campanella's poetry, 351
Coronado, Francisco, 333n
Cortese, Giulio, 24, 32, 34
Costo, Tommaso, 76
Counter Reformation: Campanella's influence on, 73; clergy of, 283n, 284–85; hierarchical authority of, 272; image of Machiavelli in, 182; imperialism of Church in, 247–

60; religion of, 195; Spanish role in, 213
Covarrubias, Diego, 267, 268
Cremonini, Cesare, 150
Crotonists, 17

D'Ailly, Pierre, 66, 67
Dal Pozzo, Cassiano, 101
Dante, 285; Campanella's use of, 56, 57, 270, 297, 343
De auxiliis controversy, 323
Decembrio, Pier Candido, 300, 301
deception: as political expedient, 188–89
Della Porta, Giambattista: and Inquisition, 27–28; *Magia naturalis,* 23, 24; occultism of, 65, 145, 165, 349; *L'Olimpia,* 24; his patronage of Campanella, 24–25
Della Porta, Gian Ferrante, 22–23
Della Porta, Gian Vincenzo, 22
Della Porta family, 19, 22
Del Tufo, Mario, 21–22, 44, 119n, 215
De Mattei, Roldolfo, 205
Democritus, 29
Descartes, René, 339; his reading of Campanella, 90, 125, 137, 138
De Soto, Domingo, 201, 266–67, 309, 336
Diodati, Elias, 121, 122, 160n
Diodorus of Tarsus, 321n
Diogenes Laertius, 333
discipline: as pastoral function, 248–51
disputatio: meaning of, 174, 175n
divination: Campanella's study of, 18, 19
divorce, 310
Dominican order: Campanella on, 141, 286, 288, 290, 291–93, 337; Campanella's entry into, 14–15; enemies of Campanella among, 26; global evangelization of, 317; missions of, to Japan, 51; at Naples, 20–21; Parisian, 155; predestinarian theology of, 106, 131, 241; reformation of, 45; Spanish, 131, 285; on universal monarchy, 201
Doni, Anton Francesco, 301
Doria, Paolo Mattia, 218
Dosio, Giovanni Antonio, 60
doubt: Campanella on, 35–36, 90
Du Bray, Jean, 136
Dubray, Toussaint, 128
Duchhardt, Heinz, 232n
Ducros, François, 56, 63, 64
Dupuy, circle of, 120, 126, 134, 153, 229

Dutch: naval power of, 202n, 225, 228; in New World, 233

Ecclesiastes, 175n; knowledge in, 173–75
ecclesiastical state: in *Aforismi Politici*, 261; in *Monarchia messiae*, 260–61, 269–71; Thomas Aquinas on, 262–63; as utopia, 280. *See also* universal theocracy
education: in *La Città del Sole*, 342–43; Jesuit, 289–90; in *La Monarchia di Spagna*, 215–16, 220
egalitarianism, 291
Elliott, John, 203
Elzevir, Louis, 86, 226; on Spanish monarchy, 208–9
Empedocles, 150
empiricism, 24, 160; in Campanella's works, 91, 95, 145, 151, 162, 167, 179, 344–45; of Galileo, 161, 162, 165, 167, 179; and magic, 164; of Mersenne, 124. *See also* experience
England: absolutism in, 255; Campanella's readership in, 207; Catholic restoration in, 160n; civil war in, 135, 354; intellectual life of, 159–60; in *La Monarchia di Spagna*, 224; naval power of, 202n, 223, 224, 225; Puritanism in, 316
Epiphanius, Saint, 308
epistemology: in Campanella's works, 89, 90, 91, 342, 344; of forms, 164
Erasmus, Desiderius, 281, 322; on pastoral theology, 250
Ernst, Germana, xxiv, 133, 207n, 336n; and *Le Monarchie della natione*, 231
eschatology, 195, 196; and divine initiative, 249; of New World, 337
eugenics: Campanella on, 31, 44; in *La Città del Sole*, 215, 220, 299–301, 303, 312, 313; and hispanization, 219; Huarte on, 302; and monarchy, 215; in *Quaestiones . . . De politicis*, 309–10
Eurocentrism, 323, 348; of Campanella, 328–29, 337, 338
Europe, early modern: Campanella's place in, xix; and exploitation of America, 221; hispanization of, 214–15, 217, 219–21, 224; intellectual community of, 302; millenarianism of, 40, 42; prisons of, 49–51, 99; revolution in, 35; socioeconomic problems of, xx; sovereign states in, 198; unification of, xxi

evangelization: Bernard of Clairvaux on, 330; in Japan, 330, 333
evangelization, global, xx, 317–37; Campanella on, 319, 323, 328–37, 352. *See also* New World; salvation, Christian; universal theocracy
experience: autoptic, 344n; in Campanella's works, 81, 91, 95, 145, 162, 164–65, 325, 342, 344, 353
experimentation, scientific, 23, 148; and Christian philosophy, 150; of late Renaissance, 155; and magic, 66
exploration: in Campanella's works, 216, 343

Faber, Johann, 70, 205; Schoppe's correspondence with, 69, 74, 75, 100
Failla, Pietro Giacomo, 97, 101, 105, 176–77
Fama fraternitatis, 77
Fancan, François de Langlois (sieur de), 244
Fanzago, Cosimo, 60
Feilding, Basil, 207
Felice, Felice De, 60
Ferdinand I (Holy Roman emperor), 243
Ferdinand II (Holy Roman emperor), 71, 74, 75, 214; and use of heretics, 238
Ferdinand I de' Medici, 27, 136, 180
Ferdinand II de' Medici, 136
Ferraro, Giacomo, 48
Ferrier, Jeremy, 245
Ficino, Marsilio, 20, 320, 345; astrology of, 66, 67; *De Christiana religione*, 316, 319; *De vita coelitus comparanda*, 108; Platonism of, 342
Firpo, Luigi, xxiii; on *Antiveneti*, 272; on Campanella's lost works, 193n; on Campanella's poetry, 56; and *Documenta ad Gallorum nationem*, 231
Fisher, John, 251
Flanders: Spanish loss of, 233
Florence: Campanella at, 27; Platonism of, 27, 319, 347, 349; prisons of, 49
Formula of Concord, 77
Forstner, Christoph von, 100–101, 129
Foscarini, Paolo Antonio, 173
Fozio, San Giustina da, 321n
France: alliance of, with Turks, 245; intellectual life of, 117–18, 124–26, 137–38; invasion of Italy by, 194, 195; natural

frontiers of, 241; Spanish army in, 228–29. *See also* Bourbon dynasty, French
Francis, Saint, 301
Franciscans, 289, 293; global evangelization of, 317
Frankfurt Book Fair, 352
Frederick II (Holy Roman emperor), 9
freedom: intellectual, xxi, 150; of scientific investigation, 172–77; of will, 141, 273
freedom, sexual: Campanella on, 42, 43, 44, 300; among early Christians, 313n
Fugger, Georg, 71; and aid to Campanella, 73–74, 75

Gadol, Joan Kelly, 245n
Gaffarel, Jacques, 116, 118, 122
Gagliardo, Felice, 65
Galilei, Galileo: and Adami, 82; astrology of, 97n; Campanella on, 64, 326–27; Campanella's correspondence with, 41, 95–98, 104, 112–14, 148, 165–66, 167; comparison with Columbus, 326, 327n; condemnation of, 103, 111n, 117, 158, 307; in *De Gentilismo*, 161; empiricism of, 161, 162, 165, 167, 179; relationship with Campanella, 27, 97, 161–62, 171–72, 179; research methods of, 98; on scripture, 178; telescopic discoveries of, 150, 168, 179; two Books imagery of, 177; use of patristic texts, 171, 172. Works: *The Assayer*, 166–67; *Dialogue on the two Great World Systems*, 109n, 112–13, 168, 322, 341, 342; *Letter on Sunspots*, 69; *Letter to the Grand Duchess Christina*, 171, 172–74, 177–78; *Siderius Nuncius*, 53, 95, 148, 161, 165. *See also* Campanella, Tommaso. Works: *Apologia pro Galileo*
Galilei, Roberto, 119
galleys: as prisons, 50
Gallicanism, 135, 256
Garnica, Juan de, 200
Gassendi, Pierre, 114, 156, 339; atomism of, 119, 121; and Campanella, 118, 119, 123; *Observationes*, 115
Gentiles, 147; in *Quod reminiscentur*, 333–34
Gentilism, 146n, 181
Germany: Campanella's influence in, 77, 78, 84–89; and overthrow of Spain, 233
Geronimo, Giovanni, 21–22
Giacomo II Milano, 21

Gilbert, William, 95
Ginzburg, Carlo, 324
Giovanni, Biagio di, 166
Girón, Pedro (duke of Osuna), 99–100
Giustiniani, Tommaso, 149
Gnosticism, 309, 312, 313
God: Campanella's perception of, 59–60, 72, 89, 90; existence of, 132; occult aspects of, 65
Godefroy, Jacques, 118
Goldast, Melchior, 201
González de Mendoza, Juan, 225n
Granvelle, Antoine de, 199
Gratian, 307
Greek texts: recovery of, 17, 152
Gregory the Great, Saint, 248n, 252
Gregory V (pope), 269
Gregory IX (pope): on Aristotle, 153, 154; bull of 1231, 154n, 155, 156, 157, 158; Campanella on, 159; and Fifth Lateran Council, 154
Gregory XV (pope), 101, 317, 331; death of, 283
Gregory, Tullio, 133
Guicciardini, Francesco, 84, 139, 192; on *mutazione*, 35n
gynaecea, 220n

Habsburg dynasty, 282; branches of, 198, 201; Lutheran succession to, 236, 238
Habsburg dynasty, Austrian, 238, 239–40
Habsburg dynasty, Spanish: Army of Flanders, 228–29; as *brachium* of God, 275; Elzevir on, 208–9; global policies of, 223–24; and Jesuit order, 317; Kingdom of Naples under, 9–13, 218, 275–76, 277, 279; and loss of Flanders, 233; and Lutherans, 198–99; military of, 13, 214, 234; subordination of, to papacy, 212, 213, 239–40, 245, 246; in Thirty Years' War, 128; as threat to central Europe, 214; as universal monarchy, xix, 3–4, 34, 40, 198–228, 243, 282, 328. *See also* Campanella, Tommaso. Works: *La Monarchia di Spagna;* universal monarchy
Hadrian (pope), Adrian of Utrecht, 269
Harriot, Thomas, 173n
heat and cold, Telesian theory of, 16, 23, 81, 82, 93, 164, 168, 220
heliocentrism: Campanella on, 82–83

Henrietta Maria (queen of England), 133, 134, 160n
Henry IV (king of France), 202, 225; absolutism of, 254
heresy: Catholic Church's treatment of, 29n, 43
heretics: Campanella on, 267, 326; in *Documenta ad Gallorum nationem,* 235-39; political use of, 232, 234-38, 243-45
Hermes Trismegistus, 315-16, 350; Campanella's use of, 17, 18, 64, 84
Hermeticism: French interest in, 126; of late Renaissance, 347; Mersenne on, 124
hispanization: of early modern Europe, 214-15, 217, 219, 224; of Native Americans, 223, 328-29; role of intermarriage in, 220, 221-22
Hobbes, Thomas, 4, 147n, 339; on Greek metaphysics, 160; on pastoral office, 257; on *saecula,* 257-59
Holstenius, Lucas, 153
Holy Office: Campanella's denunciation to, 36; condemnation of Copernicanism, 111-12; extradition of Campanella, 98, 99, 102, 106; imprisonment of Campanella, 29-30; prisons of, 50; restriction on Campanella, 101, 102, 104; sentencing of Campanella, 48-49
Holy Roman Empire: Campanella's influence in, 77; Spanish encroachment on, 4, 201; territorialization of, 199, 245; as universal empire, 198
Houssaye, Denis, 136
Huarte, Juan (Juan de Dios), 302
Huguenots, 135
Hulliung, Mark, 191n
humanism, 350; Christian, 250; Church's reaction to, 149
hylomorphism, Aristotelian, 16, 93, 164n

Immaculate Conception, 276, 292
Imperato, Ferrante, 24, 65, 165
Ingoli, Francesco, 134, 135, 318
Innocent VIII (pope), 349
Inquisition: arrest of Campanella, 29; and Calabrian conspiracy, 44; on Campanella's heresy, 43, 46, 47; confiscation of Campanella's manuscripts, 27; and G. B. della Porta, 27-28; investigation of Campanella's works, 104-5; surveillance of Campanella, 32
inventors: in Campanella's works, 59, 343

Italy: destruction of, by Antichrist, 297; economic decline in, 12, 13; French intervention in, 194, 195, 240; philosophical leadership of, 165; political illegitimacy of, 194; Spanish domination of, 3-4, 9, 200, 213, 233; in Spanish universal monarchy, 222, 227

James I (king of England), 255
Jansenist controversy, 132
Japan: evangelization in, 330, 333
Jesuits, 288; Campanella's agreement with, 320n, 323; in China, 320; miracles by, 330n; as missionaries, 290-91, 317, 318; Patronato Real of, 317, 318; and predestination, 131; schools of, 221, 289-90
Joachim of Fiore, Abbot, 13; Campanella's use of, 40, 64, 286, 294-95; on millennia, 293, 294, 295, 296-97; on Rome, 298
John Chrysostom, Saint, 140; on Church authority, 248, 269; on monasticism, 287, 288, 306; on property, 308-9; on salvation, 322, 323
John of Leyden, 184
Justin Martyr, 133, 156, 321n

kairos, 241; Botero on, 212. See also *occasione*
Kepler, Johan, 67, 173n, 345-46; on universal order, 87
Koyré, Alexandre, 349, 350
Kristeller, Paul Oskar, 133; *Eight Italian Philosophers of the Renaissance,* xxiii; *Iter Italicum,* 203, 204n, 207

La Milletière, Théophile, 135-36
Langlois, Denis, 136
language: in *Monarchia di Spagna,* 215, 217; persuasive power of, 242, 324
La Rochelle: fall of, 114, 237
Las Casas, Bartolomeo de, 333, 334, 335
Lateran Council, Fifth, 149, 151, 153; Campanella on, 159, 177; and Gregory IX, 154; on scripture and nature, 161, 170
Launoy, Jean de: on Aristotle, 155-57; and Campanella, 153, 158, 162; *Syllabus rationum,* 158
Laurentian Library, 180
law: canon, 280; in *Monarchia di Spagna,* 215, 217

Le Huen, Nicole, 325n
Lemos, Don Fernandez Ruiz de Castro, 6th count of (Spanish viceroy), 46, 99
Lenoble, Robert, 155
Leo III (pope), 269n
Leowitz, Cipriano, 35
Lerma, Francisco de Sandoval y Rojas, duke of, 226
libertas philosophandi, xxi, 172, 173n; in *Apologia,* 176–77. *See also* freedom
libertinism, 181; French, 133
Lincean Academy, 117, 148
Lipsius, Justus, 15; on universal empire, 86–87
Lombardo, Marco, 52, 285
Longo, Ottavio, 29
Louis XIII (king of France), 114; as *brachium* of God, 233; Campanella's memorials to, 233, 234n, 235, 241n; his reception of Campanella, 120, 126–27
Louis XIV (king of France), 130–31, 210; Campanella's Eclogue on, 130, 299, 335; horoscope of, 246
love: in Campanella's works, 57, 92; communal, 142, 310; as justification for power, 268; and papal primacy, 251; and universal theocracy, 247. *See also* primalities, doctrine of
Lucan, Marcus Annaeus, 54
Lucretius (Titos Lucretius Carus), 20, 149
Ludovisi, Ludovico ('il Cardinal Padrone'), 284
Lull, Raymond, 126, 216
Luther, Martin, 326; on Ecclesiastes, 173n; on German empire, 236n; on monasticism, 286; on *pasce oves meas,* 251–52, 256; as precursor of Antichrist, 294, 296; on St. Bernard, 250
Lutheranism: occult in, 77; Orthodoxy of, 69, 77, 89; prophecy in, 316; and Spanish monarchy, 198–99, 207–8
Lutherans: and aid to Campanella, 77–84; Charles V's policy on, 236
Lycurgus, 188; on eugenics, 215n

Machiavelli, Niccolò: in *Antiveneti,* 193; Campanella on, 71–72, 180, 181, 183–84, 193, 234, 327; and concept of civic virtue, 182; *Discourses,* 194; manuscripts of, 180; on *mutazione,* 35n; on the papacy, 192–93, 273, 279; *Prince,* 182, 183, 193, 194; on uses of religion, 186–87, 191, 285

Magalotti, Filippo, (cardinal), 113
magic: Campanella's study of, 18, 64–69, 108, 116, 138, 164–65, 316, 319; and empiricism, 164; Mersenne on, 124; in millenarianism, 316; naturalization of, 65–66; as privatization of knowledge, 351n; in Renaissance culture, 155, 179, 315, 349; and scientific experimentation, 23–25
Malvenda, Thomas, 296n
Malvezzi, Virgilio, 200
mankind: common origin of, 333–35; transmigration of, 332; unity of, 351–52, 353
Manuel, Frank, xxi, xxiii
manuscripts: circulation of, 204; confiscation of Campanella's, 27, 73, 261; of *Discorsi ai principi d'Italia,* 203; of Machiavelli, 180; of *La Monarchia di Spagna,* 204n, 206, 207; Schoppe's conveyance of, 70–71, 73, 205, 261
Mark, Saint, 311
Marlowe, Christopher, 181
Marnix van Saint Aldegonde, Philippe de, 198
Marsilius of Padua, 267
Marta, Giacomo Antonio, 17, 26
Martello, Geronimo, 13, 14
Martin, Edmund, 156
Martinez, Cipriano, 276
Mary Queen of Scots, 33
Massimi, Innocenzo de', 102
Mazarin, Jules (cardinal), 127–28, 354
Medici, Cosimo de', 241
Medici family: Platonism of, 27, 136, 152
Medina Sidonia, Don Alonso Pérez de Guzmán, 7th duke of, 201
Meinecke, Friedrich, 181
Melchisedech: pope as, 249, 255, 259, 262, 265, 268, 270
mendicant orders, 288, 290, 296, 316; global evangelization of, 317
Mersenne, Marin, 77, 124–26, 138; and Galilean science, 339
metaphysics: Greek, 159; hylomorphic, 164n; of late Renaissance, 347
microcosm: man as, 90, 93, 351
Middle Ages: end of, 340, 341
Milan, 4; benefices of, 213
military: in *Monarchia di Spagna,* 215, 219; seminaries for, 221, 222–23
military, Spanish, 214; foreign officers in, 234; in Naples, 13

millenarianism: in *Articuli prophetales*, 293–94; astrology in, 316; in Calabrian rebellion, 39–40; of Campanella, 37, 63, 293–98, 316; of seventeenth century, 88n. *See also* apocalypse
millennia, 293–98; Hobbes on, 257–59. *See also* worlds: plurality of
minting: imagery of, 152n
miracles: by missionaries, 330
missionaries: Campanella on, 331–34; Jesuits as, 290–91, 317, 318; methods of, 330; in New World, 289, 296
modernity, 345, 353
Molfetta, Hyacinth Petronius, bishop of, 104
Monarchia Sicula, 254, 275, 279
monarchy: and eugenics, 215; Hellenistic ideas of, 86. *See also* Bourbon dynasty, French; Habsburg dynasty; universal monarchy
monasticism, 140, 142; apostolic origins of, 311; Campanella on, 261, 285–89, 306n, 311–13, 342; in church history, 306–9; community in, 306n; Luther on, 286; and prisons, 49
monotriad. *See* primalities, doctrine of
Montaigne, Michel de, 349
moon: habitation of, 165
More, Thomas, 250–51; *Utopia*, 307, 340
Morin, Jean-Baptiste, 126, 156
Muentzer, Thomas, 60
Muhammad, 188
Muhammad III (Turkish sultan), 36
mutazione: in Calabrian revolt, 39–40; celestial, 67, 83–84, 110; in political literature, 35n; of states, 32; of worlds, 25
mysticism, 341

Naples, Kingdom of: overtaxation of, 9, 12–13; and papal states, 244; *Seggi* of, 12–13; under Spanish viceroy, 9–13, 218, 275–76, 277, 279; uprisings in, 3, 12, 13
Naples (city): architecture, 10, 11; benefices of, 213; cultural life of, 19–20, 22; population of, 10; travelers' accounts of, 11–12; urbanization of, 9
nationalism: absence of, 197
natural philosophy: in *Apologia*, 175; of Aristotle, 16; of Campanella, xvii, xxi, xxiii, 25, 93, 151, 162, 168, 319–20, 343; Catholic Church's rulings on, 152–53; and Christian theology, 153; and experimentation, 23–25; Neoplatonic, 302; non-Aristotelian, 16, 17; Renaissance, 162, 346
Nature, Book of, 79, 150, 151, 162, 166, 179; in Campanella's poetry, 163–64; in *Metaphysics*, 325; in *On Gentilism*, 159, 160, 171–72; in *Theologia*, 169, 177. *See also* Scripture, Book of
Naudé, Gabriel, 98, 122, 123, 129, 272; and aid to Campanella, 115–16; on Machiavelli, 181
Navagero, Andrea, 243
navigation, 202n; Dutch, 225, 228; English, 223, 224, 225; Spanish, 224–25, 323, 326, 327, 329, 335; as subject of poetry, 343
Neoplatonism, 17, 64, 347; in *Atheism Conquered*, 191; Campanella's use of, 91, 93; natural philosophy of, 302; revival of, 349
Neopythagoreanism, 179
Netherlands: Spanish influence in, 217
New World: apocalyptic significance of, 326, 338; Campanella on, 324–28; in Campanella's *Poetics*, 325, 351; discovery of, xix; Dutch in, 233; eschatalogical significance of, 337; exploitation of, 221, 222–23; impact of, on Renaissance, 348–49; mendicants in, 290, 296; migration of Church to, 297, 329; missionary orders in, 289, 296; natural law in, 336; religion and state in, 184; Spanish domination of, 224, 226–27, 323, 335; and world community, 338, 349. *See also* evangelization, global
Nicolaites, 309, 310, 313n
Nifo, Agostino, 149
Noailles, Charles (bishop), 120
Noailles, François (comte de), 117, 118, 120
nobility: imprisonment of, 50–51; in *Monarchia di Spagna*, 215, 218–19; titles of, 284
nobility, Neapolitan, 9–10; Campanella on, 33n, 41, 219, 264; corruption of, 218, 219, 288; factions in, 12
Nogarola, Ludovico, 302
nominalism, 341, 343
Numa (king), 188

occasione: Campanella's perception of, 212, 213, 223, 241, 242
occult: in Alexandrian literature, 347, 349–50; Campanella's study of, 19, 65, 95; of Della Porta, 145; French interest in, 126;

of late Renaissance, 347; in Lutheranism, 77; Mersenne on, 124
Ocellus Lucanus, 20, 22; on procreation, 302
Olivares, Gaspar de Guzmán (count of), 207, 226, 329; library of, 203; and siege of La Rochelle, 237n; support of Campanella, 102
ontology: in Campanella's *Metaphysics*, 89, 90, 91, 138
Origen: Campanella's use of, 17, 151, 321, 350; on world renewal, 28n, 322

Padua: Campanella at, 27–28; University of, 341
Paganini, Gianni, 133
Palazzo Pucci, 50
Panofsky, Erwin, 345
Panoptic State, 51
panpsychism, 90–91
pansensism: in Campanella's works, 92, 162–63, 165
papacy: as *conditor juris,* 269; global imperialism of, 225n; Hobbes on, 258; imperial role of, 247–60; indirect power of, 255, 258, 267, 268, 271; influence of, in Kingdom of Naples, 12; intervention of, in French monarchy, 242; Italian income of, 213; Machiavelli on, 192–93, 273, 279; in *Le Monarchie delle natione,* 239; pastoral duties of, 249–50, 270, 278; and right of intervention, 240, 242, 243; and right of *translatio imperii,* 239, 243, 269; as stabilizing factor, 282; subordination of Spanish monarchy to, 212, 213, 239–40, 245, 246; temporal power of, 267–68, 279; Thomas Aquinas on, 269. *See also* Catholic Church; evangelization, global; *pasce oves meas;* universal theocracy
papal states, 4, 262, 280; and Kingdom of Naples, 244
Paracelsus, 80, 81, 347
paradise: location of, 329
Paris: Campanella at, 119-37, 354
Paris, University of, 126; Aristotle at, 155, 156; and Galileo's condemnation, 158; use of astrology at, 215, 303
Parmenides, 79
Pascal, Blaise, 320, 353
pasce oves meas (John 21:17), 268; Bellarmino on, 256–57; Campanella on, 259–60, 262; interpretation of, 247; Luther on, 251–52, 256; Reformation interpretations of, 248n; St. Bernard on, 249; and temporal power, 267–68
Pater Noster: in Campanella's poetry, 58
Patin, Guy, 121
Patrizi, Francesco, 4, 145, 316
Patronato Real (of Jesuits), 317, 318
Paul IV (pope), 137, 238, 243; enmity of, to Habsburgs, 244
Paul V (pope), 51–53, 100, 110, 261, 280–81, 331
Peace of Augsburg, 236
peasantry, Calabrian, 33
Peiresc, Nicolas-Claude Fabri de, 117, 147; patronage of Campanella, 118–25
Pelagianism, 105, 131, 132
Percy, Henry (earl of Northumberland), 50–51
Persio, Antonio, 53, 95, 96, 148
Petrarch, Francesco, 340
Petrolo, Domenico, 43
Pflug, Christoph, 70
Philip II (king of Spain), 199–200; claims of, in central Europe, 214; hispanism under, 235
Philip III (king of Spain), 36–37, 75; Campanella's correspondence with, 43, 52, 54; global monarchy under, 200; golden age under, 202; marinal seminaries of, 225
Philip IV (king of Spain), 200
Philolaus, 17, 167, 325
philology: development of, 353
philosophers: Calabrian, 3, 17, 30, 167, 333; classical, 15, 45, 54–55, 145, 149, 181
philosophers' stone, 24
Piarists, 289–90
Pico della Mirandola, Gianfrancesco, 147, 148, 149
Pico della Mirandola, Giovanni, 14, 94–95, 345
Pignatelli, Tommaso, 116
Pinelli, Gian Vincenzo, 28
Pisa, University of, 27
planets: populated, 96, 165, 179
Plato: Campanella on, 44, 54, 57, 314; community in, 289; loss to Western civilization, 152; priest-rulers in, 266, 267; revival of interest in, 145. Works: *Laws,* 268; *Republic,* 299–301, 303n, 304, 306n; *Symposium,* 92

Platonism, 17; in *Atheismus Triumphatus,* 106; Christian, 17; Florentine, 27, 319, 347, 349; Renaissance, 93, 315; Roman purge of, 4n
pleroma, 93
pluralism: Campanella on, 191; in Spanish political thought, 201; of worlds, 15, 96, 168
pneuma (Stoicism), 16, 163
poetry: Campanella's use of, 55–64; Church's ban on study of, 149
Poland: government of, 279
politics: autonomy of, 190, 191; relationship of, to religion, xxi, 181–83, 187–88, 191, 194–96
Poliziano, Angelo, 350
polledro (torture machine), 38
Pomponazzi, Pietro, 149–50, 185
Ponzio, Dionisio: in Calabrian conspiracy, 36, 37, 42, 43, 44, 45; meeting of, with Campanella, 15; release of, from prison, 61
Ponzio, Pietro, 56
Porrée, Gilbert de la, 153
Postel, Guillaume, 126, 316
poverty, 289–90
power: in Campanella's works, 57, 92, 353; as function of love, 268; and monasticism, 142; and universal theocracy, 247. *See also* primalities, doctrine of
predestination, 131, 132, 134; Campanella on, 321–23; Dominican order on, 106, 241
priest-rulers, 279; in *Aforismi Politici,* 275, 277; in Plato, 266, 267
primalities, doctrine of, 90, 92, 166, 353; in Campanella's poetry, 57, 63; in *La Città del Sole,* 303; influence of Augustine on, 90, 92. *See also* love; power; wisdom
printing: invention of, xix–xx, 315, 323, 350; Neapolitan, 22n
prisoners: living conditions of, 50–51; self-integrity of, 56
prisons: of early modern Europe, 49–51, 99
procreation: in *La Città del Sole,* 22, 299–300; in *La Monarchia di Spagna,* 220; Ocellus Lucanus on, 302; in Second Isaiah, 302–3
Prodi, Paolo, 252, 253
property, community of, 309; in Campanella's works, 288, 304, 308; early Church on, 301, 310

prophecy: Campanella's use of, 31, 34, 39–40, 45, 54–55, 61, 68, 139, 298–99, 342; decrease of interest in, 340; and Lutheranism, 316; in Renaissance culture, 353; and Spanish universal monarchy, 228
prostitution, 49
providentialism, Spanish, 210n
Prynne, William, 190, 206, 208, 212
Psalms: Campanella's use of, 57
Pseudo-Dionysius: Campanella's use of, 17
Ptolemy of Alexandria, 347n
Ptolemy of Lucca, 290; and community of wives, 300n; *De regimine principum,* 265, 267, 268–69; republicanism of, 262, 274
Pucci, Francesco, 31; imprisonment of, 29, 30
Puritanism, English, 316
Pythagoras, 13, 167; Campanella's use of, 17, 54, 79, 178; and use of deception, 188

Querengo, Antonio, 52, 94, 163
Quevedo y Villegas, Francisco de, 76
Quintilian, Marcus Fabius, 152
Quirini, Vincenzo, 149

ragion di stato, 195; Campanella on, 184–85; of Machiavelli, 181–83; and religion, 194. *See also* Botero, Giovanni
Raleigh, Sir Walter, 51
Reeves, Marjorie, 340
Reformation, Protestant, 312, 315
religion: Campanella's redefinition of, 186; in civil society, 194–95; coercion in, 248–49; fusion of, with politics, xxi, 181–83, 187–88, 191, 194–96; Machiavelli on, 186–87, 191, 285; meaning of, in seventeenth century, 185; in *Monarchia di Spagna,* 187; multiplicity of, 186; naturalism in, 315–16; quatripartite division of, 332n; social need for, 189. *See also ragion di stato*
Renaissance: as cultural movement, 339–41; empiricism in, 341; end of, 339–40; eugenics programs of, 301; humanist/rhetorical tradition of, 341, 344, 353; impact of New World on, 348–49; republicanism of, 272; universal monarchy in, 197–98
Renaissance culture: antiquity in, 341; astrology in, 67–68, 315, 349, 353; chemical/medical studies in, 23; credulity in,

350; French, 242; magic in, 155, 179, 315, 349; of Naples, 19–20; natural philosophy of, 162; prophecy in, 353; in works of Campanella, xxii, 339
Renaudot, Theophraste, 126
republic: Campanella on, 31, 263–66, 274, 291
Republic of Letters: Campanella in, 124, 126
Riccardi, Niccolò (Il Mostro), 104, 105, 109, 112; Campanella on, 113, 131; on Campanella's *Theologia*, 322
Richelieu, Armand Jean du Plessis (cardinal): pamphleteers of, 244n; relationship of, with Campanella, 126, 127–30, 229, 230, 232, 242–43; and Spanish invasion, 228–29; in Thirty Years' War, 128; his use of astrology, 246; his use of heretics, 237
Ridolfi, Niccolò, 105, 109, 112, 131
Rinaldi da Nocera, Fra Serafino, 21
Rinaldis, Maurizio, 39, 43
Rohan, duc de, 243
Roman Academy, 103
Rome: as Babylon, 297–98; cultural life of, 103; political influence of, 4
Rosicrucianism: demise of, 84, 87; Hermetic features of, 77; Mersenne on, 124; Naudé on, 115
Royal Society: Campanella's influence on, 216, 343

Sacchi, Andrea, 110
saecula. See millennia
Sagredo, Giovanni Francesco, 341
Salazar, Juan de, 200, 207
salvation, Christian, 42, 44, 105; limitations on, 322; for savages, 336–37; for Turks, 105. See also evangelization, global
Salviano, Orazio, 21
San Domenico di Cosenza (convent), 15; Campanella in, 26; library of, 16n
San Domenico Maggiore (Naples), 20
Sandys, Sir George, 10–11
San Giorgio Morgeto (convent), 14, 15, 21
Santa Maria della Sanità (convent), 20–21
Santa Maria di Jesû at Stilo (convent), 33, 34, 38
Santa Maria sopra Minerva (convent), 30, 104, 131, 285
Santa Sabina: Campanella at, 30, 44
Sarpi, Paolo, 27, 28, 267, 273
Savonarola, Girolamo, 184, 340

Scaglia, Desiderio (cardinal), 105
Scheiner, Marcus, 114
Schmitt, Charles, 147
Schoppe, Kaspar, 51, 100, 151; advocacy of Campanella, 74–77; conversion of, 69; conveyance of Campanella's manuscripts, 70–71, 73, 205, 261; *Ecclesiasticus*, 73; and *Monarchia di Spagna*, 211
Sciarra, Marco, 33
science: Campanella's commitment to, 161; Church's acceptance of, 170-71, 178–79; effect of, on religion, 186; Galilean, xxii, 24, 167; reconstruction of, xix, 199
Scripture, Book of, 79, 150, 151, 162, 179; in Campanella's poetry, 163–64; in *On Gentilism*, 159, 160, 172; in *Theologia*, 169, 177. See also Nature, Book of
self-consciousness: individual, 91, 346, 349
seminaries: educational role of, 215, 219, 220–21; Jesuits, 221; military, 222–23; for women, 223
Seneca, Lucius Annaeus, the Younger, 55
sensism: of Campanella, 29, 81, 84, 89–90, 145
Simon, Cardinal, 156
sixteenth century: apocalypse in, 195; as end of Middle Ages, 340
Sixtus V (pope), 317; and establishment of congregations, 282–83
skepticism: in scientific enquiry, 155
society: clericalization of, 291–92
Socrates: Campanella on, 53; in Plato's *Republic*, 300
Spain: in Antarctica, 273, 329; domination of Italy by, 3–4; domination of New World by, 224, 226–27, 323, 335; naval strength of, 202, 223, 224–25, 323, 326, 327, 329, 335; population of, 226, 227, 234, 287, 328. See also Habsburg dynasty, Spanish; universal monarchy
spheres, revolution of, 186n
Spini, Giorgio, 111n, 196n
Spitz, Lewis, 352
Squillace: castle of, 37
states, territorial: consolidation of, 4, 198, 206; emergence of, 195, 346; role of papacy in, 252–53
Stelliola, Colantonio (Stegliola), 24, 25, 32, 34, 82
Stoicism, 319, 320; concept of *pneuma*, 16, 163; pantheism of, 124; plurality of worlds

Stoicism (cont.)
  in, 15, 96; rationality in, 323; revival of, 315, 349; Thomas Aquinas on, 146
Stubbe, Henry, 216, 343
subjectivity, human, 345–46
Sylvester I (pope), 265
Sylvester II (pope), 152n

Tacitism, xviii n
Talmudists, 188
Tampach, Gottfried, 82
Tasso, Torquato, 343
Telesio, Bernardino: Adami on, 79; Campanella's use of, 15, 26–27, 29, 89, 145, 325; del Tufo's support of, 22; *De rerum natura,* 15–16, 28; detractors of, 145; doctrine of heat and cold, 16, 23, 81, 82, 93, 164, 168, 220; Mersenne on, 124
Termoli, bishop of, (Alberto Drago), 46
Tertullian, Quintus Septimus Florens, 288, 308
Theophilus (patriarch of Alexandria), 36
Thirty Years' War, 128, 202; and universal monarchy, 87
Thomas Aquinas, Saint, 14–15; on Aristotle, 17, 75, 146, 157–58; on astrology, 66, 67; in Campanella's works, 146, 157, 162, 239, 319, 321; on doubt, 35–36; on ecclesiastical state, 262–63; natural theology of, 337; on the papacy, 269; on Plato, 152; primalities in, 92
Thou, Jacques-Auguste de, 120–21
Three Impostors, 184
Timaeus, 13, 167, 325; Campanella's use of, 17
Torquemada, Juan de, 267
Tragagliola, Alberto, 29, 38, 45, 46; death of, 47, 48
translatio imperii, 239, 243, 269
Trebizond, George of, 301
Trejo y Paniagua, Gabriel de (cardinal), 203, 275, 292; Campanella's correspondence with, 276–79
Trent, Council of, 177–78, 285
Trevor-Roper, Hugh Redwald, 352
trigons: astrological, 67, 68, 130
Trinity: doctrine of, 92
Troeltsch, Ernst, 290, 345
Tübingen, University of, 208
Turks: alliance of, with France, 245; in Calabrian rebellion, 39; *devshirme* of, 218,

220; extirpation of, 86; Lutheran ambivalence toward, 88; raids in Calabria, 9, 11, 32; salvation for, 105; threat of, 4, 213, 222; threat to Naples, 36
Two Sicilies, Kingdom of, 3, 275

Ultramontanism, 135
universal monarchy, xix, xx; administration of, 217–18; Aristotle on, 266, 267; astrology in, 228; Besold on, 86–87; of Bourbon dynasty, xix, 228–46; Campanella's commitment to, 197, 202, 245; decay of, 246; in *Discorsi ai principi d'Italia,* 88; effect of Thirty Years' War on, 87; intermarriage in, 219, 220, 221–22; national versions of, 198; prophecy in, 228; role of ecclesiastical power in, 213; Spanish monarchy as, 198–228, 328; Spanish-papal, 34, 40, 63, 199, 200, 239–40, 329. See also Campanella, Tommaso. Works: *La Monarchia di Spagna*
universal theocracy, xxi; Campanella on, 31, 142, 192, 194, 243, 259, 261, 273, 281–82, 319, 337; communitarianism in, 264; in *Discorsi universali del governo ecclesiastico,* 262–63, 279–80; John Fisher on, 251; Hobbes on, 258–59; limits on, 271; and pastoral role of church, 247–60, 270, 278; and state formation, 252–53. See also evangelization, global; papacy; *pasce oves meas*
universities, medieval, 216
Urban I (pope), 306
Urban VIII (pope), 101, 131; anti-Habsburg policy of, 89; Campanella's memorials to, 235, 239; election of, 283; and Galileo, 111n; patronage of arts, 103; *Poëmata,* 110, 111; state formation under, 252; support of Campanella, 106–10, 112, 193n
utopias, xxi; Anabaptist, 306; German, 77, 88

Valentinus, 93
Valla, Lorenzo, 250, 350
Valori, Baccio, 180
veglia, la (torture machine), 3, 47–48, 141
venality, 218
venatio (experimentation), 23
Venice: Campanella on, 28; confiscation of Campanella's manuscripts in, 73, 261; as ideal republic, 45; mercenaries of, 274; pa-

pal authority in, 273; papal interdict against, 52, 254, 255, 256, 271; penal servitude in, 49; republicanism of, 272. *See also* Campanella, Tommaso. Works: *Antiveneti*
Vernalione, Giovanni Paolo, 24, 32, 34
Vespucci, Amerigo, 325
Vesuvius: explosion of, 115
Vienne, Council, 216
Villani, Giovanni, 152
virginity, 312; Campanella on, 286
Vitoria, Francisco, 323, 327, 330, 336; *De Indis*, 352

Walker, D. P., 108
Welser, Mark, 69–70, 76
Wense, Wilhelm von, 77, 80
Wicquefort, Jacques, 208
Widdrington, Roger, 256
Wilkins, John, 96n
wisdom: in Campanella's works, 57, 92. *See also* primalities, doctrine of

witchcraft, 349, 350
women: community of, 44, 299–301, 304–5, 308–11, 313–14; in *La Monarchia di Spagna*, 220, 223; in Plato's *Republic*, 299–300; seminaries for, 223
workers: Campanella on, 189
workhouses: for women, 220, 223
world: renewal of, 28n, 67, 96; transformation of, 83, 141. *See also* millennia
world monarchy. *See* universal monarchy
worlds: astral, 165; inhabited, 179; plurality of, 15, 96, 168, 257–59
World Soul, 125

Xarava, Luis de, 33, 37, 38

Yates, Frances, xxiii

Zabarella, Giacomo, 150
Zumárraga, Fray Juan de (bishop), 289

ABOUT THE AUTHOR

John M. Headley is Professor of History at the University of North Carolina at Chapel Hill. He has authored studies of Luther, Thomas More, the Emperor Charles V, and San Carlo Borromeo.